The Emergen[...]
Delhi Sul[...]
1192–1286

For Anjali

The Emergence of the Delhi Sultanate 1192–1286

SUNIL KUMAR

permanent black

in association with

ASHOKA UNIVERSITY

Published by

PERMANENT BLACK
'Himalayana', Mall Road, Ranikhet Cantt,
Ranikhet 263645
perblack@gmail.com

in association with

ashoka
UNIVERSITY

Distributed by

ORIENT BLACKSWAN PRIVATE LTD
Bangalore Bhopal Bhubaneshwar Chandigarh Chennai
Ernakulam Guwahati Hyderabad Jaipur Kolkata
Lucknow Mumbai New Delhi Patna
www.orientblackswan.com

First published in hardback 2007
First paperback printing 2010
Sixth impression 2020

ISBN 81-7824-306-7

Printed and bound by Sapra Brothers, New Delhi 110092

Contents

CHARTS

TABLES

MAPS

HEDGEHOG AND FOX

ashoka UNIVERSITY HISTORY SERIES

"The fox knows many things, but the hedgehog knows one big thing"

GENERAL EDITOR RUDRANGSHU MUKHERJEE

Steven I. Wilkinson
ARMY AND NATION

Thomas R. Trautmann
ELEPHANTS AND KINGS

Partha Chatterjee, Sudipta Kaviraj, Nivedita Menon
THE INDIAN IDEOLOGY

Nayanjot Lahiri
ASHOKA IN ANCIENT INDIA

Nicholas B. Dirks
AUTOBIOGRAPHY OF AN ARCHIVE

Vasudha Dalmia
HINDU PASTS

Dipesh Chakrabarty
THE CALLING OF HISTORY

Sunil Agnani
HATING EMPIRE PROPERLY

Mahesh Rangarajan
NATURE AND NATION

Bhavani Raman
DOCUMENT RAJ

Sumit Guha
BEYOND CASTE

Iqtidar Alam Khan
INDIA'S POLITY IN THE AGE OF AKBAR

Linda Hess
BODIES OF SONG

Charu Gupta
THE GENDER OF CASTE

Ajay Skaria
UNCONDITIONAL EQUALITY

Velcheru Narayana Rao
TEXT AND TRADITION IN SOUTH INDIA

Uday Kumar
WRITING THE FIRST PERSON

Chinya V. Ravishankar
SONS OF SARASVATI

Christian Lee Novetzke
THE QUOTIDIAN REVOLUTION

B.D. Chattopadhyaya
THE CONCEPT OF BHARATVARSHA AND OTHER ESSAYS

Sumit Sarkar
ESSAYS OF A LIFETIME

INDIAN HISTORY CLASSICS

Ranajit Guha
A RULE OF PROPERTY FOR BENGAL

Ranajit Guha
THE SMALL VOICE OF HISTORY

Romila Thapar
THE PAST BEFORE US

Muzaffar Alam
THE LANGUAGES OF POLITICAL ISLAM IN INDIA *c.*1200–1800

Asok Sen
ISWAR CHANDRA VIDYASAGAR AND HIS ELUSIVE MILESTONES

Rosalind O'Hanlon
CASTE CONFLICT AND IDEOLOGY

Arvind Krishna Mehrotra, ed.
A CONCISE HISTORY OF INDIAN LITERATURE IN ENGLISH

Ramachandra Guha
AN ANTHROPOLOGIST AMONG THE MARXISTS

Partha Chatterjee
DEAD MAN WANDERING

Partha Chatterjee
EMPIRE AND NATION

Partha Chatterjee
THE BLACK HOLE OF EMPIRE

M.S.S. Pandian
BRAHMIN AND NON-BRAHMIN

Nayanjot Lahiri
FINDING FORGOTTEN CITIES

Iqtidar Alam Khan
THE MUGHAL NOBILITY

Srinath Raghavan
WAR AND PEACE IN MODERN INDIA

HISTORICAL SOURCEBOOKS IN CLASSICAL INDIAN THOUGHT

Patrick Olivelle, ed.
A DHARMA READER

Sheldon Pollock, ed.
A RASA READER

Preface

The Sultans of Delhi have attracted the attention of scholars and lay persons for generations. Their history is filled with romance, conquerors, and tragic heroes. It was a time of mystery when the Qutb Minar was constructed, a Queen ruled from Delhi, and capricious monarchs moved capitals back and forth. Their courts were awe-inspiring and ceremonial. They reduced prices or introduced a 'token' currency. In the hands of master raconteurs, the lives of these monarchs and their courts made for some fabulous, captivating stories that occupied students like me for days on end.

I discovered during my long graduate career, however, that there was more to the Delhi Sultanate than grand stories, but little which could be satisfied by the existing literature on the subject. The histories of scholars like Muhammad Aziz Ahmad and Khaliq Ahmad Nizami were paraphrased summaries of Sultanate chronicles, complete with an appendix on the character of the monarch.[1] Another historian of this period, A.B.M. Habibullah, provided more questions than answers: How could the Delhi Sultanate be 'founded' by Turks if the invasions were led by the Shansabanids who were from Ghur in Afghanistan? What were the traditions that influenced the making of the Delhi Sultanate: Ghurid, Turkish, slave, or Muslim? How, if at all, were they interrelated? If the Sultanate was constantly besieged by 'Hindus' waiting to recapture their homelands, how did it manage to survive? How could Balban be obsessed with Turkish racial purity

[1] Muhammad Aziz Ahmad, *Political History and Institutions of the Early Turkish Empire of Delhi* (Lahore: Research Society of Pakistan, University of the Punjab, 1987, reprint); Khaliq Ahmad Nizami, 'Foundation of the Delhi Sultanat', 'The Early Turkish Sultans of Delhi', in *A Comprehensive History of India: The Delhi Sultanat* (Delhi: People's Publishing House, 1982 reprint).

if he deployed Afghans all around Delhi?[2] These were admittedly small positivist questions, but they serve to explain the chill that ran through a well-meaning student testing the waters of the Early Middle Ages in Indian history.

As I delved deeper into the history of the early Delhi Sultanate, various such questions concerning the period became even more fundamental: Why do economic historians of the Delhi Sultanate pass hurriedly over the thirteenth century and into the fourteenth?[3] How can slaves be nobles?[4] If the Sultanate had a bureaucracy, chief ministers, and so on, how is it that a civil service did not administer the state?[5] When I decided to look at some of these questions in greater detail, I came across the only major disagreement amongst scholars writing on the Delhi Sultanate. Peter Hardy warned students that the medieval chronicles would not contain answers to the questions with which they approached their sources, but Khaliq Nizami and Irfan Habib assured readers that this was not the case: Ziyā' al-Dīn Barani, for example, was a scientific, reliable historian.[6]

As a young graduate student in the 1980s my sense of being out of my depth was profound. It was fortunate, therefore, that I was firmly

[2] A.B.M. Habibullah, *The Foundation of Muslim Rule in India* (Allahabad: Central Book Depot, 1945, 1976 revised edition).

[3] W.H. Moreland, *The Agrarian System of Moslem India: A Historical Essay with Appendices* (Delhi: Oriental Books Reprint Corporation, 1929, 1968 reprint); Irfan Habib, 'Agrarian Economy', 'Non-Agricultural Production and Urban Economy', in *The Cambridge Economic History of India, vol. 1, c. 1200–1750* (Delhi: Orient Longman, 1984 reprint).

[4] S.B.P. Nigam, *Nobility under the Sultans of Delhi* (Delhi: Munshiram Manoharlal, 1968); Kanwar Muhammad Ashraf, *Life and Conditions of the People of Hindustan* (Delhi: Munshiram Manoharlal, 1935, 1988 reprint).

[5] Ishtiaq Husain Qureshi, *The Administration of the Sultanate of Delhi* (Delhi: Oriental Books Reprint Corporation, 1942, 1971 edition); R.P. Tripathi, *Some Aspects of Muslim Administration* (Allahabad: Central Book Depot, 1978 reprint).

[6] Peter Hardy, *Historians of Medieval India: Studies in Indo-Muslim Historical Writing* (London: Luzac and Company, 1966 reprint); Khaliq Ahmad Nizami, 'Ziya-ud-din Barani', in M. Hasan, ed., *Historians of Medieval India* (Delhi: Jamia Milia Islamia, 1968), pp. 37–52; and Irfan Habib, 'Barani's Theory of the History of the Delhi Sultanate', *Indian Historical Review*, vol. 7 (1981), pp 99–115.

led away from the Delhi Sultanate and spent some years studying Islam, the early evolution of the Muslim community, and the history of Iran, Europe, and modern India. The historiography in these fields had its own set of problems with anachronism, teleology, and reification, but the mere fact that scholars recognized them as legitimate historiographical concerns was a major learning step for a student raised on a diet of consensual opinions on what happened in India's Middle Ages.

The 1980s and 1990s proved to be exciting years to rethink medieval Indian history. The work of scholars such as Simon Digby, John Richards, Sanjay Subrahmanyam, Muzaffar Alam, B.D. Chattopadhyaya, Dirk Kolff, Richard Eaton, Ebba Koch, Iqtidar Alam Khan, Chris Bayly, Ronald Inden, Bruce Lawrence, Carl Ernst, Stewart Gordon, Frank Perlin, Ashin Das Gupta, André Wink, Peter Jackson, Richard Barnett, Michael Fisher, Chetan Singh, and Stephen Blake textured and complicated the range of questions that historians were bringing to their materials. Although the Delhi Sultanate was still very much out of the purview of contemporary research, there was much to learn from historians who had started reflecting on the texture and narratives of their 'sources' rather than merely interrogating and pillaging them for 'facts'. I still remember the sense of excitement and relief with which I first read Simon Digby's article on the Qalandars, reassured that historians could profitably ask new questions of Sultanate literary materials read and re-read by countless historians in the past.[7]

Persian chroniclers crafted the history of the early Delhi Sultanate in the thirteenth century itself, a subject that was revisited by a variety of authors with differing agendas in subsequent years. At one level, this book is part of a long tradition of histories investigating the emergence of the Delhi Sultanate. At another level, it intersects with the ways in which Persian chronicles and a later historiography remembered the past. The two are not discrete exercises. As I argue through the book, the processes involved in the creation of the Sultanate were not as transparently narrated in the Persian chronicles as

[7] Simon Digby, 'Qalandars and Related Groups: Elements of Social Deviance in the Religious Life of the Delhi Sultanate of the Thirteenth and Fourteenth Centuries', in Yohanan Friedmann, ed., *Islam in Asia, volume 1, South Asia* (Boulder: Westview Press, 1984), pp. 60–108.

imagined in modern historiography. And they were frequently misconstrued in translation from a medieval lexicon of politics to a more modern one. Certainly, the Delhi Sultanate created and was, in turn, imbricated in power relationships with a lasting impact on social hierarchies, settlement patterns, and ideologies touching on morality, social conduct, and public service. The literature that reported on the Sultanate was not just sensitive to the politics that was an inherent part of the age; it was also implicated in perpetuating or challenging its structures. These accounts elided as much as reported on the politics of the thirteenth century. My history of the early Delhi Sultanate therefore moves constantly between an examination of the accounts that describe the politics of the period and a discussion of the ways in which these narratives need to be interrogated to comprehend the politics of the thirteenth century.

This going back and forth has also burdened my narrative and I must apologize to the uninitiated reader who will find this book replete with (unfamiliar) names, phrases, and terminologies in Persian. This is not because of any empirical overindulgence, however. Since it is hardly possible to grasp the social contexts of elite politics without a history of people, it has sometimes been necessary to get into the nitty-gritty of who was related to whom, and who was what, where, at what time. The need to keep an accurate track of individuals is the reason for the tables and charts in the book and an important consideration in the use of diacritics (see below for details): they help, for example, in distinguishing between Nāṣir al-Dīn and Naṣīr al-Dīn. Citations of Persian terminologies were equally necessary to clarify contextual meanings and I have always provided English translations. Unless otherwise mentioned, all translations are my own. I have provided two sets of dates for greater precision: the Hijri oblique the Common Era (607/1210, for example).

This book has had a long gestation period and it is wonderful to finally part with the script. I have had a long graduate career, and the opportunity to work with many teachers. Muhammad Amin of St Stephen's College kept me riveted with his stories about the Delhi Sultanate and sparked a curiosity about the period that eventually changed my life. Dr D.E.U. Baker showed by example what teaching commitment is all about. Professor Stanley E. Brush of the University of Bridgeport introduced me to the history of Islam and the central Islamic lands. My wife and I will always remember the warmth with which he and Beverley supported our academic and personal ventures as young foreign graduate students in an alien land. I am grateful to Professor John Woods for the training he gave me in Persian diplomatics and the skills in researching the history of the central Islamic lands. This work could not have progressed but for his help. Professors C.M. Naim and the late Barney Cohn of the University of Chicago were always sources of encouragement years after our formal academic relationship had come to an end.

In its original incarnation this book was defended as a doctoral dissertation at Duke University. The support and encouragement of the members of its history department exceeded my wildest expectations. In my years of experience as a student and teacher I have yet to see a university department make as concerted an attempt to gear its organization to the needs of its students. I can hardly individually thank the many friends that I made there, but let me record the help that was always forthcoming from members of my dissertation committee: Professors John F. Richards, Charles Young, Kristen Neuschel, David Gilmartin, Jan Ewald, and the late Jack Cell.

I really do not know how to acknowledge the support that I received from John Richards. I was extraordinarily fortunate that he was both my supervisor and a concerned friend. He taught me how to formulate my questions, to research with care and rigour, and he gave me the confidence to articulate my ideas. He provided generous support that made it possible for my family to accompany me to Durham and complete my dissertation in Delhi in relative comfort.

The University of Delhi was kind enough to give me a two-year sabbatical to study at Duke University. The Department of History where I teach at Delhi University is a unique centre: thin on resources but brimming with research, energy, and political activity. It is a special place because of the contribution of historians like Sumit Sarkar, never my teacher but always a mentor. Dilip Menon, Shahid Amin, Arup Banerjee, Denys Leighton, B.P. Sahu, and Nayanjot

Lahiri provided collegiality and intellectual sustenance during long departmental meetings. Working with my editorial colleagues at the *Indian Economic and Social History Review* (*IESHR*) has been an exciting educational experience and I am grateful to Sanjay, Bala, Dilip, and Tirtho for all the support and companionship they have provided over the years.

My friends watched my slow progress towards completion with considerable anxiety. To Sanjay Subrahmanyam a special thanks for always being there. The words of encouragement and care from Muzaffar Alam, Ebba Koch, Steven Wilkinson, G. Balachandran, and my sister Nita Kumar helped more than they will ever know. Rukun Advani's perseverance and editorial care finally eased my residual fears.

Some of the themes in the book were presented at different times at seminars and conferences. I am grateful to the discussions and responses from the audience at Jawaharlal Nehru University, at the history seminars at St Stephen's, Ramjas, Indraprastha, Lady Shri Ram and Jesus and Mary—colleges all at the University of Delhi. Discussions in seminars at the Aligarh Muslim University, the École des Hautes Études en Sciences Sociales in Paris, Oxford University, NIAS in the Netherlands, Oberlin College, Lewis and Clark College, University of Illinois at Urbana-Champaign, University of Chicago, and the East-West Center at the University of Hawaii were equally useful. My graduate students at the history department at Delhi University were a captive audience for the many ideas worked out in this book. They will be familiar with its contents; thank you for bringing them to some semblance of lucidity. Many of my students are now my colleagues and friends. Pankaj Jha's intellectual companionship has been a special source of joy over the years and I am extremely grateful to him for taking time out to prepare the index. At the final stages of revision Jyoti Gulati provided invaluable support by converting all my ancient files into Word documents. She proofed the typescript, checked the diacritics, and set a pace without which I would still be working on the fifth chapter! Without her help a larger number of errors would have crept into the final typescript.

For a long time it was politically incorrect to discuss my progress with the book at home. My in-laws, Robin and Usha, provided my family with emotional and material security in Delhi. I wish I could share the joys of the completed book with them. Likewise my father, Naresh Kumar, would ask after my work only with the greatest of love and care. It would have been a real pleasure to see this book in his hands. He and my mother Suniti always supported the intellectual aspirations of their children during their darkest moments. I am grateful to them for their faith in all our endeavours, their support and guidance.

If Anjali did not disagree with my opinions so much I would have put her as the coauthor of this book. We have discussed and argued about many of the ideas presented here. Without her willingness to share the burden of the enterprise I could never have written this book. She worked, parented, read, and reread countless drafts and allowed me the space to retreat into my ivory tower. I will be forever indebted to her. Shefali and Sikandar have wondered if my book would ever be history. If sheer force of will could prevail, my children would have had it completed years ago. I am grateful to them for making the present such a joyous and sublime moment in my life.

For the better part, I have followed the transliteration system of F. Steingass, *A Comprehensive Persian–English Dictionary* (Delhi: Munshiram Manoharlal, 2000 edition). I have departed from Steingass in marking the *iẕāfat* with a hyphen, *ahl-i kalam* rather than *ahli kalam*, for example. In Arabic-Persian combinations I have retained the article *al* followed by a hyphen: Rukn al-Dīn rather than Ruknu'd-dīn, the form followed by Steingass. I have provided full diacritics for the Persian forms, G͟haznawī, G͟hūrī for example, but not their English derivatives, Ghaznavid, Ghurid. Note also the distinction between terms such as *Shaik͟h*, *K͟hān*, *Sulṭān* in their Persian form, and Shaykh, Khan, Sultan in their English usage, without diacritics.

Turkish names have been a bit of a problem because their orthography is never clear in the Persian chronicles. I have adopted the Turkish form when a name was evidently clearer in that form—Ai-Beg (Moon Prince), rather than Aybak, for example.

CHAPTER 1

Writing a History of the Delhi Sultanate

The conquest of Delhi in 587/1192 by the Afghan ruler of Ghazni, Mu'izz al-Dīn Ghūrī (d. 602/1206), marked the establishment of the Delhi Sultanate. This was the beginning of a political formation that left its impression on the history of the Indian subcontinent for the following three and a half centuries. In the early decades of the sixteenth century, the founder of the Mughal dynasty, Ẓahīr al-Dīn Bābur (d. 937/1530), provided a reading of this past:

> The capital of all Hindustan is Delhi. After Shihāb al-Dīn Ghūrī's reign [569–602/1173–1206] until the end of Sulṭān Fīrūz Shāh's [d. 790/1388], most of Hindustan was under the control of the Delhi Sulṭans.[1]

Indeed, similar reports of the power and significance of the Sultanate of Delhi impressed people distant from it in time and space. In a Tamil folktale of Tanjavur—a town located in the southern extremity of the peninsula—the story of the 'Subahdar of the Cot' recognized Delhi as the ultimate political centre in India. In this articulation of local political identity within the Nāyaka culture of power relations (sixteenth through the early eighteenth centuries), it is the respectful acknowledgement of status by the courtesan of the Delhi Sultan, and

[1] Ẓahīr al-Dīn Bābur, *Bābur Nāma*, translated by Wheeler M. Thackston, *The Baburnama: Memoir of Babur, Prince and Emperor* (New York: Oxford University Press, 1996), p. 330.

not merely that of Vijayanagara, which transforms the 'Subahdar's' regal illusion into substantive reality.[2]

This book studies the emergence of the Delhi Sultanate during the first century of its turbulent history, *circa* 580–690/1190–1290. These were years when short periods of political stability and consolidation were followed very quickly by years of rebellion and loss of territory. The Delhi Sultans not only survived the political stresses of this period but went on to expand and annex most of the subcontinent in the fourteenth century, with the Sultanate reaching its apogee at this time, its frontiers almost mapping the contours of the modern nation state. The small, relatively inconsequential city of Delhi was transformed over this period into the capital of a powerful state, a role it would often occupy in the following centuries.

Not surprisingly, then, the history of the Delhi Sultanate is dominated by narratives of the high points of its achievements under a handful of powerful monarchs. The complicated social and political developments of the thirteenth century are thus pared down to teleological studies wherein an assembly of frontier garrison towns evolves almost seamlessly into a subcontinental empire.[3]

The kingdom of Delhi was originally one of several appanages distributed by Mu'izz al-Dīn Ghūrī to his military commanders in north

[2] For an account and discussion of this folktale, see Velcheru Narayana Rao, David Shulman, and Sanjay Subrahmanyam, *Symbols of Substance: Court and State in Nāyaka Period Tamilnadu* (Delhi: Oxford University Press, 1992), pp. 13–22. For another perspective, see Phillip B. Wagoner, 'Harihara, Bukka, and the Sultan: The Delhi Sultanate in the Political Imagination of Vijaynagar', in David Gilmartin and Bruce B. Lawrence, eds, *Beyond Turk and Hindu: Rethinking Religious Identities in Islamicate South Asia* (Gainesville: University of Florida Press, 2000), pp. 300–26.

[3] Historians often frame a linear evolution of political institutions and revenue regulations in an ascending order of complexity and disciplinary rigour through the Turks (thirteenth century), the Khalajīs and the Tughluqs (fourteenth century), the Mughals (sixteenth–seventeenth centuries), and down into the modern nation state. From different historiographical traditions, see for example the works of R.C. Majumdar, W.H. Moreland, R.P. Tripathi, and Irfan Habib. Full citations of such works are given later and in the bibliography.

India. Its annexation of rivals and seizure of their urban settlements in the mid-620s/late-1220s transformed this small principality. In just over forty years after the first Mu'izzī campaigns in north India, Delhi's authority expanded to include a diverse collection of people resident in areas as far away as Sindh in the west and Bengal in the east. The urban residents of these provinces had experienced several decades of stable political and economic life under their respective commanders. They had few ties with Shams al-Dīn Iltutmish (607–33/1210–36), the new and very distant Sultan of Delhi. The problems of consolidating these newly conquered territories and subjects within a composite Sultanate of Delhi were further complicated when cities in north India started receiving a flood of immigrants from eastern Iran, Khurasan, Transoxiana, and Afghanistan. 'Muslims' from diverse ethnic, 'class', and regional backgrounds, fleeing from the invasions of Chingīz Khān and his military commanders, began to make their way into the domain of the Delhi Sultan. While resisting the challenge of political peers as well as establishing a cadre of dependent subordinates through whom he could marshal his military forces and consolidate his authority, Iltutmish faced the formidable task of integrating his new subjects into a body politic that could gloss over their regional and cultural differences. Iltutmish's subjects had to be socialized into accepting the authority of the Delhi monarch and his political agents.

Many of these problems manifested themselves again later, in the thirteenth century. During the reign of Sultan Ghiyāṣ al-Dīn Balban (664–85/1266–87) the challenge of integrating the kingdom of Delhi was once more on the political agenda. But this time it was framed in a remarkably different form. In the intervening half century or so, the social profiles of many of the participants, elites, and subjects had altered. Many of the old elites and immigrants (and their descendents) were now entrenched in political and social networks that extended beyond the old urban environs. Their establishments were rooted in local contexts and their stability made them quite resilient against the authoritarian interventions of the Delhi Sultan.

The long duration and complicated interlinkages between these transformations is one reason why I study the 'emergence of the

Delhi Sultanate' as a historical process which continued through the thirteenth century. However, the term 'emergence' carries the sense of a linear development, a perception conventionally associated with an incremental increase in might and influence—in this case of the Delhi Sultans, their administrative institutions, and the formation of a centralized state. Being fully cognizant of the enormous transformations which occurred in the structure of the Delhi Sultanate and the social groups over which it ruled through the thirteenth century, I use the term 'emergence' in a sense far more impermanent and discontinuous. Over long periods, it often seemed as if the Sultanate had come to an end, its resurrection more in the nature of a reincarnation, its bodily form different from that of its precursor.

In order to understand these transformations better, one aspect of my book deals with the nature of political relationships between various elites as they jostled for power and influence. I am interested in studying the changing contexts of the praxis of power; the manner in which patronage ennobled some people and marginalized others over time; and the cultural meanings given to service and loyalty by different groups who did not necessarily abide by the Sultanate's definitions of legitimate authority. Much of my research resides upon a prosopographical study of elites, the attempt being to understand the social and ideological contexts of notables involved in the political world of the Sultanate in the thirteenth century. Rather than focusing on Sultanate administrative institutions and prescriptive bureaucratic norms, my study highlights individuals and groups, and the conditions in which they held public responsibilities.

I found this approach helpful in bridging the conventional historiographical divisions between politics and society. By placing political elites in their larger social contexts my study argues, for example, that the military commanders of the Delhi Sultans honoured with the title of *Amīr* or *Malik* were not necessarily regarded with concomitant respect by their subjects. An *amīr* often lacked the qualities possessed by a *sharīf*, an individual or 'nobleman' who was cultured, learned, often had independent sources of income, and possessed a high social pedigree.[4] Devoid of the social recognition that ought in theory to

[4] Persian and Arabic do not possess a term that carries the full implication of the Latin/English 'nobilitas'/'noble'. For a further discussion, see Sunil

have complemented his political-military status, the *amīr's* authority was, therefore, crucially undermined and limited. Social elites—those whom the Muslim subject population regarded as their leaders and guides—were in fact centres of disciplinary formations that intersected in both supportive and contentious ways with Sultanate authority. In enlarging upon the nature and content of these alternative disciplinary formations in the thirteenth century, I also hope to expand the existing historiographical understanding of political life by taking it beyond the narrow ambit of the ruler's court and the impact of his administrative policies on his subjects.

Although the Delhi Sultans and their agents are an extremely important focus in my work, my research thus takes a more decentred approach. It underlines the competitive character of the political world of the thirteenth century, a domain within which the rulers of Delhi were only some among the many protagonists of this period, and who emerged paramount only occasionally.

But if highlighting the fragmentary and discontinuous political world of the Delhi Sultanate was the only agenda of my book, I would have preferred to use as its title the clumsier but perhaps more accurate plural form: 'the history of the north Indian Sultanates'. Such a title might indeed be thought to reflect more precisely some of the political complexities and discontinuities of the period. On the other hand, while it may seem valuable to move away from the unicentric and synchronic image of a single and relatively stable political formation lording over the destiny of north India during the thirteenth century, it is impossible to disregard the presence of a vast amount of narrative evidence arguing for the uninterrupted historical presence of a dominant Delhi Sultanate.[5]

My specific usage of both 'emergence' and 'Sultanate' (rather than 'Sultanates') is clarified by my study of the ideologies that gave meaning to the political formation called the Sultanate of Delhi. The creation of this political formation did not entail merely the ruler's political and administrative ability to command and appropriate the

---

Kumar, 'When Slaves were Nobles: The Shamsī *Bandagān* in the Early Delhi Sultanate', *Studies in History*, 10 (1994), pp. 23–52.

[5] For a discussion of the sources on the Delhi Sultanate, see the section 'Reading the Persian Evidence' of this chapter, and the Appendix.

surplus produce of subjects. It also implied the construction of an *idea* of a unitary dominion wherein, it was suggested, subjects were protected, and law as well as an orderly social equilibrium maintained.

This idea of a unitary political terrain was composed of several intersecting strands and involved different groups of people. At its most obvious level, the writings of court chroniclers provided a history and rationale for the existence of the protective and disciplinary agencies of the Delhi Sultan. More discreet were the voices of some jurists and preachers—the censors of public morality—whose visions of an ideal Muslim community envisaged a people united in belief and conduct. Such moralising groups may have been inspired by aspirations and fears different from those of the Persian chroniclers, but the promise of a stable and composite universe within a united Sultanate appealed to them as well, albeit for different reasons. Together, they comprised a socially important and articulate people who, despite their differing agendas, seized upon the idea of a political regime that protected and maintained their vision of a prosperous Muslim community. This *idea* of a Sultanate had its coercive side as well; it defined appropriate conduct and belief for Muslims, punishing dissenters as hypocrites or apostates.

It is therefore my argument that the Sultanate was a political structure which, perhaps ironically, was the creation of a variety of people, not just of the Sultans of Delhi. Since the Sultanate received support from agents who were, crudely speaking, not always its servants, material life in fact reflected a stability that was incongruous in the context of the political uncertainties of the thirteenth and fourteenth centuries. Put in a different way, the structures upon which the Delhi Sultanate resided managed to survive even when its Sultans did not. This also meant that dissent against the structures of the Delhi Sultanate was not always directed towards Delhi or its Sultan. There was wide-ranging contestation against the Delhi Sultanate and what it represented to different people, but in the thirteenth century dissent never managed to obscure the emergence, and eventual embellishment, of the idea of a unitary dominion constituting the Sultanate. Through the century Delhi reached a pre-eminence quite out of keeping with its economic and strategic advantages: this was evident from the seriousness with which many political aspirants sought to seize the city in their bid to gain more than provincial significance.

My understanding of the Delhi Sultanate relies upon evidence contained largely in Persian chronicles, epigraphs, and coins produced during the thirteenth and fourteenth centuries. These materials have been used by earlier scholars, but my understanding and deployment of this evidence differs considerably from those of my predecessors. I have reserved a discussion of the source material used in this book for the appendix. To better contextualize my own research I felt it more important to first provide an account of how scholars have reconstituted information from the thirteenth and fourteenth centuries into their historical narratives on the Delhi Sultanate. Secondary writings on the Sultanate have today accumulated into a voluminous mass, inchoate insofar as their major intellectual lineages have not been distinguished. In an effort to provide a more coherent context for my own analysis, the next two sections consider the manner in which our current knowledge of the thirteenth century is composed by the existing historiography of the Delhi Sultanate.

Historiography of the Delhi Sultanate

There is no dearth of writing on the Delhi Sultanate. A casual survey of the *Index Islamicus*, a reference bibliography of European-language articles on the world of Islam, confirms that the history of the Delhi Sultans is relatively well served by historians.[6] The most important historiographical intervention in the study of this period, one which is still extremely influential in the making of university syllabi and trends in research, was made by Mohammad Habib in a series of articles published intermittently through the 1920s and 1950s.[7] Unlike

[6] J.D. Pearson, ed., *Index Islamicus* (Cambridge: Cambridge University Press, 1958–).

[7] In a long historical introduction to a new edition of the second volume of Elliot and Dowson's *History of India as Told by its Own Historians*, Habib sketched out what he believed were the major changes introduced in north Indian society with the establishment of Sultanate rule in the thirteenth century. It was a fitting context to rewrite the history of the early Delhi Sultanate; much of medieval Indian history written in the English language over the last century bore the impress of Elliot's translations and interpretation of the Persian chronicles. See Mohammad Habib, 'Introduction to Elliot and Dowson's History of India, vol. II', in K.A. Nizami, ed., *Politics and Society in Early Medieval India: Collected Works of Professor Mohammad Habib* (New Delhi:

his predecessors and peers, Habib chose not to get involved in a history of events centred around 'Hindu' or 'Muslim' protagonists.[8] In a brief theoretical digression he explained the influence of the writings of Marx and Engels on his work, which was as follows: social relations were determined by a person's relationship to the prevalent mode of production, which alienated the slave, serf, peasant, and proletariat from the surplus value of his or her labour. Material relationships created a larger superstructure of law, religion, the state, and these consolidated class distinctions between the exploited and the ruling class. History recorded the dialectical relationship between these classes, and there were cycles of revolutions which altered social relationships to the forces of production.[9]

With this understanding of history, Habib argued that the doctrine of Islam during the period of Muḥammad and the 'rightly-guided' Caliphs (11–40/632–61) introduced a social and economic revolution of global dimensions. Islam's egalitarian ideals altered, for the moment, the basis of all class relationships within the central Islamic lands. But these ideals did not last; a governing class and a state with new hierarchical and administrative systems emerged. By the eighth century the original inspiration of the Qur'ānic revelation was lost, the hierarchy present in the new Caliphal and Sultanate courts followed pre-Islamic models and a docile class of religious specialists was no longer the keeper of the original egalitarian ideals of Islam. The only exceptions were dispersed groups of mystically minded Muslims of ascetic inclinations who shunned state service.[10]

People Publishing House, 1952, 1974 reprint.), vol. 1, pp. 33–110. Habib's acute observations on how edited translations were responsible for much of the communal 'mischief' present in the historiography of his day did not, unfortunately, extend to a comment on how the publication of select manuscripts of court chronicles by the Asiatic Society of Bengal and their easier accessibility might have shaped interpretation of the Middle Ages.

[8] For a general introduction to this historiography, see Peter Hardy, *Historians of Medieval India*, pp. 1–19. 122–31.

[9] Mohammad Habib, 'Introduction to Elliot and Dowson', pp. 38–43.

[10] Ibid., pp. 43–59. This idea was further elaborated by Mohammad Habib in 'Shaikh Nasīruddīn Maḥmūd Chirāgh-i Dehlī as a Great Historical Personality', *Islamic Culture*, 20 (1946), pp. 129-53; idem, 'Chishti Mystic Records

The implications of this argument for north Indian history were, to begin with, a reconsideration of the Ghaznavid and Ghurid invasions. Here, rather than religious zeal directed at punishing idolaters, material gain—plunder—was rationalized as the primary motivation for the military campaigns into India.[11] The establishment of Ghurid rule in India, however, had repercussions of its own. Two factors were important: first, the state's ambition to mobilize increasing resources; and second, the egalitarian ideology of Islam. Within the caste-ridden context of 'Hindu' society, the ostracised low castes and untouchables saw in 'Muslim' society an opportunity to participate in the urban economy of the new state. Muslim rulers welcomed their participation because it consolidated the economic base of the state and improved its revenue resources. This was facilitated by an Islamic ideology that disregarded Hindu caste divisions. Hence, in Mohammad Habib's opinion, the Ghurid invasion 'was not a conquest' of India but 'a turn over of public opinion . . . a revolution of Indian city-labour led by Ghurian Turks'.[12]

Although the Ghurid conquests ushered in a period of great artisanal activity whereby low-caste converts, together with skilled immigrants from the central Islamic lands, revitalized trade and urban economies, the revolution itself remained unfinished because it did not go beyond the cities. Outside Sultanate control the countryside was under a 'Hindu' landed elite whose caste and fiscal privileges made it the immediate exploiter of the peasantry. The feudal nature of this society was destroyed by the military campaigns and revenue policies of 'Alā' al-Dīn Khalajī (695–715/1296–1316). This was a 'rural revolution' that destroyed caste inequities in the countryside, removed exploitative Hindu intermediaries, and brought the peasantry in direct contact with the Delhi Sultanate. Habib wanted his readers

---

of the Sultanate Period', *Medieval India Quarterly*, 1 (1950), pp. 1–42; idem, *Ḥaẓrat Niẓāmuddīn Auliyā: Ḥayāt aur Ta'līmāt* (Delhi: Department of Urdu, Delhi University, 1970).

[11] For an earlier articulation of this, see Mohammad Habib, 'Sultan Mahmud of Ghazni', in K.A. Nizami, ed., *Politics and Society during the Medieval Period: Collected Works of Professor Mohammad Habib* (New Delhi: People's Publishing House, 1927, 1981 reprint), vol. 2, pp. 36–104.

[12] Mohammad Habib, 'Introduction to Elliot and Dowson', pp. 72-3.

to appreciate the magnitude of this revolution, hence his analogy: 'Alā' al-Dīn 'liquidated the intermediaries as effectively as Chairman Mao-Tse-tung and the Communist Party have liquidated feudalism in China. [As a result] . . . India would never again become a land of caste-privileges it had been for some centuries past.'[13]

Writing at a time when 'Hindu–Muslim' conflict and a narrative of the wars, diplomacy, and administration of the different Sultans of Delhi were the main features of Sultanate historiography, Mohammad Habib's foregrounding of larger social and economic changes in the history of Indian society seemed to challenge the manner in which the thirteenth century was interpreted. But, in fact, in at least three interrelated points, Habib's contribution left the field undisturbed. The first concerned the disparate body of immigrants fleeing into India from Afghanistan, eastern Iran, and Transoxiana. In the historiography of the Delhi Sultanate these immigrants, collectively and individually, were always described as 'Muslims', as part of a larger, monolithic community.[14] Habib paid little attention to the denominational background of immigrants into India, and he did argue that Muslim social and political identities were formed by a shared urban culture within which occupational and class differences were important. But, having said that, Habib provided a brief historical survey of Islamic ideologies that bound Muslims together through a shared past.[15] As a result,

[13] Ibid., p. 94, and, more generally, pp. 84–94 for the 'rural revolution'.

[14] See from a vast selection, the following examples: Sir Wolseley Haig, ed., *The Cambridge History of India, vol. III, Turks and Afghans* (Cambridge: University Press, 1928); Stanley Lane Poole, *Medieval India under Muhammadan Rule (A.D. 712–1764)* (New York: Haskell House, 1903, 1970 reprint); W.H. Moreland, *The Agrarian System of Moslem India*; A.B.M. Habibullah, *The Foundation of Muslim Rule in India*; R.P. Tripathi, *Some Aspects of Muslim Administration*; Aziz Ahmad, *Studies in Islamic Culture in the Indian Environment* (Oxford: Clarendon Press, 1964); K.A. Nizami, *Some Aspects of Religion and Politics in India during the Thirteenth Century* (Delhi: Idarah-i Adabiyat-i Delli, 1961, 1974 reprint); K.M. Ashraf, *Life and Conditions of the People of Hindustan*; M. Mujeeb, *The Indian Muslims* (Montreal: McGill University Press, 1967); and, more recently, André Wink, *al-Hind: The Making of the Indo-Islamic World, vol. II: The Slave Kings and the Islamic Conquest, 11th–13th Centuries* (Leiden: E.J. Brill, 1997).

[15] Mohammad Habib, 'Introduction to Elliot and Dowson', pp. 47–59, 95–100.

despite his attempts at historicization, Habib's understanding of the Muslim community stressed its underlying unifying principles, resulting at bottom in an essentialization that did little to disturb interpretations of Muslim society as singular or monolithic.

The second assumption widely prevalent amongst scholars concerned the history of the 'Muslim community', which they believed could only be charted through the history of the 'Muslim Sultanate'; these two not merely merged into a monolith but were also congruent. At one extreme this led to the argument that the iconoclastic, militaristic character of Islam and Muslims determined the nature of the Sultanate and its rulers; these were regarded as positive or negative attributes, depending upon who was narrating the history.[16] At the other extreme, it led to the production of histories by secular minded and progressive historians such as Mohammad Habib who saw in the arrival of Islam and the foundation of the Delhi Sultanate the appearance of new ideologies and modes of production that transformed society and politics in India for the better.[17] Since these ideas were 'foreign' to 'Hindu' society, their novelty could only be grasped through the early history of 'Islamic' state formations in the Arabian peninsula, Iran, and Transoxiana. That was the collective pre-history of Muslims in India, and it needed the Delhi Sultanate to create the social and political preconditions for the import of these new ideas into the subcontinent.[18] Even while Habib argued for the

[16] For an early contrast see James Mill, *The History of British India*, 3 vols (New Delhi: Associated Publishing House, 1817–18, 1972 reprint, 2 vols); and Mountstuart Elphinstone, *The History of British Power in the East* (London: Murray, 1842, 1887 reprint). See also R.C. Majumdar, ed.,*The Struggle for Empire: The History and Culture of the Indian People, vol. V* (Bombay: Bharatiya Vidya Bhavan, 1957). More recently, see André Wink, *al-Hind, vol. II: The Slave Kings*, pp. 294–333.

[17] For Habib's reflections on the introduction of new technologies by Muslim immigrants in India, see 'Introduction to Elliot and Dowson', pp. 68–9.

[18] Habib explained: 'The relation of the culture of Ajam to Indo-Muslim culture is extremely simple. The whole of the science and culture of Ajam, briefly surveyed above, was bodily imported into India by the first quarter of the thirteenth century. . . .' Ibid., p. 59. Note also the long introductory chapter, 'The Asiatic Environment' authored by Habib in the volume edited by him and K.A. Nizami, *A Comprehensive History of India, vol. 5: The Delhi Sultanat, A.D. 1206–1526* (New Delhi: People's Publishing House, 1970, 1982 reprint),

distance between the religion of Islam and its political manifestations, the history of the Muslim community in India could not be told without the context of an Islamic state. Thus, the paradox: while Chishtī saints abhorred service with the state because of its materialistic, hierarchical attributes, this same state challenged the caste-based stratifications of Hindu society. Nor was the urban character of Muslim society entirely accidental: the towns were the centres of religious training and culture. They were also its major centres of production. And they flourished because they received state patronage and were the hub of Sultanate government and economy.[19]

The third assumption concerned the other face of the Muslim state: an undifferentiated 'Hindu' subject population. For a large number of historians the seizure of Delhi by 'Muslims' marked the beginning of a period when 'indigenes' were ranged in opposition to 'foreign' invaders; a 'Hindu' community juxtaposed and in conflict with the 'Muslim'. A.B.M. Habibullah worked this theme with complete confidence into his text: the only threat to the 'foundation of Muslim rule in India' was occasioned by 'Hindu aggression'.[20] In Mohammad Habib's formulation the Muslim–Hindu divide operated at the level of social organizations: one was casteist and hierarchical, the other was egalitarian. Just as normative juridical and hagiographical texts had enlarged on the qualities of Muslim society, al-Birūnī and the

---

pp. 1–131. Sub-sections in the chapter reviewed individual dynasties and rulers and were introduced by an account titled, 'Rise of Monarchy and the Governing Class among the Musalmans'. Until very recently this was the standard textbook (also available in Hindi) prescribed to undergraduate students and published under the auspices of the Indian History Congress.

[19] Mohammad Habib, 'Introduction to Elliot and Dowson', pp. 36, 43–7, 74–80, and especially pp. 84–94. For a different interpretation, see Richard M. Eaton, 'The Political and Religious Authority of the Shrine of Bābā Farīd', in Barbara Metcalf, ed., *Moral Conduct and Authority: The Place of Adab in South Asian Islam* (California: Berkeley University Press, 1984), pp. 333–56, reprinted in Richard M. Eaton, *Essays on Islam and Indian History* (Delhi: Oxford University Press, 2000), pp. 203–24. Also see idem, *The Rise of Islam and the Bengal Frontier, 1204–1760* (Delhi: Oxford University Press, 1997 reprint).

[20] Note the title of Habibullah's book: *The Foundation of Muslim Rule in India*, and chapter 6, 'Hindu Aggression: 1235–1265'.

Manū Smritī summarized the features of 'Hindu' society. Caste differences in 'Hindu' society implied differing reactions to the Muslim Delhi Sultanate; the low castes, first in the towns and then in the countryside, saw the Muslim Sultanate as a liberating force, while the upper castes, the rulers, and the rich peasantry had to be destroyed by 'Alā' al-Dīn Khalajī.[21] The differing responses of 'Hindus' to the Sultanate notwithstanding, the nature of the conflict between the two was built into the supposedly compelling logic of antithetical Hindu and Muslim social structures.

The shared terrain between the more traditional historiography and Mohammad Habib's formulations made it difficult for Habib's colleagues and students to make a serious contribution to Sultanate studies. For the better part, historians like K.A. Nizami and I.H. Siddiqui remained within Habib's conclusions, with all of their problems.[22] Others, like Peter Jackson, ignored his theoretical framework altogether and returned instead to earlier formulations in which the Delhi Sultanate was postulated as 'the sole bastion of Muslim power in the Indian subcontinent'.[23]

For the longest time, W.H. Moreland was the only historian whose focus on the relationship between the state and the peasantry remained outside the fold of Sultanate historiography. Moreland argued that the revenue collection functions of the Muslim state in India were 'the most potent factor in the distribution of the national income; while its action in regard to distribution inevitably reacted on production, so much so that we are justified in concluding that, next only to the weather, the administrator was the dominant fact in the economic life

[21] Mohammad Habib, 'Introduction to Elliot and Dowson', pp. 61–7, 71–80, and 91–4.

[22] K.A. Nizami, *Some Aspects of Religion and Politics*; idem, *Studies in Medieval Indian History and Culture* (Allahabad: Kitab Mahal, 1966); and Mohammad Habib and K.A. Nizami, *A Comprehensive History of India, vol. 5: The Delhi Sultanat*. From his recent publications, see I.H. Siddiqui, 'Social Mobility in the Delhi Sultanate', in Irfan Habib, ed., *Medieval India 1: Researches in the History of India, 1200–1750* (Delhi: Oxford University Press, 1992), pp. 22–48.

[23] Peter Jackson, *The Delhi Sultanate: A Political and Military History* (Cambridge: University Press, 1999), p. xiii.

of the country.'[24] Moreland's work was a mixture of extremely awkward anachronisms (note his discussion of 'Hindu–Muslim' social and revenue systems and on the office of *wazīr*), balanced by some very nuanced readings and translations of Persian texts and terminologies (see especially the discussion on his use of the term 'Province' and 'Governor').[25] Although rooted in the limited and biased context of a colonial administrator's experience in the *mufaṣṣil*, many of Moreland's observations had a resonance in Mohammad Habib's ideas on 'Alā' al-Dīn Khalajī's rural revolution.[26] More specifically, even if his economic history was ignored, Moreland's emphasis on Sultanate institutions and administrative structures impressed a generation of scholars trained in British universities. R.P. Tripathi's work on the theories and institutions of kingship and the *Wizārat*, I.H. Qureshi's book on Sultanate administration with chapters on the 'legal' and the 'actual' sovereign, the royal household and ministers, reflected the impact that constitutional and administrative histories of the United Kingdom had on studies of the Sultanate.[27]

It was not until the mid-1960s and 70s that Moreland's economic and institutional histories were extensively used and redeployed within a more rigorous Marxist framework by Irfan Habib.[28] To be

[24] W.H. Moreland, *The Agrarian System of Moslem India*, p. xii.

[25] Ibid., p. xiv (*wazīr*); pp. 1–20 (revenue systems); pp. 22–6, 216–23 (Province and Governor).

[26] See, for example, Mohammad Habib, 'Introduction to Elliot and Dowson', pp. 92–3.

[27] R.P. Tripathi, 'Some Aspects of Muslim Administration', a London University thesis with acknowledgements to Harold Laski and Moreland; I.H. Qureshi, *The Administration of the Sultanate of Delhi* (New Delhi: Oriental Books Reprint Corporation, 1942, 1971 reprint), a revised Cambridge University dissertation with acknowledgements to Moreland and R.B. Whitehead. More recently, the impact of this historiography is also visible in the work of Peter Jackson, *The Delhi Sultanate*.

[28] Moreland's research was resurrected and redeveloped by Irfan Habib first in his *The Agrarian System of Mughal India* (Delhi: Asia Publishing House, 1963) and subsequently in different contexts in his 'An Economic History of the Delhi Sultanate—An Essay in Interpretation', *Indian Historical Review*, 4 (1978), pp. 287–303, and in 'Agrarian Economy' and 'Non-Agricultural Production and Urban Economy' in Tapan Raychaudhuri and Irfan

sure, Irfan Habib clarified that there would be no actual departure from his father Mohammad Habib's ideas in his work because, 'in very broad terms . . . the two major changes that Professor Habib had ascribed to the Sultanate, namely, an advance in urbanization and a reduction in the power of the local hereditary rural potentates are substantiated by actual evidence'.[29] In Irfan Habib's argument, urbanization in the Sultanate period was a result of the increasing immigration of craftsmen fleeing into India from the Mongol invasions of eastern Iran and Afghanistan. These migrants brought with them technologies of production unknown in the subcontinent. They received sanctuary in the Delhi Sultanate, whose urban centres were replete with a huge slave population seized in plunder campaigns. The conjuncture of new technologies, artisanal skills, a safe sanctuary, dishoarded wealth, and a plentiful supply of slave labour increased craft production and transformed Sultanate towns.[30] Irfan Habib's arguments concerning the processes of urbanization under the Sultanate—centred on enhanced commodity production—remained within the broad parameters of Mohammad Habib's understanding of the 'urban revolution'. His emphasis on material and technological fact-

---

Habib, eds, *The Cambridge Economic History of India, vol. 1*, pp. 48–93.

[29] Irfan Habib, 'An Economic History of the Delhi Sultanate', p. 297.

[30] Ibid., p. 292. On the introduction of new technologies in the subcontinent, see also Irfan Habib, 'Technological Changes and Society, Thirteenth and Fourteenth Centuries', *Proceedings of the Indian History Congress*, 31 (1969), pp. 139–61; and idem, 'Medieval Technology: Exchanges between India and the Islamic World', *Aligarh Oriental Series*, no. 6 (1985). On slave labour, see also idem, 'Slavery in the Delhi Sultanate, Thirteenth and Fourteenth Centuries: Evidence from Sufic Literature', *Indian Historical Review*, 15 (1988–9), pp. 248–56. Several general studies focused on the extractive taxation system of the Delhi Sultanate: Irfan Habib, 'Social Distribution of Landed Property in Pre-British India', *Enquiry*, New Series, 2 (1965), pp. 21–75, reprinted in idem, *Essays in Indian History, Towards a Marxist Perception* (New Delhi: Tulika, 1995), pp. 59–108; idem, 'The Peasant in Indian History', *Proceedings of the Indian History Congress*, 43 (1982), pp. 1–53, reprinted in *Essays in Indian History*, pp. 109–60; idem, 'Agrarian Economy' and 'Non-Agricultural Production and Urban Economy', in *The Cambridge Economic History, vol. 1*, pp. 48–93.

ors, however, eased the awkward emphasis in the latter's work on the release of new social forces because of Islamic egalitarian ideals.

But when it came to the 'rural revolution', Irfan Habib stayed very close to his father's arguments. Through a series of detailed studies on agricultural production and taxation, Irfan Habib correlated the increasing systematization of the Sultanate fiscal regime with the decline in status and influence of the rich peasantry and rural chieftains. They sank in status from aristocrats with rights to impose their own cesses, to intermediary functionaries oscillating between the Sultanate and the peasantry. In Irfan Habib's argument, as in Mohammad Habib's, it was not until the reign of 'Alā' al-Dīn Khalajī that a uniform land tax was systematically imposed at the cost of the economic and political privileges traditionally enjoyed by the superior rural classes.[31] Since the tax on land was collected in cash over the larger part of 'Alā' al-Dīn's dominion, the economy was increasingly monetized while the authority of the richer peasantry and rural aristocracy substantially diminished. Because of this 'rural revolution' the prosperity of the Sultanate and its agents, resident in the cities of the Sultanate, was in marked contrast to the plight of the rural aristocracy.[32] In Irfan Habib's argument, 'Alā' al-Dīn's fiscal measures were hardly akin to Mao's rural revolution, and they certainly failed to liberate the toiling peasants. But their interventionist character altered rural society in the long duration and contributed towards the establishment of the agrarian base of the Sultanate and a successful implementation of the harsh market regulations of the Delhi Sultan.[33]

[31] This argument was made by Habib in all his general essays, for example in his 'Social Distribution of Landed Property' and in his chapter, 'Agrarian Economy' in *The Cambridge Economy History, vol. 1*, pp. 48–76. It received its most detailed exposition in idem, 'Price Regulations of 'Alā'uddīn Khaljī: A Defence of Ziā' Baranī', *Indian Economic and Social History Review*, 21 (1984), pp. 393–414.

[32] Idem, 'Price Regulations of 'Alā'uddīn Khaljī', pp. 408, 410.

[33] Ibid., pp. 397–404. The significance of 'Alā' al-Dīn's taxation system in the history of India was underlined elsewhere by Habib. He noted: ''Alā'u'ddīn Khaljī's taxation system was probably the one institution from his reign that lasted the longest, surviving indeed into the nineteenth or even the twentieth century. From now on, the land tax (*kharāj* or *māl*) became the principal form in which the peasant's surplus was expropriated by the ruling class'. Idem, 'Agrarian Taxation', *The Cambridge Economic History, vol. 1*, p. 62.

The degree of internal coherence within Irfan Habib's arguments set his work aside from that of his peers. If one understood the implications of the introduction of new technologies, Habib argued, then the presence of the Persian wheel enhanced agricultural productivity; its introduction in the Punjab region and the peasantization of pastoral Jat lineages in the area could be analysed as interlinked processes.[34] Furthermore, the impact of new technologies on the artisanal economies of the Sultanate urban centres was most noticeable amongst weavers. The introduction of the spinning wheel enhanced production while markets created by the ruling classes of the Sultanate increased demand. Technological advancement and increased demand led to an increase in artisanal population and, with it, pressure on the rigid caste system as a larger number of low castes now took to weaving. As Habib noted, 'It was, perhaps, this social environment, the visible breaches in the walls of the caste system, and the economic temptation to break its rules, that lay behind the artisans' fervour for monotheism'.[35] It was also an important reason for monotheism's appeal amongst other marginalized sectors of society, such as the Jats of Punjab. They were already seeking a new identity as peasants and found amongst the ideological strands of the monotheistic movements of the *Sants*, the inspiration to break away from a 'heritage that demeaned them in relation to other peasant communities'.[36]

Irfan Habib carried many of his father's ideas to their logical conclusion—and with them several problems as well. Although there is considerable persuasiveness within his argument about technological diffusion during the medieval period, its historicity still needs to be worked out very carefully. For, as Habib's more detailed analysis of the Jats and monotheistic movements suggests, the impact of new technologies was not felt until the fifteenth and sixteenth centuries. It is therefore unclear—except in the most rudimentary, determinist interpretation—how the introduction of the spinning wheel, for example, impacted on urbanization or commerce in the

[34] Idem, 'The Jatts of Punjab and Sind', in Harbans Singh and N. Gerald Barrier, eds, *Punjab Past and Present: Essays in Honour of Dr. Ganda Singh* (Patiala: Punjab University, 1976), pp. 92–103.

[35] Idem, 'The Historical Background of the Popular Monotheistic Movement of the 15th–17th Centuries', mimeograph, p. 11.

[36] Ibid., p. 14.

thirteenth century. There are other problems in Habib's argument as well: on the basis of his research on medieval Punjab, Chetan Singh demonstrated that ecological conditions did not favour the introduction of the Persian wheel in precisely the region where, according to Irfan Habib, its deepest impact was felt by the Jats.[37]

Indeed, although Habib was sensitive to the problems in Marx's arguments about a static, widely prevalent 'Asiatic mode of production', his own argument on the impact of technological innovations introduced into India by immigrants carried with it the implication that structural ennuï in Indian society could be overcome only through *external* stimuli.[38] Irfan Habib's argument derived its credibility from the observations of al-Birūnī, whose reliability had already been defended by Mohammad Habib. But his conclusions also militated against research by Andrew Watson which underscored the flow of technological skills from South Asia into the Middle East—multi-cropping techniques learnt by the early Arabs in the Sindh region diversified and improved agricultural yields in the Tigris–Euphrates basin.[39] Nor does the recent work of B.D. Chattopadhyaya and others confirm Habib's characterization of a static, or regressive, 'feudal' condition prevalent in South Asia in the pre-Sultanate period.[40] In fact, to comprehend the implications of Irfan

[37] Chetan Singh, 'Well-irrigation Methods in Medieval Panjab: The Persian Wheel Reconsidered', *Indian Economic and Social History Review*, 22 (1985), pp. 73–87.

[38] See Irfan Habib, 'Classifying Pre-Colonial India', *Journal of Peasant Studies*, vol. 12 (1985), p. 51, where the author recognized the tensions in his argument. Habib notes, '. . . "Indian Feudalism" very obviously did not undergo a breakdown: it was overwhelmed by external conquest, which supplanted it by a new formation, in which its survivors had a definite, though subordinate, place. Such a radical consequence of an external intrusion may strike one as somehow non-dialectical; but such events are numerous in history. One cannot naturally use modern political frontiers to demarcate the external from the internal; but even to assume that all social change must come as a result of the internal contradictions of a formation alone would be a grave error.'

[39] Andrew M. Watson, *Agricultural Innovation in the Early Islamic World (The Diffusion of Crops and Farming Techniques, 700–1100)* (Cambridge: Cambridge University Press, 1983).

[40] B.D. Chattopadhyaya, *The Making of Early Medieval India* (Delhi: Oxford

Habib's arguments we have to follow them to their conclusion: if a static Indian society was transformed by 'outside' technological interventions in the thirteenth century, then the institutions on the basis of which a centralized state mechanism appropriated the surplus from the countryside, the *iqṭā'* and the *kharāj*, were also honed in Iran and Afghanistan. It may not have been Islamic egalitarian ideas that 'revolutionized' Indian society in the thirteenth century; it was now conquerors and immigrants from outside the pale of South Asian systems of exchange and production that revitalized a dormant society and economy. Both these remain extremely problematic, overlapping statements.

Many of Irfan Habib's rich insights were diluted by his generalizations. He was, for example, very careful in stating that the subjects of the Delhi Sultans included a variety of different social groups, often with contradictory economic and political interests. But his research also diminished the importance of this heterogeneity by underlining that the fundamental class contradiction in the 'medieval Indian system' was binary: between the subjects on the one hand and a rapacious ruling class on the other.[41] In this social formation it was the land revenue imposed by the state and its ruling elite that marked the great dividing line between producers and consumers of goods and capital. The intensity of the contradiction and the relative strength of one class fluctuated in relation to the other. The ability of the state to impose its coercive tax demand on its subjects was the index which was used to determine the relationship between two protagonists, polarised as two monolithic social units placed along a class divide. Unfortunately, it is almost impossible to ignore the fact that this class divide cuts a path not far removed from Mohammad Habib's communitarian divisions, where the ruling class is Muslim and the subjects Hindu.

University Press, 1994, 1997 reprint). See also the collection of articles on the subject in B.P. Sahu, ed., *Land System and Rural Society in Early India* (Delhi: Manohar, 1997).

[41] For the context in which Habib used the term 'medieval Indian system'; see his 'Economic History of the Delhi Sultanate', especially p. 298, and 'Classifying Pre-Colonial India', pp. 44–53, especially pp. 49–52.

The shifts in theoretical reasoning in the historiography of the Delhi Sultanate are slighter than they sometimes appear. But the nuanced differences are important as well. The next section suggests the moments of convergence and divergence in this historiography as it studies the manner in which different scholars use the literary materials available to them from the thirteenth and fourteenth century as historical sources.

Reading the Persian Evidence

One of the main reasons why historians treat the establishment of the Delhi Sultanate as an important new development in Indian history is that the evidence from the thirteenth century onwards is markedly different from that of earlier periods. Historians of the sixth through the twelfth centuries rely primarily on epigraphic, numismatic, and archaeological sources. Of these, donative and commemorative inscriptions are most used by historians, but their fragmentary character does not facilitate the writing of narrative or chronological accounts of large regions. Attempts to overcome some of this lacuna, especially with regard to a political history of these early centuries, by reconstituting genealogies from texts in the *itihāsa-purānic* tradition into dynastic lists, and seeking corroboration for these in epigraphic and numismatic evidence, have, however, remained extremely superficial and unreliable.[42] Problems of 'reliability' in literary texts have forced historians towards epigraphic and numismatic sources to produce histories of the social and political life of small communities. Efforts at generalizing from this data have been more difficult; contradictory conclusions have generated some fierce historiographical debates.[43] To a large extent, therefore, the source material available for the period prior to the establishment of the Delhi Sultanate has encouraged

[42] David P. Henige, 'Some Phantom Dynasties of Early and Medieval India: Epigraphic Evidence and the Abhorrence of a Vacuum', *Bulletin of the School of Oriental and African Studies*, 38 (1975), pp. 525–49. For a useful discussion of this problem, see Cynthia Talbot, *Precolonial India in Practice: Society, Region, and Identity in Medieval Andhra* (Delhi: Oxford University Press, 2001), pp. 11–16.

[43] For a representative of the pan-Indian, epicentric interpretation of this period, see R.S. Sharma, *Indian Feudalism c. A.D. 300–1200* (Delhi: Macmillan India Ltd., 1963, 1980 reprint); idem, *Urban Decay in India (c.300-c. 1000)*

the writing of a history that studies material culture and local communities in the *longue durée*, one that is amenable to structuralist analysis and generalization through relatively static models.[44]

The Persian chronicles of the thirteenth century provide evidence which is quite the opposite in quality to the epigraphic–archaeological. These histories, *ta'rīkh* (plural, *tawārīkh*), narrate events which have the courts of the rulers and their capitals as their major focus (see Appendix). In other words, the history of all of 'Hindustan'—the Punjab and Ganga–Jamuna plain—is observed through what is usually a very narrow prism. Interesting vignettes, together with broad generalizations, obscure the small human experience on which the authors of the *tawārīkh* of the Sultanate period usually base their narratives. Indeed, modern practitioners of the trade further whittle down this information to produce narratives of gripping wars and administrative policies. Despite their larger historiographic canvas, these histories remain quite skeletal in comparison with the details on local conditions collated from inscriptions of the time prior to Sultanate rule. But, in contrast with an earlier time period within which the historiographic world was more circumscribed, the *tawārīkh* of the Delhi Sultans have facilitated the production of narratives of state formation and institutions that are usually interpreted as providing the robust structures characteristic of this period.[45]

(Delhi: Manohar, 1987); for a regional, processual interpretation see B.D. Chattopadhyaya, *The Making of Early Medieval India*; and for a decentred, 'segmentary' interpretation that distinguishes between a 'ritual' imperial centre and 'real' power at the local level, see Burton Stein, *Peasant State and Society in Medieval South India* (Delhi: Oxford University Press, 1980).

[44] It is, therefore, not altogether surprising that a historian whose work is strongly influenced by these debates should organize articles in his book on state formations along different 'models': the Asiatic mode of production model, the Indian historiographical model, Indian feudalism, segmentary state, the patrimonial state and the 'integrationist paradigm'. See Hermann Kulke, ed., *The State in India 1000–1700* (Delhi: Oxford University Press, 1995, 1997 reprint); and idem, 'Fragmentation and Segmentation versus Integration? Reflections on the Concepts of Indian Feudalism and the Segmentary State in Indian History', *Studies in History*, 4 (1982), pp. 237–63.

[45] The expansive canvas of Persian chronicles has effectively relegated epigraphic, numismatic, architectural, and archaeological evidence to a secondary, corroborative role in the work of most historians. Barring John S. Deyell,

As a result, the general conviction once prevalent amongst historians of the Delhi Sultanate—that the twelfth century marked the beginning of a 'Muslim' period—is hardly diminished by the more recent practice of referring to these years as 'medieval'. The presence of Persian source materials that draw upon textual traditions, worked out in the central Islamic lands from the eighth century, has helped to confirm the impression that the Ghurid conquests introduced novel political, social, economic, and religious systems into the subcontinent. The argument for a dramatic change, an economic and commercial resurgence, brought about by a centralized Sultanate state that ruled over large areas, is consolidated by a scholarship that argues that the earlier period was feudal, politically fragmented, and regressive in its social and economic aspects.[46] But even as the feudal model is undergoing revision, interpretation of the Delhi Sultanate and the historiographical intersection with Persian evidence—as we have already seen in Irfan Habib's work—has remained remarkably stable.

This is surprising because there are actually fairly dissimilar perceptions concerning the nature and value of the chronicles available for a study of the Delhi Sultanate. On the one hand, Peter Hardy has

---

Living Without Silver: The Monetary History of Early Medieval North India (Delhi: Oxford University Press, 1990)—and he uses textual materials very selectively—few scholars show any confidence with numismatic or epigraphic information. Note, for example, the contrast between the works of Y. Subbarayalu, *Political Geography of the Chola Country* (Madras: State Department of Archaeology, Government of Tamilnadu, 1973); James Heitzman, *Gifts of Power: Temples, Politics and Economy in Medieval South India* (Delhi: Oxford University Press, 1997); and Cynthia Talbot, *Precolonial India in Practice*, on the one hand, and Pushpa Prasad, *Sanskrit Inscriptions of Delhi Sultanate, 1191–1526* (Delhi: Oxford University Press, 1990), on the other. While Subbarayalu, Heitzman, and Talbot 'mapped' their epigraphic information spatially and temporally to indicate regional variations and historical change, Pushpa Prasad organized all the Sanskrit inscriptions from the modern state of Uttar Pradesh chronologically, as if they were a linear [textual] narrative. Without re-indexing Pushpa Prasad's monograph along more specific geographical and temporal contexts, the reader is unable to grasp the history of local conditions—precisely the area where inscriptional evidence can be particularly valuable.

46 A dominant idea in the research of Irfan Habib (references cited above), and *The Cambridge Economic History, vol. 1*, p. xiii.

warned that medieval texts used by modern scholars do not contain answers to their presentist questions. To paraphrase his arguments: since documentary evidence was absent, and Sultanate texts in prose and poetry fell far short of modern standards of objectivity, these eulogies, these works of romance, adventure, and theology cannot be used to write serious political, and economic histories.[47] Literary texts provide insights into the metaphysical, subjective realm of ideas, attitudes, and perceptions, not into the material structures of society and state. Historians like Irfan Habib, Khaliq Nizami, and Harbans Mukhia disagree with Peter Hardy.[48] Indeed, in their opinion, some texts are biased, whereas others are extraordinarily sound in their marshalling of information and causative reasoning. For example, according to Irfan Habib, Ẓiyā' al-Dīn Baranī's 'factual account [was] correct in all substantive matters' and his 'analysis [was] . . . sound'.[49] And, writing centuries before Marx, Baranī astutely anticipated ideas of dialectical materialism: he 'is a believer in the reality of class conflicts', Habib noted, 'stand though he may on the wrong side of the barricades'.[50] Although Hardy and Habib were diametrically opposed to each other in their conclusions about the merits of Ẓiyā' al-Dīn Baranī's works as a source, both evaluated these texts from a positivist, literalist methodology. According to one, Baranī's biases made him an unreliable source; according to the other, despite his own social predilections, Baranī's analysis was sound. At one level, the methodologies of the two scholars do not differ; the parameters against which they evaluate reliability do.

Hardy's doubts about the credibility of the Persian evidence were enabling: they allowed him to make innovative suggestions on how historians could critically use narrative sources. Hardy had criticized scholars who expected their 'source [to] supply us with information ready made' but his own recommendation to scholars was that they

[47] Peter Hardy, *Historians of Medieval India.*

[48] Irfan Habib, 'Baranī's Theory of the History of the Delhi Sultanate'; Khaliq Ahmad Nizami, 'Ziya-ud-din Barani'; and Harbans Mukhia, *Historians and Historiography during the Reign of Akbar* (New Delhi: Vikas Publishing House, 1976), pp. 1–40.

[49] Irfan Habib, 'Price Regulations of 'Alā'uddīn Khaljī', p. 393.

[50] Idem, 'Baranī's Theory', p. 101.

should try 'to gain an insight into the mentality of people unlike [our]self' because that is what the 'authors reveal, explicitly or through deduction . . .'.[51] If, in his emphasis to stay close to the evidence, Hardy's position remained naively empirical in the 1960s, by the 1990s he felt that even this exercise was impossible. Impressed by extreme postmodernist interpretations of reality, as individuated, Hardy now suggested that texts were 'representational of, rather than cognitive of, reality', that the historian could never access an 'unmediated "real world" '.[52] The suggestion that 'reality' may have slipped away amidst its many representations was perhaps an inevitable conclusion from a historian who remained dissatisfied with the quality of sources on the Delhi Sultanate.

The difference between the researchs of Hardy and Irfan Habib can perhaps be best explained by their differing approaches to the study of the moment of conquest and establishment of the Sultanate at Delhi. Hardy's attempt to understand the nature of authoritative relationships that were established with the conquered elite in the thirteenth century was frustrated because he could not go beyond what appeared to be formal stylistic tropes of describing political participants, negotiations, and engagements.[53] The actions of the Ghurid military commanders, for example, were described in the Persian chronicles in a style very similar to the one used a century earlier for the Ghaznavid lords. But Hardy carried out no independent investigation to verify whether Ghaznavid and Ghurid commanders shared organizational features. Nor, for that matter, did the depiction of Ghurid military lords as neo-Ghaznavids lead Hardy to ask if this

[51] Peter Hardy, *Historians of Medieval India*, p. 131. It needs to be stressed that Hardy's notion of 'mentality'—religious, ethical, and aesthetic ideas—was very distant from the *Annales* understanding of *mentalité*.

[52] Peter Hardy, 'Approaches to Pre-Modern Indo-Muslim Historical Writing: Some Reconsiderations in 1990–91', in Peter Robb, ed., *Society and Ideology: Essays in South Asian History presented to K.A. Ballhatchet* (Delhi: Oxford University Press, 1994 reprint), p. 70.

[53] Peter Hardy, 'Growth of Authority over a Conquered Political Elite: Early Delhi Sultanate as a Possible Case Study', in John F. Richards, ed., *Kingship and Authority in South Asia* (Delhi: Oxford University Press, 1998 reprint), pp. 216-41.

'make-over' by the Persian chroniclers glossed over some uncomfortable aspects of the Ghurids. For the better part, Hardy noted the discursive stance present in his sources but never moved beyond them.

Irfan Habib, on the other hand, also noted that the Ghaznavid and Ghurid political systems differed, but, having said that, he assumed a linear transmission of institutions from an earlier to a later regime. Habib argued that since the 'institution' of the *iqṭā'*, a military assignment, was previously known to the Ghaznavids, Mu'izz al-Dīn Ghūrī 'must have become familiar at Ghaznīn with the traditions of the empire of which that city had been the capital'.[54] In fact, Habib argued for an even longer history for the *iqṭā'*: it was a term, 'Arabic in origin [that] represents [a] long-established institution . . . of the polity of Islamic countries'.[55] To take Habib's interpretation seriously we would have to ignore three facts: first, that the history of *iqṭā'* is quite discontinuous—whereas the term in fact carried a host of different meanings before the usage of the Buyid and Seljuqid regimes in Iran and Iraq in the tenth and eleventh centuries gave it the meaning of a revenue-military assignment.[56] Second, that even under the Buyids and Seljuqids the meaning of *iqṭā'* was not stable; normative prescriptions did not coincide with political practice. The advice of the

[54] Irfan Habib, 'Formation of the Sultanate Ruling Class of the Thirteenth Century', *Medieval India 1*, p. 7.

[55] Idem, 'The Social Distribution of Landed Property', *Essays in Indian History*, pp. 59–108, see especially p. 82.

[56] In particular see the writings of Claude Cahen on the *iqṭā'*: Claude Cahen, 'L'évolution de l'Iqṭā' de IXe au XIIIe siècle', *Annales: Economies, Sociétés, Civilisations*, 8 (1953), pp. 25–52; idem, 'Au seuil de la troisiẹme année: réflexions sur l'usage du mot "Féodalité" ', *Journal of the Economic and Social History of the Orient*, 3 (1960), pp. 2–20; idem, 'Iḳṭā'', *Encyclopaedia of Islam* (Leiden: E.J. Brill, second edition, 1956–), s.v. See also, A.K.S. Lambton, 'Reflections on the *Iqṭa*', in George Makdisi, ed., *Arabic and Islamic Studies in Honour of H.A.R. Gibb*, Leiden; idem, *Landlord and Peasant in Persia: A Study of Land Tenure and Land Revenue Administration* (London: Oxford University Press, 1953); and C.E. Bosworth, 'Military Organisation under the Būyids of Persia and Iraq', *Oriens* 18–19, pp. 143–67, also reprinted in his *The Medieval History of Iran, Afghanistan and Central Asia* (London, Variorum Reprints, 1977).

Seljuqid *wazīr*, Niẓām al-Mulk, on the rights and responsibilities of those who were 'granted' *iqṭā*'s needs to be located in the context of his efforts to restrain the traditional claims of the Seljuqid ruling family and their dependents to appanages and autonomous territories.[57] Finally, we would also need to ignore the strong evidence which suggests that the *iqṭā*' was *not* used by the Ghaznavids as a mode of payment to military Governors, especially after 388/998 and Maḥmūd's accession. The question of their influence on the Ghurids does not, therefore, arise.[58] The representation of autonomous territories and governorships as *iqṭā's* under the Ghurids in a thirteenth-century text, such as Jūzjānī's *Ṭabaqāt-i Nāṣirī*, raises a separate set of historiographical problems that cannot be obviated by a simple collation of terms which actually carry a variety of different contextual referents.

But let us leave these facts aside for the moment and concentrate on Habib's argument. For Habib the *iqṭā*' was an important institution that enabled political centralization. Decontextualizing Niẓām al-Mulk's advice, Habib froze it as an ideal model and interpreted it as one of the primary institutions through which 'Islamic states' collected revenue resources from the peasantry and distributed them amongst military commanders in exchange for service. It then became a part of his systemic analysis of medieval political formations wherein the interests of a parasitic ruling class were, in different degrees, protected by the institutions of the state. Although Habib's account was impeccably logical within a Marxist framework of analysis (and,

[57] Niẓām al-Mulk, *Siyāsat Nāma*, translated by Hubert Darke, *The Book of Government or Rules for Kings* (London: Routledge and Kegan Paul, 1978 reprint), p. 32. Compare his remarks here with those on pp. 99–100, 102. See also W. Barthold, *Turkestan down to the Mongol Invasion* (London, E.J.W. Gibb Memorial Trust, Luzac and Company, 1977 reprint), pp. 309–10 and A.K.S. Lambton, 'The Internal Structure of the Saljuq Empire', in J.A. Boyle, ed., *Cambridge History of Iran, vol. 5: The Saljuq and Mongol Periods* (Cambridge: University Press, 1968), pp. 218–19, 231–5; and idem, *Landlord and Peasant*, pp. 53–76. As a contrast, note Irfan Habib's interpretation: 'Iqṭā's: Distribution of Revenue Resources among the Ruling Class', *The Cambridge Economic History, vol. 1*, pp. 68–75.

[58] Niẓām al-Mulk, *Siyāsat Nāma*, pp. 99–100. See also Clifford Edmund Bosworth, *The Ghaznavids: Their Empire in Afghanistan and Eastern Iran, 994–1040* (Beirut: Librairie du Liban, 1973 reprint), pp. 66, 124–5.

ironically, very close to Moreland's views on the subject), it was impossible to sustain because the 'institution' that Habib identified lacked any internal coherence. Habib therefore found it difficult to explain why the institution of the *iqṭā*' altered its character from one regime to another. Contradicting his own argument that the *iqṭā*' enabled centralization, Habib suggested elsewhere that the form of the institution varied either because of the inherent nature of the individual polity—the Ghurids and the Lodis, for example, were clannish and the *iqṭā*' reflected this trait—or because of the individual predilections of the monarch—'Alā' al-Dīn Khalajī's authoritarian interventions in the administration of the *iqṭā*' were in contrast to Fīrūz Shāh Tughluq's timid concessions to the nobility.[59] The confusion in Habib's work was caused not by the Persian evidence but by the interpretive structures into which he sought to mould it. Even as he argued for the factual accuracy of his arguments, Habib reconstituted information on the *iqṭā*'*s* until they were far removed from the social contexts of power and authoritative relationships in which they were located.

I have focused specifically here on Peter Hardy and Irfan Habib only because their work serves to illustrate some of the historiographical problems that have much wider currency. Inability to move beyond the categories of depiction and analysis present in literary texts is as widespread as its obverse: a priori arguments that are often teleological or anachronistic and cannot be sustained by the evidence. It is ironic that while conventional political history on the Delhi Sultanate has shown few signs of change, there is much that historians can learn from recent research on mysticism.

Indeed, a large part of the conventional historiography on mysticism shares an empiricist bent also present in political history; whether it was Mohammad Habib weeding out 'genuine' from 'fabricated' records of conversations between mystic saints, *malfūẓāt*, or P.M. Currie searching for the historical Mu'īn al-Dīn Chishtī.[60] But over the last few years mystic records—both *malfūẓāt* and biographical

59 Irfan Habib, 'Iqṭā's'. For further comments see Sunil Kumar, 'When Slaves were Nobles', pp. 28–9.

60 Mohammad Habib, 'Chishti Mystic Records', P.M. Currie, *The Shrine and Cult of Mu'in al-Din Chishti of Ajmer* (Delhi: Oxford University Press, 1989).

encyclopaedias or *tazkirāt* (singular, *tazkira*)—have started to be read more carefully for their rhetorical significance. The work of Carl Ernst and, more recently, Bruce Lawrence, has paid attention to the stylistic form, content, and narrative intent of *ṣūfī* texts to show how important they were in the constitution of a Shaykh's authority. Other than a 'historiographical' approach to the sources, Ernst also emphasized the need for a micro-study, 'an intensive study of a tightly circumscribed field', to better grapple with the several perspectives of different accounts from a central location.[61]

Since the style, rhetorical content, and contextual provenance of the *tawārīkh* of the Delhi rulers is so different from *ṣūfī* texts, Carl Ernst's methodology cannot be simply transposed into a study of the Sultanate. The twin vectors of his analysis—the need to pay attention to the narrative content of texts together with an intensive study of a tightly circumscribed field—however, urges us away from the study of large 'ready-made topics'—such as state, society, and administration—to a study of their components. What is required is an effort to go beyond the narratives of the Persian chronicles, which seldom waver from their preoccupation with the King, his court, and events that affected these.

Certainly, in a text like the *Ṭabaqāt-i Nāṣirī* the dominance of the state in the social and political world of north India was quite unproblematically narrated. Baranī's *Ta'rīkh-i Fīrūz Shāhī*, on the other hand, was only slightly more complicated in first denying the state any doctrinal legitimation and then allowing for its hegemony under the plea of the 'welfare' of the Muslim community, *maṣlaḥa*.[62]

[61] Carl Ernst, *Eternal Garden: Mysticism, History, and Politics at a South Asian Sufi Center* (Albany: State University of New York Press, 1992), p. xxviii and chapters 4 and 5, pp. 62–93. Bruce B Lawrence, 'Biography and the Seventeenth-century Qadiriyya of North India', in A.L. Dallapicola and S.Z. Lallemant, eds, *Islam and Indian Regions* (Stuttgart: Steiner, 1993); and Marcia K. Hermansen and Bruce B. Lawrence, 'Indo-Persian Tazkiras as Memorative Communications', *Beyond Turk and Hindu*, pp. 149–75.

[62] The philosophic foundations of statecraft informing the *Ta'rīkh* were developed by Baranī in his *Fatāwā-yi Jahāndārī*, edited by Afsar Saleem Khan (Lahore Research Society of Pakistan, University of the Punjab, 1972). On the subject of *maṣlaḥa*, see the elaborate advice of Baranī in the *Fatāwā*, pp. 219–20. This sentiment is more obliquely incorporated by Barani in his *Ta'rīkh*.

Baranī's disingenuous intellectual resolution has its roots in the more complicated efforts of jurists to legitimize the emergence of Sultanates in the late 'Abbāsid period and it remained a parody of classic normative texts like al-Ghazālī's *Naṣīḥat al-Mulūk*.[63] But ultimately, the opinions of both Jūzjānī and Baranī remained utterly derivative in delinking the hegemony of the state from the politics of its subjects and carrying a rejection of all revolutionary change. In turn, careful, empirically-minded scholars like Peter Jackson were bound by the narratives of the Persian *tawārīkh* and the great divide between state and society. Their work therefore remained a 'political and military history' of the state.[64]

It is possible, however, to go beyond the statist discourse of the Persian chronicles. A careful scrutiny of their narratives on the hegemonic state reveals, for example, niggling inconsistencies and contradictions, efforts made by different authors to gloss over awkward bits of information. Sometimes, these contradictions can be enlarged by information from other types of sources. But to go beyond the narrative discourse in these *tawārīkh* we need to disaggregate their information and study the components of the subjects that they mention without reifying them into an anachronistic modern usage.

In Jūzjānī's *Ṭabaqāt-i Nāṣirī*, for example, information on political elites under the early Delhi Sultans is included in three different contexts. The single largest record of military commanders is in the twenty-second section of the *Ṭabaqāt*, where the author provides relatively elaborate biographical accounts of the military slaves,

---

See, for example, Ẓiyā' al-Dīn Baranī, *Ta'rīkh-i Fīrūz Shāhī* edited by Sayyid Ahmad Khan (Calcutta: Bibliotheca Indica, 1860–2), pp. 41–4; edited by Shaykh Abdul Rashid (Aligarh: Dept. of History, University Press, 1957), vol. 1, pp. 49–53. For its reference in the advice given by Sultan Balban to his younger son Bughra Khān, see ibid., edited by Khan, p. 103; edited by Rashid, vol. 1, p. 120.

[63] al-Ghazālī, *Naṣīḥat al-Mulūk*, translated by F.R.C. Bagley (London: Oxford University Press, 1971 reprint). See also Peter Hardy, 'Unity and Variety in Indo-Islamic and Perso-Islamic Civilization: Some Ethical and Political Ideas of Ḍiya' al-Dīn Baranī of Delhī, of al-Ghazālī and of Naṣīr al-Dīn Tūsī Compared', *Iran*, 16 (1978), pp. 127–36.

[64] Peter Jackson, *The Delhi Sultanate.*

bandagān (singular, *banda*) of Sultan Shams al-Dīn Iltutmish.[65] There are also taciturn lists of nobles and military commanders at the end of the reign of Mu'izz al-Dīn Ghūrī and Iltutmish, and at the beginning of Nāṣir al-Dīn Maḥmūd's reign.[66] Finally, there are random references to military commanders throughout the detailed chronology of wars, rebellions, and conspiracies that constitutes the bulk of the *Ṭabaqāt-i Nāṣirī*.

No simple collation of this evidence is possible because we need to remain cognizant of the deliberate manner in which Jūzjānī marshalled his information. The biographies of the Shamsī slaves in the twenty-second section of his text were provided by Jūzjānī as a gift, a 'memorial' for the many favours he had received from these notables at different times in his life.[67] Moreover, although all the individuals mentioned were military slaves, they were not necessarily contemporaries, and their experiences in training and upbringing had made some *bandagān* very different from others. Still more complicated are the lists of nobles at the end and the beginning of the reigns of the Sultans. Jūzjānī nowhere explains his reasons for including some military commanders and excluding others, and there is little unity amongst those mentioned in these lists. In Mu'izz al-Dīn and Nāṣir al-Dīn's case, military commanders were mentioned together with relatives and others who were close to the monarch, *aqribā'*.[68] For Iltutmish, some manuscripts carried a separate list of his children.[69] In the case of all three, free military commanders of various backgrounds jostled with the occasional mention of slaves.

Finally, the largest number of references to military commanders and other notables is dispersed throughout Jūzjānī's narrative. These random references are extremely important because, by the standards of the Delhi Sultanate, the *Ṭabaqāt-i Nāṣirī* is an unusually detailed

[65] Minhāj-i Sirāj Jūzjānī, *Ṭabaqāt-i Nāṣirī*, edited by Abdul Hay Habibi (Kabul: Anjuman-i Tarikh-i Afghanistan, 1963-4, 2 vols.), vol. 2, pp. 3–89.

[66] Ibid., vol. 1, pp. 405–7, 450–1, 475–7.

[67] Ibid., vol. 2, p. 3.

[68] Ibid., vol. 1, pp. 405–6, 475–7. The editor provides alternative readings of names in the footnotes to the respective lists. These are extremely important in deciphering individuals and their identities.

[69] Ibid., vol. 1, pp. 450–2 and the relevant footnotes.

(and dry) chronicle. It mentions a large number of individuals in the context of significant events that occurred in the reigns of the respective Sultans. The fragmented nature of the *Ṭabaqāt* (see Appendix for details) also meant that Jūzjānī provided a narrative of the same event from the perspective of different protagonists within the various sections of his chronicle.[70] Thus, if an individual was overlooked in one context, he could be mentioned in another, even if only in passing. It is curious, therefore, to find that the narrative does not carry even a fleeting reference to some of the great military commanders included in the list of notables at the end of Iltutmish's reign. Was this, as some scholars have suggested, a consequence of Jūzjānī's bias against specific individuals?[71] If so, how did exorcising them from his narrative help when the author was forced to acknowledge their eminence in his list of the Sultan's elites? Other than trying to work out Jūzjānī's disposition towards particular notables, should we perhaps ask whether an individual's social renown automatically translated into political patronage under Iltutmish? In other words, Iltutmish's court was certainly a sanctuary for many social luminaries fleeing from Mongol invasions. Their presence leant splendour to his court and Jūzjānī would have found it profitable to broadcast this fact in his chronicle. But, given the nature of the early Sultanate, was it equally politic for Iltutmish to grant these distinguished people important positions of command in his fledgling state? Would their political marginalization explain why Jūzjānī's narrative of events ignored some of them?

Questions of this nature demand a detailed investigation of the composition of Sultanate elites, their deployment, the types and varying content of patronage, the cultural meaning of service, and the construction of authoritative relationships. This would also take us into more general problems that cannot be posed simply as the biases of one author, the institutional structures of the state, or the royal

[70] On the *ṭabaqāt* genre of history see Tarif Khalidi, *Arabic Historical Thought in the Classical Period* (Cambridge: Cambridge University Press, 1994), pp. 46–8.

[71] Peter Jackson, 'The *Mamluk* Institution in Early Muslim India', *Journal of the Royal Asiatic Society* (1990), pp. 340–58; and Irfan Habib, 'Formation of the Sultanate Ruling Class', pp. 1–21.

'policies' of a monarch. Since the composition of elites, patronage, and the cultural context of service changed according to the time and location of the various political participants, every facet of this investigation would also need to be located temporally and spatially within the history and geography of the Delhi Sultanate. Perhaps, most critically, disaggregating the information on political elites in this manner allows historians the opportunity of investigating the social and ideological contexts in which Sultanate political structures were embedded.

The state-centred organization of information in chronicles, in South Asia as well as in the central Islamic lands, has seriously deterred research in this direction. In fact, an influential body of work on early Muslim society and polity has argued for a remarkable chasm between the political and social worlds during the Caliphates of the Umayyads, the 'Abbāsids, and the succeeding Sultanates. Taking their extreme reliance on personnel of 'servile' origin and/or military slaves into consideration, these scholars suggested that the early Islamic polities created a 'conquest society', one of whose features was a distancing of social elites from the 'formal' trappings of power.[72] The central juxtaposition between 'formal' and 'informal' power has also carried the assumption that the state was the only legitimate locus of authority. Any disciplinary formation outside it showed little internal coherence—which is why it remained 'informal'. It had, at best, a residual power, evident when the state was in decline.

Many of these assumptions have been challenged by scholars studying the histories of urban communities in Islamdom. Their research is not just reliant on the *tawārīkh* of the court. They use local histories where available, and *tazkirāt*, biographical dictionaries

[72] For a sophisticated arguing of this point see Patricia Crone, *Slaves on Horses: The Evolution of the Islamic Polity* (Cambridge: University Press, 1980), especially pp. 82–91. See also Daniel Pipes, *Slave Soldiers and Islam: The Genesis of a Military System* (New Haven: Yale University Press, 1981). Earlier versions of the argument can be found in N.J. Coulson, 'Doctrine and Practice in Islamic Law: One Aspect of the Problem', *Bulletin of the School of Oriental and African Studies*, 18 (1956), pp. 211–26; and H.F. Amedroz, 'The Office of Kadi in the *Ahkam Sultaniyya* of Mawardi', *Journal of the Royal Asiatic Society* (1910), pp. 761–96.

of urban notables: poets, religious scholars, sufis, and, more generally, the *ahl-i qalam*, people of the pen—socially eminent people through whom a region gained fame as a cultural centre. In reconstructing the histories of urban elites, scholars like Bulliet, Bosworth, Lapidus, Cahen, Chamberlain, Frye, and Petry developed the idea of a close association between social status and *'ilm*, knowledge.[73] This was knowledge gained through an education in *madrasas* and/or through a peripatetic schooling from a variety of masters in far-flung areas. 'Education' included a specialized knowledge of the religious sciences and law, but it also meant embracing a cultural code of comportment that was an intrinsic part of the transformative exercise of 'schooling'. As a result, it was not merely in appreciation of an individual's scholarly accomplishments—a possession of 'formal' knowledge, as it were—that an urban notable was distinguished from his (and, more rarely, her) peers. One did not need to be terribly well read to belong to the circle of urban notables; descent from a family of *'ulamā'*, or administrative control of a mosque or *madrasa*, were also eminent qualifications. Family pedigree, wealth, comportment, and social

[73] Richard W. Bulliet, *The Patricians of Nishapur: A Study in Medieval Islamic Social History* (Cambridge: Harvard University Press, 1972); idem, *Islam: The View from the Edge* (New York: Columbia University Press, 1994); Clifford Edmund Bosworth, *The Ghaznavids*, pp. 145–202; Ira Lapidus, *Muslim Cities in the Later Middle Ages* (Cambridge: Harvard University Press, 1967); Claude Cahen, *Pre-Ottoman Turkey*, translated by J. Jones-Williams (New York: Taplinger, 1968); Michael Chamberlain, *Knowledge and Social Practice in Medieval Damascus, 1190–1350* (Cambridge: University Press, 1994); Richard Frye, *Bukhara: The Medieval Achievement* (Norman: University of Oklahama Press, 1965); and Carl Petry, *The Civilian Elite of Cairo in the Late Middle Ages* (Princeton: University Press, 1981). Other than local histories and *tazkirāt*, records concerning charitable endowments, *waqfnāma*, have also been used to chart the histories of urban communities by some of the above-mentioned historians, and by Jonathan P. Berkey, *The Transmission of Knowledge in Medieval Cairo: A Social History of Islamic Education* (Princeton: University Press, 1992). Also see, more generally, Marshall G.S. Hodgson, 'The A'yān-Amīr System', in idem, *The Venture of Islam: Conscience and History in a World Civilization, vol. II, The Expansion of Islam in the Middle Periods* (Chicago: University Press, 1974), pp. 91–135 and Roy P. Mottahedeh, *Loyalty and Leadership in an Early Islamic Society* (Princeton: University Press, 1980).

decorum, as much as scholastic qualification—together and separately—gained public esteem, and they were crucial signifiers in any local acknowledgement of elite status.

The history of urban communities in the central Islamic lands emphasizes the importance of these notables in the social and political life of towns as dispersed as Nishapur, Bukhara, Damascus, Cairo, and pre-Ottoman Anatolia.[74] But the political importance of urban notables in the city was equally dependent upon a number of (inconstant) variables: the social composition of the city's residents, the internal coherence of its elite groups, their investments—moral and economic—in the city, their success in mobilizing public support, the strategic importance of the town to the economy and politics of the region, and the ability of elite groups to impress their importance upon the local military ruler. Certainly, up to the Mongol invasions in the thirteenth century, the degree of autonomy that the notables negotiated for themselves worked to the credit of the city as well. Although fraught with uncertainties and a careful balancing of interests amongst factions of the urban elite, these notables were frequently able to ensure long stretches of social and economic stability in the midst of the political misfortunes that plagued ruling dynasties.

In South Asia the conquest of urban centres by Ghurid commanders went almost apace with the immigration of a wide variety of people from the eastern regions of the *Dār al-Islām*. Although the ruling elites encouraged and patronized this immigration, it would be a mistake to assume that there was any internal coherence amongst these immigrants or between them and the ruling elite. The fashioning of composite societies in the Ghurid towns has a history that is as tumultuous as the processes involved in the making of the Sultanate of Delhi. And an intrinsic part of the consolidation of recently annexed territories was the negotiation of new relationships between dispersed urban communities and Delhi.

How does one study these processes? Unlike the central Islamic lands, there are no local histories of urban settlements in South Asia from the early thirteenth century and hence no accessible narrative on social and political developments within local communities. The first

[74] Ibid.

tazkira, the *Siyar al-Awliyā'* of Amīr Khwurd, was completed sometime in 751/1350, and the systematic production of such texts began only in the sixteenth century.[75] The late development of this genre of Persianate literature in the early Delhi Sultanate may be related to the relatively brief experience of many cities as settlements with 'Muslim' residents. But their precocious intellectual and social dynamism was captured in the *malfūẓ* literature, a genre unique to the subcontinent.[76]

The *malfūẓāt* record the discourses of *ṣūfi* Shaykhs to a large mixed assembly of *ṣūfi* adepts, novitiates, and casual visitors. These were rhetorical, didactic texts organized to impress readers with the spiritual merits of their protagonists (see Appendix). Noteworthy amongst the early authors of *malfūẓāt* were Amīr Ḥasan Sijzī and Ḥamīd Qalandar, who were extremely successful in advertising the excellent qualities of Niẓām al-Dīn Awliyā' (died 725/1325) and Naṣīr al-Dīn Chirāgh (died 757/1356) in their respective texts.[77] The authors argued for the superlative stature of their protagonists by comparing them favourably with other pious individuals of renown. This authority was always contingent upon the ability of the Shaykhs and their panegyrists to successfully relate their narratives to socially accepted norms of spirituality and to the historical memory of individuals who were regarded as the repositories of these ideals. These two aspects were crucially interlinked because the elaboration and

[75] Amīr Khwurd, *Siyar al-Awliyā'*, edited by Sayyid Mahdi Ghuri (Lahore: Markaz-i Tahqiqat-i Farsi Iran wa Pakistan, no. 23, Mu'assi-yi Intisharat-i Islami, 1978). This edition is exactly the same as the Delhi, Muhib-i Hind Press, 1302/1885 lithograph. The only difference is in the pagination: the table of contents and introduction have added exactly ten pages to the Lahore edition.

[76] The roots of this literary tradition are obscure. For an interesting argument, see Ishtiaq Ahmad Zilli, 'The Production of Early Malfuzat: Fact and Fiction', in the forthcoming proceedings of the conference 'Patronage in Indo-Persian Culture' Paris, 2001. For a further discussion see the Appendix.

[77] For Niẓām al-Dīn Awliyā', see Amīr Ḥasan Sijzī, *Fawā'id al-Fu'ād*, edited by Khwaja Ḥasan Thani Nizami Dihlawi (Delhi: Urdu Academy, 1990). This reproduces the Lahore edition of M.L. Malik (Lahore: Malik Siraj al-Din and Sons, 1966) exactly, including the pagination and critical commentary. For Naṣīr al-Dīn Chirāgh, see Ḥamīd Qalandar, *Khair al-Majālis*, edited by Khaliq A. Nizami (Aligarh: Department of History, Aligarh University Press, 1959).

canonical justification of the mystical path of the great Shaykhs implied the displacement of some interpretations of Islam and the valorization of others. In particular, the literal, scripturalist interpretation of the *Sharīʿa* by many *ʿulamāʾ* and some *ṣūfis* came under sharp indictment. The teachings of others were hegemonized in the elaboration of a mystical path that was clearly larger and superior to its contemporaries. At the same time there were some individuals whose piety was venerated—people who constituted a fraternity of like-minded individuals and who were regarded as honoured associates of the Shaykhs. The particular discursive stance in the evaluation of individual piety notwithstanding, the *malfūẓāt* contain a considerable amount of detail on the exegesis of 'belief' and a rare account of their exponents—a multitude of jurists, religious scholars, and *ṣūfis*, all trying to enlarge and consolidate their respective constituencies. They inhabited a competitive arena where canonical disputations had far-reaching social and political resonances.[78]

It is certainly possible to refer to these individuals as a 'religious elite' because they were all authoritative figures involved in the realm of the sacred and the spiritual. The prefix of 'Muslim' can also be applied to this elite group, since they were all Muslims invested in studying, practising, and teaching Islam.[79] But a terminology of this

[78] Simon Digby, 'The Sufi Shaikh as a Source of Authority in Medieval India', *Purusartha (Islam and Society in South Asia)*, 9 (1986), pp. 57–77; idem, 'The Sufi Shaikh and the Sultan: A Conflict of Claims to Authority in Medieval India', *Iran*, 28 (1990), pp. 71–81; Bruce B. Lawrence, 'The Earliest Chishtiya and Shaikh Nizam al-Din Awliya', in R.E. Frykenberg, ed., *Delhi Through the Ages* (Delhi: Oxford University Press, 1986), pp. 104–28; Carl Ernst, 'The Textual Formation of Oral Teachings in the Early Chishti Order', and 'The Interpretation of the Sufi Biographical Tradition in India', *The Eternal Garden*, pp. 62–93; and Sunil Kumar, 'Assertions of Authority: A Study of the Discursive Statements of Two Sultans of Delhi', in Muzaffar Alam, *et al.*, eds, *The Making of Indo-Persian Culture: Indian and French Studies* (Delhi: Manohar, 2000), pp. 37–65.

[79] From a large volume of writing wherein *ʿulamāʾ* are described as theologians or clerics, see, as an example, K.M. Ashraf, *Life and Conditions of the People of Hindustan*, p. 102. Ashraf notes that 'the religious class of Islam [*sic*] was composed of a number of important groups, namely the theologians, the ascetics, the Sayyids, the Pirs and their descendants.'

nature also suggests an exclusive, homogeneous world with a relatively neat differentiation between the 'religious' and the 'political'. Perhaps even more crucially, the term occludes any further attempt at problematizing what Islam meant to a dispersed body of Muslims resident in the urban centres of north India in the thirteenth century, synthesising them instead in convenient, but anachronistic and analytically weak communal and cultural typologies. The *malfūẓāt* require us to study instead the social milieu of the early Sultanate, where doctrinal differences did not exist in abstraction from their proponents or their strategies to promote the merits of their teaching. The dominant self-representation of the ruler, carried in his epigraphs, coins, and eulogistic histories, portrayed him as the 'protector of the *Sharī'a*', responsible for constructing schools, mosques, and other public monuments where Muslims could be taught and socialized into accepting an orthopraxis aligned to a scripturalist interpretation of Islam. Although this interpretation had a large body of adherents, there were others who looked to a variety of different Shaykhs as votaries of an alternative disciplinary order legitimated by their own understanding of Islam. Although the *Sharī'a* was equally central in the organization of this order, its interpretation was always uniquely tempered by the special, intuitive genius of its teachers. In the thirteenth century neither Islam nor the Muslim community were monolithic, and the various self-affirmations of piety were articulated as cogent, historical constructions, each championed at the local level by Muslims of varying hues and number.[80]

The political initiative to create coherent forms of administrating these urban communities of Muslims did not lie entirely with the Sultanate. To begin with, in the early thirteenth century, Delhi's authority was relatively novel within select parts of north India. Some cities were under Ghurid control. These had already experienced at least a generation of rule under Mu'izzī lords who had maintained ties

[80] See Sunil Kumar, 'Assertions of Authority'; and Marcia K. Hermansen and Bruce B. Lawrence, 'Indo-Persian Tazkiras as Memorative Communications'. For a more general Islamicate perspective, see Michael Chamberlain, *Knowledge and Social Practice*, and Jonathan P. Berkey, *Popular Preaching and Religion in the Medieval Islamic Near East* (Seattle: University of Washington Press, 2001).

with Ghazni, not Delhi. In those halcyon years, and in the following decades, the military commander who administered an *iqṭā*‘ could not guide his subjects on matters concerning morality and law. Instead, as the *malfūẓāt* clarify, Muslims looked for guidance to the pious in their congregations, ascribing them with honorifics such as *buzurg*, a great man, a learned elder. It was through the acknowledgement of the local congregation that the *‘ulamā’* and *ṣūfī* Shaykhs achieved a respectable status, and the state ignored these local sentiments only at its peril.[81]

The complex manner in which local and imperial assertions of authority intersected can never be charted institutionally. An insight into some of the difficulties involved can be elaborated through the ‘office’ of the *Shaikh al-Islām*, a nebulous figure who seems to have been quite generally a guide, an adjudicator, a keeper of the moral conscience of Muslims under his charge. He checked on teaching imparted in schools and in public discourses, and maintained standards of probity in conformity with the *Sharī‘a*. He was a powerful appointee of the Delhi Sultan and was the cause of much public harassment of *ṣūfīs* in the capital. But the title of *Shaikh al-Islām* was also an honorific conferred by residents of a town to a locally venerated individual. For example, in towns such as Multan and Ajudhan, in the Sindh and Punjab regions, it was these ‘informal’ political figures—pious *ṣūfī* Shaykhs in both instances—who were referred to as *Shaikh al-Islām* and who commanded ‘real’ authority rather than the *qāẓī*.[82] Any consolidation of political authority by the Delhi Sultanate in these regions required careful negotiation with individuals who commanded the allegiance of large congregations which were sometimes extremely jealous of their autonomy. And, despite its representations, this was not a synchronic universe. Through the thirteenth century, both the discourse as well as the relationships between these individuals and the urban communities changed. Nor were these developments

[81] This subject has been little investigated, but for some insightful remarks see Simon Digby, ‘The Sufi Shaikh as a Source of Authority’, and from a slightly different perspective, Richard M. Eaton, *Rise of Islam*; and idem, ‘The Political and Religious Authority’. See also Chapter 4 for details.

[82] For a survey of the early history of the *Shaikh al-Islām* see Richard Bulliet, ‘The Shaykh al-Islam and the Evolution of Islamic Society’, *Studia Islamica*, 35 (1972), pp. 53-67; and Chapter 4 below.

unrelated to transitions in the character of the state and the composition of its ruling elites.[83]

A more carefully nuanced study of local contexts of power also helps to complicate our understanding of Sultanate authority. Take, for example, the well-commented-upon deployment of military slaves by the Delhi Sultans in the thirteenth century. While the dispensation of high offices to *bandagān* has been noticed by several historians, its usage in north India is narrated as a simple extension of political traditions present amongst the Sultanates of the central Islamic lands. It was, in other words, merely a part of a larger 'Muslim tradition' of which the Delhi Sultanate was an adjunct—a formulation that belies any further historical investigation.[84] But in a world where questions of social status were based upon subjective evaluations of an individual's learning, pedigree, and comportment, how did 'Muslims', we are left to wonder, respond to a slave military elite functioning as Governors and military commanders?[85] This question is

[83] This point needs to be underlined, if nothing else to distance it from the synchronic elements present in André Wink's arguments about *fitna*, a system of shifting relationships, sustained negotiations, and strategic alliances amongst local elites and the state through which imperial formations were always constructed in South Asia. In Wink's analysis, the material contexts that had produced a system of fickle loyalties and monetized honours in the cosmopolitan Islamic world over the last millennia were: a highly sophisticated fiscal system, advanced monetization of the economy, extensive trade networks, and a dualist bureaucracy of separate military and fiscal departments. This was in contrast to the sturdy tiers of dependence characteristic of backwater feudal and post-feudal Europe. André Wink, *Land and Sovereignty in India: Agrarian Society and Politics under the Eighteenth-century Maratha Svarājya* (Cambridge: University Press, 1986), pp. 31–4, 153–5, 377–88; and idem, *al-Hind, vol II: The Slave Kings*, p. 183. For a clearer, but equally synchronic, argument on the merits of using *fitna* as a heuristic device to explain and contrast Islamicate systems of power and honour from West European ones, see Michael Chamberlain, *Knowledge and Social Practice*.

[84] Peter Jackson, 'Mamluk Institution'; and Irfan Habib, 'Formation of the Sultanate Ruling Class'.

[85] The classic study of W.H. Moreland, 'Feudalism (?) in the Moslem Kingdom of Delhi', *Journal of Indian History*, 7 (1928), pp. 1–8, revised and reprinted in his *Agrarian System of Moslem India*, pp. 216–23, only developed the uniqueness of political traditions in 'Muslim' India by contrasting the prebendal regimes of the Delhi Sultanate with feudal Europe. The passage of

further complicated if we recall the large number of émigré aristocrats present in the Delhi Sultanate, free individuals of reputed lineages whose presence leant splendour to the court, but who were very circumspectly patronized by the Delhi Sultan. While social stature was given considerable regard in some contexts, it was, apparently, given short shrift in others. It would be a mistake to assume, however, that these were fixed categories. Many military slaves consolidated their political positions and established influential households through the duration of the thirteenth century. They then postured, with a few notable successes, as aristocrats of long standing.[86]

In any study of an emerging Sultanate wherein both society and politics saw considerable flux, the complicated composition of Muslims resident in north India is a subject that has to be carefully historicised. Who were these people? What were their endogenous histories? How did they appraise and interact with each other? How were the contours of an exogenous identity and of '*a*' Muslim community shaped, and what were the kinds of reservations against efforts at homogenization?[87] It is astonishing how little we know about the making of individual and collective identities in the medieval period. Its complicated textures have been reduced to a study of 'Hindu–Muslim' relations, to the prehistory of a communal difference that bisects India afresh today.

Some of the problems in the study of identities in the pre-modern period originate from a genre of literature that Aziz Ahmad described

---

years has not shifted this focus. See, for example, André Wink, *al-Hind, The Making of the Indo-Muslim World, vol. I: Early Medieval India and the Expansion of Islam, 7th–11th centuries* (Delhi: Oxford University Press, 1990), pp. 12–13. By way of contrast see Sunil Kumar, 'When Slaves were Nobles'.

[86] On the households of the *mawlāzādagān*, sons of slaves, and their aristocratic pretensions in the late thirteenth century, see Baranī, *Ta'rīkh*, edited by Khan, p. 134, edited by Rashid, p. 155, and the elaborate lineages provided for Iltutmish and Balban by Jūzjānī, *Ṭabaqāt*, vol. 1, p. 441, vol. 2, pp. 47, 220–1 and Baranī, *Ta'rīkh*, edited by Khan, p. 39, edited by Rashid, p. 47.

[87] Surprisingly enough, this is a line of inquiry that has never been systematically explored for the pre-Mughal period. Richard M. Eaton has posed some of these questions in his *Rise of Islam*. Unfortunately, his work is far richer and more nuanced on the Mughal rather than the pre-Mughal years.

as the 'epics and counter-epics' of conquest and resistance.[88] Persian chronicles routinely valorised the campaigns of the 'armies of Islam' and Sultanate conquests over infidels. This literature also led to the production of 'counter-epics' that focused on the heroic nature of Rajput resistance and demonized Muslim conduct. Exceptions to these narratives notwithstanding, there were some remarkably motivated readings of these materials to vindicate communalist arguments of innate differences between Hindus and Muslims and a long, violent history of conflict between the two communities.[89] But, if we recall, Mohammad Habib's interventions in the early 1920s already looked beyond the 'holy warrior' discourse present in the chronicles narrating Maḥmūd Ghaznawī's campaigns. Many of Habib's insights came from his reading of Persian texts but they were never theorized sufficiently in his larger arguments and were, therefore, completely missed by later generations of scholars.[90] Instead, Weberian essentializations received a fresh lease of life in André Wink's work,

[88] Aziz Ahmad, 'Epic and Counter Epic in Medieval India', *Journal of the American Oriental Society*, 83 (1963), pp. 470–6. See also, Richard Davis, *Lives of Indian Images* (Delhi: Motilal Banarsidass Publishers, 1999 reprint), pp. 88–112.

[89] See for example, Sita Ram Goel, *Hindu Temples: What Happened to Them? vol. 1: A Preliminary Survey* (New Delhi: Voice of India, 1990); *vol. 2: The Islamic Evidence* (New Delhi: Voice of India, 1991).

[90] Habib noticed, for example, that, in the thirteenth century, 'To the people at large the Turkish slave-officer appeared presumptuous, self-assertive, brutish and tyrannical . . . A great and impassable chasm divided the Governors from the governed . . .' ('Introduction to Elliot and Dowson', p. 108). In his explanation, the collective qualities of the crude and unattractive Turks made them unpopular and the regime ultimately collapsed. Because low-caste converts were present amongst the Khalajī nobility, Habib argued for a greater degree of integration between the state and society after 'Turkish' rule. Ironically this rather mundane exegesis became a popular theme for comment amongst later scholars, but it obscured Habib's more interesting remarks regarding perceptions by the 'people at large' of their Governors. Habib did not dilate on how historians could investigate this, and the subject was never further developed. Elsewhere, regarding the *ṣūfīs*, Habib noted, 'The *silsilahs* quarrelled with each other; there was no co-ordination even between the Shaikhs of the same *silsilah*, who acted independently and often appointed rival successors to the same territory' (ibid., p. 56). These observations

where an 'Islamic theology of iconoclasm' explained temple destruction in India under the Muslim Sultans.[91]

By contrast, in her study of medieval Andhra Pradesh, Cynthia Talbot historicized the production of different kinds of representations of a Telugu or Hindu 'we-hood' through the framing of the qualities of the 'Other'—Turk or Muslim 'them-hood'.[92] In Talbot's work the framing of these identities was an interesting textual strategy by elites who sought to cohere fragmented political groups within a homogeneous ethnicity marked by a shared linguistic, regional, and (apocryphal) history. It was a slow, non-linear process spanning the fourteenth through seventeenth centuries. Talbot developed and textured Habib's arguments when she argued that textual materials relating to the qualities of a demonized 'Other' were politically motivated and could not be separated from processes involved in the construction of the identity of the 'self'. Unfortunately, since her work was limited to a study of identity formation that occurred through political and cultural exchanges across the frontier, it always faced the risk of becoming reduced into 'a recognition of the fact that much of modern Hindu identity is rooted in the history of the rivalry between Hinduism and Islam [and this] will enable us to correctly gauge the strength of communalist forces and wage war against them'.[93]

---

escaped the attention of his principal colleagues, including K.A. Nizami who wrote extensively on the *ṣūfis*. Decades later, quite independently, Simon Digby focused upon these questions in his '*Ṭabarrukāt* and Succession among the Great Chishtī Shaykhs of the Delhi Sultanate', *Delhi Through the Ages*, pp. 63–103. These observations aside, it needs to be borne in mind that Habib also argued rather naively for the veracity of al-Birūnī's reportage on the nature of Hindu society (see above for citations, and 'An Introduction to the Study of Medieval India (A.D. 1000–1400)') in K.A. Nizami, ed., *Politics and Society during the Early Medieval Period*, vol. 1, pp. 25–32.

[91] André Wink, *al-Hind, vol. II: The Slave Kings*, pp. 294–333.

[92] Cynthia Talbot, 'Inscribing the Other, Inscribing the Self: Hindu–Muslim Identities in Pre-Colonial India', *Comparative Study of Society and History*, 37 (1995), p. 720.

[93] David N. Lorenzen, 'Who Invented Hinduism?', *Comparative Study of Society and History*, 41 (1999), p. 631. For an earlier, more sophisticated version of the argument, see Sheldon Pollock, 'Ramayana and Political Imagination in India', *The Journal of Asian Studies*, 53 (1993), pp. 261–97.

Less developed in Talbot's work was a recognition that elite processes of framing self-identities were also intrinsically violent and hierarching exercises. The making of a Telugu ethnicity within the Andhra region required both appropriate communicative mediums—monumental, inscriptional, textual, and ritual—and socially important agents who were invested in its dissemination.[94] These agents upheld and represented the new social and moral order and ranked collaborators, shirkers, and dissidents appropriately. This was hardly a consensual exercise. Instead, these processes created multilayered identities that had their own local, contextual politics usually obscured by grander accounts of Hindu–Muslim engagements and state formations. Talbot was entirely correct, of course, in remarking that much of the process of introspection and creation of collective identities was 'pre' rather than 'post-colonial', but in breaking away from one periodization Talbot shifted perilously close to the older metanarrative, where Ancient/Hindu and Medieval/Muslim juxtapositions shaped political and social organizations.[95]

The histories of social identities as endogenous processes has suffered because of inadequate information on local communities. The quality of records available on the Rajputs, however, makes them an important exception. Research here has pointed out how the *rājputra* fashioning of a *kshatriya* status or the reference to a *Rāmrājya* mytheme of ideal rule were both framed in the local contexts of political competition amongst *rā'īs* and *rānās* some years *before* the tenth century and Ghaznavid or Ghurid invasions.[96] The subsequent 'finessing' of a Rajput, from a more generic *kshatriya* identity, occurred from the fourteenth through sixteenth centuries. Through this

[94] To be fair, Cynthia Talbot devoted considerable attention to 'communicative mediums' in the creation of a regional Telugu ethnic identity in her *Precolonial India in Practice*. But this work also eschewed—in a manner very reminiscent of structuralist-functionalist interpretations of an earlier generation—any reference to political violence or resistance to inclusion within new identities and hierarchies.

[95] This was more apparent in her 'Inscribing the Other, Inscribing the Self' than in her *Precolonial India in Practice*.

[96] See B.D. Chattopadhyaya, 'Origin of the Rajputs: The Political, Economic and Social Processes in Early Medieval Rajasthan', in *The Making of Early Medieval India*, pp. 57–88; and his rejoinder to Sheldon Pollock's, 'Ramayana

entire period, the narration of elaborately embroidered accounts of battles between Rajput lineages, Sultanate, and Mughal forces were together and separately important components that went into the creation of the myth of Rajput honour and valour, important ingredients in the self-image of this caste.[97] Ultimately, in the eighteenth and nineteenth centuries and thereafter, this self-image was not derived from frontier conflict; it had an autonomous presence all its own, and later processes of 'Rajputization' were not always framed with reference to Muslim rule or aggression.[98]

The point, however, is not simply the need to historicize political processes, locate interactions between different groups of people, and study the impact of their engagements more carefully. Important as these exercises might be, the significant point is surely the need to contextualize the production of discursive texts for their attempts to frame the history of India within large civilizational and political-cultural entities.[99] Historians of the Delhi Sultanate can use Talbot's observations to understand how Persian historians relied upon their narratives of conflict with idolaters to underline both the unique qualities inherent in a 'Muslim', and how these attributes were shared within a larger membership that constituted the community of Islam. But to go beyond Talbot's work would imply recognizing that such

---

and Political Imagination in India', in idem, *Representing the Other? Sanskrit Sources and the Muslims* (Delhi: Manohar, 1998), pp. 98–115.

[97] See Dirk H. Kolff, *Naukar, Rajput and Sepoy: The Ethnohistory of the Military Labour Market in Hindustan, 1450–1850* (Cambridge: University Press, 1990); and Norman P. Ziegler, 'Rajput Loyalties during the Mughal Period', *Kingship and Authority in South Asia*, pp. 242–84.

[98] Surajit Sinha, 'State Formation and Rajput Myth in Tribal Central India', *Man in India*, 42 (1962), pp. 35–80, reprinted in Kulke, ed., *The State in India*, pp. 304–42.

[99] An important subject on which little work has been done. But see the important contributions of Marcia K. Hermansen and Bruce B. Lawrence, 'Indo-Persian Tazkiras as Memorative Communications'; Shantanu Phukan, ' "Through Throats where Many Rivers Meet": The Ecology of Hindi in the World of Persian', *The Indian Economic and Social History Review*, 38 (2001), pp. 33–58; and Velcheru Narayana Rao, David Shulman, and Sanjay Subrahmanyam, *Textures of Time: Writing History in South India, 1600–1800* (Delhi: Permanent Black, 2001).

communitarian identities also empowered specific definitions of Islam and their exponents—an authority that was constantly tested and challenged.[100]

The thirteenth century, the years of the early Delhi Sultanate, occupies an important period in the history of India: not just for the synergetic social and economic processes that it is supposed to have released, but also because in the modern consciousness of Indians these were the years regarded as the 'foundation of Muslim rule in India', the beginning of a historical interaction between people that has had such a tragic, divisive impact on the nation. The writing of a history of this period requires the historian to be conscious not just of the politics that produced the source materials of the thirteenth century but, equally, the politics of the modern world that filters the reading of this past. It is my hope that the following chapters will bring a different focus to the reading of this history, problematize some longstanding interpretations, and provoke alternative sets of questions which will complicate future research.

[100] See also, Sunil Kumar, 'Qutb and Modern Memory', in Suvir Kaul, ed., *The Partitions of Memory: The Afterlife of the Division of India* (Delhi: Permanent Black, 2001), pp. 140–82; reprinted in idem, *The Present in Delhi's Pasts* (Delhi: Three Essays Press, 2002), pp. 1–61.

CHAPTER 2

The Sultanates of North India: The Mu‘izzī Maliks in Hindustan

Finally in the year 602/1205–6 he [Mu‘izz al-Dīn Ghūrī] . . . [decided once again] . . . to make a beginning by an inroad into India for the purpose of mending the affairs of his retainers and followers, who had lost all their gear and accoutrement during the last few years of campaigning in Khurasan. Upon arriving in India, he was able by one victory that God granted him to repair all the deficits of treasury and army.[1]

‘Alā’ al-Dīn ‘Aṭā Malik Juwainī made these rather innocuous remarks nearly a half-century after the event, in his history of the Mongol invasions of Iran. The fortunes of the Ghurid dynasty were peripheral in Juwainī's history; what is interesting about this passage is the author's confident narration, especially when he seems to have got his facts, at best, only partially correct. Mu‘izz al-Dīn's urgent need to campaign in north India in 602/1205–6 was more likely provoked by certain pastoralist Khokar tribesmen's challenge to Ghurid establishments in the Punjab; plunder, this time, was probably only an incidental consideration.[2]

Factual inaccuracies aside, Juwainī's account is interesting for the mechanical, almost commonplace, explanation of the reasons for Mu‘izzī campaigns in north India. It is significant that Juwainī linked

[1] ‘Alā’ al-Dīn ‘Aṭā Malik Juwainī, *Ta’rīkh-i Jahān-Gushā*, translated by John A. Boyle, *The History of the World-Conqueror* (Manchester: Manchester University Press, 1958), vol. 1, pp. 325–6.

[2] Jūzjānī, *Ṭabaqāt-i Nāṣirī*, vol. 1, pp. 403–4.

the fortunes of the Ghurid dominions in Khurasan and India; plunder from the latter, his narrative suggests, sustained the costs of administration and military campaigns in the former. That Juwainī made these connections is not terribly surprising. The example of Sultan Maḥmūd Ghaznawī (338–421/998–1030), great hero and patron of Persian litterateurs and paradigmatic despoiler of infidel temples in the subcontinent, was most immediately before him, for it was this Sultan's rule in Afghanistan and Khurasan that was partially sustained by iconoclastic expeditions into India. Maḥmūd Ghaznawī's raids had, of course, also transformed pre-existing images of the wealth of India into epic proportions, and these had remained untarnished with the passage of time.[3] As Juwainī's account stated most impressively, the plundering of north Indian hoards restored lost fortunes in a twinkle.

At least as far as Juwainī was concerned, political systems—either Ghaznavid or Ghurid—based in Afghanistan and abutting the riches of the Indian subcontinent, were equally lacking in internal resources: hence these plundering raids into the neighbouring El Dorado. But synthesizing the two regimes hardly did justice to either; for in fact the political systems constructed by the Ghaznavid and Ghurid dynasties were quite distinct. The ruling family of the former were military slaves of Turkish background, perhaps of Qārlūq tribal origin, who fled into eastern Afghanistan from the Samanid capital of Bukhara.[4] They had few local ties with the regions under

[3] C.E. Bosworth, *The Ghaznavids*; idem 'Maḥmūd of Ghazna in Contemporary Eyes and in Later Persian Literature', *Iran*, 4 (1966), pp. 85–92, and 'The Development of Persian Culture under the Early Ghaznavids', *Iran* 6 (1968), pp. 33–44, reprinted in idem, *The Medieval History of Iran, Afghanistan and Central Asia* (London: Variorum Reprints, 1977). See also the recent work of Sunil Sharma, *Persian Poetry at the Indian Frontier: Mas'ūd Sa'd Salmān of Lahore* (Delhi: Permanent Black, 2001), pp. 6–67, 136–64 and the re-evaluation of Sultan Maḥmūd's raid on the temple of Somnath in Richard H. Davis, *Lives of Indian Images*, pp. 88–112.

[4] On the Ghaznavids see C.E. Bosworth, *The Ghaznavids*, his collection of articles published as *The Medieval History of Iran, Afghanistan and Central Asia*; M. Nazim, *The Life and Times of Sulṭān Maḥmūd of Ghazna* (Cambridge: Cambridge University Press, 1931); idem, 'The Pand-Nāmah of Subuktigīn', *Journal of the Royal Asiatic Society* (1933), pp. 605–28.

their control and sought to maintain their distance from these by creating an extremely authoritarian political regime. More than with Afghanistan, the Ghaznavids consolidated their ties with Khurasan in eastern Iran. As their political influence and ambitions increased, they made successful efforts to transform their capital into a centre of Persian culture and learning, metamorphozing this backwater province in Afghanistan into a region that could, for the moment, overshadow Samanid Khurasan and Transoxiana.[5]

By contrast, the rulers of Ghur, the Shansabanids, were humble pastoral chieftains from one of the least developed regions of Afghanistan. Their inaccessible hilly tract of land lay some distant to the west of Ghazni but closer, to the east of Herat. Agriculture was possible in the relatively fertile valleys of Ghur and their residents also reared horses and cattle. Yet overall Ghur was a poor and isolated region, even by the standards of Afghanistan, and was 'Islamicized', after a fashion, only under the Ghaznavids in the late-tenth and early-eleventh century. It had no urban settlements of significance and only small, dispersed political formations centred around mountain outposts. From these hill forts, local chiefs commandeered the neighbouring population into raids upon infrequent caravans which hazarded the journey through their inhospitable terrain.[6] The high cultural achievements of the Ghaznavids had passed Ghur by, and an anonymous report from the end of the tenth century described the residents of the region as 'bad-tempered, unruly [*nā-sāzanda*], and

[5] For citations see the work of Bosworth and Sharma mentioned above, fn. 4.

[6] For an early account of the Ghurids and a geographical survey of the region near their capital, see A. Maricq and G. Wiet, *Le Minaret de Djam, la Découverte de la Capitale des Sultans Ghorides (XIIe–XIIIe siçles)* (Paris: Memoires de la Délégation Archéologique Franȩise en Afghanistan, 1959), vol. 16. Many of these conclusions were disputed by Lorenz S. Leshnik, 'Ghor, Firuzkoh and the Minar-i Jam', *Central Asiatic Journal*, 12 (1968–9), pp. 36–49. For more general but valuable surveys, see, C.E. Bosworth, 'The Early Islamic History of Ghur', *Central Asiatic Journal*, 6 (1961), pp. 116–33, reprinted in his, *The Medieval History of Iran, Afghanistan*; A.D.H. Bivar, 'Gh̲ūr', *Encyclopaedia of Islam*, edited by H.A.R. Gibbs *et al.* (Leiden: E.J. Brill, second edition, 1956–), vol. 2, p. 1096 (hereafter referred to as *EI*²); and C.E. Bosworth, 'Gh̲ūrids', *EI*², vol. 2, pp. 1099–103.

ignorant'.[7] Far removed from the Persianate world of Iran and parts of Afghanistan, their dialect was distinct from the language spoken in Ghazni and, in his campaigns into Ghur, Sultan Mas'ūd Ghaznawī (421–32/1031–41) carried interpreters with him.[8] Even at the height of their power, at the end of the twelfth century, the Shansabanids did not wholly assume forms of governance that the earlier Ghaznavid regime had imposed to centralize their rule.[9] Instead, the Shansabanids left a huge amount of local initiative with the military commanders of their administrative provinces. The traditions of honouring all male relatives of a ruling family by giving them titles and governorships, virtually as autonomous Sultans, continued without a hiatus even during the period of this dynasty's greatest political success.[10]

If there was any resemblance between the two regimes, it arose out of their similar interest in north India. It is more than clear that neither the Ghaznavids nor the Shansabanids (nor Juwainī for that matter!) shared the impression of some modern historians that north India was at this time witnessing a 'decay of commerce and decline of towns, which seems to have continued down to the eleventh century'.[11] Rather, to contemporary observers and military personnel—and one can assume they had more than an impressionistic experience of medieval Indian economic conditions—India personified wealth. Despite the extreme attention in Persian and Arabic accounts to

[7] Anonymous, *Ḥudūd al-'Ālam: The Regions of the World, a Persian Geography*, translated and explained by V. Minorsky (London: Luzac and Company, E.J.W. Gibb Memorial Series), p. 110.

[8] Abū' al-Fazl Baihaqī, *Ta'rīkh-i Mas'ūdī*, edited by Ghani and Feyyaz, p. 117, cited by C.E. Bosworth, 'Early Islamic History of Ghūr', p. 118. The passage of time may not have eased some of the unique qualities present in the dialect(s?) spoken in the Ghurid region. Jūzjānī, *Ṭabaqāt-i Nāṣirī*, occasionally reports on the general distinctiveness of their language, *bar lughat-i Ghūr*. See vol. 1, pp. 325, 349, 353.

[9] Jūzjānī, *Ṭabaqāt-i Nāṣirī*, vol. 1, p. 333, on the fragmented, contentious political environment at Ghur during the eleventh and twelfth centuries.

[10] See Chart 1 and discussion below.

[11] Irfan Habib, 'The Peasant in Indian History', p 138; and for the general exposition on this subject, R.S. Sharma, *Indian Feudalism* and Simon Digby, 'Economic Conditions before 1200', in *The Cambridge Economic History*, vol. 1, pp. 45–7.

moral and material considerations in waging iconoclastic raids into India and seizing hoarded precious metals from temples, we should not ignore the variety of plunder available to 'warriors in the cause of Islam' (*ghāzīs*) in the subcontinent. As the early thirteenth century normative work of Fakhr-i Mudabbir reminds us, the spoils of war, *ghanīma*, included horses, camels, cattle, goats, slaves, valuables, and arms, *asp wa ushtur wa gāo wa gosfand wa barda wa matā' wa silāḥ.*[12] The availability of these riches in the subcontinent far outstripped resources that could be plundered from other neighbouring regions; which is no doubt why Juwainī assumed that Mu'izz al-Dīn Ghūrī sought to recoup his losses in northern Afghanistan by campaigning in India.

These shared economic attractions aside, Ghaznavid interventions in north India differed from those by the Shansabanids. For the better part of his reign, Maḥmūd Ghaznawī was not interested in territorial gains in the subcontinent. If he had any serious interests at all on this front, these lay in the Sindh region and in expelling the *Shī'i* Fāṭimid influence from Multan. The garrisoning of Lahore happened late in his reign; nor was control of the Punjab pursued systematically. The lack of any serious Ghaznavid interest in long-term territorial investments in India was apparent in 431/1040 when, after suffering a reversal at Dandanqan, Sultan Mas'ūd considered fleeing from the Turkmen Seljuqs and shifting his capital to Lahore. Mas'ūd's subordinates were appalled at the idea and rather than accepting a rough life on the frontier marches, they deposed the monarch. It was only the unremitting pressure exerted by the nomadic Ghūzz, and the expanding authority of the Shansabanids, that finally drove the Ghaznavids to move their capital to Lahore, but only over a century later, in 558/1163.[13]

[12] Fakhr-i Mudabbir, *Ādāb al-Ḥarb wa al-Shajā'ā'a*, edited by Aḥmad Suhaili Khwansari (Teheran: Iqbal, 1968), p. 398.

[13] C.E. Bosworth, *The Ghaznavids*, pp. 229–30; idem, 'The Political and Dynastic History of the Iranian World (1000–1217)', in J.A. Boyle, ed., *The Cambridge History of Iran, vol. 5, The Saljuq and Mongol Periods* (Cambridge: Cambridge University Press, 1968), pp. 157–63; idem, *The Later Ghaznavids: Splendour and Decay: The Dynasty in Afghanistan and Northern India, 1040–1186* (New York: Columbia University Press, 1977), pp. 9–20, 111–31; and Peter Jackson, 'Lahawr', *EI*², vol. 5, pp. 597–8.

One reason why modern historians often overstress a link between the Ghaznavids and the Ghurids is because the latter's interventions in India also occurred from their base in Ghazni.[14] Sultan Ghiyāṣ al-Dīn Ghūrī (558–99/1163–1203) seized the city from the Ghūzz in 569/1173 and appointed his younger brother Mu'izz al-Dīn (569–602/1173–1206) as the Governor of Ghazni, making him the monarch's most powerful ally. Mu'izz al-Dīn supported his older brother in his campaigns within Afghanistan and into Khurasan and Khwarazm. But he had his own agenda as well. And this related to consolidating his rule in Ghazni through plunder remitted from secure territorial bases strategically dispersed in north India.

A summary description of Mu'izzī conquests will suffice to convey the extent of the new domain. Control over trade routes through much of western Punjab was completed when the remnant Ghaznavid principality of Lahore was seized by Mu'izz al-Dīn in 582/1186. In 587/1191 Tabarhind (modern Bhatinda) was occupied and, after the second battle of Tarain (588/1192) against the Chāhamāna (Chauhān) ruler Prithvīrāja, Mu'izz al-Dīn seized Kuhram, Mīrat (modern Meerut), Hansi, and Delhi. In 590/1194, Kōl (modern Aligarh) was seized, and after the defeat of the Gāhaḍavāla King Jāyachandra, Benaras was occupied. Subsequently, in 591/1195 Ajmer, and in 592/1196 Thangir/Bayana, were captured. The year 593/1197 saw raids into Gujarat against the Rā'ī of Nahrwala, Ujjain, and Khalajī raids into Bihar and Bengal, culminating with the seizure of Lakhnauti from the Sena ruler. In 594/1197–8 Budaun was occupied, and the next year Qanauj. In 597/1200–1 Gwalior, and in 599/1202 Kalinjar, were seized from the Chandellas. Subsequently, itinerant plunder and consolidatory raids continued—as in the case of Budur in 600/1203–4, or in the Kūh-i Jūd (Salt Range) in 602/1205–6—but the Mu'izzī expeditions of conquest had apparently come to an end. Mu'izz al-Dīn was assassinated during the Kūh-i Jūd expedition but, significantly, his previous campaign had occurred quite some time before this, in 592/1196, against Bayana. In other words, Mu'izz al-Dīn had stayed away from the north Indian marches for ten years (the years 592–602/1196–1206), leaving the management of his conquests

[14] See Habib, 'The Formation of the Sultanate Ruling Class', p. 7; and Jackson, *The Delhi Sultanate*, pp. 8–9.

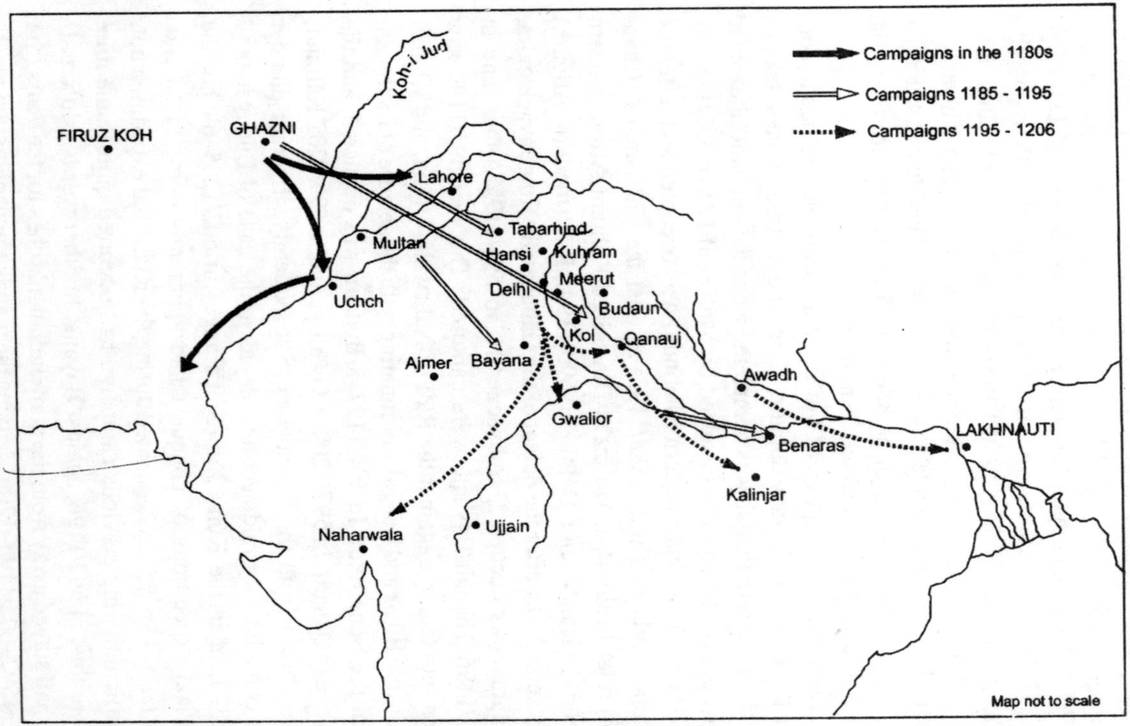

Map 1: Mu'izzī Campaigns into Hindustan

and the extension of his dominions to military subordinates stationed in the subcontinent. During this period, he was getting increasingly involved in the politics of Afghanistan and Transoxiana, a commitment accentuated by his brother's death in 600/1203.

The systematic territorial extension of Mu'izzī rule over distant areas in north India is a clear contrast with the Ghaznavids. But what was the nature of their rule and how was it manifest in north India? Here historians are less precise, even if they do provide a cursory account of the important features of Shansabanid rule in Ghur.[15] The larger question of how Shansabanid traditions were manifest within their north Indian possessions has remained ignored.[16] Mu'izz al-Dīn's principality of Ghazni was only one part of the larger dominion controlled by the Shansabanid family, and his rights to governance were derived from the fact that he was a grandson of Sultan 'Izz al-Dīn Ḥusain, also entitled *Abū al-Salāṭīn*, the 'father of Sultans'. Mu'izz al-Dīn operated within the traditions of the Shansabanid family, and the extent to which these guided and inflected the manner of his management of the Ghaznavid principality, with its extensions in north India, is worth investigating.

In the twenty years or so of active military intervention, Mu'izz al-Dīn captured several urban centres in north India and garrisoned these towns with troops and commanders from his army. The Sultan made his presence felt in these dominions only occasionally, leaving his personnel considerable independent initiative. Yet, during the period 582–602/1186–1206, the areas garrisoned by Mu'izzī forces in north India were also an inherent part of the Ghurid political system. To what extent did the parent Shansabanid system of governance influence their administrative organization? The origins of the

[15] On early accounts on Shansabanid traditions of governance in Afghanistan, see Mohammad Habib, 'Shihabuddin of Ghur', in *Politics and Society*, vol. 2, pp. 105–43; R.P. Tripathi, *Some Aspects of Muslim Administration*. On Shansabanid governance in north India, see A.B.M. Habibullah, *The Foundation of Muslim Rule*; Peter Jackson, *The Delhi Sultanate*; Irfan Habib, 'Iqṭā''; idem, 'The Formation of the Sultanate Ruling Class'.

[16] Compare, for example, Mohammad Habib's analysis of 'Shihabuddin of Ghur' with the 'Heritage of the Slave Kings' in *Politics and Society*, pp. 144–8.

Delhi Sultanate lay within these Mu'izzī territories in India, and it was their garrison towns that received immigrants fleeing from eastern Iran and Afghanistan in the wake of Mongol invasions. The following sections of this chapter analyse the making of these political and social formations; in other words, the immediate prehistory of the Sultanate of Delhi.

The Shansabanid Sultanate and North India

The fame and importance of Sultan Ghiyāṣ al-Dīn and his brother Mu'izz al-Dīn in the politics of twelfth-century Afghanistan and eastern Iran was disproportionate to the humble origins of their family. Shansab, the eponymous founder of the Shansabanids, and his descendants were fairly insignificant tribal chieftains whose early history is lost in myth.[17] A recognizable transition in the prominence of the family was noticeable from the chieftainship of 'Izz al-Dīn Ḥusain, whose reign (493–543/1100–46) coincided with the period of decline of the Ghaznavid and Seljuq Sultanates. In the emerging power vacuum, three of 'Izz al-Dīn Ḥusain's sons were, in turn, able to succeed their father and improve the position of the Shansabanid family in central Afghanistan.[18]

'Izz al-Dīn's successors can be distinguished into two separate groups in accord with their descent and privilege. The marginalized group were the children of Turkish mothers whose poor social status precluded their sons from gaining senior positions in the family. The more favoured children were the five sons of a Princess of the Shansabanid lineage, and the future Sultans of Ghur belonged to this conjugal union (see Chart 1). A system of horizontal succession rights to the supreme office of chieftainship prevailed within the members of this group. Sultan Saif al-Dīn Sūrī (died 544/1149) was succeeded by his brothers Bahā' al-Dīn Sām (died 544/1149) and

[17] The main chronicler for the Shansabanids is Jūzjānī. For their early history, see *Ṭabaqāt-i Nāṣirī*, vol. 1, pp. 318–33.

[18] Ibid., pp. 334–8. C.E. Bosworth, 'Notes on the Pre-Ghaznavid History of Eastern Afghanistan'; *Islamic Quarterly*, 9 (1965), pp. 12–24, reprinted in his, *The Medieval History of Iran, Afghanistan*; idem, 'Ghūrids', *EI*[2].

'Alā' al-Dīn Ḥusain (died 556/1161). This also indicated the presence of corporate rights to inheritance; the patrimony of the father, 'Izz al-Dīn, was not the sole inheritance of any one son but belonged to all of them. This principle of coparcenary inheritance was recognized at 'Izz al-Dīn's death and the Ghurid patrimony was distributed amongst his sons. While Sultan Saif al-Dīn Sūrī retained Istiah as his capital, Bahā' al-Dīn Sām received the ancestral lands of Mandesh, 'Alā' al-Dīn the territory of Wajiristan, while Nāṣir al-Dīn Maḥmūd received Madin, and Jarmas was given to Shujā' al-Dīn 'Alī. After Shujā' al-Dīn's premature death, Jarmas passed to his son 'Alā' al-Dīn. These were all uterine brothers.

Although the lower-ranking group of half-brothers was excluded from succession to the supreme chieftainship of the Shansabanid family they were not alienated from rights of inheritance to land and nominal authority. The eldest brother, Fakhr al-Dīn Mas'ūd, son of a Turkish concubine, *kanīzak*, received Kashi, to which Sultan 'Alā' al-Dīn Ḥusain (544–56/1149–61) added Bamiyan. Quṭb al-Dīn, the son of a harem servant, was given the appanage of Warsar and he proceeded to construct his capital at Firuz Koh.[19] The two half-brothers were obviously dissatisfied with the extent of their inheritance. As a result, Quṭb al-Dīn revolted and fled to the Ghaznavid court, where he was killed; and Fakhr al-Dīn was placated by a subsequent increase in the size of his dominions.[20]

[19] Jūzjānī, *Ṭabaqāt-i Nāṣirī*, vol. 1, pp. 335–6, 340, 385. Jūzjānī's father had served the Bamiyanid family and Jūzjānī was circumspect in mentioning the maternal ancestry of his family's patrons: see, vol. 1, p. 380. By contrast, the author was hardly bashful when recounting details about Quṭb al-Dīn's mother.

[20] It is likely that Fakhr al-Dīn's appanage was gradually increased. Jūzjānī only mentions Kashi: ibid., vol. 1, p. 336, but clarifies on p. 385 that after Sultan 'Alā' al-Dīn Ḥusain's victorious campaigns in the region of Tukharistan, the throne of Bamiyan, *takht-i Bāmiyān*, was given to Fakhr al-Dīn. The later addition to the half-brother's appanage may have been provoked by fear of his dissatisfaction (like that of Quṭb al-Dīn) with the earlier dispensation. Jūzjānī also noted that Malik Fakhr al-Dīn Mas'ūd did not support Ghiyāṣ al-Dīn's succession to the throne of Firuz Koh. The Malik felt that since he was the oldest of the seven sons of 'Izz al-Dīn Ḥusain and none of his brothers were alive [*hīch bāqī na-māndeh*], the throne of Firuz Koh was rightfully his. Ibid.,

Other than via appanaging, a sense of the prevailing tradition of corporate solidarity within the family was evident from the large number of marriages within branches of the lineage. The descendants of Bahā' al-Dīn Sām ibn 'Izz al-Dīn Ḥusain about whom we have the most information, received or gave brides to all the collateral lineages barring Quṭb al-Dīn Muḥammad and his descendants (see Chart 1). No apparent seniority amongst the lineages in bride-giving or bride-taking seems to have existed, and this complements the general sense of corporate egalitarianism that existed within the Shansabanid family.

The formation of the far-flung Ghurid state during the reign of Ghiyāṣ al-Dīn ibn Bahā' al-Dīn Sām (558–99/1163–1203) might have provided an opportunity for the exclusion of some collateral lineages within the Shansabanid family and the creation of a more centralized state apparatus. But this does not seem to have happened. Changes due to attrition did take place within the Shansabanid kin group. Quṭb al-Dīn (d. *circa* 543–4/1148–9) and Saif al-Dīn (d. 544/1149) had no male successors and therefore their claims lapsed in favour of their affinal relatives (see Chart 1). Neither did the establishment of the head quarters of the lineage in Firuz Koh by 544/1149 serve to create a more centralized structure of governance for the Ghurid dominions. Through the long reign of Ghiyāṣ al-Dīn Muḥammad, 558–99/1163–1203, the appanaging of territories to collateral lineages continued. The descendants of Malik Fakhr al-Dīn Mas'ūd became associated with the principalities of Bamiyan and Tukharistan, which appeared, in time, as the patrimonial property of this branch of the family. On Fakhr al-Dīn Mas'ūd's death, his oldest son, Shams

vol. 1, pp. 355–6, 359–60. In the ensuing conflict Ghiyāṣ al-Dīn and Mu'izz al-Dīn defeated Fakhr al-Dīn. See also ibid., vol. 1, p. 386. It was some years later that the brothers cultivated Shams al-Dīn Muḥammad ibn Fakhr al-Dīn Mas'ūd. Subsequently, the Bamiyanid cousin lineage again became ambitious, and it was in part because of an attempt to neutralize them that another cousin, Ẓiyā' al-Dīn, received so much attention from the two brothers. After Ghiyāṣ al-Dīn's death (599/1203) his brother Mu'izz al-Dīn, based in Ghazni, retained lordship over the Ghurid dominions for himself, and appointed Ẓiyā' al-Dīn, now honoured by the title of Sultan 'Alā' al-Dīn, to the appanage of Firuz Koh. Ibid., vol. 1, pp. 369–72, and discussion below.

al-Dīn, succeeded to the territory, not by appointment of the Ghurid Sultan but according to the will of his father, *ba wasiyat-i pidar.*[21] In fact, all the evidence points to the fact that Ghiyāṣ al-Dīn encouraged the process of appanaging of the Shansabanid patrimony amongst the remaining members of the kin group. The grandson of Malik Shihāb al-Dīn Muḥammad, Shihāb al-Dīn 'Alī, was allowed to continue undisturbed in Madin; and out of new conquests in Khurasan, the appanage of Nishapur was created for Malik Ẓiyā' al-Dīn Muḥammad Abū 'Alī and Sarakhs for Tāj al-Dīn Zangī ibn Fakhr al-Dīn Mas'ūd (see chart 1). Through the alliances formed by the grants of these new appanages, Ghiyāṣ al-Dīn hoped to placate and win the affections of collateral Shansabanid lineages.

The most important appointment in Ghiyāṣ al-Dīn's reign was that of his brother Mu'izz al-Dīn to the appanage of Ghazni in 569/1173. The Ghūzz were cleared from the region and Mu'izz al-Dīn given the right to govern the lands of the Ghaznavid Sultanate in eastern Afghanistan and western Punjab.[22] Mu'izz al-Dīn helped Ghiyāṣ al-Dīn on some of his campaigns in Khurasan and Khwarazm, but, at least at the outset, his major concern was consolidating and enlarging his appanage which included north India. The hierarchy and degree of mutual autonomy between the two brothers were reflected on the sigilla on their coins. Ghiyāṣ al-Dīn, as the senior brother, was *Sulṭān al-'aẓam*, the supreme Sultan, and his name and title were stamped on one side of the coin. The younger brother's name and title figured on the reverse of the same coin, where he was identified as *Sulṭān al-mu'aẓẓam*, the great Sultan.[23] Despite the paramount position occupied

[21] Ibid., vol. 1, p. 387.

[22] Ibid., vol. 1, p. 396.

[23] John S. Deyell, *Living without Silver*, p. 359, coin nos 238, 239. Although Mu'izz al-Dīn would occasionally use the title *Sulṭān al-'aẓam* (see nos 240, 242, 245), he apparently never presumed to do so when his brother's name was also included on the coins. Prior to the appointment of Mu'izz al-Dīn to Ghazni there was some competition and discord between the two siblings, the younger of the two feeling marginalized. See Jūzjānī, *Ṭabaqāt-i Nāṣirī*, vol. 1, pp. 354, 395-6 for details; and William Spengler, 'Some new Numismatic Evidence regarding Royal Nomenclature and Titulature in the Ghurid Period', *Numismatics and History* (Nasik: Indian Institute of Research in Numismatic Studies, Inaugural Seminar, 1984), pp. 106–16.

Chart 1: The Shansabanid Lineage

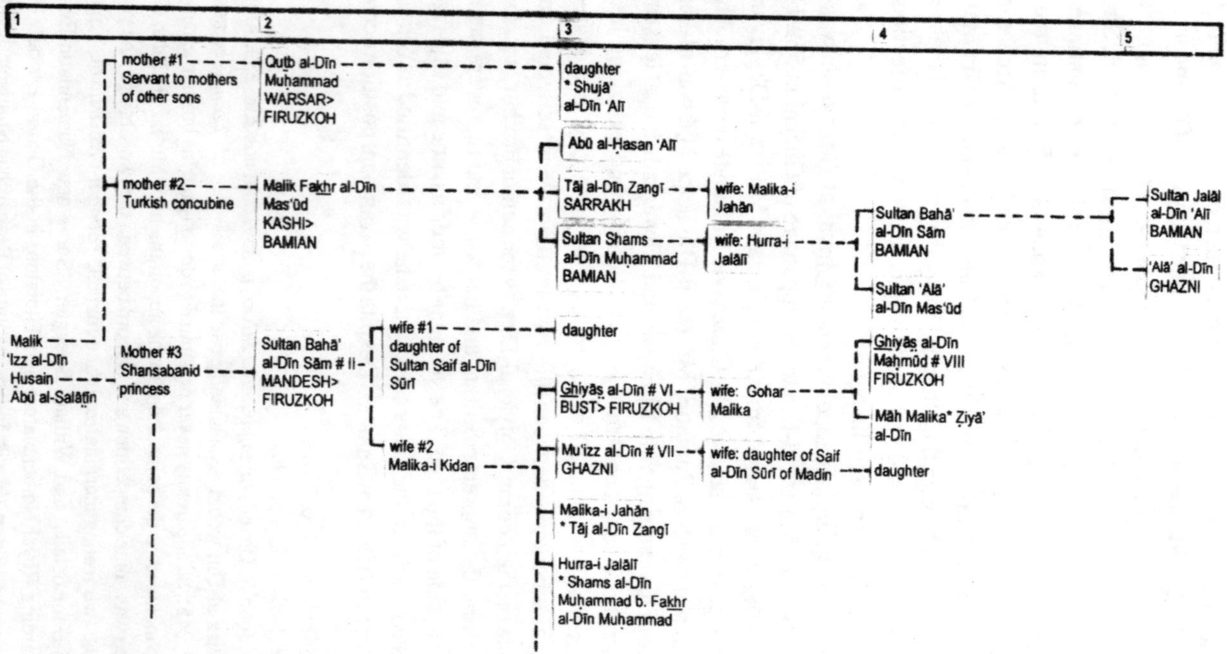

Continued on Next Page

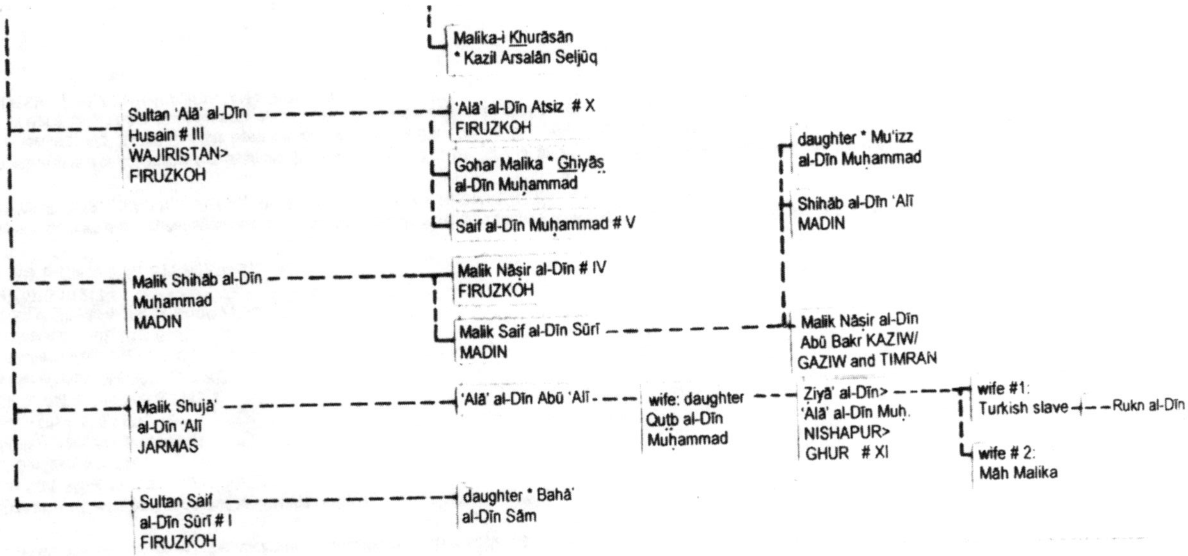

INDEX TO CHART 1

1 etc. in the top horizontal bar indicates generations within the family of 'Izz al-Dīn Ḥusain. The rights of the family of Shansab were preserved by his descendent Amīr Banjī who dispossessed the lineage of Shīsh. After an indeterminate number of descendents from Amīr Banjī, Amīr Sūrī controlled Ghur. Malik 'Izz al-Dīn Husain *Abū al-Salāṭīn* (Father of Sultans) was a descendent in the 6th generation from Amīr Sūrī.

Continued on Next Page

* indicates daughter: [daughter] * married to 'x'.

Mother #1 etc. : Jūzjānī reports that the seven sons of Malik 'Izz al-Dīn Ḥusain (1st generation) had three different mothers. Of the three mothers we can only be confident that mother #3, a Shansabanid, was a wife of the Malik. Of the others, one was a concubine, and the other a servant. The social status of the mothers did not cause their sons to be disinherited. I have therefore indicated the women as mothers with the additional information about their social background.

 # I etc. refers to Shansabanids who were regarded as Sultans of the Ghurid dominions:
I Sultan Saif al-Dīn Sūrī, 540-4/1146-9.
II Sultan Bahā' al-Dīn Sām, 544/1149.
III Sultan 'Alā' al-Dīn Ḥusain, 544-56/1149-61.
IV Malik Nāṣir al-Dīn G͟hur, 556/1161.
V Malik Saif al-Dīn b. 'Alā' al-Dīn, 556-8/1161-3.
VI G͟hiyāṣ al-Dīn Muḥammad, 558-99/1163-1203.
VII Mu'izz al-Dīn Muḥammad, 599-602/1203-6.
VIII G͟hiyāṣ al-Dīn Maḥmūd, 602-9/1206-12.
IX Bahā' al-Dīn Sām b. G͟hiyāṣ al-Dīn, 609-10/1212-3.
X 'Alā' al-Dīn Atsiz, 610-1/1213-4.
XI Ẓiyā' al-Dīn b. 'Alā' al-Dīn Abū 'Alī, 611-2/1214-5.

GHUR etc. : All upper case names are appanages held by members of the Shansabanid lineage. The important ones mentioned in this genealogical chart are: FIRUZ KOH; BAMIAN; MANDESH; GHUR; WAJIRISTAN; MADIN; JARMAS; GHAZNI; TUKHARISTAN; NISHAPUR.

> indicates a transition in title or appanage. For example: (i) When Malik Ẓiyā' al-Dīn ibn Alā' al-Dīn Abū 'Alī (4th generation) was given the appanage of Nishapur and the title of Sultan, he was also given a new title: 'Alā' al-Dīn. This has been indicated as: Ẓiyā' al-Dīn > 'Alā' al-Dīn. (ii) On Quṭb al-Dīn Muḥammad's death (2nd generation) his unfinished capital of Firuz Koh was occupied by Bahā' al-Dīn Sām. Subsequently when 'Alā' al-Dīn succeeded his brother he also transferred his capital to Firuz Koh. These transitions in appanages have been indicated as: MANDESH > FIRUZ KOH; WAJIRISTAN > FIRUZ KOH.

by the Ghurid Sultanate in eastern Iran and Afghanistan in the late twelfth century, and the honour bestowed upon it by the 'Abbāsid Caliph, the Shansabanid government never made the transition from being other than a loose patrimony of autonomous principalities led by a senior kinsman. Theoretically, each kinsman was supreme in his own appanage, with some possessing greater autonomy than others.

This system of governance and distribution of power influenced the level of Shansabanid participation in north India. Mu'izz al-Dīn's rights to north India were seen as an extension of his appanage of Ghazni and, just as the descendants of Malik Fakhr al-Dīn Mas'ūd of Bamiyan protected their inheritance,[24] Mu'izz al-Dīn guarded the rights to his assignment jealously. Perhaps it was the fear of an attack from his relatives in Afghanistan that compelled Mu'izz al-Dīn to spend a large amount of his time at his base in Ghazni. He led military campaigns into north India but, after the initial invasions, left further campaigns, organization of the conquered areas, and remission of plunder in the charge of his subordinates.

Mu'izz al-Dīn's efforts at retaining control over his appanage and monopolizing the wealth of north India also decisively curtailed kin participation in raids into the subcontinent. Jūzjānī's history makes a fleeting reference to only one Shansabanid in India: Malik Ẓiyā' al-Dīn Muḥammad Abū 'Alī. Although Jūzjānī seems quite familiar with the personal history of this Malik, his narrative is surprisingly confused.[25] The *Ṭabaqāt-i Nāṣirī* records the presence of Malik Ẓiyā' al-Dīn at the first battle of Tarain, 587/1191. Curiously, this record

[24] Amongst other reasons to jealously guard their region's autonomy, the Shansabānī lineage controlling Bamiyan profited from its abundant mineral wealth. See Jūzjānī, *Ṭabaqāt-i Nāṣirī*, vol. 1, p. 384. An anecdote in Niẓāmī 'Arūzī Samarqandī, *Chahār Maqāla*, translated by E.G. Browne (London: Luzac and Co. Ltd., E.J.W. Gibb Memorial Series o.s. XI.2, 1978 reprint), p. 87, recounts how Sultan Fakhr al-Dīn Mas'ūd of Bamiyan rewarded the author with the grant of a lead mine at Warsa. 'Arūzī noted in passing that his workers 'melted so much of the ore, so that in seventy days twelve thousand maunds of lead accrued to me'.

[25] Jūzjānī's family was closely attached to Malik Ẓiyā' al-Dīn's wife, the daughter of Ghiyāṣ al-Dīn Muḥammad (see further on this relationship below). The intimacy notwithstanding, the author provided confusing accounts of the Malik's parentage. In two different places Jūzjānī noted that Ẓiyā' al-Dīn was

does not occur, as we would expect, in the chapter on the reign of Sultan Mu'izz al-Dīn, where a full account of the first battle of Tarain is narrated. There is no mention of the Malik in this section. He figures, instead, in the chapter devoted to the history of Malik Ẓiyā' al-Dīn, where his diverse services, *khidmat*, to the Sultan are extolled.[26]

Although this does introduce some uncertainty about Ẓiyā' al-Dīn's presence in India, the asymmetrical relationship between the Malik and the two brothers remains unambiguous. There were affinal ties between the two cadet branches of the family: Māh Malika, the daughter of Sultan Ghiyāṣ al-Dīn Muḥammad was married to Malik Ẓiyā' al-Dīn.[27] It was through his services to the two brothers that the Malik eventually won a prestigious appanage for himself. After the successful campaigns in Khurasan in 596/1199–1200, Ẓiyā' al-Dīn was given Nishapur as his principality and the title of 'Alā' al-Dīn.[28]

---

the son of Shujā' al-Dīn, the son-in-law of Ghiyāṣ al-Dīn Muḥammad and the cousin (uncle's son) of the two brothers (Ghiyāṣ al-Dīn and Mu'izz al-Dīn). Jūzjānī, *Ṭabaqāt-i Nāṣirī*, vol. 1, pp. 369, 360. But in a third context, where the author provided a detailed account of the Malik's lineage, Ẓiyā' al-Dīn was mentioned as the son of 'Alā' al-Dīn Abū 'Alī and the grandson of Shujā' al-Dīn 'Alī. This would make Ẓiyā' al-Dīn the nephew, not the cousin (the uncle's grandson, not son), to Ghiyāṣ al-Dīn and Mu'izz al-Dīn. Ibid., vol. 1, p. 340 and Chart 1. This narrative also carries an account of Malik Ẓiyā' al-Dīn's mother, the daughter of Quṭb al-Dīn Muḥammad, and a report of his pilgrimage to Mecca which won him such high regard in the Shansabanid family and the title of Malik al-Hājī. Despite the contradictions, all accounts agree that Ẓiyā' al-Dīn was Ghiyāṣ al-Dīn's son-in-law and was distinguished by the title Malik Hājī.

[26] Ibid., vol. 1, p. 370. In this context, Jūzjānī also listed Ghiyāṣ al-Dīn's participation in the battle of Tarain, a curious inclusion not mentioned anywhere else by the author. Neither Ẓiyā' al-Dīn nor Ghiyāṣ al-Dīn are mentioned in the fuller account of the conflict: vol. 1, p. 399. Furthermore, in his account of Ghiyāṣ al-Dīn, vol. 1, pp. 353–69, Jūzjānī does not mention a single instance of the Ghurid monarch's march into India.

[27] Ibid., vol. 1, pp. 369, 383. Her title was *Jalāl al-Dunyā wa al-Dīn*. Ẓiyā' al-Dīn had a son from a Turkish servant and did not apparently consummate his marriage with Māh Malika.

[28] This would have meant that father and son were both titled 'Alā' al-Dīn, a possible reason for later copyist errors.

The degree of confidence existing between Mu'izz al-Dīn and Ẓiyā' al-Dīn was further displayed at the death of Sultan G͟hiyāṣ al-Dīn Muḥammad in 600/1203. Mu'izz al-Dīn could have co-opted Ghur within his own appanage or, more appropriately, appointed his brother's son, Bahā' al-Dīn Sām, to his father's principality. Instead, the Sultan assigned Firuz Koh to Ẓiyā' al-Dīn, a relative of high pedigree and a steadfast ally.[29] Thus, even if Jūzjānī's report is correct and Ẓiyā' al-Dīn was present at the battle of Tarain, it is worthwhile to notice that the exceptional reference to a Shansabanid in north India occurred in the context of a clearly dependent relative.

After his brother's death in 600/1203, Mu'izz al-Dīn was the most powerful member in the Shansabanid family. He now assumed the right to dispense appanages to kinsmen. It is in this context that the evidence regarding the exclusion of family members from principalities and governorships in north India appears particularly striking. Without doubt, the control of plunder from the north Indian marches was an extremely important factor in tilting the precarious balance of power within the Shansabanid family in Mu'izz al-Dīn's favour. It is not surprising, therefore, that the Sultan ignored Shansabanid coparcenary rights and refused to share these resources with any of his kinsmen. Unlike the process of appanaging from new conquests which continued apace during the apogee of Ghurid power, conquests in north India were not apportioned amongst the Shansabanids. The entire region was regarded as a part of Mu'izz al-Dīn's principality, an exclusive Ghaznavid preserve.

While the resources generated by north Indian plunder forced Mu'izz al-Dīn to guard his appanage from his kinsmen, the opportunity of making a quick fortune attracted a diverse body of soldiers into the Sultan's service. Over the twenty-eight years of the Sultan's campaigns in India (574–602/1178–1206), the nature of his expeditions as well as the composition of his soldiers and commanders altered considerably. Amongst his near contemporary chroniclers, Jūzjānī kept a fairly detailed record of these early campaigns, but his

[29] Ibid., vol. 1, pp. 360, 369–72.

narrative was quite unreflective in relation to the composition of and historical transitions within the body of Mu'izzī military personnel present in north India. The major distinctions within the armed personnel this author chose to recount were what we might loosely call ethnic, linguistic, and regional: there were military commanders from Ghur; others who were Persian speakers, *tājiks*, presumably from eastern Iran, Khurasan, and Khwarazm; there were Khalaj tribesmen from different parts of Afghanistan; and finally, soldiers and Amirs of Turkish ethnicity.

Sometimes, Jūzjānī clarified that the Turks he was referring to were military slaves; at other times the context and incidental details regarding their names and histories happened to reveal their social backgrounds. Closer study of other Mu'izzī military commanders reveals that Jūzjānī's categorization of Ghurid, Khalaj, or *tājik* Amirs as composite social groups was also an inadequate gloss. There were significant differences amongst these military commanders: some possessed lands and armed personnel of their own. Others, of more humble origin, were involved in a variety of short-term alliances as they explored opportunities of service and upward mobility. Elites and underprivileged military personnel were also deployed in different ways by Sultan Mu'izz al-Dīn. And, of course, the contrasting social backgrounds of these soldiers meant that their investments in the frontier marches differed sharply from each other.

In the following sections of this chapter I have differentiated Mu'izzī personnel within two very broad categories: notables who were free are distinguished from those who were slaves or of slave origin. Whereas these distinctions underline crucial differences between two very general groups of Mu'izzī notables, I use this categorization to also develop the considerable complexity within the internal composition of free and slave notables. As the following sections show, a collation of their life-histories elaborates on the character of the Shansabanid presence in India. This was a presence shaped equally by the political traditions used and adapted by Mu'izz al-Dīn to consolidate his appanage, and by the social backgrounds, alliances, and ambitions of the various and varying notables present in north India. The following few pages are dense with the information they carry, but only through such detail can we move from clichés to a more precise contextualization of the various Amirs as well as their individual and collective commitments to serve on the north Indian frontier.

Mu'izzī Free Amirs and Jurists in North India

At least in his early campaigns into the Punjab and north India, Mu'izz al-Dīn seems to have welcomed free military commanders from Ghur into his army. He needed to raise an armed retinue and welcomed commanders who would strengthen his forces by bringing their own troopers into his service. It is important to recall the monarch's precarious political condition at the time of his accession. He had actually been briefly in disfavour with his elder brother Ghiyāṣ al-Dīn before his appointment to Ghazni.[30] When he was finally given Ghazni in 569/1173, it was a territory that had suffered terribly for twelve years or so at the hands of the pillaging Ghūzz .[31] With the support of the Ghurid Amirs, Mu'izz al-Dīn cleared the Ghaznavid region of the Ghūzz, countered the Qarāmiṭa-Ismā'īlī centres in the Sindh region, and went on to challenge the residual Ghaznavid Sultanate in the Punjab with its capital at Lahore.

Amongst the Ghurid Amirs who joined Mu'izz al-Dīn in his early campaigns into north India, some—like Malik 'Izz al-Dīn Ḥusain ibn Kharmīl—were also participants in the larger Shansabanid endeavour for political paramountcy in eastern Iran and Khwarazm. Malik 'Izz al-Dīn, for example, was obviously a celebrated commander and Jūzjānī included him in the list of 'Maliks and kindred, *aqribā*' ', appended to his account of Sultan Mu'izz al-Dīn.[32] He reported that 'Izz al-Dīn Kharmīl was installed in Sialkot after the annexation of Lahore in 582/1186.[33] 'Izz al-Dīn was also a leading participant in the

[30] For a fleeting mention of the incident, see ibid., vol. 1, p. 396; and for a further discussion see William F. Spengler, 'Some New Numismatic Evidence', pp. 106–16.

[31] Ibid., vol. 1, pp. 243, 357–8, 396; Fakhr-i Mudabbir, *Ta'rīkh-i Fakhr al-Dīn Mubārak Shāh*, p. 19; and for a discussion of Ghūzz presence in Ghazni, see also C.E. Bosworth, *The Later Ghaznavids*, pp. 124–5.

[32] Jūzjānī, *Ṭabaqāt-i Nāṣirī*, vol. 1, pp. 405–6.

[33] Ibid., vol. 1, pp. 397–8.

campaign against Rā'ī Jāyachandra that led to the occupation of Benaras in 590/1194.[34] But there are no further references to Kharmīl's activities in north India, and this is in marked contrast to his important political profile in Afghanistan.

Jūzjānī reports that 'Izz al-Dīn Kharmīl was one of the Maliks of Gurzawān and had his own retinue of soldiers and followers. In 601/1204–5 these soldiers comprised the van of Mu'izz al-Dīn's army against the Qarā Khitā'ī forces at Andkhud. Sensing Mu'izz al-Dīn's weak military position, 'Izz al-Dīn Ḥusain withdrew from the imperial camp with his followers just before the battle where the Ghurid forces suffered a disastrous defeat.[35] After the death of Mu'izz al-Dīn in 602/1206, 'Izz al-Dīn continued to occupy a prominent place in Ghur as the Governor, *walī*, of Herat. His increasing disenchantment with Ghurid political fortunes was evident from his vacillation between joining the Khwārazm Shāh or remaining in the service of the Shansabanids.[36]

Malik 'Izz al-Dīn is also interesting for his social background. Together with the lineage of Shīsh, the descendants of Kharmīl came closest to forming an aristocratic class in Ghur. While the lineage of Shīsh derived its stature from their legendary political competition with the Shansabanids (honourably settled in the memorialisation of this conflict by none other than the 'Abbāsid Caliph, Hārūn al-Rashīd, 170–93/786–809), the lineage of Kharmīl gained social and political privileges through the selfless conduct and sacrifice of its ancestors in the service of the Ghurid monarch.[37] Given 'Izz al-Dīn Kharmīl's social standing in Ghur, it is not surprising that he worked

[34] Ibid., vol. 1, p. 417.

[35] Ibid., vol. 1, p. 402.

[36] Ibid., vol. 1, pp. 307, 412–13, and Juwainī, *Ta'rīkh-i Jahān Gushā*, translated by Boyle, vol. 1, pp. 328–9, 333–4.

[37] On the Kharmīl ancestors, Kharmīl Sām Ḥusain and Kharmīl Sām Banjī, the two brave warriors, *pahlawānān*, of Sultan 'Alā' al-Dīn Ḥusain (544–56/1149–61), see Jūzjānī, *Ṭabaqāt-i Nāṣirī*, vol. 1, p. 342. It is possible that the Kharmīls were distantly related to the Shansabanids through Amīr Banjī Nahārān; ibid., vol. 1, pp. 324–7. If so, then the mother of the two Sultans, Ghiyāṣ al-Dīn and Mu'izz al-Dīn, who was from the Banjī family (ibid., vol. 1, p. 353), provided an additional bond between the two families. On the Shansabanid conflict with the lineage of Shīsh, see ibid., vol. 1, pp. 324-7, 351-2, 354-5 and below.

so hard to consolidate his influence in the heartland of the Ghurid state rather than suffer the risk of political marginalization on the peripheries of the north Indian frontier.

Another individual, about whom we have far less detail, was Malik Ḥusām al-Dīn 'Alī Karmākh. It is not clear when Malik Ḥusām al-Dīn was appointed as the *walī*, Governor, of Multan, but in 582/1186 Mu'izz al-Dīn gave him charge of Lahore.[38] As the Governor of Multan, 'Alī Karmākh checked *shī'i* influence in the Sindh region. But Lahore was even more prestigious: this was the newly captured capital of the Ghaznavids.[39] 'Alī Karmākh was indisputably an honoured and trusted personage in Mu'izz al-Dīn's court and belonged to the aforementioned lineage of Shīsh, a family renowned for its military commanders, *pahlawānān*.[40] It is hardly surprising, therefore, to find Jūzjānī including him in the list of the *aqribā'* of Sultan Mu'izz al-Dīn.[41] Unfortunately, we have no information about Malik Ḥusām al-Dīn 'Alī Karmākh's subsequent career. Reportedly, he occupied no other command in north India and may, like 'Izz al-Dīn Kharmīl, have returned to Afghanistan where his family had a longstanding political claim.[42] Certainly, when Quṭb al-Dīn seized Lahore in 602/1206, it was not from 'Alī Karmākh.

[38] Ibid., vol. 1, p. 398. Mu'izz al-Dīn captured Multan in 571/1175–6 (ibid., vol. 1, p. 396). It is not clear, however, if Malik Ḥusām al-Dīn was appointed to Multan at this time. According to Jūzjānī, Mu'izz al-Dīn stopped at Multan during his campaign into Gujarat in 574/1178–9, but there were two other campaigns into the Sindh region as well: in 572/1176–7 against the Sanqurān and in 578/1182–3 into Dewal (ibid., vol. 1, p. 397). We cannot discount the possibility that Malik Ḥusām al-Dīn was given charge of Multan during one of these later campaigns.

[39] 'Alī Karmākh must have constructed the tomb of 'Khālid Walīd' (as it is remembered today) at Kabirwala near Multan some time during his service in the Punjab. Although the inscription framing the *mihrāb* ascribed the foundation of the tomb to 'Alī Karmākh, the identity of Khālid Walīd remains obscure. See Finbarr B. Flood, 'Ghūrid Architecture in the Indus Valley: The Tomb of Shaykh Sadan Shahid', *Ars Orientalis*, 31 (2001), p. 130; and Taj Ali, 'The Mehrab-Inscription of the so-called Tomb of Khalid Walid near Kabirwala (Khanewad District)', *Ancient Pakistan*, 7 (1991), pp. 39–46.

[40] Jūzjānī, *Ṭabaqāt-i Nāṣirī*, vol. 1, p. 327.

[41] Ibid., vol. 1, p. 405.

[42] The silences about his career in Afghanistan are unusual. It is always likely, of course, that Karmākh met an early, perhaps accidental, death. If that

Ḥasan Niẕāmī provides us with further examples of Ghurid elites active on the north Indian frontier. He mentions Naṣīr al-Dīn Ḥusain amidst a group of commanders who were part of an expeditionary force sent to Ajmer, *circa* 591/1195, to relieve Quṯb al-Dīn.[43] Naṣīr al-Dīn also figures in Jūzjānī's list of the *aqribā'* of Sultan Mu'izz al-Dīn. Here Jūzjānī describes him as the officer in charge of the hunt, the *amīr-i shikār*, at the Ghurid court in Ghazni.[44] He may have also participated in some other campaigns into north India, and Jūzjānī mentions at least one where Malik Naṣīr al-Dīn accompanied Quṯb al-Dīn Ai-Beg in the Nahrwala campaign into Gujarat in 593/1197.[45] Naṣīr al-Dīn returned to Ghazni immediately after the campaign, where, Jūzjānī makes quite clear, the Amir commanded considerable influence by the Sultan's death in 602/1206.

In the uncertain years after Mu'izz al-Dīn's death, the appanage of Ghazni managed to protect its autonomy from Ghur through the efforts of Naṣīr al-Dīn, who defeated and killed Sultan 'Alā' al-Dīn ibn 'Alā' al-Dīn Ātsiz (610-11/1213–14) of Ghur. Together with the Mu'izzī slave Tāj al-Dīn Ildūz, and the *wazīr*, Mu'ayyid al-Mulk Muḥammad 'Abd Allāh Sistāṇī, Naṣīr al-Dīn completed the triumvirate that wielded political power in Ghazni. The condominium was of short duration, however, and the increasing ambitions of the partners led them into a conflict where Tāj al-Dīn Ildūz managed to defeat and kill Naṣīr al-Dīn and the *wazīr* Mu'ayyid al-Mulk.[46]

---

had occured while he was at Lahore the chances of his 'martyrdom' being reported would have been greater.

[43] Ḥasan Niẕāmī, *Tāj al-Ma'āẕir*, translated by Bhagwat Saroop (Delhi: Saud Aḥmad Dehlavi, 1998), p. 217; translated by Elliot and Dowson, *The History of India as told by its Own Historians* (Allahabad: Kitab Mahal, 1963 reprint), vol. 2, p. 229. The other commanders were Jahān Pahlawān Asad al-Dīn, Asad al-Dīn Arsalān Kalij, 'Izz al-Dīn ibn Mu'ayyid al-Dīn Balkhī, and Sharaf al-Dīn Jarah. Excluding Naṣīr al-Dīn Ḥusain, there is no further information on any of these individuals, nor do they figure again in any of the accounts of Ghurid expedition into north India.

[44] Jūzjānī, *Ṯabaqāt-i Nāṣirī*, vol. 1, p. 405. Habibi writes the name as Nāṣir al-Dīn in his text, but in his citations in fn. 9 notes a variant manuscript where the name is spelt Naṣīr al-Dīn. Elsewhere, for example, vol. 1, pp. 381, 442, Habibi uses the form Naṣīr al-Dīn.

[45] At the end of the expedition both returned to Ghazni; ibid., vol. 1, p. 442.

[46] Ibid., pp. 381, 413.

In his brief military experience with north India, Naṣīr al-Dīn behaved much like the other *aqribā'* that we have just discussed. These were all individuals of considerable standing in Ghur, of honourable lineage and social networks, with their own armed retinues and followers. They occasionally participated in campaigns in north India with their troops, and the Sultan sometimes honoured them with military assignments. But these members of the Ghurid elite apparently found little to interest them in north India on a long-term basis. They eventually returned to Afghanistan and Shansabanid politics, the domain of their primary concern. The management of Mu'izzī conquests was left to people from a completely different social background, individuals who had more to gain by perpetuating their contact with the north Indian marches.

This larger body of people does not figure in Jūzjānī's list of *Malik wa aqribā'* of Mu'izz al-Dīn. Many of these commanders were also from Ghur, but there is no account of their participation in the high politics of the Shansabanid court at Firuz Koh or Ghazni. They were of humbler social background, minor commanders seeking their fortune in north India, and trying therefore to consolidate their positions by establishing themselves as leaders of small bodies of kindred groups.[47] Their relative political insignificance also meant that the chroniclers of the time seldom recorded their histories, and so we only chance upon incidental references to their careers on the frontier. One such individual was Malik Ẓiyā' al-Dīn Qāẓī Tūlak Muḥammad 'Abd al-Salām Nisāwī Tūlakī, the son of Qāẓī Majd al-Dīn Tūlakī. We know of him because he was Jūzjānī's maternal grandfather's brother, *pisar-i 'amm-i jadd-i mādarī*, and hailed from Tulak, where the author had many relatives and friends, *aqribā' wa ikhwān*.[48] In 587/1191, before Mu'izz al-Dīn's reversal at Tarain,

[47] I use the term 'kindred group' to suggest a corporate association of people that is 'egocentric'. It extends beyond cognatic relationships and is animated through a personal relationship that can encompass bonds of region and associations through past service. For a helpful discussion of 'kindred groups' in the study of early medieval social formations, see Alexander C. Murray, *Germanic Kinship Structure, Studies in Law and Society in Antiquity and the Early Middle Ages* (Toronto: Pontifical Institute of Medieval Studies, Studies and Texts, 1983), pp. 1–6.

[48] Jūzjānī, *Ṭabaqāt-i Nāṣirī*, vol. 1, p. 399 and vol. 2, p. 135.

Malik Ẓiyā' al-Dīn was appointed by the Sultan to the fort of Tabarhind. The Malik must have lacked the resources and personnel to adequately garrison Tabarhind because Jūzjānī notes that at Ẓiyā' al-Dīn's request, *ba iltimās-i o*, 1200 cavalrymen from Tulak were chosen from the forces of 'Hindustan and Ghazni' and added to his cavalry, *khail*. The Tūlakīs were beseiged by Prithvīrāja Chauhān after his victory over the Mu'izzī forces at Tarain, and without aid from the Sultan they held out for thirteen months.[49] But what is significant is that Malik Ẓiyā' al-Dīn marshalled the defence of Tabarhind around co-residents of Tulak, warriors specially deployed in the region because of a shared natal bond, and they adhered in defence of their charge.

There are similarities between Malik Ẓiyā' al-Dīn Qāẓī Tūlak and Malik Bahā' al-Dīn Muḥammad, the commander of Sangwan near Multan. Ḥasan Niẓāmī has a fleeting reference to Malik Bahā' al-Dīn in his narrative, and he does not indicate the year of his appointment to Sangwan.[50] Like Malik Ẓiyā' al-Dīn, who was supported by a cavalry consisting of kindred from Tulak, Bahā' al-Dīn relied upon siblings and local residents to protect his command. This alliance for local self-preservation took place when Sultan Mu'izz al-Dīn—involved in campaigns against the Khwārazm Shāh and the Qarā Khitā'ī in Khurasan (601/1204–5)—could not come to their defence during the Khokar attack on Multan and its environs.[51] The attack of the Khokars was challenged by Malik Bahā' al-Dīn and his brothers (who held military assignments, *iqṭā'*, in the neighbourhood), and they were 'accompanied by many of the chief people [*ra'is*], of the city'. The Malik and his brothers had consolidated their position in local society until, in the absence of royal aid from Ghazni, the 'chief people of the city' participated with the Maliks in domestic defence.

This banding together of military personnel on the frontier into kindred groups sharing geographical or genealogical links was also evident amongst the Khalajīs in north India. Although sharing ethno-linguistic affinities, the Khalaj were not a composite group of people

[49] Ibid., vol. 1, p. 400.

[50] Ḥasan Niẓāmī, *Tāj al-Ma'āṣir*, translated by Elliot and Dowson, vol. 2, pp. 233–4, translated by Saroop, pp. 253-4.

[51] This event can be situated at some time between Mu'izz al-Dīn's reversal at Andkhud, 601/1204-5, and his murder at Damyak in 602/1206.

in the late twelfth century. They were a humble pastoral people located in the Garmser-Zamindawar region of the Afghanistan plains to the south of Ghur and Ghazni. Through the eleventh century many of the Khalaj had dispersed from this region in search of military service under a variety of patrons. They had, on occasion, served with the Ghaznavid armed forces and were also recruited by the Ghurids and the Khwārazm Shāhs.[52] The Mu'izzī campaigns provided them with an attractive opportunity for service and upward mobility, and some Khalaj must have already been present in north India at the first battle of Tarain in 587/1191, when a Khalajī youth saved Mu'izz al-Dīn's life.[53] Examples of exceptional service notwithstanding, Mu'izz al-Dīn is not reported to have honoured any Khalaj warrior with independent command. Instead, the example of Muḥammad Bakhtiyār Khalajī, the most celebrated Khalajī commander of the time, underlines the indigent circumstances of many members of the Khalaj and the discrimination that they often faced in Ghazni and north India.

Strictly speaking, Muḥammad Bakhtiyār Khalajī was not a Mu'izzī Amir: the Sultan's muster-master in Ghazni found him unqualified for service, *mukhtasar*, and refused to recruit him. Bakhtiyār Khalajī persisted in his search for fortune through military service and came

[52] This dispersal meant that they sometimes served opposing sets of patrons. For service under the Ghaznavids see Bosworth, 'Khaladj', *EI*², vol. 4, p. 918; and; idem, *The Ghaznavids*, p. 111; under the Ghurids see Jūzjānī, *Ṭabaqāt-i Nāṣirī*, vol. 1, pp. 346, 373 and below; under the Khwārazm Shāh see Juwainī, *Ta'rīkh-i Jahān Gushā*, trans. Boyle, vol. 2, pp. 414, 462–4; Jūzjānī, *Ṭabaqāt-i Nāṣirī*, vol. 1, p. 420; and Peter Jackson, 'Jalāl al-Dīn, the Mongols, and the Khwarazmian Conquest of the Panjāb and Sind', *Iran*, 28 (1990), pp. 49, 51. For the Khalaj see also the anonymous, *Hudūd al-'Ālam*, pp. 111, 347–8; Vladimir Minorsky, 'The Turkish Dialect of the Khalaj', *Bulletin of the School of Oriental (and African) Studies*, 10 (1940), pp. 426–34; R. Dankoff, 'Kashghari on the Tribal and Kinship Organization of the Turks', *Archivum Ottomanicum*, 4 (1972), pp. 32–3; C.E. Bosworth and Gerard Clauson, 'Al-Xwarazmi on the Peoples of Central Asia', *Journal of the Royal Asiatic Society* (1965), pp. 8–9. From a different, Afghan nationalistic perspective see A.H. Habibi, 'Khaljis are Afghan Tarak or Turk', *Afghanistan*, 24 (1971), pp. 76–88; and Irfan Habib, 'Formation of the Sultanate Ruling Class', pp. 2–4, 7–8, who follows Habibi. For further comments, see Sunil Kumar, 'When Slaves were Nobles', p. 31, fn. 26.

[53] Jūzjānī. *Ṭabaqāt-i Nāṣirī*, vol. 1, p. 399.

to Hindustan. But, in Delhi as well, the *ṣāḥib-i diwān-i 'arẓ* found him so apparently without virtue, *jamālī na dād*, that he was rejected. Bakhtiyār Khalajī was poor, possessed rude armaments, and was not urbane enough (both *mukhtasar* and *jamālī na dād* carry the associated, contextual sense of coarseness) to warrant recruitment. In this sense, this Khalajī 'reject' did not qualify as a soldier, far be it an Amir, even of so 'middling' a standing as Malik Bahā' al-Dīn Muḥammad, commander of Sangwan.

The expanding Mu'izzī frontier in India, however, needed armed personnel—even rude, ill-accoutred ones. Rejected in Ghazni and Delhi, Bakhtiyār Khalajī eventually made his way to the eastern peripheries of Mu'izzī control in Hindustan. He found service with the Mu'izzī commander at Budaun and met with some military success, acquired horses, arms, and some wealth. Opportunities for independent action and amassing wealth here were still limited for a poor military entrepreneur, so he travelled further east: moving from the service of Hizabr al-Dīn Ḥasan Arnab at Budaun to Ḥusām al-Dīn Ughul-beg at Awadh. This was not a simple exchange of patrons; the migration also took him further from the fulcrum of Mu'izzī military initiatives in north India, to spaces where he could operate without supervision.[54]

The definitive transformation of the humble soldier into an Amir occurred with the conquest of Bihar and Bengal, but only sometime around 593/1197. As the fame of his military success and wealth spread, it attracted other migrants to his service. These included a variety of people—including scholars, *dānishmandān*, who had apparently opted for soldiering—but the group that seized the attention of observers of the time were the Khalajīs, adventurers not different from Bakhtiyār Khalajī himself. A large number of these Khalaj were already seeking their fortunes in north India and, lured by accounts of Bakhtiyār Khalajī's success, migrated to the eastern frontier and joined his service, *jamā'at-i Akhlāj az aṭrāf-i Hindūstān rūy bado āwardand.*[55] Some of these Khalajī migrants eventually became

[54] For an account of Bakhtiyār Khalajī's background and career, see ibid., pp. 422–3.

[55] Ibid., p. 423. In 582/1186 *Hindūstān* was a euphemism for the western Punjab–Haryana region under the erstwhile control of the late Ghaznavids, but

important military commanders in Bengal, but, as Jūzjānī brings out, their social origins were often as nondescript as their leader's.[56] Nor did success erase the stigma of low origins; jealous of Bakhtiyār Khalajī's success, Jūzjānī reports how the valiant, if simple, Amir was needled, humiliated, and provoked by the Mu'izzī *umarā'* in one of his rare visits to Delhi.[57] Class and cultural distinctions might have distanced the Khalajī migrants in Bengal from their compatriots in Hindustan, but, together with the shared vicissitudes of the frontier, it also brought the dispersed Khalaj together around a leader whose experiences and ambitions seemed to embody their own aspirations. For the moment, these were important cohering sentiments, particularly significant because the leaders of these Khalaj groups had little immediate experience of operating together as a political unit. In fact, by the time of Bakhtiyār Khalajī's assassination in 602/1206, this cohesion was already fast disappearing and subordinate Khalajī chieftains staked their claim to different parts of Bengal.[58]

The rare details that we possess regarding Bakhtiyār Khalajī and the larger Khalaj presence in Bengal fleshes out the opportunities that military service in north India opened for a wide spectrum of social groups in Afghanistan. Certainly, the evidence before us is very scanty, yet it is remarkably consistent in suggesting that class differences inflected the varying responses of the *aqribā'* and the humbler military commanders to the fabled wealth of the subcontinent. Elite Amirs served in north India but kept their networks in Afghanistan alive. After a stint in the marches they returned 'home' and capitalized on their interim gains to further their interests in Ghaznavid politics. The humbler Amirs migrated to north India, sometimes with their families, and sought to consolidate their networks through alliances with other military entrepreneurs of similar background. Hindustan

by the turn of the century the term encompassed areas of the Ganga–Jamuna *do-āb* into Budaun and Awadh. See Chapter 6.

[56] See in particular Jūzjānī's account of Ḥusām al-Dīn 'Iwaz Ḥusain Khalajī's origins, ibid., vol. 1, pp. 435–6.

[57] Ibid., p. 424.

[58] Ibid., pp. 432–6.

was a land of opportunity to these people, and Mu'izz al-Dīn's objectives in securing control of these regions was supported by the individual ambitions of these personnel.

To suggest, however, that notables in the service of the Mu'izzī regime in India faced the dilemma of balancing possible political marginalization in their homelands with realistic social and material profits available on the frontier carries the assumption that they had an option to choose the nature and area of their service—that they were, as the sub-title of the section notes, 'free Amirs' exercising their preferences. It is important to underline this point because, in the historiography of the early Delhi Sultanate, the title *Amīr* is frequently, and rather confusingly, translated as a noble who functioned somewhat like a bureaucrat. Devoid of any historical agency, these 'nobles' were reportedly 'transferred' from one appointment to another.[59] This was manifestly untrue in the case of 'Izz al-Dīn Ḥusain Kharmīl and Bakhtiyār Khalajī: free notables, but of divergent social backgrounds. It is only when we interrogate the nature of the 'freedom' possessed by some of these Amirs in choosing their preferred areas of service that we discern the importance of their world of kinship networks, privileges, and avenues of social mobility—the factors that made some individuals more powerful Amirs than others and complicated their relationship with the Sultan. Beyond the examples already provided, the case of Maulānā Sirāj al-Dīn Minhāj, Jūzjānī's father,

[59] Probably the most confused usage of 'noble' is to be found in the work of S.B.P. Nigam, *Nobility under the Sultans of Delhi*. According to him, the status of the 'nobility' was not determined by birth (pp. 2, 97), or feudal privileges (pp. 93–103), but the author does not find it necessary to explain why the individuals he was describing should then be referred to as nobles. To add to the confusion, Nigam goes on to add that the nobles also constituted one element of the 'bureaucratic' organization, of the Sultanate (see pp. 106–10). K.A. Nizami, 'The Early Turkish Sultans of Delhi' in *A Comprehensive History of India, vol 5: The Delhi Sultanat*, pp. 224–6, goes further and refers to 'an all-India military-cum-administrative service manned entirely by foreigners . . . Turkish slave officers and *Tazik*'. For a similar interpretation see also Mohammad Habib, 'Introduction to Elliot and Dowson's History of India, vol. 2', pp. 103–10; and Irfan Habib, 'The Formation of the Sultanate Ruling Class', p. 5.

provides a wonderful illustration of both the nature of service on the north Indian marches and the manner in which social backgrounds textured individual commitments to Mu'izz al-Dīn.

Maulānā Sirāj al-Dīn Minhāj belonged to a family of scholars and jurists who had shifted to Ghazni at the end of the eleventh century.[60] Although Jūzjānī extolled his father's achievements and honours in the *Ṭabaqāt-i Nāṣirī*, Sirāj al-Dīn Minhāj was not included in his son's list of eminent jurists, *qāẓīs*, of Mu'izz al-Dīn's realm.[61] Nor did he receive, his many travels notwithstanding, any significant office in Afghanistan. This was despite his seemingly enviable imperial connections: he was associated through his wife with the Princess Māh Malika, daughter of Sultan Ghiyāṣ al-Dīn of Ghur.[62] These connections seem to have made no significant impact on Sirāj al-Dīn Minhāj's early career. After an initial period of wandering, during which he delivered some sermons—apparently in search of patronage—in the Bamiyanid court, he was included in the second embassy sent by Ghiyāṣ al-Dīn to the 'Abbāsid court.[63] Ultimately, Sirāj al-Dīn accepted Mu'izz al-Dīn's offer to serve in Lahore together with Malik Ḥusām al-Dīn 'Alī Karmākh. This was some time after the capture of the city in 582/1186. While on the frontier in Lahore, Sirāj al-Dīn Minhāj performed the functions of the itinerant 'judge of the army of Hindustan', the *Qāẓī-i lashkar-i Hindūstān*, and had twelve camels assigned to aid him in fulfilling his responsibilities.[64]

[60] See Jūzjānī, *Ṭabaqāt-i Nāṣirī*, vol. 1, p. 239, for an early account of the family.

[61] Ibid., vol. 1, p. 405.

[62] Ibid., p. 369. The author spent his childhood in the Princess's harem.

[63] Ibid., p. 361. For the Maulānā's early connections with Bahā' al-Dīn Sām of Bamiyan, see pp. 388–9.

[64] Ibid., p. 398. The office of the *qāẓī-i lashkar-i Hindūstān* was much like the early Ayyubid and Ottoman office of *qāẓī-i 'askar* in that he had judicial responsibility and supervisory functions over a specific unit of the army. In the early Ottoman state the *qāẓī'yi askar* was also responsible for appointing subordinate *qāẓī*s in areas under his jurisdiction. See Uriel Heyd, *Studies in Old Ottoman Criminal Law* (Oxford: Clarendon Press, 1973); Halil Inalcik, *The Ottoman Empire: The Classical Age 1300–1600* (London: Weidenfeld and Nicolson, 1975); and *EI*², s.v. 'Ḳāḍi 'Askar'.

Although the fortunes of the 'army of Hindustan' over which Maulānā Sirāj al-Dīn Minhāj adjudicated between 582/1186 and 591/1195 were rapidly improving, it is not clear if his own responsibilities increased commensurately. Certainly, the passage of time did little to excite him about future prospects in Hindustan, and he responded with alacrity to better offers. After spending nine years on the frontier, around 591/1195, Maulānā Sirāj al-Dīn Minhāj's contacts in the Bamiyanid court finally came good. He was secretly enticed from Lahore and Mu'izzī service to the court of Sultan Bahā' al-Dīn Sām of Bamiyan (588–602/1192–1206). Here the Sultan's largesse made the Maulānā's previous responsibilities of *Qāẓī-i lashkar* appear modest. Jūzjānī reported that his father was now appointed to the dignity of the 'chief judge of the realm', the *quẓā-i mamālik*, and was given, in addition, the position of preacher to the victorious army, the *kh̲aṭābat* of the state, and responsibility as 'censor of public morals' [*iḥtisāb bā kull umūr-i shar'ī*]. Leaving aside possible exaggerations in reportage, the son clarified that, on a more material level, his father was also given two *madrasas* together with their immunities, *in'ām*, and revenue assignments, *iqṭā'*.[65]

For a relatively well-connected jurist, the early period of the Maulānā's life without an appointment in Afghanistan must have been extremely frustrating. By contrast, his appointment as *qāẓī-i lashkar* in Lahore was a huge honour. Now he had status and a share in the proceeds of the spoils from plunder campaigns; an enviable lot for many people. Yet, if comparable or better opportunities were to open up within the central Islamic lands, individuals looking for social mobility (like the Maulānā), with patronage networks in Afghanistan, could easily be enticed 'home'. Sirāj al-Dīn returned to Bamiyan, to what was certainly a less arduous life, without so much as informing and getting the permission of the Ghurid Sultan [*bī ijāzat-i Sulṭān G̲h̲iyaṣ al-Dīn bā ḥaẓrat-i Bamiyān raft*].[66]

Certainly, the 'push and pull factors' favouring service in north India at the turn of the twelfth century remained unappealing to social elites and the more ambitious jurists in Afghanistan. Instead, the

[65] Ibid., vol. 1, pp. 388–9. On Jūzjānī's life see also the appendix in Habibi's edition, vol. 2, p. 233, and Raverty's translation, vol. 1, pp. xxi–xxii.

[66] Ibid., vol.1, p. 389.

1190s saw the emergence of new opportunities for elite groups within the Shansabanid homelands in Afghanistan. These were the years when the forces of Ghur, Ghazni, Bamiyan, and Sistan opened a new military front in the northern territories of Ghur against the Khwārazm Shāh.[67] The area around Merv was seized in 588/1192 and an ambitious thrust into Transoxiana was initiated with the capture of Nishapur in 596/1199–1200.[68] These were years of high achievement, a moment when Ghur appeared on the threshold of becoming a dominant political power in Iran. It was during this period of intense political activity in Afghanistan that the withdrawal of the elite free Amirs from service in the north Indian marches becomes noticeable.[69] They reappear in the history of Ghur, where they were engrossed in consolidating their individual political fortunes.

Nor were the less privileged free Amirs and jurists untouched by the opening up of new frontiers and opportunities in the 1190s. Some, like Maulānā Sirāj al-Dīn, rushed to a new appointment in Bamiyan from Hindustan. Others, like Bakhtiyār Khalajī, chose to stay in north India even as they migrated eastwards into Lakhnauti and away from the second wave of Mu'izzī campaigns. These had led to the capture of cities like Delhi, Mīrat (modern Meerut), Hansi, Kōl (modern Aligarh), Benaras, Bayana, Awadh, and Kalinjar. Only the Ghaznavid army was involved in these campaigns, but, in contrast with the period 569–88/1173–92, Mu'izz al-Dīn gave the command of the newly annexed north Indian urban centres to his military slaves.[70] After 588/1192 they were the dominant military commanders of Mu'izzī dominions in north India.

The context of the withdrawal of the Ghurid free elites after 588/1192, or thereabouts, carried with it its own paradox: henceforth, Mu'izz al-Dīn reserved high offices in the north Indian marches largely for individuals who were 'unfree'. For the entrenched elite commanders of Ghur, the gradual attrition of lucrative possibilities in

[67] Jūzjānī, *Ṭabaqāt-i Nāṣirī*, vol. 1, pp. 359–60.

[68] Ibid.

[69] For a different interpretation of these developments, see Irfan Habib, 'The Formation of the Sultanate Ruling Class', pp. 6–7.

[70] For references to the appointments of Mu'izzī military slaves, see below. In the campaigns over 569–88/1173–92, Sialkot, Multan, and Lahore were held at different times by free Amirs; see above for references.

the north Indian marches coincided with the increasing allure of political opportunities available in the Ghurid homelands. As we will see in the following sections, the appointment of military slaves, *bandagān* (singular, *banda*), in the world of the north Indian marches made eminent sense from Sultan Mu'izz al-Dīn Ghūrī's perspective. Indeed, for the remaining years of the Sultan's reign, these *bandagān* pursued the cause of their master and were the vital element in consolidating his conquests in north India.

Mu'izzī Slaves and the *Bandagān-i Khāṣṣ*

While it is quite clear that the bulk of the conquests after 588/1192 and the military administration of the annexed urban centres in north India were entrusted to Mu'izz al-Dīn's *bandagān*, even these slaves were not a homogeneous body. The Mu'izzī corps of military slaves was led by an elite personnel of largely Turkish ethnic background. Although most of Mu'izz al-Dīn's *bandagān* remain anonymous to us, some of the elite cadre of slaves were extensively described by Jūzjānī and Fakhr-i Mudabbir. In the *Ṭabaqāt-i Nāṣirī*, Jūzjānī described this elite corps as the *bandagān-i khāṣṣ* (the senior, literally, the special slaves). These *bandagān-i khāṣṣ* were given strategic military and administrative assignments by Mu'izz al-Dīn and they participated in the Sultan's campaigns. He also deployed them, together with some free Amirs, within the central contingent, *qalb*, of his armed retinue, where they were supposed to protect the monarch during his campaigns. By reputation, at least, during moments of military crisis, they stood by their master and were the last to retreat.[71]

According to Jūzjānī, Mu'izz al-Dīn was apparently obsessed, *īlā'*, with the idea of purchasing Turkish slaves.[72] This was not an entirely unusual obsession for the time. Merchants brought Turkish slaves from the central Asian steppes to the Transoxianian slave markets at Bukhara and Samarqand, where they were sold at exorbitant

[71] On the *bandagān-i khāṣṣ*, their Turkish origins, their deployment within the qalb, and loyalty to their master during a time of crisis, see Jūzjānī, *Ṭabaqāt-i Nāṣirī*, vol. 1, p. 403, and the description of the Andkhud campaign. For a slightly later reference, see ibid., p. 456.

[72] Ibid., p. 410.

prices to a rich clientele throughout the central Islamic lands.[73] They commanded a high price, in part because of their fearsome reputation as warriors. In the ninth century, Jāhiz had eulogized the qualities of Turkish slaves to the 'Abbāsid *wazīr* in the following manner:

> If a thousand of their [Turks] horse join battle and let off a single shower of arrows, they can mow down a thousand [Arab] horse. No army can withstand this kind of assault. The Kharijites and the Bedouin have no skill worth mentioning in shooting from horseback, but the Turk can shoot at beasts, birds, hoops, men, sitting quarry, dummies and birds on the wing, and do so at full gallop to fore or to rear, to left or to right, upwards or downwards, loosing ten arrows before the Kharijite can nock one . . . and if they do turn their back, they are to be feared as much as deadly poison and sudden death; for their arrows hit the mark as much when they are retreating as when they are advancing.[74]

Reports such as Jāhiz's eulogy helped in disseminating the great reputation enjoyed by Turkish slaves; their actual deployment, however, varied in the different Sultanates. The Ghurid armed forces, for example, were largely infantry, and although they had a large contingent of cavalry and archers, we cannot be sure that the Turkish slaves performed these roles.[75] More to the point, we do know that the Turkish *bandagān-i khāṣṣ* were often deployed as Mu'izzī Governors and commanders of armies. But this seems to have occurred at a relatively late period: it is only in the nineteenth year of Mu'izz al-Dīn's reign that the first deployment of a military slave as a Governor is mentioned by Jūzjānī. Quṭb al-Dīn's appointment as the commander

[73] See C.E. Bosworth, 'Recruitment, Muster, and Review in Medieval Islamic Armies', in V.J. Parry and M.E. Yapp, eds, *War, Technology and Society in the Middle East* (London: Oxford University Press, 1975), p. 65.

[74] C.T. Harvey Walker, 'Jahiz of Basra to al-Fath ibn Khaqan on the "Exploits of the Turks and the Army of the Khalifate in General", *Journal of the Royal Asiatic Society*, 23 (1915), p. 666; and J.D. Latham, 'The Archers of the Middle East: The Turco-Iranian background', *Iran*, 8 (1970), p. 97. See also E. McEwen, 'Persian Archery Texts: Chapter Eleven of Fakhr-i Mudabbir's *Adab al-Harb*', *The Islamic Quarterly*, 18 (1974), pp. 76–99.

[75] The inconclusive nature of the evidence is brought out in a useful discussion by Peter Jackson, *The Delhi Sultanate*, pp. 11, 16–19.

of Kuhram in 588/1192 was almost certainly preceded by Tāj al-Dīn Ildūz's assignment to Karman and Sanquran, perhaps as early as, or soon after, 582/1186.[76] But even this would have been thirteen years into the Sultan's reign.

Certainly Mu'izz al-Dīn's weak economic and military standing in 569/1173 must have hampered his ability to procure expensive slaves.[77] Moreover, slaves segregated for military service could not be deployed immediately; they were carefully vetted, trained, and only gradually given the responsibilities that came with military command. Some slaves, like the Turk Tāj al-Dīn Ildūz or Iltutmish, were purchased when they were very young [*khurd sāl būd*].[78] The Sultan then raised Ildūz up the ranks [*buzurg gardānīd*], step by step [*pas martaba*], and eventually gave him charge [*sarwar*], of the Turkish slaves. When he was older [*chūn buzurg shud*], he received a command and governorship [*amārat wa wilāyat rasīd*]. At Mu'izz al-Dīn's death in 602/1206, he was the chief [*mihtar*], of the Turkish Maliks and the most distinguished of the slaves, *buzurgtar-i bandagān*.[79] Similarly, the slave Bahā' al-Dīn Tughril was raised in status

[76] Jūzjānī, *Ṭabaqāt-i Nāṣirī*, vol. 1, pp. 401, 411 for Ai-Beg and Ildūz's respective appointments. Although Jūzjānī does not provide any details, it is likely that Ildūz, the favourite slave of Mu'izz al-Dīn, received the commission to guard the staging posts for invasions into India around the time of the capture of Lahore in 582/1186. This would have facilitated Mu'izzī campaigns into Hindustan, which started almost immediately afterwards.

[77] In contrast to his humble condition at his accession (see above), the lesser half of the hoard in Mu'izz al-Dīn's treasury at the time of his death in 602/1206 was reported as 250 camel loads of gold, jewel-studded articles, and vessels of gold and silver. Much of this wealth accrued from the Sultan's campaigns in north India and from remittances sent to him by his slave commanders. Ibid., vol. 1, pp. 408–9. See also John F. Richards, 'Outflows of Precious Metals from Early Islamic India', John F. Richards, ed., *Precious Metals in the Later Medieval and Early Modern Worlds* (Durham, NC: Carolina Academic Press, 1983), pp. 183–205, especially p. 193.

[78] Jūzjānī, *Ṭabaqāt-i Nāṣirī*, vol. 1, pp. 411, 441. For an exception, note the case of Quṭb al-Dīn Ai-Beg who was purchased as a youth (ibid., p. 416), but eased into a command only once he had matured in service and displayed his trustworthiness. See below.

[79] Ibid., p. 411.

[*buzurg gardānīda būd*], after (appropriate) training, *batarbiyat*.[80] There is greater detail about Ai-Beg. After Mu'izz al-Dīn raised him above the rest of the newly purchased slaves and made him serve in the royal court, his was a faster rise in the ranks: from a leader of troops, *sar-i khail*; to amir of the stables, *amīr-i ākhūr*; to incharge of the foragers on campaign, *bar sar-i . . . 'ulafgī*, until he was given the assignment, *iqṭā'*, of Kuhram in the Punjab.[81]

There are meaningful points of comparison between the processes of appointment and promotion within the Ghurid slave corps and the normative system of slave deployment described by the Seljūq *wazīr* Niẓām al-Mulk in his *Siyāsat Nāma*. The *wazīr* noted:

> This is the system which was still in force in the time of the Sāmānids [204-395/819–1005]. Slaves were given gradual advancement in rank according to their length of service and general merit. Thus after a slave was bought, for one year he was commanded to serve on foot at a rider's stirrup . . . when he had done one year's service with boots, the tent leader spoke to the chamberlain and he informed the King; then they gave him a small Turkish horse . . . in his third year he was given a belt to gird on his waist. In the fourth year they gave him a quiver and bow case. . . . In his fifth year he got a better saddle and a bridle with stars on it. . . . In the sixth year he was made a cup-bearer or water-bearer. . . . In the seventh year he was a robe bearer. In the eighth year they gave him a single apex, sixteen-peg tent and put three newly bought slaves in his troop. . . . Every year they improved his uniform and embellishments and increased his rank and responsibility until he became a troop-leader and so on until he became a chamberlain.[82]

[80] Ibid., p. 421.

[81] Ibid., pp. 416–17.

[82] Niẓām al-Mulk, *Siyāsat Nāma*, pp. 103-4. It is useful to compare this process of training with the experiences of other slaves in the Delhi Sultanate. We have the greatest amount of information concerning the slaves of Shams al-Dīn Iltutmish summarized in Table 1. For an interesting account of Sultan Ghiyāṣ al-Dīn Balban's experience (664–85/1266–86), see Ibn Baṭṭūṭa, *Rehla*, translated by Mahdi Ḥusain (Baroda: Oriental Institute, Gaekwad Oriental Series, no. 122, 1976 reprint), pp. 36–7. For a rare account by a *banda* of his early experiences as a slave, see M. Nazim, 'The Pand-Namah of Subuktigin',

Ghurid practice was not nearly as structured as Niẓām al-Mulk might have wanted it to be, but the process of training, evaluation, and gradual advancement was one that all military slaves—irrespective of their age and ethnic background—went through. The intention was to create a new identity for the slave where his dependence upon his master was absolute. To achieve this, the alienation of the slave from his natal surroundings and the related absence of social moorings in his new environment were crucial.[83] In their stead, newly fostered ties and opportunities in the service of the monarch enticed the slave into an exotic world.

The Sultan sought to ensure that his dependents from foreign cultural environments fit into their new social and religious surroundings. As a result, together with training in arms and deployment with the army, it was important that the slaves be acculturated into the religion and etiquette of his new world. This religious instruction was provided to both captured and purchased slaves segregated for military service. At least in the case of those slaves purchased by the Sultan, the slave-merchant or a previous master sometimes carried out this aspect of the training. A slave, who possessed preliminary military and religious training commanded an excellent price in the slave market. Quṭb al-Dīn's value, for example, accrued from the religious training that he had received earlier from the Ḥanafī jurist Fakhr al-Dīn 'Abd al-'Azīz Kūfī.[84] This preliminary introduction to the Islamic world was of enormous value, for it implied that the slave possessed the rudimentary etiquette to attend the imperial court, enabling the Sultan to interact with his slave without social discord.[85] A secondary effort was also

---

pp. 605-28, especially p. 623. Also see, more generally, Niẓām al-Mulk, *Siyāsat Nāma*, pp. 102–17.

83 On the significance of natal alienation and social death in slavery within the Islamicate context, see Ibn Khaldūn, *The Muqaddimah*, translated by F. Rosenthal, edited and abridged, N.J. Dawood (Princeton: Bollingen Series, Princeton University Press, 1974 reprint), pp. 103–5. For a theoretical discussion of its implications, see Orlando Patterson, *Slavery and Social Death* (Cambridge: Harvard University Press, 1982).

84 Jūzjānī, *Ṭabaqāt-i Nāṣirī*, vol. 1, p. 416; and Fakhr-i Mudabbir, *Ta'rīkh-i Fakhr al-Dīn Mubārak Shāh*, pp. 21–2.

85 In addition to their training, what further endeared the youth of the Central Asian steppe to the Sultan, as in the case of Ildūz and Iltutmish, was their

directed to seduce the loyalty of the slaves by holding out the promise of wealth and high office in the service of the monarch. This helped draw the contrast between the lives of the slaves in their former environment, while they were free, and as slaves in the service of the Sultan. Fakhr-i Mudabbir presented the imperial case faithfully. Referring solely to Turkish slaves, he noted that in the steppes the Turks were nondescript, indistinguishable from each other in power and wealth; but when they came within the Muslim world, 'the further [the Turk slaves] are taken from their hearth, their kin and their dwellings [*har chand az khāna wa aqribā' wa wilāyat-i khud dūrtar uftad*] the more valued, precious and expensive they become [*qadr wa qīmat wa bahā'ī-yi o ẓiyādat gardad*] and they become commanders and generals [*umarā' wa sipahsālārān shawand*].'[86]

The ideal distance between the steppe and the Islamic world that Fakhr-i Mudabbir was hinting towards was not merely spatial but also cultural. At least, according to that author, the ability to renounce heathen practice and natal root was an ethnic quality peculiar to the Turks. He noted that 'when their hearts turn to Islam [*chunān dil Musalmānī banihand*] they do not really remember their homes, their places of origin or their kinsmen [*khāna wa jāy wa aqribā' besh yād nakunand*].'[87]

I am sure, however, that not all Turks were quite able to see the experience of enslavement as a chance to make good in new surroundings. Fakhr-i Mudabbir, writing for Quṭb al-Dīn Ai-Beg, a patron of Turkish slave antecedents, definitely overstated his case; there were examples of discord in the imperial court from the Ghaznavid period caused by Turk slaves who lacked sufficient decorum.[88]

---

comeliness, their fairness [*jamāl*], and agreeable manners. Jūzjānī, *Ṭabaqāt-i Nāṣirī*, vol. 1, pp. 411, 442. Such youth were prized possessions and were kept in close proximity to the monarch. Nevertheless, while pedarasty might endear a young slave to his master, this did not necessarily improve the slave's political status. Quṭb al-Dīn Ai-Beg, for one, possessed no apparent beauty, *ba ẓāhir-i jamālī nadāsht* (vol. 1, p. 416). This, of course, did not prevent his subsequent rise to political prominence.

[86] Fakhr-i Mudabbir, *Ta'rīkh-i Fakhr al-Dīn Mubārak Shāh*, p. 36.

[87] Ibid.

[88] Note the examples of Asïghtigin/'Asaftigin Ghāzī and Eryaruq/Aryāruq for the Ghaznavids. See C.E. Bosworth, *The Ghaznavids*, p. 57. According to

Yet Fakhr-i Mudabbir was correct within a more limited context. The process of training was certainly aimed at creating a *banda* who was at home within a Perso-Islamicate context, was loyal to his master, and grateful for the avenues of promotion that opened up for him in imperial service. And there were notable successes. Among such slaves, some certainly did learn the etiquette of their master quickly enough, so that the Sultan felt comfortable in their company, and it was through a process of careful screening that qualified cadets gradually made their way into the ranks of the *khāṣṣ* slaves.

It is here that slaves of Turkish origin had an advantage. Since they were a financial investment (in contrast to war booty), the merchants and their masters made careful attempts to train this group. Quṭb al-Dīn is a good example here. Purchased with prior training, he had a head start over many of his peers and leapfrogged as many ranks within a couple of years as Niẓām al-Mulk might have ideally stretched over half a decade.[89] It was thus from this smaller group of expensive slaves purchased from slave brokers that most of the more privileged *bandagān-i khāṣṣ* originated.[90]

'Awfī, Iltutmish was also concerned about the impetuosity [*tahawwur*], of the Turkish slave and preferred the Persian secretary to handle delicate fiscal investigations. 'Awfī, *Jawāmi' al-Ḥikāyāt*, British Library ms. Or.2676, fol. 263b, cited by Peter Jackson, *The Delhi Sultanate*, p. 65 and fn. 29. See also M. Nizamuddin, *Introduction to the Jawāmi' u'l-Ḥikāyāt wa Lawāmi' u'r-Riwāyāt of Sa'dīu'd-Dīn Muḥammad al-'Awfī* (London: E.J.W. Gibb Memorial Series, 1929), p. 228.

89 In 587/1191, at the time of the Ghurid campaigns in Khurasan against Sulṭān Shāh, brother of the Khwārazm Shāh Tekish, Quṭb al-Dīn was the Commander of the Stables, *amīr-i ākhūr*. During the campaigns he received additional charge as leader of the foragers. In the very next year, 588/1192, the military assignment, *iqṭā'*, of Kuhram was entrusted to him. See Jūzjānī, *Ṭabaqāt-i Nāṣirī*, vol. 1, pp. 398, 416–17.

90 Although Jūzjānī (see vol. 1, pp. 411, 415, 442) only gives us direct information about the purchase of Ildūz, Ai-Beg, and the inconclusive financial negotiation regarding the price of Iltutmish, it is not hard to surmise that the other Turkish slaves were also purchased. The Shansabanid territories in the 1170s and 1180s, decades when Mu'izz al-Dīn was raising his slave retinue, did not have a frontier with central Asia. As a result, the Sultan remained dependent upon slave brokers for the periodic supply of qualified, and hence expensive, *bandagān*.

The starting point to a position of trust and command for the *bandagān-i khāṣṣ* was an opportunity to personally serve the monarch. During this period the slave would display his personal worth and ability to follow the instructions of his master. The master in turn would establish close personal ties with his subordinate and win his trust and affection through kindness and choice rewards. This was a period of nourishing or fostering a slave, and the Persian chronicles used the verb *parwardan*, to foster, and *tarbiyat*, educating or nourishing, to indicate the process through which slaves were regarded, in time, as foster sons. Fakhr-i Mudabbir noted that, after a period of close association, Mu'izz al-Dīn 'adored [Quṭb al-Dīn] as a beloved, precious son [*farzand-i 'azīz girāmī baparward*] [and] went to extremes in his rearing [*wa dar tarbiyat-i o mubālaghat namūd*]'.[91]

The ties of relationship established between the *bandagān-i khāṣṣ* and the Sultan were complemented by similar ties between the slaves themselves. Niẓām al-Mulk had explained that a slave's appointment as the commander of a province with a military retinue should occur only after his 'suitability, skill and bravery' were apparent and, most crucially, after he had been 'found to be considerate to his fellows and loyal to his master'. These were the qualities, Jūzjānī suggested in an elaborate anecdote, that brought Quṭb al-Dīn to the attention of Sultan Mu'izz al-Dīn.

Jūzjānī reported that Mu'izz al-Dīn sometimes held convivial gatherings and parties [*baṭarab wa 'aish*], and during one such engagement he ordered the distribution of precious gifts amongst his (attendant) slaves. Quṭb al-Dīn received his share of the Sultan's largesse, but he came out of that party and proceeded to share his portion with the slaves outside: the Turks, the pages in charge of the curtains, those responsible for pitching the imperial tents and laying the carpets, and sundry other workers [*az majlis bīrūn āmad, tamām ān māl baturkān wa pardahdārān wa farrāsh wa dīgar kārdārān bakhshīd*]. These junior slaves in training in the Sultan's court were, like Quṭb al-Dīn himself, deployed as attendants. At any rate, as Jūzjānī's anecdote concludes, when Quṭb al-Dīn's conduct was reported to the Sultan, he rewarded the slave and employed him in the court and kept him close at hand. This marked the slave's rise to favour.[92]

[91] Fakhr-i Mudabbir, *Ta'rīkh-i Fakhr al-Dīn Mubārak Shāh*, p. 22.
[92] Jūzjānī, *Ṭabaqāt-i Nāṣirī*, vol. 1, p. 416.

Jūzjānī deployed this anecdote as a powerful narrative device to draw attention to Quṭb al-Dīn Ai-Beg's unique qualities; debating its veracity might make us miss the purpose it was supposed to serve in his history. According to Jūzjānī, Quṭb al-Dīn Ai-Beg was rewarded by his master because he had inadvertently shown a degree of corporate solidarity with those of his less fortunate slave 'brethren' who happened to be absent from the Sultan's soirée. This concern for his companions indicated leadership qualities in the slave, a disposition that the astute master (together with the reader of the anecdote) needed to appreciate.

It worked in the interest of the monarch if the slave corps were bonded by a sentiment of common interest and sympathy. Muting hierarchical distinctions between the older slaves and the newly purchased ones, by incorporating them within a patrimonial lexicon, meant that ties other than a formal chain of command united the group. In fact, Mu'izz al-Dīn seems to have taken considerable care to develop a sense of corporate solidarity amongst his *bandagān-i khāṣṣ*. In a manner that paralleled the cousin marriages of the Shansabanid imperial lineage, the Sultan ordered affinal relations between some of his *bandagān-i khāṣṣ*. The Sultan commanded that the daughters of Ildūz should marry Quṭb al-Dīn Ai-Beg and Qubācha; two daughters of Quṭb al-Dīn were married, one after the death of the other, to Qubācha.[93] Mu'izz al-Dīn sought to tie his slaves not merely to himself through his affection, close association, and via the political and economic opportunities proffered to the select, he also wanted them to bond with each other through a unity of interests and social interdependence. There might have been a degree of stratification amongst the larger corps of slaves where the older, trained *bandagān-i khāṣṣ* guided the newly acquired pages. But within the *khāṣṣ* group, Mu'izz al-Dīn wanted to introduce an element of corporate egalitarianism where he would be the linchpin in these relationships. The Sultan dispensed favours that determined the honour and responsibilities appropriate to all of his slaves.

As in the case of Quṭb al-Dīn, it is likely that Mu'izz al-Dīn sought to ascertain the competence and loyalty of his military slaves before

[93] Ibid., pp. 411, 418.

he appointed them to independent command in north India. Hence the 'delay' in the appointment of the *bandagān-i khāṣṣ* to independent military assignments: they had to qualify for this honour. In the far-flung, hostile, yet lucrative frontier zone in north India, it seems that these *khāṣṣ* Mu'izzī slaves were the ideal, closely drilled, military personnel who could be most trusted with independent initiative to pursue and manage Mu'izz al-Dīn's programme of conquest and plunder. Certainly, as the second wave of Mu'izzī invasions started in north India in the 590s/1190s, the Sultan assigned the majority of his new conquests to his elite slaves.

The Dispersal of the Mu'izzī *Bandagān-i Khāṣṣ* in North India

Despite the importance of the Mu'izzī *bandagān-i khāṣṣ* in the consolidation of their master's authority in north India, we are not equally well informed about all of their careers. Given the nature of the available sources, this uneven coverage is hardly surprising. All extant texts produced in the early thirteenth century were dedicated to the rulers of Delhi: Quṭb al-Dīn Ai-Beg or the lineage of his slave, Shams al-Dīn Iltutmish.[94] The Quṭbī and Delhi-centred provenance of the surviving texts from this period shaped their discourse, diminishing, indeed obscuring, the activities of the other Mu'izzī *bandagān-i khāṣṣ* in north India.

Amongst the Mu'izzī *bandagān-i khāṣṣ*, other than the great hero of the early Persian narratives, Quṭb al-Dīn Ai-Beg, with his charge of Kuhram, and later, in 588/1192, Delhi and Tabarhind (modern Bhatinda), we have the clearest information about Tāj al-Dīn Ildūz, Governor of Karman and Sanquran, strategically important sites for organizing campaigns into north India.[95] Jūzjānī, discoursed at length on Ildūz because, after the death of Mu'izz al-Dīn, this slave became the most important political figure in Ghazni. Jūzjānī also informs us that the Sultan assigned Uchch and Multan at an uncertain date to

[94] Fakhr-i Mudabbir presented his *Ta'rīkh* to Quṭb al-Dīn and his *Ādāb al-Ḥarb* to Iltutmish. Ḥasan Niẓāmī and Jūzjānī dedicated their respective texts to Iltutmish and his youngest son Nāṣir al-Dīn Maḥmūd. See also Appendix.

[95] For references, see above.

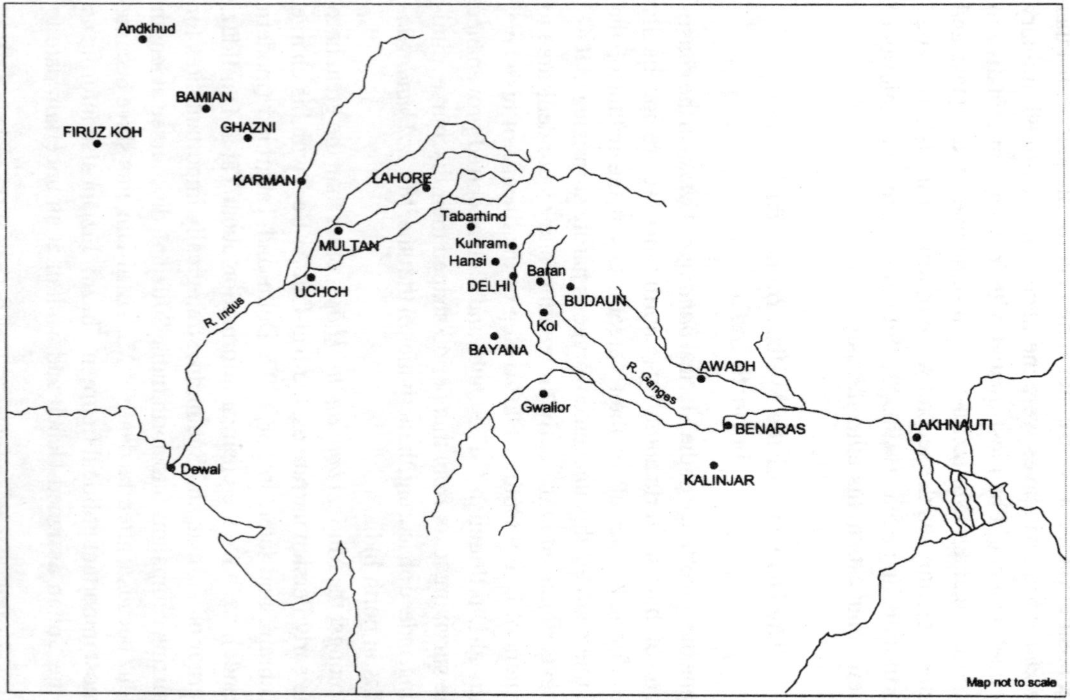

Map 2: The Mu'izzī *Bandagān* in Hindustan

Nāṣir al-Dīn Ai-Temur and, upon his death in 601/1205, to the slave Nāṣir al-Dīn Qubācha.[96] Although Jūzjānī provides no details about Nāṣir al-Dīn Ai-Temur he could hardly ignore Qubācha; the Amir was the patron of many émigrés, including the author. Less discussed in the records of the time was the assignment of Thangir, in the district of Bayana. This was given by Mu'izz al-Dīn to Bahā' al-Dīn Tughril in 592/1196, and of special interest to us is the manner in which its annexation was treated in the Persian chronicles.

Jūzjānī mentioned the conquest of Thangir in three separate sections in his history: in his narrative concerning Mu'izz al-Dīn, and then in his respective accounts of Quṭb al-Dīn and Bahā' al-Dīn. In the first two instances Jūzjānī records rather laconically that Quṭb al-Dīn seized Bayana and incorporated it within his territory.[97] There is no mention at all of Bahā' al-Dīn in these notices. It is in Jūzjānī's brief historical account of Bahā' al-Dīn Tughril that the author acknowledges Thangir's annexation by none other than Mu'izz al-Dīn himself. Here the author also reveals that the Sultan appointed Bahā' al-Dīn, not Quṭb al-Dīn, as its Governor.[98] Ḥasan Niẓāmī corroborated this information and remained, in this instance, remarkably lucid about the sequence of events.[99] By contrast, Fakhr-i Mudabbir more ambiguously placed Thangir within the areas captured by Quṭb al-Dīn.[100]

It is important to keep in mind that without Jūzjānī's brief narrative on Bahā' al-Dīn Tughril's career we might well have trusted his other references concerning Thangir's assignment to Quṭb al-Dīn. This was, after all, confirmed by Fakhr-i Mudabbir's brief but otherwise chronologically reliable account. Ḥasan Niẓāmī's reference to Tughril's governorship of Thangir would have remained unsupported,

[96] Jūzjānī, *Ṭabaqāt-i Nāṣirī*, vol. 1, p. 419. Habibi writes Qubācha's predecessor's name as Ai-Tam; Raverty has 'Aetamur' (vol. 1, pp. 531-2). The orthography is unclear and I have adapted Raverty's (and Peter Jackson, *The Delhi Sultanate*, p. 27 and fn. 16) transcription.

[97] Jūzjānī, *Ṭabaqāt-i Nāṣirī*, vol. 1, pp. 401, 417.

[98] Ibid., p. 421.

[99] Ḥasan Niẓāmī, *Tāj al-Ma'āṣir*, translated by Elliot and Dowson, vol. 2, p. 227, translated by Saroop, pp. 196-202.

[100] Fakhr-i Mudabbir, *Ta'rīkh-i Fakhr al-Dīn Mubārak Shāh*, p. 23.

its integrity suspect because it was not in harmony with Niẓāmī's otherwise fulsome eulogy of Quṭb al-Dīn's command of Mu'izzī territories in north India.[101] The Persian evidence, in other words, is remarkably ambiguous about Bahā' al-Dīn Tughril's independent command of Bayana, suggesting instead that it was under Delhi and Quṭb al-Dīn Ai-Beg's control.

We are fortunate to glean some information on Bahā' al-Dīn Tughril and Bayana; in many other cases the fleeting notices given to Mu'izzī slave commanders makes it difficult to decipher their service relationships at all. Take the case of Ḥusām al-Dīn Ughul Beg, for example. Was he a Mu'izzī *bandagān-i khāṣṣ*, or, as Ḥasan Niẓāmī would suggest, a subordinate of Quṭb al-Dīn?[102] In the early years of Mu'izzī expansion into the Jamuna–Ganges basin, Ughul Beg was given the command of Kōl (modern Aligarh) in 590/1194,[103] to which the region of Awadh was added soon after. He must have lost this

[101] For a positivistic reading of Ḥasan Niẓāmī's text, see I.H. Siddiqi, 'The Thirteenth and Fourteenth Century Farmans concerning the Conduct of the Governors under the Sultans of Delhi', in idem, *Perso-Arabic Sources of Information on the Life and Conditions in the Sultanate of Delhi* (Delhi: Munshiram Manoharlal Publishers Pvt. Ltd., 1992), pp. 168–9.

[102] Jūzjānī, *Ṭabaqāt-i Nāṣirī*, vol. 1, pp. 423, 451, who does not mention his master; Ḥasan Niẓāmī, *Tāj al-Ma'āṣir*, translated by Elliot and Dowson, vol. 2, 224, translated by Saroop, p. 177, suggests that Ughul Beg was a dependant of Quṭb al-Dīn. Together with Irfan Habib, 'The Formation of the Sultanate Ruling Class', p. 6 and fn. 30, Peter Jackson (*The Delhi Sultanate*, p. 26 and fn. 13) accepts Niẓāmī's account. There is little consistency in the reading of the officers's title. According to Habibi, the various manuscripts of the *Ṭabaqāt-i Nāṣirī* have variants of the Turkish title Ughul-Beg (see vol. 1, p. 423, fn. 1.). Al-'Awfī, *Jawāmi' al-Ḥikāyāt wa Lawāmi' al-Riwāyāt* also mentions the name as Ḥusām al-Dīn Ughul-Beg; M. Nizamuddin transliterates this as Aghlabek. See M. Nizamuddin, *Introduction to the Jawāmi'u'l-Ḥikāyāt*, p. 228. I.H. Siddiqi reads Ughul Beg as 'Alaik. Siddiqi, 'Lubab-ul-Albab and Jawami-'ul-Hikayat', *Perso-Arabic Sources of Information*, pp. 32–3. Raverty transliterated the title Aghul-Bak (translated by Raverty, vol. 1, pp. 549, 627). See also the commentary of S.H. Hodivala, *Studies in Indo-Muslim History: A Critical Commentary on Elliot and Dowson's History of India* (Bombay: Popular Book Depot, 1939, 1957, 2 vols) vol. 1, pp. 180–1. Peter Jackson (see above for references) reads the title as Oghulbeg.

[103] This would be only two years after Quṭb al-Dīn's own appointment to Kuhram and, eventually, Delhi.

position to Quṭb al-Dīn's appointee Qaymāz Rūmī some time around Mu'izz al-Dīn's death in 602/1206.[104] In the years after 607/1210 and Quṭb al-Dīn's death, Ḥusām al-Dīn and Rūmī had contrasting runs of fortune. During the early years of Sultan Shams al-Dīn Iltutmish's reign (607–33/1210–36), 'Awfī's evidence suggests that Ug͟hul Beg was assimilated into the Sultan's retinue together with some other Mu'izzī's.[105] On the other hand, Iltutmish fought and defeated the Quṭbī commander Qaymāz Rūmī at Ranthambhor in 623/1226.[106] It is when we take their possible rivalry into account and juxtapose their careers in the longer duration—Ḥusām al-Dīn seems to have prospered in the dispensation of authority by Mu'izz al-Dīn and survived to serve Iltutmish, whereas Qaymāz Rūmī profited during the Quṭbī dispensation and battled with Iltutmish—that we get an insight into their possible affiliations to different patrons. Whether Ḥusām al-Dīn Ug͟hul Beg was a Mu'izzī or a Quṭbī subordinate is of some importance, because these political associations reflect degrees of autonomy: as part of a Mu'izzī dispensation of power Ḥusām al-Dīn Ug͟hul Beg would have a dyadic, binary relationship with his master, the Ghurid monarch. It is because of this dependent relationship that Ug͟hul Beg received the command of Kōl and Awadh. This connection between the master and the slave was, in turn, quite distinct from Quṭb al-Dīn's association with Mu'izz al-Dīn, and it also meant that their respective commands were discrete from each other.

But beyond Ḥusām al-Dīn Ug͟hul Beg, there were other military commanders about whom we would like to know more: Sipahsālār Hizabr al-Dīn Ḥasan Arnab assigned to Budaun in 594/1197-8,[107] for

[104] Jūzjānī, *Ṭabaqāt-i Nāṣirī*, vol. 1, pp. 432–3 and below for further details. There is no reference to Qaymāz Rūmī in Ḥasan Niẓāmī.

[105] See M. Nizamuddin, *Introduction to the Jawāmi'u'l-Ḥikāyāt*, p. 228, and I.H. Siddiqi, 'Lubab-ul-Albab and Jawami-'ul-Hikayat', pp. 32–3. Habibi has not included Ḥusām al-Dīn in his list of Shamsī notables but his name figures in variant manuscripts: Jūzjānī, *Ṭabaqāt-i Nāṣirī*, vol. 1, pp. 451-2 and fn. 6. See also Chapter 3 for details on the nature of Mu'izzī and the Quṭbī alliances at Iltutmish's accession.

[106] Jūzjānī, *Ṭabaqāt-i Nāṣirī*, vol. 1, p. 452 and the list of Iltutmish's conquests.

[107] For Ḥasan Arnab's command of Budaun see ibid., p. 422, and for the probable date of the event: Fak͟hr-i Mudabbir, *Ta'rīk͟h-i Fak͟hr al-Dīn Mubārak Shāh*, p. 24. He was subsequently moved to Kalinjar in 599/1202–3 by Quṭb

example; or the mysterious 'Izz al-Dīn 'Alī who figures as the commander of Nagaur in some manuscripts but not in others.[108] The report on these individuals is ambiguous at best, and, if carefully read, suggests a degree of autonomy that the Persian evidence did not want to countenance. If we take the Delhi-centred provenance of the early-thirteenth-century chroniclers into account, it is hardly surprising that they hesitate to recognize the presence of multiple sites of Mu'izzī power in north India.[109] Fakhr-i Mudabbir, for example,

---

al-Dīn, an appointment that would suggest that Arnab was a dependant of Quṭb al-Dīn, not Mu'izz al-Dīn. See Ḥasan Niẓāmī, *Tāj al-Ma'āṣir*, translated by Elliot and Dowson, vol. 2, p. 232, translated by Saroop, p. 244. At Arnab's appointment to Kalinjar, Budaun must have come under the control of Quṭb al-Dīn's slave Shams al-Dīn Iltutmish: see Jūzjānī, *Ṭabaqāt-i Nāṣirī*, vol. 1, p. 443. It is hard to relate the chronology of these events to the political relationships described in these accounts. Iltutmish, for example, is portrayed by Jūzjānī as one of Quṭb al-Dīn's senior slaves but his first assignment, that of Gwalior, only took place in 597/1200–1, some three years *after* Ḥasan Arnab's deployment in Budaun. This would make Ḥasan Arnab senior, in fact, to Iltutmish. Moreover, in his account of Mu'izz al-Dīn's reign, Jūzjānī (vol. 1, p. 401) narrates the sequential subjugation of Nahrwala, Thangir, Gwalior and Budaun by Quṭb al-Dīn. Some of this is evidently hyperbole: Nahrwala was raided not subjugated and Quṭb al-Dīn never controlled Thangir. Other parts seem chronologically inaccurate: Gwalior was seized in 597/1200–1 after Budaun in 594/1197–8. Or was Jūzjānī suggesting that just as Quṭb al-Dīn seized Gwalior in violation of Mu'izz al-Dīn's wishes, he also captured Budaun, displacing Ḥasan Arnab, an earlier appointee of Mu'izz al-Dīn? There is merit in this speculation because Mu'izz al-Dīn's preoccupation with affairs in Khurasan forced him to ignore affairs in India during the years 597–602/1200–6. These were the years that Quṭb al-Dīn profitably used to extend his own influence (see below for a fuller discussion). There is no ambiguity regarding any of these questions in Irfan Habib, 'The Formation of the Sultanate Ruling Class', p. 6, and fn. 31. Habib follows Ḥasan Niẓāmī in identifying Arnab as a dependant of Quṭb al-Dīn and reads the name as Artab. S.H. Hodivala, *Studies in Indo-Muslim History*, vol. 2, pp. 53–4, argues for Arnab as the correct reading. Peter Jackson, *The Delhi Sultanate*, p. 26 and fn. 13, follows Hodivala's reading of the name and Ḥasan Niẓāmī's account in making him Quṭb al-Dīn's deputy.

[108] Habibi does not include this Amir's name in his edition but notes that variant manuscripts do mention him. Jūzjānī, *Ṭabaqāt-i Nāṣirī*, vol. 1, p. 422, fn. 5. See also Peter Jackson, *The Delhi Sultanate*, p. 27.

[109] The historiographical intersection with this evidence has also varied.

wants his readers to appreciate that Quṭb al-Dīn was the chosen commander, the viceroy if you wish, of Sultan Mu'izz al-Dīn in India:

> This hero and world conqueror of Hind [Quṭb al-Dīn] was addressed as Malik,[110] and was made the heir apparent [*walī 'ahd*], to Hindustan, and the lands from the gates of Peshawar [Parshūr] to the limits of Hind were given to him, and the [authority] to appoint and remove [literally, 'unfasten and bind, *ḥall wa 'aqd*'], the remaining commanders was entrusted with him [*badū mufauwaz gardānīd*]. [Mu'izz al-Dīn] left [Quṭb al-Dīn] as his deputy and heir in the capital of Hindustan [*qā'im maqām wa walī 'ahd-i khud badār al-mulk-i Hindūstān baguẕasht*], and sent him back to Delhi.[111]

Fakhr-i Mudabbir and, for that matter, Ḥasan Niẓāmī, had little inhibition eulogizing Quṭb al-Dīn's status. But even Mudabbir's discourse wore thin on occasion, and the author's dissimulation was apparent in the fleeting recognition he paid to the presence of other prominent military commanders:

> And although [*agarcheh*], all the victories which God gave [Quṭb al-Dīn Ai-Beg] are clearer than the sun, and well known to all the world: nevertheless [*ammā*], the details of the care and assistance [*tarbiyat wa wilā*] of the *Sipahsālār* Ḥusām al-Dīn Aḥmad 'Alī Shāh, who is the slave of long service [*banda wa khidmatgārī qadīm ast*] to the King of Islām [Mu'izz al-Dīn], and who was never absent from his stirrup, and was present at these victories and battles, are [also] known and recorded. [Indeed] all the commanders of this court [*jumla-i khidmatgārān-i īn dargāh*], were gifted, skilful and noble [*fāẓil wa hunarmand wa buzurgzādand*], and each was distinguished for his courage [*har yak dar mardāngī mustaṣnīand*], and they received an ample share of

---

Historians like A.B.M. Habibullah, *Foundation of Muslim Rule in India*, pp. 51, 74 and Habib, 'The Sultanate Ruling Class', p. 6, have argued that Quṭb al-Dīn at Delhi was Mu'izz al-Dīn's viceroy. For important dissenting opinions, see K.A. Nizami, 'The Early Turkish Sultans of Delhi', *A Comprehensive History of India, vol. 5: The Delhi Sultanat*, p. 198; R.P. Tripathi, *Some Aspects of Muslim Administration*, p. 23; and Peter Jackson, *The Delhi Sultanate*, pp. 26–7.

[110] *'īn pahwān (?) wa jahāndār-i Hind rā Malik khiṭāb farmūd'*. *'Pahwān'* in the Persian edition of the *Tā'rīkh* must be a mistake for *'pahlawān'*.

[111] Fakhr-i Mudabbir, *Tā'rīkh-i Fakhr al-Dīn Mubārak Shāh*, pp. 28–9.

the good fortune and prosperity of the King of Islam, and to all of them his patronage and favour [brought] prominence and fame [*har yak rā banawākht wa tarbiyat m'arūf wa mashhūr gardānīdast*]. To some of these servants he gave high commands, guards, pavilions, drums, standards and districts, and each performed fine acts of service, and was duly praised . . .[112]

As his name suggests Ḥusām al-Dīn Aḥmad 'Alī Shāh was probably a free Amir and one of Fakhr-i Mudabbir's early patrons. In acknowledging his importance even while he glorified Quṭb al-Dīn and Mu'izz al-Dīn throughout his text, Fakhr-i Mudabbir showed how the pressures of patronage often created a variety of tensions in the narratives of thirteenth-century Persian chroniclers. Although the author was judiciously ambiguous in avoiding uncharitable disclosures regarding Quṭb al-Dīn, it is possible to tease such ambiguities into revealing the very conditions their authors sought to obscure. Fakhr-i Mudabbir's stray references to the other 'commanders' of the King of Islam—in the plural—*all* of whom received the monarch's patronage and favour, complicated his attempts to portray Quṭb al-Dīn as the sole hero of his narrative. As the author lets slip, the Sultan's 'viceroy', who busily dashed around offering assistance to beleaguered garrisons in India, had a variety of peers, and they commanded considerable authority and respect.

Jūzjānī was slightly more complicated in his efforts at dissembling. In one part of his text, where he narrated the account of Quṭb al-Dīn's reign, he was very direct and mentioned that, after his master's death, Quṭb al-Dīn received the title of Sultan from his successor, Sultan Ghiyāṣ al-Dīn (602–9/1206–12).[113] But elsewhere, in a slightly more elaborate account of Sultan Ghiyāṣ al-Dīn's reign, Jūzjānī suggested that there were several commanders in India, not just Quṭb al-Dīn, and they all received the right to independent command from Mu'izz al-Dīn's successor:

[112] Ibid., pp. 25–6. The translation is by E.D. Ross, with some minor changes: E.D. Ross, 'The Genealogies of Fakhr al-Din Mubarak Shah', in T.W. Arnold and R.A. Nicholson, ed., *'Ajab Nāmah: A Volume of Oriental Studies presented to E.G. Browne on his 60th Birthday* (Cambridge: Cambridge University Press, 1922), p. 399.

[113] Jūzjānī, *Ṭabaqāt-i Nāṣirī*, vol. 1, p. 417.

Sulṭān Tāj al-Dīn Ildūz and Sulṭān Quṭb al-Dīn Ai-Beg and the other Turkish Maliks and Amirs [*dīgar mulūk wa Umarā'-yi Turk*] who were Mu'izzī slaves [*bandagān-i Mu'izzī būdand*] each one [*har yak*] sent a reliable emissary [*m'arūfi*] to attend his [the Sulṭān Ghiyāṣ al-Dīn Maḥmūd's] court and they petitioned [*iltimās namūdand*], for letters of manumission and mandates [*khaṭūṭ-i 'itq wa miṣāl*], to the kingdom of Ghazni and Hindustan.[114]

It is likely that, rather than 'letters of manumission', Jūzjānī was alluding to formal mandates of governance, a legal permission for the manumitted slaves to continue in public office after their master's death. That Mu'izzī slave commanders were already free for quite some time before 602/1206 is suggested by the fact that they had manumitted slaves during the lifetime of their master.[115] Certainly, these were prerogatives available only to free men. And yet, within an Islamicate context, manumission did not alter the subordinate condition of the freedman; he remained dependent on his master as a client, a *mawālī*.[116] Manumission preserved all the old personal and

[114] Ibid., p. 373.

[115] See the discussion below for details and citations to the purchase of slaves by the Mu'izzī *bandagān*. That Quṭb al-Dīn was manumitted by Mu'izz al-Dīn some time earlier during his reign (perhaps in 587-8/1191-2 when he was appointed Governor of Kuhram and Delhi) is also unwittingly suggested by Jūzjānī (vol. 1, p. 444). The author described how Quṭb al-Dīn had freed his slave, Iltutmish, at the recommendation of Mu'izz al-Dīn sometime in 601–2/1205–6. This was hardly likely because, according to the author, Quṭb al-Dīn was still a slave at this time and a slave could hardly 'possess' a slave, far from manumitting one.

[116] Since the status of *mawālī* did not alter the subordinate condition of the slave or his ties with the monarch, I have continued to describe them as *bandagān*. We have, in any case, little precise information regarding the dates of manumission of Mu'izzī slaves. Moreover, manumission notwithstanding, the term, *banda* captures the nature of the subordination of these personnel more precisely. For a valuable discussion of the ties between the freed slave and his patron see, Paul G. Forand, 'The Relation of the Slave and Client to the Master or Patron in Medieval Islam', *International Journal of Middle East Studies*, 2 (1971), pp. 59–66. For its manifestation in Egypt, see David Ayalon, 'Studies in al-Jabartī I: Notes on the Transformation of Mamluk Society in Egypt under the Ottomans', *Journal of the Economic and Social History of the Orient*, 3 (1960), pp. 283–8. For the technical position of the freed slave in

emotional ties that bonded master and slave. At the master/patron's death, however, the *mawālī* had to relinquish all their public responsibilities unless they were reconfirmed by the heir. Keeping these juridical aspects in mind, it seems likely that the *bandagān* were seeking a legal confirmation of their right to continue as Governors after Mu'izz al-Dīn's death. That is why they sent emissaries to the court of his successor, Sultan Ghiyāṣ al-Dīn Maḥmūd.

Although Jūzjānī does not mention it directly, he provides enough information to clarify that, aside from Tāj al-Dīn Ildūz and Quṭb al-Dīn Ai-Beg, Mu'izzī slaves were not just manumitted but also freed of their *mawālī* obligations after their master's death. The example of the slave Bahā' al-Dīn Tughril, commander of Thangir, substantiates this inference. At his death, which occurred some time after Mu'izz al-Dīn's, Jūzjānī notes that his descendants disposed of their father's slaves.[117] Neither slaves, nor *mawālī*, nor their progeny possessed these social rights. These were prerogatives available only to individuals of free origin or manumitted slaves absolved by their master or his heirs from a status of client dependence.

Persian and Arabic scholars often touched upon the question of manumission in the context of slaves controlling political authority in India.[118] This was perhaps expected of a jurist such as Jūzjānī, for

---

Islamic law, see Joseph Schacht, *Origins of Muhammadan Jurisprudence* (Oxford: Clarendon Press, 1975), p. 161; and in *EI*², s.v.: A.J. Wensinck, I. Goldziher, and P. Crone, 'Mawlā'; R. Brunschvig, ''Abd', and D. Sourdel, C.E. Bosworth and Peter Hardy, 'Ghulām'.

[117] With the increasing political competition between elites in the early years of Sultan Iltutmish's reign, the fortunes of Bahā' al-Dīn's descendants declined. Bahā' al-Dīn's sons felt the need to sell his slave, Naṣīr al-Dīn Ai-Tamar al-Bahā'ī (and possibly Malik 'Izz al-Dīn Tughril Bahā'ī), to Sultan Iltutmish. See Jūzjānī, *Ṭabaqāt-i Nāṣirī*, vol. 1, p. 451, vol. 2, pp. 2–3. It is important to point out here that, unless legally manumitted, the descendants of male slaves inherited their father's unfree status. The slave's descendants, slaves themselves, could hardly sell *bandagān* that their father never legally 'possessed'. See Forand and citations in *EI*² mentioned above.

[118] The question of slaves as Governors and rulers becomes important once again when Quṭb al-Dīn's slave, Shams al-Dīn Iltutmish, challenged his master's son and usurped the throne. It is also significant that it was Ibn Baṭṭūṭa, another jurist who travelled in the subcontinent during the early

resolving the question of manumission would have eased, if not completely resolved, the more uncomfortable ethics involved in slaves functioning as Governors ruling over Muslims of free origin. And yet, the relatively slight impact of this situation on actual 'master–slave' relations was evident in the temporal vagueness with which the author placed these events.

In the following section we will have occasion to discuss the extent of independent political initiative possessed by Mu'izzī slaves. But, as we unravel the nature of the Mu'izzī polity, let us for now keep in mind Jūzjānī's grudging recognition of the presence of *other* Mu'izzī *bandagān-i khāṣṣ*—slaves other than Quṭb al-Dīn Ai-Beg and Tāj al-Dīn Ildūz, that is—who were also important political agents in north India.

The Mu'izzī *Bandagān-i Khāṣṣ* and their Appanages

The deployment and ability of the Mu'izzī *bandagān-i khāṣṣ* to chart their autonomous domains in north India becomes clearer when we study their efforts to establish viable military and administrative centres of governance. At the time of their appointment, the military slaves were already commanders of armed contingents, bodies of troops apportioned them by their master. These slave commanders augmented their forces through independent recruitment. The engagement of humble soldiers like Bakhtiyār Khalajī by Ḥusām al-Dīn Ughul Beg and Hizabr al-Dīn Ḥasan Arnab indicates the shortage of manpower—the proverbial scraping the bottom of the barrel—that some commanders on the eastern frontier faced. By contrast, Quṭb al-Dīn Ai-Beg was far more selective: he recruited Bakhtiyār Khalajī only after the latter had achieved some measure of success.

Skilled and sometimes well-accoutred, military personnel were also available nearer at hand and the Ghurid commanders apparently did not hesitate to ally with local chieftains and their subordinates. Fakhr-i Mudabbir notes the presence of *rātkān (rānāgān) wa tākrān*

---

fourteenth century, who focused on these questions. See Chapters 3 and 4 for a full discussion and references.

in the service of Quṭb al-Dīn Ai-Beg.[119] These terms refer to *rānās* and *thākkurs* in the Sanskrit inscriptions of the time: the former were local chieftains, the principal military subordinates of the King; the latter were commanders in the service of the *rānāgān*. Both belonged to the broad range of a *sāmanta* aristocracy which was dominant in the twelfth-century north Indian political milieu.[120] These *rānāgān* and *thākkurs* remain shadowy individuals in the Persian literature of the period because the chroniclers hardly wanted to draw attention to the presence of 'Hindus' in the 'army of Islam' engaging in wars they euphemistically described as *g̱hazw*, or holy war against infidels.

Many of these service relationships were, however, of short duration, typically cobbled for a specific campaign. The *bandagān-i k̲h̲āṣṣ* therefore also needed a far more stable cadre of service personnel, and to this end, they established slave retinues of their own. Jūzjānī mentions the names of two of Bahā' al-Dīn Tug̱hril's slaves: Naṣīr al-Dīn Ai-Tamar and 'Izz al-Dīn Tug̱hril Bahā'ī.[121] Quṭb al-Dīn Ai-Beg also purchased military slaves and we have references to two, Shams al-Dīn Iltutmish and Tamg̱haj, bought after the 593/1197 Nahrwala campaign. Iltutmish was, as we noted earlier an expensive slave, trained by the merchant who sold him, and it was not long before Quṭb al-Dīn deployed him as a commander: first at Gwalior in 597/1200–1, soon after in the *qaṣaba* of Baran (modern Bulandshahar),[122] and eventually at Budaun in 599/1202–3.[123] The accumulation of slaves by the *bandagān-i khāṣṣ* was carried out with the full cognizance of Mu'izz al-Dīn, and Jūzjānī provides a long, embellished account of

[119] See Fak̲h̲r-i Mudabbir, *Ta'rīk̲h̲-i Fak̲h̲r al-Dīn Mubārak Shāh*, p. 33, where *rātkān* should be read as *rānāgān*.

[120] On the *rāuta*, *thākkur*, and *Sāmanta*, see R.S. Sharma, *Indian Feudalism*, pp. 127–69; B.N.S. Yadav, *Society and Culture in Northern India* (Allahabad: Central Book Depot, 1973), pp. 136–200; B.D. Chattopadhyaya, *The Making of Early Medieval India*, pp. 57–88, 183–222.

[121] Jūzjānī, *Ṭabaqāt-i Nāṣirī*, vol. 1, p. 451, vol. 2, pp. 7–8.

[122] While he was at Baran, Iltutmish seems to have started accumulating a slave retinue of his own. Jūzjānī provides biographies of two of these slaves: Malik Ik̲h̲tiyār al-Dīn Ai-tegin and Tāj al-Dīn Sanjar Qutluq. Ibid., vol. 2, pp. 22, 25.

[123] Ibid., vol. 1, p. 443. Tamg̱haj was previously assigned to Tabarhind but at an indeterminate date. He was killed in battle, *circa* 604/1208.

how the Ghurid Sulṭān appreciated Iltutmish's valour and recommended him for manumission.[124]

Beyond the military retinue, the *bandagān-i khāṣṣ* hired secretaries to handle their diplomatic and other chancellery affairs. Malik Niẓām al-Dīn Muḥammad, for example, was the *wakīl* of Quṭb al-Dīn Ai-Beg. He was the individual deputed by Quṭb al-Dīn to conclude the details of Iltutmish's purchase in Ghazni. The Mu'izzī *bandagān-i khāṣṣ* were essentially military men and so they seem to have required 'men of the pen' to pursue their more delicate diplomatic negotiations.[125] As we have already noticed, their skills were used by the elite slaves to negotiate with Sulṭān Ghiyāṣ al-Dīn Maḥmūd (602–9/1206–12) for a continuation of their political privileges after Mu'izz al-Dīn Ghuri's death. According to Jūzjānī, 'each one, *har yak*' of the Mu'izzī slaves sent a reliable emissary, *m'arūfi*, to Sulṭān Ghiyāṣ al-Dīn Maḥmūd's court. Quṭb al-Dīn had his case represented by the aforementioned *wakīl*, Malik Niẓām al-Dīn Muḥammad.

The recruitment of military personnel and administrators indicates some of the measures taken by the Mu'izzī *bandagān-i khāṣṣ* in north India to develop the capacity to defend and govern their respective dominions. There is additional evidence that can flesh out their efforts at consolidation, but to get a proper perspective we should not forget the extremely circumscribed dominions of the Mu'izzī commanders at the turn of the twelfth century. The conventional administrative terminology to describe Mu'izzī territories in the Persian chronicles was *iqṭā'* or *wilāyat*, a military assignment or a province.[126] The vague dimensions of these 'provinces and assignments' are apparent in Jūzjānī's incidental and quite unsystematic references to

[124] Ibid., p. 444, for the description Mu'izz al-Dīn's campaign against the Khokars (after the defeat at Andkhud 601/1204–5), where the forces of Quṭb al-Dīn and his slave Iltutmish were also present. Mu'izz al-Dīn was sufficiently impressed by Iltutmish that he commended the slave to Quṭb al-Dīn and 'commanded that they should write and prepare [Iltutmish's] deed of manumission [*bafarmūd tā khaṭṭ-i 'itq o dar tahrīr āwardand*]'. Also note the discussion above on the question of manumission.

[125] For a fuller discussion of the qualities of the 'men of the pen', the *ahl-i qalam*, see Chapter 4.

[126] For a review of this information see Irfan Habib, 'Iqṭā'' and his 'The Formation of the Sultanate Ruling Class'.

the territories of the early Sultanate commanders.[127] Sometimes he uses variations of the phrase *shahr wa qaṣaba wa muẓāfāt*, 'the town, its neighbouring encampments and suburbs', to convey the territorial extent of areas charged to the Mu'izzī Amirs.[128] Rather than conveying the control of large provinces, Jūzjānī's comments suggest the 'urban-centred' nature of these commands and the extremely uncertain influence their commanders had over the interior tracts of the country. Periodic military expeditions and the constant infusion of plunder were vital in sustaining these garrison centres. While a portion of the plunder was remitted to the Ghurid Sulṭān in Ghazni, the residue was distributed amongst the Amir and his dependents in north India.[129] The Amir and his dependents invested some of their wealth in the purchase of slaves, war materials (including horses), the maintenance of troopers, and the embellishment of the court of the local commander.

The restricted, urban character of these regimes also meant that their sustenance relied upon the establishment of stable supply routes and commercial links with local trading marts, and with the more

[127] Peter Jackson has detailed this aspect of the problem very well. See *The Delhi Sultanate*, pp. 95–102.

[128] From several examples, see in Jūzjānī, *Ṭabaqāt-i Nāṣirī*, vol.1, p. 443: *qaṣaba-i Baran wa muẓāfāt;* vol. 1, p. 419: *qil'a wa qaṣabāt wa shahrhā-i mamlakat-i Sindh;* vol. 2, p. 4: *qil'a wa shahar-i Uchch wa muẓāfāt wa nawāhī-yi ān*; vol. 2, p. 5: *shahar wa ḥiṣār-i Multan wa qaṣabāt wa aṭrāf wa nawāḥī-yi ān.* Not all of these references are to Mu'izzī commanders, some include Quṭbīs and Shamsīs as well, but they all refer to conditions in the first two decades of the thirteenth century.

[129] The ratio according to which the plunder was divided is unclear for this time. In the case of the four melons/drums of gold seized from Ranthambhor, Quṭb al-Dīn sent all four to Ghazni. Of the four, Mu'izz al-Dīn remitted one to his (senior) brother Ghiyāṣ al-Dīn at Ghur. Elsewhere, Fakhr-i Mudabbir, *Ta'rīkh-i Fakhr al-Dīn Mubārak Shāh*, p. 23, elaborates on how this apportioning was carried out after the Nahrwala campaign. He noted that after the conquest 'the army of Islam carried away a lot of booty mostly in red gold and valuable cash. All of this [Quṭb al-Dīn] distributed amongst the soldiers. Thirty-two incomparable elephants were [also] brought away [from Nahrwala] and sent to the Sultan [Mu'izz al-Dīn].' It seems that extremely valuable or unique pieces of plunder (and this certainly included strategic war material) were usually reserved for the Sultan, the rest were shared between the commanders and the troopers descending in rank and influence.

distant slave and horse markets in the central Islamic lands. Jūzjānī describes how Bahā' al-Dīn Tug͟hril invited merchants, *tujjar*, and men of repute, *ma'ārif-i rūy*, from different parts of Hindustan and Khurasan to Bayana. To further encourage trade within the region, all merchants were granted accommodation and material support, *jumla rā k͟hāna wa asbāb mībak͟hshīd.*[130] In stabilizing the economy of these frontier cantonments the Mu'izzī *bandagān* recognized that limited territorial control, plunder, and trade were interdependent ingredients.

Beyond the long-distance trade, the army camps had to have stable relationships with their hinterlands. The Persian textual evidence, however, seldom departs from a single-minded narrative of hostilities and the conflictual nature of Mu'izzī relationship with the local non-Muslim 'infidel' population. Mu'izzī coins struck from the captured mints of the local *rājās,* however, point to efforts at establishing a more enduring relationship with local communities resident in the vicinity of these Mu'izzī camps. Many of these coins carried sigilla which clearly proclaimed a local element within the identity of the new conqueror. The Mu'izzī Amirs were introduced as Shrī Hammira: the same title, but in the locally comprehensible devnagari script. In fairly clear terms, the local population was being informed of the presence of a new political formation in their vicinity. But other aspects of these coins seem to implicitly ease the insecurities caused by these transitions. With very few exceptions, the newly minted Mu'izzī coins harmonized with the earlier Rajput currency in weight and metallic purity. Rather than introducing monetary reforms, Mu'izzī currency sought to nestle within pre-existing mediums of exchange.[131]

As interesting were the efforts to ground the new regimes within an older semiotics of power and respect: the Mu'izzī coins sometimes carried the image of Shiva's revered vehicle, the Nandi bull, and the visage of the Rajput horseman with a lance. An even better exam-

[130] Jūzjānī, *Ṭabaqāt-i Nāṣirī*, vol. 1, p. 421.

[131] See Edward Thomas, *The Chronicles of the Pathan Kings of Delhi* (Delhi: Munshiram Manoharlal, 1967 reprint), pp. 15–20; H. Nelson Wright, *The Coinage and Metrology of the Sultans of Delhi* (Delhi: Oriental Books Reprint Corporation, 1974 reprint), pp. 6–12; John S. Deyell, *Living Without Silver*, pp. 195–206; and A.B.M. Habibullah, *The Foundation of Muslim Rule in India*, pp. 235–6.

ple of continuity in sigilla was evident to the local audience from the gold coins minted at Benaras and Bayana after their conquest. On one side of the Mu'izzī coins was the outline of the Goddess (of wealth) Lakshmi, and on their reverse a devnagari inscription broadcast Mu'izż al-Dīn's name as the new lord, *Mahamada bini Sama*. That the coins of the Mu'izzī Governors were fully assimilated within an economic world that crossed political frontiers is evident from the fact that the Nandi bull and horseman type billon coins of the Mu'izzī Governors Ildūz and Qubācha were found in a hoard in Haryana—distant from the areas of their control—together with the coins of rulers ranging from the Tomara Kings of Delhi: Sallakshana Pāla, Ananga Pāla, and Madan Pāla; the Chauhāns of Ajmer: Somesvara, Chahada, and Prithvirāja; and the ruler of Budaun, Amrita Pāla.[132] Mu'izzī coinage had a circulation that went beyond the strict confines of their dominions; and since they were equal in value and iconic representation to other mediums of exchange, the local inhabitants used and hoarded these coins.

Mu'izz al-Dīn's *bandagān-i khāṣṣ* were well aware of their master's brief: they were to remit wealth to Ghur. The practice of this agenda meant in the long duration that their urban outposts in north India needed to be stable entities maintained by resources generated from their local contexts. The decision of the Mu'izzī *bandagān* to continue with older ratios of precious metals and weights in their coinage, together with a deliberate invocation of old, familiar, regal, and sacred motifs reveal their efforts to locate their domains within a larger material world of production and exchange.[133] The economy

[132] John S. Deyell, *Living without Silver*, pp. 195–206, and Appendix E, hoard no. 25. See also hoard nos 27–32. The gold Lakshmi type coin of the Gāhaḍavāla ruler Govinda Chandra (coin no. 145) can be compared with Mu'izz al-Dīn's coin (no. 252) in the plates at the end of the book.

[133] John Deyell's research on this subject is important. Deyell mapped the findspots of the bull and horseman and the gold Lakshmi type coin hoards (Map 9, p. 204). The mapping clarified the extent of circulation of the bull-horseman billon coinage in areas around the appanages of the Mu'izzī *bandagān*. More problematic was the manner in which Deyell contrasted the dispersal of the findspots of these hoards with those from the ninth century Gurjara Pratihara period (Map 2, p. 29). He felt that, in contrast to the Gurjara

of the Mu'izzī principalities needed trade and plunder if they were to flourish, so they mimed pre-existing fiscal regimes to attract and trap precious metals as far as they could. Nor were these attempts at local consolidation pursued only by Delhi; the Mu'izzī *bandagān-i khāṣṣ*—Qubācha in Sindh and Tughril in Bayana, for instance—made earnest attempts to transform their appanages and capitals into flourishing mercantile centres, alluring migrants.

Even a Delhi-centric chronicler such as Jūzjānī was forced to recognize these developments: he noted that Bayana had profited from the many beneficial monuments, *āṣār-i khair bisyār*, constructed by the Mu'izzī slave Bahā' al-Dīn Tughril.[134] His patronage of trade and commerce had made the province rich and powerful enough to warrant the construction of a new capital—Sulṭānkōt, a new capital to go with his improved circumstances.[135] But Jūzjānī's taciturn admissions do not capture Bahā' al-Dīn's drive to embellish his capital in a form befitting his ambitions. The recent research of Mehrdad and Natalie H. Shokoohy on the mosques constructed by Bahā' al-Dīn in his appanage in Bayana shows this aspect somewhat more clearly.[136]

These authors studied three constructions of Bahā' al-Dīn Tughril: the Chaurasi Khamba Masjid at Kaman, the mosque of Ukha Mandir,

---

Pratihara dispersal of coins in the eastern areas of the Gangetic plain and central India there was a greater bias towards Delhi, the Punjab and into Afghanistan in the Mu'izzī period. This evidence, he concluded rather conventionally, suggested a huge transposition of wealth from India into Ghurid dominions as plunder. Another part of his conclusion—'The pay of the Central Asian and Ghaznavid troopers of the Ghurid army in India was probably issued in local coinage, and *although much of it would have been spent in India*, a goodly percentage must have found its way back to the soldier's homes in the west' (p. 205, my italics)—remained understated. The problems with his conclusions notwithstanding, the presence of economic integration in areas in and around Mu'izzī control can be gleaned from the author's painstakingly accumulated materials regarding bull and horseman coin hoards discovered in the Delhi, Budaon, Haryana, Punjab, and the northern Rajasthan regions.

[134] Jūzjānī, *Ṭabaqāt-i Nāṣirī*, vol. 1, p. 421.

[135] Ibid.

[136] Mehrdad and Natalie H. Shokoohy, 'The Architecture of Baha al-Din Tughrul [*sic*] in the Region of Bayana, Rajasthan', *Muqarnas*, 4 (1987), pp. 114–32.

and the *'īdgāh* in Bayana at the Amir's newly built capital of Sulṭān-kōt. According to Mehrdad and Natalie Shokoohy, these mosques were constructed at the turn of the twelfth century and were contemporaneous with the Delhi congregational mosque. Both the mosques in Bayana—respectively 36.58 x 24.24 m. and 37 x 27 m—were slightly smaller than the Delhi *masjid* (43.2 x 33 m.).[137] All three, however, were alike in that they were constructed by reusing temple material. In the mosque at Kaman, the garlands, rosettes, pot, and foliage motifs on the stonework are still visible. As in the case of the Delhi mosque, the constructors had defaced some of the idols and deliberately inverted a number of the reused temple columns in the mosques. Other than the similarity in the material and its utilization, the three mosques also shared the common architectural style of a rectangular courtyard surrounded by colonnaded bays with the main gate to the east. Architectural solutions to construction problems were dealt with in an identical fashion in all three mosques. To achieve the required height in the colonnaded bays, temple pillars were placed one on top of the other. As in the Delhi *masjid-i jāmi'*, only the corbelled arch and dome were used, and the form of construction mirrored Ghurid aesthetics strongly impressed with 'Indic' traditions. As recent research has revealed, these stylistic forms were common for the period in buildings located in the Afghanistan, Gujarat, and Sindh regions.[138]

[137] For information on Bahā' al-Dīn's constructions in Bayana, see ibid. There seems to be a misprint concerning the measurement of the *masjid-i jāmī'* in Bayana which was recorded as 37 x 17 m. on p. 122. The authors mention that the subsequent addition to the mosque was *narrower*, measuring only 19 m. (p. 126), hence the original mosque must have been wider than 17 m. On the basis of the proportions available on the maps provided in the article, I have assumed that 17 m. stands instead for 27 m.

[138] For Ghurid aesthetics, see Finbarr B. Flood, 'Ghurid Architecture in the Indus Valley'; idem, 'Refiguring Islamic Iconoclasm: Image Mutilation and Aesthetic Innovation in the Early Indian Mosque', in Anne McClanan and Jeffrey Johnson, eds, *Negating the Image* (Ashgate Press, forthcoming). For Indic traditions see Alka Patel, 'Towards Alternative Receptions of Ghurid Architecture in north India (late Twelfth–early Thirteenth century CE), *Archives of Asian Art*, 54 (2004), pp. 35–61; and idem, *Building Communities in Gujarat: Architecture and Society during the Twelfth through Fourteenth Centuries* (Leiden: E.J. Brill, 2004).

What is striking about the mosques built by Quṭb al-Dīn Ai-Beg and Bahā' al-Dīn Tughril is the similarity in the kind of statements that they were making. In their inscriptions, composition, and arrangement of material in these congregational mosques both commanders eulogised their conquest over idolaters, their creation of a sanctuary for Muslims. Both structures carried the 'text' of their patrons to the Muslim congregation, informing it of the accomplishments of rulers as conquerors, iconoclasts, and morally upright Muslims who abided by and protected the *Sharī'a*. The *masjids* defined the probity of the individual military commander, and their message to the local Muslim population and immigrants was unequivocal: as with political authority, there were many centres of Muslim civilization in north India, each protected and patronized by an Amir aware of his responsibilities to the faithful. But if Quṭb al-Dīn Ai-Beg drew the attention of visitors to the Delhi *masjid-i jāmi'* and his military and moral accomplishments as the *Sipahsālār* and *Amīr al-Umarā'* of Sulṭān Mu'izz al-Dīn Ghūrī, the visitors to the mosques in Bayana were similarly entertained by Bahā' al-Dīn Tughril's epigraphs. In an inscription on the eastern gate of the Chaurasi Khamba mosque that must date to sometime after Mu'izz al-Dīn's death, Tughril had appropriated regal pretensions: he introduced himself not as *Sipahsālār* but as the exalted monarch, *Pādshāh wa al-Sulṭān Jahān Pahlawān Tughril al-Sulṭānī.*[139] The discourse of a monolithic Islam was displaced by that of a more complicated political realm in which there were multiple lords claiming to be the leaders of the Muslim community.

Consolidation and Expansion

The processes of consolidation and expansion of Mu'izzī territories in north India hardly appear to be linear, beset as they were by the

[139] Both Quṭb al-Dīn's and Bahā' al-Dīn's inscriptions were placed on the most strategic site on the eastern gate, the main entrance, to their respective congregational mosques. For Quṭb al-Dīn's inscription, see J.A. Page, *An Histoical Memoir on the Quṭb* (Calcutta: Memoirs of the Archaeological Survey of India, no. 22, Government of India Central Publication Branch, 1926), p. 29; and J. Horowitz, 'The Inscriptions of Muḥammad ibn Sam, Qutbuddin Aibeg and Iltutmish'. *Epigraphica Indo-Moslemica* (1911–12), p. 13; for Bahā' al-Dīn's undated inscription in the 'Chaurasi Khamba' mosque in Kaman, see Mehrdad and Natalie H. Shokoohy, 'Baha al-Din Tughrul', p. 115.

seemingly contradictory interests of the Mu'izzī commanders. A more textured interpretation of the history of these developments is possible through a detailed study of two such sets of 'contradictions'. The first concerns the iconoclastic statements of a triumphant Islam present in the mosques at Delhi and Bayana, where the great Muslim conquerors consecrated their victories by sacralizing the profane conquered lands of idol worshippers. The semiotics in these statements do not reside very comfortably with the iconic representations of the Nandi bull, the horseman with the lance, and the Goddess Lakshmi placed as sigilla on the coins of these Mu'izzī victors. The second contradiction concerns Tughril's assumption of the title of *Pādshāh* and *Sulṭān*, an exalted title suggesting an independent authority in keeping with the efforts of the Mu'izzī *bandagān* to make much of their local autonomy. But why did Tughril display the regal *Pādshāh* honorific in an epigraph where his title also carried the *nisba*, *al-Sulṭānī*, a deliberate statement of self-abnegation, a public acknowledgement that he was (nothing but) the slave of the Sultan? How did independent political authority coexist with a self-reflective acknowledgement of slave status?

Theoretically, the issue of 'contradictory statements' becomes a challenge only if historians expect their sources to be relatively seamless and internally coherent. This is hardly ever the case, however. As we have already seen frequently, the facts deployed by medieval chroniclers are often challenged by the narratives they are meant to support. Certainly, in the context of the discursive claims that we are evaluating at present, the seemingly contradictory disposition of the Mu'izzī *bandagān* towards non-Muslims forces us to go back and re-examine the modes of representing different groups of people in the early Sultanate sources. 'Hindus and Muslims', for example, are presented in a deliberately homogenized and synchronic manner in a lot of the records of this period. These completely obliterate divergent modes of self-representation, internal stratification, and competition within such juxtaposed groups. Shifting to a diachronic mode of analysis certainly helps us read identity formations historically—in resolving, for instance, irreconcilable elements in the titles of Mu'izzī Amirs, where meanings are layered and which shift with the passage of time. 'Contradictions', in other words, sometimes provide valuable insights into complex historical processes that may otherwise remain glossed over.

In this context, it is important to keep in mind that the statements of an iconoclastic, triumphant Islam were present in both the Persian chronicles of the time and in the architectural constructions of the Sultans. In South Asia, these sources tend to reify the Sultanate into a composite body of 'Muslims' opposed by an equally undifferentiated body of infidel 'Hindus'. It is quite easy to read textual and architectural materials together, as if one corroborated the other in the articulation of an 'Islamic theology of iconoclasm' contained in the genus of all Muslims.[140] The history of temple desecration cannot be teleologically read back into a primordial inspiration provided by the 'great text' of a particular community. The practice of temple desecration in north India (and elsewhere) pre-dates and is quite unconnected with the migration of 'Muslims' and the arrival of Sultanate forces. As the research of Richard Davis has shown, victorious 'Hindu' Kings of the subcontinent routinely despoiled the temples of their vanquished opponents and redeployed sacred relics as signs of victory in their temples.[141] Temple desecration, in other words, was not an 'Islamic' innovation within the subcontinent. It had a local history that was familiar to the political participants of the time.

The nature of Sultanate desecration of Hindu temples did however differ from its precedents. Unlike Hindu monarchs, among whom the episode of destruction and reconstruction of temples was carried out within ritually homologous forms of Hindu kingship, Quṭb al-Dīn Ai-Beg and Bahā' al-Dīn Tughril naturally did not construct temples as a statement of their victory; they made a *masjid-i jāmi'*. This act signified the arrival of alternative traditions of governance in Delhi and Bayana. The event carried larger social and moral implications for the constitution of authority in the region, since royal temples were also the sites of redistributive and transactional relationships

140 Thus André Wink, *al-Hind, vol. 2: The Slave Kings*, pp. 313–16.

141 Richard Davis, 'Indian Art Objects as Loot', *Journal of Asian Studies*, 52 (1993), pp. 22–48. See also, Richard Eaton, 'Temple Desecration and Indo-Muslim States', *Beyond Turk and Hindu*, pp. 246–81.

between the King, his subordinate chieftains, and the larger subject population. The construction of a *masjid-i jāmi'* terminated these alliances. Yet it did not imply a concomitant distancing of the subordinate echelons of rural chieftains from the newly emerging structures of Sultanate authority in north India.

In the late twelfth century, when the Shansabanids first appeared in the north Indian political arena, 'Muslims' and Sultanate traditions of governance were not unfamiliar to local rulers. The Ghaznavids had inhabited the Punjab and Haryana regions from the eleventh through the twelfth centuries. As B.D. Chattopadhyaya, Romila Thapar, and Carl Ernst have discussed at great length already, Brahmanical orderings of the social universe had already cast the Ghaznavid commanders as a demonic, destabilizing 'Other'.[142] Indeed, there is a great deal of reportage on the levels of hostility and widespread conflict within the Persian chronicles and Sanskrit epigraphs of the time, but the entirety of the late-twelfth and early-thirteenth-century experience cannot be summed up through the extremely narrow filters of the state and their political elites invested in preserving the status quo. In order to show greater sensitivity to the open frontiers of these times, scholars need to pay more attention to the trade, migration, and settlement manifest in the region at all levels. Historians like Jūzjānī occasionally gesture to the presence of this permeable political and social terrain in incidental remarks concerning, for example, the ease with which Ba<u>kh</u>tiyār <u>Kh</u>alajī marched into Lakhnauti. The latter's presence was hardly demonic to the people en route his march into Lakhnauti and they did not attempt to stop him. He appeared as a horse trader, *bāzargānand wa asp bahā'-yi āwardand,* like so many others before him and, therefore, quite harmless.[143] Information sometimes appears in entirely unexpected areas. A tombstone epitaph dated 633/1236 informs us of a mystic who had travelled from Akhsi in Farghana, Central Asia, and settled in Damoh in Malwa, decades

[142] Romila Thapar, 'The Tyranny of Labels', *The IX Zakir Husain Memorial Lecture*, 1996, reprinted in her collection of essays titled *Cultural Pasts: Essays in Early Indian History* (Delhi: Oxford University Press, 2000), pp. 990–1014; B.D. Chattopadhyaya, *Representing the Other?* and Carl Ernst, *Eternal Garden*, pp. 47–55.

[143] Jūzjānī, *Ṭabaqāt-i Nāṣirī,* vol. 1, p. 426.

before Sultanate intrusion in the area. The *Bābā* resided in Damoh for a while and then moved to Petlad, where he died. The inscription on his tombstone in Petlad carries his name: Bābā Arjun Shāh, an individual obviously venerated by local 'Muslims' and non-Muslims alike, whose piety, like his name, penetrates through modern binary and communitarian typologies.[144]

A more careful reading of the establishment of Shansabanid power in north India helps to historicize and crucially supplement early impressionistic accounts of the movement of people, the tensions and hostilities these generated, and larger processes of settlement and regional integration within which the Sultanate insinuated itself. The Mu'izzī annexation of territories in north India was a slow conquest rather than an abrupt transition from one set of regimes to another. It occurred in different forms. The events surrounding the seizure of Gwalior, for example, carry within it many of the elements whose different details also appear in other contexts. Mu'izz al-Dīn and Quṭb al-Dīn had forced the ruler of Gwalior, Rā'ī Solankh Pāla(?) to capitulate for the first time in 592/1196. At that time, they had reinstated the Rā'ī after accepting tribute.[145] Subsequently, in 597/1200, Gwalior was besieged by the forces of Bahā' al-Dīn Tughril. After continued resistance proved impossible, Rā'ī Solankh Pāla(?) resigned the fort to Quṭb al-Dīn Ai-Beg. We have no further information on the Rā'i and his descendant from the region of Gwalior, but it is obvious that the ruling lineage perceived the loss of their capital as only a temporary set back. It is not clear when they regained Gwalior, but Jūzjānī informs us that the fort had to be reinvested by Iltutmish, and reconquered from Rā'ī MILK (?) Deo only after a protracted seige, 629–30/1232–3.[146] Despite two reversals, in *circa* 603/1206,

[144] See G. Yazdani, 'Inscriptions in the Tomb of Baba Arjun Shah, Petlad (Baroda State)', *Epigraphica Indo-Moslemica* (1915–16), pp. 15–18 and Plate XIV.

[145] Fakhr-i Mudabbir, *Ta'rīkh-i Fakhr al-Dīn Mubarak Shāh*, p. 23. Ḥasan Niẓāmī, *Tāj al-Ma'āsir*, translated by Elliot and Dowgon, vol. 2, pp. 227–8, translated by Sartoop, pp. 203–8, provided the details for this expedition and noted the name of the ruler as Rā'ī Soiankh Pāla. Jūzjānī, *Ṭabaqāt-i Nāṣirī*, vol. 1, pp. 400, 417, referred to this expedition, but provided no details or dates.

[146] Jūzjānī, *Ṭabaqāt-i Nāṣirī*, vol. 1, p. 421, on the events leading to the second invasion of Gwalior to which Fakhr-i Mudabbir, *Ta'rīkh-i Fakhr al-Dīn*

the ruler of Gwalior continued to reside in the adjoining tracts, persisting in his resistance until he met with success. Embedded within the episode was a brief period when the local King was the vassal of the Mu'izzī Governors, a transitory moment prior to a renewed Sultanate assault.

The hiatus in the push towards annexation was also evident in the context of Mu'izzī campaigns against the Chauhāns and the Gāhaḍavālas. Although Prithvīrāja Chauhān was defeated at Tarain in 588/1192, Mu'izz al-Dīn did not apparently annex Delhi immediately; the local Chauhān Governor, Govind Rā'ī's son, was appointed vassal and Quṭb al-Dīn seized the town from him later in the year. Similarly, Sultanate forces seized Qanauj, the capital of the Gāhaḍavālas, only in 595/1198, although its ruler was defeated and killed nearly five years earlier. Rather than a summary conquest, Shansabanid annexation of territories in north India transpired slowly, sometimes including moments when individuals from old lineages were installed as vassal rulers, or after a period of intervening campaigns in the neighbourhood.[147]

As in the Gwalior episode, defeated chieftains did not simply disappear from the political scene; sometimes they migrated a short-distance, planning a revanche, at other times making a definitive shift and establishing new political centres away from Sultanate political activity. John Richards and Kashi N. Singh have drawn attention to how the diaspora phenomenon evident in the histories of proto-Rajput lineages, continued into the years of Sultanate political formation.[148] Internecine clan conflicts drove Rajput lineages from their

---

Mubārak Shāh, p. 24, provides the date. For Iltutmish's campaign and seige, see Jūzjānī, *Ṭabaqāt-i Nāṣirī*, vol. 1, p. 448. The name of the ruler MILK is unclear; A.B.M. Habibullah, *The Foundation of Muslim Rule in India*, pp. 85, 94, fn. 93, cited Hiraman Munshi's, *Gwalior Nāma*, B.M. Add. 16842, f. 11, to suggest that the ruler's name might be Malayavarmadeva.

[147] A.B.M. Habibullah, *The Foundation of Muslim Rule in India,* pp. 50–6, brings out the gradual nature of these annexations very well.

[148] See R.L. Singh and K.N. Singh, 'Evolution of the Medieval Towns in the Saryu-Par Plain of the Middle Ganga Valley: A Case Study', *The National Geographical Journal of India,* 9 (1963), pp. 1–11; Kashi N. Singh, 'The territorial basis of Medieval Town and Village Settlement in Eastern Uttar

homelands, and the insertion of Sultanate political authority in the competitive politics of the Punjab and Gangetic belt further complicated these processes. Jūzjānī's account of the Sena ruler at Lakhnauti underlines the familiarity that ruling groups had with strategic migration. The author noted that the Sena King Rā'ī Lakshmanasena (written as Lakhmanī'a by Jūzjānī) was 'advised by the astrologers, brahmans and counselors of the kingdom [*munajjimān, brahmanān, wa hukmā'-yi mamlakat*] . . . [that] . . . since the prophecy of Turkish conquest was at hand the Rā'i should agree to transfer himself and all of his people from this territory so that we may remain safe from the havoc of the Turks [*az fitna-i turkān basalāmat mānand*].'[149] Despite its hyperbolic rendition of the tale, Jūzjānī's account was accurate enough in so far as the Sena King did retreat into east Bengal without offering serious military resistance to the Khalajī invaders.

Sanskrit epigraphs also record this as the response of other local chieftains to Mu'izzī incursions. An undated Gāhaḍavāla inscription from Etawah in eastern Uttar Pradesh, recounted the events of the last decade of the twelfth century (*circa* 1195),[150] in a manner that paralleled Jūzjānī' account:

> Salute to the Goddess! In the honour of the images of Canḍikā, Durgā and Śiva [in the city] installed by the wise Mahārāja Ajaysiṁha who performed the sacrifice after [?] his father's brother Jaichandra of Qanauj. Today, I, his *ācārya* as well as priest, performed the Mahayoga of Canḍikā. The statue of Durgā was previously installed on the boundary, or outer wall of the fort. My rationality has been destroyed

Pradesh, India', *Annals of the Association of American Geographers*, 58 (1968), pp. 203–20; and John F. Richards, 'The Islamic Frontier in the East', *South Asia*, 4 (1974), pp. 107–8. Also crucial to the study of these historical processes is B.D. Chattopadhyaya, 'The Origin of the Rajputs: The Political, Economic and Social Processes in Early Medieval Rajasthan', in idem, *The Making of Early Medieval India*, pp. 57–88.

[149] Jūzjānī, *Ṭabaqāt-i Nāṣirī*, vol. 1, p. 425.

[150] The inscription records the death of Rājā Jaichandra, the paramount Gāhaḍavāla overlord (died, 590/1194) and the sacrifice performed by his nephew (brother's son) 'Mahārājā' Ajaysiṁha. See 'II: 18 Etawah Fort Inscription', translated by Pushpa Prasad, in idem, *Sanskrit Inscriptions of Delhi Sultanate*, pp. 93–4.

> because of my fear of the *Mleccha* [literally, the unclean, i.e., the Muslims]. With great sorrow, touching her with my head [to honour her], I place this Durgā, the dweller of the fort and destroyer of bad luck, into this pit, till the god Skanda turns their [*Mleccha*] glory [Sun] to dust. When ill fate meets the *Yavanas* [literally the Greeks, a euphemism for foreigners] she might re-appear, or manifest herself again amidst uproar. Until that time, I am a fool like a drunkard. [However] let not fear enter you; the gods will quickly return [with victory] along with you.[151]

In the defeat of the Gāhaḍavāla ruler, the *ācārya* lost all his social and political privileges—his doubts about the new order are understandable—but did the Gāhaḍavāla dominion and the secondary rank of chieftains suffer an equal dislocation? If we recall Fakhr-i Mudabbir's observation, Quṭb al-Dīn Ai-Beg sometimes retained local chieftains, the *rānāgān* and their subordinates, the *thākkurān*, in his campaigns. They may not have received any space in his court, but they were important allies, especially since the 'Hindu' political domain was open to considerable negotiation amongst a myriad of potential allies and competitors. The regional lord, *rājā/rā'ī* was the lynchpin of an assembly of local chieftains and officers—the *sāmanta*, *rānākas*, *rāutta*, *thākkura*—where all the participants also possessed considerable independent political resources and ambitions.

After the Mu'izzī conquest of Qanauj in 595/1198-9, members of the Gāhaḍavāla ruling lineage and *rānākas* continued to reside in the vicinity of the Mu'izzī camps. Three inscriptions ranging from Samvat 1253/1197 to Samvat 1273/1217 from the neighbourhood of Benaras and Jaunpur, the eastern portion of the Gāhaḍavāla realm, present us with information which helps understand how local elites reacted to Mu'izzī and later Sultanate intrusion. From the two inscriptions dated Samvat 1253/1197 it is evident that, at least at the initial stage, the institutional process of royal grants and ritual recognition of authority suffered no dislocation with the death of the ruler; instead of Jāyachandra the inscriptions recorded the name of his son Harishchandra as the new ruler.[152] By Samvat 1273/1217, however,

[151] Ibid.

[152] See inscription no. II: 5 'Belkhara Pillar Inscription', translated by R.D. Banerji (?) and inscription no. II: 6 'Machchlishahr Copper-plate Inscription', translated by Pushpa Prasad, in ibid., pp. 56–7, 58–70.

the reference to the ruler was absent, yet the principal military subordinates, the *rānāka* and the *rāutta*, continued to occupy rights to their property which the latter mortgaged for loans.[153] The participants in the mortgage agreements, including the four *rāutta* witnesses, seem to have been unaware of any change in customary traditions governing fiscal obligations and had enough confidence in the future to participate in long-term financial transactions. They pledged cultivable lands in exchange for a monetary loan, utterly oblivious of any possible threat of military expulsion from Sultanate commanders in the neighbouring cantonments of Benaras and Kara. Nor was their confidence misplaced. Ten years later, socially well-placed individuals within the erstwhile Gāhaḍavāla domains were still concluding similar mortgage agreements. But there was a significant difference: the mortgage agreement of Samvat 1283/1227 from Kasrak, in the region of Kather (near the old Gāhaḍavāla capital of Qanauj), between a *rāutta* and three Brahmins, recognized Sultan Iltutmish as the paramount ruler of the land.[154]

It is pertinent that the acknowledgement of the Delhi Sultan from the region of Kasrak in the Samvat 1283/1227 inscription pre-dates the first recognition in the Persian evidence of direct Sultanate administrative control in the region from the city of Qanauj. According to Jūzjānī's evidence, it was only some time around 634/1236 that Malik Tamar Khān was given Qanauj as his military assignment (*iqṭā'*). In the interim, it is entirely possible that there were (several?) unrecorded military expeditions into the areas around Kasrak and Jaunpur, but, as the inscriptional evidence from the region brings out, these did not displace the local landed elites or create any sense of crisis in their material lives. Nevertheless, the cumulative pressure—*circa* two decades in the case of Qanauj—forced local elites to eventually acknowledge Sultanate authority.

One aspect of this pressure was the emergence of Mu'izzī camps as centres of trade and authority, a development that saw the penetration

[153] See inscription no. II: 9 'Jaunpur Brick Inscription', translated by V.S. Agarawal in ibid, pp. 78–9.

[154] See inscription no. II:11 'Mahoba Fort Copper-Plate Inscription', translated by Pushpa Prasad in ibid., pp. 80–9. For a different usage of some of these inscriptional materials, see Irfan Habib, 'Rural Classes', *The Cambridge Economic History*, p. 56.

of local markets through restrained monetary reforms, local political alliances, and judiciously directed aggressive military campaigns. The conquest of the region over the long duration also implied the reorientation of political power to new centres of authority, allowing old ones to atrophy. Qanauj languished, for example, while Awadh and Kara prospered.[155] This relocation of political authority did not mean a degeneration in the economic life of the region; instead, old fiscal and transactional relationships continued even as the Mu'izzī Amirs sought to insinuate their appanages within their orbits. The capitulation of local elites to Sultanate authority in the countryside was a product of multiple forces whose pressure increased over time. And the fleeting reference to the *rānāgān* and the *thākkurān* in the Quṭbī armies, the desecration of temples, and the confessionally ambiguous sigilla on the coinage of the *bandagān* are not internally inconsistent statements. They are, together, vestiges of the complicated forces deployed over the long duration to enable regional consolidation of Mu'izzī appanages in north India.

Mu'izz al-Dīn Ghūrī obviously felt that his *bandagān-i khāṣṣ* were the ideal subalterns via whom he could consolidate his access to the wealth of India; hence their wide-scale deployment after 588/1192. Their deracinated nature, coupled with the programme of instruction (*tarbiyat*) and fosterage (*parwarish*), made them a dependent, indoctrinated cadre that the Sultan could trust as Governors over his dispersed

[155] This is indirectly suggested by the fact that by the 1220s and 1230s Qanauj was not regarded as an important enough appointment for a senior military commander. Tamar Khān, one of Sultan Iltutmish's distinguished slaves (see Table 1 for details), was appointed to Qanauj in 634/1236 and quickly moved to the nearby more strategic commands of Kara and then Awadh: Jūzjānī, *Ṭabaqāt-i Nāṣirī*, vol. 2, p. 17. Notice also that during the campaigns of 645/1248 in the Qanauj region, Sultan Nāṣir al-Dīn had his headquarters at Kara, where he received his brother Jalāl al-Dīn Mas'ūd Shāh based at that time in Qanauj (idem, vol. 1, p. 482). Less detail is available for other regions (like Ajmer, the Chauhān capital, for example), but see the case of Bengal where Bakhtiyār Khalajī moved away from the old Sena capital of Nadiya to Lakhnauti. In a similar fashion, Bahā' al-Dīn Tughril captured Thangir but eventually moved and established his capital at Sulṭānkōt. Ibid., vol. 1, pp. 421, 427 and above for details. This was, of course, in marked contrast to other areas like Lahore or Delhi, where the political centre did not shift.

territories in north India. In turn, the *bandagān* recognized that it was their servile status, their absolute dependence on their master and their adherence to his commands, that had, quite paradoxically, raised them to the position of Governors. This seems to have also restrained them from assuming any regal airs or titles while their master was alive. On the contrary, the *bandagān-i khāṣṣ* proclaimed their unfreedom without any reticence whatsoever: they incorporated *nisbas* such as *al-Sulṭānī* or *al-Mu'izzī* in their titles and displayed it on their inscriptions and coins.

Certainly, the paternalistic (and patriarchical) discourse of the court chronicles diluted the meaning of slavery and, especially if the man were a Turkish slave, transformed the enslaved into a recipient of high honours. The Seljuq *wazīr* Niẓām al-Mulk had recommended to the Sultan:

> A slave whom one has brought up and promoted, must be looked after, for it needs a whole lifetime and good luck to find a worthy and experienced slave. Wise men have said that a worthy and experienced servant or slave is better than a son. On this subject the poet says:
>
> One obedient slave is better
> than three hundred sons;
> for the latter desire their father's death,
> the former his master's glory.[156]

Slaves, in other words, would be like sons to their master without all their manifest problems. These sentiments of Niẓām al-Mulk were redirected in a very interesting way by Jūzjānī to focus on the unique attributes of Mu'izzī dominions and the deployment of slaves. Jūzjānī used an apocryphal conversation between a favourite at Mu'izz al-Dīn's court [*muqarrabān-i ḥaẓrat-i Sulṭanat*], to express regret to the monarch that the King of Islam did not have male heirs. The King deserved many sons, the confidant observed, so that each one of them could inherit a kingdom from the kingdoms of the world [*tā har yak az īshān wāriṣ-i mamlakatī būdandī az mamālik-i gītī*].[157] Jūzjānī placed the conversation in the account of the slave Tāj al-Dīn Ildūz, where

[156] Niẓām al-Mūlk, *Siyāsat Nāma*, translated by Darke, p. 117.
[157] Jūzjānī, *Ṭabaqāt-i Nāṣirī*, vol. 1, p. 410.

the slave's service to his master was extolled. Jūzjānī narrated the following as Mu'izz al-Dīn's reply:

> [While] other rulers may have one or two sons, I have many thousand sons, in other words [my] Turkish slaves, and my dominions will be their inheritance. After my death they will preserve my name in the Friday sermons [read] in my dominions. [*Digar Salāṭīn-rā yak farzand ya dū farzand bāshad, marā chandīn hazār farzand ast, ya'nī bandagān-i Turk, ki mamlakat-i man mirāṣ-i īshān khwāhad būd, b'ad az man khuṭba-i mamālik bā ism-i man nigāh khwāhand dāsht.*][158]

Jūzjānī went on to conclude that Mu'izz al-Dīn's wishes did indeed come true. After his death, his slaves honoured their master's memory: they recalled his name on their inscriptions and coins, and, apparently, in Friday sermons as well. But what is striking is Jūzjānī's expression of an ideal world. In a 'perfect' world, each of the sons (*har yak az īshān*) of the King of Islam should inherit a kingdom from the kingdoms of the world. This was somewhat unusual because coparcenary traditions of inheritance were quite foreign to normative Persianate tradition of governance, where kingship was never divided. In a properly ordered world the senior son—either the oldest or the son of the favoured queen—or the seniormost male relative of the deceased monarch should become the successor to the composite patrimony. Jūzjānī, however, was not following any of these ideas. In his interpretation, the state consisted of many dominions and these should become the inheritance of each of the sons. The sharing of the patrimony amongst multiple heirs was, strictly speaking, a rarer occurrence. It was a tradition with which Jūzjānī at least, with his long service with the Shansabanids, was intimately familiar.

The logic in Jūzjānī's fictional dialogue was actually quite linear. The author first regretted that Mu'izz al-Dīn Ghūrī would not be able to fulfill the destiny that he rightfully deserved. He may have been the 'King of Islam' but he would never be an *Abū al-Salāṭīn*, the father of Sultans. This was the title, if we recall, borne by the monarch's grandfather, all of whose sons received dominions and high honour. Three of them had succeeded each other as head of the family. The distribution of appanages to all the male descendants of Malik 'Izz al-Dīn

[158] Ibid., pp. 410–11.

Ḥusain seems to have crystallized into a normative tradition of sovereignty for the family. Certainly, all the succeeding Shansabanid monarchs abided by these traditions, a family prerogative to appanages that Mu'izz al-Dīn and his brother Ghiyāṡ al-Dīn also followed (see Table 1). It was as a corollory of these traditions that some lineages tried to monopolize regions: Fakhr al-Dīn Mas'ūd and his descendants made Bamiyan their home province, and, during his lifetime, Mu'izz al-Dīn excluded his family from his Ghaznavid dominions and their extension into north India.

What is intriguing in Jūzjānī's anecdote is the concern that Shansabanid traditions could not be followed by Mu'izz al-Dīn Ghūrī since he had no sons. That this was merely a rhetorical device is apparent from the manner in which the author managed the denouement. Jūzjānī had Mu'izz al-Dīn himself remind readers of the *Ṭabaqāt-i Nāṣirī* that he indeed had heirs: his slaves, who were, in fact, preferable to real sons because they were more trustworthy. When the authorial voice of Jūzjānī reappears in the narrative, it is to confirm Mu'izz al-Dīn's claim. History had vindicated the monarch; his slaves had shown greater respect to their master than most sons proffer to their father. Their deployment had brought all the advantages that able and loyal Princes may bring to the state without carrying any claims of birthright to weaken the patrimony. And it was through their filial respect that the monarch's memory was properly perpetuated.

Embedded in this conversation was a rather remarkable analysis of how Mu'izz al-Dīn followed Shansabanid traditions of governance in the organization of his dominions in north India. In a form that mirrored Shansabanid practice in Ghur, Jūzjānī's account suggested, Mu'izz al-Dīn distributed appanages amongst his *bandagān-i khāṣṣ* as if they were his progeny. The appanaging of Mu'izzī dominions in north India was, therefore, only to be expected; Mu'izz al-Dīn would, after all, follow—and creatively manipulate—traditions of governance that were closest and most familiar to him. Jūzjānī provided enough details in the *Ṭabaqāt-i Nāṣirī* to confirm that the Mu'izzī *bandagān-i khāṣṣ* were indeed deployed like Shansabanid Princes with autonomous principalities—they were given dominions, the prerogative to raise armies, wage war, construct alliances, collect tribute, disburse funds, embellish their capitals, and patronize commerce. Yet, even if there was considerable merit in comparing Shansabanid traditions in Ghur with those implemented in Hindustan, it was transparently flimsy in its proposition that the Shansabanid polity, with its baggage of competing kinsmen, could serve as a paradigm for a wonderfully stable regime.

Jūzjānī was actually hardly circumspect in narrating the levels of tension and conflict that existed within the Shansabanid family in Afghanistan. He described in some detail how the two brothers, Mu'izz al-Dīn and Ghiyāṣ al-Dīn, were in frequent conflict with the Bamiyanid side of the family. There was, for the larger part, not a whisper of dissension amongst the Mu'izzī *bandagān-i khāṣṣ*—forget conflict—in Jūzjānī's account of their deployment in India. That is, until we come to the years 592–601/1196–1205. These were the years between Mu'izz al-Dīn's annexation of Bayana and his defeat at the hands of the Khwārazm Shāh at Andkhud. During this time period, Mu'izz al-Dīn never campaigned in the subcontinent. If we follow the accounts of Ḥasan Niẓāmī and Jūzjānī, Ghurid expansion into Khurasan and Khwarazm seems to have absorbed all of the Sultan's attention. As a result, for almost a decade the monarch's *bandagān-i khāṣṣ* in north India remained largely unsupervised. It was precisely during this period that they expanded and consolidated their control over their principalities. These were the years that witnessed a new phase of military expansion: there were plunder raids into Gujarat in 593/1197, Khalajī excursions into Bihar and Bengal, Budaun was occupied in 594/1197–8, Qanauj in 595/1198, Gwalior in 597/1200–1, and in 599/1202 Kalinjar was seized. This was also the time when Quṭb al-Dīn Ai-Beg built the Delhi congregational mosque and Bahā' al-Dīn Tughril established his new capital at Sulṭānkōt. The infusion of wealth and exploitation of new political opportunities strengthened the individual *bandagān-i khāṣṣ*, but it also introduced competition amongst them. The events surrounding the annexation of Gwalior bring this out very well.

Gwalior was a strategically important fort that straddled the trade routes into northern Rajasthan, Malwa, and Gujarat. It also brought access to Bundelkhand with its resources of war elephants, particularly important for the army. Mu'izz al-Dīn was interested in gaining a foothold in the area and, after the capture of Thangir-Bayana, had marched towards Gwalior. He had retired without accomplishing his mission, entrusting the future campaign to Bahā' al-Dīn Tughril, promising him the territory upon its capitulation. Bahā' al-Dīn postponed his campaign for about four or five years and marched against Gwalior only after he had consolidated his control over the Bayana region, around 597/1200–1. The conquest of Gwalior would have added to his resources, a development unacceptable to Quṭb al-Dīn Ai-Beg in Delhi. As a result, Quṭb al-Dīn disregarded his master's wishes, marched into the region, negotiated with the ruler of Gwalior, promising him favourable terms. When Gwalior finally capitulated, it was to the forces of Quṭb al-Dīn and not Bahā' al-Dīn. The former confirmed his control over the region with the appointment of his slave, Shams al-Dīn Iltutmish, as its commander. Jūzjānī, who narrated this incident, was, as usual, very circumspect. He concluded rather diplomatically that as a result of the Gwalior episode there was (not) a little dislike between Bahā' al-Dīn Tughril and Quṭb al-Dīn, *miyān Malik . . . wa Sulṭān andak ghubārī būd.*[159]

Bahā' al-Dīn Tughril was not the only Mu'izzī Malik in Hindustan to suffer the effects of Quṭb al-Dīn's growing ambition. The case of the Mu'izzī commanders Ḥusām al-Dīn Ughul Beg and Sipahsālār Hizabr al-Dīn Ḥasan Arnab, moved from their original commands by Quṭb al-Dīn, consolidates the general impression that the commander of Delhi wanted to impress his influence over wide areas of north India. In fact, Ḥasan Niẓāmī's text carries a fictional and extremely patronizing homily on good governance that Quṭb al-Dīn supposedly delivered to Ḥusām al-Dīn Ughul Beg.[160] This was deployed by the author to underline the growing assymetrical relationship between the two Mu'izzī *bandagān*.

[159] Ibid., p. 421. Readers should also note the deliberate attempt to convey inequality between the two Mu'izzī slaves: Jūzjānī used the title of Malik for Bahā' al-Dīn and Sultan for Quṭb al-Dīn.

[160] Ḥasan Niẓāmī, *Tāj al-Ma'āṣir*, translated by Saroop, pp. 178–82. See also I.H. Siddiqui, 'The Thirteenth and Fourteenth Century Farmans concerning the Conduct of the Governors under the Sultans of Delhi', in *Perso-Arabic Sources of Information*, pp. 168–9. Siddiqui suggests that, rather than a didactic passage, this was an edited transcript of a *parwāna/farmān* sent by Quṭb al-Dīn to Ḥusām al-Dīn Ughul Beg.

Mu'izz al-Dīn's reactions to Quṭb al-Dīn's growing influence in north India are relatively unclear. Fakhr-i Mudabbir notes rather laconically that in 598/1201–2, Quṭb al-Dīn visited the monarch in Ghazni. This was after he had seized Gwalior.[161] No other chronicler writing in or around this time noticed this visit. In the next century, however, 'Iṣāmī put an interesting spin on the whole story. According to him, rumours of Quṭb al-Dīn's growing insubordination had reached Mu'izz al-Dīn and this provoked the monarch to recall his slave. Despite the doubts surrounding 'Iṣāmī's chronologically distant and eulogistical report of Quṭb al-Dīn's reception in Ghazni, the apprehensions that had led to the slave commander's summons to Ghazni appear to possess a credible core.[162] The slave must have managed to successfully reassure his master of his continuing loyalty; all the reports convey how Mu'izz al-Dīn's regard for Quṭb al-Dīn did not decline in the long duration. Assuredly, in the absence of his master's intervention in the affairs of his *bandagān* in north India, by 598/1201 Quṭb al-Dīn was fast emerging as the dominant Mu'izzī commander in north India.

Quṭb al-Dīn's increasing influence over some of the *bandagān* in north India does not coincide with the qualities of collegial comradeship that he had displayed in his youth. If we recall, the process of training slaves was intended to promote fidelity to the master and a close companionship within the cadre of slaves. The spirit of corporate egalitarianism amongst the corps of slaves was supposed to further accentuate the sentiment of comradeship. In a refrain that would be articulated later, all the *bandagān* were equal since they were the 'slaves of the same master' and the Sultan had established exclusive, dyadic, binary relationships with each of them.[163] The emergence of

[161] Fakhr-i Mudabbir, *Ta'rīkh-i Fakhr al-Dīn Mubārak Shāh*, p. 24. According to the author, it was to seek the Sultan's permission to campaign in Khurasan and bring the region under the monarch's rule in a manner similar to Hindustan.

[162] 'Iṣāmī, *Futūḥ al-Salāṭīn*, edited by A.S. Usha (Madras: University of Madras, 1940), pp. 85–9. 'Iṣāmī's report, more than a century and a half after the event, is quite vague in its chronology of Quṭbī campaigns. But for Fakhr-i Mudabbir's unambiguous dating of the event there would be strong reasons to doubt its veracity.

[163] On the sentiment of 'slaves of the same master, *khwāja tāsh*' see Ẓiyā'

one to a dominant position over others introduced asymmetrical interpersonal relations, a development that disturbed the precariously balanced political system. Jūzjānī's taciturn remark about the 'dislike' between Bahā' al-Dīn Tughril and Quṭb al-Dīn marked the extent to which the author wanted to comment upon the impact of a more aggressive Delhi on its peers. What he did not wish to develop was how the discord caused by the actions of the ambitious Delhi commander mirrored the tensions introduced within the Shansabanid polity by the domineering presence of the brothers Ghiyāṣ al-Dīn and Mu'izz al-Dīn. Not merely did the two political structures share the common features of a horizontally dispersed network of family/slave commanders with autonomous appanages, they were also similar in their hostile responses to increasing stratification introduced in such a delicately balanced political order by one of its members.

With the death of their master in 602/1206, the flagrant competition between the Mu'izzī *bandagān* could not be ignored even by Jūzjānī. Hostilities started when Tāj al-Dīn seized Ghazni in what appears a bid by the slave to usurp his erstwhile master's pivotal role in the affairs of the Shansabanid polity.[164] The sigilla on Ildūz's coins stated his ambitions clearly enough. He appropriated the title *Sulṭān al-mu'azzam*, the great Sultan, a claim to authority that tried to gain credence by acknowledging his dead master, Mu'izz al-Dīn, as the *Sulṭān al-'aẓam*, the supreme Sultan, on the same coin.[165] Interestingly enough, although Jūzjānī makes much of Ildūz's protestations of support and loyalty to the reigning Ghurid monarch, Ghiyāṣ al-Dīn Maḥmūd at Firuz Koh, no public declaration of his allegiance is present on any extant coin.[166]

Quṭb al-Dīn resisted Ildūz's efforts to dominate the Shansabanid dominion and extend his influence towards Lahore. In response to Ildūz's challenge, Quṭb al-Dīn had already shifted his headquarters

---

al-Dīn Baranī, *Ta'rīkh-i Fīrūz Shāhī*, edited by Khan, p. 28, edited by Rashid, p. 33, and Chapter 5 for a full discussion.

[164] Jūzjānī, *Ṭabaqāt-i Nāṣirī*, vol. 1, pp. 411–12.

[165] See Edward Thomas, *The Chronicles of the Pathan Kings*, pp. 29–31; Nelson Wright, *The Coinage and Metrology of the Sultans of Delhi*, pp. 12–13; and John S. Deyell, *Living without Silver*, p. 361.

[166] Jūzjānī, *Ṭabaqāt-i Nāṣirī*, vol. 1, p. 412.

to the old Ghaznavid capital and, around 604/1208, defeated Ildūz and seized Ghazni. This was only a fleeting victory, however. Faced with a renewed attack from Ildūz, together with the hostility of the local population, Quṭb al-Dīn was forced to relinquish his master's capital.[167] For the remainder of his life Quṭb al-Dīn (d. 607/1210) reigned from Lahore, commanding the extensive appanage of Lahore–Delhi that had areas such as Kuhram, Tabarhind, Budaun and Gwalior under its control.

Increasing stratification and conflict within the Ghurid political system after Mu'izz al-Dīn's death did not mean that older traditions of coparcenary rule were completely displaced. It did marginalize some members of the ruling circle but others used the moment of stress to seize power. This was apparent amongst the Bamiyanid circle of the Shansabanid family members in the Ghurid homelands; it was equally manifest amongst the Mu'izzī *bandagān-i khāṣṣ* in north India. Although Bahā' al-Dīn Tughril, Ḥusām al-Dīn Ughul Beg, and Sipahsālār Hizabr al-Dīn Ḥasan Arnab suffered Quṭb al-Dīn's aggressive interventions, they continued as important Mu'izzī military commanders in north India. Amongst the Mu'izzī *bandagān-i khāṣṣ*, it was Nāṣir al-Dīn Qubācha, the commander of Multan and Uchch, who used the disturbed conditions of the first decade of the thirteenth century most effectively to his advantage. As we will see in the following two chapters, he rose rapidly to power, became the dominant commander, and eventually emerged as a threat to both Ghazni and Delhi.

The impact of these commanders on the histories of their respective commands sometimes continued to be manifest years after their demise. The influence of Bahā' al-Dīn's successors, for example, did not decline in the Bayana region even after Quṭb al-Dīn's successor, Iltutmish, annexed the region in the early 1230s.[168] Affinal relations

[167] Ibid., pp. 412–13, 417.

[168] If we recall, Bahā' al-Dīn's successors sold their father's slaves to Iltutmish. There is no explicit date mentioned for the event. In fact, in Habibi's edition of the *Ṭabaqāt-i Nāṣirī*, Thangir is not included in the list of Iltutmish's conquests. But see vol. 1, p. 452, fn. 5, where the editor notices its presence in other manuscripts, as also the edition of W. Nassau Lees, p. 179, where it is

with Bahā' al-Dīn's family in the second generation still served to improve an individual's status, and Sultan Iltutmish married one of his trusted manumitted slaves, Tāj al-Dīn Sanjar Arsalān Khān, to Bahā' al-Dīn's daughter. Because of his marriage into Bahā' al-Dīn's family, Jūzjānī notes, Tāj al-Dīn Sanjar Arsalān was appointed to Bayana in Sultan Nāṣir al-Dīn Maḥmūd's reign (644–64/1246–66).[169] Clearly, despite challenges to their authority, nearly fifty years after their progenitor's death, Bahā' al-Dīn's descendants still possessed familial claims upon portions of the Bayana region.

Quṭb al-Dīn's rise to political dominance in north India, in other words, did not erase the dispensation of power constructed by Mu'izz al-Dīn. Despite Jūzjānī's restrained comments on the subject, it is perhaps important to underscore how competition and tension amongst the constituent members of the Shansabanid political system was not a corrupt development but a vital aspect of its coparcenary political traditions. The effort to maintain a balance of power within the ruling circle and the contradictory impulse towards the segregation of authority remained a characteristic feature of the Shansabanid state, a feature equally manifest in its collateral Mu'izzī dominions in north India.

After Mu'izz al-Dīn's death, many of his *bandagān-i khāṣṣ* publicly took on the title of Sultan. Ildūz and Qubācha displayed it on their coins, Tughril on an inscription in his congregational mosque[170] And although we have no extant inscriptional or numismatic evidence for Quṭb al-Dīn's assumption of this title, Jūzjānī, Ḥasan Niẓāmī, and Fakhr-i Mudabbir did not hesitate to retrospectively use it in their

---

mentioned. Elsewhere, Jūzjānī records that Gwalior was (re-)captured in 630/1232 and Juzjānī mentions that in 632/1234–5 the Shamsī slave, Malik Nusrat al-Dīn Tā'īsī, was appointed to the command, *iqṭā'*, of Bayana/Thangir and the superintendence, *shahnagī*, of the region of Gwalior. Ibid., edited by Habibi, vol. 2, p. 10.

169 Ibid., p. 34.

170 For Ildūz, see references cited above; for Qubācha see Edward Thomas, *The Chronicles of the Pathan Kings*, p. 101, undated silver and copper coin no. 87; and for Tughril see Mehrdad and Natalie Shokoohy, 'The Architecture of Baha al-Din Tughrul', p. 115.

references to the ruler of Delhi. But these were not outright assertions of authority; even when the *bandagān* claimed the status of monarchs, they were careful to state that their rights to authority flowed from their close and dependent relationship with their master. One of Tāj al-Dīn Ildūz's coins stated that he was *Sulṭān al- mu'aẓẓam* while Mu'izz al-Dīn was *Sulṭān al-'aẓam*. Another coin carried the title of the dead monarch within a square frame, the exalted *Sultan Mu'izz al-Dunyā' wa al-Dīn abū al-Muẓaffar Muḥammad ibn Sām*. At the edge of the coin, around the square, was Ildūz's title: *'abd wa mawlā* (the slave and client) *Tāj al-Dunyā wa al-Dīn Ildūz al-Sulṭānī* (the slave of the Sultan).[171] When Bahā' al-Dīn Tughril took on the title of *Pādshāh* with a simultaneous acknowledgement of his slave status (*al-Sulṭānī*) he was placing on record his career of service to his master, a service of self-abnegation that had gained his master's trust and raised his status. He and the other *khāṣṣ* slaves were closer to Mu'izz al-Dīn than anybody else, and it is this proximity that Jūzjānī praised as filial respect. After their master's death, the *bandagān-i khāṣṣ* recognized their connections to him in their coins, an affiliation which they deployed to confirm their inheritance as independent Sultans.[172] Over 602–7/1206–10 the political landscape of Mu'izzī dominions in north India was not very far from Jūzjānī's description: Mu'izz al-Dīn's *khāṣṣ* slaves had emerged as Sultans, and, even as they competed and partitioned their master's patrimony, each asserted their right to rule because they were his trusted slaves. Stresses within the Shansabanid patrimony notwithstanding, its final dismember-

[171] Deyell, *Living Without Silver*, p. 361, no. 262, and for an alternative version see Edward Thomas, *The Chronicles of the Pathan Kings*, p. 30, no. 23.

[172] In contrast to the efforts to retain their links with their master, note the estampage on the coinage of 'Alī Mardān Khalajī, a free Amir, commander of Lakhnauti, with no bonds to Mu'izz al-Dīn. The sigillum on the reverse of one of his coins carried the title: the Sultan and Support of the world, the victorious 'Alī Mardān (*al-Sulṭān al-'Alam Rukn al-Dunyā wa al-Dīn Abū al-Muẓaffar 'Alī Mardān),* with no reference to the Ghurid monarch at all. See Deyell, *Living without Silver*, p. 364, coin no. 298. Deyell dates the coin to 600/1204, which is curious because Jūzjānī states quite clearly that 'Alī Mardān took the title of Sultan 'Alā' al-Dīn at the death of Quṭb al-Dīn. Jūzjānī, *Ṭabaqāt-i Nāṣirī*, vol. 1, p. 434.

ment would take place only after the death of Quṭb al-Dīn and the other Mu'izzī *bandagān*.

Conclusion

The Mu'izzī political structure in north India was influenced by two overlapping factors. The first was the Shansabanid system of governance operating through the lineage and slave systems where coparcenary traditions were very strong. The second was the rich, and yet terribly insecure environment of the frontier north Indian marches, attractive enough to Ghurid elites for short durations of service but not permanent settlement. It is important to emphasize the provenance of the early Sultanate social and political traditions because neither 'Muslim' nor 'Turkish' captures the unique qualities that the Shansabanids and Mu'izz al-Dīn imparted to their regime in north India. While there is a huge currency to the terms 'the Muslim/Turkish Sultanate' in modern historiography, it is important to recognize the ahistoricism implicit in these characterizations.[173] There were very precise historical conditions that gave form and character to the early Sultanate regime in north India and these are accessible to the historian; the reductive ascription of essentialized confessional and ethnic qualities makes the historian's task quite redundant.

Ghurid expansion into north India occurred during the reigns of the two brothers Ghiyāṣ al-Dīn and Mu'izz al-Dīn, a time that marked the apogee of that Sultanate's power. The two brothers worked in rare harmony and dominated their family, the eastern Iranian world, and the marches of north India. The unanimity of interests between the two siblings should not obscure the fact that the Ghurid domain was extremely fragmented amongst members of the Shansabanid family, within which conflict to protect presumed familial rights within the kin group was quite common. That the Ghurid Sultanate managed to preserve a stable exterior was dependent, in part, upon a balance of power that definitely favoured the two brothers in Firuz Koh and Ghazni. Mu'izz al-Dīn was also extremely energetic in consolidating his position within his own appanage. He preserved his rights within

[173] See Chapter 1 for a detailed discussion.

the Ghaznavid territory in Afghanistan and north India through a large deployment of *bandagān* led by a judiciously selected elite slave cadre.

The death in rapid succession of the two brothers destabilized the balance within the Shansabanid patrimony. The descendants of Fakhr al-Dīn Mas'ūd and 'Alā' al-Dīn Ḥusain grappled with the Mu'izzī slaves and the heirs of Ghiyāṣ al-Dīn over Firuz Koh. Within the Ghaznavid appanage, Mu'izz al-Dīn's north Indian domains devolved to his *bandagān-i khāṣṣ* and, to a lesser extent, free military commanders, specifically the Khalaj on the Bengal frontier. Some historians have argued that without the backing of vaster resources several of these Mu'izzī territories in north India were recaptured by local chieftains, and some diminished in size as Ghurid forces were driven closer to their garrison towns.[174] The evidence does not support this conclusion. After Quṭb al-Dīn Ai-Beg's death, and in the unstable first years of Iltutmish's reign, the areas that devolved to local chieftains, with the exception of Gwalior, were those that were only nominally under Mu'izzī suzerainty. Areas such as Ranthambhor, Malwa, and Nahrwala had been plundered, not settled as a part of Mu'izzī territory. In some of these places, local chieftains were reinstalled in exchange for tribute. The crisis in the Mu'izzī dominions in north India came with the death of the Sultan, when his slaves competed with each other to retain or extend their appanages.

The *bandagān-i khāṣṣ* and the Khalaj Amirs managed to hold their own very well in the absence of any direct Mu'izzī supervision. The *bandagān* had much to thank Mu'izz al-Dīn for the rigorous military training that he imparted to his slaves. As we have noticed, the Mu'izzī *bandagān-i khāṣṣ* organized their own armed retinues around similarly trained military slaves. Schooled in the martial arts and drilled together, these military slaves possessed an *esprit de corps* that was often more coherent in the battlefield than the more decentralized clan and lineage *levees* of the 'Rajputra' chieftains.

[174] See the forceful argument of Habibullah, *The Foundation of Muslim Rule in India*, pp. 83–7.

They were a formidable fighting machine and proved to be a bulwark against the aspirations of many local chieftains to recapture their lost territories.

The military resilience of these Mu'izzī appanages complemented their economic viability. Although infusion of plunder was important for their sustenance, slave Governors also tried to develop the replenishable resources of their urban commands through trade and commerce. Merchants were given preferential treatment, for they were avenues through which exotic goods as well as the necessities of their profession—warhorses and slaves—were supplied. Although the textual evidence can be sometimes misleading on the subject, numismatic materials are far clearer in suggesting that efforts to build up a viable resource base for the Mu'izzī appanages implied reassuring local communities and integrating urban garrison towns in the material life of their hinterlands. Plunder and trade, military engagements and negotiating alliances, iconoclasm and figural depiction on coinage were adroitly reconciled by the Mu'izzī Governors in their efforts to expand and consolidate their territories.

The degree of consolidation achieved by the Mu'izzī appanages was reflected by increasing immigration into north India. Although the push and pull factors were not in favour of service in India in 588/1192, with the passage of time larger number of émigrés made their way into the region. While Lahore had already profited as the capital of the Ghaznavids and it was not quite the frontier any longer, further afield even Delhi and Bayana possessed their congregational mosques, *masjid-i jāmi'*. Suffice it to say that by 607/1210 the factors influencing a choice either to stay in eastern Iran and Afghanistan or to serve in one of the wealthier appanages in north India were balanced very slightly in favour of the central Islamic lands. Any individual misfortune could tilt the balance in favour of India. Larger disturbances, such as the Khwarazmid invasion of the Ghurid domains in Afghanistan or the Chingiz Khanid invasions of Khurasan and Afghanistan in the next decade, started a flood of migrations. The Mongol destruction in Khurasan and Afghanistan was only partly responsible for this migration into north India. After all, migrants could still flee westwards towards Iraq, as did the monarch of Khwarazm, Sultan

Jalāl al-Dīn Mingbarnī (617–28/1220–31). That a large number of people chose to come to north India was only because the region had gained a reputation as a sanctuary for Muslims seeking patronage.

This reputation was possible only because, by the first decade of the thirteenth century, the umbilical cords connecting north India to Ghazni were gradually severed. The Mu'izzī *bandagān-i khāṣṣ* had transformed their appanages into what I would call the 'Sultanates of north India'. They were self-governing, prosperous, and powerful dominions under ambitious rulers. There was a long history of competition between these rival Sultanates. Yet, the emergence of Quṭb al-Dīn Ai-Beg to political prominence, even over the years 602–7/1206–10, did not succeed in displacing many of the Mu'izzī *bandagān-i khāṣṣ* from their centres of power. The establishment of the paramount Sultanate of Delhi under Shams al-Dīn Iltutmish was still in the future, and, as we will see in the next two chapters, its establishment would be at the cost of these rival north Indian principalities.

CHAPTER 3

The Shamsī Dispensation and the Political Paramountcy of Delhi

With the death of Mu'izz al-Dīn (602/1206) and Quṭb al-Dīn Ai-Beg (607/1210) in rapid succession, even Jūzjānī, the chronicler of the Delhi Sultans, was forced to recognize the fragmentation of the Mu'izzī patrimony into separate domains where Delhi, far from being the paramount province, struggled to retain its autonomy from its neighbours. He explicitly noted the division of the Mu'izzī patrimony in north India into four dominions: Ghazni ruled by Tāj al-Dīn Ildūz, Sindh under Nāṣir al-Dīn Qubācha, Delhi governed by Shams al-Dīn Iltutmish (607–33/1210–36), and the domains of Lakhnauti controlled by the Khalaj Sultans and Maliks.[1] Both Jūzjānī and Ḥasan Niẓāmī described the conflict for paramountcy that occurred between these states. While I discuss the details of these conflicts later in this section, suffice it to note for now that of the four principalities, Delhi may well have been the weakest and had, in 607/1210, a slim chance of political survival.[2]

[1] Jūzjānī, *Ṭabaqāt-i Nāṣirī*, vol. 1, p. 418. The presence of several states and individuals in authority in Bengal is evident from Jūzjānī's usage of the plural, *mamālik-i Lakhnautī muluk wa salāṭīn-i Khalaj, dar ẓabṭ āwardan*, the dominions of Lakhnauti were seized by the Khalaj Maliks and Sultans.

[2] For details on the conflict with Ildūz and Qubācha, see below and Jūzjānī, vol. 1, pp. 413, 419, and 445–7; and Ḥasan Niẓāmī, *Tāj al-Ma'āṣir*, translated by Elliot and Dowson, vol. 2, pp. 239 and 241–2. The British Museum manuscript, also used by Elliot and Dowson, covered events until 626/1229. The

The death of Quṭb al-Dīn removed the overweening presence of one of the more powerful and ambitious military commanders from north Indian politics but it also cast into doubt the future integrity of his domain. During his lifetime Quṭb al-Dīn had consolidated his rule through the deployment of his slaves and some free Amirs. Of the two, it was his slaves that Jūzjānī and Ḥasan Niẓāmī described as the principal political actors in the realm. More interesting was the fact that Quṭb al-Dīn also had a son, Ārām Shāh, an individual who the contemporary chroniclers preferred not to dwell upon even as they extolled the achievements of his father. At Quṭb al-Dīn's death all three—the Quṭbī *bandagān*, the free Amirs, and the son—competed, together and separately, to control their master's patrimony. This was an unusual 'war of succession' because although there was only one 'legal' heir, the reports of the event sought to diminish his rights to the throne while inflating those of the usurper. But, beyond the narrow concern with individuals, the succession conflict was embedded in the political system of the time and provides a useful entry into the study of political relationships, questions of inheritance, and the making of Sultanate authority. What kinds of contending groups did the Mu'izzī political system produce in the second generation, and what kinds of alliances and hostilities were generated through their differing aspirations?

Dynastic Change in the Lahore–Delhi Appanage, 607/1210

In fundamental ways the deaths of Mu'izz al-Dīn and Quṭb al-Dīn created analogous sets of problems in the respective domains of the two monarchs. It is difficult to refer to the 'dilemma' of 602/1206 or 607/1210 within the Ghaznavid or the Lahore–Delhi principality as

---

manuscript used by B. Saroop terminates at 614/1217–18. It mentions the conquest of Lahore 613/1217 but has scant information after that event: translated by Saroop, pp. 321–2. For a description of Ḥasan Niẓāmī's work, see also Mumtaz Ali Khan, *Some Important Persian Prose Writing of the Thirteenth Century A.D. in India*, (Aligarh: Department of History, Aligarh Muslim University, 1970), pp. 70–86.

one posed purely by a problem of succession. The term 'succession' assumes that there were specific rights, prerogatives and powers that could be transferred, or could continue as the estate of an heir. Within the Mu'izzī political system, where seniority was already a bone of contention amongst the *bandagān-i khāṣṣ*, the choice of perpetuating the life of the principality by seeking a successor was only *one* of the options open to Mu'izzī subordinates. As we have already noticed, the alternative recourse of opting out of the principality and seeking an independent path was one that many Governors had already exercised when their master, Mu'izz al-Dīn Ghūrī, died in 602/1206. By Quṭb al-Dīn Ai-Beg's death in 607/1210, the movement towards the further fragmentation of the Mu'izzī patrimony had gathered strength and Benaras and Awadh joined Bayana, Sindh, Lahore, and Lakhnauti in having little to do with Lahore–Delhi.[3]

Within the Lahore–Delhi principality, notables who had been elevated through the dispensation of office during the reign of Quṭb al-Dīn fought to perpetuate their rights to command. In his account of the events of 607/1210, Jūzjānī identified the two contending groups for power as members of rival political dispensations, the Mu'izzīs and the Quṭbīs. Neither the Mu'izzīs nor the Quṭbīs were quite as homogeneous as their names suggest. Although the Mu'izzī Amirs dominated the north Indian political landscape (they constituted what I described earlier as the 'north Indian Sultanates'), those resident in the Lahore–Delhi appanage were not nearly so influential. As we will see, members within the group waffled in their alliances, moving back and forth between contenders they assumed were most likely to win in the forthcoming conflict.

The Quṭbīs were also a fragmented group.[4] On the one hand there were the senior military slaves, commanders like Shams al-Dīn

[3] Benaras and Awadh were under the command of the Quṭbī slave Qaymāz Rūmī. Although there is no information about the slave commander's participation in the succession conflict, he remained unreconciled to Iltutmish's succession. See section three below, and Chapter 2, for details. Bayana was under the Tughril family, Sindh under Qubācha, Lahore was seized by Ildūz, and Lakhnauti was in the control of the Khalajī commanders.

[4] Modern scholars have sometimes collapsed the internal differences amongst the Quṭbīs, suggesting that the conflict was a simple one between

Iltutmish, Governor of Budaun. On the other there were soldiers and commanders who were a part of the central contingent of the royal army, the *qalb,* based in Lahore, led by a body of senior slaves apparently not yet deployed as Governors by Quṭb al-Dīn. The names of two of their leaders mentioned by Ḥasan Niẓāmī also suggest that they were Turkish slaves: *sar-i jāndār* (leader of the guards) Turkī and Aq-Sunqar Khitā'ī.[5]

The response of the Quṭbī slaves to their master's death differed. The main supporters of Quṭb al-Dīn's son, Ārām Shāh, for example, were members of the central contingent, the *qalb,* located in Lahore. This was, on the face of it, hardly surprising. Acknowledging the heir of the master was the legal duty incumbent upon slaves, whether they were manumitted or not: as commodities, the slaves were a part of the bequest inherited by their master's successor. As *mawālī*, manumitted slaves, they were still tied to their master by ties of association that continued their subordinate, dyadic relationships. As we have already noticed, manumission did not alter the conditions under which slaves held public responsibility, and on Mu'izz al-Dīn's death the Mu'izzī slaves had requested special patents from his heir to allow them to continue in their posts. Their subordinate relationship and links with their master's successor continued, even if their's was only a normative subordination rarely, if ever, enforced.

The juridical reasons that led Quṭbī slaves in Lahore to recognize Ārām Shāh as their new master were reinforced by two more pragmatic considerations. Jūzjānī explained the first: the Quṭbī Turks and Amirs [*Turkmān wa Umarā'-yi Quṭbī*], upheld the cause of Ārām Shāh to 'restrain rebellion and [promote] the comfort, [*ārāmish*], of the people and the confidence, [*itmi'nān*], of the soldiers of the *qalb*'.[6]

Quṭbīs and Mu'izzīs. See Irfan Habib, 'The Formation of the Sultanate Ruling Class', p. 9; and Peter Jackson, *The Delhi Sultanate,* p. 29.

[5] Ḥasan Niẓāmī, *Tāj al-Ma'āṣir*, translated by Elliot and Dowson, vol. 2, p. 237, translated by B. Saroop, pp. 297–8. The orthography of *sar-i jāndār* Turkī's name is not clear: Saroop has Tatar in his translation, Peter Jackson, *The Delhi Sultanate*, p. 29, fn. 29, reads the name as Berki, and Elliot and Dowson as Turkī.

[6] Jūzjānī, *Ṭabaqāt-i Nāṣirī*, vol. 1, p. 418.

Jūzjānī's telling comments—restrain rebellion . . . promote comfort and confidence—underlines how, in raising Ārām Shāh, the Quṭbī slaves were not as consumed by the need to enforce the son's legal rights of inheritance as they were in managing public order to the benefit of their own group. Certainly, the 'comfort' and 'confidence' of the Quṭbī commanders in Lahore envisaged a further promotion of their personal ambitions and their emergence as the real executors of authority under the nominal command of Ārām Shāh.

The second reason why the Lahore-based Quṭbī Amirs sprang to Ārām Shāh's support was the developments further away. According to Jūzjānī, in Delhi the judge (*amīr-i dād*) 'Alī Ismā'īl, together with some other judges, *ṣudūr,* and military commanders of the city, invited the senior Quṭbī slave Shams al-Dīn Iltutmish to succeed to the throne.[7] Given the presence of the legal heir and successor, it is astonishing that these jurists invited the slave to succeed his master. As we will see later, this was another instance of a remarkable dissembling by Jūzjānī to suit the interests of Iltutmish, his slave patron. Jūzjānī and Niẓāmī's biases notwithstanding, both authors provided enough details from Quṭb al-Dīn's reign to confirm Iltutmish's powerful position within his master's retinue. Purchased in 593/1197, he was one of Quṭb al-Dīn's oldest *bandagān,* and had already held the position of *sar-i jāndār* and *amīr-i shikār* (commander of the hunt) in his court. In 597/1200–1 the charge of Gwalior was given to Iltutmish immediately after its annexation, followed by Baran (modern Bulandshahr), and on his master's death he was the Governor of the important command of Budaun.[8]

Iltutmish had a vast retinue of soldiers and military slaves, years of military experience and was an altogether formidable presence within the Quṭbī contingent.[9] His authority was very similar to the influential positions that Ildūz and Quṭb al-Dīn Ai-Beg had created for themselves within Mu'izz al-Dīn Ghūrī's retinue during the latter years of their master's reign. And the response of the Quṭbīs to Iltutmish's attempts at garnering supreme control over their master's

[7] Ibid., p. 444.

[8] Ibid., p.443.

[9] For references on Iltutmish's military retinue, see section 4 below.

dispensation was as abhorrent to his peer group as Ildūz and Ai-Beg's challenge to their compatriots in a prior generation. The legality of a slave usurping power from the master's heir was only part of the problem. It was also extremely difficult for the Quṭbī *bandagān* to accept a fellow slave as their new lord and master, a peer who was sure to enhance stratification within the cadre by displacing them with members of his own retinue. This was an important reason why they had supported Ārām Shāh at all, and not chosen a member of their own group as Sultan. Iltutmish's claim to the throne went completely against the sentiments of equality present in the idea of *khwāja tāsh*, 'slaves of the same master'. As we have already noticed, military slaves resurrected this idea whenever they felt that stratification was threatening the fragile corporate character of their cadre. Iltutmish's bid for the throne forced the Lahore-based Quṭbī commanders to advance towards Delhi, and their forces were augmented by other Quṭbīs from different provinces. At this time, some of the Mu'izzī commanders located in the city also joined them [*jam'īyat kardand*].[10] It was a futile move; their combined forces were defeated by Iltutmish and he emerged as the next Sultan of Delhi.

[10] Jūzjānī, *Ṭabaqāt-i Nāṣirī*, vol. 1, p. 444. Habibi's edition has the following passage: *chun Turkān wa umarā'-yi Quṭbī az aṭrāf baDehlī jam'a shudand wa ba'ze az Atrāk wa umarā'-yi Mu'izzī bā īshān jam'īyat kardand wa ṭarīq-i makhālifat sapurdand wa az Dehlī bīrın raftand wa dar ḥawālī jam'a shudand wa 'isiyān wa kharūj āghāz nihādand.* I cannot agree with the translation of this passage in Irfan Habib, 'The Formation of the Sultanate Ruling Class', p. 9 and fn. 50, and, following him, Peter Jackson, *The Delhi Sultanate*, p. 29 and fn. 29. I translate it as: 'When the Turks and Quṭbī Amirs gathered from the provinces at Delhi, some of the Turks and Mu'izzī Amirs joined with them and committed themselves to the path of resistance. They went out of Delhi and assembled in its environs and began their rebellion and insurrection.' The 1864 edition of the *Ṭabaqāt-i Nāṣirī*, edited by W. Nassau Lees, p. 170, has the underlined portions different from the Habibi edition, and it quite alters the meaning: *ba'ze az Atrāk wa umarā'-yi Mu'izzī bā īshān jamī'at nakardand.* This was followed by S.A.A. Rizvi, *Aadi Turk Kalin Bharat* (Aligarh: Department of History, Aligarh Muslim University, 1956), p. 25, whose reading is very close to that of Habib and Jackson. As it happens, Raverty translates this passage quite accurately, *Ṭabaqāt-i Nāṣirī*, translated, vol. 1, p. 606.

The resolution of the intra-dispensational conflict between the Quṭbīs and their associated groups in favour of Shams al-Dīn Iltutmish also implied that the centre of political authority gravitated from Lahore to Delhi. Although the defeat of the Lahore-based Quṭbī Amirs was important for Iltutmish, the victory did not mean that his position was secure. Not merely did Quṭbī opposition continue, the remaining Mu'izzī commanders in the 'North Indian Sultanates' were even more threatening.

Iltutmish's precariousness was evident from the way he and his ideologues tried to gloss over the dynastic change entailed in his accession. The circumstance of a slave succeeding his master was not without precedent in the history of the Sultanates within the central Islamic lands, but it was still a development regarded with considerable ambivalence. Jūzjānī himself had mentioned the case of Tughril Bozan (?) who had murdered his master Sultan 'Abd al-Rashīd in 444/1053 and seized the throne. The chronicler had in fact described the slave as *Tughril al-mal'ūn*, 'Tughril, the accursed', because of his disloyalty and ingratitude to the household of his patrons.[11] By contrast, he was the soul of discretion when reporting any controversy raised by Iltutmish's succession, glossing over Iltutmish's violent seizure of royal privileges and obvious display of disloyalty to the memory of his master. Instead, Jūzjānī's Persian chronicle dwelt upon the honourable conduct of his patron and the seamless continuity of the Sultanate from one lineage to another.

It is unlikely that discussions concerning the legality of Iltutmish's actions disappeared so easily in the thirteenth century. In what is an extremely unusual account of Sultan Iltutmish from the fourteenth century, the Moroccan traveller Ibn Baṭṭūṭa, narrated how the *qāẓīs* of Delhi appeared before Iltutmish immediately after his accession to the throne of Delhi.[12] Iltutmish realized that they doubted the legality

[11] Jūzjānī, *Ṭabaqāt-i Nāṣirī*, vol. 1, p. 236, and his was not a minority opinion. Other chroniclers referred to Tughril as *kāfir-i ni'mat*, the ingrate, or *maghrūr makhzūl*; the arrogant and contemptible. See C.E. Bosworth, *The Later Ghaznavids 1040–1186*, p. 41.

[12] Ibn Baṭṭūṭa, *Rehla*, translated by Agha Mahdi Hussain, p. 33. The Moroccan is usually believed to have worked and travelled in India between 734/1333

of his accession and the slave, therefore, showed them his deed of manumission. Since only a free individual could hold a position of public responsibility and command over other free Muslims, it was only after they had perused the document that the jurists rendered their oath of allegiance to the new monarch.[13]

What is interesting about the reports of Ibn Baṯṯūṯa and Jūzjānī are the references in common to the different roles of jurists and the pious. In the tale of the travelogue, the *qāẓīs* appeared to scrutinize the legality of the (freed) slave's accession. In the Delhi chronicler's account, the [freed] slave was *invited* to the throne by the jurists (*amīr-i dād* and the *ṣudūr*) of Delhi. It is extremely doubtful that Ibn Baṯṯūṯa, himself, was deliberately inverting Jūzjānī's text; his narrative carries no evidence of his ever reading, or of having any of the Sultanate chronicles read to him.[14] He composed his history on the basis of a variety of oral reports from diverse informants. Some of these were of indiscriminate provenance; others we know he received from friends and acquaintances like the chief *qāẓī* of Delhi, Kamāl al-Dīn Muḥammad, or the Suhrawardi Shaykh Rukn-i 'Ālam.[15] It is curious that, nearly a century after the event, of all the things that Ibn Baṯṯūṯa recalled, it was his informants' account of the interrogation of the slave's usurpation of high office by jurists that stuck in his memory. That it was reported to him from this perspective is also striking, because Jūzjānī was extremely careful not to cast any aspersions whatsoever upon the slave's accession to office. Ibn Baṯṯūṯa's report provides a wonderful insight into how, years after the event, the

---

and 743/1342. Peter Jackson, 'The Mongols and India 1221–1351', Cambridge University: Ph.D. dissertation, 1976, pp. 219–30, pushes back the date of Baṯṯūṯa's departure from India to about 747/1346.

[13] Ibn Baṯṯūṯa, *Rehla,* p. 33.

[14] Ibid., p. 39, and the note to the *Liqā' al-Sa'dain.* As Mahdi Hussain pointed out, this is probably an incorrect reference to Amīr Khusrau's *Qirān al-Sa'dain,* about which the traveller may have been informed. There is nothing in the travelogue to suggest that he was familiar with the content of this or another Sultanate chronicle.

[15] Ibid., pp. 32, 47, 55 for references to the *qāẓī* and the Shaykh. See also p. 39, where Ibn Baṯṯūṯa notes more ambiguously: 'An Indian narrated to me . . .'.

seizure of authority by a slave continued to circulate amongst jurist informants of the traveller, if not within a more universal 'public' arena.

It was in an attempt to defuse the bad press that followed his conflict with Ārām Shāh that Shams al-Dīn married the daughter of Quṭb al-Dīn Ai-Beg. This matrimonial union was a departure from past practice. Hitherto, within the Shansabanid family and the Mu'izzī *bandagān-i khāṣṣ*, brides were given either to peers or to lineages that were socially superior.[16] In effect, through such asymmetrical matrimonial union between the slave and the lineage of the master, Iltutmish sought to obscure dynastic change.[17] Thus, while on the one hand Iltutmish started the process of taking apart the political dispensation of his master, on the other hand he emphasized continuity with the previous order by claiming an affinal right to succession. For an individual operating within a *mamlūk* environment, this was in many ways a rather predictable response. Within a corporate group of slave dependants, the only way that a slave could hope to achieve pre-eminent status was by suggesting that he had a special relationship with his master. It was exactly such an exclusive claim that the Quṭbī slaves had sought to neutralize by supporting Ārām Shāh.

Certainly, when this succession struggle was narrated in late-sixteenth-century accounts by the Mughal historians Niẓām al-Dīn Aḥmad and 'Abd al-Qādir Badā'ūnī, the conflict was between equals: on the one hand there was the son, Ārām Shāh, on the other there was

[16] Note the Shansabanid genealogical chart and the discussion concerning the exchange of brides between Tāj al-Dīn Ildūz, Quṭb al-Dīn Ai-Beg, and Nāṣir al-Dīn Qubācha in Chapter 2. Iltutmish's innovation would set a precedent which Shamsī slaves would subsequently follow; see Chapter 5.

[17] Jūzjānī, *Ṭabaqāt-i Nāṣirī*, vol. 1, p. 417, makes two references to the marriage of Quṭb al-Dīn's daughter to Iltutmish. The first reference suggests that Iltutmish was a son-in-law before Quṭb al-Dīn's death. The second reference mentions the order of events more clearly, although it leaves Iltutmish's initiative in seeking the marriage quite vague. Iltumish's affinal relationship with Quṭb al-Dīn's family was linked by Jūzjānī to the degree of trust reposed in the slave by his master. He noted, vol. 1, p. 443, that Quṭb al-Dīn called Shams al-Dīn his son, *Sulṭān Quṭb al-Dīn Ai-Beg o rā farzand khwānd wa bakhud nazdīk gardānīd.*

Shams al-Dīn Iltutmish, the slave and son-in-law who was (also) called 'son' by Sultan Quṭb al-Dīn.[18] Mughal historians, inexperienced with the functioning of slave-based military elites, were already reifying the 'war of succession' as a fratricidal conflict familiar to them, ignoring the act of usurpation and the dynastic change introduced by Iltutmish's succession. In the twentieth century, in a development that would have certainly pleased Jūzjānī, modern historians reviewed all this material and expressed doubt over whether Ārām Shāh was at all the 'real' son of Quṭb al-Dīn Ai-Beg.[19] At the same time, there was an acknowledgement that Iltutmish was such a wonderful, attentive, loyal slave that his master thought of him as a 'son', made him his son-in-law, and, quite logically, his heir. The trauma of Quṭb al-Dīn's death and the nature of Iltutmish's succession are, ironically, captured in the efforts of historians to elide and explain the event away.

Competitors and Military Paramountcy in North India, 607–33/1210–36

Iltutmish's precarious political authority was evident in 607/1210 itself, when the autonomy of Delhi was challenged by the Mu'izzī slave Ildūz. He sent Iltutmish a ceremonial parasol and staff acknowledging the Delhi commander as his subordinate [*Ildūz az Lawhōr wa*

[18] Khwāja Niẓām al-Dīn Aḥmad, *Ṭabaqāt-i Akbarī*, edited by B. De, (Calcutta: Bibliotheca Indica Series no. 223, Asiatic Society of Bengal, 1927), vol. 1, p. 55: *ki banda wa dāmād wa pisar khwanda . . . būd.* See also, 'Abd al-Qādir Badā'ūnī, *Muntakhab al-Tawārīkh*, (Calcutta: Bibliotheca Indica Series, n.s. no. 131, 1868), vol. 1, p. 61.

[19] See, Muḥammad Aziz Aḥmad, *Political History and Institutions of the Early Turkish Empire of Delhi*, (Lahore: University of the Punjab, 1987 reprint), pp. 152–5; R.P. Tripathi, *Some aspects of Muslim Administration*, pp. 24–5; A.B.M. Habibullah, *The Foundation of Muslim Rule in India*, pp. 76–7; S.L. Rathor, 'A Plea Against the Charge of Usurpation by Iltutmish', *Islamic Culture*, 32 (1958), pp. 262–7; Gavin Hambly, 'Who were the *Chihalgani*, the Forty Slaves of Sultan Shams al-Dīn Iltutmish of Delhi', *Iran*, 10 (1972), p. 60; and, most recently, Peter Jackson, *The Delhi Sultanate*, p. 29; and idem, 'Ḳuṭb al-Dīn Aybak', EI^2, vol. 5, p. 546.

Ghaznīn bā o 'ahd bast, o rā chatr wa dūrbāsh farmūd].[20] This loss of status was driven home immediately after Quṭb al-Dīn's death, when Iltutmish's competitors seized control of vast areas of the Lahore–Delhi appanage. In 607/1210 Ildūz had reportedly already occupied Lahore, which marked the beginning of a conflict over the city between Tāj al-Dīn and Nāṣir al-Dīn Qubācha (now Sultan of Sindh). Between the years 607/1210 and 613/1217, Lahore seems to have exchanged hands several times between Ildūz and Qubācha, but was nominally under the control of Ghaznavid forces.[21] Between 607/1210 and 613/1217, however, Qubācha had seized Multan, Tabarhind, Kuhram, and Sursuti (modern Sirsa) from Iltutmish.[22]

The same period saw the presence of new competitors in the north-west as well. In 612/1215–16, driven out of Khwarazm by the Mongols, Jalāl al-Dīn Khwārazm Shāh seized Ghazni, and made his presence felt in the north Indian marches. From 618/1221 onwards, the Khwārazm Shāh, his subordinates, Saif al-Dīn Ḥasan Qārlūq,

[20] Jūzjānī, *Ṭabaqāt-i Nāṣirī*, vol. 1, p. 444.

[21] Ibid., vol. 1, p. 444. Elsewhere Jūzjānī also noted the conflict between Ghazni and Sindh over Lahore; see ibid., vol. 1, p. 418. When he mentioned, p. 419, that Qubācha seized Lahore several times, *Lawhōr rā chand karrat bagirift*, (obviously losing it several times as well) it was from the forces of Tāj al-Dīn Ildūz who treated it as a part of their domain. Jūzjānī noted quite clearly (vol. 1, p. 419) that previously (*az pīsh*) Qubācha's forces had been defeated in the environs of Lahore by Ildūz's *wazīr*, Mu'ayyid al-Mulk Sanjarī. Since the *wazīr* was killed by the Turkish Maliks and Amirs of Ghazni *before* 612/1215–16 (Jūzjānī, vol. 1, p. 413), the conflict with Qubācha, obviously, preceded this date. From 607/1210 Lahore seems to have exchanged hands several times, and, going by the number of times Jūzjānī mentions the defeat of Qubācha's forces, it is likely that the region was under the nominal control of Ildūz's forces. After the defeat of Ildūz at Tarain in 612/1215–16, Lahore lapsed into Qubācha's control, from whom it was subsequently seized in 613/1217 by Shams al-Dīn Iltutmish. See Ḥasan Niẓāmī, *Tāj al-Ma'āṣir*, translated by Elliot and Dowson, vol. 2, pp. 239–41. There is no evidence to suggest that Lahore was held by Qubācha and was seized by Tāj al-Dīn only in 612/1215–16; as suggested by Peter Jackson, 'The Mongols and India', p. 69, Muḥammad Aziz Aḥmad, *Political History and Institutions of the Early Turkish Empire of Delhi*, p. 165; and A.B.M. Habibullah, *The Foundation of Muslim Rule in India*, p. 77.

[22] Jūzjānī, *Ṭabaqāt-i Nāṣirī*, vol. 1, p. 419.

Uzbeg-bei, and the Khalajīs under Malik Khān Khalaj, together with Chingīz Khān and the Mongol commanders Dorbei Doqshin and Mengutei, constituted a powerful political presence in the north-west.[23] In effect, almost immediately after his accession, Shams al-Dīn Iltutmish had lost Lahore and the western wing of the Lahore–Delhi appanage. Together with Lahore's past antipathy towards Iltutmish's accession, its loss to military competitors merely underlined the emergence of Delhi as the capital of a new, truncated principality in north India.

In 607/1210, however, Iltutmish's competitors challenged his authority not just on the north-west frontiers of his principality, but in and around Delhi, the core area of his domain. Jūzjānī was characteristically vague in reporting details that might sully the image of his patron's father. Nevertheless he noticed that 'on several occasions from different parts of [north] India [*dīgar dar aṭrāf-i mamālik-i Hind*], he was in opposition to the Amirs and Turks [*bā Umarā' wa Atrāk mukhālafat uftādsh*] . . . and all those who revolted or sowed dissension [*khurūj mīkard ya 'iṣyān mībarzīd*] against [Iltutmish] were reduced [*maqhūr mīgasht*].[24]

Jūzjānī goes on to note that through these campaigns Iltutmish managed to annex different parts of the kingdom, *aṭrāf-i mamālik*, specifically Budaun, Awadh, and Benaras, the suburbs, *muẓāfāt*, of Delhi, and the Siwalik territories.[25] The arrangement of Jūzjānī's narrative suggests that chronologically these events occurred before 612/1215–16,[26] although we have to turn to Iltutmish's list of victories, *dā'ira-i futūḥ-i o*, for information concerning the identity of the involved protagonists.[27] Here, Jūzjānī reports that Benaras was seized

[23] On the career of Jalāl al-Dīn Khwārazm Shāh and the Chingīz Khanids in north India see the useful dissertation of P. Jackson, 'The Mongols and India', pp. 71–86; and idem, 'Jalāl al-Dīn, the Mongols and the Khwarazmian Conquest of the Panjāb and Sind', *Iran*, 28 (1990), pp. 45–54.

[24] Jūzjānī, *Ṭabaqāt-i Nāṣirī*, vol. 1, p. 444.

[25] Ibid., p. 445.

[26] Ibid., pp. 444–5 where the campaigns are sandwiched between the events of 614/1217 and 612/1215 (in that order), and the contexts suggest a date prior to 612/1215.

[27] Ibid., pp. 452–3.

from Qaymāz Rūmī, but to this we can also add Awadh which, the author noted elsewhere, was also under Qaymāz's control.[28] In a variant manuscript of the *Ṭabaqāt-i Nāṣirī,* Jūzjānī mentions Husām al-Dīn Ug͟hul Beg as the Governor of Awadh, and it is likely that at this time Iltutmish returned the Amir to his old command so unceremoniously snatched from him by Qaymāz Rūmī in Quṭb al-Dīn's reign.[29] The scant available information is frustrating, and it is also in the list of Iltutmish's victories, in a variant manuscript, that we find a reference to the seizure of Thangir-Bayana from Bahā' al-Dīn's successors.[30]

The seizure of territories previously controlled by members of the Quṭbī dispensation and some recalcitrant Mu'izzīs allowed Iltutmish to consolidate his core territories.[31] The campaigns also included clearing the suburbs of some of these territories from predatory groups: the campaigns in Budaun against Rā'ī Mān in the environs of Delhi and the Siwalik region protected crucial trade routes to the cantonments. Yet it is Jūzjānī's efforts at obfuscating intra-appanage conflict that underlines Delhi's precarious status in 607/1210. The chronicler of the Delhi Sultans did not want to dwell upon the history of conflicts that resurrected memories of a period when Delhi was little more than one appanage amongst many in north India—and not even the most important or powerful.

With the settlement of the core areas of the Delhi principality, Iltutmish could respond to the larger challenge posed by his more powerful Mu'izzī adversaries. In 612/1215–16 Ildūz was defeated, imprisoned and killed during his attempted march upon Delhi. In

28 Ibid., pp. 433, 452.

29 Ibid., pp. 450–1, fn 6. Ug͟hul Beg could only have been appointed to Awadh in the early years of Iltutmish's reign because in 623/1226 the Sultan gave its command to his eldest son, Nāṣir al-Dīn. Ibid., p. 453.

30 See Chapter 2 for details and references.

31 Exceptional for this time period was the Sultan's Jalor campaign. Ḥasan Niẓāmī, *Tāj al-Ma'āṣir*, translated by Elliot and Dowson, pp. 238–9, translated by B. Saroop, pp. 303–20, provides the details on this expedition. Niẓāmī places it before Iltutmish's conflict with Ildūz in 612/1215–16. Habibi mentions that a reference to Jalor exists in a variant manuscript of the *Ṭabaqāt-i Nāṣirī*, vol. 1, p. 452, fn. 5, which was also used by Raverty in his translation (vol. 1, p. 627).

613/1217 Lahore, Tabarhind, and Kuhram were seized from Nāṣir al-Dīn Qubācha, and Iltutmish's eldest son, Nāṣir al-Dīn Maḥmūd, was appointed Governor of the region in 614/1217.[32] The north-west frontier was hardly stable in these years, and control over Lahore would fluctuate at least until 620/1223 between Iltutmish, Qubācha, and the Khwārazm Shāh. Yet, over this time, Iltutmish's confidence had increased sufficiently for him to challenge Sultan Jalāl al-Dīn Khwārazm Shāh at Lahore in 618/1221 and divert him into Sindh and Qubācha's territory.[33] This success was followed by a string of campaigns that brought Lakhnauti, Bihar (622/1225),[34] Ranthambhor (623/1226), and Mandor (623/1226) under his control. These were transitory victories however, and some of these territories, like Lakhnauti (in 628/1231), would have to be reconquered soon enough. Nevertheless, these initial campaigns did reflect the change in the military potential of Delhi and its ability to coerce or conquer some of the hitherto autonomous Mu'izzī appanages. As important was the decline in power of Iltutmish's competitors, a result of the campaigns of the Khwārazm Shāh in Sindh; not merely did he keep Qubācha's attention diverted, but by the time Jalāl al-Dīn withdrew into Kirman and western Iran in 620/1223, he had also weakened the Sultan of Sindh enough to change the balance of power between Delhi and Multan.

The defeat of Qubācha after a string of campaigns through 625/1227–28 brought the Sindh provinces of Uchch, Multan, Bhakar, and Dewal under the command of the Delhi Sultan and, more crucially,

[32] For details see Ḥasan Niẓāmī, *Tāj al-Ma'āṣir*, translated by Elliot and Dowson, vol. 2, pp. 239–41, translated by B. Saroop, pp. 321–39; and Jūzjānī, *Ṭabaqāt-i Nāṣirī*, vol. 1, p. 445.

[33] Jūzjānī, *Ṭabaqāt-i Nāṣirī*, vol. 1, p. 445. See also the comments of Peter Jackson, 'The Mongols and India', p. 72.

[34] Bihar is not included in the list of Iltutmish's victories. In the narrative of the reign of Ḥusām al-Dīn 'Iwaz Khalajī, however, Jūzjānī notes that Iltutmish seized and appointed his own Amirs in Bihar. The seizure of Bihar was associated with Iltutmish's first campaign into Lakhnauti, at which time Iltutmish's eldest son held the governorship of Awadh. Bihar may have been under the supervision of Awadh and Lakhnauti. Subsequently Malik Yaghāntut was appointed to the province of Bihar, some time between 630/1232 and 631/1233–4. Jūzjānī, *Ṭabaqāt-i Nāṣirī*, vol. 1, pp. 437–8, 453–4, vol. 2, p. 9.

marked the end of the Mu'izzī challenge to Iltutmish's authority. Significantly, it was only in 626/1229, after the removal of Iltutmish's competitors, when there were no other rival Sultans in north India comparable to the Delhi monarch in effective military potential, that al-Mustanṣir, the 'Abbāsid Caliph in Baghdad (623–40/1226–42), recognized Sultan Iltutmish as Sultan.[35]

Whether Iltutmish sought to realize in practice these theoretical claims of sovereignty over north India or not, in the remaining seven years of his reign (626–33/1229–36) he commenced campaigning against territories that had rebelled against the authority of the Delhi Sultan. Western Bengal was reconquered from Balka Khalaj̱ī in 628/1230–1, and Gwalior from Rā'ī Milk (?) Deo in 629–30/1232–3. Plunder campaigns were launched against Malwa in 631/1233–4 and the campaigns in the last years of his life (632/1234–5) were directed against the subordinates of Jalāl al-Dīn Khwārazm Shāh in Banian and Karman, the remnants of one of Iltutmish's original competitors for control over north India.

The Shamsī Dispensation

Through a series of campaigns over a twenty-six-year reign Iltutmish managed to successfully vanquish, co-opt, or simply keep at bay competitors to the authority of Delhi. A concurrent effort was made to establish a body of supporters through whom the Sultan of Delhi could, in fact, govern his domain. Jūzjānī had not missed Iltutmish's efforts to recruit a following:

> To all sorts of people [*aṣnāf-i khalq*] from learned jurists [*dastār-band*], Princes [*kulāh dār*], landlords [*dahāqīn*], traders [*tujjār*], to travellers from foreign cities [*ghurabā'-yi amṣār*] his grants [*in'ām*] were universal. From the beginning of his reign, the dawn of his power, he spent more than a hundred lakhs [of tankas?] each year on the community of eminent learned scholars [*ijtimā'yi 'ulamā'-yi bā*

[35] The implication of Caliphal investiture to rule is discussed by H.A.R. Gibb, 'Some Considerations on the Sunni Theory of the Caliphate' and 'al-Mawardi's Theory of the Caliphate', in Stanford J. Shaw and William R. Polk, eds, *Studies on the Civilization of Islam*, (London: Routledge and Kegan Paul, 1969), pp. 142–65.

> *nām*],[36] respected Sayyids, Maliks, Amirs, Sadrs and great men. He gathered together in Delhi—which is . . . the centre of Islam . . . the sanctuary (*qubba*, literally dome, arch) of Islam in the eastern hemisphere—people from all sides of the world.[37]

Through the patronage and recruitment of émigrés of such eminence from eastern Iran, individuals with training in and experience of governance, Iltutmish managed to create a body of dependent followers, multiplying the numbers with whose help he had gained the throne. Yet, immigrants were by no means the only group recruited by Iltutmish, nor necessarily the most important in his dispensation of offices and privileges. We are fortunate that Jūzjānī included biographies of twenty-five slaves of Shams al-Dīn Iltutmish in the twenty-second section of his chronicle. As the details in the author's narrative clarify, not all of these slaves were important in the Sultan's reign; Jūzjānī's account was the grateful offering of the author of dues [*adā'-yi ḥuqūq*], owed to his powerful benefactors.[38]

Faced with potential political disaster at the moment of his accession, Iltutmish had to be extremely selective in his recruitment of subordinates. The transformation in the power and position of the Delhi Sultan occurred very gradually, and to study the content and nature of this change we must be clearer about the composition of the social groups who were patronized by Iltutmish, the types of political responsibilities entrusted to them, and the nature of their relationship with the monarch as well as with each other.

[36] The printed text has *istijmā'* (?), which seems to be a mistake for *ijtimā'*, community, group. Jūzjānī, *Ṭabaqāt-i Nāṣirī*, vol. 1, p. 440.

[37] Ibid., vol. 1, pp. 440–1. These migrations were provoked by the Mongol invasions into Khwarazm and eastern Iran from 615/1218 onwards. This immigration was also commented upon in the mid-fourteenth century by Baranī, *Ta'rīkh-i Fīrūz Shāhī*, edited by Khan, p. 27, edited by Rashid, p. 32. 'Iṣāmī, *Futūḥ al-Salāṭīn*, pp. 114–15 added a rhetorical touch when he stated that all kinds of people, from every class, ethnicity, town and country [of the world] migrated to Delhi. 'Iṣāmī included different types of artisans, *kāsibān*; embroiders, *naqshbandān*; craftsmen, *ṣan'atgarān*; jewel merchants, *jawāhir-firoshān*; and physicians *ḥakīmān, ṭabībān* in his list of migrants. For migrations into north India in the early thirteenth century, see also the conclusion to Chapter 2, the discussion below, and Chapter 4.

[38] Jūzjānī, *Ṭabaqāt-i Nāṣirī*, vol. 2, p. 2.

In the previous chapter, the nature of the Shansabanid and Mu'izzī political systems in north India were studied through an analysis of the ruling lineage, as well as the internal differences between and amongst free Amirs and slaves. But we have richer information on the personnel recruited by Iltutmish and can detail the categories of our research more sharply. In the following section I have studied the patronage given by Iltutmish to free military commanders, individuals who were sometimes conventionally described as part of the *ahl-i saif,* people of the sword. This analysis will therefore exclude the group of people also rather conventionally described as the *ahl-i qalam,* people of the pen, whom I study separately in the following chapter.

The binary distinctions that I have proposed collapse very quickly in the context of the general militarization of medieval society in north India and because of the number of occasions upon which 'people of the pen' also served as generals in the armies of their monarch. These caveats notwithstanding, distinctions between people of the pen and the sword are germane in the context of skills—a specialized training and a body of experiences—carried by these émigrés. A secretary, for example, possessed educational qualifications and experience to man administrative posts in which a knowledge of accountancy, mathematics, and diplomatics was essential. He could command an army as well, but his value as a general was incidental to his proficiency and value as a keeper of records, an expertise that military commanders rarely possessed. On the other hand, potential military commanders were also evaluated by their qualifications: amongst other things, as a military strategist, by the charismatic ability to lead men into war, and by an appropriate genealogy which spoke of generations of valorous conduct on the battlefield. The varying backgrounds and qualifications of these émigrés had a huge impact on the direction of royal patronage.

The value of a study of patronage and deployment transcends its static, functional limitations if it is cognizant of the cultural and historical implications of political empowerment. Shams al-Dīn Iltutmish's choice of personnel for the construction of his political authority informs us of the kind of political system he envisaged and the adjustments that a host of contingent factors forced on him. But his patronage also had its own history. The deployment of personnel with special characteristics also shaped the cultural and political milieu of the Sultanate into forms not always anticipated or envisaged by the Delhi Sultan. As a beginning to the study of these historical processes, the following section studies the free military commanders included in Iltutmish's political dispensation.

(a) Free Military Commanders Subordinate to Iltutmish

When looking at the Mu'izzī military expeditions into north India, we noticed that it was not the entrenched elite class from Afghanistan that chose to stay on in north India after plunder campaigns in the insecure marches of the frontier. Instead, individuals of a humbler social background, who had little to lose in their homeland sought the opportunity to improve their stock here. Subsequently, the efforts of the Mu'izzī *bandagān-i khāṣṣ* to consolidate their appanages and the 'pull' of their patronage led to an increase in migrations into north India over the first decade of the thirteenth century.

The subsequent wave of migrations occurred after the upheaval caused by Chingīz Khān's conquest of Transoxiana, and campaigns into Afghanistan in pursuit of Jalāl al-Dīn Khwārazm Shāh, 616–18/ 1219–21. The resulting migrations were distinguished by the presence of social elites from the central Islamic lands who, expelled from their homelands, turned to north India for sanctuary and new opportunities. The court of Shams al-Dīn Iltutmish was, however, only one of the destinations for the migrants fleeing Mongol destruction, and in the early1220s it was not the most popular choice. Despite gratitude for the patronage received from the Delhi Sultans, Jūzjānī still recognized the pull of the Sindh court on notables, *akābir*, from Khurasan, Ghur, and Ghazni who received grants, *in'ām*, and numerous rewards, *ikrām-i wāfir*, from Sultan Nāṣir al-Dīn Qubācha.[39]

Amongst migrants who made their way to Delhi, a large group consisted of military commanders. That a number of these immigrant military commanders were of high social standing from Khwarazm and Ghur is evident from the titles (*laqabs*) or *nisba* of affiliation attached to their names: Malik 'Alā' al-Dīn Jānī *Shāhzāda* (Prince) of

[39] Ibid., vol. I, p. 419 and details in Chapter 4.

Turkistan, Malik *Ghūr* 'Izz al-Dīn Muḥammad Shāh Mahdī, Malik Nāṣir al-Dīn Mādīnī Malik *Ghūr*, Malik Quṭb al-Dīn Ḥasan 'Alī *Ghūri*, Malik Fīrūz Shāh Iltutmish *Shāhzāda* of *Khwārazm*, Malik Tāj al-Dīn Ināltegin *Shāhzāda* of *Khwārazm*.[40]

A privileged background in the central Islamic lands, however, did not automatically translate into an important military position in Iltutmish's dispensation. Malik Quṭb al-Dīn Ḥasan 'Alī Ghūrī, for example, was forced to flee to north India in 620/1223 because of the recalcitrance of his subjects in Tulak in the face of Mongol pressure. Jūzjānī, who was also from the region of Tulak, knew the military commander well and provided an account of his career in Saifrud and Tulak prior to a very vividly described flight into India and eventual immigration to Iltutmish's court.[41] Despite his social position, Jūzjānī did not mention him once in his narrative of Iltutmish's reign, nor does he figure in any of the biographies of the Shamsī slaves. The silence is intriguing because Jūzjānī was hardly biased against Quṭb al-Dīn and details how the amir rose to importance after 633/1236 in the reign of the Sultan's successors.[42] In 639/1241 Quṭb al-Dīn

[40] See Jūzjānī's list of Iltutmish's Maliks, vol. 1, pp. 450–2. For the evidence from variant manuscripts see ibid., p. 450, fn. 6 and for complete titles for 'Izz al-Dīn Muḥammad and Quṭb al-Dīn Ḥasan, see ibid., p. 476 in the list of Sultan Nāṣir al-Dīn's (644–64/1246–66) notables.

[41] Ibid., vol. 2, pp. 134–5 for his career in Saifrud and Tulak, and pp. 140–1 for a description of his immigration.

[42] Ẓiyā' al-Dīn Baranī noted in passing that Quṭb al-Dīn was the *wakīl-i dar* of Sultan Iltutmish; *Ta'rīkh-i Fīrūz Shāhī*, edited by Khan, pp. 31, 39, edited by Rashid, pp. 37, 46. The information was provided in the context of an apocryphal story where Iltutmish was portrayed as an ideal sovereign. In the same context Baranī also mentioned 'Izz al-Dīn Muḥammad Salārī. These references were used by Peter Jackson and Irfan Habib to argue that free notables were important in Iltutmish's reign, but Jūzjānī, who was biased in favour of the *bandagān*, chose to ignore them. See Peter Jackson, 'The *Mamluk* Institution in Early Muslim India', *Journal of the Royal Asiatic Society*, (1990), p. 344, and fn 17; idem, *The Delhi Sultanate*, p. 42; and Irfan Habib, 'The Formation of the Sultanate Ruling Class', p. 13. Although Jūzjānī did not provide a biography of Quṭb al-Dīn, as he did of the Shamsī slaves, he hardly ignored the free amir who belonged to the same town as the author (on Tulak see references in the previous footnote and Chapter 2 regarding information on Ẓiyā' al-Dīn Qāẓī Tulak). It is unlikely that Jūzjānī would have failed to recognize Quṭb al-Din if

became *nā'ib-i mulk*, deputy of the realm.[43] It is possible that during Iltutmish's rule Quṭb al-Dīn occupied a position in the Sultanate very similar to that of Malik Tāj al-Dīn Ināltegin, *Shāhzāda* of Khwārazm. Malik Ināltegin immigrated to north India in 596/1199 together with his cousin Malik Fīrūz Shāh Iltutmish, also a Shāhzāda. There seems to have been no rapid promotions for Malik Ināltegin, who, twenty-one (lunar) years later, still held a subordinate post under Malik Karīm al-Dīn Ḥamzah at Nagaur. In 617/1220 Ināltegin killed Khwāja Najīb al-Dīn, stole an elephant, migrated to Uchch, and came to Qubācha's court. He later joined the retinue of Sultan Jalāl al-Dīn Khwārazm Shāh and left Sindh for Kirman to become in 622/1225 the ruler of Sistan.[44] Curiously enough, despite their social status and in marked contrast to their subsequent achievements, neither of the Maliks enjoyed high posts within Iltutmish's dispensation of power. At least one of them preferred service with Qubācha, the Sultan of Sindh, over Delhi.

Even those free Maliks who were fortunate enough to receive important positions could find themselves suddenly deprived of their posts, and the absence of further information about their deployment suggests that their subsequent appointments gave them less political prominence. A good example is that of Malik 'Alā' al-Dīn Jānī Shāhzāda of Turkistan who was appointed Governor of Lakhnauti, only to be dismissed, *ma'zūl shud*, sometime between 629–30/1231–3, with the Shamsī slave Saif al-Dīn Ai-Beg appointed in his place.[45] 'Alā' al-Dīn Jānī's case is very similar to that of Sipahsālār Rashīd al-Dīn who was appointed as *kotwal*, commander, of Gwalior in 630/1233. Rashīd al-Dīn's appointment to Gwalior was only for a short duration;

---

he had been an influential personality in Iltutmish's reign; he had no hesitation in giving 'Izz al-Dīn Salārī his due. Quṭb al-Dīn was certainly important in the post-Iltutmish period and Jūzjānī records his activities despite the fact that the Malik was often at odds with his patron (see Chapter 5). As in the case of Balban (on whom, see the next section), Baranī telescoped the career of Quṭb al-Dīn, assuming that the commander's later importance originated from his eminence in previous generations as well.

[43] Jūzjānī, *Ṭabaqāt-i Nāṣirī*, vol. 1, p. 468.

[44] Ibid., pp. 284–5, and vol. 2, pp. 184–5

[45] Ibid., vol. 1, p. 448, vol. 2, pp. 9–10. For a discussion of the amir's later deployment see below.

in 632/1234–5 the Shamsī slave Nuṣrat al-Dīn Tā'īsī al-Mu'izzī was given the military command over Bayana-Sulṭānkōt and, in another example of a *banda-i khāṣṣ* taking over charge from a free notable, the superintendence, *shaḥnagī*, of Gwalior.[46]

It would hardly be safe to conclude from the little information that we possess that Iltutmish refused patronage to émigré notables of eminence. Indeed, the patronage given to Malik 'Izz al-Dīn Muḥammad Sālārī suggests the opposite. Malik 'Izz al-Dīn was Iltutmish's *amīr ḥājib* (Chamberlain) in 625/1228, and participated in the Uchch campaign together with the slave Tāj al-Dīn Sanjar Kazlak Khān.[47] His importance apparently did not diminish at the accession of Iltutmish's successor, Sultan Rukn al-Dīn (633/1236), when the Malik reportedly occupied the important military assignment, *iqṭā'*, of Budaun.[48] It is possible that the deployment of 'Izz al-Dīn indicates the patronage that Iltutmish was willing to give to choice free military commanders pushed into north India by the Mongol campaigns in the central Islamic lands.

The information we have on the free amirs is sometimes extremely difficult to contextualize. Jūzjānī reports that during the brief reign of Rukn al-Dīn Fīrūz (633–4/1236), 'Alā al-Dīn Jānī held the command of Lahore and another free amir, Amir Saif al-Dīn Kūchī, had the *iqṭā'* of Hansi.[49] It is possible, as one historian has suggested, that these were appointments made by Iltutmish towards the end of his reign. Yet there is also some reason for doubt: after dismissing 'Alā al-Dīn Jānī from Lakhnauti, for example, it is unlikely that Iltutmish honoured him with the enviable post of Lahore, a command previously occupied by the monarch's son.[50] On the other hand, it is very likely that on his accession Iltutmish's son, Rukn al-Dīn, wanted to win over disgruntled notables to counter the challenge posed to his authority by his father's powerful military slaves. The appointment of 'Alā al-Dīn Jānī to

[46] Ibid., vol. 2, p. 10.

[47] Ibid., vol. 1, p. 446.

[48] Ibid., p. 455.

[49] Ibid., p. 456.

[50] See Irfan Habib, 'The Formation of the Sultanate Ruling Class', p. 13, keeping in mind that there is nothing in Jūzjānī to corroborate Habib's inference that the two Maliks were appointed to their respective posts by Iltutmish.

Lahore was, in this context, not a solitary incident. On his accession the Prince had appointed the disgraced slave Kabīr Khān Ayāz, pensioned off to Palwal by Iltutmish, to the prestigious post of Sunam, and Saif al-Dīn Kūchī's appointment to Hansi probably belongs to this time as well.[51]

We may never be able to iron out some of these ambiguities, but the materials that we possess caution us against any assumption about the uniform liberality of the monarch. Jūzjānī described Iltutmish as a patron who was a hundred times more generous than his predecessor, Quṭb al-Dīn Ai-Beg, the latter famous as *lak-bakhsh*, the giver of a hundred thousand (presumably the silver coin, *tanka*), as bountiful as the legendary Ḥātim al-Tā'ī.[52] Yet a high social status and a privileged background—which would have included useful experience of military command—in the central Islamic lands did not immediately guarantee these free commanders a commensurate political appointment under Iltutmish. Some, like Rashīd al-Dīn 'Alī, did receive such appointment, only to be later dismissed; others, like Quṭb al-Dīn Ḥasan, remained politically obscure only to rise to prominence after Iltutmish's reign. While the patronage of the monarch was forthcoming in many cases, Iltutmish was hardly impressed with social status if notables like 'Alā' al-Dīn Jānī gave him cause for displeasure. Iltutmish might honour individuals with an enviable

[51] In his narrative on Rukn al-Dīn's reign the author merely notes that Kabīr Khān Ayāz, 'Alā' al-Dīn Jānī, and Saif al-Dīn Kūchī respectively held the commands of Multan, Lahore, and Hansi; none of the dates of their appointments are mentioned (Jūzjānī, vol. 1, pp. 455–6). It is only because the author provided a separate biography on Kabīr Khān Ayāz that we have the more precise information that he was appointed by Rukn al-Dīn (idem, vol. 2, p. 6). Here the author clarifies that rather than Multan, Rukn al-Dīn gave Ayāz the command of Sunam. During Sultan Rukn al-Dīn's reign the three, Malik Jānī, Kūchī, and Ayāz, allied together against the monarch. For further details see Chapter 5.

[52] Ibid., vol. 1, p. 440, and also pp. 413, 415. This account has been uncritically followed by (amongst others) Muḥammad Aziz Aḥmad, *Political History and Institutions of the Early Turkish Empire of Delhi*, p. 157; R.P. Tripathi, *Some Aspects of Muslim Administration*, p. 26; and K.A. Nizami, 'Sultan Shamsuddin Iltutmish', *A Comprehensive History of India, Vol V: The Delhi Sultanat,* pp. 225–6; K.A. Nizami, *Religion and Politics in India*, p. 127; and, most recently, Peter Jackson, *The Delhi Sultanate*, p. 41; Irfan Habib, 'The Formation of the Sultanate Ruling Class', p. 14.

genealogy, even employ them, but not automatically raise them to important commands within his dispensation.

Years later, Iltutmish's court was favourably reviewed for its ability to attract so many distinguished people,[53] and it is in this context that the case of the Shansabanid Prince of Madin, Malik Nāṣir al-Dīn Abū Bakr, is telling. He migrated to Iltutmish's court, received respect and affection, *ikrām wa 'awāṭif*, from the monarch at Delhi but no command.[54] Having aristocrats seek sanctuary in the Delhi Sultanate added lustre to the Sultan's court and later authors eulogized the monarch for his generosity, but these social elites could also be a nuisance. The danger of some émigrés emerging as centres of inimical political alliance against the Sultan was very real, and that is why Iltutmish refused to provide succour to Sultan Jalāl al-Dīn Khwārazm Shāh.[55] On the other hand, Iltutmish chose to favour the 'socially dead'—individuals who did not possess, or make much of their *nisba* or *laqab*—with strategic posts. Without any social recognition and alternative ties, the monarch was more confident of their dependence and loyalty. As long as the Delhi monarch had the capacity to purchase and deploy slaves he could afford to be particular about recruiting free military commanders to the highest posts within the Sultanate. This was evident from the hiatus in the careers of several free amirs as they made the passage to India. Hence the complicated political arrangement within the Shamsī dispensation: even though increasing numbers of social elites sought patronage and were honourably received by the Sultan, only some were promoted to positions of influence. Instead, smaller groups of the socially unfree, the *bandagān-i Shamsī*, were given dominant political roles in the Sultanate.

(b) Slave Subordinates of Shams al-Dīn Iltutmish

Much like the organization of the Mu'izzī slaves, the Shamsī *bandagān* were separated in rank; there was an older elite cadre who were

[53] For a fairly conventional record, see Baranī, *Ta'rīkh-i Fīrūz Shāhī*, edited by Khan, p. 27, edited by Rashid, p. 32.

[54] Jūzjānī, *Ṭabaqāt-i Nāṣirī*, vol. 1, pp. 340, 451.

[55] See Peter Jackson, *The Delhi Sultanate*, p. 33; and idem, 'Jalāl al-Dīn, the Mongols and the Khwarazmian Conquest of the Panjāb and Sindh'.

regarded with far greater favour by their master than the newly purchased slaves. In his narration of Shams al-Dīn's reign, Jūzjānī, in fact, does not use the term *bandagān-i khāṣṣ* to describe the senior slaves of Sultan Iltutmish, although he does distinguish between *bandagān* of long standing occupying important offices and newly purchased slaves who served as pages in the court. He identified the senior Shamsī *bandagān* as slaves of the dynasty [*bandagān-i daulat*], who were close to his royal majesty (Iltutmish) [*baḥaẓrat-i salṭanat-i o qurbatī dāshtand*].[56] The sense of a larger corps of slaves within which there was an elite cadre privileged by the trust reposed by the Sultan is well brought out in the mid-fourteenth-century chronicle of Ẓiyā' al-Dīn Baranī. The latter noted that Sultan Ghiyāṣ al-Dīn Balban (664–85/1266–87) was one of the Shamsī slaves [*banda az bandagān-i Shamsī būd*], and was manumitted together with the 'forty' Turkish slaves [*wa dar miyān-i bandagān-i turk-i chihalgānī āzād shud*].[57] Manumission, of course, did not alter the juridical tie of dependence, *walā'*, or the emotional bond of association that tied the slave to his master.[58] Instead, it was a reward given to only some [*bandagān-i turk-i chihalgānī*] from the larger body of slaves [*bandagān-i Shamsī*] in return for faithful service. The *banda-i khāṣṣ*, the future Sultan Shams al-Dīn Iltutmish, had been thus rewarded by Quṭb al-Dīn Ai-Beg, and, according to Baranī, Ghiyāṣ al-Dīn Balban, together with the other *chihalgānī*, belonged to a similar privileged category.

Gavin Hambly was the first scholar to see the *chihalgānī*, the corps of forty slaves, as a privileged cadre within the larger retinue of the *bandagān-i Shamsī*.[59] Hambly argued that the *bandagān-i Shamsī*

[56] Jūzjānī, *Ṭabaqāt-i Nāṣirī*, vol. 1, p. 458. Elsewhere (vol. 1, p. 444), he had more vaguely referred to *khadam-i khāṣṣ*, senior/special servants of the King.

[57] Ẓiyā' al-Dīn Baranī, *Ta'rīkh-i Fīrūz Shāhī*, edited by Khan, p. 25, edited by Rashid, p. 30.

[58] Paul G. Forand, 'The Relation of the Slave and the Client', and Joseph Schacht, *Origins of Muḥammadan Jurisprudence*, p. 161, "'Abd" and "Ghulām" ', *EI*², s.v.

[59] Gavin Hambly, 'Who were the *Chihalgānī*', pp. 57–62. The author also provides (pp. 57–8) a fairly clear survey of the early historiography on the subject, which I have chosen not to repeat.

included in the twenty-second section of Jūzjānī's *Ṭabaqāt-i Nāṣirī* were twenty-five of the forty members of the *chihalgānī*. He based this conclusion on the argument that since Jūzjānī chose to narrate their biographies they must have been important slaves of Iltutmish. Moreover, most of them shared the essential qualities attributed to the *chihalgānī* by Baranī: 'Turks, Shamsī slaves, holders of high offices and titles'.[60] He goes on to add that since two of the *chihalgānī* identified by Baranī, Ghiyāṣ al-Dīn Balban and Shīr Khān, also had their biographies in Jūzjānī, then the *bandagān* in the *Ṭabaqāt-i Nāṣirī* must be a part of the 'forty' elite slaves of Iltutmish.

The basic presumption in Baranī's statement was that those Shamsī slaves (like Balban) who held high offices and titles in the reign of Sultan Nāṣir al-Dīn Maḥmūd (644–64/1246–66) must have also held posts of equal status in Iltutmish's reign.[61] Hambly based his argument on the same false assumption. If we refer to Table 1, which presents the information from Jūzjānī on the career of the *bandagān-i Shamsī*, it becomes immediately apparent that of the twenty-five Shamsī slaves, eight (numbers 11, 16, 17, 19, 22, 23, 24, and 25) held no positions of privilege during Iltutmish's reign. Ulugh Khān, the future Sultan Ghiyāṣ al-Dīn Balban (number 25), around whom hangs Baranī's tale of the 'forty' slaves, was purchased only in 630/1232–3, which was towards the very close of Iltutmish's reign (died, 633/1236). It is not likely that he was manumitted during the remaining three (lunar) years of Shams al-Dīn's life, and he was certainly not given the responsibilities entrusted to a senior Shamsī slave. At the end of Iltutmish's reign he was still only a *khāṣadār* (falconer) and received his first advancement only in Sultan Raẓiyya's service (633–40/1236–40). Nor could someone like Malik Ikit[62]

[60] Ibid., p. 62.

[61] If we recall the discussion in the previous section, Baranī had made a similar assumption in the case of the free Amir Quṭb al-Dīn Ḥasan 'Alī Ghūrī.

[62] Habibi read the name of the slave as Bat (BT?) Khān Saif al-Dīn Ai-Beg Khitā'ī and also recognized the existence of different readings in the various manuscripts including Ikin (AIKN). See Jūzjānī, *Ṭabaqāt-i Nāṣirī*, vol. 2, p. 28, and vol. 1, p. 476 and fn. 11. I have followed Jackson's reading of the name as Ikit Khān. Peter Jackson, 'The Mongols and India', p. 92, fn. 137; and idem, *The Delhi Sultanate*. p. 73, fn. 76.

Table 1: Shamsī *Bandagān* in Iltutmish's Reign

Jūjānī, Ṭabaqat-i *Nāṣirī*, edited by Habibi, vol. 2, pp. 1–89

Serial No. Habibi ed.	Name of Shamsī Slave Ethnic Background	Purchased from	Deployment of Notable in Iltutmish's Service >indicates change in the slave's career
1 II: 3-5	MALIK TĀJ AL-DĪN SANJAR KAZLAK KHĀN ? ; probably of Turkish origin	Khwāja 'Alī Bāstābadī	Bought in Ai-Beg's reign> grew up with Nāṣir al-Dīn> *chāshnīgīr*> *amīr-i ākhūr*> 625/1228 *wilāyat* of Wanjrut in Multan> *iqṭā*' of Kuhram> *maḥrūsa*, garrison town, of Tabarhind.fort, town and suburbs of Uchch> d.629/1231–2.
2 II: 5-7	KABĪR KHĀN AYĀZ AL-MU'IZZĪ Rūmī ; Turk from Anatolia	heirs of Naṣīr al-Dīn Ḥusain *Amīr-i Shikār*	Slave of Naṣīr al-Dīn Ḥusain Amīr-i Shikār> sold to Iltutmish by Nasīr al-Dīn's heirs> 625/1227-8 town, fort, *qaṣabāt*, market towns, and territory of Multan> circa 1231 Palwal for his maintenance>
3 II: 7-8	MALIK NASĪR AL-DĪN AI-TAMAR AL-BAHĀ'Ī ? ; Probably of Turkish origin	heirs of Bahā' al-Dīn Tughril of Bayana	Slave of Bahā' al-Dīn Tughril> sold to Iltutmish by Bahā' al-Dīn's heirs> *sar-i jāndār*> *iqṭā*' of Lahore> after 625/1227–8 *wilāyat* of Siwalik, Ajmer, Lawah (?), Kasli, Sambharnamak and grant of elephant> killed during *ghazw* in Bundi region.
4 I: 8-9	MALIK SAIF AL-DĪN AI-BEG-I UCHCH Of Turkish origin	Jamāl al-Dīn	Purchased by Iltutmish before his accession as Sultan> *sar-i jāndār*> *iqṭā*' of Narnaul> Baran> Sunam> Uchch after Tāj al-Dīn Kazlak Khān's death in 629/1231–2>

5 II: 9–10	MALIK SAIF AL-DĪN AI-BEG YAGHĀNTUT Khitā'ī Turk	heirs of Ikhtiyār al-Dīn Chust Qaba	*Amīr-i majlis*> by 625/1227-8 *wilāyat* of Sursuti/ Sirsa as *iqṭā'* > Bihar> after 'Alā' al-Dīn Jānī's removal: Lakhnauti and title of Yughāntut> died in 631/1233–4.
6 II: 10–13	MALIK NUṢRAT AL-DĪN TĀ'ĪSĪ AL-MU'IZZĪ Of Turkish origin	? a slave of Sultan Mu'izz al-Dīn	Slave of Mu'izz al-Dīn> *ca.* 625/1225–8 *iqṭā'* of Jind, Barwala> *ca.* 630/1233 Bayana, Sulṭankōt and *shaḥnagī* of Gwalior> *ghazw* into Kalinjar>
7 II: 13–18	MALIK 'IZZ AL-DĪN TUGHĀN KHĀN TUGHRIL Qarā Khitā'ī	?	*Sāqī-yi khāṣṣ*> *sar-i dawātdār*> *chāshnīgīr*> *amīr-i ākhūr*> in 630/1232 *iqṭā'* of Budaun> *wilāyat* of Bihar when Malik Yaghāntut received Lakhnauti> 631/1233–4 and Yaghāntut's death, became *muqti'* of Lakhnauti>
8 II: 17–18	MALIK TAMAR KHĀN A Qipchaq Turk	Asad al-Dīn Mankalī	A member of the *ghazw* contingent against Rā'ī Chandwāl> *nā'ib-i amīr-i ākhūr*> after 630/1232 and Tughan Khān's appointment to Budaun became *amīr-i ākhūr*>
9 II: 18–19	MALIK HINDŪ KHĀN MU'AYYID AL-DĪN MUBĀRAK AL-KHAZĪN 'Hindū'	Fakhr al-Dīn Isfahānī	Purchased by Iltutmish before his accession as *Sultan*> *Yuzbān*> *mash'aldār* (while Iltutmish in Baran)> *tashtdār* (while Iltutmish in Budaun)> *tashtdār* + *khazīnadār*>
10 II: 19–20	MALIK IKHTIYĀR AL-DĪN QARĀQUSH KHĀN AI-TEGIN Qarā Khitā'ī	?	An old slave of Iltutmish> *sāqī-yi khāṣṣ*> *iqṭā'* of Barihun (?) and Darnakwan (?)> *shaḥna* of *khālisa* of Tabarhind> after Malik Kabīr Khān: *iqṭā'* of Multan and title Qarāqush>

11 II: 20–22	MALIK IKHTIYĀR AL-DĪN ALTŪNIA-I TABARHIND ? ethnic origin	?	*Sharābdārī*> *sar-i chatrdār*>
12 II: 22–23	IKHTIYĀR AL-DĪN AI-TEGIN Qarā Khitā'ī Turk	Amīr Ai-Beg Sanamī	*Sar-i jāndār*> *iqṭā'* of Mansurpur> Kujat and Nandanah>
13 II: 24–25	MALIK BADR AL-DĪN SUNQAR AL-RŪMĪ Rūmī; Turk from Anatolia	?	*Tashtdār*> *bahladār*> *shaḥna* of the *zarrādkhāna*, the armoury, of Badaun> *nā'ib-i amīr-i ākhūr*>
14 II: 25–27	MALIK TĀJ AL- DĪN SANJAR QUTLUQ Qipchaq Turk	Khwāja Jamāl al-Dīn Nadīmān	*Sar-i jāndār*> *shaḥna-i ākhūr*>
15 II: 27–28	MALIK TĀJ AL- DĪN SANJAR KURET KHĀN Qipchaq Turk	?	*Shaḥna-i bahar wa kishtīhā*>
16 II: 28	MALIK İKIT/BAT KHĀN SAIF AL- DĪN AI-BEG KHITĀ'Ī Khitā'ī	?	*Jāndār*>
17 II: 28–29	MALIK TĀJ AL- DĪN SANJAR TARKHĀN Karakhī Turk	?	?>
18 II: 30–33	MALIK IKHTIYĀR AL-DĪN YUZBEG TUGHRIL KHĀN Qipchaq Turk	?	*Nā'ib-i chāshnīgīr* during Gwalior siege (*ca.* 629/1231–2)>
19 II: 33–35	MALIK TAJ AL-DĪN SANJAR ARSALĀN KHĀN AL-KHWĀRAZMĪ ? ; probably Khwārazamī Turk.	Ikhtiyār al-Mulk Abū Bakr Habshī	*Khāṣadār*>

20 II: 36–40	MALIK 'IZZ AL-DĪN KUSHLŪ KHĀN AL-SULṬĀNĪ Qipchaq Turk	From a merchant at Mandor	Purchased at Mandor (*ca.* 623/1226)> *sāqī*> *sharābdār* at Gwalior (*ca.* 629/1231–2)> *iqṭā'* of Barhamun (?)> Baran>
21 II: 40-42	MALIK SAIF AL-DĪN ARKALĪ DĀḌ BEG Qipchaq Turk	Khwāja Shams al-Dīn 'Ajamī Malik al-Tujjār	?> sent as ambassador/courier (*bamuhimmāt-i buzurg baitrāf-i mamālik*)>
22 II: 42–43	MALIK BADR AL-DĪN NUSRAT KHĀN SUNQAR SŪFĪ Rūmī; Turk from Anatolia	?	?>
23 II: 43–44	MALIK NUṢRAT AL-DĪN SHIR KHĀN Ilbarī (Yimak) Turk	?	?>
24 II: 45–47	MALIK KISHLĪ KHĀN SAIF AL-DĪN AI-BEG AL- SULṬĀNĪ MALIK AL-ḤUJJĀB Ilbarī (Yimak) Turk	Ikhtiyār al-Dīn Abū Bakr Ḥabash	A slave in the *dargāh-i khāṣṣ*>
25 II: 47–89	AL-KHĀQĀN AL-MU'AẒẒAM AL-KHĀN AL-'AZAM BAHĀ' AL-ḤAQQ WA AL-DĪN ULUGH KHĀN BALBAN AL-SULṬĀNĪ Ilbarī (Yimak) Turk	From Khwāja Jamāl al-Dīn Basrī	Bought by Iltutmish in 630/1232-3> *khāṣadār*>

Khān Saif al-Dīn Ai-Beg Khitā'ī (number 16) have been a Shamsī *bandagān-i khāṣṣ*. He was a lowly guard, *jāndār*, in Iltutmish's reign, and had progressed to the post of chief guard, *sar-i jāndār*, in 'Alā' al-Dīn Mas'ūd's dispensation (639–44/1242–6). If the Shamsī *bandagān-i khāṣṣ* like the *chihalgānī* were senior, privileged slaves, holding important commands because of Sultan Iltutmish's trust and patronage, then at least all of Jūzjānī's 'twenty-five' slaves, including Balban, were not Baranī's 'forty'.

Years ago, Mohammad Habib explained that forty was merely 'a formal number', and that the actual number of slaves that comprised the '*chihalgānī*' was probably far lower.[63] What Habib was alluding to was the fact that within Biblical and Qur'ānic contexts, 'forty' was a synonym for 'many' and should seldom be taken literally. There are innumerable examples of the usage of 'forty' in this context, and, in a form much like the *chihalgānī*, the *Book of Dede Korkut* referred to Dirse Khān's 'forty warriors'.[64] In both cases 'forty' should be understood as a metaphor for 'a large (unspecified) number' and Baranī's usage of the term *chihalgānī* is clearer when interpreted in this sense.[65] Baranī was accurate in defining the *chihalgānī* as an

[63] Mohammad Habib, 'Introduction to Elliot and Dowson's History of India, vol. 2', p. 107. Mohammad Habib's point was misrepresented by Aziz Aḥmad, 'The Early Turkish Nucleus in India', *Turcica, Revue d'etudes Turques,* vol. 9 (1977), p. 102, fn. 19.

[64] *The Book of Dede Korkut*, translated by Geoffrey Lewis, (New York: Penguin Books, 1982 reprint), p. 28 and fn. 3.

[65] There have been several interesting efforts to account for the 'forty' notables of Iltutmish. The most imaginative exercise is by Khurram Qadir, 'Amiran-i Chihalgan of Northern India', *Journal of Central Asia*, 4 (1981), p. 97, who calculated that 'Iltutmish had four qazis, two wazirs, twenty one Amirs and ten offsprings [*sic*. Iltutmish, in fact, had nine children. See Table 2 for details]. If one were to include the three Mu'izzī contenders for the throne of Ārām Shāh, the list of individuals thus involved in the power struggle during Iltutmish's reign comes to forty'. Peter Jackson's comments in his dissertation, 'The Mongols and India', p. 208, fn. 82, need to be taken more seriously. He suggested that rather than 'forty slaves' the 'use of the distributive numeral [*ganī*] suggests . . . that each [slave] was [a] commander of a company of 40 *mamlıks*. In Egypt the royal *mamlıks* were divided into groups of fifty.' Subsequently, in '*Mamlūks* in Muslim India', Jackson was more cautious: 'This can only be a matter of conjecture, but we should notice in passing that

elite cadre within the *bandagān-i Shamsī*, effectively a group of Shamsī *bandagān-i khāṣṣ*. These would be a group of slaves, trusted and commended for their actions, raised above others by Shams al-Dīn Iltutmish, and manumitted as a reward for their service. Baranī, however, was inaccurate in suggesting that Balban was a member of this group and subsequent scholars are mistaken in interpreting his usage of 'forty' too literally.[66]

The steps through which slaves rose to prominence and influence within the Shamsī slave corps has been detailed by Jūzjānī and this information has also been incorporated in Table 1. From this information it is clear that most Shamsī slaves were purchased and went

---

in Egypt the royal *mamlūks* were divided into groups of forty, each under an *amīr ṭablkhāna* . . .' (p. 346). In *The Delhi Sultanate*, p. 66, after recalling the case of Mamlūk Egypt, Jackson notes: 'we should perhaps conclude that the *Chihilgānīs* formed a parallel group of commanders within the ranks of Iltutmish's Shamsī slaves.' I am not sure how the comparison with the Mamlūks of Egypt helped Jackson's analysis, since he does not elaborate further on the character or the composition of the *chihalgānīs*. See Sunil Kumar 'When Slaves were Noble', pp. 26–8, for further comments. But if we were to seriously pursue the question of numerical commands within the early Delhi Sultanate army, as suggested by Jackson in his dissertation and later writings, it is inexplicable why Jūzjānī, who paid considerable attention to the careers of the *bandagān-i Shamsī*, ignored them altogether. For that matter, it seems too far-fetched to assume that Fakhr-i Mudabbir, Ḥasan Niẓāmī, and Amīr Khusrau would all ignore such a system of hierarchical commands until Baranī, writing more than a hundred years after Iltumish's reign, mentioned it in passing. On the other hand, a near contemporary of Baranī, 'Iṣāmī, *Futūh al-Salāṭīn*, p. 122, also mentioned 'forty turkish slaves' during the reign of Iltutmish. 'Iṣāmī did not use the distributive numeral with forty. He mentioned the slaves as '*chihal banda-i turk* . . .' and the context made it clear that the author implied not forty but an indeterminate number.

[66] Baranī was attempting to explain the process through which the *bandagān-i Shamsī* had managed to prolong their power by removing other competitors during the interregnum between Iltutmish and Balban. Balban had excelled in this politics of manipulation, and had come to effectively control power within the Sultanate from 647/1249. One way of explaining Balban's influential position was by suggesting that he had always been in the circle of power as a *banda-i khāṣṣ*. Baranī was wrong on some of his facts but his analysis of the organization of the Shamsī slave system was accurate.

through stages of training and service in the household of the monarch in the same manner as had the Mu'izzī slaves. The slave Malik Tāj al-Dīn Sanjar Kazlak Khān (number 1 in Table 1), for example, had been bought as a child and was brought up and nourished (*parwarish*) in the royal residence, together with the eldest Prince Nāṣir al-Dīn Maḥmūd.[67] He was then appointed as the supervisor of the Sultan's kitchen (*chāshnīgīr*), and was promoted thereafter to the commander of the horses (*amīr-i ākhūr*).[68] Similarly, the slave Malik 'Izz al-Dīn Tughān Khān Tughril (number 7 in Table 1) graduated from being senior cup bearer (*sāqī-yi khāṣṣ*), to senior keeper of the royal writing case (*sar-i dawātdār*), to supervisor of the Sultan's kitchen (*chāshnīgīr*), to commander of the horses (*amīr-i ākhūr*), until he finally received a military and administrative assignment, *iqṭā'*.[69] The length of time spent in close association with the Sultan and the nature of his subsequent deployment were two fairly reliable indicators of the seniority of the *banda* within Iltutmish's slave corps. Without doubt, some of the Shamsī *bandagān-i khāṣṣ* were individuals like Malik Tāj al-Dīn Sanjar Kazlak Khān; Malik Saif al-Dīn Ai-Beg; Malik Hindū Khān Mu'ayyid al-Dīn Mubārak al-Khāzin and Malik Ikhtiyār al-Dīn Qarā Qush (numbers 1, 4, 9, and 10 in Table 1). All of these slaves had been bought, and trained by Iltutmish before he became Sultan. Because of this early bonding and service it is also not surprising that, when their master became Sultan, they were trusted and deployed by him in some of the most crucial posts (in Uchch, Multan, and as the treasurer) within his realm.

The time spent together in the household of the monarch also created a sentiment of corporate affiliation amongst the Shamsī slaves. Sometimes, matrimonial relations within slave families sought to achieve these ends, as in the case of Malik Timur Khān, who was married to Malik Saif al-Dīn's daughter.[70] Years after Iltutmish's death, in *circa* 648/1250 during the conflict between the Shamsī slaves Malik 'Izz al-Dīn Kushlū Khān and Malik Nuṣrat al-Dīn Shīr Khān over Uchch, Malik Kushlū Khān sought to resolve the

[67] Jūzjānī, *Ṭabaqāt-i Nāṣirī*, vol. 2, p. 4: *bā o* (Malik Nāṣir al-Dīn Maḥmūd) *yak jā dar ḥujra-i daulat parwarish yāft*.

[68] Ibid.

[69] Ibid., p. 13.

[70] Ibid., p. 18.

hostilities through negotiations, placing confidence in the fact that they were both from one house, *az yak khāna*, and one threshold, *az yak astāna*.[71] As with the Mu'izzī *bandagān*, vertical linkages between Shams al-Dīn and his slaves were as important as the horizontal links within the slave corps itself. The sense of a corporate 'Shamsī' identity leant coherence to the military elite and consolidated the master–slave dyad crucial to the functioning of the regime.

The Mu'izzī and Shamsī deployment of *bandagān* indicates how important it is not to understand these politically influential commanders as 'nobles', or individuals who possessed a social status determined by genealogy *and* a code of conduct associated with their aristocratic position.[72] The *bandagān* were commodities, like all other slaves (*barda*, domestic, *kanīzakhā*, concubines), and their deployment, importance, and privileges were derived from and dependent upon

[71] Ibid., p. 38. Malik Kushlū Khān's confidence was misplaced and he was imprisoned by Shīr Khān. The recognition of the sentiment of corporate solidarity amongst slaves is in itself important, as is its dissolution after the death of Iltutmish, on which see Chapter 4.

[72] For useful overviews of current research on nobility in Western Europe, see Lawrence Stone, 'Prosopography', in F. Gilbert and S. Graubard, eds, *Historical Studies Today*, (New York: Norton, 1972), pp. 107–40; George Beech, 'Prosopography', in James M. Powell, ed., *Medieval Studies: An Introduction*, (Syracuse: Syracuse University Press, 1976), pp. 151–84, Bernard S. Bachrach, 'Some Observations on the Medieval Nobility: a Review Essay', *Medieval Prosopography*, 1 (1980), pp. 15–33. Two collections of essays provide an introduction to the major issues of interest in the field: Timothy Reuter, ed. and trans., *The Medieval Nobility*, (Amsterdam: Europe in the Middle Ages, selected studies, vol. 14, North-Holland Publishing Company, 1978); and Georges Duby, *The Chivalrous Society*, translated by Cynthia Postan, (Berkeley: University of California Press, 1977). I use the term 'noble' in the twelfth- and thirteenth-century sense of the term. A useful comparison can be made between the *ministerialis* and the military slaves to highlight how 'unfree' individuals were used to segregate authority in German and Islamic societies. Such a comparison would also serve the useful purpose of emphasizing dissimilarities in the two medieval societies whereby the *ministerialis* managed to improve their social position over a period of time but the *bandagān* could not. On the *ministerialis* see—other than the articles in Reuter—Benjamin Arnold, *German Knighthood 1050–1300* (Oxford: Clarendon Press, 1985), and John B. Freed, 'Nobles, Ministerials, and Knights in the Archdiocese of Salzburg', *Speculum*, 62 (1987), pp. 575–611.

the will of their owner. Yet the fact that trusted slaves were often expected to play crucial, strategic, and unsupervised roles within the Sultanate drew the attention of contemporaries who emphasized the normative code of loyalty and obedience owed by the slave to his master. From the early ‘Abbāsid period itself, the conduct of the *ghulām/mamlūk/banda* was idealized as the paradigm of obedience and selfless loyalty.[73] Thus, by a rather perverse irony, the trusted slaves were not judged by values applicable to commodities but by their ‘noble’, selfless conduct in the service of their master.

There were other similarities between Mu‘izzī and Shamsī slave systems. The information on the ethnic origins of the slaves mentioned by Jūzjānī indicates that Iltutmish favoured the practice of his day by buying slaves of central Asian origin. Of the twenty-five slaves about whom we have fairly complete data in Jūzjānī's biographical section, twelve were Turks from different tribes (numbers 3, 6, 8, 14, 17, 18, 20, 21, 23–5 in Table 1); Qipchaqs predominated, and then the Ilbarīs,[74] three were from Rūm who, as their names indicate, were

[73] al-Ṭabarī, writing in the ninth century, recalled the ‘Abbāsid Caliph al-Mahdī's sentiments: ‘The *mawālī* [freed slaves] deserve such a treatment, for only they combine in themselves the following qualities. When I sit in public audience, I may call a *mawlā* and raise him and seat him by my side, so that his knee will rub my knee. As soon, however, as the audience is over, I may order him to groom my riding animal and he will be content with this and will not take offence. But if I demand the same thing from somebody else, he will say: ‘I am the son of your supporter and intimate associate’ or ‘I am a veteran in your [‘Abbāsid] cause (*da‘wā*)’ . . . And I shall not be able to move him from his [obstinate] stand.’ Cited by David Ayalon, ‘Preliminary Remarks on the *Mamluk* Military Institution in Islam’, in V.J. Parry and M.E. Yapp, eds, *War, Technology and Society in the Middle East*, (London: Oxford University Press, 1975), p. 49.

[74] Jūzjānī noted that both Sultan Iltutmish and Balban were Ilbarī Turks, and there has been considerable speculation about the background of these Ilbarīs. There is no reference to an Ilbarī tribe or clan in Kāshghari, *Dīwān-i Lughāt al-Turk*, (see R. Dankoff, ‘Kashghari on the Tribal and Kinship Organization of the Turks’, *Archivum Ottomanicum*, 4 (1972), pp. 29–35), nor in the Anonymous, *Ḥudūd al-‘Alam*, or in Fakhr-i Mudabbir, *Ta'rīkh Fakhr al-Dīn Mubārak Shāh*. It is possible that ‘Ilbarī’ is an orthographic mistake in the surviving manuscripts of Jūzjānī's text or a Persianized rendering of the Turkish name for the tribe. Jūzjānī noted that Shams al-Dīn Iltutmish's father's title was Il-Khān (in a

probably Turks purchased in or around Anatolia (numbers 2, 13, 22), five were described as Qarā Khitā'ī, two in all probability Turks (numbers 5, and 12), and three Mongols (7, 10 and 16),[75] four were of unmentioned origin (numbers 1, 3, 11, 19) but at least two of their names were identifiably Turkish (numbers 1, 3), and one, in all likelihood, was a Turk from Khwarazm (number 19). Finally, one was of South Asian origin captured in the region of MHR/Maihar in

---

variant manuscript: Ilam Khān), which translates literally as subordinate chief; vol. 1, p. 441. One possible inference from this information can be that the Ilbarīs were a subordinate clan, *batn*, or branch of a larger Turkish tribe or confederacy. That the inference is probably accurate is suggested by Jūzjānī's concluding verse, *qiṭ'a*, in the *Ṭabaqāt-i Nāṣirī*, vol. 2, pp. 220–1, where Balban is eulogized as the 'Khān of the Ilbarīs and Shāh of the Yimak, *Khan-i Ilbarī ast wa Shāh-i Yimak*.' The Yimak were a tribal confederation historically associated with the Kimak and Qipchaq confederacies. On the basis of information in Amīr Khusrau, *Nuh Sipihr*, edited by M. Wahid Mirza (London: Oxford University Press, 1950), p. 173, one can conclude that (enslaved) members of the Yimak were present in north India in the thirteenth and fourteenth centuries. If Jūzjānī's information is correct, and there is no reason to doubt it, the Ilbarīs were probably a subordinate clan of the Yimak and associated with the larger Qipchak, Qanqalī, and Kimak confederacies, some of whom had migrated or were enslaved and sold in India in large numbers, especially after the start of the Mongol invasions. The link between these tribes and their presence in India is also suggested by Jūzjānī, who is fairly precise about associating the Ilbarīs with the related tribes of Qipchaq, Qanqalī, and Yimak. See vol. 2, pp. 175–6. Interestingly enough, Juwainī, *Ta'rīkh-i Jahān Gushā*, translated by Boyle, vol. 1, p. 107, described the process of enslavement of Qanqalī youths in Khwarazm and Afghanistan and their sale in north India and Egypt. The coherence with which the tribal context of the Ilbarīs is narrated in the Sultanate sources is remarkable and it is now externally corroborated by P.B. Golden, 'Cumanica II, The Ölberli (Ölperli): The Fortunes and Misfortunes of an Inner Asian Nomadic Clan', *Archivum Eurasiae Medii Aevi*, 6 (1986), pp. 5–29. As Golden shows, the Ölberli/Ölperli were a Turkic group associated with the Yimak-Kimak-Qanqalī-Qipchaq confederacies. The significance of these tribal groups in the history of the Sultanate is developed in my forthcoming work 'The Ignored Elite: Turks and Mongols in the Early Delhi Sultanate'.

[75] It is not clear how Jūzjānī used the term Qarā Khitā. The Qarā Khitā confederacy located in Balasaghun (Hu-ssu Ordo) were of Mongol antecedents, which would lead one to assume that the slaves mentioned in Jūzjānī as Khitā'i were of Mongol ethnic background. It is more likely, however, that Jūzjānī used

northern Bundelkhand (number 9).[76] Thus, in all, twenty-two of the twenty-five slaves mentioned by Jūzjānī were of central Asian background.

Yet, unlike the Mu'izzī slaves, not all the Turk and other *bandagān* of Shams al-Dīn were recently enslaved. From Jūzjānī's biographies it is evident that at least three slaves had served previously in Afghanistan and north India and were sold to Iltutmish by the heirs of their masters. Kabīr Khān Ayāz al-Mu'izzī had been a slave of the

---

Qarā Khitā in a geographical sense to mean the lands occupied by the Western Liao. Jūzjānī clarified occasionally that some of the slaves from this geographical region were Turks: note the examples of Maliks Saif al-Dīn Ai-Beg Yaghāntut and Ikhtiyār al-Dīn Ai-Tegin described as Khitā'ī Turks. See vol. 2, pp. 9, 22 and Table 1. On the Qarā Khitā'ī, see Karl A. Wittfogel and Feng Chia-Sheng, 'Appendix V: Qara Khitay', in idem, *History of the Chinese Society: Liao (907–1125)* (Philadelphia: Transactions of the American Philosophical Society, 1946), vol. 36, pp. 619–74; and C.E. Bosworth, 'Ḳarā Khitāy', *EI*², vol. 4, pp. 580–3. The Qarā Khitā' ī dynasty ruled over an extraordinarily diverse body of people in the steppe and its tolerance of ethnic and religious minorities made it a sanctuary for many immigrants. The dynasty's traditions of governance and succession patterns need to be separated from the social usages of the subjects under their rule. It is significant that Jūzjānī did not provide a tribal identification to the Qarā Khitā Shamsī *bandagān*. The deracinated slaves were 'Turks', perhaps from different tribes, belonging to the Qarā Khitā *region.* Whether their shared geographical provenance (as in the case of the three *bandagān* from Anatolia) implied any cultural or social affinities is doubtful. Jackson argues otherwise in his 'Sultān Raḍiyya bint Iltutmish', in Gavin R.G. Hambly, ed., *Women in the Medieval Islamic World: Power, Patronage, Piety*, (New York: Palgrave, 1998), pp. 81–97. See also Chapter 5.

[76] The printed text of Jūzjānī, *Ṭabaqāt-i Nāṣirī*, edited by Habibi, has the place where Hindū Khān was enslaved as MHR, without any vowels: Jūzjānī, *Ṭabaqāt-i Nāṣirī*, vol. 2, pp. 11, 18, 44, 62. Irfan Habib, 'The Formation of the Sultanate Ruling Class', p. 10, fn 60, (and following him, Shadab Bano, 'The Acquisition and Trade of Elite Slaves in the Thirteenth Century', *Proceedings of the Indian History Congress*, Patiala, 59 (1998), pp. 229–36) suggests MHR was Mathura because ''Mahūr' in Persian with the diacriticals dropped is really Mathūr or Mathurā'. One can assume that the long vowel 'waw' was dropped in transcription by a later scribe, but Jūzjānī also referred to MHR as a *qaṣaba*, a term used for a small town, a definition that would hardly apply to Mathura, already an important pilgrimage centre in the thirteenth century (on

Mu'izzī notable, Naṣīr al-Dīn Ḥusain Amīr-i Shikār,[77] and Malik Nāṣir al-Dīn Ai-Tamar al-Bahā'ī[78] had been a slave of the Mu'izzī *banda-i khaṣṣ* Bahā' al-Dīn Tughril. Finally, Malik Nuṣrat al-Dīn Tā'īsī al-Mu'izzī had apparently been a slave of Mu'izz al-Dīn himself, sold to Iltutmish under unclear circumstances.[79]

---

the *qaṣaba* see also Chapter 5). In contrast, Raverty read MHR as 'Mahir, Mihar and Mihir' and placed the town at Lat. 24°16' and Long. 80°49', in the Sagar and Narmada territories (*Ṭabaqāt-i Nāṣirī*, translated by Raverty, vol. 2, p. 744, fn. 9 and s.v. index). That MHR was probably on the frontier of Sultanate territories towards Bundelkhand and was often associated with the governorships of regions as dispersed as Kōl, Mahavan, and Gwalior emerges from Jūzjānī's narrative of Malik Nuṣrat al-Dīn Tā'īsī's campaign in 631/1233 (vol. 2, p. 11). The Malik commanded military contingents from Qanauj, MHR, and Mahavan from Gwalior on plunder expeditions into Chanderi and Kalinjar. MHR is most likely Maihar (at the precise location identified by Raverty), an area with urban centres dating from the tenth-century Kalacuri period, on which see, B.D. Chattopadhyaya, 'Urban Centres in Early Medieval India: An Overview', *Making of Early Medieval India*, pp. 155–82, and map, p. 171. It was an attractive region to seek slaves and plunder (Malik Tā'īsī's expedition into Kalinjar reportedly yielded a hundred and twenty five lakh [*tankas?*]). It is certainly likely that one of the early campaigns in northern Bundelkhand led to the enslavement of Malik Hindū Khān. To read the *qaṣaba* of MHR as Mathura is, however, extremely questionable.

[77] Malik Kabīr Khān's name is also included in the list of Iltutmish's notables as 'Izz al-Dīn Kabīr Khān without the al-Mu'izzī *nisba*. Jūzjānī noted explicitly in Kabīr Khān's biography (Jūzjānī, vol. 2, p. 5) that he was a slave of Naṣīr al-Dīn. Traditionally, the slave, manumitted or otherwise, included in his own name the name of his master as the *nisba* of affiliation or belonging. Thus, Iltutmish did not hesitate to publicly proclaim himself *al-Quṭbī*. See from many examples the inscription of Iltutmish dated 608/1211: M.M. Shu'aib, 'Inscriptions from Palwal', *Epigraphica Indo-Moslemica* (1911–12), p. 3. But then why did Malik Kabīr Khān the slave of Naṣīr al-Dīn use the *nisba* Mu'izzī?

[78] Habibi reads the name as Ai-Tam? (AITM) Bahā'ī, and the Malik's name is also included in the list of Iltutmish's notables (vol. 1, p. 451) as Malik Nāṣir al-Dīn AITM Bahā'ī. In the list of Iltutmish's nobles Habibi also mentions the alternate reading Ai-Tamar in a variant manuscript. I have preferred the Turkish reading Ai-Tamar. See Jūzjānī, *Ṭabaqāt-i Nāṣirī*, vol. 1, pp. 450–1 and fn. 6. In the list of Iltutmish's notables (vol. 1, p. 451) another dependant of Bahā' al-Dīn Tughril is also mentioned: Malik 'Izz al-Dīn Tughril *Bahā'ī*.

[79] Ibid., vol. 2, p. 10.

Through these purchases Iltutmish went against the traditional practice of buying slaves that were natally and socially alienated.[80] These three slaves had already established political and social ties with individuals in the area of their deployment and because of their connections they were not as dependent upon their new master for privileges. Significantly enough, Malik Kabīr Khān Ayāz al-Mu'izzī provides the only example of a Shamsī *banda-i khāṣṣ* who was punished and had his privileges reduced. In 625/1227–8 he was appointed as commander of the town of Multan, its fort, together with its surrounding territory and towns, *qaṣabāt*. Multan was a plum appointment; the city straddled the major trade routes into Sindh, Afghanistan, and eastern Iran, and it was also a strategic frontier outpost against Mongol incursions into the Delhi Sultanate. Circa 629/1231,[81] however, Malik Kabīr Khān was removed from Multan and given (the town of?) Palwal for his personal maintenance, *ba-wajh-i mā-yaḥtāj-i ḥāl*. Kabīr Khān's loss of power and privileges would only be reversed in the reign of Rukn al-Dīn Fīrūz Shāh (633–4/1236).

Clearly an 'imperfectly' recruited slave corps defeated the purposes for which it had been raised, and there was a swift response to Malik Kabīr Khān's insubordination. However, rather than casting doubt upon the effectiveness of the *bandagān-i Shamsī*, the case of Malik Kabīr Khān enlarges upon the pressures that faced Shams al-Dīn to not pay any particular attention to tradition in the purchase of his *bandagān*. It must be remembered that the Shansabanid Sultan Mu'izz al-Dīn had ignored the normative system advised by the Seljuqid *wazīr* in his *Siyāsat Nāma* in much the same way. The urgency with which Iltutmish sought to recruit and deploy military personnel, especially just before and right after his accession, might also explain the surprising presence of Malik Hindū Khān as a *banda-i khāṣṣ*. Malik Hindū Khān, to my knowledge, was the first indigene to be advanced to the status of a senior slave since Tilak, the slave of Sultan Mas'ūd Ghaznawī (421–32/1031–41),[82] and would be followed

[80] On the significance of natal alienation and social death in slavery, see Orlando Patterson, *Slavery and Social Death*, (Cambridge: Harvard University Press, 1982).

[81] Jūzjānī, *Ṭabaqāt-i Nāṣirī*, vol. 2, p. 6, notes that his removal from Multan took place after two or four (lunar) years of his appointment.

[82] On Tilak see C.E. Bosworth, *The Ghaznavids 994-1040*, pp. 101, 127-8.

subsequently by the slave Malik Kafūr Hazārdinārī of Alā' al-Dīn Khalajī and Khusrau Khān Barwarī, elevated by Mubārak Shāh Khalajī (716–20/1316–20).[83] The circumstances influencing Hindū Khān's recruitment and promotion differed from the other examples of elite slaves of subcontinental provenance, as did his conduct which, unlike that of Khusrau Khān Barwarī, showed loyalty to his master in an exemplary degree.

It was because the Sultan trusted his *bandagān* that they were widely deployed in his realm. The information in Table 1 on the careers of the *bandagān-i Shamsī* also details the areas under their command. Taking them together and synchronically for a moment serves to clarify the areas in the Sultanate that came under their supervision at one time or another through the reign of Iltutmish. In the north-west and Sindh regions, senior Shamsī slaves had appointments in Multan, Wanjrut (near Multan), Uchch, Mansurpur, Lahore, Nandana, and Kuja (? probably Kajakot, north-west of Nandana, south of the Indus). In the Punjab, between Lahore and Delhi, slaves had assignments in Tabarhind, Hansi, Barwala, Jind, Kuhram, Sunam, Sursuti (Sirsa). In the biographical twenty-second section of his chronicle Jūzjānī mentioned that in the region west and south-west of Delhi and north Rajasthan, Gwalior, Ajmer, Sambharnamak (the town Sambhar on the Sambhar salt lake), Kasli, Narnaul, Bayana-Sulṭānkōt, and Palwal were held by Shamsī slaves. In the narrative on Shams al-Dīn's reign (section twenty-one), Ranthambhor and Mandor were also mentioned as areas conquered by the Sultan's

[83] I have deliberately excluded from the category of Shamsī *bandagān-i khāṣṣ* the example of the eunuch, *khwāja sarā*, 'Imād al-Dīn Raihān, also of subcontinental origin. Jūzjānī recognized 'Imād al-Dīn Raihān's prominence in the politics of the Delhi Sultanate only in 650/1252, during the reign of Sultan Nāṣir al-Dīn Maḥmūd. There is no information, however, concerning his enslavement and early service. His importance in the early years of Nāṣir al-Dīn's reign (644–64/1246–66) suggests that he was purchased, like his rival Balban, sometime in the last years of Iltutmish's reign. As a result, he would have been too young to have been a Shamsī *banda-i khāṣṣ*. His rise to prominence, unlike that of Tilak or Khusrau Khān, was not a result of the favour and trust of the monarch. 'Imād al-Dīn rose to power, much like Balban, through his successful ability to utilize opportunities for political manipulation in the unstable years of Iltutmish's successors. See Chapter 5 for a full discussion.

slaves.[84] Although both arcas were subsequently garrisoned, perhaps by these slaves, these were not definitive conquests and the areas eventually lapsed to local chieftains. In the eastern Gangetic plain, military and administrative assignments were held by slaves in the Bihar corridor and the province of Lakhnauti. In Uttar Pradesh, north-east of Delhi, slaves occupied posts in Baran and Budaun. The area under the direct control of royal slaves in the area of modern Uttar Pradesh was perhaps greater than that suggested by the information in Jūzjānī.[85] Writing in the mid-fourteenth century Baranī supplied the additional information that two or three thousand members of the *qalb*, the central contingent of Iltutmish's army in which slaves were predominant, also had *iqṭā's* in the Ganga-Jamuna *do-āb*.[86]

The dispersal of the Shamsī *bandagān-i khāṣṣ* over the newly annexed regions is a telling indicator of the impact of Iltutmish's conquests and the methods used to integrate the Sultanates of north India within a politically paramount Delhi Sultanate. While, as we have seen in the last chapter, remnants of the conquered elite might continue to reside in their old principalities—like Bayana-Sulṭānkōt—the making of a new political structure seems to have been contingent on the creation and deployment of a deracinated elite. The deployment of the *bandagān* followed the string of campaigns of the Sultan in the first half of his reign, and the final scale of their control over annexed territories in north India becomes quite visible by the late 1220s.

The charges held by the Shamsī slaves were described by Jūzjānī as *iqṭā'*, *wilāyat*, or a town, *shahr*, together with its environs, *muẓā-fāt* and neighbouring towns, *qaṣabāt*. We do not have information

[84] Ibid., vol. 1, pp. 445–6.

[85] Towns such as Kōl, Jalesar, Mahavan, Meerut, Patiali, MHR/Maihar, Hansi, Benaras, Qanauj, and Kara were also under Shamsī subordinates. We have little information on the social background of commanders who were given charge of most of these towns. Some of these towns were under slave military commanders (for example, Patiali), others were, for a time, under royal Princes (for example, Hansi, Awadh).

[86] See Baranī, *Ta'rīkh-i Fīrūz Shāhī*, edited by Khan, p. 61, edited by Rashid, p. 72. Khan mentions 2000 horsemen from Shams al-Dīn's *qalb* retinue with *iqṭā's* in the Ganga-Jamuna *do-āb*; A. Rashid's edition mentions 2000 or 3000 horsemen.

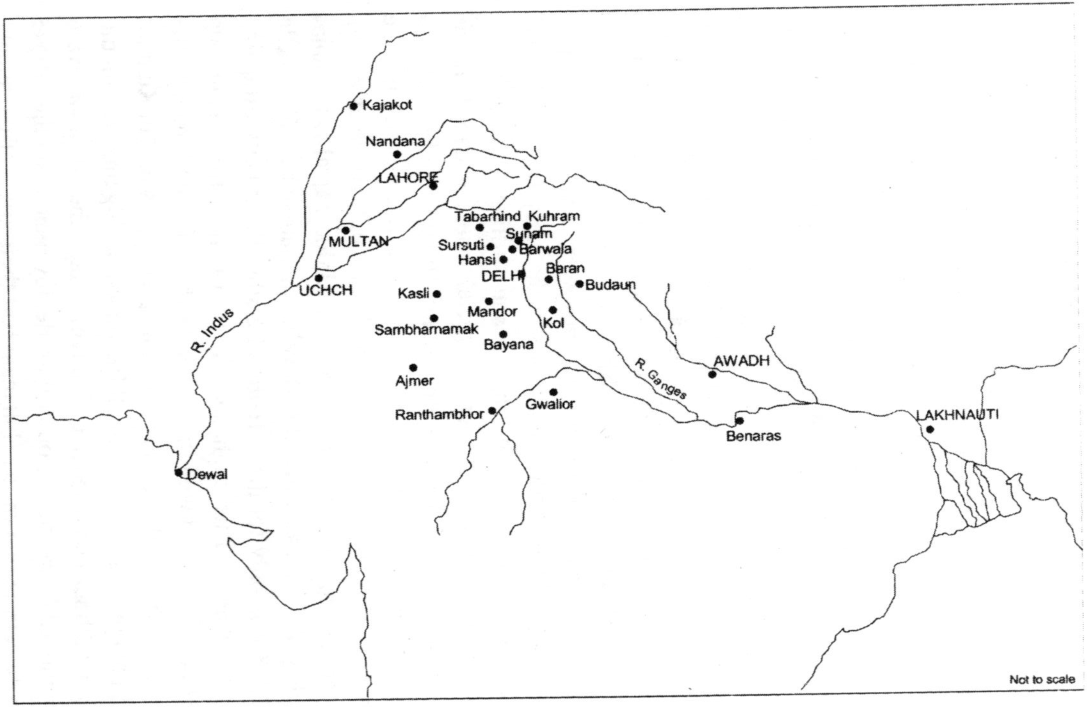

Map 3: The Deployment of Shamsī *Bandagān*

concerning the functional demands made on appointees to these areas, but the geographical and strategic context of each appointment must have made a difference. Multan, Uchch, Lahore, Budaun, and Lakhnauti, for instance, were important appointments at this time, and even here the responsibilities of the Governor of Multan must have differed from that of Budaun and Lakhnauti.

It is not difficult to forget that the high political offices occupied by elite slaves were in direct contradiction to their menial social stature. This factor needs to be kept in mind as we study the processes that allowed for the consolidation of Sultanate authority in north India. Several scholars have suggested that one reason why Iltutmish managed to stabilize his realm was that he 'transferred' his Governors frequently, without giving them a chance to strike 'roots'.[87] On the face of it, this would have further underlined the deracinated nature of many of the slave commanders, and a quick glance at Jūzjānī's information, included in Table 1, does suggest that military assignments were not made in perpetuity; elite Shamsī slaves were moved around periodically. We have to be cautious, however, in assuming the presence of proto-bureaucratic traditions in the early Delhi Sultanate. Disaggregating Jūzjānī's information and shifting to a diachronic reading of the evidence provides the crucial context that explains the movement of slaves. For example, Iltutmish appointed slaves to a specific command while the area was the scene of conflict. Once the campaigns were over, the Sultan moved other military commanders into the region. Jūzjānī's biography of Malik Tāj al-Dīn Sanjar Kazlak Khān indicates that the slave's appointment to Wanjrut in 625/1228 was only for the duration of Sultan Iltutmish's campaign against Qubācha. This might have been a part of the cleaning-up operations associated with the campaign, because subsequently the Sultan gave the Malik the older and more prestigious post of Kuhram as his charge. Wanjrut was, in all likelihood, amalgamated with the larger neighbouring province of Multan. In fact, the *bandagān* were rarely moved from one region of their deployment to another: those in the eastern region of the Sultanate had their areas of movement located within the Awadh–Bihar–Lakhnauti axis (numbers 5, 7);

[87] For references, see fn. 91 below.

those in the Haryana, Punjab, and Sindh regions (numbers 1, 2, 4, 10, 12) usually stayed within that locale, and another circuit included north Rajasthan, the Siwaliks, and north Bundelkhand (numbers 3, 6).

Otherwise, too, the peripatetic careers of many Shamsī *bandagān* were associated with different stages in the processes of their training and bear a remarkable similarity to the model proposed by the Seljuqid *wazīr* Niẓām al-Mūlk. After some time of service as a domestic in the court, they were given limited responsibility, usually as *sar-i jāndār* (head of the guards), *amīr-i ākhūr* (in charge of the stable), or *amīr-i shikār* (in charge of the hunt). As they graduated from being pages to junior slaves, their deployment seems to have been the occasion when they won their spurs in positions of limited responsibility, such as *shaḥna* or superintendent.[88] This was when the Sultans detailed slaves to specific tasks under their close supervision. The slave was made an officer through whom the master maintained control over certain establishments or over crucial functions of government. Before his appointment to the command of Multan and receipt of the title Qarā Qush, Malik Ikhtiyār al-Dīn (number 10 in Table 1) was the *shaḥna* of the *khāliṣa* in the vicinity of Tabarhind, the revenues of which were reserved for the Sultan. While the presence of unalienated *khāliṣa* lands itself indicated an attempt by the Sultan to increase his revenue from taxation on the produce of land (in contrast to an income largely from commerce or plunder and tribute), it is significant that the administration of these lands was under the command of a *shaḥna* who would eventually become one of the Sultan's *bandagān-i khāṣṣ*. Junior slaves were also appointed as *shaḥnas* to the armoury, *zarrād khāna*, of Budaun

[88] Although there is insufficient evidence to draw a parallel, there are certain features common between the areas where *shaḥnas* were used in the Seljuqid state and the early Delhi Sultanate. For the Seljuqids, see Ann K.S. Lambton, 'Internal Structure of the Seljuq Sultanate', in J.A. Boyle, ed., *The Cambridge History of Iran*, (Cambridge: Cambridge University Press, 1968), pp. 244–5. The office itself is of a Chinese origin (*shao-chien*) and was introduced into the central Islamic lands by the Qarā Khitā'ī. See Gerhard Doerfer, *Turkische und Monglische Elemente im Neupersischen*, (Weisbaden: Franz Steiner Verlag, 1967), vol. 3, pp. 320-1, s.v. 'sihna'.

(number 13 in Table 1), of the river and the boats, *shaḥna-i bahr wa kishtihā* (number 15 in Table 1), of the imperial stable, *shaḥna-i ākhūr* (number 14 in Table 1). In other words, there was a correlation between the increase in the *banda's* responsibilities, his years of service, and the greater bonding between master and slave. The Sultan's increasing confidence in the abilities of some of his junior slaves was reflected in their employment to positions of greater responsibility and political initiative.

The appointments of some *bandagān* to select military assignments were seen as the apogee of a *banda's* career. These assignments were seemingly 'reserved' as commands for the most trusted slave officers, and some *bandagān* served in these regions for long periods of time. Uchch, for example, was conquered in 625/1228 and, when the royal forces withdrew, its charge was handed over to the Shamsī slave Malik Tāj al-Dīn Sanjar Kazlak Khān (number 1 in Table 1). Malik Tāj al-Dīn's governorship came to an end with his death in 629/1231–2, upon which another slave, Malik Saif al-Dīn Ai-Beg-i Uchch (number 4 in Table 1), was appointed Governor of the region. Malik Saif al-Dīn remained Governor of Uchch through the remaining portion of his master's reign. The case of Multan was identical. After its conquest, its charge was handed over to the slave Malik Kabīr Khān Ayāz al-Mu'izzī (number 2 in Table 1). After Iltutmish removed him in disgrace, *circa* 629/1231, the charge of Multan was handed over to the slave Malik Ikhtiyār al-Dīn Qarā Qush Khān Ai-tegin (number 10 in Table 1), who continued as Governor through the remainder of Iltutmish's reign. The strategic locale of both Uchch and Multan seemed to necessitate the appointment of trusted subordinates from the very outset. As Table 1 also reveals, interestingly enough, three of the four Amirs (numbers 1, 4, and 10) appointed to Multan and Uchch were old slaves of Iltutmish dating back to a period before he had succeeded in becoming Sultan. Not accidentally, the seniormost slaves of Shams al-Dīn were appointed to positions of trust from which—with the exception of Kabīr Khān—they were never removed during the lifetime of their master.

The close nexus between strategic commands and the deployment of senior slaves is also well brought out by the case of Lakhnauti. Here, unlike the case of Uchch and Multan, it was the free Amir 'Alā' al-Dīn Jānī who was appointed Governor of Lakhnauti after the death of Prince Nāṣir al-Dīn Maḥmūd in 628/1230-1.[89] Subsequently, some time in 629–30/1231–3, Malik 'Alā' al-Dīn Jānī was dismissed, *ma'zūl shud*,[90] and in his place the slave Malik Saif al-Dīn Ai-Beg (number 5 in Table 1) was appointed. Unlike Malik Jānī, Malik Saif al-Dīn's governorship was a huge success and the Sultan appreciated his remission of elephants to Delhi enough to reward him with the title Yaghāntut. Saif al-Dīn established the new tradition for Lakhnauti for the remainder of Iltutmish's reign. After Saif al-Dīn's death in 631/1233–4, governorship of the province passed into the hands of the slave Malik 'Izz al-Dīn Tughan Khān Tughril (number 7 in Table 1).

The Shamsī *bandagān* were the most favoured group in Iltutmish's dispensation precisely because, contrary to established historical opinion, they were not a slave or a Turkish 'bureaucracy'.[91] Rather than professional service regulations between an officer and the

[89] Jūzjānī, *Ṭabaqāt-i Nāṣirī*, vol. 1, pp. 438, 448, 453–4. The date of Prince Nāṣir al-Dīn Maḥmūd's death is not clearly mentioned by Jūzjānī. In his account of the Prince he mentions that Nāṣir al-Dīn died in 626/1229 (vol. 1, p. 447). Later in his chronicle (vol. 1, p. 454) he mentions that the Prince died in Lakhnauti a year and a half after (*b'ad az yak sāl o nīm*) the arrival (626/1229) of the Caliphal envoys in Delhi. In other words he died around 628/1230–1. This seems to be the more likely date for the Prince's death. The inscription on the door of the Prince's mausoleum in Delhi notes the date of construction as 629/1231–2. See J. Horowitz, 'The Inscriptions of Muḥammad ibn Sam, Qutubuddin Aibeg and Iltutmish', p. 24, and S.A.A. Naqvi, 'Sultan Ghari, Delhi', *Ancient India* 3 (1947), p. 5. Nāṣir al-Dīn's death probably occurred the year before the construction of the mausoleum, in early 628/1230. This date coincides with Jūzjānī's latter statement and the date of Iltutmish's campaign into Lakhnauti against Balka Khalajī (628/1230–1) whose rebellion Jūzjānī mentioned (vol. 1, p. 448) as occurring immediately after the Prince's death. Iltutmish appointed 'Alā' al-Dīn Jānī as the Governor of Lakhnauti at the termination of this expedition.

[90] Jūzjānī, *Ṭabaqāt-i Nāṣirī*, vol. 2, pp. 9–10.

[91] See for example, Mohammad Habib, 'Introduction to Elliot and Dowson's *History of India, vol. 2*', pp. 103–10; K.A. Nizami, 'The Early Turkish Sultans of Delhi', *A Comprehensive History of India, Vol. V: The Delhi Sultanat*, pp. 224–6 ('an all-India military-cum-administrative service manned entirely by foreigners . . . Turkish slave officers and Tazik'); idem, *Religion and Politics in India*, pp. 128–33 (where the Turkish nobles constituted one element of the bureaucratic organization of the Sultanate); and S.B.P. Nigam, *Nobility*

state, dyadic bonds created through careful fostering, *parwarish,* and education, *tarbiyat,* influenced relationships between master and slave. 'Promotions', when they were given, were rewards for 'approved/agreeable service', *khidmat pasandīda karda būd,*[92] and while there might be a range of 'approved actions', these were ultimately judged against the cultural expectations of a slave's selfless service in the cause of his master. If we argue, as some historians have done, that the appointment to a particularly important *iqṭā'* reflected the rank and status of the subordinate in Iltutmish's dispensation, we would ignore the relationships on the basis of which 'ranks' were constituted.[93] Irrespective of the high positions occupied by some of the favoured *bandagān*, whether they were manumitted or not, their careers were entirely dependent upon their *relationships* with their master. Kabīr Khān Ayāz, for example, one of the more powerful military commanders, could be swiftly pensioned off by the Sultan. And for that matter, despite Niẓām al-Mulk's advice to the contrary, there were no time-bound promotions within this cadre. Some slaves seemingly languished with the same responsibilities for years; even when Malik Hindū Khān (number 9 in Table 1) was appointed *khīzānadār*, treasurer, he continued as *ṭashtdār*, ewer-bearer, a position he did not give up until the end of Iltutmish's reign.[94] Jūzjānī presented this information as evidence of the affection for the master by the slave and the honour given to the *banda*, who was allowed such close proximity and intimacy, *qurbat tamām dāsht*, with the Sultan over an extended period of time. Malik Hindū Khān's career languished only if we understand this notion from the anachronistic perspective of a bureaucratic system and assume that the commands of *iqṭā's* alone constituted rank and status.[95]

---

under the Sultans of Delhi, pp. 2, 93–103, 106–10. Irfan Habib carries the same ambiguity of usage in his 'The Formation of the Sultanate Ruling Class', when he refers to the manner in which 'nobles' were 'transferred'.

[92] From many examples, see in Jūzjānī, *Ṭabaqāt-i Nāṣirī*, vol. 2, pp. 9, 10.

[93] Irfan Habib, 'The Formation of the Sultanate Ruling Class', p. 11.

[94] Jūzjānī, *Ṭabaqāt-i Nāṣirī*, vol. 2, p. 19: '*tā ākhir'umr dast az ṭasht dārī nadāsht.*

[95] Certainly, Hindū Khān's example forces us to question Irfan Habib's emphatic point: 'Iltutmish's Turkish slaves are not known to have occupied a single of the highest central or court offices at his death . . .', 'Formation of the

Since the relationships of master and slave determined deployment, seniority, and service conditions to such an extent, they should also inflect the manner in which historians consider the relationship between the 'centre' and its 'provinces'. As Peter Jackson has detailed, Persian chronicles used a variety of terms to carry the sense of 'province' (*iqṭāʻ, wilāyat, iqlīm, diyār*) and, as we will see, the administration of these areas with each other and the capital (almost uniformly termed, *ḥaẓrat-i Dehlī*) became increasingly complex. The *bandagān* had considerable political initiative as Governors but the relationship between the 'province and the centre' was not between temporal, administratively defined spaces; it was finally delineated and determined by the relationship that existed between its Governor and the Sultan. This was not a depersonalized state functioning through institutionalized structures, but a careful balancing of assigned privileges and responsibilities. Iltutmish relied upon his personal relationships with his slaves to cohere his distant cantonments under the Sultanate, but he also put into place different agencies that surveyed their activities. These were not always integrated into the entourage of the *bandagān* but they were important in the administration of their commands.

The retinues of the Shamsī *bandagān* were, like the preceding Muʻizzī commanders, fairly substantial in size, including people that the slaves recruited themselves and others that the Sultan associated with their commands. Jūzjānī provides us with little information about these retinues from Iltutmish's reign, but evidence from a slightly later period suggests that the Shamsī *bandagān* must have had military slaves like Qara Jamāq, a *banda-i khāṣṣ* of Balban, and free men who performed administrative duties for them like Khwāja Ṣāliḥ, who was the *nā'ib* and *kōtwāl*, deputy and commander, of Uchch for Hindū Khān. Elsewhere, Jūzjānī mentioned that in Nāṣir al-Dīn's reign Balban had administrators and servants [*mutaʻalliqān wa khuddām*], to look after his *iqṭāʻ*.[96] Amongst these administrators was an individual called the *khwāja*. It is unclear how widespread the

---

Sultanate Ruling Class', p. 12. It is also worth pointing out that offices such as *amīr-i majlis, sar-i jāndār* or *amīr-i ākhūr* gave their holders rare access to the Sultan and great influence in Sultanate administration.

[96] See Jūzjānī, *Ṭabaqāt-i Nāṣirī*, vol. 2, pp. 61, 67, 170.

appointment of *khwājas* in *iqṭā's* might have been, but the casualness with which Jūzjānī provides us with the one instance from Nagaur, where Malik Karīm al-Dīn Ḥamzah and Khwāja Najīb al-Dīn functioned together in *circa* 618/1221, suggests that it was already a common practice.[97] The presence of the *khwāja* as an accountant and administrator together with the military commander in Iltutmish's reign makes it necessary, however, for us to correct Habib's argument that the pairing of the two officers was first noticeable only in Balban's reign (664–86/1266–87).[98]

The primary task of the *khwājas* needs to be related to the urban character of the *iqṭā's* and the functioning of the provincial garrisons. Although the Shamsī *bandagān* carried out periodic incursions into

[97] Ibid., vol. 1, p. 284. Although in the context of Nagaur Jūzjānī did not clarify the functions of the *khwāja*, he was far more specific when he described the administration of Tulak. In Tulak, Jūzjānī noted, the Malik Tāj al-Dīn Muḥammad, son of Quṭb al-Dīn Ḥasan 'Alī Ghurī, was in charge of the armed forces, and Qāẓī Jalāl al-Dīn Majd al-Mulk Aḥmad Uṣmān Hākim Nishāpurī as the *khwaja* (who was also the *mutaṣarif*) was responsible for the administration of the area. See ibid., vol. 2, p. 134. This reference also clarifies that the term *khwāja* referred to an officer whose duties were more specific than that of a general administrator, *mutaṣarif*, and probably more like that of a *mustaufī*, or accountant. This is also evident from the fact that *khwāja* was used much like the titles *qāẓī* and *mustaufī*, as an honorific to indicate certain professional, socially commendable accomplishments of an individual. The best example of such a usage is that of Sultan Mu'izz al-Dīn Bahram Shāh's (637–9/1240–2) *wazīr* Muḥammad 'Iwāz, to whose name Jūzjānī sometimes added the title *mustaufī* and at other times *khwāja* (ibid., vol. 1, pp. 463, 465). Note also the name and title of Malik Bahā' al-Dīn Ai-Beg Khwāja (ibid., p. 482, vol. 2, p. 58). Other than the Sultan, evidently the military notables also appointed *khwājas* as accountants in their own commands (note the example of Hindū Khān's deputy Khwāja Ṣāliḥ mentioned above).

[98] In Ghiyāṣ al-Dīn Balban's reign there is a solitary reference to the presence of the two officers, the *khwāja* and *muqṭi'* within an *iqṭā'*. See Baranī, *Ta'rīkh-i Fīrūz Shāhī*, edited by Khan, p. 36, edited by Rashid, p. 43. Habib (following R.P. Tripathi, *Some Aspects of Muslim Administration*, p. 251) has argued that this might be the first reference to the presence of the accountant (*khwāja*) who was now auditing the collection and expenditure of revenue in (some?) military assignments and perhaps remitting excess sums to Delhi. See Irfan Habib, 'Iqṭā's', p. 70; and Peter Jackson, *The Delhi Sultanate,* p. 100.

the countryside, control over the interior of the provinces, and between the *iqṭā'ṣ* remained in most cases in the hands of local rulers. Although the change from the Mu'izzī to the Shamsī dispensation did not alter the character of Sultanate interventions in the countryside and the military cantonments of the Sultanate still sought to sustain themselves within local circuits of commercial exchange, the military pressure on local chieftains increased through the 1220s. As Jūzjānī's history suggests, campaigns against these chieftains were incessant and they certainly generated considerable revenue as tribute and plunder within the *iqṭā'ṣ*. A unique Shamsī coin from the region of Qanauj celebrated the success of one such engagement that led to the gradual recognition of Sultanate authority in mortgage agreements within the Gāhaḍavāla dominion.[99]

The deployment of the *khwājas* makes sense in this context: they kept an account of the tribute and treasure troves seized by the *muqṭi's* and they were responsible for its subsequent distribution amongst the fighting forces and the notables, as well as for the remission of the fifth portion as *khums* to the Sultan in Delhi. In a reference to the apportioning of plunder, *ghanā'im* (singular, *ghanīma*), and setting aside the fifth, *khums*, for Iltutmish, Jūzjānī noted that the Shamsī slave Malik Tā'īsī's campaign into Kalinjar in 631/1233–4 had netted vast sums of booty—such that in fifty days the Sultan's fifth was noted as 2,500,000 (*tankas?*) [*bīst o panj lak khums Sulṭānī dar qalam āwarad*]. Elsewhere, Jūzjānī contradicted himself and noted that the Sultan's share was 2,200,000 (*tankas?*), [*khums-i*

[99] See Nelson Wright, *The Coinage and Metrology of the Sultans of Delhi*, p. 20, no 52, pp. 71–2. The silver coin dated *circa* 632/1234–5 refers to tribute/plunder gained from the environs of Qanauj, an area which had passed from Mu'izzī to Shamsī control in the beginning of Iltutmish's reign. The marginal estampage on the reverse of the coins reads: '*min kharāj-i Qanauj wa kufr*', and Wright's translation presents the sense correctly 'out of the tax (*kharāj*) levied on Qanauj and infidels'. Wright translated *kharāj* as a capitation tax, synonymous with *jizya*, and more recent research suggests this to be an accurate understanding. See Peter Hardy, 'djizya, Hind', *EI*², s.v., and Irfan Habib, 'Agrarian Taxation', in *The Cambridge Economic History of India*, vol. 1, pp. 60–2. See Chapter 2 for the early history of Sultanate interaction in the area of Qanauj and a review of the epigraphic evidence from the region.

Sulṭānī dar īn muddat nazdīk-i bīst o dū lak ḥāṣil shuda būd].[100] The discrepancy in the figures could make us doubt Jūzjānī's report, but that would miss the value of the author's observations. The fact that Jūzjānī sought to provide a precise monetary figure of the actual *khums* (the seized plunder was not cash; it may have been precious metal or other goods seen as valuta)[101] only lends credibility to the systematic division of booty that was practised and the role of secretaries and accountants in performing the related complex mathematical computations.

It is unlikely that Jūzjānī was recording here a normative juridical statement on the division of spoils amongst Muslims,[102] especially when he had made no such statement in his narrative on Mu'izz al-Dīn, Quṭb al-Dīn Ai-Beg or Bakhtiyār Khalajī. Indeed, he had always been extremely vague when it came to the division of plunder during Mu'izz al-Dīn and Quṭb al-Dīn's reigns and this was probably closer to reality in a situation where subordinates enjoyed considerable autonomy.[103] The movement, towards identifying a formal *khums*, the Sultan's fifth, was a transition where the monarch's claim was more clearly stated and apportioned. While there must have been instances of collusion between the *muqṭi'* and *khwāja*,[104] this does not detract from the intent of the scheme, which implied greater

[100] See Jūzjānī, *Ṭabaqāt-i Nāṣirī*, vol. 2, pp. 11, 62.

[101] See Fakhr-i Mudabbir, *Ādāb al-Ḥarb*, p. 398, who lists horses, camels, cattle, goats, slaves, weapons, and armour as treasure from which *khums* should be set aside for the Sultan before distribution amongst soldiers.

[102] For normative statements on the distribution of war booty written in the north Indian context, see ibid. pp. 398–9; and idem, *Ādāb al-Mulūk wa kifāyat al-Mamlūk*, edited by Muḥammad Sarwar Maulavi (Teheran: Haidari, 1976), p. 23 (on the *mushrif* who apportioned the *khums*). From a later period (*circa* 760/ 1359), see 'Abd al-Ḥamīd Muharrir Ghaznawī, *Dastūr al-Albāb fī 'ilm al-Ḥisāb*, translated by S.A. Rashid, *Medieval India Quarterly*, 1 (1950), pp. 64–5.

[103] Concerning the distribution of plunder after the conquest of Bengal, for example, Jūzjānī noted very generally that Bakhtiyār Khalajī sent a large portion (?) of the plunder to Quṭb al-Dīn Ai-Beg [*az ān ghanā'im wa amwāl-i bisyār bā khidmat-i Sulṭān Quṭb al-Dīn firistād*]. See Jūzjānī, *Ṭabaqāt-i Nāṣirī*, vol. 1, p. 427; and Chapter 2.

[104] For an example from the middle of the thirteenth century see Baranī,

knowledge of the financial resources generated in the *iqṭā'*s and the expenses incurred by military commanders.

These details were crucial for the proportionate division of tribute and spoils amongst the Sultan and those who participated in the campaign. But to accomplish this task the *khwājas* must have also maintained a register of the fighting forces of the *muqṭi'*. Other than musters organized by the Sultan, the provincial commanders also reviewed their forces and occasionally raised extraordinary levees for campaigns which required additional armed personnel. Although evidence of these musters does not exist from Iltutmish's period, Jūzjānī referred to them during the reigns of the Sultan's sons, where they were not described as novel exercises. The office of the *Dīwān-i 'Arẓ-i Mamālik* is mentioned and, on another occasion, the *Ṣāḥib-i Dīwān-i 'Arẓ-i Mamālik* as a reference to individuals responsible for the royal musters.[105] More indirect references exist for occasions when provincial commanders mustered/prepared (*isti'dād*) their forces to participate in campaigns at the direction of Delhi. The evidence for extraordinary levees from the *muqṭi'*s is suggested by Jūzjānī's references to occasions when he recited a *tazkīr*, an exhortation, mobilizing 'people to enrol in the army for fighting with the infidels'.[106] It is consistent with Iltutmish's concerns with military administration to have kept records of his armed forces and certainly Fakhr-i Mudabbir provided a detailed account of how such musters should be organized.[107]

None of these aspects of military governance, not the *bandagān*, the *khwājas*, the *khums*, nor the muster were unique inventions of Shams al-Dīn Iltutmish. They had long histories in the central Islamic lands, and it would be a huge mistake to incarcerate them into a

---

Ta'rīkh-i Fīrūz Shāhī, edited by Khan, pp. 60, 61–4, edited by Rashid, pp. 70, 72–6.

105 Jūzjānī, *Ṭabaqāt-i Nāṣirī*, vol. 1, p. 493, vol. 2, p. 83. He also described two occasions (vol. 2, pp. 75, 83) when the *'arẓ* (muster) was held to impress visitors with the might of the accumulated forces of the Sultanate.

106 Ibid., vol. 2, pp. 70, 76. For a useful interpretation of the *tazkīr* see A.B.M. Habibullah, *The Foundation of Muslim Rule in India*, p. 219; and S.H. Hodivala, *Studies in Indo-Muslim History*, vol. 1, p. 211.

107 Fakhr-i Mudabbir, *Ādāb al-Ḥarb*, pp. 276–80.

Weberian typology that would see in their presence in north India a continuation of 'Muslim' traditions of governance. Iltutmish relied upon methods of governance that were old and familiar but he re-deployed them, just as he used the skills available amongst his personnel to create a state that responded to the challenges of a thirteenth-century post-Shansabanid political milieu seriously disturbed by the Mongol holocaust. It also led to the creation of a Shamsī dispensation of order which was already shifting dramatically from its Mu'izzī precursor.

Although the Shamsī slaves, like the Mu'izzīs, were given commands over territories for long periods of time, and though like the Mu'izzīs the Shamsī *bandagān* possessed a great amount of local initiative, they could not disturb the organization of their master's dispensation of power in ways that Quṭb al-Dīn Ai-Beg had tested in a previous generation. Greater surveillance over the acquisition of plunder, the disbursement to soldiers and remittance of the King's share existed together with dyadic relations to cohere the territories in the charge of the *bandagān* with the 'centre'.

Perhaps the most important distinction between the Mu'izzī and Shamsī regimes related to their dissimilar responses to members of the royal family. While the Mu'izzī *bandagān* were deployed to protect the Sultan's territories and exclude members of the Shansabanid family, the Shamsī slaves were expected to serve the monarch and his sons. Although his notables occupied some of the highest and most powerful positions in the state, they were still slaves whose inferior position to the members of the master's family was underlined in a variety of ways. And yet, in the long term there was a contradiction between reliance upon *bandagān*, by definition a 'one-generation-nobility', and dynastic succession, which implied a fresh dispensation of power under the new monarch. The contradictions in this structure of political relationships were apparent after the death of Quṭb al-Dīn Ai-Beg, when the Quṭbī dispensation fragmented in favour of different candidates. The problem would recur again with the death of Iltutmish, because the Delhi Sultan clearly envisaged the continuance of power within his family and associated his adult sons in the governance of his principality. While the deployment of the Shamsī *bandagān* and the Princes served the immediate purpose of consolidating Iltutmish's power in relation to his rivals, the slaves and Iltutmish's sons had divergent long-term interests which drew them into eventual conflict.

(c) *The Deployment of the Shamsī Princes*

We are less then well informed about Iltutmish's descendants, and even the list of the Sultan's sons provided by Jūzjānī is not present in all the manuscripts of the *Ṭabaqāt-i Nāṣirī*. The Shamsī lineage presented in Chart 2 accounts for Iltutmish's descendants into the third generation. In all probability the genealogy is less than comprehensive, especially with regard to the Sultan's daughters.[108] Yet, on the basis of the information provided by Jūzjānī, a reconstruction of the deployment and role of the Shamsī Princes during Iltutmish's reign can be attempted.

At least superficially there was a similarity in the deployment of the royal Princes and the Shamsī *bandagān*. Like the slaves of the monarch, the Princes were entrusted with territorial commands in the most strategic areas of the Delhi Sultanate. Again, in conformity with the practice followed with slaves, these commands were not given in perpetuity; Iltutmish periodically reorganized the principalities under the responsibility of the royal Princes. Iltutmish's oldest son, Nāṣir al-Dīn Maḥmūd, for example, was given the charge of Lahore in 614/1217, when Shamsī control was hardly confirmed over the region. He was subsequently given Hansi, and then moved to Awadh in 623/1226.[109] In 624/1227 Prince Nāṣir al-Dīn captured Lakhnauti and was appointed Governor of the province until his death in 628/1230.[110] Similarly Rukn al-Dīn was given the command of Budaun in 625/1228 and was moved to Lahore in 631/1233, which he governed until

[108] The manuscript used by Habibi did not include the list of the Sultan's sons. Habibi, however, incorporated this information in a footnote. See Jūzjānī, *Ṭabaqāt-i Nāṣirī*, vol. 1, pp. 451, fn. 6; and idem, translated by Raverty, vol. 1, p. 625. For one reference to a daughter of Iltutmish, see Jūzjānī, *Ṭabaqāt-i Nāṣirī*, edited by Habibi, vol. 1, p. 463, where a uterine sister [*hum-shir*], of Mu'izz al-Dīn Bahrām Shāh is mentioned in the narrative only because of her husband's opposition to the reigning Sultan.

[109] Jūzjānī, *Ṭabaqāt-i Nāṣirī*, vol. 1, p. 453.

[110] Ibid., pp. 438, 447, 454.

Chart 2: The Shamsī Lineage

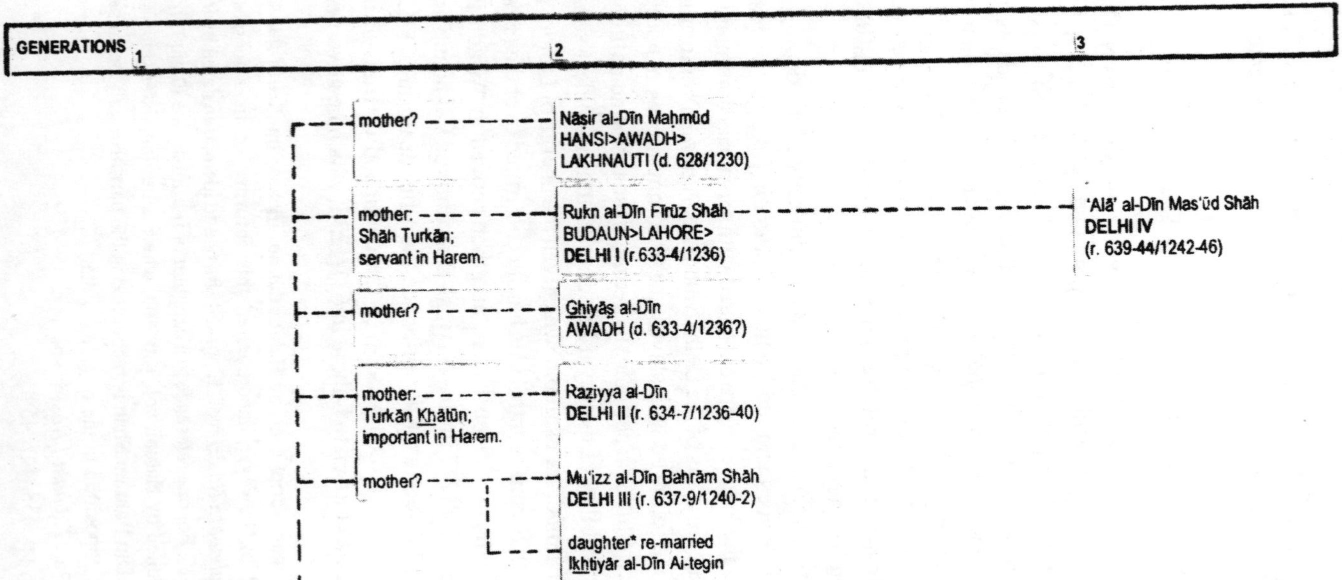

Continued on Next Page

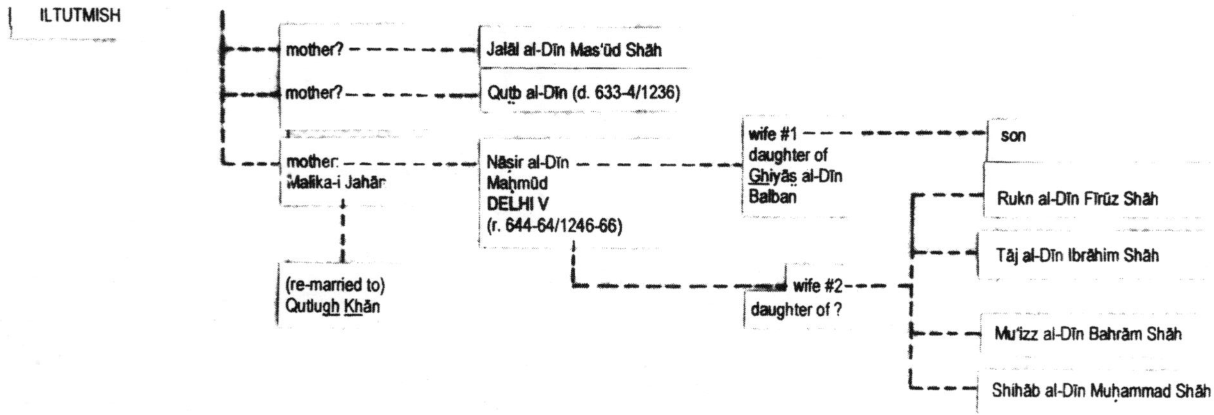

NOTE:

DELHI I etc.:	Indicates sequence of succession to the throne of Delhi.
* :	Indicates marriage.
mother:	Indicates the wives of Iltutmish and the mother of his children.
AWADH etc:	Indicates commands given by Iltutmish to his sons. No subsequent appointments are shown on this chart.
d.:	Date of death.
r.:	Regnal years.

633/1236.[111] We have uncertain information about the administrative charges held by the other descendants of Iltutmish. Jūzjānī does suggest that Prince Ghiyāṣ al-Dīn was old enough for military command by 633/1236, when he seized treasures from Lakhnauti bound for Delhi. In that year Ghiyāṣ al-Dīn either had the command of Awadh or of a neighbouring region.[112]

The social and political prestige that accrued to members of the royal lineage were, however, clearly different from that of the *bandagān*. The military slaves had close, individualized relationships with the master and although there may have been variations in the military strength and responsibilities possessed by the various slaves, the Sultan sought to create fraternal bonds between the *bandagān* where there was no element of social seniority. While both the older Princes must have possessed their own personal subordinates and military retinues like the *bandagān-i khāṣṣ*,[113] in a clearer departure from privileges given to military slaves the Princes were given occasional commands over other notables of the realm in addition to their territorial charges. The seniority of the royal lineage was clearly in evidence when the Governor of Awadh, Prince Nāṣir al-Dīn, was given supervisory powers over notables appointed in the Bihar corridor. It was for this reason that Malik 'Alā' al-Dīn Jānī appealed to

[111] Ibid., p. 454.

[112] Ibid., vol. 1, p. 455. The sequence of events mentioned by Jūzjānī, vol. 2, pp. 12–13, concerning the appointment of the slave Nuṣrat al-Dīn to the command of Awadh, *circa* 634/1236, suggests that the Malik was appointed to Awadh only after the death of Prince Ghiyāṣ al-Dīn. This would suggest that Ghiyāṣ al-Dīn did hold charge of Awadh in the last years of Iltutmish's reign. A few of the other children were too young to be given independent commands or, like the daughter Raẓiyya, stayed in Delhi. Some young Princes might have stayed with their mothers in neighbouring garrisons. The 'junior' Nāṣir al-Dīn was brought up by his mother in the small town, *qaṣaba*, of Luni near Delhi (ibid., vol. 1, p. 472).

[113] See ibid., vol. 1, p. 490, vol. 2, p. 29, where the author mentions Malik Beg Timur Orkhān-i Ruknī who, as his *nisba* of affiliation (*Ruknī*) suggests, must have been a slave of Rukn al-Dīn. There is no way to ascertain, however, if Malik Beg Timur had been acquired while Rukn al-Dīn was Prince or Sultan. Logically, however, if Shamsī *bandagān-i khāṣṣ* organised their independent military retinues, one would expect Shamsī Princes to have done the same.

the Prince for help when attacked by Sultan Ghiyāṣ al-Dīn 'Iwaz of Lakhnauti.[114] It is also from the 624/1227 campaign into Lakhnauti that we have evidence of Shamsī notables being ordered by the Sultan to serve under his son. Jūzjānī noted that the troops of Hindustan were placed under the Prince at the command of Iltutmish, together with famous notables, *mulūk-i nāmdār*, like Bulan and Malik 'Alā' al-Dīn Jānī.[115] In this sense, the royal Princes were additional 'agents' used by Iltutmish to consolidate his authority over dispersed provinces, neutralize competitors, and provide a check on the conduct of subordinates.

It is important to bear in mind, however, that while Iltutmish conceded that his sons should receive territorial commands, these commands were never organized as autonomous appanages. Iltutmish was the eponymous progenitor of the Shamsī lineage and his seniority was not disputed by any kinsman of his generation. As a result, the Delhi Sultan avoided the problems of a fragmented dominion where power was shared within a corporate kin group. Nor did he favour the development of these traditions. Because of the frequent reorganization of the territorial charges under Nāṣir al-Dīn and Rukn al-Dīn, none of his sons could claim a geographical portion of his father's dominion as his share of the inheritance; unlike the Shansabanid Sultanate of Ghur, the Sultanate of Delhi was not apportioned amongst the Princes.

Instead, without diminishing the prestige of the imperial lineage, Iltutmish emphasized a horizontal integration within his dispensation where rights and privileges emanated from the Sultan. The Delhi Sultan deliberately sought to create close ties between some of his important subordinates and his elder sons in an effort to enhance cohesion within the Shamsī dispensation, and perhaps strike a balance between its important constituent elements. The slave Tāj al-Dīn (number 1 in Table 1) was bonded to the elder Nāṣir al-Dīn through the experience of being brought up and fostered, *parwarish*, together.[116] When Rukn al-Dīn was entrusted with the charge of

[114] Ibid., p. 438.
[115] Ibid., p. 453.
[116] Ibid., vol. 2, p. 4.

Budaun he was also given the experienced *wazīr* 'Ain al-Mulk Ḥusain Ash'arī as a guide.[117] Although Jūzjānī presented no further information on the fate of 'Ain al-Mulk, it is likely that the notable Bahā'ī al-Mulk Ḥusain Ash'arī, who served Rukn al-Dīn when he became Sultan, was an associate of the erstwhile *wazīr*.[118]

The position of the royal Princes in relation to other members of the Shamsī dispensation and the Sultan can be clarified by a comparative study of their respective titles. The eulogistic inscription on the doorway of Nāṣir al-Dīn's mausoleum, inscribed no doubt with Iltutmish's approval, referred to the Prince as the Malik of Maliks of the East, *Malik-i Mulūk al-Sharq*.[119] While *Malik al-Sharq* was a traditional encomium, the inscription clarified further that the status of the Prince, as 'Malik of Maliks', had been senior to the other notables of the Sultan. One such notable was the slave Farrukh, who extolled himself as *Iftikhār al-Umarā' al-Mulūk al-Sharq*, or the 'Glory of the Amirs and the Maliks of the East'.[120] In effect, the slave Farrukh claimed that while being one of a body of Amirs and Maliks,

[117] Ibid., vol. 1, p. 453. 'Ain al-Mulk's role may well have been that of a tutor-father. Similar roles had been played by other *wazīrs* in the Islamic world. Closest to time and space to the Delhi Sultanate is the example of the Seljuqid *wazīr*, Niẓām al-Mulk, and his relationship of *atābeg* (father-commander) to the Sultans Alp Arsalān (455–65/1063–72) and Malik Shāh (465–85/1072–92). For the relationship between the Barmakid *wazīrs* and the early 'Abbāsid Caliphs, see S.D. Goitein, 'The Origin of the Vizierate and Its True Character', in idem, *Studies in Islamic History and Institutions* (Leiden: E.J. Brill, 1968), pp. 168–96. Goitein emphasized that the term *wazīr* meant 'burden-bearer', 'helper' and 'assistant', which would be closer to the sense in which Jūzjānī uses the word. 'Minister', 'finance minister', or 'prime minister' reify the functions and role of the subordinate and endow the term an extremely inaccurate, anachronistic meaning.

[118] For a reference to Bahā'ī al-Mulk Ḥusain Ash'arī, see Jūzjānī, *Ṭabaqāt-i Naṣīrī*, vol. 1, p. 456.

[119] J. Horowitz, 'The Inscriptions of Muḥammad ibn Sam, Qutubuddin Aibeg and Iltutmish', p. 24, no. 22, Plate XVI, no. 1 (inscription on the gateway, tomb of 'Sultan Ghari', Malikpur); and S.A.A. Naqvi, 'Sultan Ghari, Delhi', p. 5.

[120] J. Horowitz, 'The Inscriptions of Muḥammad ibn Sam', p. 23, no. 20, Plate XXVIII (inscription on the northern wall of the courtyard of the Sayyid Wara mosque, Bilgram).

he was the most glorious. While the publicly proclaimed status of the Prince was senior to that of Farrukh, both the Maliks still operated and identified themselves on separate levels as (great) notables within the Shamsī dispensation of Maliks and Amirs. If there were any uncertainties about seniority in this order, Iltutmish allayed all doubts by personally claiming the title Sultan of the East, *Sulṭān al-Sharq*.[121] The singularity of Iltutmish's position rested on the fact that he was not the Sultan of the Sultans of the East; according to Iltutmish he was a Sultan without peer.

It was consistent with Iltutmish's concern to maintain a united domain that he strove to overcome divisive tensions which could originate over the question of succession to the throne of Delhi. In 626/1229, at the height of his power, Iltutmish sent one of the robes he had received from the Caliph together with a red parasol to Nāṣir al-Dīn, then Governor of Lakhnauti, and recognized him as his heir to the Delhi Sultanate. Two facts need to be noted here: first, in nominating Nāṣir al-Dīn as heir, Iltutmish confirmed that he did not envisage a division of the Delhi Sultanate; Nāṣir al-Dīn was the future Sultan of Delhi, and not Bengal. Second, the recognition of Nāṣir al-Dīn as the heir to Delhi implied subsidiary positions for the Sultan's other sons. While Iltutmish's second son, Rukn al-Dīn, continued as Governor of Budaun, his position as subordinate to Nāṣir al-Dīn was evident in that he only received a green parasol.[122]

As it turned out, Nāṣir al-Dīn predeceased Iltutmish in 628/1230, but this did not detract the Sultan from his attempt to resolve all ambiguities concerning succession to the Delhi throne. Jūzjānī suggests that Iltutmish's subsequent choice of successor was Raẓiyya, his eldest daughter. But just before his death in 633/1236, it is clear that Iltutmish had settled upon Rukn al-Dīn as his heir apparent and brought the Prince to Delhi from Lahore to ensure a smooth transition of power.[123]

Unlike the crisis in the Lahore–Delhi appanage with the death of Quṭb al-Dīn in 607/1210, when the very existence of the principality

[121] Ibid., p. 30, no. 32, Plate XXIII (inscription on the central arch, *Arhāī din kā Jhonprā*, Ajmer).

[122] Jūzjānī, *Ṭabaqāt-i Nāṣirī*, vol. 1, p. 454.

[123] Ibid., pp. 454–5, 458 and Chapter 5 for further details.

was in doubt let alone the hoary problems of succession, one would not have expected the death of Iltutmish to plunge members of the Shamsī dispensation into mutual conflict. Iltutmish had after all subordinated competing Sultanates in north India, placed his own subordinates in command, and designated his heir before his death. Yet the members of the Shamsī dispensation failed to provide support to Iltutmish's successors. They envisaged a role for themselves which was substantially different from that of a mere prop to the sons of their master.

Conclusion

The state of the existing evidence makes it impossible to graph the transition in power from the Sultanates of north India to the paramountcy of the Delhi Sultanate. We are especially poorly informed on the reactions of the regional military elites to their conquest. Certainly by the late 1220s, with Iltutmish's string of political and military successes, the resources available to the Delhi Sultan's competitors started to decline. Diminishing resources would be suggested if, for example, a political authority was forced to divest itself of strategically crucial assets to raise money. That this was indeed the response of Iltutmish's Mu'izzī competitors can be inferred from the example of Naṣīr al-Dīn Ḥusain Amīr-i Shikār's heirs who were forced to sell their father's slave Kabīr Khān Ayāz to Iltutmish. In similar fashion, the successors of Bahā' al-Dīn Tughril, Sultan of Bayana, sold their father's slaves Naṣīr al-Dīn Ai-Tamar and 'Izz al-Dīn Tughril to the Delhi Sultan.[124] Trained slaves commanded an excellent price and while their sale might have helped in overcoming the immediate financial difficulties of Naṣīr al-Dīn's and Bahā' al-Dīn's successors, this must have been achieved only at the cost of a diminished military potential. In this context the fact that the military slaves were purchased by none other than the Delhi Sultan, the main competitor of Naṣīr al-Dīn and Bahā' al-Dīn, suggests not merely that Iltutmish possessed the financial resources to mop up the *bandagān* retinues of his competitors, but also that these opponents could be pressurised to sell their slaves to him.

[124] See Table 1 and Jūzjānī, *Ṭabaqāt-i Nāṣirī*, vol. 2, pp. 5, 7, and vol. 1, p. 451 for the reference to 'Izz al-Dīn Tughril.

By the 1230s the primacy of Iltutmish in the political world in and around the urban centres of north India was complete. Unquestionably, this was made possible by a period of slow conquests (including reversals no doubt, although these are glossed over) and the deployment of military slaves as an exclusive corps of dependants over newly annexed territories. The free military commanders were also a large element within Iltutmish's body of subordinates, but few of them were elevated to positions of political authority primarily because their dependence upon the Sultan was suspect. Although lacking an administrative system in the bureaucratic, anachronistic sense of the term, Iltutmish possessed extreme control over his subordinates and was to the end capable of manipulating their careers.

There is little doubt about the fact that Iltutmish dispensed hierarchy and political status to such individuals as he chose while he reigned, a prerogative which he wished his sons to inherit. But the inherent tensions within such an enforced political regime, although ignored by Jūzjānī and other chroniclers, were certainly present and became explicit in their narration of events after the death of the Sultan. To some extent, the presence of simmering hostilities and the yearning for lost office can be traced in the manner in which disgraced notables like 'Alā' al-Dīn Jānī and Kabir Khān Ayāz quickly manipulated themselves back to prominence after Iltutmish's death. Similarly, the exclusion from power of émigrés such as Quṭb al-Dīn Ḥasan Ghūrī during Iltutmish's reign seems hardly to have been successful in delimiting their political and social power bases; soon after Iltutmish's death many free military commanders possessed sufficient support to become an important group in the conflict for political power.

The social and political dimensions of the conflict in the post-Shamsī period will be dealt with more fully in the fifth chapter. More relevant at this stage is to draw attention to another important change which had occurred between 607/1210 and 633/1236, to developments which were best contrasted by Jūzjānī. In 607/1210 he had noted the presence of four contending dominions in north India: Ghazni, Sindh, Delhi, and Lakhnauti. *Circa* 635/1237, two lunar years after Iltutmish's death, Jūzjānī presented an astonishing mental map of the Delhi Sultanate. The author noted that in Sultan Raẓiyya's reign (634–7/1236–40), 'the kingdom was at peace [*ārām girift*], and the extent of the state apparent [*daulat rā bastat ẓāhir shud*], and from the domain of Lakhnauti to Diwal [*az mamālik-i Lakhnautī wa Diwal*] all the Maliks and Amirs submitted [*hama Mulūk wa Umarā' inqiyād namūdand*].'[125]

Jūzjānī credited Sultan Iltutmish with the creation of an integrated dominion, consisting of urban centres and their adjoining environs linked to each other by overland routes. In his statement there was an implied link between the consolidation of a dominion and the submission of local notabies to the authority of Delhi, measures which, as we have seen in this chapter, Iltutmish accomplished during his reign. Yet it does need to be remembered that the north Indian Sultanates conquered by Iltutmish had built up successful material and political bases for themselves, and the Delhi Sultan's major definitive conquests—that of Sindh and Lakhnauti—dated only from 625/1228, which was very late in his reign. Despite the political integration of these provinces with the Delhi Sultanate in the last eight years of Iltutmish's reign, it is apposite to question whether this integration was sufficient to diminish longer established regional identities. Surely creating the idea of a contiguous Sultanate of Delhi had to depend upon more than just political subordination of the north Indian Sultanates and their control through trustworthy slave subordinates.

It is important to recognize that Iltutmish's achievements of conquest and consolidation were significant because they coincided with far-reaching structural transformations in eastern Iran and Afghanistan. As north India was coming under a paramount military power, the societies of the central Islamic lands were suffering dislocation and destruction because of the campaigns of Jalāl al-Dīn Khwārazm Shāh and then Chingīz Khān. The increasing migration of displaced Muslims from Iran and Afghanistan into the urban settlements of north India implied that a large number of émigré elites had little sense of regional loyalties. Excluding the military commanders, who were indeed recruited in the various Sultanates and therefore had a stake in their preservation, for the larger number of émigrés physical security and productive commercial relationships were more immediate concerns which the campaigns of Delhi did not threaten. More

[125] Jūzjānī, *Ṭabaqāt-i Nāṣirī*, vol. 1, p. 459.

significantly, the response of the leaders and opinion-makers amongst the Muslim community, the *ahl-i qalam* (people of the pen) and piety-minded Muslims, to the trauma of their dispersal from their homelands made them anxious to promote a composite character for the Muslim community in north India. A large number of them accepted grants and positions of public responsibility from Iltutmish, and they did provide ideological support to the ideal of a unitary domain for the faithful. Jūzjānī's map of a politically contiguous Delhi Sultanate during Raẓiyya's reign may have been hyperbole, but, in imagining such a geographic configuration at all, it is worth investigating if Jūzjānī was representing a view formulated and disseminated by people of his background.[126]

Together with (an uneven) political integration of the lands between 'Lakhnauti and Diwal' there were other forces at work which made the notion of a contiguous domain meaningful to Jūzjānī's readership. The next chapter explores the nature of the change which occurred in the Muslim society of north India in the early thirteenth century, and of the agents involved in creating the *idea* of an entity such as the Delhi Sultanate.

[126] It is surprising, for instance, that 'Iṣāmī writing a century and a half after Iltutmish should share Jūzjānī's estimation of the Delhi Sultan's accomplishment in establishing a unitary dominion encompassing much of north India. See 'Iṣāmī, *Futūḥ al-Salāṭīn*, pp. 115–16, 124. This is particularly interesting for 'Isāmī was writing his history in the rival Deccani Bahamanid court and had no reason to present a flattering picture of the court of the Delhi Sultan as the sanctuary and axis of Islam in India. The author noted (pp. 115–16) that the city of Delhi profited from the number of immigrants from the central Islamic lands and was purified by the sacred *zamzam* waters from Mecca, which were mixed with the waters of the reservoir constructed by the Sultan (*ḥauẓ-i Sulṭānī*). The image of the Delhi Sultanate extending from the Bay of Bengal to the Indus river is also mentioned on p. 124.

CHAPTER 4

The *'Ulamā'* and the Emergence of Delhi as the Sanctuary and Axis of Islam in North India

The defeat and death of Qubācha in 625/1228 may well be regarded as a turning point in the making of the Delhi Sultanate. Other than the fact that the death of the Sultan of Sindh marked the removal of Iltutmish's most powerful adversary, the mid-620s/1220s was also the time when increasing number of refugees fled the central Islamic lands in the face of Mongol raids. Eastern Iran, Khwarazm, and Afghanistan had already felt the brunt of their plundering campaigns, but in the mid-1220s the Mongols also made their presence felt in the Indus plain and Sindh. The establishment of a politically paramount Sultanate in north India with its headquarters in Delhi coincided with the influx of migrants from the neighbouring urban centres of Muslim culture and civilization. Because of the new political realignment in north India and the Mongol 'push', émigrés increasingly moved towards eastern Punjab and the Gangetic plain. Although there is no quantitative evidence through which one can judge the actual growth in population, this increase is suggested by the fact that old towns such as Budaun, Baran, and Kara became more important, and that there were increasing references to settlements such as Sirsa, Nagaur, Patiali, and Maihar.

The character and nature of the growth of urban settlements in north India was strongly influenced by the overwhelming military character of Sultanate society and the prominence of the military elite. The small urban settlements referred to as *qaṣabāt* (singular, *qaṣaba*) in the early-thirteenth-century literature, for example, did not possess the commercial, rural-urban market functions which were to become among their distinguishing characteristics at a later time period. Nor did the term contain the connotations of 'chief town' ascribed to it in the Maghreb and north Africa. In this period the *qaṣaba* was a fortified encampment, sometimes independent, at other times associated with a town with military subordinates of the Sultan or his commanders.[1] It is therefore not surprising that one way to trace the transformation of a *qaṣaba* into a town (*shahr*) is by following the careers of Shamsī military commanders. During Mu'izz al-Dīn's reign, Baran (modern Bulandshahr), was described as a *qaṣaba* when Iltutmish received its charge.[2] During Iltutmish's reign two *bandagān-i Shamsī* were appointed to Baran (numbers 4 and 20 in Table 1). The subsequent rise to importance of the *qaṣaba* can be gauged from the frequent appointment of Shamsī slaves to the town between the years 633/1236 and 644/1246.[3] Already by 644/1246 Baran was important enough for its commander, Malik Ikit Khān (number 16 in Table 3), to possess a prominence enabling his appointment as *wakīl-i dar*, or deputy in the court of Sultan Nāṣir al-Dīn Maḥmūd (644–64/1246–66). This appointment was no accident; subsequent to Ikit Khān, in 654/1256, another commander from Baran, Malik Tāj al-Dīn Sanjar Tarkhān, was appointed *wakīl-i dar* (number 17 in Table 3). The *qaṣaba* must have grown to become a relatively important urban centre with its command, by the middle of

[1] For the connotations of 'chief town' ascribed to the *qaṣaba* in the Maghreb and north Africa, see G. Deverdun, 'Ḳaṣaba', *EI*[2] s.v. In the early thirteenth century both the *qaṣaba* and the *shahr* shared military–administrative functions. This was evident in the case of the *qaṣaba* of Luni which also possessed a fort, *qil'a* (Jūzjānī, *Ṭabaqāt-i Nāṣirī*, vol. 1, p. 472) and subordinates of the military commander. Note Jūzjānī's description (Jūzjānī, vol. 2, p. 61) of his journey through the *wilāyat* of Ulugh Khān (in 647–8/1249–50), during which the author received aid from subordinates of Ulugh Khān who were resident in each *qaṣaba*, *shahr*, and *qil'a*. According to Jūzjānī (vol. 2, p. 5), in Iltutmish's reign his slave Kabīr Khān Ayāz was given command of the town and citadel of Multan and its associated towns and regions: *shahr wa ḥiṣār-i Multan wa qaṣabāt wa aṭrāf wa nawāḥ-i ān*.

[2] Jūzjānī, *Ṭabaqāt-i Nāṣirī*, vol. 1, p. 443.

[3] See numbers 1 [illegible]4, 15, 16 in Table 3, Chapter 5.

the thirteenth century, being given to two of the more important military commanders in the Delhi Sultanate.

Although historians now regard increases in population and urbanization as indicators of historical change and 'progress', the agents of this transformation in the early thirteenth century—the military elite—were not universally appreciated by their contemporaries. Both Jūzjānī and the *ṣūfī* Niẓām al-Dīn Awliyā' recognized the role of military personnel and the patronage of the Sultan as an important ingredient in the process of urbanization, yet in contrast with Jūzjānī, Niẓām al-Dīn's response to the activities of the ruling elite was entirely negative. He described Ghiyāṣpur, his choice of residence, as an unknown, sparsely populated village [*mauẓa'ī majhūl būd wa khalq andak*].[4] According to Niẓām al-Dīn, with Kaiqubād's (686–9/1287–90) establishment of a fort and residence in the neighbouring region of Kīlūkhrī, the coming and going of notables to the Sultan's court commenced, a city and congregational mosque were constructed. And since Ghiyāṣpur was close by, the number of visitors to see the Shaykh also increased. Niẓām al-Dīn complained that, because the Sultan's residence was in Kīlūkhrī, Ghiyāṣpur also became uncomfortably busy and loud, until its bustle almost drove him away.[5]

While Niẓām al-Dīn's was an entirely personal, and perhaps deliberately exaggerated, response to the disturbance introduced in his environment by the existing political regime,[6] his comments nevertheless draw attention to the need to study the reaction of local Muslim

[4] Amīr Ḥasan Sijzī, *Fawā'id al-Fu'ād*, p. 243. Compare Niẓām al-Dīn's comments with the fulsome praise of Jūzjānī, *Ṭabaqāt-i Nāṣirī*, vol. 1, p. 421 (for Bahā' al-Dīn Tughril and Bayana), p. 436 (for Ḥusām al-Dīn 'Iwaz and Basankot-Lakhnauti), pp. 440–1 (for Shams al-Dīn Iltutmish and Delhi), and vol. 2, p. 52 (for Ulugh Khān and the *iqṭā'* of Hansi).

[5] Amīr Ḥasan Sijzī, *Fawā'id al-Fu'ād*, pp. 242-3. See also Amīr Khwurd, *Siyar al-Awliyā'*, pp. 110–11. Niẓām al-Dīn's experience of moving his residence to Kīlūkhrī was also repeated by Ḥāmid Faẓl Allāh Jamālī, *Siyar al-'Ārifīn* (Delhi: Rizwi Press, 1311/1893), pp. 63–4.

[6] Niẓām al-Dīn's account of his decision to move to Ghiyāṣpur was faithfully reproduced in all later *ṣūfī* biographical compilations. All of these note that Ghiyāṣpur was a wilderness and that Kīlūkhrī prospered after Sultan Kaiqubād's decision to live there. Ẓiyā' al-Dīn Baranī, *Ta'rīkh-i Fīrūz Shāhī*, edited by Khan, p. 130, edited by Rashid, p. 151, describes the increase in population and prosperity of Kīlūkhrī in similar fashion. Kīlūkhrī, however, had already been

communities to the political structures of governance constructed by the Delhi Sultans. We are still quite unaware whether, or to what extent, or in which manner, local urban Muslim communities supported or participated in the political life of the Delhi Sultanate. Especially during the years of rapid political and demographic change concurrent with the reign of Iltutmish, not merely were new regions conquered but large numbers of Muslims were also very recent migrants into the Delhi Sultan's domains. Together with dispensing power to carefully considered notables, Iltutmish sought to integrate local Muslim urban communities into a homogeneous body of the Delhi Sultanate. Iltutmish's success in this endeavour is debatable, and we will have more to say about it later in this chapter. But 'actual' success or failure notwithstanding, the very presence of a map of a contiguous territory in the Delhi Sultanate by the end of Iltutmish's reign suggests the introduction of a new idea which few would have found acceptable at the beginning of the Sultan's reign. In fact, together with the absence of any political unity, it was the lack of homogeneity between rulers and the ruled, and within the Muslim community which was most obvious during the better part of Iltutmish's reign.

Ethnic Differences within the Muslim Community in North India

In the previous chapters we have seen how, with Mu'izz al-Dīn's campaigns and the subsequent consolidation of his conquests under his subordinates, there was an increase in the number of individuals of Turkish background in positions of power and influence in north India. Until the 620s/1220s, and the Chingīz Khanid invasions in eastern Iran and Afghanistan, most of the Turks were military slaves, many of the older ones being the elite *bandagān-i khāṣṣ*. Subsequently, free Amirs of Turkish origin also made their way into north India,

---

a fortified residence of Sultan Rukn al-Dīn Fīrūz (633–4/1236); see Jūzjānī, *Ṭabaqāt-i Nāṣirī*, vol. 1, p. 456. Although the 'new city' certainly declined after that monarch's death, it is unlikely that Kīlūkhrī relapsed to become quite the desolate place described by Niẓām al-Dīn Awliyā' and others (for a reference to Kīlūkhrī in 655/1257–8, see ibid., p. 493). This exaggeration was useful to emphasize Niẓām al-Dīn's own spiritual and ascetic personality.

although few of them received influential commands: the *bandagān-i khāṣṣ* continuing as favoured subordinates. In short, by the end of Iltutmish's reign the influence of the Turkish *bandagān* on the political structure of the Sultanate was disproportionate with their number and social status.

Although these Turks had undergone the trauma of natal alienation and, as part of their training, had been introduced to the Islamic creed and the decorums of court, they retained their Turkish ethnicity. This was to be expected, for they had only just been uprooted from their homes in the Central Asian steppes. Fakhr-i Mudabbir, whose *Ta'rīkh* has a large section on the Turks, never travelled in central Asia. Much of his information must have been culled from travellers and merchants, but parts of the author's observation on languages, scripts, and religious beliefs of the Turks came either from direct observation or were received firsthand from Turks in north India.[7] Fakhr-i Mudabbir's account suggests that, in the first decade of the thirteenth century, the Turks maintained their racial affinity in north India and retained at least some elements of their cultural identity. This is also suggested by the fact that in this period Turkish was a flourishing language in the Delhi Sultanate. Fakhr-i Mudabbir explained that

> after the Persian language [*tāzī*] none is finer and more dignified [*bahtar wa bā-haibattar*], than Turkish. And now-a-days the Turkish language is more popular than it ever was before [*imroz rughbat-i mardmān bazabān-i Turkī besh az ān ast*]. This is due to the fact that the majority of Amirs and Commanders [*sipahsalārān*] are Turks. And it is the Turks who are most successful and most wealthy; and so all have need of that [language] [*wa daulat baīshān ast wa naᶜmat wa zar wa sīm dar dast-i īshān ast, wa jumla'i khalā'iq ra badān hājat ast*]. And grandees of the highest pedigree [*asīlān wa buzurgān wa buzurg-zādgān*], are in the service of the Turks . . . [and from their success derive] . . . peace, prosperity and honour . . .[8]

[7] See Fakhr-i Mudabbir, *Ta'rīkh-i Fakhr al-Dīn Mubārak Shāh*, pp. 38–42, where the description of Turkistān was probably culled from the reports of travellers and merchants. The account of the language, poetry, and religious beliefs, pp. 43–6, is fleshed out by the information received from émigrés.

[8] Ibid., pp. 43–4. I have followed E.D. Ross's translation of this passage,

Other than suggesting that the Turks maintained a composite racial, cultural, and linguistic identity, Fakhr-i Mudabbir also noted the social and political prominence of this group in north India. That this prominence led 'the grandees of the highest pedigree' to seek patronage from the powerful Turkish lords of the realm is also interesting. But Fakhr-i Mudabbir's statement is particularly significant because it draws our attention to the considerable distance which separated the lords from the members of the realm that they governed, so much so that Persian-speaking secretaries had to master a 'foreign' language to function as their subordinates. Fakhr-i Mudabbir's statement should not be taken to mean that the Turkish slaves of the Delhi Sultans knew no Persian (see for example, the case of the Turk slave Malik Saif al-Dīn who functioned as a judge and must have known at least some Persian and Arabic), but that, in the early Delhi Sultanate, for a Persian subordinate to prosper in a Turk's service knowledge of the Turkish language would be an advantage.[9]

Turkish ethnicity was to some extent deliberately preserved in north India amongst the Turk *bandagān* by the Delhi Sultans, who were themselves Turks. As part of the process of divesting old relationships and creating new identities and bonds for the slaves, the *bandagān* were renamed by the Sultans. Rather than giving Turkish slaves Muslim names or naming them after Persian folk heroes, the slaves were, without exception, given new Turkish names by Quṭb al-Dīn and Iltutmish. Quṭb al-Dīn gave his slave Ai-Beg, a compatriot of Iltutmish, the name Tamghaj, and all the Turk *bandagān-i Shamsī*

---

barring minor modifications. See E.D. Ross, 'The Genealogies of Fakhr-ud-Dīn, Mubārak Shāh', p. 405.

[9] For the details on Malik Saif al-Dīn, see Jūzjānī, *Ṭabaqāt-i Nāṣirī*, vol. 2, pp. 40–2. The later testimony of Amīr Khusrau confirms Fakhr-i Mudabbir's observations on the efforts by the *Tāziks* to learn Turkish. See Amīr Khusrau, *Dībācha-i Dīwān Ghurrat al-Kamāl*, edited by Sayyid Ali Haidar (Patna: Institute of Postgraduate Studies and Research in Arabic and Persian Learning, 1988), p. 40: 'I have seen many Persians, not Turks [*chandīn tāzik na Turk*], who have learnt Turkish studiously and industriously [*bata'allum wa kasb*], in Hindustan. And they speak [Turkish thus] that [when] the eloquent speakers of that language [*fuṣaḥā'-yi ān ṭā'ifa*], come from [Turkistan; *az bālā baāmadand*, literally: 'come from the upper lands'], they are astonished [*firo-māndand'*].

mentioned in Jūzjānī's twenty-second section were given Turkish names and titles by Sultan Shams al-Dīn Iltutmish.[10]

What seems to have prevailed in the early Delhi Sultanate was a phenomenon similar to the one described by David Ayalon for the Mamlūks of Egypt. There, the Turkish slaves 'attached supreme importance to the name-barrier . . . [which separated] . . . them from the local Muslim population. . . . [It] served as an almost watertight proof of their belonging to the Mamlūk ruling class and as a most distinctive mark of their superiority over all outsiders.'[11] There is much to commend Ayalon's analysis: the systems of military slavery in north India and Egypt were similar inasmuch as the *bandagān* in both regions were an exclusive, deracinated military elite which controlled power and privilege. Unlike the Mamlūks of Egypt, however monopolistic control of power within the *bandagān* corps in the Delhi Sultanate was not based solely upon a shared Turkish ethnicity. All Shamsī *bandagān-i khāṣṣ*, Turk and non-Turk, had a close rapport with the Delhi Sultan. A shared Turkish ethnicity served to establish an additional bond between the Turk *bandagān-i khāṣṣ* (who were in

[10] On Ai-Beg/Tamghaj see Jūzjānī, *Ṭabaqāt-i Nāṣirī*, vol. 1, pp. 442–3; on the Shamsī slaves refer to Chapter 3, Table 1, bearing in mind the fact that large numbers of the titles mentioned by Jūzjānī were given to the Shamsī slaves by Iltutmish's successors. Balban, for example, received the title Ulugh Khān, the 'Great Khān', only in 647/1249 (Jūzjānī, vol. 2, p. 60), and we have no information concerning his earlier name or title. It is also important to remember that in Turko-Mongol usage the title 'Khān' was reserved only for a member of the imperial lineage and Jūzjānī seems to have been aware that the appropriation of this title was, strictly speaking, a usurpation of 'royal' privileges. He narrated a long story of doubtful authenticity to legitimize Balban's title. In this story the great Il-Khanid monarch, Hūlāgū (654–63/1256–65), out of respect for Balban's achievements, approved of the Shamsī slave's usage of the title Ulugh Khān. See Jūzjānī, vol. 2, p. 87. It needs to be noticed in passing that one of the important historiographical accomplishments of Jackson's *The Delhi Sultanate* is a careful restoration of the Turkish names and titles of Iltutmish's and Balban's slaves. Jackson performed this task diligently without asking why Turkish names and titles were given to members of the political elite operating within a Persianate world, or why there was so much corruption in the transcription of Turkish names and titles by the Persianate literati.

[11] David Ayalon, 'Studies in al-Jabarti I', p. 152; and idem, 'Names, Titles, and Nisbas of the Mamluks', *Israel Oriental Studies*, 5 (1975), pp. 189–232.

any case a majority within the elite cadre) and the Sultan, although it did not imply the distancing of other elite non-Turkish slaves. Instead, the Sultan sometimes honoured non-Turks with Turkish titles. Iltutmish gave his *banda-i khāṣṣ,* Hindū Khān, who was, as his name suggests, of subcontinental provenance, the Turko-Mongol title of Khān and appointed him the *mihtar-i mubārak,* the overall-in-charge of his slaves.[12]

To observers like Fakhr-i Mudabbir, the deracinated character of the military elite underlined the distance between the rulers and the ruled—those with power, influence, and wealth and those who sought access to such privileges. The author also gave these material distinctions an ethnic colour, subsuming the possessors of military authority within the general category 'Turk'. While Fakhr-i Mudabbir, writing for a Turk patron, only exaggerated the positive elements and accomplishments of the Turkish race, others who served or depended upon the Turk *bandagān* also ascribed to the group a composite ethnic identity but with completely different moral qualities.

In the hands of court chroniclers reporting on the Delhi Sultanate, the political system of the 'Turks' in north India was eulogized for creating a stable sanctuary for Islam, especially when eastern Iran, central Asia, and Afghanistan were suffering the Mongol apocalypse. Sultan Iltutmish and his *bandagān-i khāṣṣ* stood united against the foes of Islam. Even as the great Sultan's political arrangements unravelled after his death, court chroniclers kept the memory of its homogeneity alive. It was for this reason that Baranī was surprised when the Khalajīs removed the Turks from political power in 689/1286. As he put it, 'people . . . wondered how the Khalajīs had replaced the Turks and seized the throne and how kingship had left the line [*aṣl*] of the Turks and gone to another'.[13] By the middle of the fourteenth century, when Baranī was composing his text, he could essentialize the years of slave dominance as a period of Turkish dynastic rule.

While court chronicles put a positive spin on their descriptions of

[12] On Hindū Khān see Jūzjānī, *Ṭabaqāt-i Nāṣirī,* vol. 2, pp. 18–19, and chapter 3. Jūzjānī described Hindū Khān as a slave especially close to the monarch, *qurbat tamām dāsht.*

[13] Baranī, *Ta'rīkh-i Fīrūz Shāhī,* edited by Khan, p 175.

this regime, its simple, monochromatic appearance also allowed its detractors relatively easy, visible targets to assault. The Chishtī *ṣūfī* saint Niẓām al-Dīn Awliyā', who never otherwise identified individuals according to their ethnicity, seldom noticed the Sultan's central Asian slaves by name, or title; to him they were just anonymous Turks. The anonymity of Turk benefactors in the *ṣūfī* literature might be explained by the fact that they were, finally, incidental agents of God's beneficence. Thus it was through God's intervention, and not the devotion or generosity of 'a Turk', that Maulānā Kaithālī was given twenty *tankas*, enough money to clear an outstanding debt.[14] Similarly, Bābā Farīd comforted Shaykh Najīb al-Dīn on his removal from the mosque, house, and office of *imām* conferred upon him by a 'Turk' because he had criticized the Turk's wasteful, selfish expenditure. Rather than celebrating the wedding of his daughter so ostentatiously, Shaykh Najīb advised his master to spend the money instead on charitable service for the Muslim community. Niẓām al-Dīn mentioned that perhaps the Turk's name was Ai-Tamar, for Bābā Farīd prophesied that 'if an Ai-Tamar departs, God brings forth an Ai-Takar (in his place)'—and indeed another Turk by the name Ai-Takar subsequently became Shaykh Najīb's benefactor.[15] Thus, even when Niẓām al-Dīn informed his audience of the identity of the Turks, he made it clear that one Turk benefactor was much like another; the alliteration in their names underlined their incidental nature. It is important to note, however, that Niẓām al-Dīn did not stereotype any other group of people. Other individuals were also 'incidental agents' of God's will on earth, but they were identified by name, or place of origin, or by their occupation: military commander (*amīr*, *malik*), merchant (*tājir*), Governor (*walī*), or judge (*qāẓī*, *ḥākim*). Only the Turks required no further form of description; the reference to their ethnicity encapsulated a host of qualities comprehensible to the saint's audience.

Niẓām al-Dīn had clarified some of these qualities through his anecdote regarding Shaykh Najīb, but Niẓām al-Dīn best described the distinction between the Turks and their subject population in a

[14] Amīr Ḥasan Sijzī, *Fawā'id al-Fu'ād*, pp. 112–14.

[15] Ibid., p. 134.

story about Khwāja Ḥamīd and the Turkish slave Tughril. Khwāja Ḥamīd was a secretary in the service of Tughril who suddenly, one day, saw a mysterious, disembodied face that taunted him. The face reappeared on several occasions and finally explained the reason for harassing the secretary: 'Oh Ḥamīd! Why are you standing before this man? . . . You are wise and he is ignorant, you are a free man and he is a slave, you are a pious man and he is an uncultured sinner.'[16]

Apparently, Khwāja Ḥamīd had never perceived his position from that perspective and he promptly left Tughril's service. Via a pithy anecdote Niẓām al-Dīn thus encapsulated all the qualities of the Turks. They were slaves, not learned in the secretarial or Islamic sciences; they were rude, bellicose, vain, and their military calling undoubtedly led to the unjust killing of innocent people. But the central conundrum in Niẓām al-Dīn's stories revolved around the fact that it was 'these Turks' that possessed power, wealth, and patronage, which attracted individuals like Khwāja Ḥamīd and Shaykh Najīb (and Fakhr-i Mudabbir and Jūzjānī for that matter) to their service.

Like Fakhr-i Mudabbir, Niẓām al-Dīn Awliyā' remembered the presence of an ethnic divide in the early thirteenth century which followed the distinction between those who held political power and wealth and those who were excluded from these. Certainly, Niẓām al-Dīn disagreed completely with Fakhr-i Mudabbir's opinion that the special qualities of the Turks made them a race superior to others, *badīn khaṣā'iṣ bar dīgar-i ṭā' ifa tarjīh dārand*, and that they used these virtues to serve and promote the cause of the Muslim community.[17] Depending upon the circumstance and the observer, the virtues of 'the Turks' differed, but to the audience of the day they did appear as a homogeneous group, powerful, rich, and very different.

Although the making of this ethnic divide was present during the governorships of the Mu'izzī subordinates, it was the arrangement of the Shamsī dispensation that accentuated the exclusive position of the Shamsī *bandagān-i khāṣṣ*. Perhaps the most significant consequence of Iltutmish's political system was that slave agents of the Sultan were distanced from local society. While this arrangement

[16] Ibid., pp. 342–3: *'Ay Khwāja Ḥamīd! tu pīsh-i īn mard chi mī'istī? . . . tu 'ālimī wa o jāhil, tu ḥurrī wa o banda, tu ṣālihī wa o fāsiq'*.

[17] Fakhr-i Mudabbir, *Ta'rīkh-i Fakhr al-Dīn Mubārak Shāh*, p. 48.

was politically useful in that it ensured the dependence of the subordinate upon the monarch, it also introduced a host of very ambiguous attitudes in the minds of the subjects towards their Governors.

It is important to note that the classical divide between the rulers and the ruled consistently posited in Sultanate studies as a relationship between the Sultan's officers on the one hand and the peasantry (*ra'āyā*) on the other, is far from clear for the early thirteenth century. As mentioned in the last chapter, Iltutmish's control between, and in the vicinity of, the urban garrisons was extremely tenuous. From the perspective of both the Amirs and the *ra'āyā*, 'ruled' or 'governed' implied little more than the occasional seizure of plunder or tribute. While this plunder and tribute was useful in sustaining the economy of the Sultanate at least as far as the political structure of the Delhi Sultanate was concerned, the peasantry were an 'occasional subject population' as yet unintegrated in its political life.

This was far from true in the urban centres of Iltutmish's domains, where the military elite and the administrators of the Sultan interacted on a daily basis with other residents of the town. It was in the *shahrs* and the *qaṣabāt* that the ruling elite had to build up support from the local communities to consolidate its power. As the evidence of Niẓām al-Dīn Awliyā' brings out, however, not all Muslims rallied behind their rulers as 'natural leaders' or nobles. Despite the numbers that were attracted to the service of the military elite, many of their subordinates considered them uncultured boors who had illegitimately monopolized power and privilege. Social, cultural, and functional differences thus separated local society from the lords of the realm, and the range of positive and negative qualities ascribed to the military elite was subsumed in a single ethnic generalization: 'Turk'.

Different Ways of being a Pious Muslim

The distinction between rulers and the ruled, was only one aspect of the lack of homogeneity within the Muslim community. In fact, generalizations such as 'Muslim community', while convenient to the historian, serve to obscure the more meaningful sentiments of corporate belonging present amongst Muslims in thirteenth-century north India. Even amongst *Sunnī* Muslims, the religious practice, affiliation, and sense of identity was prompted more by their recognition of the merits of one school of legal or theological reasoning over another, or their acknowledgement of one or the other mystic preceptor, than by any immediate sentiment of *jamā'at* solidarity. The *shī'ī* groups constituted yet another stream of piety which claimed the affiliation of many Muslims. Hodgson explained that in this period Islam presented three faces: 'one, *Sharī'a*-minded, concerned with outward, socially cognizable behaviour, accepted as their care by the *Shar'ī 'ulamā'*; the other mystical-minded, concerned with the inward, personal life of the individual, accepted as their care by the *ṣūfī pīrs*. Often the same religious leader was at once *pīr* and *Shar'ī* scholar, or at least took both sides of Islam very seriously—just as most of the Muslim public respected and took guidance from both *pīrs* and *'ulamā'*. Always, however, there were those who accepted the one face of Islam as genuine and mistrusted the other, or even rejected it as spurious . . . 'Alid loyalism with its chiliastic vision [was the third face]. Sometimes it was merged with *Sharī'a*-mindedness, in the *Shar'ī 'ulamā'* of the *Shī'a*; sometimes it contributed to *sufism*, when its esoteric notions proved illuminating; from time to time it emerged as a positive independent force.'[18] Early-thirteenth-century piety was still extremely individualistic, so that Muslims could indulge in considerable 'borrowing' from the separate Islamic streams of belief without any sense of contradiction.

It is therefore not surprising that, while all three streams of piety were in evidence in the early Delhi Sultanate, there was considerable divergence in opinions concerning the piety of each tradition. This was evident, for example, in the reports concerning the *shī'ī* Qarāmiṭa community (Qarmatians) in north India. According to Jūzjānī, the *Sharī'a*-minded chronicler of the Delhi Sultans, the Qarāmiṭas, believers in the Ismā'īliyā Imamate of the Fāṭimids, were *mulāḥida* or heretics. They had their stronghold in the urban centres of Sindh and had opposed the Ghaznavids and, subsequently, Mu'izz al-Dīn Ghurī.[19] In Jūzjānī's mind, the nefarious activities of the Qarmatians

[18] See Marshall Hodgson, *The Venture of Islam: Conscience and History in a World Civilization* (Chicago: University Press, 1974), vol. 1, pp. 359–64, and vol. 2, pp. 203–4.

[19] For the Fāṭimid affiliation of the Ismā'īlī community in Multan, see the anonymous, *Ḥudūd al-'Ālam*, translated by V. Minorsky, pp. 89, 246. For the Ismā'īlī–Ghaznavid conflict, see C.E. Bosworth, *The Ghaznavids, 994–1040*,

was always a cause of instability in the *Sunnī* community, and he blamed them, in circumstances which are not nearly so clear, for Mu'izz al-Dīn's assassination.[20]

Jūzjānī's narration of the Qarāmiṭa *mulāḥida* attack on the Delhi *masjid-i jāmi'* (congregational mosque) in 634/1236 clarified the extent to which he believed that community was organized in opposition to the majority of the *Sunnī* Muslims. According to Jūzjānī, the Qarmatians of Hindustan were incited by a 'sort of' learned man [*shakhsī dānishmand gūna*], by the name of Nūr Turk. Nūr Turk's following of common people [*khalq-i 'awām*], from Gujarat, Sindh, the environs of Delhi, and the banks of the rivers Ganges and Jamuna assembled in Delhi, affirmed loyalty to each other, and listened to

---

pp. 52–4, 76, 199–200, and 235; idem, *The Later Ghaznavids, 1040–1186*, pp. 14, 31; and S.M. Stern, 'Isma'ili Propaganda and Fatimid Rule in Sind', *Islamic Culture*, 23 (1949), pp. 298–307. See Jūzjānī, *Ṭabaqāt-i Nāṣirī*, vol. 1, p. 396, for Mu'izz al-Dīn Ghurī's capture of Multan and dispersal of the Qarmatians.

[20] Fakhr-i Mudabbir was in Lahore at that time and closest in time and space to Mu'izz al-Dīn's death. In his history, however, Fakhr-i Mudabbir mentioned the assassination of the Sultan without further elaboration. Fakhr-i Mudabbir, *Ta'rīkh-i Fakhr al-Dīn Mubārak Shāh*, pp. 29, 72. Juwainī, *Ta'rīkh-i Jahān-Gushā*, translated by Boyle, vol. 1, p. 326, credited the murder to Hindu assassins (*fidā'īs*). V.V. Barthold, *Turkestan Down to the Mongol Invasion*, p. 352, fn. 7, mentioned that in Ibn al-Aṣir, *al-Kāmil fi al-Ta'rīkh*, edited by C.J. Tornberg, vol. XII, pp. 139–40, the assassins are recorded as being Hindus and Ismā'īlīs. Like Jūzjānī, Ḥasan Niẓāmī, *Tāj al-Ma'āṣir*, p. 236, blamed the *mulāḥida* for the Sultan's murder. Interestingly enough the epithet *mulāḥida* was also used for the Niẓārī Ismā'īlīs, and they are also known as the 'Assassins'. While Mu'izz al-Dīn's murder bore evidence of the type of assassinations that had won the Niẓārī Ismā'īlīs so much infamy, it is doubtful that they were involved in Mu'izz al-Dīn's murder. It could not have been a reprisal for Mu'izz al-Dīn's campaigns against the Qarmatians because, contrary to the common assumption, there was no known connection between the Qarmatian Ismā'īlīs in north India and the Niẓārī Ismā'īlīs of Alamut. On the contrary, in the late-twelfth and early-thirteenth century there had been a falling out between the Fāṭimid Ismā'īlīs (who were linked with the Qarmatians) and the Niẓārī Ismā'īlīs. See S.M. Stern, 'Isma'ilis and Qarmatians', in *L'Elaboration de l'Islam, Colloque de Strasbourg Juin 1959* (Paris: Presses Universitaires de France, 1961), pp. 99–108; and W. Madelung, 'Ḳarmati', idem, 'Isma'iliyya', *EI*², s.v.

Nūr Turk's exhortations against the *'ulamā'* of the legal schools of Abū Ḥanīfa and al-Shāfi'ī, who were described as *nāṣibī* and *murjī'*. For an individual who was loyal to the memory of 'Ali and his descendants, *nāṣibī* were those people who ignored 'Alī's claim to the Caliphate and 'set up' (*nāṣib*) others in his stead. The *murji'a* were pious Muslims who sought to diminish the divisive impact of the 'Alī, Mu'āwiya conflict (35-40/656-61) on the Muslim community by ignoring the claims of the rival camps and postponing (*murjī'*) any decision on the validity of the actions of the two contenders to the day of judgement and God's adjudication. For the followers of 'Alī, the attempt of the *murji'a* to postpone a decision to the end of time detracted from the wrongs inflicted on the Prophet's son-in-law, which had to be redressed. In this sense the *nāṣibī* and the *murji'a* were associated together as groups with anti-'Alī sentiments and, according to Jūzjānī, Nūr Turk's exhortations against them motivated the rebels to attack the Muslims at prayer in the Delhi *masjid-i jāmi'*.[21]

Jūzjānī's account of Nūr Turk's teachings and actions were obviously coloured by his own perception of piety, and this was problematic to his near contemporary readership. In a conversation that took place on the 13th Sh'abān 718/10 October 1318, the Chishtī saint[22] Niẓām al-Dīn Awliyā' responded to Jūzjānī's accusations and clarified that Nūr Turk's faith was free from heresy.[23] In his opinion, Nūr Turk was a pious man, renowned for his sermons [o *rā sukhan gīrā būd*], who owed no allegiance to a *ṣūfī* master. Niẓām al-Dīn's portrayal of Nūr Turk was hardly that of a Qarāmiṭa heretic and the Chishtī saint clarified that it was because Nūr Turk believed (and no doubt preached) that the *'ulamā'* of Delhi were polluted by the material world

[21] Jūzjānī, *Ṭabaqāt-i Nāṣirī*, vol. 1, p. 461. The conflict between the *nāṣibīs* and the *Shī'a* was probably quite serious at this time. Sadīd al-Dīn Muḥammad al-'Awfī narrates an incident when a *shī'ī* abused 'Āyisha, the wife of Prophet Muḥammad. See M. Nizamuddin, *An Introdution to the Jawāmi' al-Ḥikāyāt wa Lawāmi' al-Riwāyāt*, p. 260.

[22] I use the term 'saint' (*walī*, plural: *awliyā'*) fully aware that there was no centralized machinery or institutionalized process of canonization in Islam. The implications of this point have been usefully clarified by P.M. Currie, *The Shrine and Cult of Mu'in al-Din Chishti*, pp. 1–19.

[23] Literally, 'he was purer than water from the heavens [*az āb-i āsmān pākīzatar būd*].' Amīr Ḥasan Sijzī, *Fawā'id al-Fu'ād*, p. 334.

[*ālūda-i duniyā*], that they in turn spread all kinds of calumnious tales about him.[24]

Niẓām al-Dīn also explained Nūr Turk's doctrinal beliefs that had provoked this 'insurrection' against the *'ulamā'*. Significantly, the Chishtī saint weeded out all evidence of 'Alid sentiments in his explanation of Nūr Turk's beliefs. He gave a taciturn explanation which made clear that *nāṣībi* meant heretical sentiments but he did not suggest that they were a part of Nūr Turk's beliefs. Niẓām al-Dīn developed in relatively greater detail two streams of *murji'a* thought. According to the Chishtī saint, the first was the conventional position of the *murji'a* teachers which emphasized that 'good faith' rather than 'good work' defined the true Muslim. According to this belief, faith alone assured a Muslim of God's mercy and ultimate salvation, even if he were a sinner. The second, and the 'less pure' [*g̲h̲air k̲h̲āliṣ*], *murji'a* opinion favoured by Niẓām al-Dīn and shared by Nūr Turk emphasized that the Muslim should believe in God's mercy as well as punishment. The fear of God's wrath should motivate Muslims to abstain from sinful actions. By introducing the conditionality of action in judging a good Muslim, Niẓām al-Dīn reserved for himself and Nūr Turk the freedom to criticize the actions of Muslims without challenging God's prerogative as the final arbiter.[25] In the Chishtī exposition, efforts were made to absolve Nūr Turk of all *shī'ī* Qarāmiṭa links, and consistent with these efforts were Niẓām al-Dīn's public statements that he shared Nūr Turk's views on matters of faith.

In his effort to exonerate Nūr Turk, Niẓām al-Dīn could have quite simply denied Jūzjānī's allegations. The fact that Niẓām al-Dīn had to explain and legitimize *murji'a* opinions on piety suggests

[24] Niẓām al-Dīn noted that, while in Hansi, Nūr Turk's impassioned sermons were famous, and on one occasion he met and praised Bābā Farīd al-Dīn Ganj-i Shakar. Some time later, when Nūr Turk was in Delhi, Sultan Raẓiyya was sufficiently impressed by his piety to offer him a cash sustenance which he spurned; ibid., pp. 334–5.

[25] Ibid., p. 334. For a further elaboration on Niẓām al-Dīn's views on the Muslim who is a sinner, and his disagreement with the *mu'tazila*, see also pp. 118–19. On the development of *murji'a* doctrine, see W.M. Watt, *Islamic Philosophy and Theology* (Edinburgh: Edinburgh University Press, 1979), pp. 27–35; A.J. Wensinck, *The Muslim Creed: Its Genesis and Historical Development* (London: Frank Cass and Co. Ltd., 1965), pp. 36–82; and J. van Ess, 'Ḳadariyya', *EI*², s.v.

that this might have been a central theme in Nūr Turk's criticism of the *'ulamā'*, and that Niẓām al-Dīn's audience was not familiar or knew only the *shī'ī* objections to *murji'* ideas. Although the evidence is not at all clear on the subject, the manner of Niẓām al-Dīn's protestations does suggest that Nūr Turk was a *ṣūfī* who gathered a sizable congregation, and they challenged the moral authority of the *Sharī'a*-minded jurists of Delhi in the last years of Iltutmish's reign. That Nūr Turk may have also had *shī'ī* leanings and was still well regarded as a mystic saint by Niẓām al-Dīn Awliyā', and by later *ṣūfī* writers like 'Abd al-Ḥaqq Mūḥaddiṣ Dehlawī, should not surprise us unduly.[26] Loyalty to the family of 'Ali could be harmonized with the special status accorded to Muḥammad by all mystics.[27] Moreover, the very fact that Nūr Turk questioned the piety of religious scholars and jurists presented grounds for a meeting of minds with *ṣūfīs*. Both criticized the conduct of the *'ulamā'*, which was believed to be never more than technically correct and frequently against the spirit of the *Sharī'a*.

On another level, there was nothing particularly exceptional about Nūr Turk; there were, as we have noticed, many ways in which Muslims could practice their piety in the early thirteenth century. The lack of agreement concerning the spiritual merits of individuals can be further thickened by reports about disagreements surrounding basic ritual practises of prayer, *namāz*,[28] or specific *ṣūfī* traditions of *samā'*

[26] 'Abd al-Ḥaqq Mūḥaddiṣ Dehlawī, *Akhbār al-Akhyār*, translated into Urdu by Maulana Muḥammad Fazil (Karachi, Madina Publishing Company, n.d), p. 164. The *Akhbār al-Akhyār* was completed in the late sixteenth century.

[27] See Annemarie Schimmel, *And Muḥammad is His Messenger: The Veneration of the Prophet in Islamic Piety* (Chapel Hill: University of North Carolina Press, 1985).

[28] Note, for example, Niẓām al-Dīn Awliyā's comments that the Suhrawardī saint Bahā' al-Dīn Zakariyā was extremely strict about the completion of the prescribed rituals associated with prayer (*Fawā'id al-Fu'ād*, p. 391). Although Bahā' al-Dīn's practice here would seem to be closer to that of the *'ulamā'*, the Suhrawardī saint disagreed with Qāẓī Quṭb al-Dīn Kāshānī over the prescribed rituals of prayer. Against Zakariyā's claim that his ritual was legitimated by his 'inner light', *nūr-i bāṭin*, Qāẓī Kāshānī argued that when such an 'inner light' contravened the dictates of the holy law [*aḥkām-i Sharī'a*], it was illegitimate [*ān ẓulmat ast*] (ibid., pp. 399–400). Similarly, in his narration of a story of Jalāl al-Dīn Tabrīzī, Niẓām al-Dīn reported that the Suhrawardī saint chided the

(invocatory singing and music).[29] Nor did this diversity of opinion concerning pious conduct follow a simple divide between mystics of competing schools of affiliation or between *ṣūfīs* and *'ulamā'*. In the early thirteenth century the Chishti *ṭarīqa* had hardly evolved, and there was a noticeable absence of consistency on matters of doctrine and conduct amongst the Suhrawardī saints.[30] For that matter, the mystic leanings of the jurist, Jūzjānī, led Niẓām al-Dīn Awliyā' to agree with the opinions of a friend that the *'ālim* should have been a *Shaikh al-Islām* and not just a *qāẓī*.[31] According to Niẓām al-Dīn it was Jūzjānī, together with the Suhrawardī saint Qāẓī Ḥamīd al-Dīn, who popularized *samā'* in Delhi.[32] Yet, Jūzjānī's piety never came under dispute, largely because the author's mystical inclinations were tempered by his *sharī'a*-mindedness and he could live his life in harmony with different types of public expectations.

ḥākim (judge) Qāẓī Kamāl al-Dīn Ja'frī of Budaun for not knowing the proper way of performing prayer, *namāz*. Jalāl al-Dīn Tabrīzī was reported to have told the Qāẓī that while the *'ulamā'* were concerned about reading *namāz* facing the *Ka'ba* in Mecca, the *ṣūfīs* did not pray until they had seen the throne of God which was their *qibla*. In other words, in contrast to the pedantic computations of the *'ulamā'* to ascertain the correct location of the *Ka'ba*, *ṣūfīs* relied upon their intuitive genius to guide them in the direction of the Almighty. Niẓām al-Dīn Awliyā' spoke approvingly of the sentiments present in Jalāl al-Dīn's comments and regarded them as evidence of his high mystical attainments (ibid., pp. 401–2).

[29] For the narration of an early dispute concerning the practice of Qāẓī Ḥamīd al-Dīn Nāgaurī and Bakhtiyār Kākī, see ibid., pp. 407–9, and from a slightly later period, p. 166. Opposition to Qāẓī Ḥamīd al-Dīn Nāgaurī's practice of *samā'* also received an exaggeratedly inaccurate notice in 'Iṣāmī, *Futūḥ al-Salāṭīn*, pp. 117–20.

[30] Note especially the critical letter written by Jalāl al-Dīn Tabrīzī to Bahā' al-Dīn Zakariyā concerning his conduct as a 'man of the world'. See Amīr Ḥasan Sijzī, *Fawā'id al-Fu'ād*, p. 172.

[31] Ibid., pp. 429–30. See below for a fuller discussion on the *Shaikh al-Islām*.

[32] Ibid., pp. 407–8. Qāẓī Ḥamīd al-Dīn's sentiments concerning the efficacy of *samā'* were not shared by his contemporary Bahā' al-Dīn Zakariyā, although Niẓām al-Dīn does report one instance where the latter also participated in (a 'closet' performance of) that mystical exercise. Ibid., pp. 234–5.

But Jūzjānī was the exception. The piety of many charismatic Muslims was disputed out of fear that they might become the source of a divisive following within the Muslim community. As was evident from the differing reactions towards Nūr Turk, the appraisal of a charismatic individual's piety was dependent upon very individualistic norms, but they provoked public and very virulent conflicts. A late Chishtī biographical encyclopaedia that otherwise venerated Bābā Farīd's memory noted the occasion when Nūr Tūrk and the *'ulamā* of Hansi misunderstood Bābā Farīd's desire to lead a secluded life in the city. They tormented him with abuse, calling him *murjī* and *nāṣibī,* allegations that the author of the *Siyar al-Awliyā'* was quick to dismiss.[33] We shouldn't miss the irony here: some years after this reported event it was Bābā Farīd's spiritual successor, Niẓām al-Dīn Awliyā, who was defending Nūr Turk from Jūzjānī's accusations of heretical conduct.

The same level of diversity in opinions and conflict over faith and praxis surrounded Najm al-Dīn Sughrā, a *Sharī'a*-minded individual who had been honoured by the post of *Shaikh al-Islām* by Sultan Iltutmish. Curiously, in the Chishtī and Suhrawardī literature Najm al-Dīn was never portrayed as a pious man. He was described instead as a petty, jealous, worldly-minded individual who used his position of *Shaikh al-Islām* to harass both Chishtī and Suhrawardī *ṣūfīs*. Najm al-Dīn's pride and pettiness were evident in his relations with the Chishtī saints Mu'īn al-Dīn and Bakhtiyār Kākī. According to the biographical compendium of Chishtī saints, *Siyar al-Awliyā'*, while there was affection, *maḥabbat*, between Mu'īn al-Dīn Chishtī and Najm al-Dīn Sughrā, the latter resented the presence of Mu'īn al-Dīn's disciple in Delhi. Apparently, Bakhtiyār Kākī would not recognize the authority of the *Shaikh al-Islām.*[34]

Najm al-Dīn also had strained relations with the Suhrawardī saint Jalāl al-Dīn Tabrīzī. The *Fawā'id al-Fu'ād* provided the first hint of a conflict when it reported disagreements and enmity between the two men and quoted Jalāl al-Dīn Tabrīzī's enigmatic remarks concerning

[33] Amīr Khwurd, *Siyar al-Awliyā'*, p. 72. I am grateful to Jyoti Gulati for drawing my attention to this reference.

[34] Ibid., p. 64.

Najm al-Dīn's responsibility in evicting him, *bīrūn kard*, from Delhi.[35] The sixteenth-century Suhrawardī author Ḥamīd ibn Fażl Allāh Jamālī substantially embellished the events leading to the departure (not expulsion!) of Jalāl al-Dīn Tabrīzī from Delhi. According to Jamālī, the *Shaikh al-Islām* of Delhi was deeply upset and envious of Jalāl al-Dīn's mystic accomplishments and Sultan Iltutmish's favour to the saint. It was this envy and insecurity that propelled Najm al-Dīn to bribe a prostitute and frame charges of adultery against Jalāl al-Dīn. These accusations were proved false at an inquest, *maḥżar*, presided over by Bahā' al-Dīn Zakariyā, with an audience consisting of mystics and scholars. Jalāl al-Dīn left the city anyway because he did not want to be further sullied by the environment of intrigue and competition present in Delhi.[36]

In this tale of competition, envy, and calumnious accusations preserved in the Chishtī and Suhrawardī sources, Shaikh Jalāl al-Dīn Tabrīzī emerged as the innocent victim, and Najm al-Dīn Sughrā anything but a paradigmatic sufi.[37] The Chishtī and Suhrawardī accounts of the conflict, however, are problematic for their contradictions. If Najm al-Dīn Sughrā was such an immoral person, these sources leave unexplained the basis upon which he built up an affectionate relationship with Mu'īn al-Dīn Chishtī. Nor do they account for Iltutmish's surprising choice of Najm al-Dīn as *Shaikh al-Islām*, an office which, despite his apparently embarrassing activities, he occupied until his death.[38] Finally, there is little reason to expect Chishtī and

35 Amīr Ḥasan Sijzī, *Fawā'id al-Fu'ād*, p. 245, recorded Niẓām al-Dīn's observation that while in Budaun Jalāl al-Dīn clairvoyantly knew of Najm al-Dīn's death in Delhi. On that occasion, Jalāl al-Dīn reportedly remarked to his followers that, just as the *Shaikh al-Islām* Najm al-Dīn had driven him out of the city of Delhi, his own *pīr* made him forsake the world [*agar Shaikh al-Islām-i Dehlī mā rā az shahr bīrūn kard, Shaikh-i mā o rā az jahān bīrūn kard*]. The story was subsequently recounted in Amīr Khwurd, *Siyar al-Awliyā'*, pp. 408, 585, and 'Abd al-Ḥaqq Mūḥaddiṣ Dehlawī, *Akhbār al-Akhyār*, pp. 102–3.

36 Ḥāmid ibn Fażl Allāh Jamālī, *Siyar al-'Ārifīn*, pp. 16, 243–7.

37 This is also the interpretation preserved in the writings of K.A. Nizami, *Religion and Politics in India*, pp. 162–4, and S.A.A. Rizvi, *A History of Sufism in India*, vol. 1, pp. 200–1.

38 This is suggested by Jalāl al-Dīn's own remarks quoted by Niẓām al-Dīn Awliyā'. See Amīr Ḥasan Sijzī, *Fawā'id al-Fu'ād*, p. 245. Iltutmish's dismissal of Najm al-Dīn Sughrā was reported by Jamālī, *Siyar al-'Ārifīn*, p. 168, and

Suhrawardī *tazkirāt* to provide a fair picture of Najm al-Dīn, especially if the Delhi *Shaikh al-Islām* had acrimonious relations with saints whose memories were venerated in these biographical compendiums.

The more recent analysis of a fifteenth-century Firdausī *tazkirāt*, however, has brought to light a completely different picture of Najm al-Dīn Sughrā and provides additional information contradicting the Chishtī and Suhrawardī reports. The *Manāqib al-Asfiyā'* reported that the *Shaikh al-Islām* of Delhi was a disciple of the famous Khwārazmī saint Najm al-Dīn Kubrā (died 618/1221). In the same source Shaykh Najm al-Dīn was unequivocally described as *mard-i buzurg, ṣāḥib-i wilāyat*, a great man, a saint. This would explain Iltutmish's rationale in appointing Najm al-Dīn the *Shaikh al-Islām* of Delhi. As Simon Digby has pointed out, 'the same source [also] sharply criticize[d] Quṭb al-Dīn Bakhtiyār for the hold he had acquired over the population of Delhi by the display of miraculous powers.'[39] Although the *Manāqib al-Asfiyā'* does not contain any information about the Najm al-Dīn–Jalāl al-Dīn imbroglio, it does provide the alternative viewpoint concerning the honourable conduct and piety of the *Shaikh al-Islām*, forcing us to assess the conflict with greater scepticism.

The ease with which the protagonist and the antagonist change in the Chishtī, Suhrawardī, and Firdausī texts certainly emphasizes the absence of any standardized norms available to judge the piety of a Muslim in the early thirteenth century. But the conflict surrounding Nūr Turk, Bakhtiyār Kākī, Jalāl al-Dīn Tabrīzī, and Najm al-Dīn Sughrā also brings out the extent of hostility between the *Sharī'a*-minded *'ulamā'* and the charismatic *ṣūfī pīrs*. For the *ṣūfī pīrs* there was a whole experiential, mystical–magical dimension to Islam which could only be intuitively explored. In a world where—

> a preacher . . . was so transported by his own eloquence that he flew away from the pulpit [*minbar*] to a neighbouring wall; . . . [where]

faithfully followed by Nizami (p. 164) and Rizvi (p. 201). But this was only a part of the author's exaggerated narration of the conflict between the *Shaikh al-Islām* and Jalāl al-Dīn.

[39] Shu'aib ibn Ḥalāl al-Dīn Manerī, *Manāqib al-Asfiyā'* (Calcutta: Nūr al-Afāq Press, 1895), pp. 121–2, cited by Simon Digby, 'The Sufi Shaikh as a Source of Authority', p. 65.

> meetings . . . [took place] . . . in deserted places with Khwāja Khiẓr who has everlasting life; . . . [where there were] various 'fairy people' . . . [*abdāls*] who physically fl[ew] above the territories which they protect from harm . . . [where] a holy man [circled] around the vault of the chief mosque at Delhi through the night till the dawn . . . [where] the [*mardān-i ghaib*] men of the unseen . . . appear[ed] and disappear[ed], and sometimes call[ed] away a mortal to join them.

Sharī'a-minded scholars did not provide all the answers for Muslims.[40] This was particularly true on Islam's eastern frontier, where the 'Muslim community' consisted of a large number of recent immigrants for whom life was indeed unpredictable, fearful, and short. There were mysteries in the lives of Muslims which only the mystic saints could explain, or reconcile, and the more charismatic *pīrs* had large followings. They were, however, also feared and regarded with suspicion by those who would seek to order society by predictable, systematized 'norms defining outward, socially cognizable behaviour'. The *Sharī'a*-minded *'ulamā'* sought to control the influence of those they regarded as charlatans—people who spread superstition, which was 'injurious to the common folk'. Nor were they alone in their quest. The political authorities were also extremely wary of *ṣūfī pīrs*, who they could not alienate outright, but whose spiritual charisma could on occasion embarrass the Sultan's more prosaic material claims to authority. At least one implication of political consolidation in Iltutmish's reign was that, together with efforts directed towards reorienting the sentiments of the dispersed communities of Muslims away from regional military lords and towards Delhi, Iltutmish also had to try and diminish the influence of alternative pietistic practices and their exponents in favour of an Islam supported by Delhi, the emerging sanctuary of Islam in India.

Towards Homogeneity: The Role of the *'Ulamā'*

Together with the military commanders, the other groups that commanded considerable social influence in north India in the early thirteenth century were the *'ulamā'* (individuals learned in the religious

[40] Simon Digby, 'The Sufi Shaikh as a Source of Authority', p. 62.

sciences) and the *ahl-i qalam* (people of the pen, which included secretaries, accountants etc.). The terms *'ulamā'* and *ahl-i qalam* did not define a social or occupational group, but denoted individuals who were believed to possess estimable qualities of piety and learning which differentiated them from the rest of the Muslim community.

Despite their ascriptive status of 'learned' and 'people of the pen', these individuals were not divorced from military activity. Iltutmish's *wazīr*, Niẓām al-Mulk Junaidī, although involved with the financial and secretarial duties of the realm also led the royal troops into Uchch and Bhakar against Qubachā in 625/1228.[41] In fact it was the jurist Jūzjānī who advised people of the need to be constantly armed and prepared to defend themselves, an advice he took to heart himself. He recorded with some pride the occasion when, with his slaves, he had repelled a murderous assault upon himself in the *masjid-i jāmi'* in Delhi.[42] Their military skills, however, were not the reasons why the *'ulamā'* and the *ahl-i qalam* won public acclaim. Instead, it was out of respect for their knowledge of the religious sciences and law, their mastery of the epistolary traditions, and their training in accountancy that the Muslim community paid the 'learned' so much deference.

Knowledge of the *Qur'ān*, *Ḥadīṣ*, the exegetical literature and the rules of legal deduction were a part of the learning, *'ilm*, of the *'ulamā'* (learned), and Fakhr-i Mudabbir had explained that the *'ulamā'* were ranked after the Prophet: indeed the 'world flourished because of the virtue of their learning, religiosity and piety and the injunctions of the *Sharī'a* and worship [were] entrusted to them.'[43] Competence over the religious sciences, however, also distinguished the adept administrator *kātib*, *dabīr*, *wazīr*, *khwāja*, *mustaufī*, etc.[44] Recounting the

[41] Jūzjānī, *Ṭabaqāt-i Nāṣirī*, vol. 2, p. 139, vol. 1, p. 447.

[42] Ibid., vol. 2, p. 139, and vol. 1, p. 468.

[43] Fakhr-i Mudabbir, *Ta'rīkh-i Fakhr al-Dīn Mubārak Shāh*, p. 10: *'jahān basabab-i barkat-i 'ilm wa diyānat wa wara'-i īshān abadan ast wa aḥkām-i Shari' wa 'ibādat bamakān-i īshān mufauwaẓ ast'*. K.A. Nizami, *Religion and Politics in India,* p. 150, also cited this passage but his references should be corrected to pp. 9–12.

[44] Although in the literal sense *ahl-i qalam*, people of the pen, should have included all those involved in scribal and learning tasks, the *'ulamā'* were usually not associated with this group. The term 'people of the pen' was normally

qualities of the *ahl-i qalam*, Niẕamī 'Arūẓī recorded that if a *dabīr* (secretary) was 'well acquainted with the *Qur'ān*, with one verse therefrom he may discharge his obligation to a whole realm.'[45] These were special accomplishments, to gain which the individual needed, together with aptitude, a lot of grit and determination.

The education of the *'ulamā'* was a strenuous exercise, achieved over years of discipleship with one or more mentors, mastering a text at a time[46] and travelling from one centre of learning to another.[47]

---

used for those involved in 'non-religious' activities, such as revenue or accounting. This sense is carried in incidental remarks like Fakhr-i Mudabbir, *Ādāb al-Ḥarb*, edited by Khwansari, p. 138, where the *wazīr* is described as the epitome of the *ahl-i qalam*.

45 For an extended recommendation to the *dabīr* to study and excel in the religious sciences, see Niẕāmī 'Arūẓī Samarqandī, *Chahār Maqāla*, p. 25, and more generally pp. 22–42. The *Chahār Maqāla* was dedicated to the Ghurid Prince of the Bamian lineage, Abū al-Ḥasan 'Alī b. Mas'ūd, and its comments enlarge upon Fakhr-i Mudabbir's more taciturn recommendations. Concerning the *barīd* (reporter, spy) Fakhr-i Mudabbir noted: 'all the learned *Ṣāḥib Barīds* were masters of composition and reporting [*ṣāḥib-i taṣnīf wa akhbār*], and on any occasion could pass unusual compositions without equal [*taṣnīfhā-yi nādir bī-miṣl*], and because the learned compositions were such, the speakers are [still] alive . . .'. Fakhr-i Mudabbir, *Ādāb al-Mulūk wa Kifāyat al-Mamlūk*, edited by Muḥammad Sarwar Maulawi, p. 27.

46 There was a considerable degree of specialization in the subjects taught by the separate scholars, and even when an *'ālim* claimed knowledge of *ḥadīṣ* he often clarified the texts on which he was competent. Furthermore, *ḥadīṣ* was only one of the subjects studied. The scholar Ẕiyā' al-Dīn, who took his classes in the Delhi *masjid-i jāmi'* by the *minār*, apparently only taught law and grammar, *fiqh wa naḥw*. According to Niẕām al-Dīn, Ẕiyā' al-Dīn was extremely apprehensive about meeting Bābā Farīd in case he was questioned on other subjects [*'ulūm-i dīgar*], outside his area of specialization. Amīr Ḥasan Sijzī, *Fawā'id al-Fu'ād*, pp. 153–4.

47 This travelling was much the accepted, even estimable, form of learning, for it allowed the student the opportunity to meet, listen, and discourse with the great scholars of the day. Because of the prestige involved with travelling in search of knowledge, religious scholars were often later accredited with voyages and educational experiences which were deliberately exaggerated. Unfortunately, there are no early *taẕkirāt* (biographical compendiums) of the *'ulamā'* through which one can follow their peregrinations in search of knowledge, but the early *ṣūfīs* were also accredited with similar kinds of travel and

Most *ahl-i qalam* did not undergo as rigorous a training in the religious sciences, their education being often a more exclusive in-house affair where they received instruction spanning several years from members of their own family. This was especially true if their learning was of a subject on which lectures were not normally given in the mosque or the *madrasa* ('college', where instruction in the religious and legal sciences was given), such as *siyāqat*, or *ḥisāb* (arithmetic and accounting), which were of particular value to an administrator. Because of the apprentice-like training of many *ahl-i qalam*, Fakhr-i Mudabbir advised that, when appointing a *mustaufī* (accountant), a person from a family of *mustaufīs* should be chosen, *az khāndān-i mustaufiyān bāshad*.[48]

It is noteworthy that when Fakhr-i Mudabbir described the qualities of the *'ulamā'* he left unexplained how an *'ālim* with 'learning, religiosity and piety' could be socially identified. In north India of the early thirteenth century there was no *madrasa* infrastructure anywhere like the latter-day ranked and institutionalized system of the Ottomans, and as a result an *'ālim* could not be recognized by the diploma of his alumnus. The *'ālim* gained a reputation as a learned man through his demeanour, by belonging to a family reputed for its knowledge of the religious sciences, by the circle of individuals that he had been associated with in the past, by his ability to expound on the texts that he had mastered or his ability to act as a guide to Muslims on matters concerning the faith. It was social esteem gained partly through an appropriate genealogy, a visibly ascertainable *ādāb* or moral conduct,

---

gained prestige from their wide circle of teachers, associates, and disciples. This posthumous search for fame has been effectively presented in the case of Mu'īn al-Dīn Chishtī in a map detailing the saint's itinerary according to different sources ranging over several centuries. See P.M. Currie, *The Shrine and Cult of Mu'in al-Din Chishti of Ajmer*, front endpaper (sketch map of Mu'in al-Din's travels according to the *Siyar al-Awliyā'*, *Siyar al-'Ārifīn*, *Siyar al-Aqtāb* and the *Hasht Bihisht*). The phenomenon of travelling in search of teachers and religious training has received a useful discussion for the central Islamic lands (where there is also richer source material) in Richard W. Bulliet, 'A Quantitative Approach to Medieval Muslim Biographical Dictionaries', *Journal of the Economic and Social History of the Orient*, 13 (1970), pp.195–211.

48 See Fakhr-i Mudabbir, *Ādāb al-Mulūk wa Kifāyat al-Mamlūk*, p. 17.

and a learning of law and theology not shared by the rest of the Muslim community.[49] Fakhr-i Mudabbir's description of the *'ulamā'* suggests the amount of respect with which Muslims regarded religious specialists. This was obviously true in the case of the relatively more qualified of the *'ulamā'* and the *ahl-i qalam*, a small group whose memory was venerated by future generations.[50] Many others had received less distinguished schooling, but even this was sufficient to distinguish them from the larger unlettered masses and, together with the *ṣūfī pīrs*, made them highly respected in the local community.

Although individuals from both levels of training had been present in north India, first in the Ghaznavid domains in Punjab and subsequently in the north Indian Sultanates, the fortunes of many pious individuals, especially in the smaller urban centres, like the Qāẓī of Tulak, must have remained unaltered during the changes in the political fortunes of the north Indian Sultanate. If we recall, the *'ulamā'*

[49] It is important to note that much of the training in the religious sciences associated with the *'ulamā'* was one that many *ṣūfīs* had also gone through. In fact, one of the striking features of Niẓām al-Dīn Awliyā's conversations was the number of occasions the Chishtī saint explained matters of creed and the *Sharī'a* to his audience, but this counsel was always tempered by the saint's personal mystic inclinations. In fact, an anecdote in the *Fawā'id al-Fu'ād*, p. 46, recalls Niẓām al-Dīn's ambitions to become a *qāẓī* and Shaykh Nājib al-Dīn Mutawakkil's admonition to become 'something else'. The differences between the *'ulamā'* and the *ṣūfī* were not so much a result of their respective scholastic qualifications but a combination of their distinctive, separate emphases upon the importance of external conduct in the lives of Muslims and their self-chosen roles in public life. The pietistic leanings of the learned were publicly known and it was the members of the local community that recognized an individual as an *'ālim* or *ṣūfī pīr*.

[50] See Fakhr-i Mudabbir, *Ta'rīkh-i Fakhr al-Dīn Mubārakshāh*, pp. 69–70, where the author's father remembered the renowned *qāẓīs* of Ghazni from his lifetime. See also Jūzjānī, *Ṭabaqāt-i Nāṣirī*, vol. 1, pp. 450–1, fn. 6, where the editor notes the presence of a list of *qāẓīs* of Sultan Iltutmish in a variant manuscript, and Nizamī 'Arūẓī, *Chahār Maqāla*, pp. 24–5, for a list of *'ulamā'*, secretaries, litterateurs, and historians, and their writings which should be studied by the secretary to improve himself. Since *'ulamā'* was an ascribed status and therefore dependent upon the norms of the observer there was, it is interesting to note, little consistency in identifying 'learned men' in contemporary literature. It was in the later biographical compilations, *tazkirāt*, that competing and dissenting claims were sometimes resolved.

of these small communities had very tenuous associations with the Sultan or the regional military commander.[51] In contrast, they had fairly stable relationships with the local communities, where the individual recognized as *'ālim* frequently fulfilled the diverse functions of adjudicator, teacher, and religious expert in the crucial life-cycle rituals of Muslims. In the *qaṣaba*, garrison town, of Patiali, for instance, there does not seem to have been a court appointed *qāẓī* or *mudarris* (teacher). The local school (*maktab*) was run instead by the calligraphist Sa'd al-Dīn Muḥammad, who also functioned as the local *qāẓī*.[52] While we do not have enough information allowing us to flesh out the relationship of the local community and the *'ulamā'* in these small towns, the *qaṣaba* of Patiali does not seem to have been an exception. Many ritual specialists in the urban centres were chosen by the local community, and the Delhi Sultan acknowledged the regard accorded to these individuals. It was as a recognition of the piety of these *'ulamā'* and in an effort to gain their good will that, out of the plunder seized from the Lakhnauti campaign of 624/1227, the eldest Prince, Nāṣir al-Dīn, bestowed grants [*bawajh-i tuḥaf in'ām firistād*], to the *'ulamā'*, the kin of the Prophet, the pious, and the learned of the capital and all the neighbouring small towns (*qaṣabāt*).[53]

The relative independence available to the *'ulamā'* has been obscured by the historiographical concern to study their relationship with the ruling elite. It needs to be remembered here that, together with income derived from their varied services as religious specialists,

[51] See Chapter 2 for the example of the Malik Ẓiyā' al-Dīn Qāẓī Tulak, hardly a ritual specialist, but referred to as *qāẓī* because his father had been one. This genealogical association alone differentiated Malik Ẓiyā' al-Dīn from his peers. From a different perspective, the example of Malik Ẓiyā' al-Dīn and Malik Bahā' al-Dīn Muḥammad of Sangwan also clarifies the tenacity with which local communities, in the absence of Sultanate support, organized themselves to defend their own interests. Changes in the political life of the court were unlikely to introduce any major upheavals in the organization of these local societies. See also Chapter 6 and the discussion on the 'debris of dispensations'.

[52] Amīr K͟husrau, *Dībācha-i Dīwān G͟hurrat al-Kamāl*, cited by Wahid Mirza, *Life and Works of Amir Khusrau*, p. 20.

[53] Jūzjānī, *Ṭabaqāt-i Nāṣirī*, vol. 1, p. 454: *'ulamā' wa sādāt wa zuhhād wa atqiyā' wa ahl-i k͟haiyir-i dār al-mulk Dihlī wa sā'ir qaṣabāt rā bawajh-i tuḥaf in'ām firistād.*

the *'ulamā'* were also involved in commerce and industry. While in Afghanistan, Jūzjānī had led embassies from Tulak and Khaisar to Kuhistan, to reopen caravan routes disrupted by Mongol raids. In 623/1226, before his immigration to India, Jūzjānī went to Farah in the Sijistan province to purchase raw silk [*abrīsham*], for the requirements of the journey to Hindustan [*bajahat-i mā-yaḥtāj-i safar-i Hindūstān*].[54] Nor was Jūzjānī, a pious man involved in trade, exceptional in any way. In 657/1259 Jūzjānī recorded the visit of the honoured and respected Sayyid Ashraf al-Dīn, son of Sayyid Jalāl al-Dīn Ṣūfī, to Delhi from Samarqand for the purposes of trade.[55] Earlier, in 648/1250, Khwāja Rashīd al-Dīn Ḥakīm Balkhī had also come from Khurasan to trade in India.[56]

These instances from the *Ṭabaqāt-i Nāṣirī* can be easily multiplied from the *Fawā'id al-Fu'ād*. Niẓām al-Dīn occasionally recounted stories of *'ulamā'* who were inclined towards trade [*nīyat-i tijārat dāsht*].[57] This 'inclination towards trade' was apparent in the *imām* of a mosque in Multan. According to the complaint of Ḥasan Afghān that was reported by Niẓām al-Dīn, this *imām* was more preoccupied with dreams of profit from the purchase of slaves from Delhi and their sale in Khurasan than he was with the rituals of prayer.[58] The slave trade yielded enormous profits and Niẓām al-Dīn Awliyā' narrated the story of a *ṣūfī* from Bihar who, after increasing his initial capital by 960 per cent through trade, was advised to trade in *bardgān* (slaves used as domestics, singular, *barda*) since they fetched an even higher rate of profit, especially when these slaves were sold in Ghazni.[59]

[54] Ibid., vol. 2, p. 184.

[55] Ibid., p. 215.

[56] Ibid., p. 177.

[57] Amīr Ḥasan Sijzī, *Fawā'id al-Fu'ād*, p. 405.

[58] Ibid., p. 15.

[59] In Niẓām al-Dīn's story, the *ṣūfī* received 500 jitals from Shaykh 'Alī Sijzī (a late contemporary of Bakhtiyār Kākī and Sultan Iltutmish). This capital was invested in trade and within a short time had increased to 30 tankas, and after reinvestment grew further to 100 tankas. Calculated at the rate of 48 jitals to the (silver) tanka, the *ṣūfī* increased his initial capital by 960 per cent in a very short period. Ibid., p. 191. There was a flourishing market for 'Hindus' in the markets of the central Islamic lands, where these slaves could be sold for a profit. Other than the information mentioned above, note also the example of Jūzjānī, who

Many of the pious were therefore also very successful businessmen. According to the *Siyar al-Awliyā'*, Niẓām al-Dīn's maternal grandfather, Khwāja 'Arab, was an extremely wealthy, established merchant [*khwāja mumakkan būd*], and he possessed numerous slaves. Some of the Khwāja's slaves were involved in manufacturing goods, while some others were involved in trading ventures on behalf of their master.[60]

Rather than frowning or suppressing information concerning pious involvement in trade, the literature of the period shows little hesitation in discussing it. In fact, the casualness with which the literature of the time supplies information about the commercial ventures of the *'ulamā'* and the pious merely emphasizes that trade was not regarded as an unusual practice, but a legitimate, and perhaps relative to other occupations even a preferred, activity. This evidence makes it difficult to accept the rather simple historiographical formula of Khaliq Nizami that the *'ulamā'* allied with the Delhi Sultan because 'they aspired for wealth and worldly prestige and did not hesitate in compromising their conscience if it served their purpose'.[61] Such

---

remitted slaves to his sister from Multan. Jūzjānī, *Ṭabaqāt-i Nāṣirī*, vol. 1, pp. 483–4, vol. 2, p. 61. The enormous overland trade in 'Hindu' slaves (*barda*, domestic, *kanīzak*, concubine) into Khurasan and Iran, which had existed from the Ghaznavid period onwards (eleventh century), has been overlooked by most scholars, but Ibn Baṭṭūta writing in the mid-fourteenth century provided a hint of its magnitude. The Moroccan traveller noted: 'Another reason for our halt was fear of the snow. For upon this road there is a mountain called Hindu-kush, which means 'the slayer of the Indians', because the slave-boys and girls who are brought from the land of India die there in large numbers as a result of the extreme cold and the great quantity of the snow. [The passage of] it extends for a whole day's march.' Ibn Baṭṭūta, *Rehla*, translated by H.A.R. Gibb (Cambridge: Cambridge University Press, Hakluyt Society, second series, no. 141, 1971), vol. 3, p. 586.

60 Amīr Khwurd, *Siyar al-Awliyā'*, p. 104. For a description of the legal position of slaves involved in domestic functions and in trade for their masters, see S.D. Goitein, 'Slaves and Slavegirls in the Cairo Geniza Records', *Arabica*, 9 (1962), pp. 1–20.

61 K.A. Nizami, *Religion and Politics in India*, p. 152. The author also distinguishes the *'ulamā'* into two groups, the *'ulamā'-i ākhirat* (otherworldly *'ulamā'*) and the *'ulamā'-i dunyā* (the worldly *'ulamā'*). In the first category

an analysis ignores the fact that, in the literature of the period, the *'ulamā'* sometimes emerge as well-to-do people whose functions as teachers and ritual specialists did not preclude either participation in commercial ventures or strong ties with the local communities. Since *qāẓīs* and *imāms* could and did function independently without falling into penury, when they did choose to associate with the Sultanate, as in Iltutmish's reign, it must have been more than 'filthy lucre' that attracted them.

Khaliq Nizami's analysis also presumes that the Delhi Sultan was happy to recruit most notables who sought his service. As the discussion in the previous chapter has explained, Iltutmish was extremely judicious in his dispensation of privileges and honours to individuals. When the Delhi Sultan did dispense his favour, it was very much with an eye to the fact that the individuals he favoured would be useful in consolidating his authority. Thus, the recruitment of *'ulamā'* and *ahl-i qalam* was, from a different context, much like Iltutmish's patronage to the *bandagān*, part of a deliberate policy of enrolling strategically important personnel. Rather than the norm, such large-scale recruitment by the Delhi Sultan was certainly the exception.

Iltutmish's lack of hesitation when it came to patronizing *'ulamā'* and the *ahl-i qalam* is particularly noteworthy since many of these had previously sought sanctuary and patronage from Iltutmish's

---

were *'ulamā'* who functioned 'as starving teachers' or 'pious preachers and scholars', in the latter were 'government servants'. The personal character and greed of the individual determined the kind of *'ālim* he would eventually become. This characterization of the *'ulamā'* is present in S.A.A. Rizvi, *A History of Sufism in India*; and Aziz Ahmad, 'The Role of Ulema in Indo-Muslim History', *Studia Islamica*, 31 (1970), pp. 2–13. Nizami *et al.* used Baranī's juxtaposition of the *'ulamā*, ignoring the rhetorical intent of the author in claiming a superior status for indigent scholars (like himself). See Baranī, *Ta'rīkh-i Fīrūz Shāhī*, edited by Khan, p. 154, edited by Rashid, p. 177. The distinctions between the *'ulamā'-i ākhirat* (otherworldly *'ulamā'*) and the *'ulamā'-i dunyā* (the worldly *'ulamā'*) was not based upon whether you served the state or not, but upon whether you were spiritually or materially inclined. As we will see later, Niẓām al-Dīn provided several examples of *'ulamā'-i ākhirat* who served as *qāẓīs* without compromising their spirituality. An excellent example, of course, was the previously considered Minhāj-i Sirāj Jūzjānī, who Niẓām al-Dīn felt should have been a *Shaikh al-Islām* and not just a *qāẓī*; but see below for other examples.

competitor, Sultan Qubachā of Sindh. In 624/1227 Jūzjānī himself had migrated to Uchch from Khurasan by way of Ghazni and Multan. In Uchch he had been given charge of the Fīrūzī *madrasa* and appointed as the *qāẓī* of the army [*qāẓī-i lashkar*], of 'Alā' al-Dīn Bahrām Shāh, son of Qubachā.[62] Jūzjānī had been preceded in the Sindh region by al-Kūfī, the translator of the *Chach nāma*, the epic of the Arab conquest of Sindh, and also by the celebrated *qāẓī* and author Sadīd al-Dīn Muḥammad al-'Awfī, who reached Uchch from Bukhara and Ghazni some time before 620/1223.[63] Both al-Kūfī and al-'Awfī had received patronage from Qubachā's *wazīr*, 'Ain al-Mulk Ḥusain al-Ash'arī.

It was only in and around the final defeat and death of Qubachā in 625/1228, when the balance of power had visibly shifted in favour of Delhi, that a larger migration of the *'ulamā'* and the *ahl-i qalam* into the Delhi Sultanate is noticeable. In contrast to those military commanders, who were also seeking sanctuary in Delhi, the Sultan and his entourage received the *'ulamā'* and the 'people of the pen' warmly and gave them immediate support and patronage. In the year of the conquest itself, Qubachā's *wazīr* 'Ain al-Mulk was employed as the *wazīr* of Iltutmish's son Rukn al-Dīn Fīrūz, Governor of Budaun [64] Almost simultaneously, Jūzjānī found favour with Iltutmish and departed with the victorious troops to Delhi. Subsequently, he accompanied the Sultan on the Gwalior campaign and at regular intervals rallied the troops with his sermons, *tazkīr*. After the fort was captured in 630/1233, Jūzjānī was appointed *qāẓī*, *khaṭīb* and *imām* (judge, preacher and religious preceptor) of Gwalior.[65] Al-'Awfī did not suffer in the change of masters; he attached himself to the Delhi *wazīr*, Niẓām al-Mulk Junaidī, and completed his magnum opus *Jawāmi al-Kalīm*, which he had begun under al-Ash'arī's patronage but which he dedicated now to Junaidī.[66]

[62] Jūzjānī, *Ṭabaqāt-i Nāṣirī*, vol. 1, p. 420.

[63] See the references to 'Awfī in E.G. Browne, *A Literary History of Persia* (Cambridge: Cambridge University Press, 1964), vol. 2, pp. 478–9; and M. Nizamuddin, *Introduction to the Jawāmi' u'l-Ḥikāyāt wa Lawāmi' u'r-Riwāyāt*, pp. 10–14, 16–18.

[64] Jūzjānī, *Ṭabaqāt-i Nāṣirī*, vol. 1, p. 454.

[65] Ibid., vol. 1, pp. 448–9.

[66] M. Nizamuddin, *Introduction to the Jawāmi' u'l-Ḥikāyāt wa Lawāmi'*

In his patronage to *'ulamā'* Iltutmish favoured the Sunnī 'scriptural' tradition but, contrary to general scholarly opinion, he seems to have supported scholars who belonged to both the Ḥanafī and Shāfi'ī-Ash'arī schools (*mazhabs*) of theology and legal interpretion.[67] Iltutmish's choice of *wazīr* for his son Rukn al-Dīn, 'Ain al-Mulk Husain al-Ash'arī, was, as his name indicates, a follower of the Ash'arī school of theological reasoning and a Shāfi'ī. So too was Rukn al-Dīn's other dependant, Bahā' al-Mulk Ḥusain Ash'arī.[68] That Shāfi'ī jurists were present in some numbers in Delhi is also suggested by Jūzjānī's report of Nūr Turk's criticism of the *'ulamā'* who were followers of Abū Ḥanīfa and Shāfi'ī.[69] This was hardly an

---

u'r-Riwāyāt, p. 20. This two-stage migration of most refugees is also suggested by the account of Fakhr al-Mulk 'Iṣāmī's passage to Delhi. According to 'Iṣāmī, his ancestor arrived in Multan and waited there until all his retinue, *khailash*, arrived. Then, while some members of Fakhr al-Mulk's retinue stayed on in Multan, the remainder made their way to Delhi. 'Iṣāmī was evidently reporting this story from hearsay and he might have telescoped the events of the journey. It seems illogical that Fakhr al-Mulk would break journey to wait for his retinue, only to have some of his dependants opt to stay on in Multan. Fakhr al-Mulk may well have sought employment in Multan and moved subsequently to Delhi, the break providing sufficient time for members of his retinue to go their separate ways. See 'Iṣāmī, *Futūḥ al-Salāṭīn*, pp. 127–8.

67 See Aziz Ahmad, 'The Role of Ulema in Indo-Muslim History', and, for the latest in this line of reasoning (Turks favoured the Ḥanafī school, Arabs the Shāfi'ī), see Andre Wink, 'Al-Hind: India and Indonesia in the Islamic World-Economy, *c.* 700–1800 A.D.', *Itinerario* 12 (1988), p. 39, and idem, *Al-Hind, vol I: Early Medieval India and the Expansion of Islam*, pp. 69–70.

68 Jūzjānī, *Ṭabaqāt-i Nāṣirī*, vol. 1, pp. 446, 454, 456. Jūzjānī also mentioned Sharf al-Mulk Ash'arī in his account of post-Shamsī Sultans; ibid., vol. 2, p. 15.

69 See above for references. Apparently the Shāfi'ī *mazhab* still had some followers at the turn of the thirteenth century because Nizām al-Dīn Awliyā' mentioned them in his conversations and compares their interpretation of *hadīs* with that of the Ḥanafīs. See Amīr Ḥasan Sijzī, *Fawā'id al-Fu'ād*, especially pp. 276–7, 312. In an intriguing tale, Amīr Ḥasan Sijzī (p. 408) noted existing hostility between the Chishtī saint Ḥamīd al-Dīn Nagaurī and a group of people mentioned as the Baḥrīs (*Bahriyān*) led by the *'ālim* Maulānā Sharf al-Dīn Baḥrī. Although the Baḥrīs were nowhere identified in the text, Bulliet noticed a family of Shāfi'ī jurists in Nishapur by the name of Bahīrī, one

innovation: the Shansabanids in a preceding generation had also favoured the Ḥanafī and Shāfi'ī legal schools after they terminated their patronage of the Karramiya.[70]

The attraction of Iltutmish's open patronage to Shāfi'ī and Ḥanafī *'ulamā'* was particularly alluring in the context of the Mongol holocaust in the adjoining lands of Afghanistan, Khwarazm, and eastern Iran. The dislocation prevailing in the lands facing the Mongol invasions was in marked contrast to the stable Delhi Sultanate, which was emerging in north India at this time. A comparison of such factors swayed Shaykh Badr al-Dīn Ghaznawī's decision to immigrate to Delhi. In the story narrated by Niẕām al-Dīn, Shaykh Badr al-Dīn Ghaznawī sought an omen [*fāl*], from the *Qur'ān* to help him decide whether he should go to Delhi from Lahore or return to Ghazni. Although Badr al-Dīn wanted to return to his family in Ghazni, the *Qur'ān* promised paradise [*bihisht*], in Delhi, while the reference to Ghazni warned of pain and punishment, [*'aẕāb*]. After reaching Delhi, and receiving a warm welcome from Iltutmish, Badr al-Dīn discovered that in the mean time the Mongols had destroyed Ghazni and killed his relatives and other inhabitants of the town.[71]

It is also important to note that Niẕām al-Dīn himself did not approve of Badr al-Dīn's close relationship with the elites of the Delhi Sultanate. His criticism of Badr al-Dīn paralleled Jalāl al-Dīn's comments concerning those 'worldly individuals' for whom it was the post of *mudarris*, *qāẕī*, or *ṣadr-i jahān* (teacher, judge or chief ecclesiastic) alone that were the chief attractions.[72] But these were criticisms concerning the personal merits of individuals and not

---

of whom participated in Maḥmūd Ghaznawī's campaigns in India. Bulliet's information about the Bahīrīs ends by 540/1145, and although the connection is tenuous, it is worth speculating whether members of this family subsequently made their way into north India and whether Baḥrī was a corrupt rendering of Bahīrī. See R. Bulliet, *The Patricians of Nishapur*, pp. 192–200.

[70] On the Karramiya and Shansabānī patronage of the Ḥanafī and Shāfi'ī *'ulamā'*, see the useful work of Finbarr B. Flood, 'Ghurid Monuments and Muslim Identities: Epigraphy and Exegesis in Twelfth-century Afghanistan', *Indian Economic and Social History Review*, 42 (2005), pp. 263–94.

[71] Amīr Ḥasan Sijzī, *Fawā'id al-Fu'ād*, p. 124.

[72] Ibid., pp. 134–5, 402.

service with the Delhi Sultan. In contrast to Shaykh Badr al-Dīn, for example, Niẓām al-Dīn narrated the story of a butcher who possessed mystic powers of making wishes come true. Niẓām al-Dīn Awliyā' reported that this butcher fulfilled Qāẓī Fakhr al-Dīn Nāqla's ambition of becoming a *qāẓī*. Another supplicant wanted the butcher to make his dream of becoming an *amīr-i dād* come true.[73] Although occupying public offices, these pious individuals were not *ulamā'-i dunyā.*

Significantly, in Niẓām al-Dīn's recounting of these stories, the ambitions of notables were not criticized. The tenor of the Chishtī saint's remarks suggested instead that these were cases where, through the 'saint-like' butcher's intercession, worthy individuals received their just rewards. When altruistic, pious individuals were given public positions as guides and teachers it was for the ultimate benefit of the Muslim community. Because service as a *qāẓī*, *imām*, etc. implied undertaking important social responsibilities, self-serving 'worldly' *'ulamā'* should not receive appointments from the Delhi Sultan. Instead, these posts of public significance should be reserved for individuals of unquestioned piety. In a narrower sense Niẓām al-Dīn suggested that serving the Delhi Sultan was not completely abhorrent; despite the relative appreciation of the merits of different individuals and their ambitions, the Chishtī saint was unequivocal about the fact that it was the service of the Sultan that appealed to a large number of (morally upright) individuals.

At least during Iltutmish's reign, this must have been a fairly strong attraction because, in agreeing to serve the Delhi Sultan, the pious *'ulamā'* also gave their acquiescence to a degree of administrative ranking and control. Niẓām al-Dīn's report of Jalāl al-Dīn Tabrīzī's criticism indicated, for example, that there was an element of hierarchy amongst the posts of *mudarris*, *qāẓī*, and *ṣadr-i jahān*, which were in an order of ascendance. This element of hierarchy was also present in Niẓām al-Dīn's statement that Jūzjānī was qualified to be a *Shaikh al-Islām* and not a mere *qāẓī*.[74] Jūzjānī's career bore evidence of this form of progression. In his initial years of service under the Delhi Sultan, Jūzjānī was very grateful to be appointed *qāẓī*,

[73] Ibid., pp. 411–12: *marā mībayad ki qāẓī shawam . . . marā mībayad ki amīr-i dād shawam.*

[74] Ibid., pp. 429–30.

imām, and *khaṭīb* of Gwalior by Sultan Iltutmish. But these offices were not as important as the charge of the Delhi *madrasa-i Nāṣirī* and the *quẓā* of Gwalior given to him by Sultan Raẓiyya, or his subsequent appointment as *qāẓī* of Delhi and the entire Sultanate, *quẓā-i ḥaẓrat wa kull-i mamālik*, in the reign of Mu'izz al-Dīn Bahrām Shah.[75] The gradations amongst these posts occupied by the *'ulamā'* must operationally have also meant differences in salaries, responsibilities, and the extent of influence and patronage available to these individuals, but the sources provide few details on this subject.[76] What seems to have had some bearing on status was the relative importance of the region in which an incumbent served. Jūzjānī's movement to Delhi from Gwalior, for example, marked a definite improvement in his career.

Irrespective of whether the *'ulamā'* were appointed by the Delhi Sultan, his notables, or the local urban community, their functional

[75] Jūzjānī, *Ṭabaqāt-i Nāṣirī*, vol. 1, pp. 448–9, 460, 466. See also vol. 2, p. 214, for Jūzjānī's term in Gwalior.

[76] Evidence from Jūzjānī's own life suggests we should be careful in making hasty generalizations. In 635/1238 Jūzjānī had been given charge of the *madrasa-i Nāṣiriyā* and the *quẓā* of Gwalior. After considerable changes in his fortune, in 643/1246 he again received charge of the Nāṣirī *madrasa* and the *quẓā* of Gwalior. This seems to have been a more privileged appointment because, on this occasion, charge of the *madrasa* included the superintendence of its endowments, *bātauliyat-i awqāf-i ān*. On the earlier occasion, somebody else must have held the post of superintendent, *mutawallī*, and Jūzjānī's importance must have been relatively lower. See ibid., vol. 1, pp. 460, 470. According to contemporary historians, the *Madrasa-i Nāṣiriyā* was constructed and endowed by the younger son of Iltutmish, Sultan Nāṣir al-Dīn. See N.N. Law, *Promotion of Learning in India during Muḥammadan Rule (by Muḥammadans)* (London: Longmans, Green and Co., 1916); S.M. Jaffar, *Education in Muslim India; Being an Inquiry into the State of Education During the Muslim Period of Indian History, 1000–1800 A.D.* (Delhi: Idarah-i Adabiyat-i Delli, 1973 reprint); Imdad Sabri, *Dihli ke qadim Madaris aur Mudarris* (Delhi: Sabri Academy, 1988), p. 64. Recently, Munibur Rahman, 'Madrasa: II In Muslim India', *EI*[2], s.v., credited Ulugh Khān with the construction of the *Madrasa-i Nāṣiriyā*. Both these ascriptions must be incorrect because, according to Jūzjānī the *madrasa* was in existence before Sultan Nāṣir al-Dīn's accession (644/1246). It is likely that the *madrasa* was built and endowed by the elder Prince Nāṣir al-Din, who died in Iltutmish's reign, hence its name *Madrasa-i Nāṣiriyā*.

responsibilities were similar in that all relied upon the *Sharī'a* for their decisions concerning legitimate conduct for Muslims. The respective *'ulamā'* differed only in terms of the extent of their influence. Thus, the *'ālim* of a *qaṣaba*, or a *shahr*, theoretically performed the same tasks in the local community as the *qāẓī* of Delhi, but a smaller body of people recognized such a person's authority and he lacked the moral force to enforce his more unpopular decisions. The *qāẓī* of Ajudhan, for example, wanted to declare illegitimate Bābā Farīd's practice of performing *samā'* and *raqṣ* in the local mosque. He, however, found himself unable to take any action against the popular *ṣūfī* saint and therefore sought the support of the more influential *'ulamā'* of Multan. In light of the Chishtī saint's stature as a *ṣūfī* saint, however, the *'ulamā'* of Multan also declined taking any action against Bābā Farīd.[77] This was in contrast to the actions of the *'ulamā'* of Delhi, who were far more forthright in their intent to curb pietistic practices seen as contrary to the *Sharī'a*. Niẓām al-Dīn Awliyā' mentioned an instance where the *samā'* practice of the Suhrawardī Qāẓī Ḥamīd al-Dīn Nāgaurī provoked the *'ulamā'* to seek *fatāwā* (legal opinions) prohibiting the holding of these music assemblies. The Chishtī saint also recorded an instance where the *samā'* session of Quṭb al-Dīn Bakhtiyār Kākī and Ḥamīd al-Dīn was interrupted and opposed by the religious scholar Rukn al-Dīn Samarqandī.[78] The ability of the *'ulamā'* of Delhi to take a more aggressive posture against conduct believed to be against the *Sharī'a* came in part from a confidence in their own eminence, but it was also inspired by the tacit support of the Sultan.

The Delhi Sultan, in turn, shared the *'ulamā's* concern regarding the imposition of the *Sharī'a* in his domains. An integral part of Iltutmish's programme of political paramountcy was to project a self-image where the Sultan appeared in the dual role of conqueror and protector of the Holy Law. The investiture from the 'Abbāsid Caliph in 626/1229 to rule as his 'helper' (*Nāṣir-i Amīr al-Mu'minīn*) was publicly proclaimed because it emphasized Iltutmish's position as the sole legitimate Muslim monarch in north India whose duty, as the lieutenant of the Caliph, was to ensure the promulgation of the

[77] Amīr Ḥasan Sijzī, *Fawā'id al-Fu'ād*, p. 166.

[78] Ibid., pp. 407–9.

Sharī'a. The timing was perfect, for it coincided with the successful conclusion of the Sultan's campaigns against all competitors.

This self-image of the monarch was publicly proclaimed on the Sultan's constructions and could hardly be missed by local Muslims. Iltutmish constructed mosques, *'īdgāhs*, or mausolea that the local Muslim community would use constantly for their ritual worship, celebration of festivals, and communal services. Although in most of the conquered areas Iltutmish and his subordinates indulged in hectic building activity—proof in itself of his paramountcy and piety—of interest are those occasions when the Sultan added to already existing structures. These were often extensive additions and were visibly planned to impress the visitor. The *masjid-i jāmi'* in Delhi was enlarged to almost double its original size and, while Iltutmish's additions were stylistically similar to the pre-existing architecture, the screen extensions in the *miḥrāb* wall were bigger and more profusely ornamented in the formal floral styles of the Islamic tradition than Quṭb al-Dīn's contribution. Even more striking was the *mīnār* within the mosque precinct which was raised to tower three additional floors above its original height.[79] Delhi's *masjid-i jāmi'*, which was rivalled in size and grandeur by the congregational mosque of Bayana in Quṭb al-Dīn's reign, was transformed in Iltutmish's rule until it had no peer. Similarly, the *Arhāī din kī Jhoprī* mosque in Ajmer was enlarged and reworked until evidence of the early structure was barely traceable.[80] By renovating monuments associated with the north Indian Sultanates Iltutmish made a very deliberate and obvious

[79] On the basis of inscriptional evidence, Iltutmish's additions probably took place only after the Delhi Sultan had defeated his major adversaries and received the patent of governorship from the 'Abbāsid Caliph. See J. Horowitz, 'The Inscriptions of Muḥammad ibn Sam, Quṭbuddin Aibeg and Iltutmish', p. 23, no. XXI, where the date 627/1229–30 is mentioned. Amongst his titles inscribed on the doorway of the second floor of the Delhi *masjid-i jāmi'* (ibid., p. 26, no. XXIV), Iltutmish recorded *Nāṣir-i Amīr al-Mu'minīn*, Helper of the Commander of the Faithful, a title given by the 'Abbāsid Caliph to the Delhi Sultan only in 626/1229. This would suggest that some, if not all, construction activity in the Delhi *masjid-i jāmi'* (or at least the *mīnār*) occurred only after this date.

[80] J. Horowitz, 'The Inscriptions of Muḥammad ibn Sam, Quṭbuddin Aibeg and Iltutmish', p. 15, nos VI, VII, noted two inscriptions dated, respectively,

statement of conquest. The new order was also proclaimed: Delhi was now the unrivalled centre of the Sultanate. The other important urban centres of the Delhi regime, containing either new or refurbished constructions, signified the presence of the new political dispensation.

The extant inscriptional record of the Sultan on his monuments in Delhi, Ajmer, Budaun, and Bilgram bears out the seriousness with which Iltutmish sought to propagate his image as protector of the *Sharī'a* and guide of the Muslim community in north India. Many of these statements were couched in the formulaic idiom of the day, 'Lord of the necks of the people . . . heir to the kingdom of Solomon . . . who renders Islam and Muslims powerful, who bestows security and protection . . .',[81] but they also contained unique statements like, 'master of the Kings of the Turks and the Persians', a sentiment particularly relevant given the ethnic composition of the Sultan's audience. The religious and Qur'ānic epigraphs of Iltutmish also seem formulaic, until one recalls the many streams of piety and the lack of homogeneity within the Muslim community in this period.

Unlike Quṭb al-Dīn's choice of Qur'ānic and religious messages, Iltutmish's inscriptions focused less on the need for Muslims to be grateful to God for victory over non-believers. While this idea was certainly present, Iltutmish's inscriptions developed other themes also present in Quṭb al-Dīn's epigraphs—the need for Muslims to remain united as a chosen community, to remember their canonical obligations to their confessor, not to stray, and to contrast their privileged status with that of hypocrites, non-believers, and idolaters

---

595/1199 and 596/1200, which prove that the original construction in the *Arhāī din kī Jhoprī* should be dated to Mu'izz al-Dīn's reign. It is impossible to define the extent of the original construction. The main features of the extant mosque conform to a later style which is associated with Iltutmish. Inscriptional evidence from the mosque confirms Iltutmish's (re-constructional) activity. See also Michael W. Meister, 'The Two-and-a-half-day Mosque', *Oriental Art*, 18 n.s (1972), pp. 57–63.

[81] These eulogistic phrases are common to almost all of Iltutmish's inscriptions. See J. Horowitz, 'The Inscriptions of Muḥammad ibn Sam, Quṭubddin Aibeg and Iltutmish', p. 22, no. XVII; p. 23, no. XXI; pp. 23–4, no. XXII; p. 26, no. XXIV; p. 27, no. XXVI; p. 27, no. XXIVA; p. 28, no. XXIVII; p. 29, no. XXIX; and p. 30, no. XXIXII.

who would suffer the wrath of God. While the ideas were the same, the difference lay in the emphasis. This was also evident from the fact that Iltutmish inscribed only two Qur'ānic verses (*sūra* 14: 29–30, and *sūra* 62: 9–10) on the *mīnār* of the Delhi *masjid-i jāmi'*, the site for those celebratory statements acknowledging God's agency in the conquest of infidels. By Anthony Welch's admission, the messages on the *miḥrāb* wall, where Iltutmish's epigraphs proliferate, stressed 'instead, the importance of worship, of adherence to the principles of Islam, and of recognition of the obligations incumbent on believers'.[82]

Iltutmish's epigraphs take for granted the indivisibility of the Muslim community and focus upon the believer's personal and social conduct as evidence of his submission to his Confessor. The *ḥadīṣ* inscribed on the second arched recess of Iltutmish's *miḥrāb* screen in the Delhi *masjid-i jāmi'*, for example, brought out the Prophet's (and Iltutmish's) emphasis upon the performance of congregational prayer and its benefits:

> The Prophet . . . said, 'whoever offered his morning prayer in congregation got his [worldly] troubles removed by Allah; and whoever offered his afternoon prayer [in congregation] got his living made plentiful by Allah; and whoever offered his late afternoon prayer [in congregation] became [as pure] as on the day he was born; and whoever offered his evening prayer in congregation is considered as if he has given away his wealth and [even] his life [in the way of Allah], and whoever offered his bed-time prayer in congregation received Allah's blessing'. [The Prophet] . . . said 'whoever observed these five prayers in congregation would have his way [to Heaven] widened by Allah.'[83]

[82] Anthony Welch, '*Qur'an* and Tomb: the Religious Epigraphs of Two Early Sultanate Tombs in Delhi' in Frederick M. Asher, and G.S. Ghai, eds, *Indian Epigraphy: Its Bearings on the History of Art* (New Delhi: Oxford and IBH Publishing Co., American Institute of Indian Studies, 1985), p. 257. Welch summarized here arguments which he presented in another, apparently still unpublished, article: 'Islamic Architecture and Epigraphs in Sultanate India', in A.K. Narain, ed., *Studies in South Asian Art and Archaeology*, forthcoming.

[83] Transcribed and translated by Maulvi Muḥammad Ashraf Husayn, *A Record of all the Qur'anic and non-Historical Epigraphs on the Protected Monuments in the Delhi Province* (Calcutta: Archaeological Survey of India, Memoirs, no. 47, 1936), pp. 109–10.

On the second floor of the *mīnār* in the Delhi *masjid-i jāmi'*, constructed by Sultan Iltutmish, *sūra* 62: 9-10 from the *Qur'ān* preached the importance of performing the obligatory rituals of prayer in the midst of one's daily activity.

> O' believers, when proclamation is made for prayer on Friday, hasten to God's remembrance and leave trafficking aside; that is better for you, did you but know.
>
> Then when the prayer is finished, scatter in the land and seek God's bounty, and remember God frequently; haply you will prosper.[84]

All these Qur'ānic and religious inscriptions were, naturally enough, in Arabic and almost always inscribed in *naskh*, an extremely difficult script to decipher for the initiated, leave alone the layman.[85] Among the largely unlettered Muslim audience of the early thirteenth century, these inscriptions would have gone unread.[86] It is likely, however, that at least the gist of the contents of the Qur'ānic and other religious statements in the mosque—if not the inscriptions themselves—were conveyed to the congregation in the sermons of the *imām*, the *khaṭīb*, and the *mutaẕakkir* who preached, harangued, and exhorted Muslims to follow the righteous path.[87] At least in terms of

[84] Ibid., p. 105.

[85] These difficulties dodged early restoration work as well. Note Horowitz's anguish that the lowest inscribed band on the *mīnār* 'has suffered much at the hands of an ignorant restorer, who replaced the different fragments in a perfectly arbitrary manner [and] it is not possible to read the whole of it . . .' .J. Horowitz, 'The Inscriptions of Muḥammad ibn Sam, Quṭbuddin Aibeg and Iltutmish', p. 16.

[86] It is truly surprising that Anthony Welch (for references see above) could argue that 'the epigraphic program of the Quṭb *mīnār* seems to have been directed towards the non-Muslim populations . . .' (p. 257). According to the author, *sūra* 48: 6, for example, was 'specifically directed towards the non-Muslim majority beyond the walls of the mosque', and since it was 'included in the epigraphic program of the Quṭb *mīnār's* first story . . . [it was on] . . . that portion of the mosque complex most visible to believers and non-believers outside the walls' (p. 260). The inscription was visible, perhaps, but if readable at all it was intelligible only to those who knew Arabic and the *naskh* script.

[87] There is some information concerning the *taẕkīr*, exhortation, given by the *mutaẕakkir*. On one occasion Jūzjānī explained that the *taẕkīr* was 'intended [the printed text has *maqsūr*, a misprint for *maqṣūd*?] to inflame [people] to

goals the *'ulamā'* and the Delhi Sultan placed an equal emphasis upon the primacy of the injunctions of the *Sharī'a* (*aḥkām-i Sharī'a*) in the lives of the Muslim community.

Although we lack details about how Iltutmish would have liked the *'ulamā'* to enforce conformity of belief and action according to the *Sharī'a*, stray references concerning the actions of the *Shaikh al-Islām* indicate that he was an individual whose specific function was to guide the conduct of Muslims in his area of jurisdiction, interact with the pious, and most crucially, scrutinize their texts and teachings. Like the *qāẓī*, the *Shaikh al-Islām* was not necessarily an appointee of the Sultan. As in the case of the Suhrawardī saint Bahā' al-Dīn Zakariyā, pious and influential individuals were sometimes given this responsibility by the local Muslim community, a decision normally abided and confirmed by the lay authority. Much like the *qāẓī*, again, the variations in his duties and functions were influenced by the individual *Shaikh al-Islām's* own pietistic inclinations, his competence as a scholar, his prestige in and the degree of support he obtained from the local community and the immediate political authority. In its normative conceptualization, the function of the *Shaikh al-Islām* in the reign of Iltutmish does not seem to have differed markedly from that of its Ghurid predecessor.[88] An anecdote in the *Chahār Maqāla* throws fortunate light on some of its features.

[participate] in *jihād* and [gain the religious] merit of *ghazwāt* [waging Holy Wars], and exert themselves [*jidd na-mūdan*] in guarding the dignity of Islam and serving the imperial court and obeying the orders of the commanders [*baimtiṣāl awāmir ulū al-amr*]'. Jūzjānī, *Ṭabaqāt-i Nāṣirī*, vol. 2, p. 76. Jūzjānī had a flair for these exhortations, and Iltutmish also required him to deliver these sermons during his campaigns (ibid., vol. 1, pp. 447–8.). The themes chosen by the *mutazakkir*, *khaṭīb*, and *imām* were all religious and the sermons were meant to move their audience to abide by the tenets of the *sharī'a* or perform meritorious actions which would benefit the community. This sermonising tone also predominated in the choice of Qur'ānic verses and *ḥadīṣ* statements inscribed in the congregational mosques of Delhi and Ajmer.

[88] Although the study of Richard Bulliet, 'The Shaikh al-Islam and the Evolution of Islamic Society', *Studia Islamica*, 35 (1972), pp. 53–67 is weak on the Ghurids and the Delhi Sultanate, it is extremely valuable in tracing the origin of the office to Khurasan and relating its evolution to social changes in the region.

> The *Shaikh al-Islām* 'Abdu'llāh Anṣārī . . . conceived a fanatical hatred . . . [towards the physician Adīb Ismā'īl] . . ., and several times attempted to do him an injury, and burned his books. Now this fanatical dislike arose from religious motives [*ta'aṣṣubī būd dīnī*], for the people of Herat believed that he could restore the dead to life, and this belief was [injurious to the common folk].[89] Now the Shaykh [al-Islam] fell ill, and in the course of the illness the death-rattle became apparent. However much the physicians treated him, it availed nothing. They were in despair . . . [and finally appealed to the physician Adīb Ismā'īl. The physician studied the symptoms and prescribed a remedy, which he sent together with this message to the *Shaikh al-Islām*] . . . 'You should study science, and not burn men's books'.[90]

Unlike many sources that ascribe persecution by the *Shaikh al-Islām* to purely personal motives,[91] the *Chahār Maqāla* goes further and explains the reason behind this fanatical hatred. The *Shaikh al-Islām* had burned Adīb Ismā'īl's books because they were understood to be the source of the heretical belief that the physician could 'restore the dead to life'. This was especially disturbing since the physician's reputed prowess had 'fooled' people and he had gained adherents within the city of Herat.

The activities of the *Shaikh al-Islām* of Delhi in Iltutmish's reign have also been recorded by several chroniclers, and these accounts range over a considerable period of time. Interestingly enough, many of these reports are clearly apocryphal; yet they all harmonize with

[89] See Niẓāmī 'Arūẓī, *Chahār Maqāla*, edited by Mohammad Qazvini and Mohammad Mu'in (Tehran: University Press, 1955–7), p. 129. For the better part I have followed the translation of Edward G. Browne. Here, however, Browne read the phrase as 'injurious to his own pretensions, [*da'wī rā'*], the version present in the BM Ms., Or. 2,955 and the Tehran lithographed edition (A.H. 1305). The translator noted however, that 'injurious to the common folk [*'awām rā'*] was the reading in the oldest manuscript, BM Ms., Or. 3,507. See Niẓāmī 'Arūẓī, *Chahār Maqāla*, translated by Browne, p. 129, fn. 2. As will be apparent from my discussion below, I believe that the oldest manuscript preserves the sense of the original passage which was also adopted by Qazvini and Mu'in in their edition.

[90] Ibid., edited by Qazvini and Mu'in, p. 129, translated by Browne, p. 129.

[91] See the above mentioned narration of the hostility between the *Shaikh al-Islām* Najm al-Dīn Sughrā and Bakhtiyār Kākī and Jalāl al-Dīn Tabrīzī in the *Siyar al Awliya'* and *Siyar al-'Ārifīn* respectively.

each other and unwittingly emphasize the *Shaikh al-Islām's* role as a guide and adjudicator of the conduct of Muslims. In Ẓiyā' al-Dīn Baranī's *Ta'rīkh-i Fīrūz Shāhī* (a mid-fourteenth-century text) the *Shaikh al-Islām* Sayyid Nūr al-Dīn Mubārak Ghaznawī was remembered by Balban as haranguing Sultan Iltutmish on how the existing customs of governance contravened the *sunna* of the Prophet and inevitably damned rulers to perdition. Subsequently, the *Shaikh al-Islām* narrated four precepts, *'amal*, for the protection of the faith, *dīn panāhī*, which rulers should follow.[92] As has been frequently remarked, Sayyid Nūr al-Dīn represents the authorial voice of Ẓiyā' al-Dīn Baranī, and, in the light of the functions of the *Shaikh al-Islām*, was seen as an apposite choice to question and voice aphorisms on moral conduct.[93] That this was no accidental choice is clarified if we recall the evidence of the sixteenth-century *Siyar al-'Ārifīn*. According to the Suhrawardī *tazkirāt*, in the inquest held to adjudicate Jalāl al-Dīn Tabrīzī's conduct, it was the *Shaikh al-Islām* Najm al-Dīn Sughrā that was the plaintiff, and the judge was the *Shaikh al-Islām* Bahā' al-Dīn Zakariyā.

Just as Adīb Ismā'īl's conduct was problematic for the *Sharī'a*-minded *Shaikh al-Islām* in Afghanistan, in the north Indian context as 'injurious to the common folk' of Delhi were Nūr Turk's preaching to the masses or Bakhtiyār Kākī's display of miraculous powers which Iltutmish's *Shaikh al-Islām*, Najm al-Dīn Sughrā, had sought to curb. In light of the responsibilities of the *Shaikh al-Islām*, Najm al-Dīn's conduct towards Jalāl al-Dīn Tabrīzī also becomes more rational. Rather than being motivated purely out of malice, it is more likely that the *'ālim's* persecution of Jalāl al-Dīn Tabrīzī followed the *ṣūfī's* failure to meet norms of conduct and doctrine acceptable to Sughrā.

It is unclear whether these examples of 'supervision and punishment' were restricted to Delhi, or if these instances were a reflection of a wider effort to 'discipline and punish', evident in the latter part

[92] Ẓiyā' al-Dīn Baranī's *Ta'rīkh-i Fīrūz Shāhī*, edited by Khan, pp. 41–4, edited by Rashid, pp. 49–52.

[93] The *Shaikh al-Islām's* aphorisms were central in Baranī's didactic 'mirror for princes', *Fatāwā-yi Jahāndārī*, where they were embellished and discussed in length. See Peter Hardy, *Historians of Medieval India*, p. 29; and K.A. Nizami, *Religion and Politics in India*, pp. 161–2.

of Iltutmish's reign. Judging by the aforementioned reports of conflict between the *'ulamā'* and *ṣūfī pīrs* over the validity of mystical practices like *samā'*, *raqṣ* and *namāz* in towns such as Budaun, Multan, and Ajudhan, Delhi does not seem to have been an isolated case. Depending upon the individual *'ālim's* confidence, conflict could occur in a *qaṣaba* as well, and Jūzjānī provided information about Qāẓī Shams al-Dīn of Maihar[pūr] who persecuted [*kofta shudan*], a Turkman dervish called Ayūb.[94] Impressionistic as the evidence may be, it does suggest that Iltutmish's reign was perhaps unique until the reign of Muḥammad Shāh Tughluq (725–52/1325–51) for the reported number of *maḥẓars* (literally, assemblies, and contextually, inquisitions) and demands for *fātāwa* (legal opinions) against Muslims whose conduct or teaching were believed to be against the *Sharī'a*. The evidence also seems to suggest that it was the *ṣūfīs* in particular that felt the brunt of this persecution in Iltutmish's reign. It is not surprising therefore for Niẓām al-Dīn Awliyā' to have said that Jūzjānī should have been a *Shaikh al-Islām* and not a mere *qāẓī*. Had Jūzjānī been a *Shaikh al-Islām*, his personal evaluation of conduct would have been influenced more by his well-known *ṣūfī* leanings rather than a 'scriptural' understanding of Islam.

This interpretation of Iltutmish militates considerably from the popular image of a pious monarch who had a special weakness for *ṣūfīs*.[95] It is indeed interesting that, as one who sought to enforce the *Sharī'a* and regulate religious practice, the Delhi Sultan managed to escape criticism in the *ṣūfī* literature. The response of the pious to Sultan Iltutmish's actions is actually not that surprising because the Delhi Sultan was never directly involved with the regulative functions of the *qāẓī* or the *Shaikh al-Islām*. Once a *Sharī'a*-minded individual with the appropriate degree of learning or social support had been

[94] Jūzjānī, *Ṭabaqāt-i Nāṣirī*, vol. 1, p. 466. This event probably took place in the last years of Iltutmish's reign or very shortly after his death, because, according to Jūzjānī, in 639/1242 Ayūb resided in Delhi, where he had gained the favour of Sultan Bahrām Shāh (637–9/1240–2) and eventually succeeded in getting Qāẓī Shams al-Dīn executed.

[95] For an uncritical collation of these sentiments see K.A. Nizami, 'The Religious Life and Leanings of Iltutmish', in idem, *Studies in Medieval Indian History and Culture* (Allahabad: Kitab Mahal, 1966), pp. 13–40.

chosen, the *'ālim* functioned according to his conscience, the Sultan intervening only to curb excesses. Obviously, this latitude for action implied that the Sultan had to be very judicious about the individual he chose to support as *qāẓī* or *Shaikh al-Islām*, but maintaining a distance helped in insulating Iltutmish from the frequently unpopular decisions of the *'ulamā'*. Iltutmish might receive representations and complaints about the *Shaikh al-Islām's* actions, but the Sultan was not made ultimately responsible for the decisions of the jurists or censors. In the account of the *Siyar al-'Ārifīn*, Iltutmish was reportedly shocked by Najm al-Dīn's actions and, therefore, dismissed the *Shaikh al-Islām*. In 'Iṣāmī's *Futūḥ al-Salāṭīn*, Iltutmish was forced to hold an inquest against Qāẓī Ḥamīd al-Dīn Nāgaurī, but, despite the prompting of the *'ulamā'*, the Delhi Sultan could not restrain showing respect and deference when the *ṣūfī pīr* appeared in court.[96]

Conclusion

Iltutmish's position was particularly difficult when it came to the question of regulating the conduct of his subjects. As a Sultan with considerable political authority, Iltutmish could demand obedience; but beyond a certain point he could not intervene as a regulator of the conduct of his Muslim subjects. His authority was circumscribed not merely because he could not function as a legislator or interpreter of the *Sharī'a*, but also because, by choice, Iltutmish had constructed a political system which derived its stability by maintaining a distance from the subject Muslim population. Moreover the 'ruled' had a very ambiguous appreciation of the moral qualities of their 'rulers'. The Amirs and Maliks were wealthy and powerful and therefore sometimes useful as patrons. But these sentiments alone were insufficient to motivate cooperation or loyalty towards Delhi from very dispersed groups of people.

On the other hand the *'ulamā'* and the *Sharī'a*-minded *ṣūfīs* commanded considerable respect amongst Muslims. They were also the one group of people that could legitimately guide and correct the actions and beliefs of ordinary Muslims. It was their authoritative

[96] 'Iṣāmī, *Futūḥ al-Salāṭīn*, pp. 117–20.

status within Muslim society that Iltutmish sought to tap and, through them, span the divide between rulers and the ruled. Rather than subvert or manipulate them, Iltutmish lent the pious his support.

This was not indiscriminate support to the piety-minded. Iltutmish may have been respectful towards the pious, but he did not encourage charismatic *ṣūfīs* who could command large followings of disciples and emerge as authoritarian figures in their own right. In contrast the *'ulamā'* did not make disciples; they commanded respect as individuals learned in the religious sciences, and guided Muslims in their endeavour to follow the teachings contained in the Qur'ānic revelation. Ideally, the *'ulamā'* were the specific group that could help Iltutmish in his goal of promoting social and political stability within his newly conquered domains—by creating the sense of a homogeneous Muslim community bound by the dictates of the *Sharī'a*.

This search for social and political stability had also driven the north Indian Sultanates and the *Sharī'a*-minded *'ulamā'* into a collaborative effort, but the scale of their efforts did not match that of the Delhi Sultan. Pious support to Iltutmish was forthcoming largely because of the Chingīz Khanid holocaust which had destroyed the vestiges of Islamic civilization dear to the *'ulamā'*. Moreover, since the fury of the Mongol invasions coincided with the establishment of the paramount Delhi Sultanate, the pious seized upon the Delhi Sultan as their final hope for the protection of the community. From the mid-1220s only the domains of the Delhi Sultan were left as the source of sanctuary for the *'ulamā'* in north India.

Coming from two completely different ends, the perceptions of the *'ulamā'* and Iltutmish coincided concerning Delhi's role in north India. Iltutmish's goal was to make Delhi the paramount power, the centre without any rival. For the *'ulamā'*, the Delhi Sultanate was a haven which could become the axis of the Muslim community, wherein the hitherto disparate and nucleated communities of north India could be integrated into a larger, comprehensive *jamā'a ummah* which abided by the *Sharī'a*. The two were complementary goals. This complementarity was apparent to the *'ālim* Jūzjānī, whose description of Delhi as the *Qubbat al-Islām* conveyed these sentiments succinctly. In its obvious sense *qubba* meant sanctuary; thus *Qubbat al-Islām* referred to the role of Delhi as the sanctuary of Islam at a time when the central Islamic lands were feeling the brunt of the Mongol invasions. *Qubba*, however, also meant, the centre, the axis, and in that sense *Qubbat al-Islām* referred to the newly gained role of Delhi as the paramount power in north India, the centre of Islam.[97] In light of their congruent aims, it is certainly not surprising that the *'ulamā'* received a warm welcome in Iltutmish's newly conquered domains, or that they cooperated with the Delhi Sultan.

If we recall the variety of pietistic practices in north India in the early thirteenth century, we can more readily appreciate the achievements of the *Sharī'a*-minded during the reign of Iltutmish. Judging by the many protests of the pious from several towns in the Sultanate, the *'ulamā'* had some success in introducing norms through which they could supervise the conduct of Muslims. Nūr Turk, Bakhtiyār Kākī, Jalāl al-Dīn Tabrīzī, and Qāẓī Ḥamīd al-Dīn Nāgaurī were all contemporaries of Iltutmish, and their protests date from the last years of the Delhi Sultan's reign. The *Sharī'a*-minded could indeed take credit for ensuring that no *ṣufī* in Iltutmish's reign succeeded in establishing a charismatic position in the Delhi Sultanate akin to Niẓām al-Dīn Awliyā' in the early fourteenth century.

By the 1230s the primacy of Iltutmish in the political world in and around the urban centres of north India was complete. The *Sharī'a*-minded *'ulamā'* were an important group of individuals whose association with the Delhi Sultan enabled him to consolidate his newly conquered domains. As the next chapter points out, however, within ten years of the Delhi Sultan's death the domains of the Delhi Sultanate were fragmented again amongst new warlords. Although political break-up did not mean the loss of sentiment helping cohere a 'Muslim community', the *Sharī'a* was not the only foundation on which it would hereafter be based. In the post-Iltutmish period, *ṣūfīs* (and not just the *'ulamā'*) gained increasing importance as keepers of the public conscience. This was, however, only one amongst a number of significant changes that took place in the nature of political relations in the Sultanate of Delhi between 633/1236 and the end of the thirteenth century.

[97] See Jūzjānī, *Ṭabaqāt-i Nāṣirī*, vol. 1, p. 441, and Ch. Pellat, 'al-Ḳubba, Ḳubbat al-Ạlam', *EI*[2], s.v.

CHAPTER 5

Social and Political Changes and a Disintegrating Shamsī Dispensation 633–64/1236–66

On Shams al-Dīn Iltutmish's death his lineal descendants succeeded to the throne of Delhi, but political power within the Sultanate devolved to the members of his dispensation. All historians have focused upon the fact that the 'nobles' controlled effective power while the Sultans, Rukn al-Dīn Fīrūz Shāh (633–4/1236), Raẓiyya (634–7/1236–40), Mu'izz al-Dīn Bahrām Shāh (637–9/1240–2), 'Alā al-Dīn Mas'ūd Shāh (639–44/1242–6), and Nāṣir al-Dīn Maḥmūd (644–64/1246–66), reigned but did not rule. Scholars have uniformly discussed their reigns as years of unmitigated disaster for the corporate character of the Delhi Sultanate. There is little doubt that the ability of the Delhi Sultans to intervene in the affairs of the ruling elites declined dramatically. What were the consequences of this decline or, to rephrase the question from a slightly less linear and teleological perspective, what was the impact of the Shamsī political organization on the Delhi Sultanate in the long duration?

The empowerment of the Shamsī *bandagān*, which led them into conflict with Iltutmish's successors, was only one part of this development. It also led them into conflict with each other, and with new groups who used the political turmoil of the period to sequester long denied advantages. These developments created new alliances and power groups. But to sustain this long-drawn-out conflict meant that these elite groups paid great attention to their military and administrative personnel, their principalities and fiscal resources. The years of conflict, in other words, went on to touch a variety of different sectors of the economy and social life of the Sultanate. It affected the *Sharī'a*-minded groups of people as well, individuals with whose collaboration Iltutmish had projected Delhi as the 'Sanctuary of Islam' in a world facing the Mongol holocaust. What happened to this vision of the Sultanate and the groups that sustained the discursive frames of Delhi's hegemony? During the post-Iltutmish years of strife, what became of the lineages of power that sustained and interrogated the definitions and enforcement of orthopraxis in the Sultanate?

There is little doubt that the years of political turmoil after the death of Iltutmish challenged the structures that had constructed the paramount authority of Delhi. And yet, the *idea* of Delhi as a cohering element survived this fractious and fragmented period. Was it therefore, just an interregnum, a momentary hiatus in the longer, uninterrupted history of Delhi's dominance of the north Indian region? This chapter argues to the contrary. It studies three vectors of change—mutations amongst the Shamsī political elites and the emergence of the Ghiyāṣī dispensation of power; the political geography of this domain and the new orientation of elites and spaces; and the role of the *'ulamā* and *ṣūfis* in the Sultanate, affected as they were, by ideological shifts in the construction of authoritative public positions in the new realm. The continued predominance of Delhi in the history of north India for another century and more tends to obliterate the fact that the Sultanate, in fact, altered considerably during the middle decades of the thirteenth century. In this chapter I try to historicize the continuities and changes that occurred through these turbulent years as precisely as possible. I start my analysis with a closer look at the transitions that occurred amongst the political elites.

Political Mutations and the Emergence of the Ghiyāṣī Elites 633–64/1235–66

The character of the conflict in the post-Iltutmish period altered as the protagonists as well as their alliances and aims shifted over time. To capture some of the changes through these years I have further distinguished the intervening decades into three periods of unequal length and contrasting character: (a) 633–9/1236–42, the period of 'inter-dispensational' conflict, when remnants of the Shamsī dispensation were in conflict with their master's successors and their military retinues; (b) 639–53/1242–55, the period of 'intra-dispensational' conflict, when members of the Shamsī dispensation were in conflict with each other; and (c) 652–64/1254–66, which saw the emergence of the new dispensation of power of the Shamsī slave Ulugh Khān, the future Sultan Ghiyāṣ al-Dīn Balban (664–85/1266–87). Although some of these periods are organized around rather simple binaries, the narrative on the different periods develops the more complex form and interconnections that were present within the fluid political terrain of the time.

(a) 633–9/1236–42: The Period of 'Inter-Dispensational' Conflict

To be able to understand the nature of the conflict in the years immediately following the death of Sultan Iltutmish we need to be aware of the composition and organization of the various groups involved, and the reasons why their mutual interests drove them into competition. The conflict in this period revolved around the heirs of the Delhi Sultan, three of whom, Rukn al-Dīn Fīrūz Shāh, Raẓiyya, and Mu'izz al-Dīn Bahrām Shāh, were deposed within six years (633–9/1236–42). Contemporary historians have followed Jūzjānī and Baranī in attributing the 'weakness' of these Sultans, and their inability to emerge as authoritative figures like their father, to the fact that they were callow striplings, lacking in moral virtue and charisma, and hence unable to command respect or obedience in their subordinates.[1] Yet, Jūzjānī's history of the period does show some of these same Sultans leading campaigns, recruiting supporters, and occasionally enforcing harsh punishments on their father's notables. It is also frequently forgotten that Iltutmish's immediate successor, Sultan Rukn al-Dīn, had served as a Governor for eight lunar years in his

[1] Jūzjānī, *Ṭabaqāt-i Nāṣirī*, vol. 1, pp. 457, Baranī, *Ta'rīkh-i Fīrūz Shāhī*, edited by Khan, p. 26, edited by Rashid, pp. 30–1.

father's dominions, first in Budaun and then Lahore.[2] There is little doubt about the fact that the rapid dethronement of the Sultans brought younger Princes into the political arena, and they had not had Rukn al-Dīn's administrative experience or the opportunity to recruit their own supporters. Yet, while the ability of the competing Shamsī notables to control and influence the Delhi Sultan increased over time, Iltutmish's heirs still had the capacity to seize the political initiative on a number of occasions.

Amongst the Shamsī notables the most powerful were the *bandagān-i Shamsī*, the military slaves of Sultan Iltutmish, already studied in some detail earlier. To recall: these were slaves who had been purchased, fostered (*parwarish*) and carefully trained until a smaller trusted group amongst them, the *bandagān-i khāṣṣ*, were given crucial territorial commands or high positions in the capital near the Sultan. Another body of the *bandagān-i Shamsī*, slightly younger than the *khāṣṣ* slaves, were under training for eventual deployment to the highest positions and were, for the moment, given intermediary administrative tasks—for example, as *shaḥnas*. A final group of the Shamsī *bandagān* included the young, newly-purchased slaves who functioned as domestics and pages at court. Because the dyadic bond between the master and these pages were hardly consolidated, they were not trusted with independent command, and their ties of association with their master were much weaker. The careers of the Shamsī *bandagān* detailed in the twenty-second part of the *Ṭabaqāt-i Nāṣirī* is summarized in Table 3. From the details in that Table, I have extrapolated information to convey a sense of seniority within the Shamsī cadre at the death of Sultan Iltutmish. Table 2, below, carries this information.

There are two important factors that we should keep in mind as we study the history of the Shamsī *bandagān* in the post-Iltutmish period. The first is the impact of time on these personnel. In its simplest form, there was attrition in the ranks of the *bandagān* cadre. At the beginning of Rukn al-Dīn's reign (633/1236), twenty-two of the twenty-five Shamsī slaves listed in the *Ṭabaqāt-i Nāṣirī* were alive;

[2] Rukn al-Dīn was appointed Governor of Budaun in 625/1228 and, some time after 631/1233, to the Governorship of Lahore. Jūzjānī, *Ṭabaqāt-i Nāṣirī*, vol. 1, pp. 449, 454. See Chapter 3 and below for further details.

by the end of Raẓiyya's reign (637/1240), four years later, only fifteen of the original twenty-five in the list survived. The rest had died in accidents and wars, and some had been executed (see Table 3).

The second relates to the more complicated aspect of relationships between the Shamsī heirs and their master's slaves. Although with Iltutmish's death the legal rights of ownership and clientship (*walā'*)

Table 2

Seniority of Service amidst Shamsī *Bandagān*, 633/1236

Bandagān-i khāṣṣ	*Bandagān-i khaṣṣ in training*	*Junior bandagān; 'pages'*
[2] KABĪR KHĀN AYĀZ AL-MU'IZZĪ[3] [4] MALIK SAIF AL-DĪN AI-BEG UCHCH [7] MALIK 'IZZ AL-DĪN TUGHĀN KHĀN TUGHRIL [9] MALIK HINDŪ KHĀN MU'AYYID AL-DĪN MUBĀRAK AL-KHAZĪN [10] MALIK IKHTIYĀR AL-DĪN QARĀ QUSH KHĀN	[6] MALIK NUṢRAT AL-DĪN TĀ'ĪSĪ AL-MU'IZZĪ [8] MALIK TAMAR KHĀN [11] MALIK IKHTIYĀR AL-DĪN ALTŪNIA-I TABARHIND [12] IKHTIYĀR AL-DĪN AI-TEGIN [13] MALIK BADR AL-DĪN SUNQAR AL-RŪMĪ [14] MALIK TĀJ AL-DĪN SANJAR QUTLUQ [15] MALIK TĀJ AL-DĪN SANJAR KURĪT KHĀN [18] MALIK IKHTIYĀR AL-DĪN YUZBEG TUGHRIL KHĀN [19] MALIK TĀJ AL-DĪN SANJAR ARSALĀN KHĀN AL-KHWĀRAZMĪ [20] MALIK 'IZZ AL-DĪN KUSHLŪ KHAN AL-SULṬĀNĪ [21] MALIK SAIF AL-DĪN ARKALĪ DĀD BEG	[16] MALIK [IKIT/BAT] KHĀN SAIF AL-DĪN AI-BEG KHITĀ'Ī [17] MALIK TĀJ AL-DĪN SANJAR TARKHĀN [22] MALIK BADR AL-DĪN NUṢRAT KHĀN SUNQAR ṢŪFĪ [23] MALIK NUṢRAT AL-DĪN SHĪR KHĀN [24] MALIK KISHLĪ KHĀN SAIF AL-DĪN AI-BEG AL-SULṬĀNĪ MALIK AL-ḤUJJĀB [25] ULUGH KHĀN BALBAN AL-SULṬĀNĪ

[3] Although Kabīr Khān Ayāz was a senior slave of Iltutmish, he did not command significant authority after his dismissal and was no longer regarded with the same sentiment by the monarch as the other *bandagān-i khāṣṣ*. Kabīr Khān was restored to high command by Iltutmish's successors, but because of his special situation I have not included him within the *bandagān-i khāṣṣ* in my discussion below.

were inherited by his successor(s), the possible ties of affection and close dyadic bond that brought together master and elite slaves were not transferable. Thus, Iltutmish's successors could never count on the reliability of the Shamsī slaves as dependable military subordinates. They had to negotiate relationships with their father's slaves with great care, especially since most of the important commands in the Sultanate were under their control.

When studying relationships between incumbent monarchs and Shamsī slaves it is important to keep in mind the existing status within the *bandagān* cadre in 633/1236, and changes that the politics of the following years introduced into these ranks. For instance, at Rukn al-Dīn's accession in 633/1236, barring Hindū Khān, Iltutmish's seniormost slaves held distant charges, over Uchch, Multan, and Lakhnauti. None of these *khāṣṣ* slaves revolted against Rukn al-Dīn, and in Raẓiyyā's reign the surviving members (numbers 7, 9, and 10 in Tables 2–3) all pledged their support to the monarch. The ties of the *bandagān-i khāṣṣ* to the master kept their loyalty alive to his lineage at a time when the rest of the Shamsī slaves were in rebellion. They followed the political arrangements that Sultan Iltutmish had wanted to perpetuate.

Amongst those who were rebelling and negotiating for advancement were slaves of several contrasting backgrounds. On the one hand was the erstwhile senior slave Kabīr Khān Ayāz, whose favour was curried in turn by Rukn al-Dīn and Raẓiyya (number 1 in Tables 2–3).[4] On the other hand were the 'middling' slaves who were often in armed insurrection against the monarch, negotiating support in exchange for high offices or creating alliances to depose the monarch. Much of the conflict of the age was generated by the ambitions of this

[4] Kabīr Khān had originally been appointed as the *muqṭi'* of Multan, but had been removed by Iltutmish and given the command of Palwal (see the discussion in Chapter 3). Jūzjānī contradicted himself when he mentioned Kabīr Khān as the *walī* (Governor) of Multan in his account of Rukn al-Dīn's reign (ibid., vol. 1, pp. 455–6). In his biography of the Shamsī notable, however, Jūzjānī noted that Kabīr Khān had received the command of Sunam from Sultan Rukn al-Dīn and rebelled some time after he had received this charge (ibid., vol. 2, p. 6). It was only in 637/1239–40 that Kabīr Khān re-acquired the command of Multan.

Table 3

Jūzjānī: Shamsī *Bandagān* in the Post-Shamsī Period

Serial No. Tabaqat 22 ed. Habibi	Name of Shamsī Slave Ethnic background	Deployment: Rukn al-Dīn (633/1236)	Deployment: Raẓiyya (634-7/1236-40)	Deployment: Bahrām Shāh (637-9/1240-2)	Deployment: 'Alā' al-Dīn (639-44/1242-6)	Deployment: Nāṣir al-Dīn (644-64/1246-66)
2 II: 5-7	KABĪR KHĀN AYĀZ AL-MU'IZZĪ Rūmī, Turk from Anatolia	*iqṭā'* of Sunam> rebelled >	*iqṭā'* of Lahore> rebelled 636/1238-9> Multan 637/1239-40>	took title: SULTĀN of Sindh and Uchch. Died 639/1241. Succeeded as ruler by son Tāj al-Dīn Abū Bakr Ayāz		
4 II: 8-9	MALIK SAIF AL-DĪN AI-BEG UCHCH	(unchanged) Uchch>	died as *muqṭi'* of Uchch.			
6 II: 10-13	MALIK NUṢRAT AL-DĪN TĀ'ĪSĪ AL-MU'IZZĪ Of Turkish origin	unchanged? Bayana, Sultankot, *shaḥnagī* of Gwalior? >	(after Ghiyāṣ al-Dīn ibn Iltutmish's death) *iqṭā'* of Awadh> Loyal to Raẓiyya> died 634/1237			
7 II: 13-18	MALIK 'IZZ AL-DĪN TUGHĀN KHĀN TUGHRIL Qarā Khitā'ī Turk	(unchanged) *muqṭi'* of Lakhnauti>	(unchanged): still occupied Lakhnauti; autonomy recognised by Raẓiyya>	(unchanged): still occupied Lakhnauti; autonomy recognised by 'Alā' al-Dīn>	seized Kara and Manikpur> lost Lakhnauti to Tamar Khan> 643/1245 received Awadh>	died 644/1246

Table 3 (*contd.*)

Serial No. Tabaqat 22 ed. Habibi	Name of Shamsī Slave Ethnic background	Deployment: Rukn al-Din (633/1236)	Deployment: Raziyya (634-7/1236-40)	Deployment: Bahrām Shāh (637-9/1240-2)	Deployment: 'Alā' al-Dīn (639-44/1242-6)	Deployment: Nāṣir al-Dīn (644-64/1246-66)
8 II: 17-18	MALIK TAMAR KHĀN Qipchaq Turk	unchanged? *amīr-i ākhūr*?>	*iqṭā'* of Qanauj> Kara in 634/1237 and death of Malik Tā'īsī: Awadh>	continued in the *iqṭā'* of Awadh	642/1245 sent to aid Tughān Khān seized Lakhnauti> in rebellion>	died 644/1246
9 II: 18-19	MALIK HINDŪ KHĀN MU'AYYID AL-DĪN MUBĀRAK AL-KHAZĪN 'Hindū'	unchanged? *Ṭashtdār*, and *khazīnadār*	loyal to Raziyya> *wilāyat* and fort of Uchch>	Jalandar> died there		
10 II: 19-20	MALIK IKHTIYĀR AL-DĪN QARĀ QUSH KHĀN AI-TEGIN	*iqṭā'* of Multan>	*iqṭā'* of Lahore> supported Raziyya against Bahrām Shāh>	*muqṭi'* of Lahore> expelled by Mongols> Bayana> imprisoned in Delhi with Ikhtiyār al-Dīn Yuzbeg>	*amīr ḥājib*> Bayana> Kara> in Lakhnauti expedition with Tamar Khan>	died in Kara 644/1246
11 II: 20-22	MALIK IKHTIYĀR AL-DĪN ALTŪNIA-I TABARHIND? ethnic origin	unchanged? *sar-i chatrdār*>	*iqṭā'* of Baran> Tabarhind> rebelled; imprisoned Sultan Raziyya>	married Sultan Raziyya and rebelled> died 637/1240		

Table 3 (*contd.*)

Serial No. Tabaqat 22 ed. Habibi	Name of Shamsī Slave Ethnic background	Deployment: Rukn al-Din (633/1236)	Deployment: Raẓiyya (634-7/1236-40)	Deployment: Bahrām Shāh (637-9/1240-2)	Deployment: 'Alā' al-Dīn (639-44/1242-6)	Deployment: Nāṣir al-Dīn (644-64/1246-66)
12 II: 22-23	IKHTIYĀR AL-DĪN AI-TEGIN Qarā Khitā'ī Turk	unchanged? *iqṭā'* of Kajakot and Nandana>	*iqṭā'* of Budaun> *amīr ḥājib*> rebelled	regent to monarch with royal paraphernalia> married Sultan's sister>murdered, ca. 637/1240		
13 II: 24-25	MALIK BADR AL-DĪN SUNQAR AL-RŪMĪ Rūmī, of Byzantine origin	unchanged? *nā'ib-i amīr-i ākhūr*	*iqṭā'* of Budaun (when Ikhtiyār Ai-Tegin appointed *amīr ḥājib*)	with death of Ikhtiyār al-Dīn: *amīr ḥājib*> rebellious> exiled to Budaun> executed		
14 II: 25-27	MALIK TĀJ AL-DĪN SANJAR QUTLUQ Qipchaq Turk	unchanged? *shaḥna-i ākhūr*?>	*iqṭā'* of Baran> Sursuti>	unchanged?>	*iqṭā'* of Budaon> murdered	
15 II: 27-28	MALIK TĀJ AL-DĪN SANJAR KURĪT KHĀN Qipchaq Turk	unchanged? *shaḥna-i bahar wa kishtīhā*?>	unchanged? *shaḥna-i baḥar wa kishtīhā*	unchanged? *shaḥna-i baḥar wa kishtīhā*	rebelled against vizier Khwāja Muḥazzib al-Dīn> *shaḥna-i pīl*> *sar-i jāndār*> *iqṭā'* of Baran> Budaun> Awadh> died in campaign at Bihar.	
16 II: 28	MALIK [IKIT/BAT] KHĀN SAIF AL-DĪN AI-BEG KHITĀ'Ī Khitā'ī	unchanged? *jāndār*?>	unchanged? *jāndār*?>	unchanged> *jāndār*?>	*sar-i jāndār*> *iqṭā'* of Kuhram and Samana> Baran> expedition against Mongols in Uchch and Multan 643/1246>	*wakīl-i dar* (after Raihān's death?)> died in Santur expedition

Table 3 (*contd.*)

Serial No. Tabaqat 22 ed. Habibi	Name of Shamsī Slave Ethnic background	Deployment: Rukn al-Din (633/1236)	Deployment: Raẓiyya (634-7/1236-40)	Deployment: Bahrām Shāh (637-9/1240-2)	Deployment: 'Alā' al-Dīn (639-44/1242-6)	Deployment: Nāṣir al-Dīn (644-64/1246-66)
17 I: 28-29 and 60	MALIK TĀJ AL-DĪN SANJAR TARKHĀN Karakhī Turk	?>	?>	*Amīr-i ākhūr*>	unchanged?> *amīr-i ākhūr*?>	*nā'ib-i amīr ḥājib*> *iqṭā'* of Jhanjhana> *iqṭā* ' of Kasmandi and Mandiana when Ulugh Khān in exile> Baran when Ulugh Khān restored> after Ikit Khān's death in 656/1256: *wakīl-i dar* and *muqṭi'* of Budaun> Awadh after Arsalān Khān

Table 3 (*contd.*)

Serial No. Tabaqat 22 ed. Habibi	Name of Shamsī Slave Ethnic background	Deployment: Rukn al-Din (633/1236)	Deployment: Raẕiyya (634-7/1236-40)	Deployment: Bahrām Shāh (637-9/1240-2)	Deployment: 'Alā' al-Dīn (639-44/1242-6)	Deployment: Nāṣir al-Dīn (644-64/1246-66)
18 II: 30-33	MALIK IKHTIYĀR AL-DĪN YUZBEG TUGHRIL KHĀN Qipchaq Turk	special confidant> *amīr-i majlis*> *shāhnagi-i pilān*> rebelled>	*amīr-i ākhūr*>	unchanged? *amīr-i ākhūr*? Imprisoned 639/ 1241-2 with Malik Qarā Qush>	*muqṯi'* Tabarhind> Lahore> rebelled> reinstated> with Jalāl al-Dīn ibn Iltumish's departure: Qanauj	Awadh> *mamlakat-i Lakhnautī*> SULṮĀN OF LAKHNAUTĪ title: SULṮĀN MUGHĪṢ AL-DĪN> killed during Kamrud campaign. Succeeded by son 'Izz al-Dīn Balban Yuzbegī
19 II: 33-35	MALIK TĀJ AL-DĪN SANJAR ARSALĀN KHĀN AL-KHWĀRAZMĪ ?; probably Khwārazmī Turk	unchanged? *khāṣadār*?>	*chāshnīgīr* > *iqṭā'* of Balaram>	unchanged? *iqṭā'* of Balaram?>	unchanged? *iqṭā'* of Balaram?>	*iqṭā'* of Bayana> *wakīl-i dar*> 651/1254 Tabarhind, conflict with Shīr Khān> Awadh, conflict with Qutlugh Khān> 657/1259 seized Lakhnauti from 'Izz al-Dīn

Table 3 (*contd.*)

Serial No. Tabaqat 22 ed. Habibi	Name of Shamsī Slave Ethnic background	Deployment: Rukn al-Din (633/1236)	Deployment: Raziyya (634-7/1236-40)	Deployment: Bahrām Shāh (637-9/1240-2)	Deployment: 'Alā' al-Dīn (639-44/1242-6)	Deployment: Nāṣir al-Dīn (644-64/1246-66)
						Yuzbegī> died (date?) succeeded by son Tatar Khan
20 II 36-40	MALIK 'IZZ AL-DĪN KUSHLŪ KHĀN AL SULṬĀNĪ Qipchaq Turk	unchanged? *iqṭā'* of Baran?> rebelled>	? imprisoned> freed?>	? honoured?> rebelled>	proclaimed himself SULṬĀN in Delhi> submitted and recognised Sultan Mas'ūd> received *bilād* of Nagaur, Mandor and Ajmer + special *muqṭi'* of Nagaur and special privileges> Nagaur and Multan	Multan and Uchch (+ forcibly retained Nagaur)> forced to give up Nagaur> lost Muitan to Qārlūqs and then Shīr Khān> lost Uchch tc Shīr Khān> given Budaun> during Ulugh Khān and Shīr Khān's exile: Multan and Uchch> when Ulugh Khān returned, sought

Table 3 (*contd.*)

Serial No. Tabaqat 22 ed. Habibi	Name of Shamsī Slave Ethnic background	Deployment: Rukn al-Din (633/1236)	Deployment: Raẓiyya (634-7/1236-40)	Deployment: Bahrām Shāh (637-9/1240-2)	Deployment: 'Alā' al-Dīn (639-44/1242-6)	Deployment: Nāṣir al-Dīn (644-64/1246-66)
						Mongol sanctuary> allied with Qutlugh Khān against Ulugh Khān> retained Multan under Mongol *shahna* protection
21 II: 40-42	MALIK SAIF AL-DĪN ARKALĪ DĀD BEG Qipchaq Turk	?>	*sahm al-Ḥashm*>	*amīr dād* of Kara>	*amīr dād* of Delhi with *iqṭā'* of office>	*iqṭā'* of Palwal and Kamah and office of *dād beg*> *iqṭā'* of Baran>Kasrak + *mīr dād*> Baran>
22 II: 42-43	MALIK BADR AL-DĪN NUṢRAT KHĀN SUNQAR ṢŪFĪ Rūmī, Turk from Anatolia	?>	?>	?>	rebelled against *wazīr* Muḥazzib al-Dīn> *amīr* of Kōl>	*iqṭā'* of Bayana> when Shīr Khān moved to Bayana then received Tabarhind, Sunam, Jhajar, Lakhwal and ferries over R.Beas>

Table 3 (*contd.*)

Serial No. Tabaqat 22 ed. Habibi	Name of Shamsī Slave Ethnic background	Deployment: Rukn al-Din (633/1236)	Deployment: Raẓiyya (634-7/1236-40)	Deployment: Bahrām Shāh (637-9/1240-2)	Deployment: 'Alā' al-Dīn (639-44/1242-6)	Deployment: Nāṣir al-Dīn (644-64/1246-66)
23 II: 43-44	MALIK NUṢRAT AL-DĪN SHĪR KHĀN Ilbarī (Yimak) Turk	?>	?>	?>	643/1246 *iqṭā'* of fort and environs of Tabarhind>	seized Multan from Qārlūqs 648/1250> seized Uchch from Kushlū Khān 649/1251> conflict with Ulugh Khān 651/1254, migrated to Mongols> conflict with Tāj al-Dīn Arsalān Khān over Tabarhind> given Kōl, Bayana, Balaram, Jalesar, Baltarah, MHR, and Mahawan

Table 3 (*contd.*)

Serial No. Tabaqat 22 ed. Habibi	Name of Shamsi Slave Ethnic background	Deployment: Rukn al-Din (633/1236)	Deployment: Raẓiyya (634-7/1236-40)	Deployment: Bahrām Shāh (637-9/1240-2)	Deployment: 'Alā' al-Dīn (639-44/1242-6)	Deployment: Nāṣir al-Dīn (644-64/1246-66)
24 II: 45-47	MALIK KISHLĪ KHĀN SAIF AL-DĪN AI-BEG AL-SULṬĀNĪ MALIK AL-ḤUJJĀB Ilbarī (Yimak) Turk	unchanged? Slave in *dargāh-i khāṣṣ*?>	unchanged? Slave in *dargāh-i khāṣṣ*?>	*sar-i jāndār*>	*amīr-i ākhūr*>	647/1249 *amīr ḥājib* + Nagaur> during Ulugh Khān's exile, 652/1254 Kara> with Ulugh Khān's return: *amīr ḥājib*> with death of Quṭb al-Dīn Ḥasan Ghūrī, 653/1255: Meerut> died 656/1259. son: 'Alā' al-Dīn made *amīr ḥājib*

Table 3 (*contd.*)

Serial No. Tabaqat 22 ed. Habibi	Name of Shamsī Slave Ethnic background	Deployment: Rukn al-Din (633/1236)	Deployment: Raziyya (634-7/1236-40)	Deployment: Bahrām Shāh (637-9/1240-2)	Deployment: 'Alā' al-Dīn (639-44/1242-6)	Deployment: Nāṣir al-Dīn (644-64/1246-66)
25 II: 47-89	AL-KHĀQĀN AL-MU'AZZAM AL-KHĀN AL-'AZAM BAHĀ' AL-ḤAQQ WA AL-DĪN ULUGH KHĀN BALBAN AL-SULṬĀNĪ Ilbarī (Yimak) Turk	?> in rebellion> imprisoned>	*khāṣadār>* *amīr-i shikār>*	through Badr al-Dīn Sunqar al-Rūmī's intervention: *iqṭā'* of Rewari> involved in plot to remove Sultan>	*iqṭā'* of Hansi> *amīr ḥājib* 642/1244-5>	*amīr ḥājib>* 647/1249 title of Ulugh Khan + *nā'ib>*651/1253 deposed from power and sent to Hansi> Nagaur> 653/1255 return to power in Delhi> death of Raihan and conflict with Qutlugh and Kushlū Khān> 664/1266 SULTAN OF OF DELHI>

group of slaves, who sometimes supported one contender for the throne only to oppose him later in the reign and eventually remove him from the throne altogether.[5] Finally, there were the juniormost slaves, whose humble status in the slave cadre belied their political ambitions. Since the ties between pages such as Ulugh Khān (number 25 in Tables 2–3) and Iltutmish—and even more so with his successors—were extremely weak, they had no hesitation in breaking away from Delhi and seeking their fortune elsewhere.[6]

But to keep Jūzjānī's information in perspective: for the majority of the Shamsī slaves, the death of Iltutmish did not mean a sudden change in fortune (see Table 3). The status quo was defended and continued for some time. For the Shamsī slaves a vigilant protection of their interests was important, but this carried the implication that the new successors to the throne of Delhi had to remain dependent upon their father's slaves. While the slaves were not necessarily motivated by any sense of deep affection for their master's successors, they accepted his heirs as Delhi Sultans so long as they did not disturb the Shamsī dispensation of power.

The free military notables, on the other hand, were very eager to alter the existing political equations. In this, their ambitions coincided with Iltutmish's successors and they were frequently patronized and given high commands. Jūzjānī recognized the presence of Maliks 'Izz al-Dīn Muḥammad Sālārī, 'Alā' al-Dīn Jānī, and Saif al-Dīn Kūchī as the respective commanders of Budaun, Lahore, and Hansi in 633/1236.[7] Their rise to high office was similar to that of Quṭb al-Dīn 'Alī Ḥasan Ghūrī, whose progression had been only slightly slower; he

[5] For details and references see below.

[6] Ibid., vol. 2, pp. 48, 51. Jūzjānī only provides information concerning Ulugh Khān. We can infer that his compatriots in rebellion were pages in the court of Iltutmish because they were resident in Delhi and not important enough to be recalled by name. Peter Jackson, *The Delhi Sultanate,* p. 69, suggested that the pages were fleeing to the court of Rukn al-Dīn's brother, Ghiyāṣ al-Dīn, at Awadh. This is possible, as is the likelihood that they were striking out on an independent path altogether, outside the ambit of the Sultanate, as was the case with the Khalajīs of an earlier generation.

[7] 'Izz al-Dīn Muḥammad Sālārī Mahdī was *amīr ḥājib* in 625/1228 (Jūzjānī, *Ṭabaqāt-i Nāṣirī*, vol. 1, p. 446; and Ẓiyā' al-Dīn Baranī, *Ta'rīkh-i Fīrūz Shāhī,* edited by Khan, p. 39, edited by Rashid, p. 46). Jūzjānī noted subsequently that

became the *nā'ib-i mulk*, deputy of the realm, in 639/1241.[8] Their service to the throne was always contingent to their perceived self-interest and their alliances shifted rapidly throughout this period. After receiving Rukn al-Dīn's patronage, the three aforementioned free amirs—Sālārī, Kūchī, and Jānī—were in almost immediate rebellion against him.

The other group of free notables were involved with the secretarial and administrative functions of the court and the Sultanate. The *ahl-i qalam* were sometimes involved in military duties and certainly possessed armed retinues.[9] The quick shifts in patronage left them constantly on the look out for strategic alliances. Rukn al-Dīn had a considerable administrative staff from his years as Governor, and they followed him to Delhi.[10] Their help to the Delhi Sultan in establishing his independent position in Sultanate politics invited the wrath of the Shamsī slaves, who decimated their ranks. The purge seems to have weakened them considerably as a group, and although the *ahl-i qalam* still made ambitious bids to improve their position in Sultanate politics, they seldom acted independently and rarely as a group.[11] Their greatest success came when they associated with the

---

in 633/1236, when 'Izz al-Dīn rebelled, he was the *muqṭi'* of Budaun. There is less information on Malik Saif al-Dīn Kūchī from Iltutmish's reign, but Jūzjānī notes that he was the *muqṭi'* of Hansi when Iltutmish died (Jūzjānī, *Ṭabaqāt-i Nāṣirī*, vol. 1, p. 456). Saif al-Dīn Kūchī's brother, Fakhr al-Dīn, is also mentioned in passing by Jūzjānī during the post-Iltutmish insurrectionary months (ibid., vol. 1, p. 459).

[8] Jūzjānī, *Ṭabaqāt-i Nāṣirī*, vol. 1, p. 468.

[9] Note for example the case of Mihtar Jattān Farrāsh, a *banda* of the *wazīr* Khwāja Muhazzib al-Dīn, who in attempting to defend his master wounded the Shamsī commander Tāj al-Dīn Sanjar Kurīt Khān (number 15 in Table 3). Ibid., vol. 2, p. 27. See also the example of Jūzjānī who had to defend himself from assassins hired by the Khwāja. For citations and details see Chapter 4.

[10] It must have been this retinue that was killed by the Shamsī slaves. Ibid., vol. 1, p. 456. S.B.P. Nigam, *Nobility Under the Sultans of Delhi*, p. 28, was correct in assuming this continuity, although his assertion that Rukn al-Dīn's *wazīr*, 'Ain al-Mulk Ash'ārī, was given the title Bahā' al-Mulk Ash'ārī, is not borne out by the evidence. The titles do suggest that they might have been kinsmen, certainly members of the same theological school; see Chapter 4.

[11] For some exceptions, see the Section, 'Relations with the Piety-Minded', below.

free military commanders, as in the case of the *wazīr* Khwāja Muhazzib al-Dīn's alliance with the free amir Quṭb al-Dīn Ḥasan Ghūrī against the Shamsī *bandagān*, although this did not preclude compacts with individual slaves as well.[12]

To a large extent the authoritarian regimen maintained by Iltutmish left the fate of all these groups in the balance when the Delhi Sultan died. While most Shamsī slaves wanted the distribution of power and office to continue unchanged, this could only be done in opposition to the interests of Iltutmish's successors, the free notables, and the *ahl-i qalam*. The biggest challenge to all the Shamsī notables, free and unfree, came from Iltutmish's heirs and their efforts to rule as independently and effectively as their father. In the traditions of the existing political system the status of notables was derived either out of their own efforts—seized outright—or had been dispensed to them by the reigning authority; there were no 'nobles'. Each generation would see conflict over authoritative rights and, after Iltutmish's death, political competition was provoked by his son Rukn al-Dīn's efforts to consolidate power.

It would appear from the accounts of Jūzjānī and Baranī that Iltutmish's sons did not pose a huge challenge to their master's slaves since they were incompetent wastrels, more given to pleasure and merriment [*lahw wa ṭarab*] than to serious affairs of governance. Rukn al-Dīn, in particular, was singled out as a Prince more generous with giving grants than any preceding monarch. This would not have been a problem in itself but for the fact that the recipients of his largesse were musicians, jesters, and catamites [*muṭribān wa maskharagān wa mukhannaṣān*]—not exactly ideals of masculinity fit to command

[12] Through the alliance between the free-born Amirs, both Khwāja Muhazzib al-Dīn and Malik Quṭb al-Dīn Ḥasan Ghūrī emerged for a while as the most powerful notables in the realm. Yet Khwāja Muhazzib al-Dīn had earlier associated with the slave Badr al-Dīn Sunqar (number 13 in Table 3). Note also the instance when the threat to the *wazīr* Niẓām al-Mulk, made him flee from the Sultan's capital and seek succour with the free Amir 'Izz al-Dīn Muḥammad Sālārī. Jūzjānī, *Ṭabaqāt-i Nāṣirī*, vol. 1, pp. 455–6, 464, 466–7.

an army, far from ruling a state.[13] Jūzjānī was generally well disposed towards Rukn al-Dīn: his generous, easygoing nature and the fact that he did not oppress people were all commendable human traits. But all his qualities were misdirected; he consorted with the base and the impure [*nājinsān wa khabīṣān*] which is why he lost his kingdom.[14]

But Jūzjānī also provided other details from the Sultan's reign that contradicted his picture of a weak-kneed, pleasure-seeking monarch. Soon after his accession, he displayed enough foresight to patronize the disgruntled slave Kabīr Khān, free amirs like Maliks 'Izz al-Dīn Muḥammad Sālārī, 'Alā' al-Dīn Jānī, and Saif al-Dīn Kūchī. When these individuals rebelled, Rukn al-Dīn did not hesitate to engage them in battle. He was ruthless enough to have his younger sibling, Quṭb al-Dīn, executed, and managed to alarm another brother, Ghiyāṣ al-Dīn Muḥammad Shāh into rebellion in Awadh; and his sister, Raẓiyya, into insurrection in the old city of Delhi.[15]

During the duration of his father's reign, Rukn al-Dīn had, as we saw, gained considerable experience as a Governor and discharged his duties creditably enough to warrant his appointment as heir. As Governor he also raised an independent military retinue. Jūzjānī provides few details of the Prince's political dispensation but we do have the intriguing reference to Beg-Timur Ōr Khān Ruknī, who was, as his 'Ruknī' *nisba* clarifies, a slave of Sultan Rukn al-Dīn.[16] Beg-Timur Ruknī may have been a part of the Prince's personal slave retinue, which certainly also included a sizeable following of Persian administrators, who we know about only from their moment of massacre at the hands of Iltutmish's slaves.[17]

Rukn al-Dīn's attempts to challenge the stifling control of his father's slaves and establish his independent political base led him into conflict with the Shamsī *bandagān* and directed the Prince's patronage into unexpected and interesting directions. In his description of Rukn al-Dīn's immoral qualities, Jūzjānī noted the great favour he

[13] Ibid., p. 457.

[14] Ibid.

[15] Ibid., pp. 455–7. Rukn al-Dīn had shifted his residence to Kilūkhrī. See Chapter 4.

[16] Ibid., p. 490; vol. 2, p. 29.

[17] Ibid., vol. 1, p. 456.

showed to mahouts (*pīlbānān*), and to the pleasure that he derived from spending time with them and riding elephants through the city. Apparently, through his gifts and kindness [*az daulat wa ihsān-i o*] their fortunes multiplied. Much to Jūzjānī's chagrin the mahouts became important in Rukn al-Dīn's court.[18]

In the wide-ranging conflict between the Ruknīs and the Shamsīs, it would be a mistake to assume that there was a simple antagonistic juxtaposition of the two dispensations. The senior Shamsīs, the *bandagān-i khāṣṣ*, did not revolt against Rukn al-Dīn, and the slaves in opposition to the Sultan seem to have come largely from the members of the *qalb,* the central contingent that had a large number of slaves of 'middling' rank. Jūzjānī does mention in passing, however, that Rukn al-Dīn approached the junior Shamsī slave, Ikhtiyār al-Dīn Yuzbeg Tughril Khān (number 18 in Tables 2-3), and tried to win him over by offering him the position of commandant of the elephants [*shaḥnagī-i pīlān*].[19] As the information in Tables 2 and 3 clarify, Malik Ikhtiyār al-Dīn was not a senior slave: he was based in Delhi and had just received a court appointment in Iltutmish's reign. He belonged to the rank of slaves who would have served in the *qalb*. Rukn al-Dīn's attempt to win a member of this otherwise recalcitrant group was consistent with his efforts to recruit select members of his father's retinue. That Ikhtiyār al-Dīn was offered the command of the elephant retinue draws further attention to the manner in which the Prince tried to establish a military following to challenge the increasingly entrenched cadre of Shamsī slaves.

The direction of the Prince's patronage to elephant drivers and the management of his elephant corps are not so perplexing once we put it in the context of their importance in the military arrangements of the Delhi Sultanate. As Simon Digby has informed us, war horses and elephants were crucial military resources in the armed forces of the Sultanate. Digby also provided considerable detail underlining the expenditure of manpower and energy by the Delhi Sultans to acquire elephants, the 'battle tanks' of medieval warfare.[20] His arguments can be pushed further: if elephants were important in the military

[18] Ibid., p. 457.

[19] Ibid., vol. 2, p. 30.

[20] Simon Digby, *War Horse and Elephant in the Delhi Sultanate: A Study of Military Supplies* (Karachi: Orient Monographs, 1971), pp. 55–82.

forces of the Sultanate, they were valuable only with their mahouts. This point was, apparently, not missed by Rukn al-Dīn.

Jūzjānī's negative portrayal of Rukn al-Dīn's character and rule does not invalidate the fact that the Prince displayed striking initiative in challenging the Shamsī forces and trying to consolidate his rule. In the middle of the fourteenth century 'Iṣāmī had very astutely understood Rukn al-Dīn's intentions: 'within three or four months, rather than following his father's customs, he followed his own conclusions [*az rusūm-i pidar Shāh-i khud rā'i gasht*] . . . I have heard that towards his father's slaves, each of whom was a world conqueror, he adopted an angry and arrogant demeanour [*khishm wa gardan-kashī sāz kard*]'.[21] In extending his patronage to mahouts Rukn al-Dīn went outside the charmed circle of personnel accustomed to high office. Unquestionably, the mahouts were menials, yet they were also an important group in the armed forces. These were individuals of little social worth, 'foreign' if you wish, to high Sultanate society, and their elevation was as pragmatic as the deployment of military slaves, individuals without any social status and roots. Like slaves, their stature was a consequence of the Sultan's patronage and, like the military slaves, their social (if not natal) alienation made them utterly dependent upon their master. Jūzjānī had described these social menials as *nājinsān wa khabīṣān*, the base and the impure, terms he would never use to describe the Shamsī Turkish slaves. But let us not forget the observations of Niẓām al-Dīn Awliyā', cited in the previous chapter: he had drawn the attention of his audience to the base, uncultured, unfree qualities of the Sultan's great Turkish commanders.

It remains to be noted that Ikhtiyār al-Dīn was not tempted by Rukn al-Dīn's offer, nor did the rest of the *qalb* respond favourably to the Prince's effort to challenge the Shamsī slaves' monopoly of power. The insurrection of the *qalb* that deposed Rukn al-Dīn placed his sister Raẓiyya on the throne, a somewhat unusual move considering there were other male siblings who could have been chosen. Raẓiyya's accession and the support of the Shamsī notables was presented by Jūzjānī as a restoration of her legitimate rights to accession prescribed in Iltutmish's will. Jūzjānī's narrative tries very hard to justify Raẓiyya's accession: her mother was of a high lineage, she possessed

[21] 'Iṣāmī, *Futūḥ al-Salāṭīn*, p. 130.

all the great qualities of leadership and, not least, her father thought she was better suited to reign than her brothers.[22] She did not, therefore, usurp the throne; her accession was merely a restoration of legitimate rights. Much of this, as we will see in greater detail later, seems to be the dissimulation of a jurist who had received his first major position in the capital through the patronage of the Princess, a jurist who still agonized over the circumstances that made a woman a ruler.

Jūzjānī's obfuscation apart, there were several advantages for the Shamsī slaves in having a Queen as a monarch. If, as Jūzjānī put it, Iltutmish favoured her 'even though she was a daughter and was in veiled seclusion [*agar-chi dukhtar būd wa mastūra*]',[23] the Shamsī Maliks must have been delighted at the nominal authority possessed by a ruler forced to work in *parda*. They would have the freedom to exercise power and maintain their monopoly over high offices.

Nevertheless, despite the disability of not 'having the good fortune of being accounted amongst men [*az ḥisāb-i mardān dar khilqat naṣībī nīufta būd*]', as Jūzjānī put it,[24] Raẓiyya was extremely successful in negotiating with, and placating, individuals like Kabīr Khān Ayāz, first with Lahore and then Multan; in neutralizing and eventually getting contumacious free-born amirs like 'Alā' al-Dīn Jānī, Saif al-Dīn Kūchī, and his brother killed, and forcing the powerful *wazīr* Niẓām al-Mulk into retirement.[25] She dispensed offices: the Shamsī slave Saif al-Dīn Ai-Beg Bhatū was given the command of the army, *niyābat-i lashkar,* and on his death she elevated Quṭb al-Dīn Ḥasan 'Alī Ghūrī to the position.[26]

This was a striking display of independent initiative which might have worried the *bandagān,* but all these appointments were still amidst a cadre of familiar personnel. It was when Raẓiyya moved outside the proverbial charmed circle and appointed her *habshī* (Ethiopian) slave Jamāl al-Dīn Yāqūt as commander of the horses, *amīr-i ākhūr,* that some of the Shamsī slaves moved to depose her.[27]

22 Jūzjānī, *Ṭabaqāt-i Nāṣirī*, vol. 1, pp. 457–8.
23 Ibid., p. 458.
24 Ibid., p. 457.
25 Ibid., pp. 459–60.
26 Ibid.
27 Ibid., pp. 460–1.

The opposition came once again from the 'middling' ranks of slaves aspiring to become *khāṣṣ,* and was led by Malik Ikhtiyār al-Dīn Aitegin, and Ikhtiyār al-Dīn Altūnia, and the insurrection later received the support of Badr al-Dīn Sunqar (numbers 12, 11, and 13 in Tables 2–3). In their aspiration for greater power this was the group which most directly felt the challenge posed by new clients introduced into the higher echelons of the political realm by the Shamsī successors. Since the political system and the form in which power was consolidated had not changed since Rukn al-Dīn's reign, the provocations which led to conflict, rebellion, and the ultimate removal of Sultan Raẓiyya were also very similar.

Nor are any obvious changes noticeable from the reign of Sultan Mu'izz al-Dīn Bahrām Shāh, Raẓiyya's brother, chosen by the rebel Shamsī *bandagān* as the new Sultan. Apparently, Mu'izz al-Dīn was too young to have held a Governorship during his father's reign and, we would assume, he lacked the kind of military retinue that had helped his elder brother, Rukn al-Dīn, fight, even if futilely, against the Shamsī slaves. Indeed, at the time of his accession, Mu'izz al-Dīn Bahrām Shāh faced the ignominy of having Malik Ikhtiyār al-Dīn Aitegin (number 12 in Tables 2–3) impose himself as his regent *and* brother-in-law (see Chart 2). The regent received support from the *wazīr*, Khwāja Muḥazzib al-Dīn, and the *amīr ḥājib*, Badr al-Dīn Sunqar (number 13 in Tables 2–3). But the condominium did not last.[28] Ikhtiyār al-Dīn was assassinated at the orders of the Sultan, Khwāja Muḥazzib al-Dīn conspired to get Badr al-Dīn Sunqar exiled and executed. [29] This marked the end of the great dominance of court politics by Badr al-Dīn Sunqar; the machinations of the *wazīr* having been intended to create conflict between the Sultan and the Shamsī slaves. That the *wazīr* was successful in his aims is a matter of detail; more relevant for the history of the time was the ability of the young Prince to successfully battle his father's slaves until two *bandagān,* Malik Ikhtiyār al-Dīn Qarā Qush and Ikhtiyār al-Dīn Yuzbeg (numbers 10, 18 in Tables 2–3), offered their services to the Sultan.

[28] Ibid., pp. 462–4.

[29] Ibid., pp. 465–6. Badr al-Dīn Sunqar was executed soon after on the Sultan's orders.

At the outset, Mu'izz al-Dīn managed to withstand the Shamsī onslaught very successfully and the conflict reveals that the young Sultan must have actually raised a substantial enough following—some of whom were Turks—to expel the Shamsī *bandagān* from Delhi.[30] Mu'izz al-Dīn's retinue was commanded by Fakhr al-Dīn Mubārak Shāh Farrukhī, whose slave status was evident in his twin *laqabs* (titles) *mihtar-i mubārak*, the leader of the slaves, and *farrāsh*, carpet spreader, janitor, the latter always used by Jūzjānī for this notable in a derogatory sense.[31] Fakhr al-Dīn's intentions to create an exclusive power base—a new Mu'izzī dispensation—for his master were unmistakable and he spurned Ikhtiyār al-Dīn Qarā Qush and Ikhtiyār al-Dīn Yuzbeg's offer of allegiance, imprisoning the two Shamsī slaves instead. Mu'izz al-Dīn himself was more than cognizant with the political dynamics of the age and had imprisoned the surviving Princes of the Shamsī lineage, possible contenders if their cause was backed by disgruntled notables.[32]

Mu'izz al-Dīn's hostility towards the overpowering influence of the different members of the Shamsī dispensation was responded to in kind. By 639/1242, the young Sultan's efforts to establish an independent base of power had alarmed all the old notables but the final conflict was waged, as in the case of the two previous monarchs, by the Shamsī slaves. And in the conflict between members of rival dispensations, Iltutmish's heir succumbed once again.

While the nature of the conflicts in the years 633–9/1236–9 suggests the persistence of preceding structures of political relationships and methods of consolidating authority, the years witnessed significant changes in the ranks of the Shamsī notables. The major protagonists in the histories of this period were not the same as in Iltutmish's reign. The influence of the old *bandagān-i khāṣṣ* declined very quickly and

[30] Two of these young slaves were responsible for the murder of Malik Ikhtiyar al-Din Al-tegun, ibid., p. 464. On the expulsion of the Shamsi slaves from Delhi, see vol. 2. p. 30.

[31] Ibid., vol. 1, pp. 467–8; vol. 2, pp. 20, 30, 163. Elsewhere, Jūzjānī had mentioned that the Shamsī slave Hindū Khān was the *mihtar-i mubārak* during Iltutmish's reign: ibid., vol. 2, pp. 18–19.

[32] This must have occurred in Mu'izz al-Dīn's reign, for Jūzjānī notes that Sultan 'Alā' al-Dīn Mas'ūd was released from imprisonment on his brother's death. Ibid., vol. 1, p. 468.

by the end of Sultan Raẓiyya's reign they were no longer the significant elements in the politics of the court. The powerful Shamsī slaves now were Nuṣrat al-Dīn Tā'īsī, Ikhtiyār al-Dīn Altūnia, Ikhtiyār al-Dīn Ai-tegin, Badr al-Dīn Sunqar, Ikhtiyār al-Dīn Yuzbeg Tughril Khān, and 'Izz al-Dīn Kushlū Khān (numbers 6, 11, 12, 13, 18, and 20 in Tables 2–3). They had been slaves waiting for deployment in the highest offices when Iltutmish died and the succession of the new monarch with his own body of followers would have meant certain political marginalization. These junior slaves acted energetically to avoid such a calamity and it is they who tried to minimize the political influence of the monarch. This political activity catapulted the likes of Ikhtiyār al-Dīn Ai-tegin and Ikhtiyār al-Dīn Yuzbeg Tughril Khān into positions of prominence until they were sometimes recipients of the Sultan's patronage or subject to his military attention. Either way, they could hardly be ignored; they were the new *bandagān-i khāṣṣ*. The crucial difference between the old and the new *bandagān-i khāṣṣ* was that the status of the parvenus was not bestowed upon them by the monarch; they reached their powerful positions by holding the Sultan hostage.

What did the emergence of these new political groups signify for the Sultanate? One fairly direct result was the presence of large bodies of military personnel in the entourage of the new *bandagān-i khāṣṣ* who were completely unattached to the Delhi Sultan and who owed allegiance only to their Shamsī slave patrons. This was more complicated than a simple case of subinfeudation, because the new political elite also patronized the 'junior' *bandagān,* the young Shamsī slaves, the least influential within the slave cadre, who had been pages in Iltutmish's court (see Table 2). Rather than seeking the help of the Shamsī successors who were attempting to create their own exclusive body of supporters, these pages sought the support of senior slave members: familiar individuals, and now powerful patrons. The rise to prominence of slaves like Ulugh Khān, who received his first command as *muqṭi'* of Rewari, occurred because of the fatherly affection [*shafaqat-i pidarāna*], of Badr al-Dīn Sunqar, in Mu'izz al-Dīn Bahrām Shāh's reign.[33] This patrimonial patronage was acknowledged by Jūzjānī, but there were others as well. In tracing the

[33] Ibid., vol. 2. p 52.

careers of the Shamsī slaves a similar link between Malik I<u>kh</u>tiyār al-Dīn Qarā Qush and I<u>kh</u>tiyār al-Dīn Yuzbeg (numbers 10 and 18 in Table 3) is also visible. These intra-*bandagān* associations further fractured the relationship between Iltutmish's successors and his father's slaves; it also marked the end of whatever corporate sentiment remained within the *bandagān-i Shamsī*.

The rise of these new slaves to important political positions introduced a group into the politics of the court which had considerable military resources and which did not share Iltutmish's vision of the structure of the Delhi Sultanate. These men carried different political expectations and increasingly individualistic ambitions for power that were consolidated through alliances with free amirs and the secretarial classes, which then introduced considerable stress and competition within the cadre of the Shamsi *bandagān*. As Ẓiyā' al-Dīn Baranī effectively managed to bring out, the rationale for this conflict lay in the very organization of the Shamsī *bandagan*:

> . . . and each one of the *bandagān-i Shamsī* was the slave of the same master [*<u>kh</u>wāja tāsh*] and [since] each of the 'forty' slaves had become great simultaneously, one would not bow to the other [*sar firo nīāwardī*] or submit [*iṭ̤ā'at*] to another. In [the disperṣal of] *iq̤ṭā's*, soldiers, honours and territories, they demanded equality and similarity with each other [*musāwāt wa muwāza'at yakdīgar ṭalabīdandī*]. . . . Yet, each would boast 'none like me'. Each would ask the other: 'what are you that I am not', and 'what have you been that I have not been' . . .[34]

Once their master was dead, it was a matter of time before the corporate sense of belonging within the slave retinue was replaced by a competition generated by the sentiment—or the illusion—of equality. The idea of being a *<u>kh</u>wāja tāsh* underlined this feeling and linked it

[34] Baranī, *Ta'rī<u>kh</u>-i Fīrūz Shāhī*, edited by Khan, p. 28, edited by Rashid, p. 33. Baranī's narrative assumed that the rise of the Shamsī slaves occurred after the destruction of the great free Amirs. See also, Irfan Habib, 'The Sultanate Ruling Class', pp. 15–16 and for an analysis of Baranī's thoughts on social stratification see Chapter 6; also Sunil Kumar, 'Service, Status and Military Slavery in the Delhi Sultanate of the Thirteenth and Early Fourteenth Centuries', in Richard Eaton and Indrani Chatterjee, eds, *Slavery and South Asian History* (Bloomington: Indiana University Press, 2006).

with the corporate character of the group. The idea of being equals and brothers was now getting fractured: a Shamsī now identified a potential competitor, not a comrade. Although political competition during the period 603–9/1236–42 was still between Shamsī heirs and Shamsī slaves, its 'inter-dispensational' nature empowered individuals who wanted to break away from their old inhibiting associations and consolidate their individual political positions. Its long-term implications were devastating for the Shamsīs as a political group.

The efforts of the parvenu *bandagān-i khāṣṣ* to translate their aspirations of upward mobility into political capital also had an impact upon their relationship with the ambitious free notables. In their bid to alter the Shamsī dispensation of power in their favour, free amirs like 'Izz al-Dīn Muḥammad Sālārī, 'Alā' al-Dīn Jānī, and Saif al-Dīn Kūchī rebelled against Delhi, and although the early conflicts were ostensibly between the free military notables and the Sultan, they were increasingly directed against the Shamsī *bandagān* who still had effective control of power within the Sultanate. The defeat and death of most powerful free notables did not curb their individual ambitions. Once the organization of the Shamsi *bandagān* began altering, free amirs collaborated with some of these slaves in their common bid to improve their fortunes.[35] In Bahrām Shāh's reign, the slaves Ikhtiyār al-Dīn Ai-Tegin and Altūnia (numbers 12 and 11 in Table 3), together with the *wazīr* Khwāja Muḥazzib al-Dīn, controlled power.[36] Later Badr al-Dīn Sunqar (number 13 in Table 3) sought to ally with the *wazīr* in a bid to depose the Sultan. The free notables had not forsaken their ambitions for final authority, but, rather than achieving this through military conflict with the Shamsī slaves, they sought to reach the same ends through their alliances, or in a more conspiratorial manner. The attempts of the *wazīr* Khwāja Muḥazzib al-Dīn and the free Amir Quṭb al-Dīn Ḥasan Ghūrī to create discord between the Sultan and the slaves was eminently successful and Bahrām Shāh was deposed.

[35] The evidence contradicts Baranī's more general statement that, because of the weakness of Iltutmish's successors, the Shamsī *bandagān* were destroying the free notables. See Baranī, *Ta'rīkh-i Fīrūz Shāhī*, edited by Khan, p. 27, edited by Rashid. p. 32.

[36] Jūzjānī, *Ṭabaqāt-i Nāṣirī*, vol. 1, pp. 462–3.

In the context of all this conflict, it is worth asking why the different members of the Shamsī dispensation persisted at all with Iltutmish's lineage. In 639/1242 all the remaining Shamsī Princes were very young and in prison. The option of moving away from the Shamsī family certainly seems to have crossed the mind of at least one slave, Malik 'Izz al-Dīn Kushlū Khān, who finally took the step that no slave had dared, and declared himself Sultan of Delhi. Yet, in an episode that has remarkable similarities to the response of the Quṭbī slaves when Iltutmish claimed the throne, a large number of 'Izz al-Dīn Kushlū Khān's slave peers opposed this development. They forced Malik Kushlū Khān to retract his claim, released Iltutmish's sons from prison, and raised Rukn al-Dīn's son 'Alā' al-Dīn Mas'ūd to the throne (see Chart 2).[37] The reason why the Shamsī lineage was continued with lies in the role that the Delhi Sultan was expected to play in a new structure of power relationships noticeable in the years between 639/1242 and 653/1255.

(b) 639–53/1242–55: The Period of 'Intra-Dispensational' Conflict

In the preceding phase the Shamsī notables, free and slave, had been in conflict with Iltutmish's successors over who should possess preeminent power in the Sultanate. Although the Shamsī slaves had, with very few exceptions, emerged victorious in these conflicts, the attempts of the Delhi Sultans to extend their influence through their circle of dependants cannot be dismissed. In contrast to the degree of influence that the Delhi Sultans had possessed in the years 633–9/1236–42, 'Iṣāmī noted about Sultan Nāṣir al-Dīn 644–64/1246–66:

> [He] sought the goodwill of the army chiefs and cordially wished each one of them well. He did not take any decision [*rā'y zādī*] without their knowledge [*be'ilm-i īshān*], or moved a foot without their orders [*na beḥukm-i īshān dast wa pā'y zādī*]. He did not drink a drop of water, nor sleep a moment without their knowledge. . . .[38]

Although 'Iṣāmī's report of Nāṣir al-Dīn's subservience to his 'masters' was undoubtedly tinged with poetic license, no preceding

[37] Ibid., p. 468; vol. 2, p. 36.

[38] 'Iṣāmī, *Futūḥ al-Salāṭīn*, p. 146.

Sultan from the Shamsī lineage had been pictured in this way. The poet's effort to communicate the decline of the Delhi Sultan's authority in the loss of domestic independence brings out a gendered emasculation which was in strong contrast to Jūzjānī's description of Sultan Raẓiyya as a 'general' [*lashkar kash būd*], not quite a decade earlier.[39]

The incarceration of the Shamsī Princes during Bahrām Shāh's reign had a great deal to do with their weak political positions as Sultans. Unlike the earlier monarchs who had their own retinues when they ascended the throne, removal from the political arena had denied 'Alā' al-Dīn Mas'ūd and Nāṣir al-Dīn the opportunity to recruit a following.[40] By contrast, a new rank of Shamsī *bandagān-i khāṣṣ* had appeared on the scene in the years of conflict after Iltutmish's reign, and their influence in Delhi was complete.

The increase in the level of competition between the military slaves was also an important reason why the Shamsī *bandagān* persisted with the lineage of their master. In a political climate where the sentiment of belonging to one house [*az yak khāna*], and one threshold

[39] Jūzjānī, *Ṭabaqāt-i Nāṣirī*, vol. 1, p. 457.

[40] By the end of his reign, 'Alā' al-Dīn Mas'ūd may have made some effort to regain command. Writing in the middle of the fifteenth century, Yaḥyā Aḥmad Sirhindī, *Ta'rīkh-i Mubārak Shāhī*, edited by M. Hidayat Hosain (Calcutta: Bibliotheca Indica, 1931), p. 34, explained that it was the Sultan's favour to Ethiopian slaves [*habshīs*] that turned the Shamsī notables against him. Jūzjānī, *Ṭabaqāt-i Nāṣirī*, vol. 2, p. 56, noted that the Sultan's disposition [*mizāj*] changed [*pazīraft*] towards the notables; he withdrew from the army and was inclined to rebellion. Elsewhere (vol. 1, pp. 471–2) he noted that some worthless people [*nakasān*] encouraged the Sultan's rebellious inclinations. 'Iṣāmī, *Futūḥ al-Salāṭīn*, pp. 143–4, concluded that the Sultan's rebellious inclinations were provoked by greater self-confidence after his success against the Mongols (643/1245–6). The evidence of Sirhindī, Jūzjānī, and 'Iṣāmī would suggest the presence of trends noticed in the last phase, but for the fact that no conflict between the Sultan's supporters and the Shamsī notables reportedly occurred. The Shamsīs replaced the Sultan with his uncle in a coup where Ulugh Khān played a dominant role. It is doubtful if 'Alā' al-Dīn had a military retinue; he was certainly unhappy with his situation and 'Iṣāmī is probably right in ascribing a greater self-confidence to the monarch after the Mongol campaigns. The Sultan's disaffection could have provoked the movement to displace him from the throne.

[*az yak āsitān*], was unable to obviate conflict between Shamsī slaves, the overriding concern was of precedence over one's peer.[41] Jūzjānī sensed the change in this period when he lamented:

> When the armies came close to each other—all brothers and friends of each other [*hama-i barādarān wa hama-i yārān:*], two battalions of one dynasty [*yak dīgar dū ḥashm-i az yak daulat*], two armies of the same capital [*dū fauj az yak ḥaẓrat*] [belonging to] the same mansion [*dū lashkar az yak khāna*], two parts of the same [saddle-?] lining [*dū jauq az yak baṭāna*]—it was impossible for there to be a more amazing case. They were all of one purse, sharers of salt, partakers of one dish and between them accursed Satan introduced much discord [*bā ham az yak kīsa wa ham namak bar yak kāsa Shaiṭān-i mal'ūn dar miyān-i īshān chunīn tafriq ẓāhir kard*].[42]

Jūzjānī had made much of the monolithic corporate character imparted to the Turkish slaves through the processes of *parwarish, tarbiyat* and matrimonial links, but, if we recall, the death of the master had led to political crisis amongst the slaves in past generations as well. Competition amongst the slaves was manifest at the death of Mu'izz al-Dīn and Quṭb al-Dīn, and once Iltutmish's successors could no longer pose a threat the Shamsī *bandagān* were in conflict amongst themselves. Their quest for pre-eminence led the Shamsī notables into conflict with each other, but the fact that there was a balance of power between the contenders, at least until the beginning of 653/1255, meant that the Delhi Sultan was still politically relevant. As long as a member of the Shamsī lineage occupied the throne of Delhi, no Amir could claim to be Sultan. Thus, Malik 'Izz al-Dīn Kushlū Khān's attempt to usurp power and become Sultan was quickly neutralized by his peers.

The last effort by the free amirs to seize independent control of the Sultanate also occurred just after 'Alā' al-Dīn's accession. In the new dispensation of authority in the capital, the slave Ikhtiyār al-Dīn Qarā Qush became the *amīr ḥājib* (number 10 in Table 3), and the free notables, Quṭb al-Dīn Ḥasan and Khwāja Muḥazzib al-Dīn, the

[41] Jūzjānī, *Ṭabaqāt-i Nāṣirī*, vol. 2, p. 38. Jūzjānī recorded these statements in the context of the conflict between Shīr Khān and Malik Kushlū Khān.

[42] Ibid., p. 73.

nā'ib and *wazīr* respectively. Such a distribution of power meant that the confederates recognized each other's authority, a presumption shown to be naïve when Khwāja Muḥazzib al-Dīn assumed regal airs and attempted to marginalize the Turk slaves.[43]

After the murder of Khwāja Muḥazzib and his supporters, the competition between the *bandagān* in Delhi turned into an open conflict for precedence. The Shamsī slaves in these conflicts can be arranged into two major groups, the first led by the *banda* Ulugh Khān (number 25 in Table 3) and the second which eventually included the Shamsī slaves 'Imād al-Dīn Raihān, Malik Kushlū Khān, and Qutlugh Khān. While Ulugh Khān's group appears in Jūzjānī's account as the more powerful one, we should not undermine the extent of 'Imād al-Dīn Raihān's support. Certainly, judging from the years that the two groups controlled power in Delhi—Ulugh Khān, 642-50/1244-52; Raihān 651-2/1253; and Ulugh Khān again from 652/1254 onwards—Ulugh Khān was the more dominant. Yet Raihān showed that he was quite capable of deposing his competitor at the height of his power. The conflict between the two camps has received considerable attention from scholars;[44] of more interest here is a study of the notables and the composition of the rival groups for what these tell us about changes in the military elites of the Delhi Sultanate.

We have fewer details about Raihān's group, but the available information suggests that it included notables cobbled together not because of any sense of loyalty to Raihān but purely because they shared the common goal of opposing Ulugh Khān. Important in the group were the Shamsī *bandagān* 'Izz al-Dīn Kushlū Khān (number 20 in Table 3), Qutlugh Khān, a junior Shamsī slave, and Raihān himself, a eunuch of about the same age as his rival Ulugh Khān. Also associated as subordinates were individuals like 'Izz al-Dīn Balban Yuzbegī, the son-in-law of Qutlugh Khān, who was appointed *nā'ib-i amīr ḥājib* when the group seized power, and Prince Rukn al-Dīn, son of Nāṣir al-Dīn, who was given the post of *amīr ḥājib*.[45] In

[43] Ibid., vol. 1, pp. 468–9.

[44] For a useful account see Peter Jackson, *The Delhi Sultanate*, pp. 70–6.

[45] Jūzjānī, *Ṭabaqāt-i Nāṣirī*, vol. 1, p. 487; vol. 2, p. 64. 'Izz al-Dīn was the son of Ikhtiyār al-Dīn Yuzbeg who was, at this time, Governor of Lakhnauti (number 18 in Table 3). It is important to note that all these individuals were

deposing Ulugh Khān and his followers, Raihān's group was successful in its goal of 'removing each of the officers who had gained privilege through Ulugh Khān's patronage'.[46] Raihān's group had several powerful Shamsī slaves, authority within the group was diffuse, and the alliance was sustained purely as a counter to a political challenge perceived by the individual notables from Ulugh Khān.

Many of the notables who united with Ulugh Khān against Raihān were very similar to their antagonists in background and motivation. They too were associated for the specific purpose of removing Raihān or the titular monarch Nāṣir al-Dīn. Amongst the original confederates were Malik Tāj al-Dīn Sanjar Arsalān Khān (number 19 in Table 3), and the Sultan's brother Prince Jalāl al-Dīn Mas'ūd. The alliance with Prince Jalāl al-Dīn was provisional; he was deployed as an alternative candidate to the throne, a threat to Sultan Nāṣir al-Dīn to discontinue his patronage of Raihān. Jalāl al-Dīn had served his purpose once Raihān was evicted from the court and exiled. He was then left to reside in Lahore, ignored by his confederates.[47] Malik Tāj al-Dīn was senior to the other supporters of Ulugh Khān and he had also been previously favoured by Raihān.[48] His loyalty to Delhi, as we will see, would continue to be uncertain.

Ulugh Khān had other supporters as well and these notables formed a very stable coalition. They included his brother Saif al-Dīn Kishlī Khān and commanders like Saif al-Dīn Ikit Khān Ai-Beg, and Tāj al-Dīn Sanjar Tarkhān (numbers 24, 16, and 17 in Tables 2–3).[49] These were all the erstwhile pages of Iltutmish's court who had gained political stature in the politics of the Sultanate only in 'Alā' al-Dīn Mas'ūd's reign, coincident with Ulugh Khān's own rise to importance in the Delhi court. Together with these Shamsī *bandagān*

---

opposed to Ulugh Khān but not allied at the same time; Malik Kushlū Khān and Qutlugh joined Raihān only after the latter's coup against Ulugh Khān had already begun.

[46] Ibid., vol. 2, p. 64: '*har shughl dārī ki batarbiyat-i Ulugh Khānī ikhtiṣāṣ dāsht, jumla rā tabdīl farmūd*'.

[47] Ibid., vol. 1, p. 489.

[48] Ibid., p. 487; vol. 2, 34.

[49] Ibid., vol. 1, pp. 488–9 on Ikit Khān's support to Ulugh Khān.

Ulugh Khān also introduced his slaves into the ranks of military elites in the Delhi Sultanate. Ikhtiyār al-Dīn Ai-tegin Mū'īdarāz was appointed the *nā'ib-i amīr-i ākhūr* (deputy commander of the horses),[50] and his *banda-i khāṣṣ*, Qara Jamāq, was entrusted with delicate diplomatic negotiations between contending Shamsī slaves.[51]

The semblance of Shamsī order was breaking down as the military notables seized political initiative. Although Shamsī slaves had always possessed the capacity for independent military action there were two important differences noticeable now. The first marked the reorientation in service of many powerful military commanders towards a new patron, Ulugh Khān, the future Sultan Ghiyāṣ al-Dīn Balban. No Shamsī Malik had been successful in introducing so many rank 'outsiders'—young slaves making the transition to *khāṣṣ* status—into the privileged circle of court elites. Ulugh Khān's supporters were very different from Raihān's associates because they had sufficient internal solidarity to start acting as a political unit. Members of this group were not dependent upon the Delhi Sultan for their position, but owed their status to Ulugh Khān. Whereas Raihān's group was bound by self interest in opposing Ulugh Khān and not by the ties of being the servant to one master, Ulugh Khān's followers thought of themselves as *khwāja tāsh*, only they did not have Iltutmish as their master in mind any more. This was more than an alliance. To join the emerging Ghiyāṣī dispensation meant that military commanders recognized that their position and influence were not gained through personal or collective endeavour but through the favour and kindness of their master. Not all the Shamsī military commanders who joined Ulugh Khān were ready to accept these service conditions, and it would be some time before the Ghiyāṣī dispensation would achieve stability and coherence. But the expectations of the patron were framed during these years of conflict: rewards and honours were distributed in the future to those who could satisfy Ulugh Khān of their commitment to his service.

[50] Ibid., vol. 2, p. 60. In the Habibi edition the name is transcribed Ikhtiyār al-Dīn Ai-Beg Mū'īdarāz, but see fn. 11 for the variant Ai-Tegin. The slave is the same as Amīn Khān Ai-Tegin Mū'īdarāz mentioned in Baranī, *Ta'rīkh-i Fīrūz Shāhī*, edited by Khan, pp. 24, 83–4, edited by Rashid, pp. 29, 98.

[51] Jūzjānī, *Ṭabaqāt-i Nāṣirī*, vol. 2, p. 67.

The second transformation related to the political geography of the Sultanate. During Iltutmish's reign Shamsī notables only led plunder raids in the areas beyond the immediate vicinity of their garrison camps. In the period between 633/1236 and 639/1242 the Shamsī slaves fought with competitors for control of Delhi and they used the moment of strife to seize and consolidate the most lucrative *iqṭā'*s. In the years between 639/1242 and 653/1255, however, Delhi started becoming immaterial to many of these *muqṭi'*s. This marked a huge shift in the organization of the Sultanate and, in a subsequent section, we will see both the efforts made by some military commanders to consolidate their territories as by others to establish autonomous principalities. The transition from the Shamsī to the Ghiyāṣī dispensation spelled disaster for many of the Shamsī elite of the time, but for many others it provided an opportunity for upward mobility and complete autonomy. Joining the Ghiyāṣī dispensation was only one of the many options available to the Shamsī notables at this time.

(c) 652–64/1254–66: The Ghiyāṣī Dispensation[52]

The eviction of Raihān from Delhi and Ulugh Khan's restoration to power in 652/1254 did not mark the end of the competition for control of Delhi. Raihān and Qutlugh Khān continued to battle for influence over the Delhi Sultan and, despite Raihān's death in 653/1255, conflict did not diminish until 655/1257. It would be a mistake to assume that Sultan Nāṣir al-Dīn and the members of his family were not implicated in the history of these developments. In fact their involvement provides useful insights into the politics of an age under transition.

In 647/1249 Sultan Nāṣir al-Dīn had married the daughter of Ulugh Khān,[53] an asymmetrical matrimonial union that must have created tensions in the relationship between master and slave. These were

[52] 'Ghiyāṣī' was the *nisba* of affiliation taken by at least one slave who identified himself in an inscription dated 684/1285 as Qutlugh Sulṭānī Ghiyāṣī. See G. Yazdani, 'The Inscriptions of the Turk Sultans of Delhi', number xv, plate xiiib (inscription from a mosque in Sakit), pp. 28–9. 'Balbanī' is the alternative form used by Baranī.

[53] Jūzjānī, *Ṭabaqāt i Nāṣirī*, vol. 1, p. 483, vol. 2, p. 59.

inadvertently highlighted by Jūzjānī when he stated that Nāṣir al-Dīn gave him the status of father [*manṣab-i pidarī mīdād*], but Balban, ever mindful of his actual position, remained more obedient and submissive to his Sultan than a thousand newly purchased slaves.[54] Nāṣir al-Dīn's unhappiness at the slave father-in-law's domineering presence at court was suggested by the actions of his son, Rukn al-Dīn (see Chart 2), who joined the group of confederates associated with Raihān. To counter his son-in-law's intransigence, Ulugh Khān had allied with Jalāl al-Dīn, Nāṣir al-Dīn's brother, threatening the Delhi Sultan with replacement by an alternative eminently eligible candidate to the throne. Jūzjānī explained very diplomatically that, in the negotiations that took place between the opposing groups, the conflict was not a consequence of animosity between the in-laws; it was a result of the hostility generated by Raihān, whose removal would reintroduce harmony within family and realm.

Raihān's exile did not quite resolve matters, however, and his powerful ally Qutlugh Khān created a momentary crisis by marrying Sultan Nāṣir al-Dīn's mother. The Delhi Sultan now had a slave step-father who was in conflict with his slave father-in-law. The city was not large enough to host the whole family, and Qutlugh Khān and his new bride were exiled. Relentless campaigns finally drove them to seek sanctuary with the Mongols and Nāṣir al-Dīn was left in the clutches of Ulugh Khān. It was with the eventual murder of Raihān and the flight of Qutlugh Khān and Kushlū Khān from the Sultanate into Mongol territory—an interesting reversal of immigration—that the wide-ranging hostilities of the last generation finally came to an end, but only by 655/1257–8.

During the course of the conflict Ulugh Khān had moved towards consolidating his authority, a course of action he could pursue more energetically from 652/1254. The backgrounds of the Shamsī slaves who were deployed by Ulugh Khān at the restoration of his authority also elaborate on the kinds of relationships he constructed with these personnel. Jūzjānī presents us with information about five Shamsīs who joined Ulugh Khān: Malik Tāj al-Dīn Sanjar Tarkhān; Tāj al-Dīn Arsalān Khān; Ulugh Khān's brother Malik Kishlī Khān; Malik Badr

[54] Ibid., vol. 2, p. 85.

al-Dīn Nuṣrat Khān Sunqar; Ulugh Khān's cousin Shīr Khān (numbers 17, 19, 24, 22, 23 in Tables 2–3). Four of these five slaves were pages in the last years of Iltutmish's reign (numbers 17, 22, 23, and 24 in Table 2), as was Ulugh Khān himself. Of the four, the careers of three (numbers 17, 23, and 24 in Table 2) had profited from Ulugh Khān's patronage and Malik Tāj al-Dīn Sanjar Tarkhān was described by Jūzjānī, for instance, as a slave 'particularly devoted to [Ulugh Khān's] interest and friendship [*bakhidmat wa hawādārī*]'.[55] All three had suffered when their patron was exiled from Delhi due to Raihān's intervention.

A fourth, Malik Badr al-Dīn Nuṣrat Khān Sunqar (number 22 in Tables 2–3), was also a page and his rise to power occurred during 'Alā' al-Dīn Ma'sūd's reign and the murder of the *wazīr* Muḥazzib al-Dīn. Although his early career seems to have followed a path independent of Ulugh Khān, his participation in the events leading to the removal of Sultan 'Alā' al-Dīn from the throne brought him closer to Ulugh Khān. Certainly, his timely assistance in neutralizing Qutlugh Khān's attempt to capture Delhi in 655/1257, displayed his commitment to Ulugh Khān's cause and he became an integral part of the future Sultan's retinue.

The history of service of the two remaining members reflects the compromises that Ulugh Khān was still required to make in recruiting reliable subordinates. The slaves Tāj al-Dīn Arsalān Khān and Shīr Khān (numbers 19 and 23 in Tables 2–3) had contrasting backgrounds: the former was from the 'middle' ranks of the Shamsī *bandagān* and the latter was a page. Arsalān Khān's seniority (number 19 in Table 3) in the ranks of the surviving *bandagān* made the transference of his allegiance from Raihān to Ulugh Khān particularly welcome. He was given Tabarhind but conflict with Shīr Khān led to a shift in his appointment to the important charge of Awadh where, despite his service against the rebellious Qutlugh Khān, the first signs of dissatisfaction with Ulugh Khān were apparent.[56] He was moved from Awadh (which was given to the trustworthy Tāj al-Dīn Tarkhān, number 17 in Table 3) and eventually received Kara as his charge.

[55] Ibid., p. 29.

[56] Ibid., pp. 34–5.

Arsalān Khān's confidence to negotiate his independent political career made his commitment to Ulugh Khān increasingly suspect and it was from Kara that he launched a secret attack on Lakhnauti, seizing the province in 656/1259 from 'Izz al-Dīn Yuzbegī (son of Malik Ikhtiyār al-Dīn Yuzbeg, number 18 in Table 3). Arsalān Khān continued as commander of Lakhnauti for the rest of his life and was succeeded by his son Tatar Khān.[57]

Shīr Khān was a cousin of Ulugh Khān, and although their blood ties were important bonds in a cadre of slaves, the two siblings were often in conflict. Shīr Khān was given the command of Tabarhind by Sultan 'Alā' al-Dīn Ma'sūd. The early part of his career was spent in consolidating and enlarging his territories in the north-west. He seized Multan from Kushlū Khān (number 20 in Table 3) and, at a time when Ulugh Khān was exiled from Delhi to the Siwaliks, came into conflict with his cousin over their shared interest in the region of Sindh. He was forced to seek sanctuary with the Mongols,[58] and returned to the Sultanate as a part of the Ghiyāṣī alliance challenging Sultan Nāṣir al-Dīn by supporting his brother Jalāl al-Dīn. The alliance also led to a (temporary) concordance between the two siblings. Tabarhind was returned to Shīr Khān where he came into conflict with Tāj al-Dīn Arsalān Khān. Ulugh Khān arbitrated between the two Amirs. Shīr Khān was mollified and Tabarhind returned in his charge. Increasing Mongol pressure finally forced him to move and he was assuaged with a large command extending from Gwalior, Mahavan, Maihar, Jalesar, Balaram, Bayana and into Kōl.[59] This was not the end of Shīr Khān's interests in the north-western territories of the Sultanate; at an indeterminate date (perhaps *ca.* 664/1266), he was again given control of the Sunam, Lahore, and Dipalpur territories. Here he remained as master until his murder, widely rumoured to have been engineered by his cousin, in 668/1270.[60]

[57] Ibid., p. 35. See also Ẓiyā' al-Dīn Baranī, *Ta'rīkh-i Fīrūz Shāhī*, edited by Khan, p. 66, edited by Rashid, p. 78.

[58] For the clearest account see Jūzjānī, *Ṭabaqāt-i Nāṣirī*, vol. 2, p. 44. The event is also described in vol. 1, p. 487.

[59] Ibid., vol. 2, pp. 34, 43–4.

[60] Ẓiyā' al-Dīn Baranī, *Ta'rīkh-i Fīrūz Shāhī*, edited by Khan, p. 65, edited by Rashid, p. 76.

In 652/1254, when Ulugh Khān resumed power, many of the fractures within his retinue were not as yet apparent. But from the delicate treatment given to some Amirs, and the types and locations of their appanages, it is clear that Ulugh Khān was willing to travel a considerable distance to mollify them. But it is with his other compatriots that the future Sultan threw up a protective military circle around the capital. The trusted Malik Tāj al-Dīn Sanjar Tarkhān (number 19 in Table 2) was given command of Budaun. Adjacent to Delhi, Ulugh Khān's brother Malik Kishlī Khān (number 24 in Table 3), the newly appointed *amīr ḥājib* (Chamberlain), was given charge of Meerut, which he extended up to Roorkee and Miapur (?, Malhipur?). To the west of Delhi, Malik Badr al-Dīn Nuṣrat Khān Sunqar (number 22 in Table 3), who had joined Ulugh Khān in the conflict with Kushlū Khān, was rewarded with the command of Tabarhind, Sunam, Jhajjar, Lakhwal (? near Dipalpur?), and the ferries over the River Beas. These were the territories that were held at one time by Shīr Khān. The areas adjacent to Delhi and to the south-west—Hansi and Rewari, Sirsa, Barwala, and Jind (the Siwalik territories)[61]—were the personal command of Ulugh Khān, where, as Jūzjānī reported, the future Sultan had administrators and servants [*muta'alliqān wa khuddām*], to look after his *iqṭā'*.[62]

Together with his Shamsī compatriots, the *khwāja tāsh,* Ulugh Khān also relied upon a secretarial class to construct his new political order. He could start with a relatively clean slate: the last important free Amir, Quṭb al-Dīn Ḥasan 'Alī Ghūrī, was murdered in 653/1255, and the jurists and secretaries who had supported Raihān, Qutlugh Khān and Kushlū Khān, were exiled in 655/1257 from Delhi. Already in 652/1254 his old supporter, Minhāj-i Sirāj Jūzjānī, was given the post of jurist of the realm, *ṣadr-i jahān,*[63] and two years later Ẓiyā' al-Mulk Tāj al-Dīn was appointed *wazīr* and the *Ṣadr al-Mulk* was given charge of *ashrāf-i mamālik*, accountant of the state.[64] The high offices

[61] The extent of Ulugh Khān's *iqṭā'* is clarified by Jūzjānī, *Ṭabaqāt-i Nāṣirī*, vol. 2, p. 71.

[62] Ibid., p. 61.

[63] Ibid., vol. 1, p. 488. Jūzjānī was given this appointment at Kōl and it was reconfirmed in Delhi the next year, p. 489.

[64] Ibid., p. 494.

of state were getting populated by the supporters of Ulugh Khān, but perhaps none of his recruits were quite as interesting as the Afghans.

This was one group of people which did not occupy the high ground in court politics, at least not yet. Information regarding the Afghans is first mentioned by Jūzjānī in his account of Ulugh Khān's 658/1260 campaigns in the Mewat region, immediately to the south of Delhi. Afghans might have been used earlier in some Sultanate campaigns but were demustered quickly enough to pass the notice of the chroniclers of the time. That they were not a regular presence in Sultanate armies is evident from the awestruck manner in which Jūzjānī described their fearful, strange presence:

> each one of them, one could say, is like an elephant with two braided manes [*dū ghazhghā*] on [their] broad shoulders [*bar kitf nihāda*], or is like a bastion [*burjī*] . . . and each one of them would seize a hundred Hindūs [whether] in the mountain or the jungle, and on a dark night would reduce a demon to helplessness.[65]

For the urbane Persian literati of the time, the Afghans were a body of 'foreigners', clearly a group that they had not associated with, and certainly not a group to which strategic combat duties were entrusted. Ulugh Khān's deployment of these personnel recalls the earlier favour shown by Sultan Rukn al-Dīn to mahouts, a humble but effective military cadre with whose support the monarch tried to consolidate his rule and withstand the attack of the Shamsī slaves. Ulugh Khān's position was far more stable than Rukn al-Dīn's had ever been, but his choice of military personnel who were certainly 'socially alienated'—if not 'socially dead' like the military slaves—was telling. Ulugh Khān already had a large slave retinue and we have already come across two of their military commanders: Ikhtiyār al-Dīn Ai-Tegin Mū'īdarāz appointed as the *nā'ib-i amīr-i ākhūr* (deputy commander of the horses) and his *banda-i khāṣṣ*, Qara Jamāq.[66] The Afghan soldiers were not as powerful or as close to Ulugh Khān as these influential slaves. But they were like the *bandagān* (and the mahouts) in that their political service and their future elevation in the

[65] Ibid., vol. 2, p. 80.

[66] Ibid., pp. 60, 67.

Sultanate would always be incongruent to their social status. Since they would be entirely dependent on their master's patronage, in the logic of ideal service relationships of the time, they had the potential of becoming reliable subordinates. And, indeed, as we will see in the next chapter, the Afghans had a bright future to look forward to in the service of the future Sultan of Delhi.

As the Ghiyāṣī dispensation was gradually deployed during the latter half of Nāṣir al-Dīn's reign, Ulugh Khān himself was the dispenser of patronage and not its recipient any more. Working within a Shamsī political order he gradually took it apart and reordered it until its constituents no longer carried their original associations and alliances. In 664/1266, twelve years after returning to power in the court, the Ghiyāṣī dispensation was ready to stand by Ulugh Khān when he seized the throne. He now took the title of Sultan Ghiyāṣ al-Dīn Balban. He was the new Sultan of Delhi.

Territorial Changes and the Political Geography of the Sultanate

Together with changes in personnel during the period 633–64/1236–66, the territories that they inhabited also altered. *Ca.* 633/1236 Jūzjānī had noticed that the domains of the Sultanate extended from Diwal in the west to Lakhnauti in the east, almost the entirety of the northern half of the subcontinent. Certainly, technological difficulties and more contingent political and geographical factors had made the connections within this domain extremely difficult. Yet, even during the brief period of his reign Iltutmish managed to cohere dispersed territories around the authority of Delhi by carefully positioning both impersonal institutional checks on fiscal management as well as slave Governors with close ties to him. The political relevance of Delhi as a centre that provided sanctuary and protected Islam was also created in the lives of its Muslim subjects, as we saw, through the agency of a variety of piety-minded jurists, scholars, and individuals with mystical inclinations, *dastārbandān*. There was considerable hostility towards the lineages of power that constituted this domain, but the *idea* of a Sultanate with Delhi as its centre had gained ground. All contestants in the future would have to challenge not just the authority of the Delhi Sultan but also its recently fashioned image as the 'axis of Islam' in the East. In the years of political turmoil after Iltutmish's death some aspects of the stature and relevance of Delhi survived, if not entirely for the original reasons, and others were whittled away and transformed.

At Iltutmish's death the loss of the eastern and western wings of the Sultanate, the provinces of the Punjab and Sindh in the west and Lakhnauti and Bihar in the east, happened very quickly. As early as 637/1240 Malik Kabīr Khān Ayāz (number 2 in Table 3) broke away from Delhi and, with his base in Multan, took the title of Sultan. Yet Kabīr Khān Ayāz, disgraced by Iltutmish, disaffected under his early successors, was a special case, and one can doubt the strength of his original attachment to the Delhi Sultanate. He established an independent, if shortlived, dynasty in the Sindh region and his son Tāj al-Dīn Abū Bakr Ayāz succeeded him to the throne.[67] Both Kabīr Khān Ayāz and his son Tāj al-Dīn's dependants continued to control areas of Sindh even after their master lost power to the encroaching Qarluqs. Jūzjānī refers to Kabīr Khān's slave Aq-Sunqar, and Tāj al-Dīn's eunuch Mukhliṣ al-Dīn, respectively, as the *amīr-i dād* and *kōtwāl* of Uchch as late as in 643/1245–6.[68] Sultanate authority in the region, already diminished thanks to Kabīr Khān and his son, was further eroded by the presence of the Mongols and the Qarluqs. Control of Lahore had effectively lapsed to the Mongols and from 639/1242 the 'intra-dispensational' conflicts in the court intruded into the region with Ulugh Khān's competitor, Malik Kushlū Khān (number 20 in Table 3), making a strong bid to bring the region under his control. The Delhi forces under Ulugh Khān frequently intervened in the region because of the Mongol threat.[69]

But despite this supervision the Shamsī slaves in Multan and Uchch were regularly in conflict with each other, without interference

[67] Ibid., pp. 6–7.

[68] Ibid., p. 54. See especially fn. 5 and Habibi's record of the reading from a variant manuscript. The variant manuscript presents the relationship of the slaves to their individual masters more clearly.

[69] Ibid., vol. 1, pp. 479, 486; vol. 2, p. 56. Campaigns took place in 643/1245–6, Rajab 644/November 1246, Sh'abān 646/November 1248, and Shawwāl 650/December 1252.

from the Delhi court. After 'Izz al-Dīn Kushlū Khān (number 20 in Table 3) lost Multan to the Qarluqs, Uchch was seized from him by Malik Shīr Khān (number 23 in Table 3). Shīr Khān was not punished for his impertinence, nor was Kushlū Khān restored to his lost command. Lest it be assumed that Shīr Khān was not chastized because he was Ulugh Khān's cousin, we need to recall Jūzjānī's information that, during Ulugh Khān's exile in Nagaur, there was conflict between the two kinsmen. This must have been serious enough to cause Shīr Khān to seek sanctuary with the Mongols and he was followed soon after by Kushlū Khān.[70] Ironically, by the late 1240s and early 1250s, political conflict between members of the Shamsī dispensation had reached such a stage that for notables like Shīr Khān, Kushlū Khān, and Iltutmish's own son Jalāl al-Dīn Mas'ūd, the Mongol dominions, and not Delhi, provided sanctuary. Certainly, in the territories of Sindh and the western Punjab, Delhi's authority was virtually non-existent.

The situation was not very different in the east where, during the period of 'inter-dispensational' conflicts (633–9/1236–42), Iltutmish's Governor of Lakhnauti, Malik 'Izz al-Dīn Tughan Khān (number 7 in Tables 2–3), ruled unchanged and in virtual autonomy. Unlike his compatriot Kabīr Khān, however, the *banda-i khāṣṣ* Tughan Khān continued to acknowledge the successors of his master who, in turn, never interfered in Lakhnauti.[71] But after 639/1242, once intra-dispensational conflict amongst the Shamsī slaves started, Malik Tughan Khān seized the territories of Awadh and Kara. These areas were still regarded as an integral part of the Delhi court, and preceding monarchs had made appointments in the region. Now, in 'Alā' al-Dīn Ma'sūd's reign, their seizure by a notable—who protested his subordination and loyalty to the Delhi Sultan—provoked no reactions from the capital at all.[72] More interestingly, when Tughan Khān did request aid from Delhi, Malik Tamar Khān (number 8 in Table 3), the leader of the relief forces, went beyond his brief. He seized Lakhnauti, deposed Tughan Khān, and between 642/1244 and 644/1246 commanded and ruled the region without check to his authority [*lashkar*

[70] Ibid., vol. 2, p. 44; vol. 1, p. 487.

[71] Ibid., vol. 2, pp. 13–14.

[72] Ibid., vol. 1, p. 469; vol. 2, p. 14.

kashī wa kām-rānī kard].[73] The ability of the Shamsī *bandagān* to seize political initiative and improve their positions was hardly a unique instance in this period, nor was the fact that this drove them into conflict with each other. But that Delhi, the *Qubbat al-Islam*, could have such little relevance in the lives of slaves raised to serve the Delhi Sultan suggested a spatial dimension to the conflict amongst the Shamsī notables. Together with the breakdown in interpersonal bonds between the slaves, the structures and sentiments that had adhered regions from Sindh to Lakhnauti were getting to be anachronistic. And indeed at a later date the slave Ikhtiyār al-Dīn Yuzbeg (number 18 in Table 3) established his independence in Lakhnauti as Sultan Mughīṣ al-Dīn Yuzbeg.[74]

The distance of Lakhnauti and Sindh from Delhi certainly provided Shamsī slaves the space to chart their own careers and Lakhnauti would eventually possess the reputation of being *bulghākpūr*, the city of insurrection.[75] But it was not just the distance from Delhi that led to cities and regions achieving notoriety as havens for rebels. Take the case of Bahraich. Nāṣir al-Dīn had resided there together with his mother soon after his release from prison in 639/1242.[76] A part of his retinue from Bahraich must have included 'Imād al-Dīn Raihān and Qutlugh Khān, an assumption that is confirmed by the long-term association of the two slaves with the town. After deposing Ulugh Khān from his authoritative position in court, they gathered their own retinues, which included Shams al-Dīn Bharā'ījī, a loyal confederate

[73] Ibid., vol. 2, p. 18.

[74] The year of Ikhtiyār al-Dīn Yuzbeg's accession is unclear, but it must have occurred some time after 644/1247 and the death of Malik Tamar Khān. A coin of Ikhtiyār al-Dīn, dated 653/1255, carries the title *al-Sulṭān al-'Aẓam Mughīṣ al-Dunyā wa Dīn Abū al-Muẓaffar Yuzbeg al-Sulṭān*. See H. Nelson Wright, *Catalogue of the Coins in the Indian Museum Calcutta Including the Cabinet of the Asiatic Society of Bengal* (Oxford: Clarendon Press, 1907), vol. 2, p. 146, and Part ii, plate I, number 6. Sultan Mughīṣ al-Dīn must have died some time before 657/1259 when 'Izz al-Dīn Yuzbegī, was defeated and deposed by Tāj al-Dīn Sanjar Arsalān Khān. See Jūzjānī, *Ṭabaqāt-i Nāṣirī*, vol. 2, p. 34.

[75] Ẓiyā' al-Dīn Baranī, *Ta'rīkh-i Fīrūz Shāhī*, edited by Khan, p. 82, edited by Rashid, p. 96.

[76] Jūzjānī, *Ṭabaqāt-i Nāṣirī*, vol. 1, pp. 470, 478–9.

to their cause, as the *qāẓī* of the realm. When they lost the conflict with Ulugh Khān, Raihān was exiled to Bahraich and Qutlugh Khān to Awadh but he eventually sought seclusion in Bahraich as well.[77] And what is important to keep in mind here is that Bahraich could only be regarded as a rebel haven by an opponent like Ulugh Khān; for Raihān and Qutlugh Khān, Bahraich would qualify as close as 'homelands' could be to deracinated slaves. This was where they had spent a part of their youthful careers and it was from this region that they drew some of their loyal accomplices. Let us not forget as well that, very much like Raihān with his interests in Bahraich, Ulugh Khān had his territory in the Siwalik, an area he had assiduously cultivated and protected even against his cousin.

During the period of intra-dispensational conflict the territory that the Delhi monarch could control contracted dramatically. Sindh, western Punjab, and Lakhnauti are obvious examples of areas that had seceded. But closer to Delhi as well, *muqṭi's* were no longer subject to 'transfers'; they were in conflict with each other, expelling peers from their commands and seizing territories, often without the cognizance or permission of the monarch. From a different perspective, it is in this period that we can see the efforts of deracinated Shamsī *bandagān* to establish roots by stabilizing control over their territories so that they could withstand the challenge of other Shamsī Amirs and, occasionally, the forces of the Delhi Sultan. One aspect of this move towards autonomy and consolidation certainly implied the raising of independent military retinues and establishing fiscal resources to manage campaigns of long duration. Money continued to pour into military establishments through plunder raids, but there were alliances as well with local chieftains through which the Shamsī *bandagān* sought to implicate their territories into the politics and economy of their local contexts. These developments must have started during the period of the intra-dispensational conflict, but they become visible only in the following years when Ulugh Khān started reasserting his authority. At that time local rulers provided support and protection to Shamsī Maliks facing the wrath of Delhi.

There is not a great deal of information on the subject of the '*Rānā-Malik*' condominium in the literature of the period, and this should

[77] Ibid., pp. 487, 490; vol. 2, pp. 64, 69.

hardly surprise us. Persian chroniclers rarely departed from their monolithic descriptions of the Delhi Sultanate as a repository of Muslim aspirations of power and grandeur. As we have already noticed in the case of Raihān and Qutlugh Khān, Shamsī rebels who went against Ulugh Khān received short shrift in Jūzjānī's account.[78] Their non-Muslim allies intrude into his narrative purely by accident. The two examples we do possess are therefore rare and important in providing an insight into the reserves of support available to recalcitrant Shamsīs as they battled the authority of Delhi.

The first example concerns Ulugh Khān's rival, Qutlugh Khān, a Shamsī Malik who, if we remember, had set up base in Awadh after his expulsion from Delhi. When Qutlugh Khān found it impossible to continue his conflict with Ulugh Khān in Awadh (655/1257), he marched into the *mawās* until he came to Santur (capital of Sirmur) in the foothills of the Himalayas. *Mawās* (plural, *mawāsāt*) was a difficult terrain, a 'natural fastness' for local chieftains outside the control of the Sultanate. As Hodivala explained: '*Mawās* was a tract or district which was a sort of sanctuary or place of refuge on account of the physical features which made it a natural fastness . . . [where] . . . indigenes had retreated . . .'.[79] Within the context of the court-centric Sultanate records, *mawās* carried with it the sense of 'disturbed, troubled territory' in the control of a rebel, which Habib, in his study of the Sultanate economy, translated as 'rebellious areas'.[80] These were, of course, 'disturbed' or 'rebellious' only from the point of view of Delhi.

After Qutlugh Khān moved into the *mawās* in the Sirmur region, he received assistance from the local non-Muslim population and

[78] The only exception to the case is, of course, their collaborator Kushlū Khān, who must have helped Jūzjānī some time during his career, because the author includes a full biography of the Malik. See number 20 in Tables 1 and 3 for a summary of his career and references.

[79] Hodivala, *Studies in Indo-Muslim History*, vol. 1, pp. 226–9. See also Jūzjānī, *Ṭabaqāt-i Nāṣirī*, vol. 2, p. 71, and the description of the *mawās* faced by Ulugh Khān on one of his campaigns: '*chūn tafriqa bar īshān rāh yāft wa jangalhā-yī Hindūstān gasht wa mazā'iq-i lorhā wa iltifāf-i ashjār-i bisyār* . . . [as their paths were separated [because] of the dense forests of Hindustan and the torrential gorges and the extremely dense woods . . .].' See also Chapter 6.

[80] Irfan Habib, 'Slavery', in *The Cambridge Economic History*, vol. 1, p. 90.

their King, Rānā Ribāl/Dibāl/ Ranbāl (?). Jūzjānī explained that it was the custom amongst these people to offer sanctuary [*'ādat-i ān jamā'at muḥāfaẓat-i multāji'ān būdī*]. He further explained that Qutlugh Khān, a powerful notable, had claims [*ḥaqūq-i ṣābit dāsht*], on all these people, so that wherever he went he received assistance.[81] Between the willingness of the local ruler to render sanctuary and the 'moral accounts' owed to the Shamsī slave, Qutlugh Khān managed to escape Ulugh Khān. Not so, however, Rānā Ribāl (?), who 'suffered a severe chastisement' as punishment for the assistance given to Qutlugh Khān, an enemy of Delhi. Ulugh Khān, plundered Rānā Ribāl's (?) capital and destroyed his market (*bāzārgāh*).[82]

This is a particularly well-documented case and it helps us enlarge upon some similar instances mentioned more briefly in Jūzjānī. After Ulugh Khān's restoration and successful campaigns against Qutlugh and Kushlū Khān, some of his supporters became anxious over his increasing authority. Prominent amongst them were the slave Tāj al-Dīn Arsalān (number 19 in Table 3) and Jalāl al-Dīn Mas'ūd Jānī (son of 'Alā' al-Dīn Jānī, referred here by his other title Qilich Khān).[83] In 656/1258 these Shamsī notables had hesitated to muster their forces in campaigns against the Mongols, and Ulugh Khān decided to lead a campaign against them before they actually rebelled. Interestingly enough, Ulugh Khān's campaigns in the Kara and Manikpur region were not initially directed against the Shamsī notables, but against the local Kings [*rānāgān*], of the region who were 'severely punished'. Faced with the punishment inflicted on the local chieftains, Arsalān and Mas'ūd Jānī did not offer resistance to the Delhi forces. They dispersed, sent their troopers and dependants into the *mawāsāt*, and then commenced negotiations with the Delhi forces.[84]

In the conflict between Shamsī notables, especially in the context of a reassertive Delhi under Ulugh Khan, the *mawās* was also a place

[81] Jūzjānī, *Ṭabaqāt-i Nāṣirī*, vol. 2, p. 71.

[82] Ibid., vol. 1, p. 491; vol. 2, pp. 72–3.

[83] Although Arsalān Khān was one of Ulugh Khān's confederates against Raihān and his associates, Shīr Khān and he were the only individuals who had advanced in their careers without Ulugh Khān's patronage. They regarded each other as peers and did not willingly accept Ulugh Khān's authority.

[84] Ibid., vol. 2, p. 76: *bazarūrat khail wa atbā' rā dar miyān-i mawāsāt firistādand*, out of necessity they sent their troops and followers into the *mawās*.

of sanctuary for Shamsī notables. Certainly, as the examples of both Qutlugh Khān and Arsalān Khān's associates suggest, in the years of conflict in the post-Iltutmish period Shamsī notables had built up personal networks of alliance to consolidate their local power. In a transformation of an earlier limited dialogue between urban cantonments and political formations in the countryside, these networks of alliance spread out to include the local chieftains, the *rānāgān*. Other than overcoming the challenge of the Shamsī notables, it was the possibility of a '*Rānā-Malik*' combine that Ulugh Khān had to counter to make Delhi paramount in north India once again.

Years ago, Mohammad Habib stressed the urban character of the early Delhi Sultanate and, in searching for the historical contexts that led to its eventual control of the territories of local chieftains in the countryside, this historian identified the importance of the reign of Sultan 'Alā' al-Dīn Khalajī, 695–715/1296–1316. In his argument, it was this Sultan's military and revenue policies that carried Sultanate authority into the interior of the north Indian countryside, bringing much of the peasantry into direct contact with the imperial administration.[85] Years afterwards, Irfan Habib had again emphasized the importance of the Sultan's reign and, even though he underlined the coercive aspects of this development, in his work the transitions in the territorial character of the Sultanate were equally sudden: from limited control of some lands held in *khāliṣa*, the Sultanate acquired a large agrarian base. In Irfan Habib's argument—and this scholar closely followed the narrative of Ẓiyā' al-Dīn Baranī here—these developments were a consequence of the revenue policies of the energetic and ambitious Delhi monarch 'Alā' al-Dīn Khalajī.[86]

To a large extent this interpretation resides on the presumption that only the Delhi Sultans and the forces under their command mobilized sufficient power and authority to introduce far-reaching change. But the fact is that during the post-Shamsī years 633–64/1236–66, political agency had moved into the hands of the Shamsī Maliks and, as

[85] Mohammad Habib, 'Introduction to Elliot and Dowson's History of India vol. II'.

[86] Amongst the author's many writings on the subject, see especially Irfan Habib, 'The Price Regulations of 'Ala al-Din Khalaji - A Defence of Ẓiā' Barani', and 'Economic History of the Delhi Sultanate—An Essay in Interpretation'.

they negotiated their relationships with Delhi, they too had constructed alliances to withstand the capital's efforts to pressurize them into submission. It was during these years that the Shamsī Maliks stepped out of the confines of their cantonments and established alliances with local chieftains and their subalterns. The 'rooting' of the Sultanate in the countryside, in other words, occurred not through the Delhi Sultan but through the agencies of those military commanders who sought to challenge and protect themselves from his authority. Its history goes back to the accommodative relationships established by the Mu'izzī *bandagān-i khāṣṣ* attempting to consolidate their respective principalities. The form that it reached now challenged the structure of the Sultanate constructed by Iltutmish, and its future organization would have to take these intervening changes into account.

Relations with the Piety-Minded and Ideological Reformulations

In the previous chapter we had considered a different condominium of interests: between the Delhi Sultan and the piety-minded of the realm—the *'ulamā*, the *qāẓīs*, the *Shaikh al-Islām*, and some of the 'people of the pen', the *ahl-i qalam*. The creation of a unitary Sultanate, protecting and creating the structures that could once again invigorate a cohesive and monolithic Muslim community was the shared vision of these people. The discursive instruments and material forms and contexts of its coercive implementation were all fashioned during the reign of Sultan Iltutmish.

The beginning of these developments can be dated to some time in the middle of the 1220s when the Mongol invasions into Khwarazm, eastern Iran and Afghanistan had commenced and the Delhi Sultan was moving towards the final annexation of the last of the north Indian Sultanates. Within a decade, or slightly more, Iltutmish was dead and succession to the throne of the Sultanate hung in the balance through the years of the interdispensational conflicts. What happened to the vision of the unitary Sultanate and the composite Muslim community in the years after one of its greatest proponents had passed away?

Certainly, the rapid dethronement of monarchs and the attempted seizure of political authority by the Shamsī *bandagān*, individuals whom Shaikh Niẓām al-Dīn Awliyā' described as 'uncouth and ignorant', challenged the careful and supportive concordance that Iltutmish had established between the lineages of temporal and sacred authority in the Sultanate. An entry into the changes that occurred in this period is provided by the enthronement in 634/1236 of Sultan Raẓiyya, the daughter of Sultan Iltutmish. The accession of a young unmarried woman to the throne was an unusual event; she was not a regent for a possible future male candidate and there were several alternative male siblings available (see Chart 2). But, as we have already discussed, for the Shamsī slaves the presumed inability of a woman in veiled seclusion to exercise independent authority as a monarch qualified her as a wonderful candidate for the throne. While Raẓiyya's accession and reign was supported and contested by various military commanders, it was not until the late sixteenth century that a jurist and scholar of *ḥadīṣ* asked the awkward question: how was it that the *'ulamā'* of the age accepted a woman as a ruler?[87] The question had not been posed so bluntly and a strange silence had prevailed around the subject. As it happened, Minhāj-i Sirāj Jūzjānī, a jurist with a strong commitment to both the Sultanate and to his faith and profession as a religious scholar, did, in fact, provide a history of Raẓiyya's reign. It is worth paying attention to his narrative for the ways in which it tried to balance his commitments and rationalize Raẓiyya's accession and reign.

Jūzjānī provided different accounts of the accession. One narrative suggested that Raẓiyya was Iltutmish's choice and the Sultan was cognizant of the objections his courtiers would raise. Yet, as Jūzjānī had him explain, the Sultan realized that she was the only one amongst his children who possessed the responsible qualities that makes a great ruler. All her male siblings were too immature to handle the onerous tasks of kingship. As a result, Jūzjānī noted, in 631/1233 Iltutmish declared Raẓiyya as his successor in his will.[88] Rukn al-Dīn's usurpation of the throne proved correct all his father's fears: the Prince and his mother dissipated the fortunes of the state on carnivals and threatened the members of Iltutmish's family. Raẓiyya

[87] 'Abd al-Ḥaqq Mūḥaddiṣ Dehlawī, *Ta'rīkh-i Ḥaqqī,* B.M. Ms. Add. 26210, fol. 9v, cited by R.P. Tripathi, *Some Aspects of Muslim Administration*, p. 29.

[88] Jūzjānī, *Ṭabaqāt-i Nāṣirī,* vol. 1, p. 457.

then rallied the *qalb* to her cause; they deposed her brother and installed her on the throne, finally honouring the terms of her father's will. In this narrative, the responsibility for the woman's succession to the throne was placed on both the father who appreciated her extraordinary qualities and the Shamsī slaves who imposed their master's will.

Jūzjānī's alternative narrative provided a completely different account of Rukn al-Dīn's accession—not usurpation. Here the author had the father systematically honouring his son—in celebration of Caliphal recognition of Iltutmish's Sultanate in 626/1229, Rukn al-Dīn was given a green parasol, second in honour to the oldest son Nāṣir al-Dīn, who predeceased the father.[89] In 631/1233 he was given the high command of Lahore and in 633/1236 brought to Delhi and recognized as heir apparent.[90] The details in this narrative are in marked contrast to the anecdotal, didactic account supporting Raẓiyya's claims to office; they carry far greater credibility.

The organization of Jūzjānī's narrative of Raẓiyya's reign is also interesting. He starts by noting all her venerable qualities and concludes with the rhetorical question: 'but in the register of creation since her account did not fall under the column of men, how did she gain from all these excellent qualities?'[91] Raẓiyya was fated to fail for no fault of her own; her destiny was predetermined by her gender. This introductory observation of the author was somewhat misleading because his account proceeded to narrate the great military and diplomatic successes that accrued to the monarch. When the kingdom was at peace and all was well, Jūzjānī introduced the elements that led to its collapse: suddenly, at the height of her success, Raẓiyya gave up the modest behaviour that befitted a woman. She stopped wearing the veil, started appearing in male clothing and headdress, and rode an elephant in full public view of men. This was when she also raised her Ethiopian slave Yāqūt to the position of *amīr-i āk͟hūr*. Insurrection then beset the kingdom and she was eventually deposed. Jūzjānī's fatalistic introductory comment makes more sense as a concluding epitaph: Raẓiyya might have continued as monarch had she not

[89] Ibid., p. 454. See Chart 2 and discussion in Chapter 3.

[90] Ibid., pp. 454–5.

[91] Ibid., p. 457. This is an idiomatic translation of the text: *ammā az ḥisāb-i mardān dar k͟hilqat-i naṣībī nīufta būd īn hama-i ṣifāt-i gazīda chi sūdash dāsht?*

departed from the decorum that God gave to women as their lot. But kingship has its own demands which women *qua* women could never fulfill. As a result, when Raẓiyya, despite all her great qualities, tried to function as a man, she met a calamitous end.

As a jurist grateful to Raẓiyya for advancement and yet trapped by the conditions of his service and his conscience, Jūzjānī was forced to ride many different horses. He could not condemn Raẓiyya outright for immodesty, nor could he criticize the Shamsī slaves for raising a woman to the throne. He was nevertheless acutely uncomfortable with the turn of events that had made a Queen a monarch. As a jurist he should have protested a woman's accession to the throne, but was constrained by the power equations of the time. His compromise was to shift responsibility entirely to Iltutmish who, responding to the exigencies of the time, chose the most qualified of his children—gender notwithstanding—as his heir. Jūzjānī's didactic comment intruded into the narrative at this point: the experiment was bound to fail because it went against the divinely ordained gendered social order. Without displaying any political responsibility towards the preservation of this Muslim social order—the duty incumbent upon all pious Muslims, especially jurists, and the reason for the sixteenth-century religious scholar's complaint against the *'ulamā'*—Jūzjānī prospered in the new political dispensation and still managed to articulate his reservations about the conditions of the age.

The difficult choice of remaining honest to his conscience or protecting his career was not unique to Jūzjānī. As we have already noticed in the last chapter, jurists, scholars, and secretaries often negotiated their service conditions and the demands of their conscience with the greatest degree of difficulty during these years. If we recall Fakhr-i Mudabbir's comment—'grandees of the highest pedigree were in the service of the Turks and derived peace, prosperity and honour from their success'[92]—patronage carried with it the compromises involved in dealing with a deracinated and lately Islamicized ruling elite.

On the other hand, the deracinated character of the *bandagān* led them to manage their careers with extreme pragmatism. They paid little attention to traditional or customary niceties. A daughter of the

[92] Fakhr-i Mudabbir, *Ta'rīkh-i Fakhr al-Dīn Mubārak Shāh*, pp. 43–4.

master could be raised to the throne and married if necessary; indeed the wife of the master could be espoused as well if it served the political interests of the slave.[93] These events were sometimes noted without comment and occasionally, as in the case of Raẓiyya, with the most convoluted didactic understatement.

As the Shamsī order collapsed the '*ulamā*' persisted with their aim of guiding the Muslim community along the path of the *Sharī'a*, but they received less help now from the Delhi Sultan. Rather than continuing with their father's grand design of associating with the '*ulamā*' to make Delhi the axis of the Muslim community, the sons of Iltutmish were involved with the Shamsī notables in retaining some

[93] One of the rebel slaves, Malik Ikhtiyār al-Dīn Altūnia (number 11 in Table 3), eventually married Raẓiyya and together they made an unsuccessful bid to recapture power. Jūzjānī, *Ṭabaqāt-i Nāṣirī,* vol. 1, pp. 462, 464; vol. 2, pp. 21–2. Note also the case of Malik Ikhtiyār al-Dīn Aitegin (number 12 in Table 3) who married the uterine sister of Sultan Mu'izz al-Dīn Bahrām Shāh, ibid., vol. 1, p. 463; vol. 2, p. 23. More startling is the case of the slave Qutlugh Khān who married Sultan Nāṣir al-Dīn's mother, Malika-i Jahān, who, together with her new husband, joined conflict with Ulugh Khān, ibid., vol. 1, pp. 489, 493; vol. 2, p. 69. Peter Jackson, 'Sulṭān Raḍiyya bint Iltutmish', pp. 81–97, has argued that Raẓiyya's accession may reflect the influence of Qarā Khitā'ī traditions carried into the Sultanate by the five Qarā Khitā'ī Shamsī slaves in Iltutmish's service (on the Qarā Khitā, see also Chapter 3, fn 76). By Raẓiyya's reign only four of these slaves were alive (numbers 7, 10, 12, and 16; number 5 died in 631/1233–4: see Tables 1 and 3) and of the four, two were Turks and two probably Mongol. It is not clear how Qarā Khitā'ī traditions affected developments in the Sultanate. In the Qarā Khitā royal lineage women occasionally held power: not as Sultans, only as regents. This may have become acceptable tradition within the Qarā Khitā'ī royal lineage, but whether it became a part of a wider customary tradition in the Qarā Khitā'ī domains is very doubtful; certainly the Turks might not have accepted Mongol traditions as easily. The further transposition of royal traditions into the Sultanate through humble and deracinated Qarā Khitā'ī slaves, who were in any case a minority within the Shamsī retinue (only two of the four were in a position to influence the succession in any way; numbers 10 and 12 in Table 3), is extremely doubtful. Central Asian traditions did manifest themselves in the Delhi Sultanate but these need to be historicized very carefully, else scholars can become trapped in rather simple Weberian assumptions wherein cultural traditions travelled mechanically through ethnic or confessional genealogies.

semblance of authority in Delhi. By 637/1240 and Mu'izz al-Dīn Bahrām Shāh's accession, the Delhi Sultans were not merely losing control of Delhi, they had also given up their father's vision of supporting the *Sharī'a*-minded *'ulamā'*. Instead, Jūzjānī noted, Mu'izz al-Dīn had been impressed by a Turkish dervish by the name of Ayūb, and he had gained the confidence [*taqarrub*], of the monarch. Under his influence the Sultan ordered the execution of Qāẓī Shams al-Dīn Maihar[pur].[94] This was a complete reversal of roles for the Delhi Sultan who, in the past, had always leaned towards the *'ulamā'* and against the *ṣūfīs*.

One can only guess at the motivations that prompted the Delhi Sultans to opt in favour of the *ṣūfīs*. Ironically, it may have been exactly the authoritarian element in Islamic mysticism that had made Iltutmish very careful in his dealings with the *ṣūfī* Shaykhs. An important aspect of sufism was the claim made by its saints to possess esoteric knowledge [*nūr-i bāṭin*] denied to the rest of the community. This knowledge also placed the mystic in a special relationship with God, where the saint could act as intercessor on the Day of Judgement; his grace [*baraka*] had curative, protective properties, and he was believed to possess miraculous powers. The disciple of the saint profited through this association and became a special person close to God, protected in his endeavours by his master's special mystical powers.

The execution of the *qāẓī* of Maihar[pur] shocked the *'ulamā'* and in 639/1241–2 they allied with the Shamsī notables to depose Sultan Bahram Shāh. Jūzjānī provides a list of confederates. These included the following important *'ulamā'* in the Delhi court: Ṣadr al-Mulk Sayyid Tāj al-Dīn 'Alī Mūsawī, Qāẓī-i Mamālik Jalāl al-Dīn Kāshānī, Qāẓī Kabīr al-Dīn, and Shaykh Muḥammad-i Shāmī.[95] Rather than maintaining their earlier association with the Delhi Sultan, as the intra-dispensational conflicts catapulted the Shamsī *bandagān* into prominence, a far closer relationship between the *'ulamā'* and the military notables becomes noticeable. Now the *'ulamā'* sought association with one or the other Shamsī commander. Balban, for instance supported Qāẓī Jalāl al-Dīn Kāshānī, who was brought from

[94] Jūzjāni, *Ṭabaqāi-i Nāsiri,* vol. 1, p. 466.
[95] Ibid., p. 464.

Awadh and appointed *qāẓī* of the realm. Upon his death in 648/1251, an old friend, Jūzjānī, was given the post.[96] Balban's rival, Raihān, had his own support from the *'ulamā'*, most notably Qāẓī Shams al-Dīn Bharā'ījī. When Raihān deposed Ulugh Khān, Qāẓī Bharā'ījī was appointed *qāẓī* of the realm.[97] The participation of the *'ulamā'* in the conflict between notables over Delhi became more obvious in later years. When Qutlugh and Kushlū Khān were on the defensive against Ulugh Khān, they received letters from Qāẓī Shams al-Din Bharā'ījī, the *Shaikh al-Islām* Jamāl al-Dīn, and Sayyid Quṭb al-Dīn who were in Delhi carrying the following invitation:

> the doors [of the city] are in our hands [*darwāẓhā-yi badast-i mā ast*], you must come to the capital, for Delhi is devoid of [Balban's] retinue [*shahr az ḥashm khālī ast*]. You are from the slaves of the court, and between [us] there is no unfamiliarity [*begānagī dar miyān nī*]. When you come to the capital, and attach yourself to the service of the crown, Ulugh Khān with all his troopers will be left outside [*baān lashkar bīrūn bamānad*].[98]

The plans of the *'ulamā'* were neutralized by the followers of Ulugh Khān, who reached Delhi in time, and the rebels were exiled. But more important for our discussion was the statement of the conspirators that Qutlugh and Kushlū Khān were 'not strangers [*begānagī . . .nī*], to them'. Although we have no knowledge about the qualities that attracted the *Sharī'a*-minded to the cause of Qutlugh and Kushlū Khān, we do know that Ulugh Khān had his own body of supporters amongst the jurists. And the conflict between the amirs had also touched the *'ulamā'* very directly. Jūzjānī complained how Raihān's paid thugs made movement difficult for him in Delhi.[99] He was safe, however, once Ulugh Khān was restored to power and with the formation of the Ghiyāṣī dispensation Jūzjānī received the post of *qāẓī* of the realm.

[96] Ibid., pp. 483–5, vol. 2, p. 62.

[97] Ibid., vol. 1, p. 487. The friendship between Raihān and Qāẓī Bharā'ījī went back to the time when Sultan Nāṣir al-Dīn, still a Prince, had been sent to Bahraich. The eunuch Raihān had probably accompanied the household at that time. For Nāṣir al-Dīn's years in Bahraich, see vol. 1, p. 470.

[98] Ibid.. p. 492; vol. 2, p. 74.

[99] Ibid., vol. 2, p. 66

Many of these developments coincided with the events that led to the death of Mu'izz al-Dīn Bahrām Shāh in 639/1242. His death led to conflicts amongst the military commanders and the greater involvement of the *'ulamā'* in these internecine quarrels, but it also curtailed the growth of *ṣūfī* influence in Delhi. Yet even if Delhi stayed relatively undeveloped as a *ṣūfī* centre, the supervision of mystical activity was not nearly so rigorous in many other regions. It was no accident that the popularity of the Chishtī *ṣūfī* saint Bābā Farīd (died *ca.* 664/1265) dates to the period of the 'intra-dispensational' conflicts and its location outside a major urban centre facilitated Bābā Farīd's ability to establish his order without undue scrutiny. The saint's hospice, *khānaqāh*, was located at Ajudhan, to begin with a deserted place on the banks of a ford across the River Sutlej. With time Ajudhan became a major stop on trade routes from Delhi to Multan, a busy place for commercial exchange and the disbursement of charity.

According to Niẓām al-Dīn Awliyā', Bābā Farīd's spiritual successor, although his master chose to live in the wilderness [*dasht wa biyābān*], innumerable people still visited the Shaykh, and the doors of the *khānaqāh* were kept open late into the night. Apparently Bābā Farīd's personal choice to live as an indigent did not apply to visitors to the *khānaqāh*, and Niẓām al-Dīn noted that

> due to the generosity of God, silver [*sīm*], food [*ta'ām*], and comforts [*ni'mat*] were present [in the *khānaqāh*], and those who came and went received a part of it, and everyone who came to his service received some good fortune [*hīch bakhidmat-i īshān nīāmadī ki o rā chīzī naṣīb na-kardī*]. It was miraculous provisionings ['*ajab qūtī*], a wonderful life ['*ajab zindagānī*] . . .[100]

Ṣūfī ideas of 'spiritual domain', *wilāyat*, and the protective grace, *baraka*, of the saint Bābā Farīd gained extraordinary currency in this time, and travellers would approach the saint for an amulet, *ta'wīz*, to guard against danger. These beliefs were reported by Niẓām al-Dīn Awliyā' in a story concerning 'Abd Allāh Rūmī, who sought *du'ā'* (benediction) from Bābā Farīd as he journeyed from Ajudhan to Multan. Bābā Farīd told him that he could provide protection in his

[100] Amīr Ḥasan Sijzī, *Fawā'id al-Fu'ād*, p. 125.

own *wilāyat* which only extended part of the way to Multan. The remainder of the distance was Bahā' al-Dīn Zakariyā's *wilāyat* where Rūmī would have to rely upon the Suhrawardī saint's grace for protection. Although these ideas were old, it is only from Bābā Farīd's time that they were being popularly invoked and relied upon.[101]

In a world where the old order was breaking down it was these friends of God, *awliyā'*, who introduced stability and provided protection. A traveller from Lahore to Budaun was quizzed by Shādi Muqrī, an old resident of Lahore, about conditions in his home town. When the traveller told him of the excessive rain and fire that were ruining the city, Shādī Muqrī asked if his *ṣūfī* master, *pīr*, resident in Lahore, was dead.[102] Not everybody was pleased with this resurgent mysticism evident in the post-Iltutmish period. Certainly not Shīr Khān, cousin of Balban, Governor of Lahore, Dipalpur, Tabarhind, Sunam, and Bhatnair, in whose territories Bābā Farīd's hospice of Ajudhan was located. Niẓām al-Dīn reported that because Shīr Khān did not believe in Bābā Farīd's charisma, *dar ḥaqq-i Shaikh al-Islām Bābā Farīd . . . i'tiqādī nadāsht*, the saint foretold future disaster for the Malik in the following verse:

Unfortunately about my grace you do not know,
Sorrow will drown you, alas, when you come to know![103]

After Bābā Farīd's death Shīr Khān's territories, naturally, suffered Mongol invasions, but not so the firm believer Balban, resident in distant Delhi. Rather than attempting to curb this resurgent mystic popularity, Balban honoured the mystic resident in the territory of his competitor. Niẓām al-Dīn reported an instance where, together with his soldiers, Ulugh Khān travelled to Ajudhan and offered gifts in cash and land to the mystic.[104] The *ṣūfī pīr,* characteristically, accepted the gifts in cash but not land.

Ulugh Khān's response to the *ṣūfīs* was in marked contrast to that of Shīr Khān, and it is important to recall the competition and mistrust

[101] Ibid., p. 236, see also Simon Digby, 'The Sufi Saint as a Source of Authority in Medieval India', pp. 62–3.

[102] Amīr Ḥasan Sijzī, *Fawā'id al-Fu'ād*, pp. 261–2.

[103] Ibid., pp. 373–4: *afsūs ki az ḥāl-i minnat nīst khabar, wa āngāh khabar shawad ki afsūskhūri!*

[104] Ibid., p. 171.

between the two cousins. Bābā Farīd's grace favoured one of the two commanders; Shīr Khān was murdered and Ulugh Khān became Sultan. But more than seeking divine benediction, Ulugh Khān showed remarkable discretion in ensuring that the greatest *ṣūfī* establishments of his time were in areas remote from Delhi, in Lakhnauti and western Punjab—areas under the control of his competitors. Within the core territories, as Ulugh Khān's collaborator, Minhāj-i Sirāj Jūzjānī never fails to remind us, the making of the Ghiyāṣī dispensation marked the restoration of a social and moral order that the interregnum of civil war had rudely disturbed. This was a theme that Ẓiyā' al-Dīn Baranī would also pick up in his history, where Balban's reign revitalized Delhi's original axial status in north India. It was a *Qubba-i Islām,* where the *Sharī'a* and the Muslim community could be assured of protection.

Conclusion

It is difficult to summarize or precisely categorize the thirty-year period 633–64/1236–66 in the history of the Delhi Sultanate. Most visibly, it was a period of rapid change among the history of the political elites and, as the Persian chronicles recount, the endless battles and goings and comings of amirs may well cause the historian to wonder about the 'real' significance of these years. Assuredly, the success and failures of individual military commanders of the time carry little historical significance within themselves. But we move into subjects of great import to the history of the Sultanate when we try to evaluate what these histories have to tell us about changes in political relationships, as well as how different types of political networks affected the spatial organization of the Sultanate and empowered different political groups and ideological positions.

It would scarcely illumine the character of the time or the changes that these years saw if we merely viewed the Shamsī *bandagān*, the free-Amirs, and the piety-minded as a monolithic 'ruling class' or a 'Muslim ruling elite'. Although the Shamsī slaves, for example, belonged to the common category of the un-free, they were at another level a deeply divided lot: in terms of their individual capacities to marshal resources at different times, their ambitions, their methods of mobilization and, not least, their relationships with their mastoi and each other. Some of these differences were temporarily clouded as the Shamsī slaves occasionally combined to withstand the threat of political marginalization when new rulers tried to deploy their own personnel. Yet the inter-dispensational conflicts themselves served to underline the multiplicity of backgrounds and interests amongst the body of slaves and other contenders. This had an impact on the next generation as well: the years of political jostling determined the participants during the intra-dispensational conflicts. Although the political contenders originated from the Amirs of a previous generation, they had only risen in stature of late and their backgrounds and relationships with each other did not replicate trends visible in an earlier period.

Bisected as they were by cross-cutting alliances, the qualitative changes that occurred within the composition of the ruling elites also affected the future political organization of the Delhi Sultanate. The mobility of personnel and the emergence of new groups within the political elite expanded the political arena, juxtaposing the interests of some members of the 'ruling class' against others. The relatively stable idea of *khwāja tāsh,* slaves of one master—an idea that had currency amongst the Mu'izzī *bandagān* as well—was subverted into an empowering ideology for junior slaves striving towards *khāṣṣ* stature and independent political agency once their master had passed away. The balance between the two contradictory impulses, the drive to acquire greater political power even while claiming equal status and rank, underlined a defining element of the intra-dispensational conflicts and the emergence of the Ghiyāṣī dispensation. The idea of *khwāja tāsh* may have remained stable but it was reoriented, in the first instance, to provide the political space for new groups to occupy dominant positions and at a subsequent moment to provide a corporate character to a new Ghiyāṣī political coterie seizing authority under the patronage of a new master.

The combination of differences amongst the Shamsī slaves and the empowering ideology for independent initiative produced new alliances with very clear temporal and spatial configurations. The period of intra-dispensational conflicts was a crucial phase—this was when the political geography of the Sultanate was decisively altered. It is sometimes difficult to notice these developments because the Persian chronicles of the thirteenth century were wedded to the history of a unitary state formation. Introducing the history of autonomous principalities and powerful political groups into their narratives entails producing a less unitary history that carries multiple genealogies of state and disciplinary formations. What, then, would become of the paramount Delhi Sultanate? As it stands, the histories of Lakhnauti and Multan only escape into light through the fissures of narratives that are primarily concerned with Delhi, and with the fortunes and misfortunes of its Sultans. But what of the '*Rānā-Malik*' alliances and of the *ṣūfī* Shaykh in Ajudhan?

In his description of Ulugh Khān's 654/1257 campaign in the Sirmur region, Jūzjānī noted with some satisfaction that the Malik's armies campaigned 'in territories where no King had ever reached and where no army of Islam had ever gained a victory'.[105] This was an astonishing observation because Ulugh Khān's campaigns in the area *followed* the Shamsī slave Qutlugh Khān into the region. Qutlugh Khān was no obscure military commander; he was no less than the stepfather of Sultan Nāṣir al-Dīn and after Raihān the major threat to Ulugh Khān. Qutlugh Khān had marched through the Sirmur area with his forces and received aid and succour from his ally, the King of Sirmur. He and his forces had obviously been in the region before, consolidating his alliances with the local King. Were the armies of Qutlugh Khān not the 'armies of Islam'? Or were the armies of the Delhi Sultan the only ones which qualified for that epithet? How should modern historians read Jūzjānī here? Were the Sultanate and Islam present in the region of sub-Himalayan tracts of Sirmur through the agency of Qutlugh Khān creating a peaceable, mutually accommodative relationship with local non-Muslim chieftains? Or should we follow Jūzjānī and record Ulugh Khān's violent intrusions into the area as the significant moment of 'Muslim' presence in the region? Who represented the Sultanate in the regions when their Governors were wont to establish their autonomy, establish local alliances, and challenge the authority of Delhi?

These questions are germane because of the relatively inflexible reading that historians sometime bring to terms such as *iqṭā*', translated

[105] Jūzjāni, *Ṭabaqāt-i Nāṣiri,* vol. 1, p. 491.

most typically as 'revenue assignment' or 'province'. In their respective analysis of the subject, both, Irfan Habib and Peter Jackson were sensitive to the manner in which the relationship of the *muqṭi'* altered from time to time with the Sultan. Yet for both these historians the constitutive authority responsible for the making of the *iqṭā'* was the Delhi Sultan and his capacity to enforce norms of a service contract ingrained in the institution. This was true up to a point. But what this analysis elided was the capacity of military commanders with *iqṭā's* to unilaterally alter the conditions of their service. It also failed to incorporate the association that certain regions came to possess for specific military commanders: Raihān in Bahraich, Ulugh Khān in the Siwalik, Kabīr Khān Ayāz in Multan, and Malik 'Izz al-Dīn Tughan Khān in Lakhnauti. Treating these examples as aberrations, as mere lapses in power that a later and more energetic Sultan would remove, involves a selective reading of the evidence to confirm the authority of the Delhi Sultan as the ultimate arbiter of political fortunes. This is very similar to the history of Jūzjānī, who noticed the presence of Qutlugh Khān in the *mawās* of Sirmur but refused to theorize on the larger historical implications of *Rānā-Malik* condominiums on the history of the Delhi Sultanate. The active agency of the amirs of the Delhi Sultan—whether or not they were 'recalcitrant'—altered the territory of the Sultanate; changes that would force the Sultanate into new directions in its efforts to re-establish control over north India. Delhi's authority barely survived the thirty years after Iltutmish's reign, and it was severely curtailed for a long period. But the conflicts of these years also marked the consolidation of new structures—not least old and new *muqṭi's*—that would alter the character of the Sultanate in the longer duration. That is the subject of the following chapter. As we will see there, the Sultanate under Balban and his successors carried the impact of the post-Shamsī years, the legacy of a political organization that left chroniclers like Baranī acutely uncomfortable.

CHAPTER 6

The End of the Seventh/Thirteenth Century: Balban and the (Re-)Emergence of the Delhi Sultanate

Jūzjānī's history ended with the events of 658/1259–60 and Ẓiyā' al-Dīn Baranī picked up the threads of the narrative six years later, with the accession of Ulugh Khān, as Sultan Balban, 664/1266. Before commencing his history, Baranī felt the need to provide the context in which the new Sultan seized power. He made two points: the first related to the traumatic years of rule under the weak Shamsī Princes when their father's *bandagān* had seized power and decimated the aristocracy carefully cultivated by Iltutmish. The second was to use the preceding years as a contrast to Balban's own achievements: this monarch restored the authority of the King, and he reinstalled the 'natural' social order that was close to, even if it did not completely match, Iltutmish's achievements.[1] In arguing for a 'restored' social and political order of the Delhi Sultanate under Balban, Baranī's account was inherently conservative. It idealized Iltutmish's reign and sought to erase the impact of the post-Shamsī years. In fact, Balban was a product of the years of 'intra-dispensational conflict with his peers and it was the vast experience that he gained finessing the 'Ghiyāṣī dispensation' as Ulugh Khān that helped him fashion his governance as a Sultan.

'Restoration' carries with it the sense of some innate quality lost and then regained; in this case, Balban regained the authority and

[1] Baranī, *Ta'rīkh-i Fīrūz Shāhī*, edited by Khan, pp. 37, 39, edited by Rashid, pp. 44, 47.

majesty that was the due of the Delhi monarch. But, as historians argue, Balban went further; he regained power and added to it, starting a cumulative process of power aggrandizement that terminated only with the reign of Sultan Muḥammad Tughluq, when a reversal of fortunes becomes noticeable. In fact, some of the greatest scholars of the period have charted the history of the Sultanate through the careers and achievements of its monarchs: the period of 'initial conquest' carried out by Quṭb al-Dīn Ai-Beg and Iltutmish, followed by a period of 'security and consolidation' under Balban. This led to military, administrative, and fiscal expansion, a period described as the 'zenith of the empire' under Sultans 'Alā' al-Dīn Khalajī and Muḥammad Shāh Tughluq, which culminated in a period of 'stasis and [eventual] decline' through the reigns of Fīrūz Shāh Tughluq and his successors.[2] This history follows the rather conventional bell-shaped origin–apogee–decline graph where the health of the state is the only coordinate worthy of tabulation. In this graph the reign of Balban falls somewhere between 'origin' and 'apogee', recapturing the dynamic velocity of the original moment and energizing it to even higher peaks of achievement in the next generation.

It might seem to some that my arguments in this book are in general agreement with this historiography. I also seem to focus on the careers of particular rulers in the fashioning of Sultanate history: Mu'izz al-Dīn Ghūrī, Shams al-Dīn Iltutmish, and now Ghiyāṣ al-Dīn Balban (née Ulugh Khān) as not the only, but certainly the 'great', patrons of the age. And in my evaluation of the nature of the late thirteenth century Sultanate, although I have substituted 'restoration' with 're-emergence', both terms carry the idea of a linear progression of a similar set of attributes from one generation to another. It would appear that the bell-graph is manifest in my narrative as well.

Despite the overt similarities, and in an effort to better situate my discussion of developments in the Sultanate in the last quarter of the Delhi Sultanate, it might be useful to highlight how my arguments help in creating a different genealogy for the history of the Delhi

[2] See the table of contents of the three most influential histories on the Delhi Sultanate: R.P. Tripathi, *Some Aspects of Muslim Administration*; A.B.M. Habibullah, *The Foundation of Muslim Rule in India*; and Peter Jackson, *The Delhi Sultanate*.

Sultanate. To begin with, I freely acknowledge that I *have* emphasized the significance of the reigns of Mu'izz al-Dīn Ghūrī, Shams al-Dīn Iltutmish, and Ghiyāṣ al-Dīn Balban for the history of the Delhi Sultanate. But equally, I must emphasize the fact that I have underlined the *difference* in the nature of their governance. The reigns of these rulers were important for their energetic construction of power relations with military elites as well as their impact on the extent of territory and nature of control over regions. The alignments of the Delhi Sultans with varied political groups also led to the fashioning of ideas and reconfiguration of ideologies that provided the authority of Delhi with a sense of commonsensical reality through the thirteenth and fourteenth centuries.

The engagements of these rulers with these larger historical processes manifest during their reigns were extremely important in the history of the Delhi Sultanate. It would be a mistake, however, to assume from this that the Delhi Sultans were the only historical agents and their world a *tabula rasa* on which they could enact their will. It would also be a mistake to assume that the only other inhabitants of the spaces occupied by the Delhi Sultanate were non-Muslims, the great 'others' in medieval Persian and modern historiographies. The Delhi Sultanate was not a monolith that revolved around its Sultans; its political elites were most certainly *not* 'military automata' designed—as one author argued for 'Abbāsid slaves—'not . . . to think, but to ride horses'.[3] The independent agency, creativity, and initiative of the military slaves and other political elites, in fact, often propelled the Sultanate in directions that its Sultans most feared.

It is extremely important to understand the contingent factors that affected the formation of the Delhi Sultanate at different moments of its history. And it is worth pausing to review some of these moments now. Briefly put, in the reign of Mu'izz al-Dīn Ghūrī some of the significant factors that had an important impact on the nature of state formation included the political traditions of the Shansabanid family, the Ghurid-Ghaznavid frontier with north India, and the opportunities and challenges this frontier presented to personnel ready (or not) to

[3] Patricia Crone, *Slaves on Horses: The Evolution of the Islamic Polity* (Cambridge: Cambridge University Press, 1980), p. 79.

invest their careers in the north Indian marches. Equally significant were long-standing traditions of political service and military slavery reinvented and creatively deployed by Mu'izz al-Dīn, and the tensions that political empowerment engendered amongst them. All of these touched upon the manner in which senior Mu'izzī *bandagān* organized their appanages in north India where—Brahmanical ideological qualifications notwithstanding—shifting political alliances and seizure of power by parvenu military adventurers was hardly unusual. A combination of these factors created the north Indian Sultanates. It would be simpleminded to conclude that this was the vision or legacy of Mu'izz al-Dīn. The monarch was an important intervening agency in the history of the moment, but larger historical factors, over some of which he had no control, affected the nature and outcome of his interventions. Mu'izz al-Dīn and his forces did capture Delhi, for example, but it is doubtful if the Ghurid monarch had envisaged a dominant role for the city in the governance of his north Indian dominions.

The reign of Shams al-Dīn Iltutmish was extremely important for the dominant role that Delhi came to eventually possess in the history of the Sultanate. But the nature of Shamsī intervention and its achievements make sense only in the context of two separate elements that were endogenous and exogenous in origin: the first was the Mu'izzī context of the Sultanate and the serious political challenges confronting Delhi and the north Indian Sultanates. The second were the Mongol invasions of the 620s/1220s and the problems posed to consolidating territories recently annexed by Delhi even as they started receiving refugees from eastern Iran, Khurasan, central Asia, and Afghanistan. The Sultan's reliance upon his sons and military slaves led to a reconfiguration of political forces in north India wherein Delhi could claim a paramount position. Equally, a condominium of interests between the piety-minded *'ulamā'*, the *ahl-i qalam*, and the Delhi Sultan provided the dispersed community of Muslims in north India with the sense of a centre, *ḥaẓrat-i Dehlī*, the majestic, sacred capital that functioned as a sanctuary, a guide, a cohering force. The conjuncture of forces that allowed for Iltutmish's political success also impressed its character on it. The Sultan's political dispensation, at once both enabling and coercive, provided a huge amount of power and resources to military slaves and the *Sharī'a*-minded *'ulamā'*, while remaining far more passively disposed towards free military commanders and *ṣūfīs*. With or without the support of the Sultan, these groups commanded important military and political resources, and some amongst them possessed considerable social stature as well. While Iltutmish's political arrangements may have unravelled at his death, the intervening changes left a configuration of forces present in north India that were absent at the beginning of the century.

The thirty years after the death of Iltutmish were some of the most dynamic moments of change in the history of the Sultanate. To a large extent, the sheer absence of a dominant political figure in the conservative historical narratives of the period makes it possible for us to appreciate other political actors, and the ambitions and resources they could marshal to subvert the great political enterprise of the Sultanate towards their own ends. The military conflicts of the time placed new personnel in power and reorganised the political terrain of the Delhi Sultanate, rooting its members in regional alliances, and implicating them in associations that had goals and aspirations quite distinct from those of Delhi. Also linked with these developments was the appearance of new piety-minded groups led by charismatic individuals with considerable ability to attract and administer to large congregations. *Ḥaẓrat-i Dehlī* was not terribly important to these congregations and regional alliances, except as an aggressive intruder — some times only one amongst many. The developments of the period introduced coherent lineages of political organization that were alternatives to the authority of Delhi but which had their origins in the old Shamsī dispensation. The historical records of the following generations, focusing as they do only on the authority of Delhi, obliterated the presence of some of these alternative lineages of power; traces of others persisted well into the following century.

Disassembling the Persian *tawārikh* of the Delhi Sultans makes it possible for us to chart the histories of some of these developments over the first half of the thirteenth century, but it also makes us sensible to continuities over this period. Notwithstanding considerable changes in political alliances, patronage networks, the cadre of the military personnel, and the spatial organization of the Delhi Sultanate, the logic that guided the choice of military personnel did not alter dramatically through this period. The value of deracinated elites for the monopolization of political authority—whether they were military slaves, mahouts, or Afghans—was well comprehended by Sultans and notables alike. Despite the rhetorical claims made by Persian chronicles for the aristocratic lineages of some of the great 'nobles', the military elite through the early half of the thirteenth century were largely of humble background. It is important to remain sensitive to the ties of service and association that animated governance because it is the nature of these dyadic relationships that communicates the political culture of the period; it also provides the more realistic context in which we need to locate the institutional checks and balances that operated in this world. This was not a political culture that appreciated the value of impersonal bureaucratic institutions; free individuals and slaves operated within a welter of social relationships and the package of skills that they carried was evaluated against their other social pre-commitments before they were recruited to serve in the public domain. The social and cultural world of the thirteenth century altered very slowly, especially relative to the political life of the period, and were distant from vicissitudes in the fortunes of individual Delhi Sultans and their military commanders. In other words, despite my emphasis on change at many different levels, there were important structural continuities that persisted through the thirteenth into the fourteenth centuries. These are factors that one cannot plot on a 'bell', nor on any similarly shaped graph.

This chapter now follows the history of the Ghiyāṣī dispensation, introduced in the previous one, as Ulugh Khān made the transition from Amir to Sultan. In my study of Ghiyāṣ al-Dīn Balban's reign, 664–86/1266–87, I continue to focus on the three vectors of change that I identified in the last chapter: change and continuity in the composition of the political elite and what these tell us about notions of service and political culture in the last half of the century; the new orientation of elites and territorial spaces in the Sultanate, in part a consequence of the preceding period of intra-dispensational conflicts; and the new configuration of relationships between the Sultanate and piety-minded groups, the *'ulamā'*, and the *ṣūfīs*. This chapter also moves beyond the reign of Ghiyāṣ al-Dīn Balban to show the afterlife of many of the developments that I have detailed here and in the preceding pages. My narrative often continues into the early fourteenth century to capture the historical significance of trends visible in the late thirteenth.

Loyalty, Service, Political Culture: The Ghiyāṣī Dispensation and the Turn of the Century

Unfortunately, we are unable to detail the events that brought Ulugh Khān to the throne. Since no source covers the crucial years between 658/1260 and 664/1266, we have to rely upon Baranī's vague statements that competition between 'Shamsī, Nāṣirī and some Balbanī Maliks' continued during the early months of Balban's accession.[4] But if we take Jūzjānī's earlier information together with Baranī's we can chart political transitions more clearly and deploy sufficient material to understand the manner in which Balban consolidated his authority.

There is little doubt that Balban gave the privileged place within his dispensation to his *bandagān*. Baranī sought to convey their status and proximity to the monarch through his descriptions of the court, where slave officers, together with junior pages, surrounded the Sultan.[5] The deployment of slaves does not seem to have varied over time: Balban used them as Governors and military commanders, and as a part of the central contingent kept in Delhi, and employed the newly purchased slaves as domestics and pages in court. Baranī describes the Sultan's penchant for hunting expeditions with his army in the winter, these being used as occasions to lead them into military manoeuvres. Falconers and those in charge of the hunting birds, *khāṣadārān wa mihtarān-i shikaradār*, were included in these 'hunting expeditions', during which field training was imparted to junior slaves.[6] Included in the hunting expeditions were also 'a thousand' senior slaves, *yak hazār banda-i qadīm*. Other than an opportune

[4] Baranī, *Ta'rīkh-i Fīrūz Shāhī*, edited by Khan, p. 119, edited by Rashid, p. 140.

[5] Ibid., edited by Khan, p. 30, edited by Rashid, pp. 35–6.

[6] Ibid., edited by Khan, p. 54, edited by Rashid, p. 64. Baranī noted that in one such 'hunting' expedition against the recalcitrant Meos near Delhi, that the *banda-i khāṣṣ* 'Yak-Lākī' was killed. Ibid., edited by Khan, p. 57, edited by Rashid, p. 67. The name seems to be a reflection of the slave's value and is a precursor of the name given to the more famous Khalajī slave Malik Kafūr Hazārdinārī.

moment to train junior slaves, these expeditions consolidated bonds within the slave cadre.[7]

Certainly, the notion of seniority within the *bandagān* cadre, based upon intimacy with the master, was apparent to Baranī. Concerning Malik I<u>kh</u>tiyār al-Dīn Begtars, Baranī reported that 'of all the slaves close to Sultan Balban none was more senior or trusted', *az Malik Begtars . . . hīch banda nazdīk-i Sulṭān <u>kh</u>awāṣṣtar wa maḥramtar na būd.*[8] Many of Sultan Balban's senior slaves must have served him while he had been <u>Kh</u>ān. The *banda* I<u>kh</u>tiyār al-Dīn Ai-tegin Mū'īdarāz was appointed *amīr-i ā<u>kh</u>ūr* in the dispersal of honours in 647/1249.[9] Unfortunately, in the absence of a chronicler like Jūzjānī, we are unable to follow the careers of the <u>Gh</u>iyāṣī slaves over a period of time. Despite this lacuna in our information, we can tell from the charges under their command that Balban, very much in the tradition of the period, reposed considerable trust in them. His old slave I<u>kh</u>tiyār al-Dīn Ai-tegin Mū'īdarāz was given the title Amīn <u>Kh</u>ān and appointed to Awadh, which was subsequently given to the slave Haibat <u>Kh</u>ān.[10] Before his death Malik Baq Baq was the *muqṭi'* of Budaun, Malik Sewinch Sar-i jāndār the commander in Sunam and Samana, and from his inscription we know that I<u>kh</u>tiyār al-Dīn Begtars commanded Garhmuktesar.[11] Finally, before the provinces were appanaged to the Princes, Tu<u>gh</u>ril had charge of the province of Lakhnauti.[12]

[7] Ibid., edited by Khan, p. 55, edited by Rashid, p. 64.

[8] Ibid., edited by Khan, p. 61, edited by Rashid, p. 71.

[9] Jūzjānī, *Ṭabaqāt-i Nāṣirī*, vol. 2, p. 60.

[10] Baranī, *Ta'rī<u>kh</u>-i Fīrūz Shāhī*, edited by Khan, pp.40, 83, edited by Rashid, pp. 48, 98.

[11] Ibid., edited by Khan, pp. 40, 85, edited by Rashid, pp. 48, 99–100; and G. Yazdani, 'The Inscriptions of the Turk Sultans of Delhi—Mu'izzu-d-dīn Bahrām, 'Alā'u-d-dīn Mas'ūd, Nāṣiru-d-dīn Maḥmūd, Ghiyā<u>th</u>u-d-dīn Balban and Mu'izzu-d-dīn Kaiqubād', *Epigraphica Indo-Moslemica* (1913-14), pp. 28–9. In his edition of Baranī's text, Rashid noted, p. 100, fn. 1, that in a variant manuscript the Malik's name is spelt SIWNJ. Although both Khan and Rashid favoured SWNJ (Sonj) as the Malik's name, I have followed Jackson, 'The Mongols and India', p. 104, in reading the Malik's name as Sewinch, which is closer to the Turkish form.

[12] Baranī, *Ta'rī<u>kh</u>-i Fīrūz Shāhī*, edited by Khan, p. 82, edited by Rashid, p. 96.

It was apparent to observers that the Ghiyāṣī *bandagān* were a powerful element in the political dispensation of the Sultan. When Baranī substantiated his statement that Balban did not distinguish between high and low when enforcing justice, he uniformly chose the examples of elite slaves to show how even the powerful were punished. Thus the slave Baq Baq, despite his power and position, was executed for a crime against a lowly *farrāsh* (janitor), and Haibat Khān escaped a similar fate by paying blood money.[13] The execution and punishment meted out to senior Ghiyāṣī slaves should not make us doubt their value as subordinate, dependable servants of the Sultan. Instead, Baranī's evidence confirms that military slaves were repositories of power and authority during Balban's reign, and his examples also serve to remind us of the extreme alienation and dependence of slaves. Since *bandagān* were property, distanced from free society and solely dependent upon their master, they had little social and legal protection other than that provided by their corporate group. This protection did not extend to save the *bandagān* from the whims of their owner, and, as in the case of the Ghiyāṣī slaves, not even from sudden and violent death. As the case of Malik Amīn Khān Mū'īdarāz brings out, the *bandagān* were ideal tools for the making of political power. Balban had raised him until he was the Governor of Awadh and one of the most powerful commanders in the Sultanate. This was at the Sultan's pleasure, however; Balban's displeasure was sufficient to warrant the slave's immediate removal and execution.[14]

While we should not diminish the important role of the Ghiyāṣī slaves in Balban's organization of political authority, we must remember that the Delhi Sultan also favoured several other groups. It would be easy to correlate the decline in the presence of Shamsī notables in the Delhi court with the rise to power of the Ghiyāṣī dispensation. But the two events were not entirely connected. Very few of the Shamsī *bandagān* were still alive three decades after Iltutmish's death. Of Balban's allies in 655/1257, Malik Kishlī Khān and Tāj al-Dīn Arsalān (numbers 24 and 19 in Table 3) were dead.

[13] Ibid., edited by Khan, pp. 40–1, edited by Rashid, pp. 47–8.
[14] Ibid., edited by Khan, pp. 82–4, edited by Rashid, pp. 96–9.

Baranī noted that the Shamsī notables feared for their lives since, after his succession, Balban was poisoning them off.[15] Despite the fact that Baranī provided only the example of Shīr Khān, who was murdered *circa* 669/1270,[16] historians have taken the diminished presence of Shamsī notables in the Ghiyāsī dispensation as negative proof substantiating Baranī's more general statements.[17] Yet, if we turn to Chapter 5 and Table 3, we notice that of the twenty-one slaves alive in 633/1236, nineteen were definitely dead by 664/1266 (I am excluding Kushlū Khān, number 20 in Table 3, from this count; he had already emigrated into Mongol territory, never to return to the Sultanate).

Even with the scanty information that we possess, it is clear that all the surviving Shamsī slaves included in the twenty-second section of Jūzjānī's chronicle had served Balban earlier and remained his allies when he became Sultan. From an inscription in Kaman we know that Balban's old compatriot Badr al-Dīn Nuṣrat Khān (number 22 in Table 3) was still alive in 669/1271 and was the *muqṭi*ʻ of Bayana.[18] Baranī remembered Shīr Khān, Tamar Khān Shamsī, and ʻAdil Khān Shamsī as important notables in the Ghiyāṣī dispensation. Of these, Jūzjānī's Malik Saif al-Dīn Arkalī Ai-Beg Shamsī'i ʻAjamī (number 21 in Table 3) was unquestionably the same as Baranī's Malik Saif al-Dīn Arkalī Shamsī'i ʻAjamī, and the author's Tamar Khān was in all likelihood Malik Tāj al-Dīn Sanjar Tarkhān (number 17 in Table 3).[19] ʻImād al-Dīn Rāwat-i ʻArẓ, a powerful Amir

[15] Ibid., edited by Khan, pp. 47, 65, edited by Rashid, pp. 56, 77.

[16] Ibid., edited by Khan, p. 65, edited by Rashid, p. 77.

[17] K.A. Nizami, 'Sultan Balban and Kaiqubad: (vi) Balban and the Turkish Nobility', *A Comprehensive History of India. Vol. V: The Delhi Sultanat*, pp. 285–6; idem, *Religion and Politics in India*, pp. 143–5; Peter Jackson, 'Mamluks in North India', p. 352; and Aziz Aḥmad, *Political History and Institutions of the early Turkish Empire of Delhi*, p. 272.

[18] G. Yazdani, 'Inscription of Sultan Balban from Bayana, Bharatpur State', *Epigraphia Indica, Arabic and Persian Supplement* (1937–50), pp. 5–6 and Plate III(a).

[19] It is important to note the variations in the orthography of this Amir's name in tne different manuscripts. Habibi reads the name as Tarkhān: Jūzjānī, *Ṭabaqāt-i Naṣirī*, vol. 2, p. 28. His footnote, vol. 2, p. 28, fn. 6, mentions Tabar/TBR as an alternative reading which could be the root for Baranī's reading of the Amir's name as Tamar.

in Balban's court, was another Shamsī slave mentioned by Baranī, but he might have been a junior slave of Ilutmish for he did not draw Jūzjānī's attention.[20] Notably, while 'Adil Khān and Tamar Khān Shamsī are both described as *khwāja tāsh*, companions of one master, Baranī clarified that this companionship did not result in competition and strife; they were *yārān-i mihtar*, special friends of the Sultan.[21] These notables continued to occupy important posts in Balban's reign. After Shīr Khān's death, Tamar Khān Shamsī was given the responsibility of supporting Prince Muḥammad from his commands at Samana and Sunam.[22] 'Imād al-Mulk was the muster master (*'arẓ-i mamālik*) of the military retinue.[23]

If we study the 655/1257 confederates of Ulugh Khān, continuities between the remnants of the Shamsī dispensation into Balban's reign are immediately apparent: when his old allies died, the Sultan allowed their children to succeed to their father's positions. Thus, Malik 'Alā' al-Dīn Chajjū succeeded his father Kishlī Khān as *Amīr Ḥājib*, and this was despite the fact that there was no warmth in the relationship between uncle and nephew.[24] Similarly, Tāj al-Dīn Arsalān Khān's son, Tatar Khān, succeeded him in Lakhnauti and Balban did recognize his tributary status.[25] Baranī noted the presence of another son of a Shamsī slave, Malik Tāj al-Dīn ibn Qutlugh Khān Shamsī, who participated in the first Lakhnauti campaign.[26] Even as Khān, Balban had appointed children of some notables that he respected to their father's positions. Jūzjānī noted that after the deaths of Jamāl al-Dīn Bustāmī, Ḥamīd al-Dīn Mārīglah, and Kabīr al-Dīn, all of whom passed away in 659/1260, their children succeeded to their posts.[27]

[20] Baranī, *Ta'rīkh-i Fīrūz Shāhī*, edited by Khan, pp. 114–17, edited by Rashid, pp. 134–7.

[21] Ibid., edited by Khan, p. 37, edited by Rashid, p. 44.

[22] Ibid., edited by Khan, p. 65, edited by Rashid, p. 77.

[23] Ibid., edited by Khan, p. 114, edited by Rashid, p. 134.

[24] Jūzjānī, *Ṭabaqāt-i Nāṣirī*, vol. 1, p. 495; Baranī, *Ta'rīkh-i Fīrūz Shāhī*, edited by Khan, pp. 24, 35–6, 113–14, edited by Rashid, pp. 29, 42–3, 132–4.

[25] Jūzjānī, *Ṭabaqāt-i Nāṣirī*, vol. 2, p. 35. See also Baranī, *Ta'rīkh-i Fīrūz Shāhī*, edited by Khan, p. 66, edited by Rashid, p. 78.

[26] Baranī, *Ta'rīkh-i Fīrūz Shāhī*, edited by Khan, p. 83, edited by Rashid, p. 98.

[27] Jūzjāni, *Ṭabaqāt-i Nāṣiti*, vol. 1, p. 495.

The nature of Balban's dispensation of power was far more complicated than Iltutmish's because of the number of diverse people that the Sultan had recruited during his extremely long political career.[28] Some, like his administrators, the *ahl-i qalam*, we know little about from Baranī, but they must have followed Balban in his transition from *nā'ib-i Mulk,* 'deputy', to Sultan. As we have already noticed, Jūzjānī is perhaps the most famous example that we possess of an *'ālim* who allied with Balban while he was still Khān. He was brought to Delhi from Lakhnauti by Balban in 643/1246 and prospered in his service.[29] His fortune was allied closely enough with Balban, and his patron's years of exile from Delhi were years of wilderness for the author as well.[30] Although Jūzjānī was alive when Balban became Sultan, Baranī merely acknowledged his presence and recorded that as *ṣadr-i jahān* Jūzjānī was one of the important *'ulamā'* in the realm.[31] In similar fashion, other old accomplices were honoured, and these included individuals like Malik Fakhr al-Dīn Kōtwāl. Although we do not know about his early years of service, the Sultan trusted him sufficiently to leave him as his deputy in Delhi during his absence.[32] By the end of his reign Balban had honoured him by referring to him as 'brother, Malik of Amirs', *barādar Malik al-Umarā'*.[33] In the intervening period Fakhr al-Dīn had consolidated his position in Delhi with a wide circle of relatives and well wishers, until in Kaiqubād's reign (685–9/1286–90) he was universally respected.[34]

The existing evidence helps to put Baranī's observations concerning the fate of the Shamsīs in some context. Baranī explained Shīr

28 Peter Jackson's argument that Balban sought to substitute Shamsī notables with his own slaves, who constituted his new power base, is a rather mechanical description of these developments. Peter Jackson, 'Mamluks in Muslim India', p. 353.

29 For evidence of his patron's generosity see Jūzjānī, *Ṭabaqāt-i Nāṣirī*, vol. 1, pp. 470, 480–1, 484–5; vol. 2, p. 61.

30 Ibid., vol. 1, pp. 487–9.

31 Baranī, *Ta'rīkh-i Fīrūz Shāhī*, edited by Khan, p. 111, edited by Rashid, p. 131.

32 This took place when the Sultan campaigned in Lakhnauti against Tughril. Ibid., edited by Khan, p. 85, edited by Rashid, p. 100.

33 Ibid., edited by Khan, p. 107, edited by Rashid, p.126.

34 Ibid., edited by Khan, pp. 107, 117–18, 131, 135–8, edited by Rashid, pp. 126, 137–8, 152, 156–60.

Khān's hesitation to come to Delhi out of fear that he might be poisoned. According to Baranī, the Amir was aware that Balban and his cohorts were murdering senior Shamsī slaves under one pretext or the other [*bandagān-i buzūrg-i Shamsī rā bahar bahāna daf' mīkardand*].[35] As we have already seen, there is sufficient reason to doubt that this was so. Baranī's statement can be placed in a clearer context when read alongside an earlier statement where the author says Balban had those Shamsī Khāns and Maliks murdered who wanted to associate in Kingship [*shurakā-i mūlk*], and obstruct the Sultan's authority, *muzāḥim takht-i khūd*.[36] This would have certainly applied to Shīr Khān, who always attempted to maintain his independence, some times in conflict with Balban. Baranī sensed the basis upon which notables could protect themselves when he noted that Shamsī notables survived [*ṣadr-i ḥayāt mānda būdand*] into the Ghiyāṣī dispensation not because of any longstanding claim on Sultan Balban, but only if they had gained his support and protection [*ḥimāyat-i Balbanī*].[37] In accepting Balban's service, the Shamsī *bandagān* had to convince their new master that they had successfully repudiated all their old social and political attachments for an exclusive, new dependence. This implied a far more subjective assessment of social alienation, but at least some of the Shamsī personnel passed Balban's careful scrutiny. Not so Shīr Khān, about whom doubts persisted, and he never quite made the transition into the new Ghiyāṣī dispensation to the monarch's satisfaction.

A structural-functionalist reading of slave–master relationships is extremely useful in capturing the rationale for the creation of political elites who were 'socially dead and natally alienated'. That framework's emphasis on the transactional nature of social relationships helps us comprehend the importance of deracination in the constitution of the Sultanate military elites. It also makes us sensitive to secondary elements through which non-slaves—social menials, for example[38]—could, like slaves, be favoured with royal patronage. The political

[35] Ibid., edited by S.A. Khan, p. 65, edited by Rashid, p. 77.

[36] Ibid., edited by Khan, p. 48, edited by Rashid, p. 56.

[37] Ibid., edited by Khan, p. 50, edited by Rashid, p. 59.

[38] The best example of social menials within a patriarchical domain would, of course, be women. Barring the case of Raẓiyya (see Chapter 5), the discussion of military elites is, unfortunately, entirely male-centred in this book.

empowerment of people of humble origin placed them in contexts that were quite alien to their social background, underlining their dependence on their master. Alienation and dependence were important factors that qualified the individual for political service. Earlier in the history of the Sultanate we have already had occasion to remark upon Sultan Rukn al-Dīn's deployment of mahouts [*pīlbānān*] who received a political prominence anomalous to their social backgrounds. Their humble social status distanced them from high Sultanate society, but, as in the case of slaves, these qualities also made their recruitment strategically useful for the Delhi Sultan.

In his *Ta'rīkh-i Fīrūz Shāhī* Baranī blamed the introduction of unstable conditions in the Sultanate to the patronage of 'cheap slaves' and social menials by the Shamsī Princes. This bleak characterization of the age was also necessary for Baranī to contextualize his own moralization on ideal governance. The peg on which the author could hang his pedagogical ruminations was Sultan Ghiyāṣ al-Dīn Balban, the one-time slave of Iltutmish. According to Baranī, one of Balban's greatest achievements was sweeping away the 'base born' [*bad aṣlī wa nā kas*] and restoring the authority of the monarchy. Baranī described how the Sultan had the genealogies of court officers scrutinized and declared that he would not associate or patronize anybody of suspect lineage and character, irrespective of their accomplishments [*hunarmandī*].[39] As Baranī put it, Balban did not want to sully the dignity of sovereignty or his own pure Afrasiyābī lineage through association with people of indiscriminate background. Ironically, Baranī presented these ideas as a part of an apocryphal conversation that the Sultan had with two of his old compatriots, individuals who were, like Balban himself, *khwāja tāsh,* or slaves of the same master.[40] Like Jūzjānī, Baranī did not consider slaves like Balban or his close associates to be 'base born' or frivolous and cheap slaves [*harzgān wa diram-i kharīdgār*].[41] They had displayed their innate high pedigree by their stated preference for a 'conventionally' stratified social order that distinguished between the 'high and the

[39] Ibid., edited by Khan, pp. 33–9, edited by Rashid, pp. 39–47.
[40] Ibid., edited by Khan, pp. 37, 39, edited by Rashid, pp. 44, 47.
[41] Ibid., edited by Khan, p. 27, edited by Rashid, p. 33.

low'. The passage of time, according to Baranī, was not kind to aristocrats, and, ever so gradually, first during 'Alā' al-Dīn's reign (695–715/1296–1316) and then Muḥammad Shāh Tughluq's (724–52/1324–51), the number of social menials increased until they held some of the highest positions in administration.[42]

In Irfan Habib's analysis, this process was described as the 'plebeianization of the nobility', when the 'sluggish nobility resting on its hereditary claims' could not keep pace with the dynamic expansion of the political sphere and complex economic life of the Sultanate under the great Khalajī and Tughluq monarchs. In his argument: 'The ambitions, fed on the immense opportunities, now brought in those who could gain the Sultan's confidence in their loyalty by their very lack of any hereditary following, and so the complete dependence upon his favours. The *plebeianization of the nobility* was an inevitable product of the political development of the Sultanate . . .'.[43] While Habib was extremely astute in noticing how the deployment of military personnel without any hereditary following worked to the advantage of Sultan Muḥammad Tughluq, he also argued that this was a result of cumulative political and economic forces set in motion by the establishment of the Delhi Sultanate. According to Habib, the medieval chronicler Ẓiyā' al-Dīn Baranī placed the conjuncture of these historical processes at the turn of the thirteenth century.[44] In resurrecting strands of evidence from the *Ta'rīkh-i Fīrūz Shāhī* to formulate a linear progression of material change and economic expansion in Sultanate history, Habib ignored the circularity in Baranī's argument. Just as Balban provided some degree of social harmony after the anarchic rule of Iltutmish's successors, Baranī argued that Fīrūz Shāh Tughluq (the best of all

[42] For a review of these materials in Baranī, see Mohammad Habib, 'Governing Class', *The Political Theory of the Delhi Sultanate*, pp. 144–51; and Irfan Habib, 'Baranī's Theory of the History of the Delhi Sultanate', pp. 104–10.

[43] Irfan Habib, 'Baranī's Theory of the History of the Delhi Sultanate., p. 109, my italics.

[44] Ibid., see also, Idem, 'The Price Regulations of 'Alā'uddīn Khalji- A Defence of Ẓiyā' Barani'.

Sultans) was the restorer of social order after the tyrannical rule of Muḥammad Shāh Tug͟hluq.[45] The negative depiction of Muḥammad Shāh Tug͟hluq's reign was vital to the didactic intent of his history, and the Sultan's patronage of the base born was integral to the creation of the Sultan's tyrannical and unbalanced character.

If we are sensitive to the discursive position of the Persian chronicles towards individuals without any 'hereditary following', then Muḥammad Shāh Tug͟hluq's appointment of people like 'Azīz K͟hammār the wine distiller, Fīrūz Hajjām the barber, Mankā Tabbāk͟h the cook, Ladhā and Pīrā the gardeners, to some of the highest positions in the state can be placed in a larger context.[46] And if we ignore Baranī's discourse on Balban's fixation with aristocrats for a moment, the Delhi Sultan's patronage of lowly Afghans can be seen as part of a systematic favour shown by the Delhi Sultans towards individuals who were, as the author put it, the 'lowest and basest of the low and base born' [*ṣifatarīn wa raẕālatarīn-i siflagān wa raẕālagān*].[47]

Jūzjānī first mentioned the deployment of Afghans in his account of Ulug͟h K͟hān's 658/1260 campaigns in the Mewat region, to the south of Delhi: he commented on their outlandish, fearsome appearance.[48] Balban's reliance upon his Afghan retinue increased after his accession. He deployed them in the strategic areas of the Ganges–Jamuna *do-āb* soon after his accession and then further afield in the areas of Haryana and western Punjab. He had forts constructed in these newly pacified areas, old military cantonments refortified, and gave charge of these important regions to the Afghans.[49] Balban gave them rent-free lands and settled them in territories encircling the capital, in areas that had seen some of the most violent engagements during the period of the intra-dispensational conflicts in the preceding decade. These were the most strategic areas in the Sultanate. In

[45] Baranī, *Ta'rīk͟h-i Fīrūz Shāhī,* edited by Khan, p. 575.

[46] Ibid., p. 505.

[47] This was Baranī's description of the kinds of people patronized by the Tug͟hluq monarch. Ibid. Khan's edition has a misprint: *razālatarīn* and *razālagān* should read *raẕālatarīn* and *raẕālagān.*

[48] See Chapter 5.

[49] For the garrisons in the *do-āb* see Baranī, *Ta'rīk͟h-i Fīrūz Shāhī,* edited by Khan, pp. 57–8, edited by Rashid, pp. 66–8 and below.

appointing Afghans to these sites Balban displayed the extent of his regard and trust towards this group, a sentiment that the residents of Delhi greeted with a far greater degree of ambivalence. Some time around 680/1280 Amīr Khusrau penned a letter to Ikhtiyār al-Dīn Begtars to convey the salient features of Afghans residing in the near vicinity of the capital:

> In this (?) fortress live the Afghans—nay man-slaying demons, for even the demons groan in fright at their shouts. Their heads are like big sacks of straw, their beards like the combs of the weaver, long-legged as the stork but more ferocious than the eagle, their heads lowered like that of the owl of the wilderness. Their voices hoarse and shrill like that of a jack-daw, their mouths open like a shark. Their tongue is blunt like a home-made arrow, and flings stones like the sling of a battering ram. Well has a wise man said that when speech was sent to men from the sky, the Afghans got the last and least share of it.[50]

Although Sultan Balban's Afghan recruits were hardly new to the Sultanate, their novel, indeed, fearsome qualities, do not seem to have waned since Jūzjānī first noted them. The Persian literati of the time looked with horror at the new military heroes of the Sultanate; these were not a body of people that could ever be ascribed the status of nobles. Yet they were systematically patronized and deployed by Balban, the one Sultan whose aversion to the low born Baranī had so satisfactorily noticed.

But they were not the only ones. Baranī provides fleeting mention of three other groups from the north-west frontier also recruited by Balban. The first of these, the impressive Sīstānī, *pahlawānān*, body-guards, we come across only in the description of the Sultan's retinue.[51] The others were the Khalaj and the Mongols, both relatively nondescript in Balban's service but who became dominant elements in the reign of Kaiqubād, Balban's successor. The Khalajīs were not unfamiliar to members of the Delhi court, but if Jūzjānī's supercilious

[50] Amīr Khusrau, *Tuḥfat al-Sighār,* IOL Persian Ms 412, fol. 50 seq., cited by Wahid Mirza, *The Life and Works of Amir Khusrau*, pp. 51–2.

[51] Baranī, *Ta'rīkh-i Fīrūz Shāhī,* edited by Khan, p. 30, edited by Rashid, p. 35.

narrative of the abilities of Ulugh Khān's emissary, Jamāl al-Dīn 'Alī Khalajī, is any guide, the urbane still regarded their most prominent members as rustics.[52] In the same way, Baranī captured the unassimilated foreignness of the Mongols by systematically using the epithet *nau-musalmān,* new-Muslims, for the group.[53] The direction of Balban's patronage was quite at odds with Baranī's efforts to herald his rule as one where birth and good breeding triumphed.

Beyond Baranī's didactic moralizing, however, it was precisely the huge social chasm between social menials and other elites in Sultanate society that made them extremely valuable military personnel for the Delhi Sultan. They could be patronized, given high political positions, but they would always remain creatures of the monarch. Like the mahouts of Sultan Rukn al-Dīn Muḥammad in an earlier generation, or the wine-distillers, gardeners, barbers, and cooks of Muḥammad Shāh Tughluq some decades later, Afghans were menial enough for the urban-based Persian literati to consider them 'the meanest of the base born'. But as a part of the culture of service and governance that ran through the thirteenth into the fourteenth centuries, it was exactly their menial quality that made them valuable to their patrons. Much to the chagrin of medieval political commentators of the age, the jurists, the piety-minded, and the aristocratic *ahl-i qalam*, political and social statuses were seldom congruent in the Sultanate. But unlike the Turkish slaves, who received such eulogistic reports in the writing of Fakhr-i Mudabbir and Jūzjānī, no effort was made to discursively reengineer the status of mahouts, Afghans, or Mongols into nobles—and the bad press lingered.

Although a structural-functionalist methodology might allow us to appreciate the logic behind these interpersonal relationships, it is also inherently synchronic and ignores the ways in which political empowerment modified the lives of deracinated groups through the thirteenth century. We need to comprehend the contexts in which slaves redeployed an inhibiting collegial anonymity—carried by the

[52] Jūzjānī, *Ṭabaqāt-i Nāṣiri*, vol. 2, pp. 86–8. See also Chapter 2 and Jūzjānī's narration of Bakhtiyār Khalajī.

[53] Baranī, *Ta'rīkh-i Fīrūz Shāhī,* edited by Khan, 133, edited by Rashid, p. 154.

sense of *khwāja tāsh,* slaves of one master—into an emancipatory slogan for self-promotion and political agency: 'what are you that I am not', they argued.

By the end of the thirteenth century, while slaves and other deracinated groups were still patronized, a large number of second-generation elites were also populating the political world of the Delhi Sultanate. The *bandagān* of the Delhi Sultans married, had children, and established households; those with high military command recruited slaves and other military personnel, hired administrators, and patronized litterateurs. As Fakhr-i Mudabbir had noted at the beginning of the century, they were the possessors of considerable wealth and power and had grandees of the highest pedigree in their service. Through the thirteenth century, many of them had translated their political accomplishments into social capital. Let us not forget the Mu'izzī *bandagān-i khāṣṣ*, Bahā' al-Dīn Tughril, appointed to Bayana in 592/1196, who took the title of *Pādshāh* about a decade after his assignment. Years after Tughril's death, after the decline in the political fortunes of the family, Iltutmish married his slave Tāj al-Dīn Arsalān to Tughril's daughter. A decade or so later Jūzjānī reported that Sultan Nāṣir al-Dīn appointed Tāj al-Dīn Arsalān to Bayana because of this matrimonial relationship. Despite the loss of political control over Bayana, Bahā' al-Dīn's family were still important and prestigious in the region and a matrimonial relationship with them worked to the advantage of the newly appointed Governor.[54]

Persian chroniclers of the time speak at length of the blood-bath that accompanied the accession of new rulers and the dispersal of honours to their followers. Yet the removal of old servants from active participation in court politics was never complete, and silences in the chronicles notwithstanding, doubts remain about the extent to which these purges displaced members of the old dispensation. Did the change of a political dispensation erase the lifetime accomplishments of a military commander? Even if they lost their lives during the maelstrom of a political transition, what became of their children and their households?

[54] See Chapter 2 for a full discussion on Bahā' al-Dīn Tughril and his family in Bayana.

In his *Ta'rīkh-i Fīrūz Shāhī*, Baranī used the term *maulāzādgān* (singular: *maulāzāda*), a neologism used by the author to describe the 'sons of [freed] slaves' of Ghiyāṣ al-Dīn Balban. As it happens, Balban must have had quite a few *maulāzādgān* in his service. He had dominated Sultanate politics for an unusually long forty years and many of his slaves died in his service. As we have already noticed, the Sultan recruited the sons of some of these slaves. But what is important to keep in mind is that they were a body of people quite distinct from the *bandagān* retinue of the Sultan. The most famous *maulāzāda* was Ikhtiyār al-Dīn 'Alī Sar-i jāndār (also known as Ḥātim Khān), the commander of Amroha and later Awadh. He had considerable influence and wealth and was a munificent patron, with enough literary discrimination to patronize Amīr Khusrau when the poet was just starting his career.[55] Similarly, despite the indiscretions of the slave Malik Baq Baq, his son Malik Qerabeg was favoured in 676/1277 with the *iqṭā'* of Sonepat.[56] These examples should not lead us to assume that any emotional attachment bound Balban to the memory of his slaves; the Delhi Sultan did not recognize status which was claimed as a birthright. As we have already noticed, he was remarkably circumspect in the selection of his subordinates, and this applied equally to the *maulāzādgān,* not all of whom won his patronage.

Balban's discretion in choosing amongst the *maulāzādgān* was apparent in the case of Kamāl Mahiyār, recommended to the office of financial administrator, *khwāja,* of Amroha. The Sultan rejected Kamāl Mahiyār's petition for the post, and Baranī suggested this was because he was the son of a Hindū *ghulām,* the context suggesting that he was not the descendant of a military slave. It is very difficult to ascertain the reasons for Balban's discrimination amongst his *maulāzādgān.* Whether it was because some of them were of 'poor lineage and background' [*kam aṣlī kam biẓā'atī*] seems, on the face

[55] Baranī, *Ta'rīkh-i Fīrūz Shāhī,* edited by Khan, pp. 24, 36, 118–19, edited by Rashid, pp. 29, 43, 138–40; and Wahid Mirza, *The Life and Works of Amir Khusrau*, pp. 66–73.

[56] Ibid., edited by Khan, p. 40, edited by Rashid, p. 48. See G. Yazdani, 'The Inscriptions of the Turk Sultans of Delhi', pp. 27–8, number XI, Plate xb (in mosque attached to the tomb of Imam Naṣīr, Sonepat).

of it, extremely doubtful.[57] There are good reasons to wonder as well whether Kamāl Mahiyār was of an altogether 'humble' background; the appointment to the office of *k̲h̲wāja* meant that the aspirant had to have knowledge of Persian, mathematics, and accountancy, not easy skills for the ordinary domestic slave to acquire.[58] Baranī's description of the event—from the rejection of Kamāl Mahiyār, the ban on recruitment of all low born to administrative positions, the recollection of Sultan Iltutmish's moralization on the issue, to the investigation and discovery of the Shamsī *wazīr* Niẓām al-Mulk Junaidī's humble weaver origins and his dismissal—are completely didactic.[59] And as we have already seen, Balban showed no hesitation whatsoever in deploying 'plebeians' throughout his reign; they were, in fact, some

[57] For this phrase see ibid., edited by Khan, p. 37, edited by Rashid, p. 44.

[58] See the discussion on the *k̲h̲wāja* in Chapter 3 and on the *ahl-i qalam* in Chapter 4.

[59] Baranī, *Ta'rīk̲h̲-i Fīrūz Shāhī,* edited by Khan, pp. 36–9, edited by Rashid, pp. 43–6. Baranī's narration of the Kamāl Mahiyār incident needs to be contextualized with the author's own negative sentiments regarding the 'base born'. The need to distance individuals of such background from political power was the theme of the twenty-first *naṣīḥat* (advice) of his normative text, *Fatāwā-yi Jahāndārī*, and Baranī transposed these didactic ideas into his history as well. Ibid., edited by Khan, pp. 29–30, 34, edited by Rashid, pp. 34–5, 40. See also Baranī, *Fatāwā-yi Jahāndārī*, edited by A. Salim Khan (Lahore: Idarah-i Tahqiqat-i Pakistan, 1972), pp. 295–304, where the ideas contained in the *Ta'rīk̲h̲* are repeated in similar episodes with new characters. Contemporary scholars have assimilated Baranī's moralizations into a 'Balban's theory of Kingship'. See for example, K.A. Nizami, 'Sultan Balban and Kaiqubad: (III) Theory of Kingship', *A Comprehensive History of India, vol. V: The Delhi Sultanat*, pp. 280–4; R.P. Tripathi, *Some Aspects of Muslim Administration*, pp. 34–7, Muḥammad Aziz Aḥmad, *Political History and Institutions of the Early Turkish Empire of Delhi*, pp. 260–3, and most recently, André Wink, *al-Hind, vol. 2: The Slave Kings*, p. 22. Peter Jackson, *The Delhi Sultanate*, p. 79 and fn. 106 doubted Baranī's account of the Kamāl Mahiyār incident as well, but for its confirmation in Sayyid Ashraf Jahāngir Simnānī, *Maktūbāt-i Ashrafī*, BL ms. OR. 267, fol. 66b. I am not questioning the veracity of the Kamāl Mahiyār incident, but the spin put upon it by Baranī. Moreover, the anecdote could have rhetorical salience for authors in different contexts across generations, as in the case of Ārām Shāh and Iltutmish or Sultan Raẓiyya and Yāqūt.

of his important subordinates. On the other hand, the rejection of Kamāl Mahiyār does serve as a salutary reminder that *all* aspirants to high political office—slaves, 'plebeians', *maulāzādgān,* or the highest lords of the land—had to gain the Sultan's support and protection [*ḥimāyat-i Balbanī*] before they could be included in his dispensation.

What is evident from these incidents is that some of the Ghiyāṣī *bandagān* successfully managed to transfer their crucial political connections to their children, enabling their recruitment into the Sultan's retinue. Others provided their descendants with the training, skills, and ambition to seek high office. Balban's slaves had established households and families, and transferred some of the opportunities of high political command into social and material capital which proved of advantage to the next generation.[60] The sons of (freed) slaves were not regarded as a part of the *bandagān* cadre; they were no longer socially dead or natally alienated and, by Balban's reign, they wanted to seize the high ground in the political affairs of the Sultanate. The *maulāzādgān* merited enough attention to be recruited by Balban's successor, Mu'izz al-Dīn Kaiqubād (685-89/1286-90), who used them to counter the baleful influence of Balban's slaves. The Sultan's patronage provided the *maulāzādgān* the space to consolidate their position, and Baranī noted that they emerged as great Maliks with large garrisons in Kaiqubād's reign.[61] Once the 'sons of slaves' had networked and established matrimonial relations with the Mongols (another new entry in Sultanate politics who had consolidated their position), they emerged as a threat to the Sultan.[62]

[60] This phenomenon was not restricted to Balban's slaves. For touching introspective ruminations by a descendant of a Shamsī slave, see Amīr Khusrau's (himself a *'maulāzāda'*) recollection of his childhood, his father, Amir Saif al-Dīn Maḥmūd, and maternal grandfather, Rāwat-i 'Arẓ 'Imād al-Mulk, both of whom were military slaves. See Wahid Mirza, *Life and Works of Amir Khusrau*, pp. 15–23, 29–35.

[61] Baranī, *Ta'rīkh-i Fīrūz Shāhī,* edited by Khan, p. 134, edited by Rashid, p. 155. The text in Rashid's edition varies, but is clearer: *b'aẓī maulāzādgān-i Sulṭān Balban ki az mulūk-i kibār shuda būdand khail khāna-i bisyār dāshtand.*

[62] Ibid.

It is important to keep in mind that Baranī used the term *maulāzādgān* in a relatively narrow context to refer only to the sons of those slaves who had served Balban. Yet his description of the *maulāzādgān* does force us to reconsider the history of the *bandagān* more generally as a social unit whose lives stretched beyond the immediate context of their master. Did they have a life of their own without a patron? Baranī himself was only concerned with the *maulāzādgān* because they remained involved and important participants in the post-Balbanid politics of the Sultanate. But what became of the *bandagān* and their families that were defeated or marginalized by new dispensations of power? Once these people were outside the realm of the court and political authority they were of little interest to Sultanate chroniclers, and we have to reconcile ourselves to fragmentary pieces of information.

If we follow the logic in Baranī's use of the term 'sons of [freed] slaves', the descendants of the aforementioned Mu'izzī slave Bahā' al-Dīn Tughril were also *maulāzāda.* But they were different in that after their father's service with Mu'izz al-Dīn they were never a part and, as far as we can tell, never tried to become members of, any subsequent Sultan's retinue. Being marginalized from court politics and incidental in the historical narratives of the time did not mean, however, that they were redundant in local politics. We can gauge their local importance from Sultan Iltutmish's efforts to link one of his slaves with them, thereby bringing together the old and new political dispensations. Iltutmish and Nāṣir al-Dīn would not, in themselves, have acknowledged and perpetuated the importance of an old slave household, unless of course the family's embeddedness in the local social milieu made the strategic choice of alliance and incorporation preferable to their marginalization or decimation.

The example of Bahā' al-Dīn directs us to social processes of political formations wherein slaves and their households emerge over time as the entrenched elite of an area. Jūzjānī provided us with information regarding Bayana and Bahā' al-Dīn from the first half of the century, and Ẓiyā' al-Dīn Baranī furnished information about the careers of Shamsī slaves and their descendants from Balban's reign. The people in question were about 2000 cavalrymen of Iltutmish's central contingent [*qalb*]. Baranī does not provide precise details about their social backgrounds, but the information from Jūzjānī consistently mentions that the central contingent of the early Sultanate army included military slaves.[63] It is also likely that at least some of the cavalrymen (their leaders certainly) were slaves because they were given military assignments [*iqṭā'*s] by Iltutmish in the strategic vicinity of the capital in, what was then, the still largely unsettled region of the Ganga–Jamuna *do-āb*. By Balban's reign these cavalrymen had aged, most were unfit to fulfill their service obligations to the state, some had died, and their sons inherited their assignments as if they were outright grants. Corruption and collusion were rife between these assignees and the officers in charge of the muster. In Baranī's narrative, Balban intervened and revoked these assignments but their emotional appeal to their past service to the Sultanate made him rescind his orders. A compromise was eventually reached between Balban and the Shamsī assignees.[64]

Baranī's passionate recounting of the incident—the plight of the Shamsī cavalrymen and its resolution—was interwoven with his own predicament. It carried a veiled appeal to Fīrūz Shāh Tughluq to abide by the great traditions of Sultan Balban and honour the service of old servants of the Sultanate such as himself.[65] But in the terms of our discussion, the case of the Shamsī cavalrymen in the *do-āb* is interesting for the manner in which members of one dispensation managed to establish their households and alter revenue assignments with specific military obligations into outright grants. They escaped

[63] For references to the *qalb*, refer to the discussion in Chapters 2, 3, and 5.

[64] For details see Baranī, *Ta'rīkh-i Fīrūz Shāhī,* edited by Khan, pp. 60, 61–4, edited by Rashid, pp. 70, 72–6.

[65] According to Baranī, when Balban revoked the grants, the old and infirm soldiers appealed to Fakhr al-Dīn Kōtwāl, who interceded on their behalf. The plea was that the Sultanate should not cast away old servants once their utility was deemed to be over. The plea succeeded in its intent. The story was very close to Baranī's own experience—he was a close confidant of Sultan Muḥammad Shāh and had lost everything when Fīrūz Shāh succeeded. The account of the Shamsī cavalrymen also carried the author's plea for patronage from Fīrūz Shāh, the Sultan to whom the *Ta'rīkh-i Fīrūz Shāhī* was dedicated. In Baranī's story, Balban was moved to tears, and, although he did demand that the young and able should perform military service, they were allowed to keep their grants. This was largely what Baranī would have liked Fīrūz Shāh Tughluq to do as well.

Sultanate scrutiny for over two decades and it was only after Balban's military intervention into the region (which saw the deployment of the Afghans) that any effort was made to discipline this group. As it happened, the effort at coercion altered into a settlement by which Balban allowed all the Shamsī servants to retain their old assignments. In Baranī's narrative this was because Balban relented on humanitarian grounds. But from a different perspective we can also appreciate the ability of the Shamsī cavalrymen to negotiate the continuation of all their inherited advantages from an aggressively inclined monarch. Certainly, contrary to traditional practices associated with *iqṭā'*s, which were always supposed to be one-generational and transferable, Balban 'enforced' a settlement whereby revenue assignments in the *do-āb* were passed from father to son.[66]

Towards the end of the thirteenth century, not very far from his capital, descendants of deracinated elites challenged the writ of the powerful Delhi Sultan, and the resurgent might of the Delhi Sultan was unable to 'restore' an old order. In the intervening years the Sultanate had changed. Baranī's and Jūzjānī's accounts of the *maulāzādgān* draw our attention to a new body of personnel in the politics of the Delhi Sultanate. These were the second generation descendants of slaves and social menials, the 'debris of [past] dispensations', who vied with old and new parvenus for the spoils of appointment. The ambitions of the *maulāzādgān* actually went much further than merely seeking office; some chose to remain outside the realm of the Delhi state and established their local bases. 'Debris' captures the distance of this group from the inner circles of authority, and the fact that they were the scattered residue of past political formations. But considering them *en bloc* is also analytically useful because it captures their shared historical background, and the impact that the recruitment of military personnel had on the Delhi Sultanate in the long duration.

In trying to write a social history of political elites in the Sultanate, the focus on the deracinated character of its servants only enlarges upon the contexts of their recruitment, training, and deployment, and

[66] Ibid., edited by Khan, p. 64, edited by Rashid, p. 76; and on the traditional practices associated with the *iqṭā'*, see Irfan Habib, 'Iqṭā'', pp. 68–9. See also Chapters 1, 3, and 5 of the present book; and Sunil Kumar, 'When Slaves were Nobles', pp. 28–9.

the authoritarian character of governance that they enabled. The narratives that emerge from a consideration of these factors are not very distant from the cyclical arguments of the fourteenth-century Arab intellectual Ibn Khaldūn, who argued for an ebb and flow in state formations and group solidarities (*aṣabīyyat*), wherein the rise and decline of authoritarian regimes depended on the transference of support from old to new groups.[67] It is this kind of restricted analysis that generates the bell-shaped graphs to which I alluded in the beginning of this chapter. The evidence on the *maulāzādgān* suggests that the history of the Delhi Sultanate was not quite that cyclical. The survival of this group depended upon their abilities to transfer the advantages gained through service to their descendants, to restore a sense of natality and social life outside the coming and going of political patrons. It points to processes whose origins lie in the earliest moment of the formation of the Delhi Sultanate, but whose history followed a genealogy that was not determined by the fortunes of the state and its rulers. It is the history of these multiple genealogies that Persian court chronicles were extremely reluctant to address—even as their histories started obtruding with increasing regularity in their narratives.

The next section tries to plot some of these emergent political groups on the map of the Delhi Sultanate.

Politics, Society, and Territorial Expansion

On the 7th of Ramaẓān, 721/ 30th September 1321, Amīr Ḥasan Sijzī was present in the hospice of the *ṣūfī pīr* Niẓām al-Dīn Awliyā' where he heard the story of how the saint Quṭb al-Dīn Bakhtiyār Kākī chose his burial site. The event must have occurred not long before 632/ 1235, the year of Quṭb al-Dīn's death. It was the month of Ramaẓān and Quṭb al-Dīn was returning from the festival ground with some disciples when he stopped at the place where his grave is now. At that time it was a deserted area outside the city with no habitation or tomb. His companions urged him to return home, but Quṭb al-Dīn lingered

[67] See Ibn Khaldūn, *The Muqaddimah*, translated by Franz Rosenthal, edited and abridged by N.J. Dawood (Princeton: Princeton University Press, 1974 reprint), pp. 123–52.

and spoke of the 'aroma of hearts' [*bū-yī dilhā*], that pervaded the region. He immediately purchased the land and asked that he be buried there. Niẓām al-Dīn concluded his discourse by weeping and commenting on the fate of that deserted place: 'See!' he exclaimed, 'all the great nobles asleep there now [*ki ānjā kiyā khufta and*!].'[68]

At one level, Niẓām al-Dīn Awliyā's story was a fairly stereotypical account of how a *ṣūfī* saint's grace attracted people even to a desolate spot, eventually altering its character. The reason why I choose to retell the anecdote, however, is not to discuss the qualities of *ṣūfī* Shaykhs, but to isolate two temporal and spatial coordinates: the passage of eighty-nine lunar years (between 632/1235 and 721/1321) and their impact on a deserted space lying about five hundred metres from the city wall of Delhi. Quṭb al-Dīn's grave site was about equidistant from the festival ground near the reservoir constructed by Iltutmish, known at this time as *ḥauẓ-i Sulṭānī*, and the city gates on the western wall leading from the congregational mosque, the *darwāzahā-yī samt-i qibla.*[69] During Iltutmish's reign this land was still deserted [*ṣaḥrā'*], a jungle of thorn and scrub. We may dispute Niẓām al-Dīn's claim and the role of Quṭb al-Dīn's grace in the transformation of this deserted jungle into a necropolis by 'Alā' al-Dīn's reign, but the point remains: by the early fourteenth century it was certainly not the outback of the city any more. A variety of different interventions over the century—and not just the monocausal one of Quṭb al-Dīn's grave site—had altered the geography of this jungle into a suburb of the city. This is a small episode showing how spaces around the capital of the Sultanate changed through the thirteenth century; but plot it on the map of north India and it becomes worth asking if this was just a discrete incident, or if there were larger changes in territories and habitations occurring at this time in the domains of the Delhi Sultans.

One of the incidental factors that Niẓām al-Dīn's story highlighted was the limited areas covered by urban habitation in the early years of the Delhi Sultanate. We have had occasion to comment earlier on how Sultanate territorial control at the beginning of the century rarely

[68] Amīr Ḥasan Sijzī, *Fawā'id al-Fu'ād,* p. 425.

[69] On the city gates on the western wall and the *ḥauẓ*, see, Baranī, *Ta'rīkh-i Fīrūz Shāhī,* edited by Khan, p. 56, edited by Rashid, p. 66.

went beyond the *shahr wa qaṣabāt wa muẓafāt,* the town, its adjoining fortified settlements and tracts. As a result, even though Sultanate domains extended from Lakhnauti to Dewal during the reign of Iltutmish, this was more in the nature of military cantonments that maintained a semblance of contiguity through tenuous and difficult-to-protect overland and riverine trade/military routes. Although the Mu'izzī *bandagān* had insinuated their appanages within local systems of trade and commerce quite successfully, the decisive breach in the city walls only occurred through the political agency of the erstwhile Shamsī subordinates during the period of the intra-dispensational conflicts after Iltutmish's death.

There were two interrelated aspects of the conflict that were particularly important, and let me quickly summarize them here. The first were the geographical areas that felt the impact of these wars. These included, on the one hand, the eastern and western wings of the Sultanate (the areas of Lakhnauti in the east and Multan and Sindh on the west) that broke away entirely from the control of Delhi, where military commanders some times appropriated the title of Sultan (see numbers 2 and 18 in Chapter 5, Table 3). On the other hand were the territories that fell between Awadh in the east, the Siwalik in the south and Samana–Sunam in the Punjab in the west. These areas and their commanders participated in some of the greatest battles during the period of the intra-dispensational conflicts. These were areas well saturated by the movements of armed forces and military personnel, chasing and fleeing from each other and looking for sanctuaries to establish as their redoubt. These were the lands that emerged as the 'core areas' of the Sultanate, deeply implicated over time in the politics of Delhi.

The second was the inter-personal aspect, which affected geographical areas as well. This was strikingly apparent in the case of the Governors of the eastern and western wings of the Sultanate. The end of their allegiance to the Delhi Sultan also sundered the links of 'Lakhnauti and Dewal' with Delhi. The period of the intra-dispensational conflicts placed military commanders in the core areas of the Sultanate—with their commitments to Delhi already at edge—in a situation where they had to consolidate their regional bases, neutralize the political competition, and seize the high ground by capturing power in Delhi. In an effort towards strengthening their individual political bases, they were amenable to moving out of their camps and establishing alliances with local chieftains. The '*Rānā-Malik*' condominium, directed against the intrusive authority of Delhi, took Shamsī personnel into regions where Sultanate armies had never traversed before. This started the process of rooting the Sultanate in the countryside, even though it was not through the agency of the Delhi Sultan but its erstwhile and now defiant servants.

With Qutlugh Khān's flight to the Mongols, Balban moved towards the restoration of Sultanate authority, but the intervening territorial changes meant that 'restoration' per se was impossible. With the changed nature of political and territorial configurations in the Sultanate, Delhi's method of annexing and administrating the western and eastern wings of its dominions differed completely from that of its core territories.

Frequent Mongol incursions forced the Delhi Sultans to keep a very close watch on their western provinces. Although by 664/1266 the great Mongol commanders were no longer leading campaigns into India, the Negüderid (referred to as the Qara'unas in Sultanate sources) pressure on the Sultanate frontier provided no respite to Delhi and its commanders.[70] Since Iltutmish's reign the frontier of the Sultanate had moved eastwards, until it lay along the River Beas. Partly through the exertions of Ulugh Khān, Delhi had regained control over areas around Lahore.[71] The need to neutralize the Negüderids, however, led Balban to open negotiations with the Il-Khanid

[70] These Mongol invasions have been detailed in the dissertation by Peter Jackson, 'The Mongols and India 1221–1351', pp. 84–112. The Negüderids were the armed forces commanded by Negüder, a subordinate of Jōchī, the Khān of the Golden Horde. On the Negüderids, see also Jean Aubin, 'L'ethnogénèse des Qaraunas', *Turcica*, 1 (1969), pp. 65–94; Beatrice F. Manz, *The Rise and Rule of Tamerlane* (Cambridge: Cambridge University Press, 1989), pp. 159–61, and Peter Jackson, *The Delhi Sultanate*, p. 328. An early recognition of the Negüderids/ Qara'unas in the Delhi Sultanate sources occurs in an elegy written on the death of Prince Muḥammad by Amīr Khusrau. Amīr Khusrau was briefly captured by a person that he described as a Qara'una; see the poet's elegy (*marṣiya*) preserved in Badā'ūnī, *Muntakhab al-Tawārīkh*, vol. 1, p. 153. See also Ibn Baṭṭūṭa, *Rehla*, p. 47.

[71] This must have occurred some time after 652/1254, when Jalāl al-Dīn Mas'ūd, son of Iltutmish and ally of the Mongols controlled Lahore. It was only after Jalāl al-Dīn retreated into the Chaghtayid domains, and Lahore came

ruler Hūlāgū (654–63/1256–65),[72] and make efforts to reorganize his western command. This had to wait until after the death of Balban's cousin, Shīr Khān (*ca.* 669/1270), the powerful Governor of Lahore, Dipalpur, Tabarhind, Sunam, and Bhatnair.[73] Subsequently, Balban gave the command of Multan to his eldest son, Muḥammad, and Samana to his younger son, Bughra Khān. The Princes received support from the slave commanders, Tamar Khān Shamsī also in Samana and Sunam, and the *banda-i khāṣṣ*, Malik Ikhtiyār al-Dīn Begtars.[74] According to Baranī, by the 15th or 16th regnal year *ca.* 679/1280, the frontier had stabilized at the Beas River, and the Mongol incursions had diminished.

Coincident with this greater stability was a reorganization of the frontier commands especially necessary when Balban left Delhi to subdue the rebel Tughril in Lakhnauti (*circa* 679–80/1280–1). At that time Prince Bughra Khān and Malik Ikhtiyār al-Dīn Begtars were removed from their commands and ordered to march east with the army.[75] Balban appointed another Ghiyāṣī notable, Malik Sewinch

---

under Shīr Khān's influence, that the Mongol presence in the region diminished; Jūzjānī, *Ṭabaqāt-i Nāṣirī*, vol. 1, p. 489; vol. 2, pp. 66–7, 44. See also Peter Jackson, 'Lahawr', *EI*², s.v. Note also Baranī's remarks concerning Balban's appointment of *gumāshtagān wa mi'mārān*, superintendents and architects, and the reconstruction and resettlement of Lahore and its neighbouring towns and villages, *qaṣabāt wa dih.* Baranī, edited by Khan, p. 61, edited by Rashid, pp. 71–2.

72 See Peter Jackson, 'The Mongols and India', pp. 100–1, for an account of these negotiations and an embassy from Berke, the Khan of the Golden Horde.

73 Baranī, *Ta'rīkh-i Fīrūz Shāhī*, edited by Khan, p. 65, edited by Rashid, pp. 76–7.

74 Ibid., edited by Khan, pp. 65, 66, 80–1, edited by Rashid, pp. 77, 79, 94–5.

75 Ikhtiyār al-Dīn Begtars eventually received the Governorship of Garhmuktesar in the northern Ganga-Jamuna *do-āb*. Peter Jackson, 'Mongols and India', p. 104, has argued that Garhmuktesar was his command at the time when he was required to support the Princes against the Mongols in the west. But this is unlikely because of the distance involved. There is an inscription of Begtars al-Sulṭānī from Garhmuktesar dated 628/1283, and the slave must have received this charge after the Lakhnauti campaign. For Begtars' participation in the Lakhnauti campaign see Baranī. *Ta'rīkh-i Fīrūz Shāhī*, edited by Khan p. 88, edited by Rashid, p. 102. For the 628/1283 inscription of Malik Begtars,

Sar-i jāndār, to Samana and Sunam and reorganized the region into smaller administrative charges [*shiqqs*], under subordinate officers.[76] But the most dramatic development was the grant of the province of Sindh and Punjab up to the River Beas as an appanage to the older Prince Muḥammad. It was from these areas that Prince Muḥammad was required to remit many choice [*chīda wa bisyār*], Baḥrī(?) and Tatārī horses to Delhi.[77] Baranī also noted that less expensive mounts were bred closer to Delhi in the regions of Samana, Sunam, Tabarhind, Thanesar, in the camps [*talwandihā*] of the Khokars, and the domains of the Jats and Mundahirs. Since Balban found them acceptable mounts for the army, he ordered the Prince to acquire and remit these to Delhi rather than become overly reliant on undependable supplies from the Mongol territories.[78]

After 680/1281 there is not a single report of the Sultan's intervention in the areas of Sindh and Multan. Baranī reported that Prince Muḥammad would come annually to Delhi with the treasures and retinue [*bā<u>kh</u>āzana wa pā'igāh*], of Multan to pay allegiance to his father.[79] The stability of the frontier may have been partly responsible for the treatment of the north-west regions as the virtually autonomous appanage of Muḥammad, and it certainly allowed the Prince to function and maintain court like a lord.[80] Muḥammad behaved with sufficient independence and impertinence to antagonize Delhi's notables.

---

see G. Yazdani, 'The Inscriptions of the Turk Sultans of Delhi', *Epigraphica Indo-Moslemica*, pp. 27–8.

[76] Baranī, *Ta'rī<u>kh</u>-i Fīrūz Shāhī*, edited by Khan, p. 85, edited by Rashid, pp. 99–100.

[77] The variant manuscripts of Baranī spell the word differently: ibid., edited by Khan, p. 53 (BHRJ̄), edited by Rashid (BḤRŪJĪ), p. 62. On the basis of the second recension of the *Ta'rī<u>kh</u>-i Fīrūz Shāhī* in his personal collection, Simon Digby argued that BḤRĪ for *baḥrī*, sea-borne, should be the correct reading. See Digby, *War Horse and Elephant*, p. 21, fn. 34.

[78] Baranī, *Ta'rī<u>kh</u>-i Fīrūz Shāhī*, edited by Khan, p. 85, edited by Rashid, pp. 99–100.

[79] Ibid., edited by Khan, p. 69, edited by Rashid, p. 81.

[80] On a description of his court, see ibid., edited by Khan, pp. 67–8, edited by Rashid, pp. 78–9. Baranī notes that he was the patron of both Amīr Ḥasan Sijzī and Amīr <u>Kh</u>usrau. See above for references to <u>Kh</u>usrau's elegy at the Prince's death.

The reason, according to Baranī, remained unclear (the author felt that it may have had something to do with women), but it did mark a distancing from the world of the Delhi court. It was because of this alienation that Muḥammad's son Kaikhusrau was an unacceptable heir to the Ghiyāṣī notables in Delhi.[81] In defiance of their master's wishes, they chose Bughra Khān's son, Kaiqubād, as the next Sultan.

Rearrangements in the control of the western provinces occurred in the context of the Ghiyāṣī slave Tughril's rebellion in Lakhnauti. Controlling the eastern provinces from Delhi had proved to be as difficult as controlling the western ones. By the last years of Nāṣir al-Dīn's reign, Sultanate authority in the east beyond Awadh had become practically non-existent. Tāj al-Dīn Arsalān had already established his independence in Lakhnauti with the title of Sultan and after his death his son Tatar Khān succeeded him.[82] Delhi interfered in these developments only in so far as it favoured competition in the region by patronizing several rivals simultaneously. Thus, Delhi supported both 'Izz al-Dīn Balban Yuzbegī and Jalāl al-Dīn Mas'ūd Jānī in their efforts to seize Lakhnauti.[83] By the time of Balban's accession Tatar Khān, son of Tāj al-Dīn Arsalān, had emerged as the master of Lakhnauti, but there was only the most tenuous of connections between the eastern provinces and the capital. Baranī described the joyous celebrations in Delhi when sixty-three elephants from Tatar Khān reached Delhi around 662–4/1264–6.[84] This was an unusual show of subordination for Lakhnauti, but it summed up the nature of the relationship that Delhi wanted to construct with the distant province: in exchange for periodic obeisance in the shape of elephants and silver, Lakhnauti's autonomy would be deemed acceptable.[85]

[81] Ibid., edited by Khan, p. 122, edited by Rashid, p. 143.

[82] Jūzjānī, *Ṭabaqāt-i Nāṣirī*, vol. 1, p. 495, vol. 2, p. 35; Baranī, *Ta'rīkh-i Fīrūz Shāhī*, edited by Khan, pp. 53, 66, edited by Rashid, pp. 63, 78.

[83] For 'Izz al-Dīn Balban Yuzbegī, see Jūzjānī, *Ṭabaqāt-i Nāṣirī*, vol. 2, p. 35; and for Jalāl al-Dīn Mas'ūd Jānī, see ibid., vol. 1, p. 495.

[84] Baranī, *Ta'rīkh-i Fīrūz Shāhī*, edited by Khan, p. 53, edited by Rashid, p. 63.

[85] For Lakhnauti's importance as a supplier of silver, see Simon Digby, 'The Currency System', in *The Cambridge Economic History of India*, vol. i.

It is not certain when Balban conquered Lakhnauti, nor when he appointed his slave Tughril as Governor. No major change seems to have occurred in Delhi's ability to control its eastern province, however, and Tughril revolted, *circa* 679–80/1280–1. On the third attempt Balban finally subdued the rebellion himself and left its governance to his younger son Bughra Khān. Balban was aware of the enormous difficulties involved in controlling Lakhnauti. During their campaigns against Tughril, the Delhi forces had to face the aggression of local chieftains who had allied with the Bengal Governor against Delhi.[86] During his own campaign Balban took the precaution of seeking the help of Bhōj Rā'ī, the ruler of Sonargaon.[87] And, after the conquest of Lakhnauti, Balban did not bring the province under the administration of Delhi; he left his younger son Bughra Khān, instead, as Governor of the region.[88]

Although Balban impressed the subordinate position of Lakhnauti on his son and underlined his duty to remit treasure to the capital, the Sultan left the eastern province with a great deal of freedom. For Balban, Lakhnauti and Delhi did not make a composite whole; the division between the two countries (*iqlīm*, literally, climates) lay along the River Saryu. Baranī presented the distinction between the two lands, *diyār*, very forcefully in an anecdote wherein Balban ordered that no soldier of the Delhi army had permission to stay in Lakhnauti, and none from Lakhnauti to migrate into Hindustan.[89] The direct supervision of the Sultan extended up to Awadh, placed under

---

pp. 96–8; and John Deyell, 'The China Connection: Problems of Silver Supply in Medieval Bengal', in *Precious Metals in the Later Medieval and Early Modern Worlds,* pp. 207–27.

86 Baranī, *Ta'rīkh-i Firūz Shāhī*, edited by Khan, p. 84, edited by Rashid, p. 98.

87 Ibid., edited by Khan, p. 91, edited by Rashid, p. 107. See also Yaḥyā Sirhindī, *Ta'rīkh-i Mubārak Shāhī*, edited by M. Hidayat Hosain, pp. 42–3, where the King's name is given as Rā'ī Dhanuj, and Balban is forced to accede to the 'Hindu' ruler's demand that the two should meet standing, on equal terms.

88 Baranī, *Ta'rīkh-i Fīrūz Shāhī*, edited by Khan, p. 53, edited by Rashid, pp. 62–3.

89 Ibid., edited by Khan, p. 106, edited by Rashid, p. 125.

the command of Malik 'Alī Sar-i Jāndār, and Baranī consistently referred to these lands as *Hindūstān*.[90] In effect, Bughra Khān was the autonomous Governor of Lakhnauti, where he established his own base of power, and Balban was the ruler of all of north India but had special interests only in *Hindūstān*. Baranī brought out the extent of Bughra Khān's eventual alienation from Delhi when he noted that the Prince, Balban's chosen successor to the Delhi throne, refused the honour, fleeing to his preferred throne of Lakhnauti.[91]

Assuredly, Balban reunited the lands from Dewal to Lakhnauti once again under the authority of Delhi, but he had obviously decided to be extremely prudent in seeking to control these newly re-annexed regions. From the information available to us today, it is clear that after 679–80/1280–1, with the defeat of Tughril and the appointment of the Princes to Lakhnauti and Sindh, the Delhi Sultan never interfered in the affairs of the two regions. These were the domains of the Princes; Balban now restricted his control to the core areas of *Hindūstān*.

Balban's interventions in the core areas continued quite seamlessly from his years as Ulugh Khān: in the former years he was in conflict with his Shamsī peers, and this some times took him into the domains of his rivals. But now, as Sultan, he could no longer allow any of his old competitors *or* their old allies to survive. It was insufficient for Balban to merely plunder their domains; he had to try to appropriate these lands and bring them into the purview of Sultanate administration. After the intra-dispensational conflicts and the alliance of the Shamsī Maliks with the local Rā'īs and Rānās, the 'restoration' of Delhi's authority demanded that Balban establish structures of governance and deploy personnel in both urban centres as well as in their more

[90] Baranī's understanding of '*Hindūstān*' appeared in a comparative mode. He some times used the term generically, when he was talking of 'Khurasan and Hindustan' (ibid., edited by Khan, pp. 66, 113, edited by Rashid, pp. 78, 133). At other times, when describing different regions in the subcontinent, he was far more precise. On these occasions he always distinguished between Lakhnauti and Hindustan (ibid., edited by Khan, pp. 83, 84, edited by Rashid, pp. 98, 99) and described the region of Sindh as Sindh and never Hindustan. See for example ibid., edited by Khan, p. 53, edited by Rashid, p. 62.

[91] Ibid., edited by Khan, p. 121, edited by Rashid, p. 142.

inaccessible hinterlands. A comparison of his interventions in the Mewat region, just south of Delhi, before and after his accession brings out the elements of difference.

Balban had campaigned in the Mewat area in 658/1260 and Jūzjānī had described the fortifications of the Meo chieftains with the greatest degree of respect. It was during these campaigns that Balban had first deployed the ferocious Afghans, and Jūzjānī described the ensuing head-hunt: whoever brought the head of a Meo received one *tanka*, whoever brought a man captive received two *tankas*.[92] Jūzjānī terminated his chronicle abruptly in the following year, and although his narrative of the Mewat campaigns was very much in the plunder-raiding mode he provided no information on the afterlife of these military interventions. When Ẓiyā' al-Dīn Baranī picked up the narrative six years later with Balban's accession, he had the advantage of hindsight—this gave the author the space to contextualize events and notice broader trends. Putting together the detailed narrative of one with the more discursive analysis of the other is extremely useful to us today.

Baranī places the Mewat campaigns in the context of unstable conditions in Delhi at Balban's accession.[93] The forests had surrounded the capital and under their cover the Meos would attack residents of the city at night. People could not safely stir abroad, domestics were harassed and molested at the nearby *ḥauẓ-i Sulṭānī* when they went to fetch water or wash clothes. As a result, the western gates of the city were shut after the evening prayers. Balban responded to these developments through military campaigns in the Mewat region. This was a predictable response, but what is more interesting is the systematic clearing of the forests that he also ordered in the areas around Delhi. With the clearing of the jungle, caravans could traverse the region in safety and the Meos were finally subjugated.[94]

Balban followed up his campaigns in the proximity of Delhi by others in the southern *do-āb*, near the towns of Kampil, Patiali, and

[92] Jūzjānī, *Ṭabaqāt-i Nāṣirī*, vol. 2, p. 80.

[93] Baranī, *Ta'rīkh-i Fīrūz Shāhī*, edited by Khan, p. 55, edited by Rashid, p. 65.

[94] Ibid., edited by Khan, pp. 56–7, edited by Rashid, pp. 65–7.

Bhojpur. Subsequently, Balban crossed the Ganges and campaigned in the areas around Budaun, Amroha, Sambhal, and Kanuri/Ganuri (?).[95] All these campaigns extended from the respective towns into the interior of the country, and each involved clearing the forest. Baranī described the large number of soldiers that he mustered for these campaigns and amongst the armed personnel was a body of people described as *tabarzan,* woodcutter(s).[96] These woodcutters cleared the paths for the army as they marched into Kather, the forested interior of the country adjoining Budaun.

In the previous chapter we discussed the geography of the *mawās* and Jūzjānī's description of the great difficulty that Sultanate armies had in penetrating these tracts. The passage of time had not altered their character, and in the early fourteenth century Ibn Baṭṭūṭa described them as places where local chieftains—

> fortif[ied] themselves in mountains, in rocky, uneven and rugged places as well as in bamboo groves. In India the bamboo is not hollow; it is big. Its several parts are so intertwined that even fire cannot affect them, and they are on the whole very strong. The infidels live in those forests which serve them as ramparts, inside which are their cattle and their crops. There is also water for them within, that is rain water which collects there. Hence they cannot be subdued except by powerful armies, who entering those forests, cut down the bamboos with specially prepared instruments.[97]

The need to carry specialized personnel to clear the *mawās* is fairly apparent from Ibn Baṭṭūṭa's description. In his account of Balban's campaign in the areas near Budaun, Baranī mentioned that the *Kathīryān*, the people of Kather, especially suffered the onslaught of Sultanate armies.[98] Hodivala identified the region as modern Rohilkand and also provided possible etymologies for the word

[95] Ibid., edited by Khan, pp. 57–60, edited by Rashid, pp. 67–70

[96] Ibid., edited by Khan, p. 59, edited by Rashid, p. 69.

[97] Ibn Baṭṭūṭa, *Rehla*, p. 124.

[98] Baranī, *Ta'rīkh-i Fīrūz Shāhī*, edited by Khan, pp. 58–60, edited by Rashid, p. 67–70. For the reference to *kathīryān*, see ibid., edited by Khan, p. 59, edited by Rashid, p. 70.

kathīr.[99] According to him the word could be a derivative of the Sanskrit, *kāstha*, wood, or the Hindi, *katherī*, woodman or carpenter. The term would refer then to the topography of the region as well as its largely pastoral, forest-dwelling people who were preying on the city. The response of urban society to the threat posed by these people required the destruction of their habitat where wood cutter(s), *tabarzan*, were an absolutely essential part of the military force. It is important to keep in mind, however, that barely a decade earlier people of an identical sociological profile in the Sirmur region had allied and protected the Shamsī Amir, Qutlugh Khān, fleeing from Ulugh Khān. The pastoralist–sedentary antagonism, was not a 'natural' juxtaposition of antithetical social and political profiles; there were important, intervening historical reasons for this animosity. And let us not forget that, in his march into Lakhnauti, Balban established alliances with local chieftains in the *mawās* and solicited the help of itinerant provenders, the *baqqāl*, to pinpoint the location of the fleeing rebel Tughril.[100]

Balban's agenda for these tracts was not simply restricted to 'clearing' forests; it included 'resettlement' as well, and once again Balban relied upon the most obtrusive tactics of sedentary societies against pastoral groups: hard on the heels of the deforestation of the *do-āb* lands came the killing and relocation of populations and the extension of an agrarian economy into the region. Balban ordered the clearing of forests, and the execution of forest-dwellers and pastoralists resident in these areas; he destroyed their cities and bazaars, enslaved infants and women, and then resettled the land with new personnel. The people that he chose to repopulate these areas with were the aforementioned Afghans, a new body of social menials to whom he gave rent-free lands [*mafrūzī*], and for whom he established military cantonments such as at Jalālī and Gopalgir.[101] Barani noted that in

[99] Hodivala, *Studies in Indo-Muslim History*, vol. I, p. 259.

[100] See above for references to Rājā Bhōj, and for the *baqqāl* see Baranī, *Ta'rīkh-i Fīrūz Shāhī*, edited by Khan, p. 89, edited by Rashid, p. 104.

[101] Baranī, *Ta'rīkh-i Fīrūz Shāhī*, edited by Khan, pp. 57–8, edited by Rashid, pp. 66–8. Bhojpur is misprinted as Bharajpur in the Rashid edition, p. 57. Hodivala tentatively identified Gopalgir as Gopalgarh on the frontier of

each *qaṣaba* Balban gave *mafrūzī* lands to Muslims and Afghans.[102] The multidimensional form of this expansion into the country also changed the character of the *qaṣaba*. It was still an armed camp, but now its role in the agrarian and commercial economy of the region was in greater evidence. The residents in the *qaṣabāt* had rights to cultivate land in the neighbourhood, and, as Barani noted after the resettlement of Kampil, Patiali, and Bhojpur, the area and trade routes leading to the cities were secure. As a result, caravans and merchants could now come and go [*kārwāniyān wa saudāgarān dar āmad-u-shud shudand*].[103] It was from Balban's reign that the *qaṣaba* acquired its urban character as a site of rural commercial exchange linking villages with a large regional economy and the *do-āb* as the agricultural heartland of the state.

This was an extremely violent and harsh intervention by the state as well as metropolitan social and political structures into the countryside. But these developments also reveal the need to acknowledge how metropolitan political structures adapted to meet the new challenge posed by the countryside. Delhi Sultans had hitherto used deracinated individuals—slaves and plebeians—in the court and the cantonments of the Sultanate; now they were an intrinsic part of settling the 'disturbed, intractable' *mawasāt*. As a consequence of the '*Rānā-Malik*' condominium, Balban innovated, but only slightly. Sultanate personnel and administration were now extended into new arenas but the nature and form of governance did not undergo any remarkable transformation; deracinated personnel deployed in metropolitan contexts were now moved into the country.

Balban's measures were inherently conservative and were always a *response* to political challenges faced by the Sultanate. The '*Rānā-Malik*' condominium led to his interventions in the countryside, Tughril's rebellions forced the territorial reorganization of the empire and, if we follow Baranī's narrative, it was only *after* the intrusive campaigns in the *do-āb* that Balban received information about the

---

the Mewati territory. S.H. Hodivala, *Studies in Indo-Muslim History*, vol. II, p. 83.

[102] Baranī, *Ta'rīkh-i Fīrūz Shāhī*, edited by Khan, p. 58, edited by Rashid, pp. 67–8.

[103] Ibid., edited by Khan, p. 57, edited by Rashid, p. 67.

Shamsī cavalrymen who had turned their *iqṭā'*s into outright grants and were ignoring their service contracts. The effort to curb this 'debris of dispensations' then followed. The establishment of the Sultanate's agrarian hinterland in the core areas of Balban's dominion occurred about the same time as the Ghiyāṣī dispensation claimed final victory over its political competitors. Just as the constitution of the Ghiyāṣī dispensation reflect the changes introduced by the intra-dispensational conflicts, so did the new territorial map of the Delhi Sultanate.

The consequences of these developments in the long duration are visible on Map 4. This plots the political geography of the Sultanate during the reign of 'Alā' al-Dīn Khalajī (695–715/1296–1316), about two decades after Balban's death. It demarcates the territory of the monarch along three coordinates: first, the area under the *khāliṣa* with their revenues reserved for the crown. These were the lands that the monarch controlled and supervised most carefully. It was the immediate hinterland of the capital, providing an important political buffer and the produce that fed residents of the city. The second area was where there was rigorous tax assessment based upon an estimation of crop yield. Next to the *khālisa,* this was the area with the greatest presence of royal administrators, with ongoing efforts to scrutinize village-level land records where state agencies demanded revenue payments in cash. The third and largest area on the map demarcates the domains of 'Alā' al-Dīn Khalajī under his military control but not acute administrative supervision.

There are some obvious correlations between 'Alā' al-Dīn Khalajī's domain as plotted on this map and the changes in Ghiyāṣ al-Dīn Balban's territories that we have just discussed. The *khālisa* lands in the *do-āb* during 'Alā' al-Dīn's reign were the areas in which there was systematic deforestation and resettlement of personnel during Balban's reign. There are only marginal shifts in this territory from Balban into 'Alā' al-Dīn Khalajī's reign. The second area, regions under the rigorous revenue collection of Khalajī administrators, were lands that had seen the worst of the intra-dispensational conflicts—the areas between Samana-Sunam, the Siwalik, and Awadh—which Balban reserved under his command, distinguishing them from the appanages created for the two Princes. These 'core areas' of the Sultanate saw increasing supervision under 'Ala' al-Dīn Khalajī, but

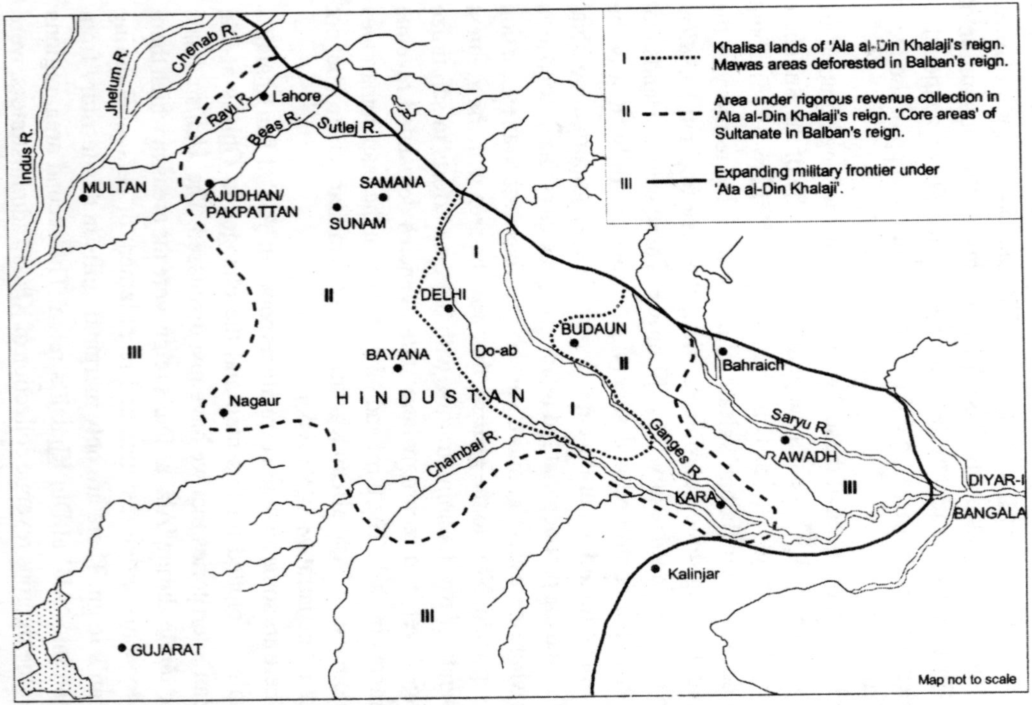

Map 4: 'Alā' al-Dīn Khalajī's Dominions

again, only slight extensions of territory into the north-west: Lahore under Balban was a part of his older son's command. The greatest change occurred in the lands that comprised the larger territory of the Sultanate: the political-military frontier, where plunder raids were still an ongoing phenomenon, saw major transitions in 'Alā' al-Dīn Khalajī's reign. This was the frontier that John Richards described as the most volatile and rapid in its expansion and contraction and which, under 'Alā' al-Dīn Khalajī's military thrust into the Deccan, expanded dramatically. By contrast the areas under rigorous Sultanate control, the heartlands of the Sultanate, remained remarkably stable through the intervening period.

Baranī described Balban as a ruler who did not want to partake in ambitious military campaigns because of the fear of Mongol invasions and the stresses on the political and economic system caused by military campaigns.[104] In his narrative of the monarch's reign, however, the author detailed the militaristic aspect of Balban's activities. And yet, since the campaigns were into the interior tracts of the core domain, the abiding impression left among readers of Baranī's history is that these were defensive, not offensive, campaigns, and there was no territorial expansion of the Sultanate during the monarch's reign. The narrative of a chronicler such as Baranī completely obscured the processes that forced Balban to intervene in the politics of inaccessible tracts in the interior of Hindustan, areas that had hitherto remained well outside the purview of Delhi's command. The 'herocentric' nature of Baranī's text treated the reigns of the separate rulers as distinct units; little effort was made to connect changes and continuities over the long duration. Hence the contexts and nature of Balban's campaigns in the *mawās,* so crucial for the later formulation of the Sultanate, remained discrete incidents unconnected with developments apparent in the period of the intra-dispensational conflicts or during the reign of 'Alā' al-Dīn Khalajī. The regnal focus of Baranī's history also made it difficult to comprehend how political agency could reside with people other than the Delhi Sultans. Whenever court narratives chose to report on the independent political initiatives of Shamsī military commanders, they were either shown

[104] Ibid., edited by Khan, pp. 50–2. edited by Rashid, p. 58–61

as supportive of or contradictory to the interests of the Delhi Sultan. There was no space available for a third or a fourth lineage of power in the court narratives; the King monopolized power and the ruling class remained composite.

We need to keep these aspects in mind, not merely to historicize long-term changes in the Sultanate more accurately, but to also re-position the Delhi Sultan more precisely in the making of this Sultanate. At one level, the clearing of the *mawās* would make little sense without the larger historical backdrop of the '*Rānā-Malik*' alliances of the preceding generation. And the imposition of 'Alā' al-Dīn's rigorous revenue collection in the core area of his domains would remain the product of the genius of the Delhi monarch if the geography of the intra-dispensational conflicts and Balban's counter-measures were not configured into the narrative. But at another, more theoretical, level, it is worth asking how the presence of the '*Rānā-Malik*' alliance or the conflict between the *Shaikh al-Islām* Najm al-Dīn Sughra and the *ṣūfī* saint Jalāl al-Dīn Tabrizī textures the mono-chromatic reportage of the Delhi Sultan as the most powerful political agent in the history of the Delhi Sultanate. Certainly, the violent nature of Balban's intervention in the *mawās* region consolidates the impression of the overwhelming might of the monarch, reconfiguring the territorial spaces of north India pretty much at his pleasure. The coercive character of this political intrusion notwithstanding, it was during the height of Sultanate authority towards the end of the thirteenth century that the emergence of regional identities seizing the high ground with their own renditions of the past becomes noticeable. These then enable a reconfiguration of chronides—like Jūzjānī's and Baranī's—which proclaimed the centrality of Delhi in the making of Sultanate authority in north India.

Regional Solidarities, the Piety-minded, and the Metropole

In the story of how Bakhtiyār Kākī chanced upon his burial site, Niẓām al-Dīn Awliyā' had concluded by wistfully reminiscing on the large number of pure souls buried in the vicinity of their *pīr*. This was a comment on the saint's grace, a spirituality that endeared him to his followers, and the high stature that they were sure he commanded in the Kingdom of God. Unquestionably, this would be of benefit to his followers on the Day of Judgement. But Niẓām al-Dīn Awliyā's story also gestured to the importance of the region rendered safe, not because of Balban's efforts at clearing the forests and the destruction of the Meo habitat, but because of the great saint's grace emanating from his grave site. This was an alternative to the more materially deterministic reasons that explained why the Sultanate capital remained a sanctuary for Muslims through the vicissitudes of the thirteenth century. The mid-fourteenth-century history of Baranī redeployed this sentiment to explain how the capital was preserved from different kinds of calamities because of the presence of Niẓām al-Dīn Awliyā' in the city.[105] After the death of the great Chishtī saints, Niẓām al-Dīn and Naṣīr al-Dīn, ruin and destruction fell upon the city and the great Delhi Sultans lost power.[106] None of these accounts were at all exceptional for the time, nor were they merely literary tropes. Cities and regions had powerful protectors venerated by large congregations: there was Bābā Farīd in Ajudhan, Bahā' al-Dīn Zakariyā in Multan, and further afield in the east in Bahraich was the shrine of Sālār Mas'ūd Ghāzī; and in Kara there was the presence of the *ṣūfī* Khwāja Gurg.

If in the early thirteenth century large mystical fraternities were still thin on the ground, and if in the general hostility between the *ṣūfīs* and the *'ulamā'* the more antinomian mystics felt the heavy disciplinarian hand of the *Sharī'a*-minded jurists, by the middle of the century their *khānaqāhs* were bustling centres of social and economic exchange and spiritual alleviation.[107] As we noticed in the last chapter, during the intra-dispensational conflicts these hospices were still located primarily at the edges of the core territory of the Sultanate where they had emerged as important centres of mystical training, producing a second generation of *ṣūfīs* sent by their master to minister to regional congregations in different parts of the Sultanate.

The process of rooting the piety-minded in north India through the thirteenth century can be evaluated in different ways. It was visible,

[105] Ibid., edited by Khan, p. 325.

[106] See Simon Digby, 'The Sufi *Shaykh* and the Sultan: A Conflict of Claims to Authority', pp. 71–81.

[107] See Chapter 5 and for a useful study of the history of Bābā Farīd's hospice at Ajudhan, see Richard Eaton, 'The Political and Religious Authority of the Shrine of Bābā Farīd', pp. 333–56.

for example, in the list of *qāẓīs* and Sayyids appended to the reigns of Balban and 'Alā al-Dīn Khalajī in the *Ta'rīkh-i Fīrūz Shāhī*. Baranī provided these lists so that readers could appreciate the glory of an age inhabited by men of such learning and eminence. His list of the pious in Balban's reign included a large number of immigrants into the Delhi Sultanate, individuals who carried the ancestry of their original residence in their names as their *nisbas*: Damishqī (Damascus), Jūzjānī (Juzjan),[108] Gāzarūnī (probably Kāzirūn in the province of Fars), and Kāshānī (Kashan). But the process of identifying with areas within north India had progressed sufficiently into Balban's reign, and Baranī could identify amongst the pious at the close of the century the important Sayyids of Kaithal, Jhajjar, Bayana, Budaun, and two pious men carrying the *nisba* of Samana: Sayyid Mu'īn al-Dīn, and Qāẓī Rukn al-Dīn Sāmāna.[109] The numbers multiply further into 'Alā' al-Dīn's reign, and Baranī noted the presence of *qāẓīs* with the subcontinental *nisbas* of Bayana, Sunam, Bhakkar, Kōl, Kara, Multan, Baran (modern Bulandshahr), Hansi, Lahore, and Luni.[110] These were *'ulamā'* who were at least second-generation migrants, but, even more, there was a confidence in the training imparted at dispersed regional centres until individuals started incorporating their subcontinental provenance with pride in their names. What is perhaps interesting to note in all of these *nisbas* is the absence of *Dehlawī*: no *'ālim* of this generation, at least as far as the *nisbas* suggest, claimed Delhi as the place of his formal training. They all moved to the capital after establishing their reputations elsewhere, and once in Delhi some of them, like Jūzjānī, had long and flourishing careers. Delhi had certainly won considerable renown as the residence of eminent *'ulamā'* by the middle of the thirteenth century, and, if we

[108] Baranī has Jūrjānī instead of Jūzjānī. Jūrjān was in the south-eastern tip of the Caspian sea; Jūzjān was on the Marghab river, north-north-east of Herat. We know that Jūzjānī belonged to the city of Tulak, which is in the province of Jūzjān and not Jūrjān. See, Guy Le Strange, *The Lands of the Eastern Caliphate: Mesopotamia, Persia and Central Asia from the Moslem Conquest to the Time of Timur* (Cambridge: Cambridge University Press, 1930), Map VIII.

[109] Baranī, *Ta'rīkh-i Fīrūz Shāh* . edited by Khan, p. 111, edited by Rashid, pp. 130–1. Khan read Jhajhar as Janjer.

[110] Ibid., edited by Khan, pp. 353-4.

respect Baranī's opinion on the subject at all, the city's regard as a residence of jurists, theologians, and litterateurs had spread into areas well outside Hindustan.[111]

The battle for power over Delhi amongst the Shamsī Amirs had drawn the regional *'ulamā'* in its wake: we have already reviewed the short but dizzying success of *qāẓī* Shams al-Dīn Bharā'ijī and his *'ulamā'* confederates when they allied with Raihān and Qutlugh Khān in 651/1253.[112] But beyond the overt gains of high office, the very presence of a jurist from the small town of Bahraich, on the Himalayan foothills, an *'ālim* of sufficient stature with the ambition and the wherewithal to become the *qāẓī* of the realm, speaks volumes for the reproduction of scholastic learning taking place at this time in the regional centres of the Delhi Sultanate.

Unlike Seljuqid Iran, no large network of *madrasas* of religious instruction like the *Niẓāmiyā* were developed under the patronage of the Sultan or his Amirs. We chance upon the names of some of the early schools, the Mu'izzī or the Nāṣirī *madrasa* in Delhi, but very little about their endowments, their premises, their teachers, or the kind of juridical and theological training imparted there.[113] Although our search for the institutional forms of a proto-Ottoman system of (religious) education for the Sultanate would be frustratingly unsuccessful, there are random references to instruction and discourses provided by eminent teachers in mosques and hospices throughout the Sultanate. We only need to peruse the quality of Shaykh Sharaf al-Dīn Manerī's letters sent from Maner in Bihar to his disciples and acquaintances all over north India to appreciate the rigour of scholarship and attention to detail present in the pedagogy of these masters.[114] Many of these teachers encompassed a role in the lives of their congregations which was much larger than that of the conventional *mudarris*, teacher; they were instead *Shaikh, buzurg*, venerable masters who taught and provided guidance in more comprehensive life-orienting ways. In the *khānaqāh* of Bābā Farīd in Ajudhan the

[111] Ibid., p. 353.

[112] Jūzjānī, *Ṭabaqāt-i Nāṣirī*, vol. 1, p. 487.

[113] See Chapter 4 for a full discussion and references.

[114] Sharaf al-Dīn Manerī, *The Hundred Letters*, translated by Paul Jackson, s.j. (New York: Paulist Press, 1980).

master taught religious texts to his students, provided exegeses, enforced decorum, punished offenders and, finally provided the accomplished with documents, *ijāzatnāmas,* permitting them to teach specific texts and/or subjects. The *khānaqāh* was more than a school and the *pīr* far more influential in the lives of his students than a teacher. It is not surprising that his followers respectfully and endearingly referred to him as *Shaikh al-Islām*, denoting the final arbiter on matters relating to pedagogy and social conduct.

Bābā Farīd was a part of the entrenched elite of Ajudhan and some times received more visitors at his hospice than he apparently wanted. Beyond Ajudhan was the hospice of Bahā' al-Dīn Zakariyā in Multan, managed by his successors after their father's death. After Shīr Khān's intransigent relationship with the *ṣūfīs* in his province and the misfortunes that apparently resulted from his arrogance, the next Governor of Sindh, Prince Muḥammad, was careful to remain on good terms with the Chishtī and Suhrawardī *pīrs.*[115] This was the moment of rapprochement at which temporal authority recognized the influence of the great *buzurgān* over their spiritual territories, *wilāyats*. Balban tried to ensure that *khānaqāhs* of this stature did not emerge in the core territories of Hindustan, but their impact was already clearly visible. Individuals from Budaun, Delhi, Hansi and Meerut were amongst the many arriving and rendering homage to Bābā Farīd in Ajudhan—now christened 'Pākpattan', the 'holy ferry', in his honour.

How did these spiritual *wilāyats* relate to Hindustan and Delhi? Bābā Farīd reportedly never liked Delhi, hating its press of people and cloistered atmosphere. After his master's death in the capital he hurried away from the city to Hansi and then to Ajudhan, but he sent his disciples to teach in Delhi, not least among whom was Niẓām al-Dīn Awliyā'. He must have arrived in the capital before his master's death in 664/1265, some time towards the end of Balban's reign. The *ṣūfī pīr* Khwāja Gurg, with his hospice in Kara, a town on the banks of the River Ganges (straddling the major riverine trade route from Hindustan to Lakhnauti), was also as uninterested in Delhi, but he

[115] Baranī, *Ta'rīkh-i Fīrūz Shāhī*, edited by Khan, pp. 67–8, edited by Rashid, pp. 79–80.

prophesied that one of his devotees would make his mark in the capital. This disciple was none other than the future Sultan 'Alā al-Dīn Khalajī, one-time Governor of Kara.

Khwāja Gurg claimed a spiritual link with the Suhrawardī saints of Multan, but his decorum and instructions were hardly those of the *Sharī'a*-minded Zakariyā family. In the biographical compendium of Khwāja Gurg, the *ṣūfī* appears as a *majzūb*, a 'madman' so 'drawn away' by divine love that he abandoned the norms of behaviour otherwise incumbent upon all Muslim believers.[116] Khwāja Gurg followed the instructions of Khwāja Khiẓr, the master of many antinomian Shaykhs, and drank wine, miraculously transformed into rosewater. It was, apparently, still a potent drink, but the Khwāja's frequently inebriated state did not interfere with his paranormal activities. He bested opponents, spiritual and temporal, as well as the forces of nature, and possessed powers that would have done an alchemist proud. Khwāja Gurg died in 700/1301 and during his life rarely travelled beyond the immediate vicinity of Kara. He loved the city, praising its climate, its habitat, even its schoolchildren whose writing abilities he thought excelled all others.

The charisma of Khwāja Gurg was associated with Kara; it protected the region which, however humble, was for its residents a special place. Kara, together with Manikpur looked towards Bihar and Lakhnauti in the east, the jungles of Mahoba and Kalinjar to the south, Awadh to its north, and the Ganga–Jamuna *do-āb* to the north-west. This was the transit point for goods coming into Hindustan from the east, as also the centre of campaigns into the *mawās* regions beyond the Ganges and Saryu rivers in the north and to the east, and into Kalinjar in the south. Khwāja Gurg must have witnessed a lot of Sultanate military activity in the region during his lifetime, as well as the rebellion of Balban's nephew Malik Chhajū in 689/1290. Although his *tazkira* suggests that he remained untouched by it all, the new

[116] See Simon Digby, 'Anecdotes of a Provincial Sufi of the Dehli (*sic*) Sultanate, Khwāja Gurg of Kara', *Iran*, 32 (1994), p. 102. Digby identified the title of Khwāja Gurg's *tazkira* as *Asrār al-Majzūbīn* ('The Secrets of those Drawn Away'). The materials on Khwāja Gurg used here are dependent on Digby's summary of the *Asrār al-Majzūbīn.*

Governor of Kara, 'Alā' al-Dīn Khalajī, appointed after the defeat of Malik Chhajū, did become his disciple.[117] As the *Asrār al-Majzūbīn* recounts, the Khalajī Governor recognized the charisma of Khwāja Gurg and brought him gifts. Although these were returned, the mystic was touched by the Governor's submissive behaviour and, in return, conferred the kingdom of Delhi upon his disciple. Khwāja Gurg mentored his disciple on how to escape from the clutches of his uncle, Sultan Jalāl al-Dīn Khalajī (689–95/1290–6), and narrated an account of the Sultan's death that was completely at variance with the narratives of Sultanate chronicles. In the story retold in the *Asrār al-Majzūbīn*, Khwāja Gurg absolved his disciple of any stigma of murder.

At one level, the *Asrār al-Majzūbīn* provides an interesting vignette into the society and beliefs prevalent in a small town on the eastern frontiers of the Sultanate. But the story picks up a pan-regional twist in its links, first with the larger Suhrawardī fraternity of saints in Multan and, subsequently, with the obeisance of the local Governor and the saint's complicity in installing him on the throne of Delhi. Nor was this merely the inebriated delusion of a *majzūb* dervish: 'Iṣāmī, the chronicler of the Delhi Sultans writing in the middle of the fourteenth century in the Deccan, was familiar with the story and reproduced its basic elements in his *Futūḥ al-Salāṭīn*.[118] But it is the manner in which Khwāja Gurg carried his affinity with the city that remained the significant point of the tale. According to the *Asrār al-Majzūbīn,* when the prophecy of Khwāja Gurg came true and 'Alā' al-Dīn, the adopted son of Kara, ascended the throne, he invited his master to Delhi. But the *majzūb* would not leave his beloved Kara. He reportedly replied:

> I am content with dry bread and vegetables;
> My appetite is not for roast meat and lamb.
> Delhi and Samarqand and Bukhara and Iraq.
> You can take them all and leave me Kara![119]

[117] On Malik Chhajū's rebellion at Kara, its suppression, and 'Alā' al-Dīn's appointment, see Baranī, *Ta'rīkh-i Fīrūz Shāhī*, edited by Khan, pp. 181–4, 187.

[118] 'Iṣāmī, *Futūḥ al-Salāṭīn,* p. 229.

[119] Simon Digby, 'Anecdotes of a Provincial Sufi', p. 103.

Ṣūfīs had also promised other Sultans the throne of Delhi, but these, as in the case of Iltutmish and Balban, had been the great Shaykhs of Bukhara.[120] Nor was Khwāja Gurg some itinerant derwish; he was the self-acknowledged *pīr* of Kara and the links of 'Alā' al-Dīn Khalajī to the city underlined the manner in which a one-time resident of the small town had gained the throne of Delhi through the intervention of his spiritual master. In this narrative, the provincial centre had seized the metropole.

The emergence of Khwāja Gurg has a historical specificity; the saint died in 700/1301. But it was also part of a longer history of settlements, migrations, regional politics, and manifestations of local pride. References to Kara multiply from the 640s/1240s as Shamsī Maliks traversed the area in conflict with each other or foraged in neighbouring forests in search of elephants and supplies. Narratives of Sultanate politics easily subvert the history of Kara until it remains no more than a provincial frontier town, whereas the history of such a region ought really to make us question the monolithic representation of Sultanate power emanating from Delhi. The history of Kara and Khwāja Gurg points to the presence of alternative sites of power in north India, not hegemonized by Delhi. These centres produced narrative accounts instead that were deeply proud of their habitat, as well as fully aware of their location in north Indian politics where they had, for the moment, seized the historical initiative. Kara was hardly exceptional in this respect; Bahraich questioned the importance of Delhi in equally fundamental and complex ways.

The background of Sultanate presence in Bahraich is nearly as murky as in Kara. It appears in Jūzjānī's narrative as the city to which Sultan Nāṣir al-Dīn was sent as Governor after his release from prison in 641/1243.[121] The city thereafter gained some notoriety in Jūzjānī's account as the homeland of a clique that sought to dominate Sultanate politics. Raihān, Qutlugh Khān, and their confederates had their political base in Bahraich and they managed to expel Ulugh Khān and his followers from Delhi in 651/1253. As we have already seen, in Jūzjānī's narrative Bahraich was a centre of strife. Local

120 For a useful collation of these stories see idem, 'The Sufi *Shaykh* and the Sultan', pp. 75–6.

121 Jūzjānī, *Ṭabaqāt-i Nāṣirī*, vol. 1, p. 470.

chieftains still controlled the forested hinterlands of the city, with whom—although a problem for Delhi—local Shamsī commanders like Qutlugh Khān, a member of the Bahraichī clique, retained very cordial relations.

Outside the narrow spectrum of Sultanate politics, there were other reasons why Bahraich was important. It had the shrine of the holy warrior Sālār Mas'ūd Ghāzī, popularly known as Ghāzī Miyān. Sālār Mas'ūd Ghāzī's history is completely lost in myth. As far as we can tell, it was provided a formal textual form in a seventeenth-century hagiography of the saint, *Mir'āt-i Mas'ūdī* by 'Abd al-Raḥmān Chishtī. This was a rather stereotypical history of a holy warrior, a *ghāzī*, who had died fighting infidels. The story was important because Sālār Mas'ūd was none other than the nephew of the great iconoclast Sultan Maḥmūd of Ghazni; it was a sad and poignant tale because the young hero was an endearing character, full of passion, unique perhaps because his pious commitment belied his youth. But the story itself was not otherwise remarkably different from accounts that glorified battles fought in the cause of Islam.

Left merely to the penmanship of 'Abd al-Raḥmān Chishtī, Sālār Mas'ūd's story may well have remained a backwater tale. But the author was attempting to historicize the legend of a shrine cult which, in the early seventeenth centuıy, was already several centuries old. The shrine must have existed in Balban's reign; it was visited by Amīr Khusrau when he was in Awadh during the reign of Sultan Kaiqubād (686–9/1287–90).[122] It was certainly a bustling pilgrimage centre when Ibn Baṭṭūṭa arrived there in 742/1341 as a part of Sultan Muḥammad Shāh Tughluq's entourage.[123] No doubt there were tales aplenty about Sālār Mas'ūd in the Middle Ages, and 'Abd al-Raḥmān's text needs to be placed in this context. He was the official historian discovering verifiable materials and trying to establish a

[122] Amīr Khusrau, *I'jāz-i Khusravī*, lithographed edition (Lucknow: Nawal Kishore Press, 1867), vol. 2, p. 155, cited by I.H. Siddiqui, 'A Note on the Dargah of Salar Mas'ud in Bahraich in the Light of the Standard Historical Sources', in Christian W. Troll, ed., *Muslim Shrines in India* (Delhi: Oxford University Press, 1992 reprint), p. 45.

[123] Ibn Baṭṭūṭa, *Rehla*, pp. 109–11.

coherent chronology. His history would provide a reasoned explanation for Sālār Mas'ūd's stature in history and the reason for his popular veneration. His account did not include everything he had heard about Sālār Mas'ūd and it certainly did not reconcile all the myths that had accrued around the saint. [124]

The strands of the vernacular tradition that were absent or severely underplayed in 'Abd al-Raḥmān Chishtī's history related to the locally endearing aspects of Sālār Mas'ūd's persona: the youth who left his wedding incomplete to fight in his last battle against a neighbouring ruler who was attacking his cowherd subjects. In the vernacular tradition much is made of his affinity with *ahir* pastoralists who brought him prestations of milk.[125] This oral tradition was given an ambiguous gloss by 'Abd al-Raḥmān Chishtī: 'The next day they were preparing, when news arrived that the enemy were driving off the cattle. The Prince sprang up like an angry lion, and beat to arms; buckling on his armour and mounting his horse, he himself put his troops into battle array, and advanced to the attack'.[126] Ironically, these traditions that lent the greatest credence to the popularity of the saint in the Bahraich region were also the most difficult to reconcile with the history of a *ghāzī* hero combating infidels.

The fleeting insight into the vernacular significance of Sālār Mas'ūd disturbs 'Abd al-Raḥmān's otherwise rather conventional account, but it points to the facility with which the regional could be quickly appropriated into the Persian cosmopolis. The fracture in 'Abd al-Raḥmān's narrative of holy war seizes our attention for two different reasons: it enables us to push elements of the oral tradition into the seventeenth century, if not earlier; and it alerts us to the possibility of regional political traditions wherein military commanders played several roles. They fought, raided, and demanded tribute from

[124] See 'Abd al-Raḥmān Chishtī, *Mirāt-i Mas'ūdī,* translated by Elliot and Dowson, *The History of India as Told by its Own Historians,* vol. 2, pp. 513–49.

[125] See Shahid Amin, 'On Retelling the Muslim Conquest of North India', in Partha Chatterjee and Anjan Ghosh, *History and the Present* (Delhi: Permanent Black, 2002), pp. 36–8.

[126] 'Abd al-Raḥmān Chishtī, *Mir'āt-i Mas'ūdī,* vol. 2, p. 543.

local rulers; their activities carried all the elements conventionally associated with holy wars against infidels. They were new immigrants to the area but chose to settle in these frontier tracts where they established resilient military bases. They sought to consolidate their political establishments by insinuating themselves in the material economy of the region, some times engaging in and reaching accommodative relationships with neighbouring pastoral groups.

It is interesting, but not altogether surprising, to note that the Persian chronicles of the Sultanate have historical dimensions very similar to 'Abd al-Raḥmān's account of Sālār Mas'ūd. Both provide renditions of different master narratives: in one case eulogies of the holy war fought against infidels, in the other the monolithic Muslim state with a composite ruling elite. And the elisions in both these varieties of texts are extremely difficult to accept without questioning. Jūzjānī's discourse of new territories where Sultanate armies had never travelled before collapses in the face of his own record of Shamsī Maliks who were in alliance with residents and rulers in the inhospitable *mawās*. And 'Abd al-Raḥmān's depiction of Sālār Mas'ūd's *g͟hāzī's* temperament is hard to reconcile with the protagonist's concern for cowherds and their cattle.

The nature of the evidence surrounding the legend of Sālār Mas'ūd makes it extremely difficult to detail the age or provenance of its several constitutive elements. But despite the problems in reportage, what we can evaluate more systematically is the political and social history of the Delhi Sultanate and the Bahraich region through the last quarter of the thirteenth century. And here there is a remarkable coincidence—of on the one hand the growing regional popularity of a *ṣūfī* shrine in the forested sub-Himalayan foothills, and on the other the presence of military elites who relied upon the local terrain and alliances to create a regional stronghold that aspired to challenge the might of the Sultanate.

As I mentioned at the beginning of this discussion, neither the emergence of Sālār Mas'ūd's shrine as a popular pilgrimage centre nor the creation of political alliances seeking to root themselves in local contexts were extraordinary events for the late thirteenth century. Kara and its local *ṣūfīs* accepted 'Alā' al-Dīn K͟halajī as their disciple, and, when the local Governor became Sultan, both honoured their relationship; the *ṣūfī* by rewriting the history of the disciple's brutal actions and the disciple by respecting and acknowledging his debt to his master.

By the end of the thirteenth century, the history of the region and its residents could not be conveniently subsumed in a narrative of Delhi's paramount authority. During Jalāl al-Dīn Khalajī's reign (689–95/1290–6), a *ṣūfī* who a half-century earlier would have suffered immediate expulsion from Delhi at the hands of Iltutmish's *Shaikh al-Islām*, established a flourishing hospice in the capital. Sīdī Muwallih had actually come to the city towards the beginning of Balban's reign, but according to Baranī it was not until his death and Jalāl-al-Dīn's accession that the rich and the famous started thronging to his residence.[127] Apparently Sīdī Muwallih, in consorting with the political elite, disregarded Bābā Farīd's advice and became fatally involved in a conspiracy to depose the Sultan. Unlike other pious offenders in the past who had similarly tried to exercise their charismatic authority in the capital. Sīdi Muwallih was executed and not exiled. In the difference with which *ṣūfī* aspirations to power were treated earlier and later lay the distance between the Sultanate of the early and the late thirteenth century.

As we have seen through this chapter, Balban's efforts to 'restore' the authority of Delhi had to be charted in territorial spaces, over social groups and political dispensations that had come to possess their own histories and stable locations. This was one reason why the processes involved in the reconstitution of the Sultanate were so violent and so unstable in monopolizing power in the long duration. The chroniclers of the Delhi Sultans were cognizant of these developments even if they did not want to theorize its implications. In their histories of the reign of 'Alā' al-Dīn Khalajī, a Sultan recognized by Baranī and Amīr Khusrau as one of the most powerful and effective rulers of the Sultanate, the authors genuflected towards both the Delhi Sultan and the reigning Sultan of Shaykhs in the city: Niẓām al-Dīn Awliyā', the disciple of the humble *ṣūfī pīr* of distant Ajudhan,

[127] Baranī, *Ta'rīkh-i Fīrūz Shāhī*, edited by Khan, pp. 208-12. On the background of the Muwallihs and Qalandars more generally see Simon Digby, 'Qalandars and Related Groups: Elements of Social Deviance in the Religious Life of the Delhi Sultanate, pp. 60–108.

who arrived in Delhi during the last years of Balban's reign. Through his ministry in the city, Delhi became the site of one of the most powerful mystical fraternities in the subcontinent. All of Balban's efforts to keep the core areas of the Sultanate free of *ṣūfī khanaqāhs* could not neutralize the changes that had occurred in the Sultanate through the thirteenth century. The province was again flexing its power in the metropole; neither its power nor its history would ever be the same again.

Conclusion

An impatient reader of this book might justifiably ask with exasperation at this moment: 'So, Sweetie, when *did* the Delhi Sultanate emerge?' This is a difficult question. Perhaps the most reasonable answer is 626/1229, the year after the definitive conquest of the 'north Indian Sultanates', when immigrants fleeing from the Mongol invasions had started arriving in large numbers in the cities of the Sultanate, also the year the investiture from the 'Abbāsid Caliph reached Delhi and the 'renovations' in the Delhi *masjid-i jāmi'* were almost finished. But this book will not please the impatient reader wanting straight answers. There are no clear linearities within complex and convoluted processes of historical change, and the instabilities and flux of our period would try the patience of a saint. The reader must therefore be warned against assuming that, after having once emerged, the Sultanate remained unchanged. This book has in fact attempted to chart how, from very small and humble beginnings, the Sultanate assumed a vast historical dimension, until its relatively circumscribed name, the *Delhi* Sultanate, hampered, rather than helped, a proper appreciation of its late-thirteenth-century character.

Having said this, it might be interesting to pursue a slightly different but related question: 'When did the Delhi Sultanate seize a historiographical space in the history of India?' The question assumes the presence of two different but immanent entities, at least in the historiographical imagination: a domain, if not a nation state, called India; and a Delhi Sultanate—a state whose history was coterminous with 'India'.

The chroniclers of the Delhi Sultans could project the domains of the Delhi Sultanate quite early on a mental map of north India, and even though Jūzjānī's formulation that Sultanate territories extended from Dewal to Lakhnauti was imprecise, it was not wholly inaccurate. Together with territorial clarity, there was also considerable chronological precision about the genealogy of the Delhi Sultanate: barring 'Iṣāmī, who placed the origins of the Sultanate in the early eleventh century, in the reign of Sultan Maḥmūd of Ghazni, all the other pre-Mughal chroniclers writing 'general histories' recognized its connections with the Shansabanid regime of Ghur. Their histories started with the campaigns of Mu'izz al-Dīn and concluded with events contemporaneous with the author's lifetime. But these histories did not try to locate the Sultanate in the subcontinent; they expanded and diminished with their King-protagonists. Jūzjānī's *Ṭabaqāt* took its readers into details of Lakhnauti, and 'Iṣāmī's *Futūḥ al-Salaṭīn* into the Deccan, but only because the author travelled or settled in the region. Some of the Persian chroniclers were certainly familiar with the extent of the subcontinent, its provinces and languages, but their texts were not histories of these regions.[128]

Sultanate histories were, therefore, the accounts of Sultans, not dominions; and, as the discussion in the appendix underlines, there were remarkable differences in style and content amongst them. Since Baranī's *Ta'rīkh* was so different in style and intent from Jūzjānī's *Ṭabaqāt,* the former did not really 'continue' the narrative of the latter. What remained from the Sultanate period were fractured, regnal accounts. Even a text like 'Iṣāmī's *Futūḥ al-Salāṭīn*, which had the greatest chronological span amongst the histories (see Appendix and Chart 3), provided a sequential genealogy of Muslim rulers from Maḥmūd of Ghazni to 'Alā' al-Dīn Bahman Shāh, not a history of the domains ruled by these monarchs.

The fundamental transitions in the historiographical representation of the Delhi Sultanate occurred during the process of consolidation of the Mughal empire in the later years of Akbar's reign (963-1014/1556–1605). The timing was important because the establishment and consolidation of the Mughal empire in the sixteenth century was

[128] For a collation of these accounts see Peter Jackson, *The Delhi Sultanate*, pp. 146–7.

the theme of a large number of 'general' histories contextualizing the larger-than-life historical persona of the Mughal *pādshāh* in a succession of past rulers. Although the flamboyant prosody and poetics of *manāqib* literature were usually preferred for eulogies of the Delhi Sultans, Akbar favoured the narrative techniques of 'general history' as the apposite medium to extol the significance of his achievements. Together with intrusive administrative innovations, history provided the grand context to appreciate the momentous departures in governance introduced by the Mughal emperor. But first the major characteristics and attributes of Akbar and his reign had to be developed, an official representation which was put together after some experimentation.

Akbar's initial statements of sovereignty were reflective of strong *Sunnī* Islamic overtones, but, as S.A.A. Rizvi and more recently Iqtidar Alam Khan and Muzaffar Alam have pointed out, there was a considerable dilution of this sentiment by the late 980s/1570s.[129] Through the 990s/1580s, with the support of the siblings Faiẓī and Abū' al-Faẓl, Akbar focused on the development of a more universalistic, confessionally ambiguous concept of authority embodied in the principles of *ṣulḥ-i kul* or 'peace with all'.

These ideological statements were provided contextual underpinnings in two different but complementary histories: Abū' al-Faẓl's *Akbar Nāma* (completed 1004/1595–6) and Niẓām al-Dīn Aḥmad's *Ṭabaqāt-i Akbarī* (completed 1001/1592–3). The *Akbar Nāma* detailed Akbar's sacred Mughal pedigree, his successful campaigns, administrative achievements, wide-ranging intellect, and other personal qualities—accomplishments which were all seen as proof of God's favour. This was not a huge 'general' history of Muslim rulers, and it therefore did not provide a history of the Delhi Sultans. Through its careful development of Akbar's qualities as a leader, however, the

[129] S.A.A. Rizvi, *Religious and Intellectual History of the Muslims in Akbar's Reign with Special Reference to Abu'l Faẓl (1556–1605)* (Delhi: Munshiram Manoharlal Publishers Pvt. Ltd., 1975); Iqtidar Alam Khan. 'Akbar's Personality Traits and World Outlook—A Critical Approach', in Irfan Habib, ed., *Akbar and His Age* (Delhi: Oxford University Press, 1997), pp. 79–96 and Muzaffar Alam, *The Languages of Political Islam* (Delhi: Permanent Black, 2004).

Akbar Nāma distinguished the Mughal emperor from all preceding rulers. Abū' al-Faẓl's description and praise of Akbar's confessional ambiguity, for example, placed his cultural pragmatism in dealing with infidel others as one of the defining traits of his regime. As Muzaffar Alam has argued, the intellectual roots of Mughal confessional ambiguity go beyond Akbar and Abū' al-Faẓl to the *a<u>kh</u>lāqī* notions of ethical practice, first expressed by Nāṣīr al-Dīn Ṭūsī in the mid-thirteenth century during the Mongol domination of Iran. In Alam's argument, the pragmatic, non-sectarian nature of *a<u>kh</u>lāqī* morality gave Mughal authors the confidence to celebrate an 'Indianess' without jeopardizing their 'Muslim, Mughal', and 'Persian' identities.[130] Although he may not have been the first or only proponent of this aspect of Mughal ideology, Abū' al-Faẓl was perhaps its most influential and lucid exponent. Because of his ability to demarcate Akbar's reign as a distinct, transitory moment in history, Abū' al-Faẓl was also able to draw the attention of the reader to the unique 'Mughal' antecedents of Akbar, a far richer heritage than the Delhi Sultans.

The specific differences between the two historical periods—the Sultanate and the Mughal—were developed in Niẓām al-Dīn Aḥmad's *Ṭabaqāt-i Akbarī*. The author's agenda was to provide a 'general' history which situated Akbar in the history of his conquered dominions. There was a dire need for such a work because, as the author explained, a fairly connected history of *Hindūstān* could be gathered from the writings of Jūzjānī and Baranī until Fīrūz Shāh Tu<u>gh</u>luq's reign (752–90/1351–88). For the subsequent years, however, political fragmentation in north India was reflected in the histories of the period: 'great disturbances have taken place in this country, the people have not had the good fortune to be ruled by any great Kings, and

[130] Muzaffar Alam, *The Languages of Political Islam*. In the late seventeenth and eighteenth centuries this sensibility allowed for the production of general histories like Banwālī Dās' (died 1085/1674–5) *Rājāwalī*, a linear account of Hindu rulers of Delhi from Yudhishtar to the Ghurids, and a briefer account of the later Sultans and Mughal *pādshāhs*. Similarly, Munshī Sujān Rāy Bhandarī's *<u>Kh</u>ulāsat al-Tawāri<u>kh</u>* (completed 1107/1695–6) carried a section on Hindu rulers, and celebrated the geography, fauna, and produce of *Hindūstān* at great length.

despite repeated searches the humble writer has only come across fragmentary histories'.[131] Disunity, dissension, and, as a result, narrow, local interests circumscribed historical imagination in the politically fragmented world of the late fourteenth and fifteenth centuries. According to Niẓām al-Dīn, the horizons could only expand during the reign of Akbar, and 'now that all the provinces and divisions of Hindustan have been conquered by the world-opening sword of His Majesty . . . and the many have been unified into the one . . . a comprehensive history', to reflect the altered political contexts was required.[132]

Niẓām al-Dīn Aḥmad accepted the challenge of providing a history of this new world. He divided his 'general' history into nine sections, *ṭabaqāt*, each relating to one of the regions incorporated by Akbar into his empire. The core of the text was the first section, which narrated the history of Delhi from Sebuktegin, Maḥmūd of Ghazni's father, to Akbar's accession. The remaining sections provided the history of the kingdoms of the Deccan, Gujarat, Malwa, Bengal, Jaunpur, Kashmir, Sindh, and Multan, from the moment of their independence from the Delhi Sultanate to their return to the parent fold. It was, in other words, a history of how the 'seven climates . . . [of *Hindūstān*] bec[a]me the abode of peace and quiet under the shadow of His Majesty's auspicious standard'.[133] This was, perhaps, the first occasion that *Hindūstān* was used to define regions beyond the 'core territories' of the Sultanate to include all of north India and the peripheral Deccan lands as well.

The *Ṭabaqāt-i Akbarī* marked the hesitant first moments of a new historiographical representation of 'Indian' history. Certainly, this was not a history of the 'people' of *Hindūstān* as modern scholars would interpret it, but, beyond this anachronistic expectation, Niẓām al-Dīn's ability to conceive the subcontinent as a geographical and political entity associated with a state far exceeded the historical imagination of his peers, who still thought in regnal units. In his argument, *Hindūstān* was conceived as a state, first under the Sultanate and, after its fragmentation, reunited once again under the Mughals.

131 Niẓām al-Dīn Aḥmad, *Ṭabaqāt*-i *Akbarī*, vol. 1, pp. 2–3.

132 Ibid., vol. 1, p. 3.

133 Ibid.

But the territorial congruence, the link in the narrative between the Delhi Sultanate and Akbar, did not detract from the huge differences between the Delhi Sultans and the Mughal monarch. Whereas the history of the Delhi Sultans was punctuated by years of instability, incompetent monarchs, and rebellions, the reign of Akbar impressed readers with its sagacity and dynamic initiative. Abū' al-Faẓl's triumphant description of Akbar's ideology of *ṣulḥ-i kul*, 'peace with all', served to underline Niẓām al-Dīn's description of a 'brave new [Mughal] world'. The Mughals were, therefore, more than just the inheritors of the Sultanate imperium; they improved it by removing its imperfections.

An even more comprehensive form to this history of *Hindūstān* was provided by Muḥammad Qāsim Firishtā in his *Gulshan-i Ibrāhīmī* (final recension completed *ca.* 1019/1609–10). Firishtā's history was written in the Deccan, in the court of the Sultan of Bijapur, Ibrāhīm 'Adil Shāh (988–1037/1580–1627), and it was dependent on the *Ṭabaqāt-i Akbarī* for a lot of its information and narrative form. Firishtā's history, however, was not simply derivative; one of its aims was to remove the imbalances and biases present in earlier histories of the subcontinent. The criticism was implicitly directed towards texts like the *Ṭabaqāt-i Akbarī* and their obsession with north India. Firishtā's account of the Deccan Sultanates of Gulbarga, Bijapur, Ahmadnagar, Telingana, Berar, and Bidar, and his shorter excerpts on Khandesh and Malabar, focused the historian's attention on a neglected area. Significantly, Firishtā's history included all those provinces that were, for the better part, still outside Mughal suzerainty. This caveat served to weaken the central theme of the inexorable progress of Mughal arms present in the history of Niẓām al-Dīn Aḥmad.

It is important to note, however, that neither the incorporation of the Deccan realms within the cognitive world of Persian 'general' histories, nor the expression of doubt concerning Mughal claims to universal hegemony, provoked Firishtā to further question the importance of Delhi advocated in Niẓām al-Dīn's history of *Hindūstān*. Instead, Firishtā's text suggested that, even prior to the Sultanate, in the earliest years of state formation in the subcontinent, Delhi possessed an axial importance in subcontinental politics. The introduction to the *Gulshan-i Ibrāhīmī* carried a report on the pre-Islamic rulers of India, a novelty, because its historical, chronological format departed from the usual cultural accounts on 'Hindu beliefs and practices' provided by historians such as Abū' al-Faẓl. Firishtā introduced his readers to the *yugas*, the ages into which Hindus divide time from eternity. The various characteristics and the number of each *yuga* was mentioned until the *Dvāpara yuga* when the author narrated the history of the Pandavas, rulers of ancient Delhi, and their conflict with the Kauravas as described in the story of the *Mahābhārat*.[134] After perambulating over subsequent conflicts and other rulers of north India, Firishtā's narrative concluded with Maldeo, the ruler of Qanauj and Delhi, after whom 'no single raja ruled over India' until the Delhi Sultans.[135] His commitment to the cause of south Indian history notwithstanding, Firishtā provided an account of the ancient past of the subcontinent without straying beyond the environs of the Gangetic plains. As a result, the Delhi Sultans could be posited as the chronological successors to the rulers of yore; these were Kings who completed the enterprise of 'Muslim' conquests initiated by the Arabs and the Ghaznavids, and went further by extending their dominion over south India. The Delhi Sultans restored both political unity within the subcontinent and authority to Delhi, accomplishments which the Mughals could not match.

The narratives of both authors gave pride of place to the Delhi Sultans in different ways. It was in their usage of information and in the framing of a Sultanate history, however, that they shared many elements and made significant departures from preceding 'general' histories. Unlike late Sultanate historians like Yaḥyā Sirhindī and Bihāmad Khānī,[136] for example, Niẓām al-Dīn and Firishtā went beyond a simple cut-and-paste methodology in their usage of information from the chronicles and histories of the thirteenth and fourteenth

[134] Muḥammad Qāsim Firishtā, *Gulshan-i Ibrāhīmī*, translated by John Briggs (Delhi: Low Price Publications, 1990 reprint), vol. 1, p. xlv.

[135] Ibid., vol. 1, p. lxiii.

[136] Yaḥyā Sirhindī, *Ta'rīkhi-Mubārak Shāhī* and Muḥammad Bihāmad Khānī, *Ta'rīkh-i Muḥammadī*, B [illegible] ms, Ot. 137, partial translation by Muḥammda Zaki (Aligarh: Centre for Advanced Study, Department of History, 1972).

centuries. Theirs was a more sophisticated effort at providing a connected narrative, paraphrasing and elucidating details and developments absent or unclear in the original 'sources'. It would be a mistake to belittle this exercise; the lacunae in information, distinct literary styles, and historical approaches of the thirteenth- and fourteenth-century Persian texts militated against the production of a connected narrative. As a result, the history of the Delhi Sultanate could hardly be 'retold' on the basis of the available 'sources'; gaps had to be bridged, their separate narrative styles had to be pruned, and 'relevant facts' identified before the contours of a Sultanate history could be defined.

In this exercise some sources were clearly more valuable in providing a coherent, workable narrative, and both Niẕām al-Dīn and Firishtā seized upon Ẓiyā' al-Dīn Baranī's *Ta'rīkh-i Fīrūz Shāhī* as a model around which the history of the Sultanate could be written. Baranī had already done much of the hard analytical work for the historian, and his text carried an even mixture of heroic personalities, impersonal institutional agencies, and divine retribution, all of which, in differing measures, were believed to have shaped the course of history in the thirteenth and fourteenth centuries. It was a readable text, short on detail but full of edifying morals which possessed a seemingly timeless, universal relevance. Since the text was already quite accessible to the historian, it merely required paraphrasing and the deletion of some of Baranī's more trenchant moral observations. For the years prior to 664/1266, which were not covered by Baranī, the two authors chose the 'authoritative source' of Jūzjānī's *Ṭabaqāt-i Nāṣirī*. Baranī, himself, had strongly recommended Jūzjānī's history and it was the only text which provided a connected narrative of the twelfth and the thirteenth centuries. Jūzjānī's text, however, needed to be edited to appear like Baranī's. Not merely did a mass of detail need to be removed and the crowd of actors cleared to identify the principal characters, but the text had to be provided a sequential chronology before a coherent narrative could emerge. This is where the intervention of Niẕām al-Dīn and Firishtā needs to be appreciated. The two authors rewrote the texts, flattening dissimilar narratives into a seamless whole. As a result, the *ṭabaqāt* and didactic forms present in the respective texts of Jūzjānī and Baranī were edited into a more conventional chronicler mode. The end product was close enough to the original works to carry the semblance of an authoritative replication, and silent enough in its editorial craftsmanship to conceal the manner in which the texts had been reworked. The *Ṭabaqāt-i Akbarī* and the *Gulshan-i Ibrāhīmī* were seemingly comprehensive in their details and, as British historians of the eighteenth and nineteenth centuries argued, far more accessible to the reader than the sources themselves.

The historiographic intervention of texts like the *Ṭabaqāt-i Akbarī* and the *Gulshan-i Ibrāhīmī* in the writing of Indian history has not been carefully studied. These were the texts, especially Firishtā's, that British colonialists appropriated as they sought to learn about India's past. Colonel Alexander Dow published the first (partial) translation of Firishtā into English in 1768,[137] followed very quickly by the translations of Jonathan Scott in 1794.[138] With our concerns, today, to trace the impact of the colonial archive on the formulation of Indian history, we tend to lose the many ways in which a prior Mughal intervention placed the Delhi Sultanate very centrally in our narratives of Indian history. The privileging of the authority of the Delhi state in the history of India had its own historical and political

[137] Colonel Alexander Dow, *The History of Hindostan from the Earliest Account of Time to the Death of Akbar; Translated from the Persian of Mahummud Casim Ferishta Together with a Dissertation Concerning the Religion and Philosophy of the Brahmins. With an Appendix Containing the History of the Mogul Empire from its Decline in the Reign of Mahummud Shau to the Present Time* (London, 1768, 2 volumes). He published a third volume in 1792 titled: *The History of Hindostan from the Death of Akbar (compiled from various writers) to the Settlement of the Empire under Aurangzebe to which are Prefixed a Dissertation on the nature of Despotism in Hindustan and an Enquiry into the state of Bengal with a Plan for Restoring that Kingdom to its Former Prosperity and Splendour* (London, 1792, vol. 3).

[138] Jonathan Scott, *Ferishta's History of Dekkan, from the First Mahummedan Conquests: with a Continuation from other Native Writers of the Events in that Part of India to the Reduction of its Last Monarchs by the Emperor Aulumgeer Aurungzebe; also, The Reigns of his Successors in the Empire of Hindostan to the Present Day: And the History of Bengal, from the Accession of Aliverdee Khan to the year 1780* (London: 1794).

compulsions for the Mughals, and its form often differed from Sultanate narratives. The politics of the reproduction of Sultanate history has a long past, and one of the defining arguments of the present book, which I hope is sufficiently evident in its writing, is that we must remain sensible to this politics within our own narratives.

APPENDIX

Persian Literary Traditions and Narrativizing the Delhi Sultanate

In contrast to the relatively sparse information for north India over the seventh through twelfth centuries, the diversity and volume of source materials increase dramatically for the thirteenth and fourteenth centuries. As in the study of earlier centuries, scholars working on the Delhi Sultanate continue to value numismatic, epigraphic, and architectural evidence. But the real transition in the writing of the history of the thirteenth and fourteenth centuries occurs because of the larger availability of Persian texts that are self-reflectively historical in character. For the modern historian, these sources introduce a representation of the past which is unmatched in continuity and focus, a perspective into the past seldom evaluated historiographically.

Chart 3 provides a list of some of the Persian texts completed in the thirteenth and early fourteenth centuries. It gives the conventional information that most historians seek about the primary sources they use: a sense of the different times in which these volumes were compiled, the various patrons for whom they were produced, and the years which their narratives span.

Not all of these texts, however, were equally used to write a history of the Delhi Sultans. To begin with, modern historians have often distinguished between what they regarded as 'historical', 'religious/hagiological', and 'literary' sources. 'Historical' sources were identified as much by their self-avowed claim as part of the 'historical' (*ta'rīkh*, plural: *tawārikh*) genre as they were by their chronological narrative style and their subjects: a concern with statecraft and with the personalities, events, and politics of Kings and their subordinates. In other words, a rather narrow understanding of political history led most modern historians to confirm some literary texts as 'historical' sources valuable for a reconstruction of the history of the Delhi Sultanate. These texts are identified in Chart 3 as ■.

Even a cursory look at this body of evidence drives home a couple of rather significant points. First, with the sole exception of 'Iṣāmī's *Futūḥ al-Salāṯīn*, completed 751/1350, all these texts were written or focused upon events from the perspective of Delhi. Second, they were all, without exception, dedicated to a royal patron. In their choice of 'historical sources', modern scholars therefore relied upon literature which possessed a singular contextual reference: a world where little existed outside the Delhi court and things touched by it.

Less obvious from the information conveyed by Chart 3 is the extreme unevenness in the details supplied by this body of literature on the affairs of the Delhi Sultans themselves. This is most clearly apparent in the lacunae in our material, namely years for which there is an absolute silence in the literary records. No chronicle, for example, covers the period 658–64/1260–6, crucial years which concern the circumstances surrounding the death of Sultan Nāṣir al-Dīn Maḥmūd and the accession of Sultān Ghiyāṣ al-Dīn Balban. For other years there is scant information: the only event recorded by Sulta-nate chroniclers from Quṯb al-Dīn Ai-Beg's reign (602–7/1206–10)—other than his death—concerned his disastrous attempt to annex Ghazni. Nor is it easy to establish a reliable chronology for huge periods of the thirteenth and fourteenth centuries. Basic inform-ation, such as the sequence of events for the reigns of Ghiyāṣ al-Dīn Balban, Mu'izz al-Dīn Kaiqubād, Jalāl al-Dīn Khalajī, 'Alā'al-Dīn Khalajī, and Mubārak Shāh Khalajī (664–720/1266–1320) exists only in the most rudimentary form.

Arranging the so-called 'historical sources' in Chart 3 according to the chronological periods of their composition and the time spans they covered helps to draw attention to some of the gaps in our material. But such an arrangement also creates the impression that these texts belonged to a common literary tradition and that their narratives flowed sequentially into each other. This is far from true. Perhaps the most significant 'fact' that Chart 3 obscures is the extent to which the texts identified as 'historical sources' constituted a patchwork of

Chart 3: Selected Sources

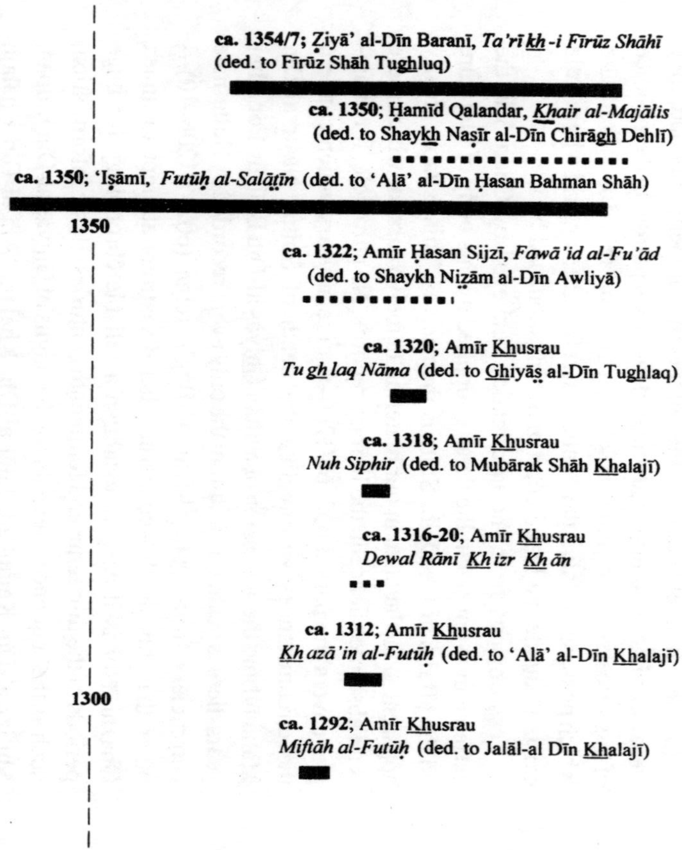

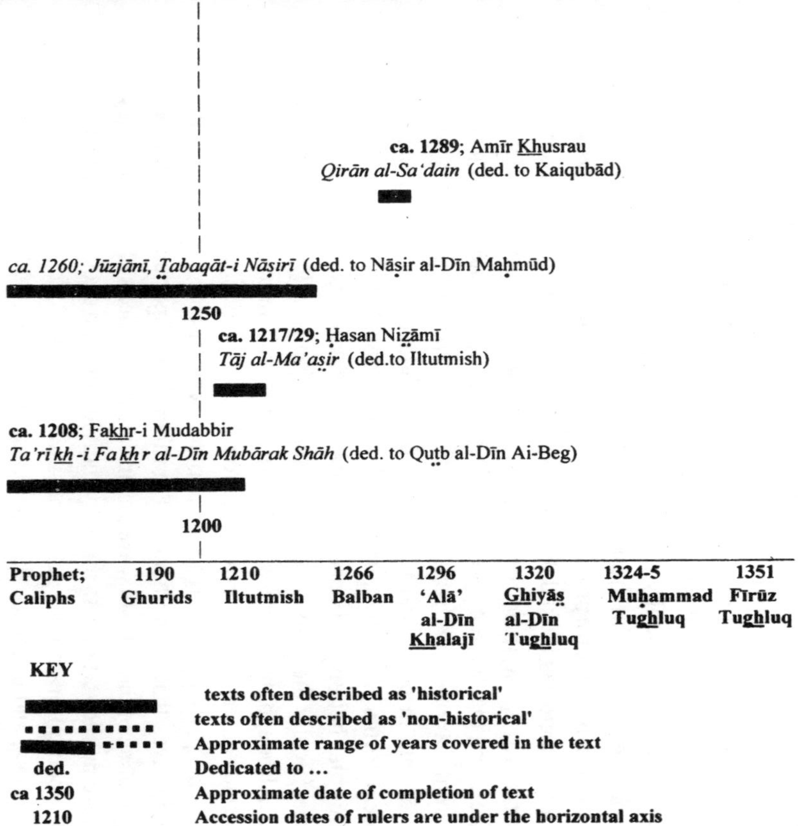
ca. 1289; Amīr Khusrau
Qirān al-Sa'dain (ded. to Kaiqubād)
ca. 1260; Jūzjānī, Tabaqāt-i Nāṣirī (ded. to Nāṣir al-Dīn Maḥmūd)
1250
ca. 1217/29; Ḥasan Nizāmī
Tāj al-Ma'asir (ded.to Iltutmish)
ca. 1208; Fakhr-i Mudabbir
Ta'rīkh-i Fakhr al-Dīn Mubārak Shāh (ded. to Qutb al-Dīn Ai-Beg)
1200
Prophet; Caliphs
1190 Ghurids
1210 Iltutmish
1266 Balban
1296 'Alā' al-Dīn Khalajī
1320 Ghiyās al-Dīn Tughluq
1324-5 Muḥammad Tughluq
1351 Fīrūz Tughluq
KEY
texts often described as 'historical'
texts often described as 'non-historical'
Approximate range of years covered in the text
ded. Dedicated to ...
ca 1350 Approximate date of completion of text
1210 Accession dates of rulers are under the horizontal axis

different narrative styles, techniques, and subject matter. There is little connection between texts even when, like Baranī's *Ta'rīkh-i Fīrūz Shāhī*, they were supposed to pick up the narrative strands of an earlier chronicle. If we were to ignore the often arbitrary distinctions between different types of sources introduced by modern historians and include, for example, texts identified as 'religious/ hagiological', then the range, variety, and complexity within the literature of this period would increase even further. It is only when we recognize the variegated nature of the literary record from the thirteenth and fourteenth centuries that we can start to appreciate the extent to which modern historiography simplified the complexity of the medieval world represented in these texts.

Persian literature produced in north India in the thirteenth and fourteenth centuries looked westwards to Iran and the Islamic traditions for its formal stylistic conventions. The four broad genres of Persian literature that were manifest in this period can be categorized as different varieties of 'general histories', *ta'rīkh*; florid, panegyrical accounts in prose and verse, *manāqib*; didactic texts enlarging on ideal norms of conduct, *ādāb*; and instructional literature concerning spiritual beliefs and conduct (broadly speaking, *ishārat* literature), specifically the conversations of *ṣūfī* teachers, *malfūẓ*.

Although the choice of narrative styles was influenced by the different personal stylistic modes favoured by each author, the preference of one particular genre over another was directed equally by the objectives that the authors had in mind. It is important to remember that none of these texts were the private ruminations of recluses; they were public statements made by individuals who occupied (or sought to occupy) prominent public positions. Their work aimed to edify, impress, and influence the manner in which their audience reflected upon their present and their past. They were interactive mediums, read aloud to an audience rather than consumed individually, trying to impress the medieval reader (and listener) with the skills of the author, educating, elucidating, and contouring the perception of their audience.

Of the four broad genres into which much of the literary output of the thirteenth and fourteenth century can be consolidated, the literary genre most read by modern historians is the *tawārīkh*. These were histories written as a long narrative of human experience, a 'general history', commencing either with Adam the first Prophet, or Muḥammad the last Prophet, and terminating in the lifetime of the respective authors with a eulogy to their patron. Within the genre of 'general' or 'universal histories' can be included the work of Fakhr-i Mudabbir and Minhāj al-Dīn Sirāj Jūzjānī. Their histories differ greatly in length and internal organization. Fakhr-i Mudabbir's history was very brief and served as an introduction to his genealogical tables, *Shajara-i Ansāb*, where only the barest outline of the early history of the Muslim community was provided. Its coverage of the early thir-teenth century and the culture of the ruling elite was only slightly denser. Only the introductory portion of Fakhr-i Mudabbir's *Shajara-i Ansāb*—the historical section—was edited and published by E.D. Ross under the incorrect title *Ta'rīkh-i Fakhr al-Dīn Mubarak Shāh.*[1] By contrast, Jūzjānī's *Ṭabaqāt-i Nāṣirī* was far more detailed, espe-cially in its narration of events after 625/1228, when the author mig-rated to Delhi.

Jūzjānī established a considerable reputation as a jurist, preacher, and litterateur in his own lifetime. His *Ṭabaqāt-i Nāṣirī* is unusual because it is not structured within a simple chronological, regnal, or dynastic framework. Instead, Jūzjānī organized his narrative around groups of people who shared, in his opinion, a common social affinity. The 'bonding' could have been a product of ties of service,

[1] For a description of Fakhr-i Mudabbir's work, see Peter Hardy, 'Some Studies in pre-Mughal Historiography', in *Historians of India, Pakistan and Ceylon*, ed. C.H. Philips (London: Oxford University Press, 1961), pp. 116–17; and, on the author, see M.S. Khan, 'The Life and Works of Fakhr-i Mudabbir', *Islamic Culture*, 51 (1977), pp. 127–40. Fakhr-i Mudabbir wrote another text, 'Customs of War and Valour', or *Ādāb al-Ḥarb wa al-Shujā'a*, ed. Suhayli Khwansari. Portions of the variant India Office manuscript, entitled, *Ādāb al-Mulūk wa Kifāyat al-Mamlūk*, or the 'Custom of Kings and Maintenance of the Subjects', was edited by Muḥammad Sarwar Maulavi. For a brief survey, see A.K.S. Lambton, 'Islamic Mirror for Princes', *Atti del Convegno Internazionale sul Tema: La Persia nel Medioevo* (Rome: Academia Nazionale dei Lincei, 1971), pp. 438–9; M.S. Khan, cited above, and Sunil Kumar, 'The Value of the *Ādāb al-Mulūk* as a Historical Source: An Insight into the Ideals and Expectations of Islamic Society in the Middle Period (945–1500)', *Indian Economic and Social History Review*, 22 (1985), pp. 307–27.

region, or kinship. The thirteenth-century Sultans of Delhi were, for example, divided into two groups, the Mu'izzī and the Shamsī Sultans. The first shared ties of service as slaves of Mu'izz al-Dīn Ghūrī and the second were descendants of Shams al-Dīn Iltutmish. In Jūzjānī's analysis, however, kinship did not automatically imply the presence of a corporate social sensibility. His account of the Shansabanid family of Ghur was divided into three separate sections and it drew the reader's attention to the manner in which collateral lineages of the family struggled to preserve their independent political spheres in their respective principalities of Ghur, Bamiyan, and Ghazni. This also implied that the *Ṭabaqāt-i Nāṣirī* sometimes covered events of the same period from the perspective of different actors and geographical regions. To arrive at a coherent account of Sultan Mu'izz al-Dīn Ghūrī's reign (569–602/1173–1206), for example, the modern historian would minimally need to read the seventeenth through twenty-third sections. These covered the history of the Shansabanid Sultans of Ghur, Bamiyan, and Ghazni, the Mu'izzī and Shamsī Sul-tans, the Shamsī Maliks, and an account of the Mongol invasions. Jūzjānī's narrative clarified how Mu'izz al-Dīn intervened on different occasions or influenced the histories of these regions. The author, however, did not merely 'repeat' events from Mu'izz al-Dīn's reign in different parts of the chronicle; he sought to place them within their own distinct spatial and historical contexts.[2]

While the *Ṭabaqāt-i Nāṣirī* provides an insight into the histories of a variety of different important personalities and regions, it remains a testament to the glory and might of the Sultans of Delhi. Here, Jūzjānī's work is very similar to that of Fakhr-i Mudabbir. The *Ṭabaqāt-i Nāṣirī* is dedicated to the exemplary Sultan Nāṣir al-Dīn Maḥmūd (644–64/1246–66), and venerated the memory and achievements of his ancestors.[3] The *Shajara-i Ansāb* is dedicated to Quṭb

[2] Thus, Harbans Mukhia, *Historians and Historiography during the Reign of Akbar*, p. 3. On the *ṭabaqāt* genre see Rosenthal, *History of Muslim Historiography*, pp. 93–5; Louise Marlow, *Hierarchy and Egalitarianism in Islamic Thought*, pp. 9–10; and Tarif Khalidi, *Arabic Historical Thought in the Classical Period*, pp. 44–9.

[3] Other than from Sultan Nāṣir al-Dīn, Jūzjānī also received support from Ulugh Khān, the future Sultan Balban (664–85/1266–86), who also received

al-Dīn Ai-Beg (regnal years, 602–7/1206–10), the possessor of all moral virtues, and the special choice of his master to govern the provinces of north India. Despite differences in internal organization, the genre of 'universal history' facilitated the production of a linear narrative wherein the prosperous and stable realm of the incumbent ruler of Delhi was the consummate glory of the history of the Muslim community.

As an alternative, texts written in a florid, stylized, panegyrical style were quite different from the rather dry *histoire evenementielle* which was the staple of the 'universal histories'. Although the Delhi Sultans (or other political elites) commissioned a large number of the texts in the *manāqib* genre, they were written in verse or extremely elaborate prose, with alliteration, metaphors, and tangential forays into philosophy and religion which left the court and the Sultans as mute witnesses in their huge, colourful canvases. There was an enormous range within these texts as well. Some were organized around specific themes: the success of Ghurid arms and the establishment of the Delhi Sultanate (Ḥasan Niẓāmī), the romantic obsession of a Prince (Amīr Khusrau), the campaigns of Jalal al-Dīn Khalajī (689–95/1290–6), and the victories of 'Alā' al-Dīn Khalajī (695–715/1296–1316) (Amīr Khusrau). Others were florid accounts produced to report a precise event: the meeting of Sultan Kaiqubād (685–9/1286–90) with his father, or the events surrounding the accession of Ghiyāṣ al-Dīn Tughluq (720/1320) (Amīr Khusrau). Exceptional within this genre was 'Iṣāmī's *Futūḥ al-Salāṭīn*, a huge historical account in verse of the Ghaznavid, Ghurid, and Delhi Sultans, covering events from the tenth through fourteenth centuries. Completed in 751/1350 at the court of Sultan 'Alā' al-Dīn Bahman Shāh in the Deccan, it emulated the great Persian epic—Firdausī's *Shāh Nāma*, in style and metre.

While appreciating the literary skills of these authors, modern historians have bemoaned the scant 'evidence' on the Delhi Sultanate provided by most of these texts. Peter Hardy's characterization of the *manāqib* genre as one which 'subordinate[s] history to art and treat[s]

---

a very favourable mention in the *Ṭabaqāt-i Nāṣirī*. See Jūzjānī, *Ṭabaqāt-i Nāṣirī*, vol. 1, pp. 479–81, 483, 486–7, 489–92, 494, 496; vol. 2, pp. 47–88.

treat[s] the past as raw material for the poetic imagination' sums up the general attitude of modern historians to these texts. The formalised, stylised treatment of heroes and villains, victory and defeat, the pleasures and vicissitudes of life, nature in all its glory, and the finality of divine judgement are developed by all these authors. This has seemed to place their writings outside the temporal context of history, so that the historiographical skills used to search for facts in the *Ṭabaqāt-i Nāṣirī* have yielded scant results. Hence, other than gleaning the odd 'fact', modern historians have not read this literature as an embodiment of the values and tastes expected of cultured Muslims trained in the classical traditions of Perso-Arabic literature and resident in north India.

Ẓiyā' al-Dīn Baranī is a good example of a sophisticated, urbane Muslim from the early fourteenth century. He was born and raised in north India, a courtier with a classical education in Perso-Arabic literature. Amongst his many works, the *Ta'rīkh-i Fīrūz Shāhī* was a unique didactic history of the Delhi Sultanate. Baranī was strongly influenced by the traditions of normative literature written in the *ādāb*, or the 'Mirrors for Princes', genre and was himself the author of one such text, *Fatāwā-yi Jahāndārī*, or the 'Principles of Government', not a very popular work judging by the near absence of surviving manuscripts and the manner in which it was ignored in later literature.[4] By contrast, the *Ta'rīkh* was an enormously popular text. In it Baranī narrated the histories of the Delhi Sultans—from Balban to the early years of Fīrūz Shāh Tughluq—as lessons from which the reigning monarch Fīrūz Shāh Tughluq (752–90/1351–88) could learn the consequences of both moral and immoral conduct. The moral exhortations present in the *Fatāwā* flowed into the *Ta'rīkh*, an

[4] It was only in 1941 that historians first used the solitary surviving manuscript of the *Fatāwā-yi Jahāndārī*, India Office Library Persian MS. 1149; see A.B.M. Habibullah, 'Re-evaluation of the Literary Sources of Pre-Mughal History', *Islamic Culture*, 15 (1941), pp. 210–13. It was Mohammad Habib who lent weight to the work and characterised it as the 'Political Theory of the Delhi Sultanate'. See the introduction to the translation of the text: Mohammad Habib and Dr. Mrs. Afsar Umar Salim Khan, *The Political Theory of the Delhi Sultanate* and Ẓiyā' al-Din Baranī, *Fatāwā-i Jahāndārī*, ed. A.U.S. Khan. Most recently, this work is discussed in Muzaffar Alam, *The Languages of Political Islam*.

exceptionally coherent history in which the author oscillated between intimate portrayals of his protagonists and more general assessments of their overall impact upon governance and the common weal.

Once again, the historical methodology used to read Ẓiyā' al-Dīn Baranī's text has seldom gone beyond a simple dredging of 'facts'. Baranī's *Ta'rīkh* has, in fact, come to be valued especially because the author displayed a sensitivity to social and 'structural' factors and their impact on the state. Whereas modern historians have been fairly quick in accepting Baranī's conclusions, still unexplored is the extent to which his analytic insights on statecraft were a part of larger medieval normative expectations.[5] Instead, historians have praised Baranī's capacity to perceive—before Marx, himself—that 'the economic basis of the Sultanate' depended upon the state's ability to appropriate the agrarian surplus from the peasantry.[6] But Baranī's text was hardly unique in this insight; works produced in the 'Mirrors for Princes' genre routinely emphasized the material dependence of the state upon the prosperity of peasantry and merchants.[7] While Baranī's literary merit lies in his attempt to structure a historical narrative of the Delhi Sultans around these general moral maxims, his analysis, like other *ādāb* texts, was synchronic.[8] Although dynastic

[5] For an early attempt at providing a larger context to Baranī's ideas see Peter Hardy, 'Unity and Variety in Indo-Islamic and Perso-Islamic Civilization: Some Ethical and Political Ideas of Ḍiyā' al-Dīn Baranī of Delhi, of al-Ghazali and of Naṣir al-Dīn Tūsī Compared', *Iran,* 16 (1978), pp. 127–35 and now Alam, cited above.

[6] Irfan Habib, 'Baranī's Theory of the History of the Delhi Sultanate', p. 113.

[7] This was a basic idea in the 'Circle of Justice' which was described in a number of texts. See Sunil Kumar, 'The Value of the *Ādāb al-Mulūk* as a Historical Source', pp. 307–27. In Fakhr-i Mudabbir's formulation it followed that 'a state cannot be possible without people [*mulk hargiz qā'im namānad magar bamardān*], and people and soldiers cannot exist without money [*bamāl*], and money cannot be gained from other than the peasants and the prosperity and tranquillity of the peasants cannot be possible without justice and [honest] governance [*wa ra'īyat-i muraffa wa āsuda nashawad magar ba'adl wa siyāsat*].' Fakhr-i Mudabbir, *Ādāb al-Ḥarb wa al-Shujā'a,* p. 120. The idea was repeated again on p. 138.

[8] Perhaps the most extensive and provocative interpretation of Baranī is to be found in Mohammad Habib, 'Life and Thought of Ziauddin Barani', in *The Political Theory of the Delhi Sultanate,* pp. 117–68. Of the competing

upheaval may have altered the circumstances of some elites, the basic structure of the Delhi Sultanate remained frozen throughout his narrative; it was the Sultans who changed and their impact on the age was deeply personalized and, therefore, innately transient.

The special characteristics of the *Tā'rīkh-i Fīrūz Shāhī,* however, cannot be ascribed purely to stylistic attributes common amongst literature in the 'Mirrors for Princes' genre. Other than the influence of the didactic element from *ādāb* literature, the author's personal predicament during Fīrūz Shāh Tughluq's reign also left its impact upon his text. Baranī belonged to a family of urban notables who had held important administrative and secretarial positions in the court of the Delhi Sultans and their Governors. He was himself a confidant of Sultan Muḥammad Shāh Tughluq (725–52/1325–51) and, in the period of uncertainty following his benefactor's death, Baranī's loyalty to the succeeding Sultan, Fīrūz Shāh Tughluq, remained suspect. On his accession Sultan Fīrūz Shāh Tughluq confiscated Baranī's wealth and threw him in prison. Although eventually released, Baranī's last years were spent in great penury. It was during this period that the author wrote his *Ta'rīkh-i Fīrūz Shāhī*, in which he severely criticized Muḥammad Shāh Tughluq and, in an effort to win the affection of Fīrūz Shāh, praised the latter as an exemplary ruler. Baranī was now a desperate man; when his history made little impression upon the Sultan, he drafted another version of the *Ta'rīkh* within which the contrast between the incumbent monarch and his predecessor was even more detailed.

Baranī's search for renewed patronage was relentless and it is fascinating to see the manner in which he used familiar tropes from *ṣūfī* and *ādāb* literature to argue the merits of his case. He whittled

interpretations on Baranī, the doubts of Peter Hardy are evident in his *Historians of Medieval India*; idem, 'The Oratio Recta of Baranī's Ta'rīkh-i-Fīrūz Shāhī—Fact or Fiction?', idem, 'Approaches to pre-Modern Indo-Muslim Historical Writing: Some Reconsiderations in 1990-1991', pp. 49–71. By contrast, enthusiastic reviews of Baranī are to be found in Harbans Mukhia, *Historians and Historiography*, pp. 19–26; in Irfan Habib, 'Baranī's theory of the History of the Delhi Sultanate', pp. 99–115; and in idem, 'The Price Regulations of 'Alā'uddīn Khaljī—A Defence of Ẓiā' Baranī', pp. 393–414. For a valuable and quite distinct approach, see Muzaffar Alam, *The Languages of Political Islam*, down complex *ṣūfī* statements concerning the virtues of *faqr*, or poverty, to imply that true piety resided only amongst those who were indigent. Given his impoverished condition, this qualification placed Baranī firmly within the ranks of the pious whom the Sultan should respect and honour, even as it excluded many individuals learned in the religious sciences, the *'ulamā'*, who were supported by the state as *qāẓīs*. In the same manner, fairly conventional ideas present in the 'Mirrors for Princes' literature were deployed by Baranī with an unmistakable personal twist. In his *Ta'rīkh*, Baranī demonstrated how the patronage of the low born by past Sultans brought ruin upon the state, a common theme in *ādāb* literature. It followed, therefore, that Fīrūz Shāh Tughluq's efforts at establishing a 'righteous gov-ernment' should also lead to the restoration of a divinely ordained social hierarchy where the pious and the cultured aristocrats, the *ashraf*, would command favour.[9] It was left for the reader to conclude how, in such a social reordering, the indigent Baranī would naturally be restored amongst the privileged elite.

Baranī's *Ta'rīkh* was an extremely unusual and complicated text, of great importance because its very subjectivity clarified how an extremely intelligent man facing a unique personal crisis in his life saw in the writing of history an opportunity to alter his circumstances. In Baranī's perception the history of the Delhi Sultanate was intertwined with that of his family and his own career, and the mid-fourteenth century crisis was thus being faced by both the Sultanate and the litterateur. In the *Ta'rīkh*, both turned to Sultan Fīrūz Shāh Tughluq as their great saviour.

If Baranī's *Ta'rīkh* was quite different from Jūzjānī's *Ṭabaqāt* or 'Iṣāmī's *Futūḥ al-Salāṭīn*, the *malfūẓ* texts possessed little apparent resemblance to any of the aforementioned 'histories'. These were texts which recorded the teachings of mystic teachers, *pīrs*, *shaikhs*, popularly venerated as saints, or friends of God, *awliyā'*. *Malfūẓāt* texts range a great deal in style, form, and content, and the *Fawā'id al-Fu'ād* of Amīr Ḥasan Sijzī (completed in 722/1322), a record of Shaykh Niẓām al-Dīn Awliyā's conversations, may well be regarded as the major innovative point in the evolution of this genre.

[9] For a useful survey of this theme in *ādāb* literature, see Louise Marlow, *Hierarchy and Egalitarianism*, pp. 128–39.

Until Sijzī's work, the *malfūẓāt* was not recognized as a suitable form for narrating the discourses of a great teacher; it was the *ishārat*, the treatises on mystical instruction, or the *tazkirāt*, the biographical narrative, which was preferred.[10] *Malfūẓāt* texts, in the form of imaginary fictional records of the discourses of *ṣūfī* masters to their disciples, were, however, an extremely popular genre of literature in thirteenth-century north India.[11] By choosing a popular mode of expression rather than the formal, conventional genre, Amīr Ḥasan Sijzī tapped into a huge pre-existing demand for this kind of literature. But Sijzī was also careful to ensure that the *Fawā'id al-Fu'ād* would distinguish itself from the mass of *malfūẓāt* in circulation. Unlike all the others, Sijzī emphasized that his text carried an authentic record of Niẓām al-Dīn Awliyā's conversations, a record which had been edited by the great Shaykh himself.[12]

This would have been insufficient to guarantee the popularity of the text, and it was here that the literary skill of the author raised the stature of the *Fawā'id al-Fu'ād* beyond that of its peers. Most *malfūẓāt* written before the *Fawā'id al-Fu'ād* were compilations of the teacher's instructions, largely flat monologues in which the master addressed his student. Sijzī, on the other hand, transformed the *malfūẓ* into an interactive record in which Niẓām al-Dīn Awliyā' responded to queries posed by members of his audience, joked, told them anecdotes, and asked individuals about their personal welfare. It was an extraordinarily intimate account, transporting the reader and the listener to the environs of the Shaykh's assemblies. The nar-rative skills of the author need to be appreciated because Sijzī man-aged to capture the 'orality', the moods and the substance of the discussion

[10] See Bruce B. Lawrence, *Notes from a Distant Flute: Sufi Literature in Pre-Mughal India* (Tehran: Imperial Iranian Acaemy of Philosophy, 1978), pp. 20–44.

[11] See Sijzī, *Fawā'id al-Fu'ād*, pp. 49, 76; and Habib, 'Chishti Mystic Records'. Sijzī's remarks on the presence of texts which carried the teachings of the early saints and Bābā Farīd, and his desire to emulate these works in his own *malfūẓ* were overlooked by Ernst, *Eternal Garden*, p. 77. In fact, Sijzī also mentions Niẓām al-Dīn's comments that these were spurious texts. See *Fawā'id al-Fu'ād*, p. 49.

[12] The point was made in an elaborate account by Sijzī, *Fawā'id al-Fu'ād*, p. 49.

in his master's assemblies.[13] It was a text which reflected the authorship of both master and pupil; the Shaykh provided the material and the disciple the literary form.

Sijzī's account of Niẓām al-Dīn Awliyā's conversations also influenced Ḥamīd Qalandar's *malfūẓ*, *Khair al-Majālis*, completed circa 751/1350. This text recorded the discourses of Naṣīr al-Dīn Chirāgh-i Dihlī, a spiritual descendant of Niẓām al-Dīn Awliyā'. By the time the *Khair al-Majālis* was written, the authority of Niẓām al-Dīn and his disciples had already become established within vast sections of the pietistic community of Muslims in north India. By the 1350s the Chishtīs were an influential, well-established mystical fraternity with a large and dispersed network of initiates. As a result, unlike the *Fawā'id al-Fu'ād*, the *Khair al-Majālis* did not need to establish the superior credentials of its protagonist in quite the same way; it had to instead establish Nasīr al-Dīn's stature as the unique heir to Niẓām al-Dīn's mystical charisma. Ḥamīd Qalandar's record of his master's conversations served a useful purpose in this context, but they also underlined their distinctive mystical bent, which was far

[13] This is well argued in the case of the *Fawā'id al-Fu'ād* by Ernst, *Eternal Garden*, pp. 63–8, 79–84. My emphasis on Sijzī's literary skill, his deliberate choice of a narrative style which appropriated a host of prestigious voices to create the authoritative persona of Niẓām al-Dīn Awliyā', contrasts with the observations of Ernst, *Eternal Garden*, pp. 78–84, where much of this is minimized. Nor am I entirely in agreement with Ernst's observation regarding the sharp decline in the 'oral' component of the *malfūẓāt* which were produced after 1400. I do not believe that such a linear development in narrative techniques occurred uniformly in the subcontinent. On the other hand, I find Ernst's qualitative differentiation of the *malfūẓāt*—as 'original' (in the sense of an 'initiatic' discourse) and 'retrospective'—far more useful (see p. 83 in particular). The oral discursive mode is especially present in the *malfūẓāt* of *ṣūfīs* attempting to elaborate the outlines of their mystical path and their 'initiatic genealogy'. Hence the parallel between Niẓām al-Dīn Awliyā' and Burhān al-Dīn's collateral Chishtī lineage in the Deccan. The retrospective *malfūẓāt*—and in this I would include as early a text as the *Khair al-Majālis*—were written when the mystical genealogy of the *silsila* already possessed form and coherence. These texts share with the *tazkirāt* a sermonizing narrative mode which overwhelms the earlier guiding, interactive, conversational tone of the 'initiatic' *malfūẓāt*.

more conventional in its pedagogical and juridical content. Neither Ḥamīd Qalandar nor Naṣīr al-Dīn could traverse the wide terrains of scholarly erudition and mystical intuitiveness with the ease and facility of Sijzī and Niẕām al-Dīn Awliyā'. The *Khair al-Majālis* remained a ponderous text that displayed some excitement when the subject of conversation turned to exegesis or grammar.

It was through the medium of the *malfūẕāt* that the respective eulogists of the *ṣūfis* dwelt upon the charismatic attributes of their teachers and provided them with a pivotal stature within a constellation of pious Muslims. Through the efforts of Sijzī and Qalandar, their respective masters could be adjudged the *Sulṭan al-mashaikh wa al-'ārifīn*, the Sultan of the Shaykhs and the pious, a distinction which the Delhi Sultans could never garner. If the discourse of the 'general' histories suggested that the reign of the incumbent Delhi Sultan was the grand culmination of a history of great rulers, the *malfūẕāt* contended that the *ṣūfi* Shaykh was the historical epitome of a succession of charismatic, pious individuals who were the special friends of God. Certainly the 'heroes' of the *malfūẕāt* were very different from those of the Persian chroniclers. Rather than Sultans and their servants, the main protagonists in the *malfūẕāt* were the Prophets of yore, the great *ṣūfi* teachers from the past, scholars of law and theo-logy, itinerant preachers, or humble, pious individuals from non-descript social backgrounds. Through an account of the lives and actions of these alternative 'heroes', the *ṣūfis* initiated spiritual adepts into the rhetoric of mystic doctrines, and introduced the laity to a *sharī'a* orthopraxis which carried the special interpretation of the Shaykhs. For the *ṣūfis* and their disciples, the histories of such indi-viduals were valuable because their character and conduct was worthy of emulation. Although the *malfūẕāt* were not organized as linear chronologies of the past, they appealed to antiquity in support of the claims of their respective protagonists through narrative stra-tegies which were very different from, but as effective as, those of the *tawārikh*. More than the exploits of the various Sultans recounted in the *tawārikh*, Muslims were here impressed by historical anecdotes which recounted the achievements of their Shaykhs. Indeed, it could well be argued that historical, didactic, and panegyric elements were all present, and reconfigured, within the *malfūẕāt* texts.

While each genre of Persian literature had its special stylistic attributes, the narrative forms of one were frequently present in the other. An embellished chronogram, a well-turned-out piece of verse, pithy aphorisms on moral conduct—these were all hallmarks of a scholar, as of tropes used by authors to display their literary talents or deliver their respective homilies. The presence of alternative stylistic forms within a text did not, however, detract from its discursive content, a rhetoric strongly influenced by the genre chosen by the author. The representation of the past portrayed in a *malfūẓ* seldom coincided with the manner in which it was depicted in a 'universal history'; these are distinctions which need to be appreciated and scrutinized because modern scholars seldom investigate the objectives the texts might have served, or the significance of authorial preference for specific narrative styles.

In fact, while the modern historian always bemoans the paucity of the available information on the thirteenth and early fourteenth centuries, it seems to me rather more necessary to acknowledge that, in their very complexity, the 'sources' provide a wonderfully variegated picture of north India for these centuries. It needs to be stressed that even in their survey and representation of affairs in the courts of the Delhi Sultans, the so-called 'historical sources' differ considerably from each other. It is also necessary to remember that, more than any other source, the literary evidence is able to provide historians with a sense of chronology and context, the information with which individuals can be identified, a sense of their lives and personalities, the construction of individual and social identities and relationships, conflicts of 'class', and ethnic and confessional interests.

The variety of information that has survived from the thirteenth and fourteenth centuries is considerable. It allows for the theoretical possibility of producing many different types of histories. This would imply, however, that historians remain open to asking a diverse body of questions and not simply follow the narratives of their sources. Unfortunately, this has been a custom more honoured in the breach than the observance.

Bibliography

Primary References

'Abd al-Ḥamīd Muḥarrir Ghaznawī, *Dastūr al-Albāb fī 'ilm al-Ḥisab*, translated by Shaikh Abdur Rashid, *Medieval India Quarterly*, 1 (1950), pp. 59–99.

'Abd al-Ḥaqq Mūḥaddiṣ Dehlawī, *Akhbār al-Akhyār*, translated into Urdu by Maulana Muhammad Fazil (Karachi, Madina Publishing Company, n.d).

'Abd al-Qādir Badā'ūnī, *Muntakhab al-Tawārīkh*, edited by Maulavi Ahmad 'Ali (Calcutta: Bibliotheca Indica Series, n.s. no. 131, 1868), vol. 1.

Abū al-Faẓl. *'Ain-i Akbarī*, translated by H.S. Jarrett and Jadunath Sarkar (Delhi: New Taj Office, 1989 reprint), 3 vols.

Abū Ḥāmid Muḥammad ibn Muḥammad al-Ghazālī, *Naṣīḥat al-Mulūk*, translated by F.R.C. Bagley (London: Oxford University Press, 1971 reprint).

'Alā' al-Dīn 'Aṭā Malik Juwainī, *Ta'rīkh-i Jahān-Gushā*, translated by John A. Boyle, *The History of the World-Conqueror* (Manchester: University Press, 1958), 2 vols.

Amīr Ḥasan Sijzī, *Fawā'id al-Fu'ād*, edited by Khwaja Hasan Thani Nizami Dihlawi (Delhi: Urdu Academy, 1990); translated by Bruce B. Lawrence (New York: Paulist Press, 1992) .

Amīr Khusrau, *Dībācha-i Dīwān Ghurrat al-Kamāl*, edited by Sayyid Ali Haidar (Patna: Institute of Postgraduate Studies and Research in Arabic and Persian Learning, 1988).

———, *Diwal Rānī-yi Khiẓr Khān*, edited by Rashid Ahmad Salim and introduced by Khaliq Ahmad Nizami (Delhi: Idarah-i Adabiyat-i Delhi, 1988).

———, *Miftāḥ al-Futūḥ*, edited by Shaikh Abdur Rashid (Aligarh: Department of Hisory, Aligarh University Press, 1954).

———, *Khazā'in al Futūḥ*, edited by M. Wahid Mirza (Calcutta: Bibliotheca Indica, 1953); translated by Mohammad Habib (Madras:

Diocesan Press, 1931); translated by M. Wahid Mirza (Lahore: National Committee for 700th Anniversary of Amir Khusrau, 1975).

———, *Nuh Sipihr*, edited by M. Wahid Mirza (London: Oxford University Press, 1950).

Amīr Khwurd, *Siyar al-Awliyā'*, edited by Sayyid Mahdi Ghuri (Lahore: Markaz-i Tahqiqat-i Farsi Iran wa Pakistan, no. 23, Mu'assi-yi Intisharat-i Islami, 1978).

Anonymous, *Ḥudūd al-'Alam*, translated and explained by V. Minorsky (London: Luzac and Company, E.J.W. Gibb Memorial Series, vol. 11, 1927).

Fakhr-i Mudabbir, *Ta'rīkh-i Fakhr al-Dīn Mubārak Shāh*, edited by E. Denison Ross (London: Royal Asiatic Society, 1927).

———, *Adāb al-Ḥarb wa al-Shujā'a*, edited by Ahmad Suhaili Khwansari (Teheran: Iqbal, 1968).

———, *Ādāb al-Mulūk wa kifāyat al-Mamlūk*, edited by Muhammad Sarwar Maulavi (Teheran: Haidari, 1976).

Ḥamid Faẓl Allāh Jamālī, *Siyar al-'Ārifīn* (Delhi: Rizwi Press, 1311/1893).

Ḥamīd Qalandar, *Khair al-Majālis*, edited by Khaliq A. Nizami (Aligarh: Department of History, Aligarh University Press, 1959).

Ḥasan Niẓāmī, *Tāj al-Ma'āṣir*, translated by H.M. Elliot and John Dowson, *The History of India as Told by its Own Historians* (Allahabad: Kitab Mahal, n.d.), vol. 2, pp. 204–43; translated by Bhagwat Saroop (Delhi: Saud Ahmad Dehlavi, 1998).

Ibn Baṭṭūta, *Rehla*, translated by Agha Mahdi Husain (Baroda: Oriental Institute, Gaekwad Oriental Series, no. 122, 1976 reprint); translated by H.A.R. Gibb (Cambridge: Cambridge University Press, Haklyut Society Series nos 110, 117, 141, 1958–1971), 3 vols.

Ibn Khaldūn, *The Muqaddimah*, translated by F. Rosenthal, edited and abridged, N.J. Dawood (Princeton: Bollingen Series, Princeton University Press, 1974 reprint).

'Iṣāmī, *Futūḥ al-Salāṭīn*, edited by A.S. Usha (Madras: University of Madras, 1940); translated by Agha Mahdi Husain (Delhi: Asia Publishing House, 1967, 1977), 2 vols.

Minhāj-i Sirāj Jūzjānī, *Ṭabaqāt-i Nāṣirī*, edited by Abdul Hay Habibi (Kabul: Anjuman-i Tarikh-i Afghanistan, 1963–4), 2 vols; edited by W.N. Lees (Calcutta: Bibliotheca Indica, 1863); translated by H.G. Raverty (Delhi: Oriental Books Reprint Corporation, 1970 reprint), 2 vols.

Muḥammad Qāsim Firishtā, *Gulshan-i Ibrāhīmī*, translated by John Briggs (Delhi: Low Price Publications, 1990 reprint), vol. 1.

Niẓām al-Dīn Aḥmad, *Ṭabaqāt-i Akbarī*, edited by B. De (Calcutta: Asiatic Society of Bengal, 1913), vol. 1.

Niẓām al-Mulk, *Siyāsat Nāma*, translated by Hubert Darke, *The Book of Government or Rules for Kings* (London: Routledge and Kegan Paul, 1978 reprint).

Niẓāmī 'Arūzī Samarqandī, *Chahār Maqāla*, edited by Mohammad Qazvini and Mohammad Mu'in (Tehran: University Press, 1955–7); translated by E.G. Browne (London: Luzac and Co. Ltd, E.J.W. Gibb Memorial Series o.s. XI.2, 1978 reprint).

Sharaf al-Dīn Manerī, *The Hundred Letters*, translated by Paul Jackson, s.j. (New York: Paulist Press, 1980).

Yaḥyā ibn Aḥmad Sirhindī, *Ta'ri<u>kh</u>-i Mubārak Shāhī*, edited by S.M. Hidayat Hosain (Calcutta: Bibiotheca Indica, 1931).

Ẓahīr al-Dīn Bābur, *Bābur Nāma*, translated by A.S. Beveridge (Delhi: Saeed International, 1989, reprint), 2 vols; translated by Wheeler M. Thackston (New York: The Modern Library, 2002 reprint).

Ẓiyā' al-Din Baranī, *Ta'rī<u>kh</u> -i Fīrūz Shāhī*, edited by Sayyid Ahmad Khan (Calcutta: Bibliotheca Indica, 1860–2); edited by Shaykh Abdul Rashid (Aligarh: Dept of History, University Press, 1957), vol. 1.

———, *Fatāwā-yi Jahāndārī*, edited by Afsar Saleem Khan (Lahore Research Society of Pakistan, University of the Punjab, 1972); translated by Mohammad Habib and Afsar U.S. Khan, *The Political Theory of the Delhi Sultanate* (Allahabad: Kitab Mahal, nd).

Secondary References

Ahmad, Aziz, 'The Sufi and the Sultan in Pre-Mughal India', *Der Islam*, 38 (1962), pp. 142–53.

———, 'Epic and Counter Epic in Medieval India', *Journal of the American Oriental Society*, 83 (1963), pp. 470–6.

———, *Studies in Islamic Culture in the Indian Environment* (Oxford: Clarendon Press, 1964).

———, *An Intellectual History of Islam in India* (Edinburgh: Edinburgh University Press, 1969).

———, 'The Role of Ulema in Indo-Muslim History', *Studia Islamica*, 31 (1970), pp. 2–13.

———, 'The Early Turkish Nucleus in India', *Turcica, Revue d'etudes Turques*, 9 (1977), pp. 99–109.

Ahmad, Laiq, 'Kara: A Medieval Indian City', *Islamic Culture*, 55 (1981), pp. 83–92.

Ahmad, Muhammad Aziz, *Political History and Institutions of the Early Turkish Empire of Delhi* (Lahore: University of the Punjab, 1987 reprint).

Alam, Muzaffar, 'Competition and Coexistence: Indo-Muslim Interaction in Medieval North India', *Itinerario*, 13 (1989), pp. 37–59.

———, 'The Culture and Politics of Persian in Precolonial Hindustan', in Sheldon Pollock, ed., *Literary Cultures in History: Reconstructions from South Asia* (Delhi: Oxford University Press, 2003), pp. 131–98.

———, *The Languages of Political Islam* (Delhi: Permanent Black, 2004).

Alam, Muzaffar and Sanjay Subrahmanyam, eds, *The Mughal State, 1526–1750* (Delhi: Oxford University Press, 1998).

Ali, Athar, 'Nobility under Muhammad Tughluq', *Proceedings of the Indian History Congress*, 42 (1981), pp. 197–202.

———, 'Military Technology of the Delhi Sultanate (13th–14th C.)', *Proceedings of the Indian History Congress*, 50 (1989), pp. 166–82.

———, 'The Mughal Polity—A Critique of Revisionist Approaches', *Modern Asian Studies*, 27 (1993), pp. 699–710.

Ali, Daud, *Courtly Culture and Political Life in Early Medieval India* (Cambridge: Cambridge University Press, 2004).

Ali, Taj, 'The Mehrab-Inscription of the So-called Tomb of Khalid Walid near Kabirwala (Khanewad District)', *Ancient Pakistan*, 7 (1991), pp. 39–46.

Amedroz, H.F., 'The Office of Kadi in the *Ahkam Sultaniyya* of Mawardi', *Journal of the Royal Asiatic Society* (1910), pp. 761–96.

Amin, Shahid, 'On Retelling the Muslim Conquest of North India', in Partha Chatterjee and Anjan Ghosh, eds, *History and the Present* (Delhi: Permanent Black, 2002), pp. 24–43.

Aquil, Raziuddin, 'Conversion in Chishti Sufi Literature (13th–14th Centuries)', *Indian Historical Review*, 24 (1997–8), pp. 70–94.

Arnold, Benjamin, *German Knighthood, 1050–1300* (Oxford: Clarendon Press, 1985).

Askari, S.H. , *Amir Khusrau as a Historian* (Patna: Khuda Bakhsh Oriental Public Library, 1992 reprint).

Ashraf, K.M., *Life and Conditions of the People of Hindustan* (Delhi: Munshiram Manoharlal Publishers Pvt. Ltd, 1988 reprint).

Aubin, Jean, 'L'ethnogénèse des Qaraunas', *Turcica*, 1 (1969), pp. 65–94.

Ayalon, David, 'The Wafidiya in the Mamluk Kingdom', *Islamic Culture*, 25 (1951), pp. 89–104.

———, *L'Esclavage du Mamelouk* (Jeruslem: Israel Oriental Society, no. 1, 1951).

———, 'Studies on the Structure of the Mamluk Army I and II', *Bulletin of the School of Oriental and African Studies*, 15 (1953), pp. 203–28, 448–76.

———, 'Studies in al-Jabartī I: Notes on the Transformation of Mamluk Society in Egypt under the Ottomans', *Journal of the Economic and Social History of the Orient*, 3 (1960), pp. 283–8.

———, 'Preliminary Remarks on the *Mamluk* Military Institution in Islam', V.J. Parry and M.E. Yapp, eds, *War, Technology and Society in the Middle East* (London: Oxford University Press, 1975), pp. 44–58.

———, 'Names, Titles, and Nisbas of the Mamluks', *Israel Oriental Studies*, 5 (1975), pp. 189–232.

———, 'Aspects of the Mamluk Phenomenon', *Der Islam* (1976), pp. 197–225 (1977), pp. 1–32.

Bachrach, Bernard S., 'Some Observations on the Medieval Nobility: A Review Essay', *Medieval Prosopography*, 1 (1980), pp. 15–33.

Bano, Shadab, 'The Acquisition and Trade of Elite Slaves in the Thirteenth Century', *Proceedings of the Indian History Congress*, Patiala, 59 (1998), pp. 229–36.

Barthold, W., *Turkestan down to the Mongol Invasion* (London, E.J.W. Gibb Memorial Trust, Luzac and Company, 1977 reprint).

Beech, George, 'Prosopography', James M. Powell, ed., *Medieval Studies: An Introduction* (Syracuse: Syracuse University Press, 1976), pp. 151–84.

Berkey, Jonathan P., *The Transmission of Knowledge in Medieval Cairo: A Social History of Islamic Education* (Princeton: Princeton University Press, 1992).

———, *Popular Preaching and Religion in the Medieval Islamic Near East* (Seattle: University of Washington Press, 2001).

Bosworth, Clifford, 'Military Organisation under the Būyids of Persia and Iraq', *Oriens*, vol. 18–19 (1965–6), pp. 143–67, also reprinted in idem, *The Medieval History of Iran, Afghanistan and Central Asia* (London, Variorum Reprints, 1977).

———, 'The Early Islamic History of Ghur', *Central Asiatic Journal*, 6 (1961), pp. 116–33, reprinted in idem, *The Medieval History of Iran, Afghanistan and Central Asia* (London: Variorum Reprints, 1977).

———, 'Notes on the Pre-Ghaznavid History of Eastern Afghanistan', *Islamic Quarterly*, 9 (1965), pp. 12–24, reprinted in idem, *The Medieval History of Iran, Afghanistan and Central Asia* (London: Variorum Reprints, 1977).

———, 'Mahmūd of Ghazna in Contemporary Eyes and in Later Persian Literature', *Iran*, 4 (1966), pp. 85–92.

———, 'The Political and Dynastic History of the Iranian World (1000–1217)', J.A. Boyle, ed., *The Cambridge History of Iran, vol. 5: The Saljuq and Mongol Periods* (Cambridge: Cambridge University Press, 1968), pp. 1–202.

———, 'The Development of Persian Culture under the Early Ghaznavids', *Iran*, 6 (1968), pp. 33–44, reprinted in idem, *The Medieval History of Iran, Afghanistan and Central Asia* (London: Variorum Reprints, 1977).

———, *The Ghaznavids: Their Empire in Afghanistan and Eastern Iran, 994–1040* (Beirut: Librairie du Liban, 1973 reprint).

———, 'Recruitment, Muster, and Review in Medieval Islamic Armies', in V.J. Parry and M.E. Yapp, eds, *War, Technology and Society in the Middle East* (London: Oxford University Press, 1975).

———, *The Later Ghaznavids: Splendour and Decay. The Dynasty in Afghanistan and Northern India, 1040–1186* (New York: Columbia University Press, 1977).

Bosworth, C.E. and Gerard Clauson, 'Al-Xwārazmī on the Peoples of Central Asia', *Journal of the Royal Asiatic Society* (1965), pp. 2–12, reprinted in idem, *The Medieval History of Iran, Afghanistan and Central Asia* (London: Variorum Reprints, 1977).

Boyle, John Andrew, *The Mongol World Empire, 1206–1370* (London: Variorum Reprints, 1977).

Browne, Edward G., *A Literary History of Persia* (Cambridge: Cambridge University Press, 1964), vol. 2.

Bulliet, Richard W., 'A Quantitative Approach to Medieval Muslim Biographical Dictionaries', *Journal of the Economic and Social History of the Orient*, 13 (1970), pp.195–211.

———, *The Patricians of Nishapur: A Study in Medieval Islamic Social History* (Cambridge, Mass.: Harvard University Press, 1972).

———, 'The Shaykh al-Islam and the Evolution of Islamic Society', *Studia Islamica*, 35 (1972), pp. 53–67.

———, *Islam: The View from the Edge* (New York: Columbia University Press, 1994).

Cahen, Claude, 'L'évolution de l'Iqtā' de IXe au XIIIe siècle', *Annales: Economies, Sociétés, Civilisations*, 8 (1953), pp. 25–52.

———, 'Au seuil de la troisième année: réflexions sur l'usage du mot "Féodalité" ', *Journal of the Economic and Social History of the Orient*, 3 (1960), pp. 2–20.

———, *Pre-Ottoman Turkey*, translated by J. Jones-Williams (New York: Taplinger, 1968).

Chamberlain, Michael, *Knowledge and Social Practice in Medieval Damascus, 1190–1350* (Cambridge: Cambridge University Press, 1994).

Chatterjee, Indrani, *Gender, Slavery and Law in Colonial India* (Delhi: Oxford University Press, 1999).

Chattopadhyaya, B.D., *The Making of Early Medieval India* (Delhi: Oxford University Press, 1997 reprint).

———, *Representing the Other? Sanskrit Sources and the Muslims* (Delhi: Manohar, 1998).

Coulson, N.J., 'Doctrine and Practice in Islamic Law: One Aspect of the Problem', *Bulletin of the School of Oriental and African Studies*, 18 (1956), pp. 211–26.

Crone, Patricia, *Slaves on Horses: The Evolution of the Islamic Polity* (Cambridge: Cambridge University Press, 1980).

Currie, P.M., *The Shrine and Cult of Mu'in al-Din Chishti of Ajmer* (Delhi: Oxford University Press, 1989).

Dankoff, R., 'Kāshghari on the Tribal and Kinship Organization of the Turks', *Archivum Ottomanicum*, 4 (1972), pp. 29–35.

Davis, Richard, 'Indian Art Objects as Loot', *Journal of Asian Studies*, 52 (1993), pp. 22–48.

———, *Lives of Indian Images* (Delhi: Motilal Banarsidas Publishers, 1999 reprint).

Dallapicola and S.Z. Lallemant, eds, *Islam and Indian Regions* (Stuttgart: Steiner, 1993), 2 vols.

Deyell, John S., 'The China Connection: Problems of Silver Supply in Medieval Bengal', in J.F. Richards, ed., *Precious Metals in the Later Medieval and Early Modern Worlds* (Durham: Carolina Academic Press, 1983), pp. 207–27.

———, *Living Without Silver: The Monetary History of Early Medieval North India* (Delhi: Oxford University Press, 1990).

Digby, Simon, *War Horse and Elephant in the Delhi Sultanate: A Study of Military Supplies* (Karachi: Orient Monographs, 1971).

———, 'The Currency System', in T. Raychaudhuri and I. Habib, eds, *The Cambridge Economic History of India* (Delhi: Orient Longman, 1984 reprint), pp. 93–101.

———, 'Qalandars and Related Groups: Elements of Social Deviance in the Religious Life of the Delhi Sultanate of the Thirteenth and Fourteenth Centuries', in Yohanan Friedmann, ed., *Islam in Asia, volume 1, South Asia* (Boulder: Westview Press, 1984), pp. 60–108.

———, 'The Sufi Shaikh as a Source of Authority in Medieval India', *Purusartha* (*Islam and Society in South Asia*), 9 (1986), pp. 57–77.

———, '*Tabarrukāt* and Succession among the Great Chishtī Shaykhs of the Delhi Sultanate', in R.E. Frykenberg, ed., *Delhi Through the Ages* (Delhi: Oxford University Press, 1986), pp. 63–103.

———, 'Hawk and Dove in Sufi Combat', *Pembroke Papers*, 1 (1990), pp. 7–25.

———, 'The Sufi Shaikh and the Sultan: A Conflict of Claims to Authority in Medieval India', *Iran*, 28 (1990), pp. 71–81.

———, 'Anecdotes of a Provincial Sufi of the Dehli Sultanate: Khwāja Gurg of Kara', *Iran*, 32 (1994), pp. 99–109.

Doerfer, Gerhard, *Turkische und Monglische Elemente im Neupersischen* (Weisbaden: Franz Steiner Verlag, 1967), 4 vols.

Duby, Georges, *The Chivalrous Society*, translated by Cynthia Postan (Berkeley: University of California Press, 1977).

Eaton, Richard M., *Sufis of Bijapur, 1300–1700: Social Roles of Sufis in Medieval India* (Princeton: Princeton University Press, 1978).

'The Political and Religious Authority of the Shrine of Bābā Farīd'. Barbara Metcalf, ed., *Moral Conduct and Authority: The Place of Adab in South Asian Islam* (California: Berkeley University Press, 1984), pp. 333–56, reprinted in idem, *Essays on Islam and Indian History* (Delhi: Oxford University Press, 2000), pp. 203–24.

———, *The Rise of Islam and the Bengal Frontier, 1204–1760* (Delhi: Oxford University Press, 1997 reprint).

———, 'Temple Desecration and Indo-Muslim States', in David Gilmartin and Bruce B. Lawrence, eds, *Beyond Turk and Hindu: Rethinking Religious Identities in Islamicate South Asia* (New Delhi: India Research Press, 2002), pp. 246–81.

———, *Essays on Islam and Indian History* (Delhi: Oxford University Press, 2002).

———, ed., *India's Islamic Traditions, 711–1750* (Delhi: Oxford University Press, 2003).

Elia, Norbert, *The Civilising Process: The History of Manners and State Formation and Civilisation* translated by Norman Jephcott (Oxford: Blackwell, 1994).

Embree, Ainslie T., ed., *Sources of Indian Tradition* (Columbia: University Press, 1988), 2 vols.

Ernst, Carl, *Eternal Garden: Mysticism, History, and Politics at a South Asian Sufi Center* (Albany: State University of New York Press, 1992).

———, *The Shambhala Guide to Sufism* (Boston: Shambhala South Asia Editions, 2000).

Ernst, Carl and Bruce Lawrence, eds, *Sufi Martyrs of Love: The Chishti Order in South Asia and Beyond* (New York: Palgrave Macmillan, 2002).

Ewing, Katherine P., ed., *Sharī'at and Ambiguity in South Asian Islam* (Delhi: Oxford University Press, 1988).

Flood, Finbarr B., 'Ghurid Architecture in the Indus Valley: The Tomb of Shaykh Sadan Shahid', *Ars Orientalis*, 31 (2001), pp. 129– 66.

———, 'Persianate Trends in Sultanate Architecture: The Great Mosque of Bada'un', in Bernard O'Kane, ed., *The Iconography of Islamic Art: Festschrift for Robert Hillenbrand* (Edinburgh: Edinburgh University Press, 2005), pp. 159–95.

———, 'Ghurid Monuments and Muslim Identities: Epigraphy and Exegesis in Twelfth-century Afghanistan and India', *Indian Economic and Social History Review*, 42 (2005), pp. 263–94.

———, 'Islam, Iconoclasm, and the Early Indian Mosque', in Sunil Kumar, ed., *Demolishing Myths or Mosques and Temples? Readings on History and Temple Desecration in Medieval India* (Delhi: Three Essays Press, forthcoming).

Forand, Paul G., 'The Relation of the Slave and Client to the Master or Patron in Medieval Islam', *International Journal of Middle East Studies*, 2 (1971), pp. 59–66.

Fox, Richard G., *Kin, Clan, Raja and Rule: State–Hinterland Relations in Preindustrial India* (Berkeley: University of California Press, 1971).

Freed, John B., 'Nobles, Ministerialis, and Knights in the Archdiocese of Salzburg', *Speculum*, 62 (1987), pp. 575–611.

Frye, Richard, *Bukhara: The Medieval Achievement* (Norman: University of Oklahama Press, 1965).

Gibb, H.A.R., *Studies on the Civilization of Islam*, eds, Stanford J. Shaw and William R. Polk (London: Routledge and Kegan Paul, 1969).

Gibb, H.A.R. *et al.*, eds, *Encyclopaedia of Islam* (Leiden: E.J. Brill, second edition, 1956–).

Goel, Sita Ram, *Hindu Temples: What Happened to Them? Vol. 1: A Preliminary Survey* (New Delhi: Voice of India, 1990); *Vol. 2: The Islamic Evidence* (New Delhi: Voice of India, 1991).

Goitein, S.D., 'Slaves and Slavegirls in the Cairo Geniza Records', *Arabica*, 9 (1962), pp. 1–20.

———, 'The Origin of the Vizierate and its True Character', in idem, *Studies in Islamic History and Institutions* (Leiden: E.J. Brill, 1968), pp. 168–96.

Golden, P.B., 'Cumanica II, The Ölberli (Ölperli): The Fortunes and Misfortunes of an Inner Asian Nomadic Clan', *Archivum Eurasiae Medii Aevi*, 6 (1986), pp. 5–29.

Gommans, Jos J.L. and Dirk H.A. Kolff, eds, *Warfare and Weaponry in South Asia, 1000–1800* (Delhi: Oxford University Press, 2001).

Gordon, Stewart, ed., *Robes and Honor: The Medieval World of Investiture* (New York: Palgrave, 2001).

———, *Robes of Honour: Khil'at in Pre-Colonial and Colonial India* (Delhi: Oxford University Press, 2003).

Habib, Irfan, *The Agrarian System of Mughal India* (Delhi: Asia Publishing House, 1963; Delhi: Oxford University Press, 1999, revised edition).

———, 'Social Distribution of Landed Property in Pre-British India', *Enquiry*, New Series, II (1965), pp. 21–75, reprinted in idem, *Essays in Indian History, Towards a Marxist Perception* (New Delhi: Tulika, 1995), pp. 59–108.

———, 'Technological Changes and Society, Thirteenth and Fourteenth Centuries', *Proceedings of the Indian History Congress*, 31 (1969), pp. 139–61.

———, 'The Jatts of Punjab and Sind', in Harbans Singh and N. Gerald Barrier, eds, *Punjab Past and Present: Essays in Honour of Dr. Ganda Singh* (Patiala: Punjab University, 1976), pp. 92–103.

———, 'An Economic History of the Delhi Sultanate—An Essay in Inter-pretation', *Indian Historical Review*, 4 (1978), pp. 287–303.

———, 'Baranī's Theory of the History of the Delhi Sultanate', *Indian Historical Review*, 7 (1981), pp. 99–115.

———, 'The Peasant in Indian History', *Proceedings of the Indian History Congress*, 43 (1982), pp. 1–53, reprinted in idem, *Essays in Indian History: Towards a Marxist Perception* (New Delhi: Tulika, 1995), pp.109–60.

———, 'Price Regulations of 'Alā'uddīn Khaljī: A Defence of Ẓiā' Baranī', *Indian Economic and Social History Review*, 21 (1984), pp. 393–414.

———, 'Slavery in the Delhi Sultanate, Thirteenth and Fourteenth Centuries: Evidence from Sufic Literature', *Indian Historical Review*, 15 (1988–9), pp. 248–56.

———, 'Classifying Pre-Colonial India', *Journal of Peasant Studies*, 12 (1985), pp. 44–53.

———, 'Formation of the Sultanate Ruling Class of the Thirteenth Century', *Medieval India: Researches in the History of India 1200–1750, 1* (1992), pp. 1–21.

———, Ziyā Baranī's Vision of the State', *Medieval History Journal*, 2 (1999), pp. 19–36.

———, 'The Historical Background of the Popular Monotheistic Movement of the 15th–17th centuries', mimeograph.

Habib, Mohammad, 'Sultan Mahmud of Ghazni', in K.A. Nizami, ed., *Politics and Society during the Medieval Period, Collected Works of Professor Mohammad Habib* (New Delhi: People's Publishing House, 1927, 1981 reprint), vol. 2, pp. 36–104.

———, 'Shaikh Naṣīruddīn Maḥmūd Chirāgh-i Dehlī as a Great Historical Personality', *Islamic Culture*, 20 (1946), pp. 129–53.

———, 'Chishti Mystics Records of the Sultanate Period', *Medieval India Quarterly*, 1 (1950), pp. 1–42.

———, 'Introduction to Elliot and Dowson's History of India, Vol. II', in K.A. Nizami, ed., *Politics and Society in Early Medieval India: Collected Works of Professor Mohammad Habib* (New Delhi: People Publishing House, 1974), vol. 1, pp. 33–110.

———, *Ḥaẓrat Niẓāmuddīn Auliyā: Ḥayāt aur Ta'līmāt* (Delhi: Department of Urdu, Delhi University, 1970).

Habib, Muhammad and K.A. Nizami, eds, *A Comprehensive History of India: Vol. 5: The Delhi Sultanat, A.D. 1206–1526* (New Delhi: People's Publishing House, 1982 reprint).

Habibi, A.H., 'Khaljis are Afghan Tarak or Turk', *Afghanistan*, 24 (1971), pp. 76–88.

Habibullah, A.B.M., *The Foundation of Muslim Rule in India* (Allahabad: Oriental Book Depot, 1976 revised edition).

Haig, Sir Wolseley, ed., *The Cambridge History of India: Vol. III, Turks and Afghans* (Cambridge: Cambridge University Press, 1928).

Hallaq, Wael B., *The Origins and Evolution of Islamic Law* (Cambridge: Cambridge University Press, 2005).

Hambly, Gavin, 'Who were the *Chihalgānī*, the Forty Slaves of Sulṭān Shams al-Dīn Iltutmish of Delhi', *Iran,* 10 (1972), pp. 57–62.

Hardy, Peter, 'The *oratio recta* of Baranī's *Ta'rīkh-i Fīrūz Shāhī*—Fact or Fiction?', *Bulletin of the School of Oriental and African Studies*, 20 (1957), pp. 315–21.

———, *Historians of Medieval India: Studies in Indo-Muslim Historical Writing* (London: Luzac and Company Ltd, 1966 reprint).

———, 'Unity and Variety in Indo-Islamic and Perso-Islamic Civilization: Some Ethical and Political Ideas of Ḍiya' al-Dīn Baranī of Delhī, of al-Ghazali and of Naṣīr al-Dīn Tūsī Compared', *Iran*, 16 (1978), pp. 127–36.

———, 'The Duty of the Sultan (in the Sultanate Period) to further the Material Welfare of his Subjects', in Wendy Doniger O'Flaherty and J. Duncan M. Derrett, eds, *The Concept of Duty in South Asia* (Delhi: Vikas Publishing House Pvt. Ltd, 1978), pp. 147–65.

———, 'Force and Violence in Indo-Persian Writing on History and Government in Medieval South Asia', in Milton Israel and N.K. Wagle, eds, *Islamic Society and Culture: Essays in Honour of Professor Aziz Ahmad* (Delhi: Manohar, 1983), pp. 165–208.

———, 'Approaches to Pre-Modern Indo-Muslim Historical Writing: Some Reconsiderations in 1990–91', Peter Robb, ed., *Society and Ideology: Essays in South Asian History Presented to K.A. Ballhatchet* (Delhi: Oxford University Press, 1994 reprint), pp. 49–71.

———, 'Growth of Authority over a Conquered Political Elite: Early Delhi Sultanate as a Possible Case Study', in John F. Richards, ed., *Kingship and Authority in South Asia* (Delhi: Oxford University Press, 1998 reprint), pp. 216–41.

Heestermann, J.C., *The Inner Conflict of Tradition: Essays in Indian Ritual, Kingship and Society* (Chicago: University of Chicago Press, 1985).

Heitzman, James, *Gifts of Power: Temples, Politics and Economy in Medieval South India* (Delhi: Oxford University Press, 1997).

Henige, David P., 'Some Phantom Dynasties of Early and Medieval India: Epigraphic Evidence and the Abhorrence of a Vacuum', *Bulletin of the School of Oriental and African Studies*, 38 (1975), pp. 525–49.

Hermansen, Marcia K. and Bruce B. Lawrence, 'Indo-Persian Tazkiras as Memorative Communications', in David Gilmartin and Bruce B. Lawrence, *Beyond Turk and Hindu: Rethinking Religious Identities in*

Islamicate South Asia (New Delhi: India Research Press, 2002), pp. 149–75.

Heyd, Uriel, *Studies in Old Ottoman Criminal Law* (Oxford: Clarendon Press, 1973).

Hillenbrand, Robert, 'Political Symbolism in Early Indo-Islamic Architecture: The Case of Ajmīr, *Iran*, 26 (1988), pp. 105–18.

Hodgson, Marshall G.S., *The Venture of Islam: Conscience and History in a World Civilization* (Chicago: University of Chicago Press, 1974) 3 vols.

Hodivala, S.H., *Studies in Indo-Muslim History: A Critical Commentary on Elliot and Dowson's History of India* (Bombay: Popular Book Depot, 1939, 1957), 2 vols.

Horowitz, J., 'The Inscriptions of Muhammad ibn Sam, Qutubuddin Aibeg and Iltutmish', *Epigraphia Indo-Moslemica* (1911–12), pp. 12–34.

Husayn, Maulvi Muhammad Ashraf, transcribed and trans., *A Record of All the Qur'anic and non-Historical Epigraphs on the Protected Monuments in the Delhi Province* (Calcutta: Archaeological Survey of India, Memoirs, no. 47, 1936).

Inalcik, Halil, *The Ottoman Empire: The Classical Age 1300–1600* (London: Weidenfeld and Nicolson, 1975).

Inden, Ronald, *Imagining India* (Oxford: Blackwell, 1990).

———, 'Hierarchies of Kings in Early Medieval India', *Contributions to Indian Sociology*, n.s. 15 (1981), pp. 99–125.

Jackson, Peter, 'The Mongols and India 1221–1351' (Cambridge: Ph.D. dissertation, 1976).

———, 'The *Mamlūk* Institution in Early Muslim India', *Journal of the Royal Asiatic Society* (1990), pp. 340–58.

———, 'Jalāl al-Dīn, the Mongols and the Khwarazmian Conquest of the Punjāb and Sindh', *Iran*, 28 (1990), pp. 45–54.

———, 'Sulṭān Raḍiyya bint Iltutmish', in Gavin R.G. Hambly, ed., *Women in the Medieval Islamic World: Power, Patronage, Piety* (New York: Palgrave, 1998), pp. 81–97.

———, *The Delhi Sultanate: A Political and Military History* (Cambridge: Cambridge University Press, 1999).

Jaffar, S.M., *Education in Muslim India; Being an Inquiry into the State of Education during the Muslim Period of Indian History, 1000–1800 A.D.* (Delhi: Idarah-i Adabiyat-i Delli, 1973 reprint).

Jha, Pankaj Kumar, 'A Table Laden with Good Things: Reading a 14th-century Sufi Text', in S. Chakravorty and A. Gupta, eds, *Print Areas II: Book History in India* (forthcoming).

Joshi, M.C., 'Some Nagari Inscriptions on the Qutb Minar', *Medieval India—A Miscellany*, 2 (1972), pp. 3–7.

Juneja, Monica, ed., *Architecture in Medieval India: Forms, Contexts, Histories* (Delhi: Permanent Black, 2001).

Kafadar, Cemal, *Between Two Worlds: The Construction of the Ottoman State* (Berkeley: University of California Press, 1995).

Khalidi, Tarif, *Arabic Historical Thought in the Classical Period* (Cambridge: Cambridge University Press, 1994).

Khan, Iqtidar Alam, 'Turko-Mongol Theory of Kingship', *Medieval India—A Miscellany*, 2 (1972), pp. 8–18.

———, 'Akbar's Personality Traits and World Outlook—A Critical Approach', in Irfan Habib, ed., *Akbar and His Age* (Delhi: Oxford University Press, 1997), pp. 79–96.

Khan, Mumtaz Ali, *Some Important Persian Prose Writing of the Thirteenth Century A.D. in India* (Aligarh: Department of History, Aligarh Muslim University, 1970).

Kolff, Dirk H., *Naukar, Rajput and Sepoy: The Ethnohistory of the Military Labour Market in Hindustan, 1450–1850* (Cambridge: Cambridge University Press, 1990).

Kulke, Hermann, ed., 'Fragmentation and Segmentation *versus* Integration? Reflections on the Concepts of Indian Feudalism and the Segmentary State in Indian History', *Studies in History*, 4 (1982), pp. 237–63.

———, ed., *The State in India 1000–1700* (Delhi: Oxford University Press, 1997 reprint).

Kumar, Sunil, 'The Value of *Ādāb al-Mulūk* as a Historical Source: An Insight into the Ideals and Expectations of Islamic Society in the Middle Period (AD 945–1500)', *The Indian Economic and Social History Review*, 22, no. 3 (1985), pp. 307–27.

———, 'When Slaves were Nobles: The Shamsī *Bandagān* in the Early Delhi Sultanate', *Studies in History*, 10 (1994), pp. 23–52.

———, 'Assertions of Authority: A Study of the Discursive Statements of Two Sultans of Delhi', in Muzaffar Alam, *et al.*,eds, *The Making of Indo-Persian Culture: Indian and French Studies* (Delhi: Manohar, 2000), pp. 37–65.

———, 'Qutb and Modern Memory', in Suvir Kaul, ed., *The Partitions of Memory: The Afterlife of the Division of India* (Delhi: Permanent Black, 2001), pp. 140–82, reprinted in idem, *The Present in Delhi's Pasts* (Delhi: Three Essays Press, 2002), pp. 1–61.

———, 'la communauté musulmane et les relations hindo-musulmanes dans l'Inde du Nord au début du XIIIe siècl: une reevaluation politique', *Annales HSC*, 60 (2005), pp. 239–64.

———, 'Service, Status and Military Slavery in the Delhi Sultanate of the Thirteenth and Early Fourteenth Centuries', in Richard Eaton and Indrani Chatterjee, eds, *Slavery and South Asia* (Bloomington: Indiana University Press, 2006).

———, 'Raziyya, Sultan', in *Encyclopaedia of Women in World History* (New York: Oxford University Press, forthcoming).

Lambton, A.K.S., *Landlord and Peasant in Persia: A Study of Land Tenure and Land Revenue Administration* (London: Oxford University Press, 1953).

———, 'Reflection on the *Iqṭa*', in George Makdisi, ed., *Arabic and Islamic Studies in Honour of H.A.R. Gibb* (Leiden: E.J. Brill, 1965), pp. 358–76

———, 'The Internal Structure of the Saljuq Empire'. J.A. Boyle, ed., *Cambridge History of Iran, Vol. 5: The Saljuq and Mongol Periods* (Cambridge: Cambridge University Press, 1968), pp. 203–82.

———, *State and Government in Medieval Islam. An Introduction to the Study of Political Theory: The Jurists* (New York: Oxford University Press, 1981).

Lapidus, Ira, *Muslim Cities in the Later Middle Ages* (Cambridge: Harvard University Press, 1967).

Latham, J.D., 'The Archers of the Middle East: The Turco-Iranian Background', *Iran*, 8 (1970), pp. 97–102.

Law, N.N., *Promotion of Learning in India during Muhammadan Rule (by Muhammadans)* (London: Longmans, Green and Co., 1916).

Lawrence, Bruce B., *Notes from a Distant Flute: The Extant Literature of Pre-Mughal Indian Sufism* (Tehran: Imperial Iranian Academy of Philosophy, 1978).

———, 'The Early Chishtī Approach to *Samā*', in M. Israel and N.K. Wagle, eds, *Islamic Society and Culture: Essays in Honour of Professor Aziz Ahmad* (Delhi: Manohar, 1983), pp. 69–93.

———, 'Early Indo-Muslim Saints and Conversion', in Y. Friedmann, ed., *Islam in Asia, Vol. 1, South Asia* (Boulder: Westview Press, 1984), pp. 109-45.

———, 'The Earliest Chishtiya and Shaikh Niẓām ud-din Awliyā', in R.E. Frykenberg, ed., *Delhi Through the Ages* (Delhi: Oxford University Press, 1986), pp. 104–28.

Leshnik, Lorenz S., 'Ghor, Firuzkoh and the Minar-i Jam', *Central Asiatic Journal*, 12 (1968–9), pp. 36–49.

Lewis, Geoffrey, trans., *The Book of Dede Korkut* (New York: Penguin Books, 1982 reprint).

Lorenzen, David N., 'Who Invented Hinduism?', *Comparative Study of Society and History*, 41 (1999), pp. 630–59.

Majumdar, R.C., ed., *The Struggle for Empire: The History and Culture of the Indian People, Vol. V* (Bombay: Bharatiya Vidya Bhavan, 1957).

Manz, Beatrice F., *The Rise and Rule of Tamerlane* (Cambridge: Cambridge University Press, 1989).

Maricq, A. and G. Wiet, *Le Minaret de Djam, la Découverte de la Capi-tale des Sultans Ghorides (XIIe–XIIIe siècles)* (Paris: Memoires de la Délégation Archéologique Franąise en Afghanistan, 1959), vol. 16.

Marlow, Louise, *Hierarchy and Egalitarianism in Islamic Thought* (Cambridge: Cambridge University Press, 1997).

Matsuo, Ara and Tsukinowa Tokifusa, 'Outline of Surveys and Studies of the Architectural Remains of the Delhi Sultanate Period', *Acta Asiatica*, 43 (1982), pp. 92–109.

McEwen, E., 'Persian Archery Texts: Chapter Eleven of Fakhr-i Mudabbir's *Ādāb al-Ḥarb*', *The Islamic Quarterly*, 18 (1974), pp. 76–99.

Meisami, Julie Scott, *Medieval Persian Court Poetry* (Princeton: Princeton University Press, 1987).

Meister, Michael W., 'The Two-and-a-half-day Mosque', *Oriental Art*, 18 n.s. (1972), pp. 57–63.

Mill, James, *The History of British India* (New Delhi: Associated Publishing House, 1972 reprint), 2 vols.

Minorsky, Vladimir, 'The Turkish Dialect of the Khalaj', *Bulletin of the School of Oriental (and African) Studies*, 10 (1940), pp. 426–34.

Mirza, Wahid, *Life and Works of Amir Khusrau* (Delhi: Idarah-i Adabiyat-i Delli, IAD Religio-Philosophy series no. 3, 1974).

Moosvi, Shireen, 'Numismatic Evidence and the Economic History of the Delhi Sultanate', *Proceedings of the Indian History Congress*, 50 (1989), pp. 207–18.

Moreland, W.H., 'Feudalism (?) in the Moslem Kingdom of Delhi', *Journal of Indian History*, 7 (1928), pp. 1–8, revised and reprinted in his *Agrarian System of Moslem India: A Historical Essay with Appendices* (Delhi: Oriental Books Reprint Corporation, 1968 reprint), pp. 216–23.

———, *The Agrarian System of Moslem India: A Historical Essay with Appendices* (Delhi: Oriental Books Reprint Corporation, 1968 reprint).

Mottahedeh, Roy P., *Loyalty and Leadership in an Early Islamic Society* (Princeton: Princeton University Press, 1980).

Mujeeb, M., *The Indian Muslims* (Montreal: McGill University Press, 1967).

———, 'The Qutb Complex as a Social Document', in idem, *Islamic Influence on Indian Society* (Meerut: Meenakshi Prakashan, 1972), pp. 114–27.

Mukhia, Harbans, *Historians and Historiography during the Reign of Akbar* (New Delhi: Vikas Publishing House, 1976).

Murray. Alexander C., *Germanic Kinship Structure, Studies in Law and Society in Antiquity and the Early Middle Ages* (Toronto: Pontifical Institute of Medieval Studies, Studies and Texts, 1983).

Nazim, M., *The Life and Times of Sulṭān Maḥmūd of Ghazna* (Cambridge: Cambridge University Press, 1931).

———, 'The Pand-Nāmah of Subuktigīn', *Journal of the Royal Asiatic Society* (1933), pp. 605–28.

Naqvi, S.A.A., 'Sultan Ghari, Delhi', *Ancient India*, 3 (1947), pp. 4–10.

Nigam, S.B.P., *Nobility under the Sultans of Delhi* (Delhi: Munshiram Manoharlal, 1968).

Nizami, K.A., *The Life and Times of Shaikh Fariduddin Ganj-i Shakar* (Delhi: Idarah-i Adabiyat-i Delli, 1987 reprint).

———, *Some Aspects of Religion and Politics in India during the Thirteenth Century* (Delhi: Idarah-i Adabiyat-i Delli, 1974 reprint).

———, *Studies in Medieval Indian History and Culture* (Allahabad: Kitab Mahal, 1966).

———, 'Ziya-ud-din Barani', M. Hasan, ed., *Historians of Medieval India* (Delhi: Jamia Millia Islamia, 1968), pp. 37–52.

Nizami, K.A., *The Life and Times of Shaikh Nizamuddin Auliya* (Delhi: Idarah-i Adabiyat-i Delli, 1991).

Nizamuddin, M., *Introduction to the Jawāmi' u'l-Ḥikāyāt wa Lawāmi' u'r-Riwāyāt of Sadīu'd-Dīn Muḥammad al-'Awfī* (London: E.J.W. Gibb Memorial Series, 1929).

Page, J.A., *An Histoical Memoir on the Qutb* (Calcutta: Memoirs of the Archaeological Survey of India, no. 22, Government of India Central Publication Branch, 1926).

Patel, Alka, 'Towards Alternative Receptions of Ghurid Architecture in North India (Late Twelfth-early Thirteenth century CE), *Archives of Asian Art*, 54 (2004), pp. 35–61

———, *Building Communities in Gujarat: Architecture and Society during the Twelfth through Fourteenth Centuries* (Leiden: E.J. Brill, 2004).

Patterson, Orlando, *Slavery and Social Death* (Cambridge: Harvard University Press, 1982).

Perlin, Frank, 'The Precolonial Indian State in History and Epistemology. A Reconsideration of Societal Formation in the Western Deccan from the Fifteenth to the Early Nineteenth Century', in Henri Y.M. Claessen and Peter Skalnik, eds, *The Study of the State* (The Hague: Morton, 1981), pp. 275–302.

———, 'State Formation Reconsidered', *Modern Asian Studies*, 19 (1985), pp. 415–80.

Petry, Carl, *The Civilian Elite of Cairo in the Late Middle Ages* (Princeton: Princeton University Press, 1981).

Phukan, Shantanu, ' "Through Throats where Many Rivers Meet": The Ecology of Hindi in the World of Persian', *The Indian Economic and Social History Review*, 38 (2001), pp. 33–58.

Pinder-Wilson, Ralph, 'Ghaznavid and Ghurid Minarets', *Iran*, 39 (2001), pp. 155–86.

Pipes, Daniel, *Slave Soldiers and Islam: The Genesis of a Military System* (New Haven: Yale University Press, 1981).

Pollock, Sheldon, 'Ramayana and Political Imagination in India', *Journal of Asian Studies*, 53 (1993), pp. 261–97.

———, 'India in the Vernacular Millennium: Literary Culture and Polity, 1000–1500', *Daedalus*, 127 (1998), pp. 41–74.

Poole, Stanley Lane, *Medieval India under Muhammadan Rule* (*A.D. 712–1764*) (New York: Haskell House, 1903, 1970 reprint).

Prasad, Pushpa, *Sanskrit Inscriptions of Delhi Sultanate, 1191–1526* (Delhi: Oxford University Press, 1990).

Qadir, Khurram, 'Amiran-i Chihalgan of Northern India, *Journal of Central Asia*, 4 (1981), pp. 59–146.

Qureshi, I.H., *The Administration of the Sultanate of Delhi* (New Delhi: Oriental Books Reprint Corporation, 1971 reprint).

Rao, Velcheru Narayana, David Shulman, and Sanjay Subrahmanyam, *Symbols of Substance: Court and State in Nāyaka-period Tamilnadu* (Delhi: Oxford University Press, 1992).

———, eds, *Textures of Time: Writing History in South India 1600–1800* (Delhi: Permanent Black, 2001).

Rathor, S.L., 'A Plea Against the Charge of Usurpation by Iltutmish', *Islamic Culture*, 32 (1958), pp. 262–7.

Raychaudhuri, Tapan and Irfan Habib, eds, *The Cambridge Economic History of India, Vol. 1, c. 1200–1750* (Cambridge: Cambridge University Press, 1982).

Reuter, Timothy, ed. and trans., *The Medieval Nobility* (Amsterdam: Europe in the Middle Ages, Selected Studies, North-Holland Publishing Company, 1978), vol. 14.

Richards, John F., 'The Islamic Frontier in the East: Expansion into South Asia', *South Asia*, 4 (1974), pp. 91–109.

———, 'Outflows of Precious Metals from Early Islamic India', in idem, *Precious Metals in the Later Medieval and Early Modern Worlds* (Durham: Carolina Academic Press, 1983), pp. 183–205.

———, ed., *Kingship and Authority in South Asia* (Delhi: Oxford University Press, 1998 reprint).

Rizvi, S.A.A., *Religious and Intellectual History of the Muslims in Akbar's Reign with Special Reference to Abu'l Fazl (1556–1605)* (Delhi: Munshiram Manoharlal Publishers Pvt. Ltd, 1975).

———, *A History of Sufism in India* (New Delhi: Munshiram Manoharlal Publishers Pvt. Ltd, 1978, 1992 reprint), 2 vols.

Ross, E.D., 'The Genealogies of Fakhr al-Din Mubarak Shah', T.W. Arnold and R.A. Nicholson, eds, *'Ajab Namah: A Volume of Oriental Studies presented to E.G. Browne on his 60th Birthday* (Cambridge: Cambridge University Press, 1922), pp. 392–413.

Sabri, Imdad, *Dihlī ke qadīm Madāris aur Mudarris* (Delhi: Sabri Academy, 1988).

Sahu, B.P., ed., *Land System and Rural Society in Early India* (Delhi: Manohar, 1997).

Saran, Parmatma, 'Politics and Personalities in the Reign of Nasiruddin Mahmud, the Slave', *Studies in Medieval Indian History* (Delhi: Ranjit Printers and Publishers, 1952), pp. 223–48.

Schacht, Joseph, *Origins of Muhammadan Jurisprudence* (Oxford: Clarendon Press, 1975).

Schimmel, Annemarie, *And Muhammad is His Messenger: The Veneration of the Prophet in Islamic Piety* (Chapel Hill: University of North Carolina Press, 1985).

———, 'Turk and Hindu: A Poetical Image and its Application to Historical Fact', Speros Vryonis jr., ed., *Islam and Cultural Change in the Middle Ages* (Wiesbaden: Otto Harrassowitz, 1975), pp. 107–26.

Sharma, R.S., *Indian Feudalism c.* AD *300–1200* (Delhi: Macmillan India Ltd, 1980 reprint).

———, *Urban Decay in India (c. 300–c. 1000)* (Delhi: Manohar, 1987).

Sharma, Sunil, *Persian Poetry at the Indian Frontier: Mas'ūd Sa'd Salmān of Lahore* (Delhi: Permanent Black, 2001).

Shokoohy, Mehrdad and Natalie H., 'The Architecture of Baha al-Din Tughrul in the Region of Bayana, Rajasthan', *Muqarnas*, 4 (1987), pp. 114–32.

Shu'aib, M.M., 'Inscriptions from Palwal', *Epigraphica Indo-Moslemica* (1911–12), pp. 1–4.

Shulman, David, *The King and the Clown in South Indian Myth and Poetry* (Princeton: Princeton University Press, 1985).

Siddiqui, I.H., 'Social Mobility in the Delhi Sultanate', Irfan Habib, ed., *Medieval India: Researches in the History of India, 1200–1750, Vol. 1* (Delhi: Oxford University Press, 1992), pp. 22–48.

———, *Perso-Arabic Sources of Information on the Life and Conditions in the Sultanate of Delhi* (Delhi: Munshiram Manoharlal Publishers Pvt. Ltd, 1992).

———, 'A Note on the Dargah of Salar Mas'ud in Bahraich in the Light of the Standard Historical Sources', Christian W. Troll, *Muslim Shrines in India* (Delhi: Oxford University Press, 1992 reprint), pp. 44–7.

———, ed., *Medieval India, Essays in Intellectual Thought and Culture, Vol. 1* (Delhi: Manohar, 2003).

Singh, Chetan, 'Well-irrigation Methods in Medieval Panjab: The Persian Wheel Reconsidered', *Indian Economic and Social History Review*, 22 (1985), pp. 73–87.

Singh, Kashi N., 'The Territorial Basis of Medieval Town and Village Settlement in Eastern Uttar Pradesh, India', *Annals of the Association of American Geographers*, 58 (1968), pp. 203–20.

Singh, R.L. and K.N. Singh, 'Evolution of the Medieval Towns in the Saryu-Par Plain of the Middle Ganga Valley: A Case Study', *The National Geographical Journal of India*, 9 (1963), pp. 1–11.

Sinha, Surajit, 'State Formation and Rajput Myth in Tribal Central India', *Man in India*, 42 (1962), pp. 35–80, reprinted in Herman

Kulke, ed., *The State in India 1000–1700* (Delhi: Oxford University Press, 1997 reprint), pp. 304–42.

Sourdel-Thomine, Janine, *Le Minaret Ghouride de Jām* (Paris: Diffusion de Boccard, 2004).

Spengler, William, 'Some New Numismatic Evidence Regarding Royal Nomenclature and Titulature in the Ghurid Period', *Numismatics and History* (Nasik: Indian Institute of Research in Numismatic Studies, Inaugural Seminar, 1984), pp. 106–16.

Sreenivasan, Ramya, 'Alauddin Khalji Remembered: Conquest, Gender and Community in Medieval Rajput Narratives', *Studies in History*, n.s. 18 (2002), pp. 275–96.

Stein, Burton, *Peasant State and Society in Medieval South India* (Delhi: Oxford University Press, 1980).

Stern, S.M., 'Isma'ilis and Qarmatians', *L'Elaboration de l'Islam, Colloque de Strasbourg Juin 1959* (Paris: Presses Universitaires de France, 1961), pp. 99–108.

Stone, Lawrence, 'Prosopography' in F. Gilbert and S. Graubard, eds, *Historical Studies Today* (New York: Norton, 1972), pp. 107–40.

Stow, A.M., 'The Road between Delhi and Multan', *Journal of the Panjab Historical Society*, 3 (1014–15), pp. 26–37.

Strange, Guy Le, *The Lands of the Eastern Caliphate: Mesopotamia, Persia and Central Asia from the Moslem Conquest to the Time of Timur* (Cambridge: Cambridge University Press, 1930).

Subbarayalu, Y., *Political Geography of the Chola Country* (Madras: State Department of Archaeology, Government of Tamilnadu, 1973).

Talbot, Cynthia, 'Inscribing the Other, Inscribing the Self: Hindu–Muslim Identities in Pre-Colonial India', *Comparative Study of Society and History*, 37 (1995), pp. 692–722, also reprinted in Richard Eaton, ed., *India's Islamic Traditions 711–1750* (Delhi: Oxford University Press, 2003), pp. 83–117.

———, *Precolonial India in Practice: Society, Region, and Identity in Medieval Andhra* (Delhi: Oxford University Press, 2001).

Thapar, Romila, 'The Tyranny of Labels', *The IX Zakir Husain Memorial Lecture*, 1996, reprinted in idem, *Cultural Pasts: Essays in Early Indian History* (Delhi: Oxford University Press, 2000), pp. 990–1014.

Thomas, Edward, *The Chronicles of the Pathan Kings of Delhi* (Delhi: Munshiram Manoharlal, 1967 reprint).

Tripathi, R.P., *Some Aspects of Muslim Administration* (Allahabad: Central Book Depot, 1978 reprint).

Wagoner, Phillip B., ' "A Sultan Among Hindu Kings": Dress, Titles and the Islamicization of Hindu Culture at Vijayanagara', *Journal of Asian Studies*, 55 (1996), pp. 851–80.

———, 'Harihara, Bukka, and the Sultan: The Delhi Sultanate in the Political Imagination of Vijaynagar', David Gilmartin and Bruce B. Lawrence, eds, *Beyond Turk and Hindu: Rethinking Religious Identities in Islamicate South Asia* (Gainesville: University of Florida Press, 2000), pp. 300–26.

Walker, C.T. Harvey, trans., 'Jahiz of Basra to al-Fath ibn Khaqan on the "Exploits of the Turks and the Army of the Khalifate in General" ', *Journal of the Royal Asiatic Society*, 23 (1915), pp. 631–97.

Watson, Andrew M., *Agricultural Innovation in the Early Islamic World (The Diffusion of Crops and Farming Techniques, 700–1100)* (Cambridge: Cambridge University Press, 1983).

Watt, W.M., *Islamic Philosophy and Theology* (Edinburgh: Edinburgh University Press, 1979).

Welch, Anthony, '*Qur'an* and Tomb: The Religious Epigraphs of Two Early Sultanate Tombs in Delhi', Frederick M. Asher and G.S. Ghai, eds, *Indian Epigraphy: Its Bearings on the History of Art* (New Delhi: Oxford and IBH Publishing Co., American Institute of Indian Studies, 1985).

———, 'Islamic Architecture and Epigraphs in Sultanate India', in A.K. Narain, ed., *Studies in South Asian Art and Archaeology*, forthcoming.

Welch, Anthony, Hussein Keshani and Alexandra Bain, 'Epigraphs, Scripture and Architecture in the Early Delhi Sultanate', *Muqarnas* 19 (2002), pp. 12–43.

Wensinck, A.J., *The Muslim Creed: Its Genesis and Historical Development* (London: Frank Cass and Co. Ltd, 1965).

Wink, André, *Land and Sovereignty in India: Agrarian Society and Politics under the Eighteenth-century Maratha Svarājya* (Cambridge: Cambridge University Press 1986).

———, *al-Hind: the Making of the Indo-Islamic World* (Leiden: E.J. Brill, 1997), 3 vols.

Wittfogel, Karl A. and Feng Chia-Sheng, 'Appendix V: Qara Khitay', idem, *History of the Chinese Society: Liao (907–1125)* (Philadelphia: Transactions of the American Philosophical Society, 1946), vol. 36, pp. 619–74.

Wolper, Ethel Sara, *Cities and Saints: Sufism and the Transformation of Urban Space in Medieval Anatolia* (Pennsylvania: Pennsylvania State University Press, 2003).

Wright, H. Nelson, *Catalogue of the Coins in the Indian Museum Calcutta Including the Cabinet of the Asiatic Society of Bengal* (Oxford: Clarendon Press, 1907), vol. 2.

———, *The Coinage and Metrology of the Sultans of Delhi* (Delhi: Oriental Books Reprint Corporation, 1974 reprint).

Yadav, B.N.S., *Society and Culture in Northern India* (Allahabad: Central Book Depot, 1973).

Yazdani, G., 'Inscriptions in the Tomb of Baba Arjun Shah, Petlad (Baroda State)', *Epigraphica Indo-Moslemica* (1915-16), pp. 15–18.

———, 'The Inscriptions of the Turk Sulṭāns of Delhi—Mu'izzu-d-dīn Bahram, 'Alā'u-d-dīn Mas'ūd, Nāṣir al-dīn Maḥmūd, Ghiyāthu-d-din Balban and Mu'izzu-d-din Kaiqubād', *Epigraphica Indo-Moslemica* (1913–14), pp. 13–46.

Ziegler, Norman P., 'Rajput Loyalties during the Mughal Period', in J.F. Richards, ed., *Kingship and Authority in South Asia* (Delhi: Oxford University Press, 1998 reprint), pp. 242–84.

Index